Therapeutic Recreation Program Design

Principles and Procedures

Fourth Edition

Norma J. Stumbo
Illinois State University

Carol Ann Peterson

PEARSON

Benjamin Cummings

San Francisco   Boston   New York
Cape Town   Hong Kong   London   Madrid   Mexico City
Montreal   Munich   Paris   Singapore   Sydney   Tokyo   Toronto

Publisher: Daryl Fox
Acquisitions Editor: Deirdre McGill
Associate Editor: Michelle Cadden
Marketing Manager: Sandra Lindelof
Managing Editor: Claire Brassert
Production Editor: Steven Anderson
Project Coordination: Matrix Productions, Inc.
Composition: TBH Typecast, Inc.
Copy Editor: Anna Reynolds Trabucco
Proofreader: Kate Petrella
Cover Designer: Yvo Riezebos
Manufacturing Buyer: Stacey Weinberger
Text and Cover Printer: Phoenix Color

Cover Photo: Getty Images

ISBN 0-8053-5497-2

Library of Congress Cataloging-in-Publication Data
Peterson, Carol Ann
    Therapeutic recreation program design : principles and procedures / Carol Ann Peterson, Norma J. Stumbo.—4th ed.
        p. cm.
    Includes bibliographical references and index.
    ISBN 0-8053-5497-2
    1. Recreational therapy.   I. Stumbo, Norma J.   II. Title.
RM736.7.G86 2003
615.8'5153—dc21   2003046052

PEARSON

Benjamin
Cummings

1   2   3   4   5   6   7—VHO—07   06   05   04   03

www.aw.com/bc

CONTENTS

Chapter 7

Chapter 8

Chapter 9

Chapter 10

Chapter 11

Efficacy Research 393

Summary 394

Student Exercises 394

References 397

Chapter 12
Accountability: Challenge for the Future 400

Useful Resources 402

Related Internet Sites 403

Summary 404

Appendix A
Relaxation: A Program System 405

Appendix B
Social Behaviors: A Program System 447

Appendix C
Therapeutic Recreation Assessment Instruments 469

Appendix D
Common Medical Abbreviations 477

Glossary 485

Index 494

From *accountability* to *wellness*. These first and last words of the text's new glossary can be a metaphor for this fourth edition of *Therapeutic Recreation Program Design: Principles and Procedures*. Although the number of quality therapeutic recreation textbooks continues to increase, there is still no equal to this *programming* text by Peterson and Stumbo. In addition to providing a solid conceptualization of a useful model of therapeutic recreation practice, this text continues to provide direction for both comprehensive and specific program development. Any therapeutic recreation practitioner who utilizes this accountable systems approach to therapeutic recreation programming will maximize the program's effectiveness and therefore clients' progress toward increased wellness and an improved quality of life.

The newly revised sections of this text add depth and contemporary language to a solid practice model for therapeutic recreation. The relationship of one's *leisure lifestyle* to three functions of therapeutic recreation practice (functional intervention, leisure education, recreation participation) is clearly described. Client and program *outcomes* are well explained. New practice *examples* and conceptual *figures* included throughout the text help students apply the information to a variety of settings. Students have the opportunity to fine-tune their learning with the new *student exercises* included in this fourth edition.

This is not an introductory text. Although professional assumptions are clearly delineated in this edition, a real benefit of this text is the opportunity for an advanced level of learning in therapeutic recreation. The comprehensive and specific program planning methods included in this text continue to withstand the trends in health care, the changing standards of JCAHO and CARF, and the professional standards of both ATRA and NTRS. I highly recommend a thorough understanding of this edition for present and prospective Certified Therapeutic Recreation Specialists.

Any therapeutic recreation professional who bases a professional practice on the content and direction provided by this text will be professionally solid and accountable. Peterson and Stumbo continue to provide the profession of therapeutic recreation with a usable and accountable text appropriate for use in both the classroom and the workplace.

Nancy H. Navar, Re.D., CTRS
Professor & Director of Therapeutic Recreation
University of Wisconsin—La Crosse

The fourth edition of *Therapeutic Recreation Program Design: Principles and Procedures* includes new, important, and timely information for therapeutic recreation students and professionals. Changes continue to happen rapidly in the world of health care and human services, and in the field of therapeutic recreation. More than ever, consumers and proponents of health care services are demanding greater accountability, more effective methods of service delivery, and a higher degree of reliable, proven client outcomes. This book aims to help students and professionals meet those demands in the new and emerging health care and human service markets.

Like the previous editions, this book is written for students preparing for the field of therapeutic recreation and professionals providing services to clients. Therapeutic recreation is concerned with the direct delivery of services to clients with disabilities, illnesses, or special needs. Delivery of these services requires an in-depth understanding of both the procedures of delivering quality programs and the content to be addressed within the programs. These two areas are interrelated and interdependent. Knowledge or expertise in one area and not the other will result in programs that are either inappropriate to clients' leisure-related needs or inadequate in terms of how the program is delivered. This text addresses both areas (process and content), utilizing a comprehensive and integrated approach. The first two chapters focus on the content underlying the delivery of therapeutic recreation services to clients. The latter nine chapters outline the process or procedures utilized to implement quality programs. Together, these two parts enable an understanding of both the content and process of therapeutic recreation programming.

This text focuses on the design, development, and evaluation of therapeutic recreation services. It is not introductory in that it presumes prior knowledge of illnesses and disabilities, service settings, therapeutic recreation as a profession, activity planning and delivery, and basic intervention techniques. Understanding of professional issues, such as credentialing, accreditation, standardization of practice, etc., is assumed. Knowledge of these concepts is important to be able to apply them within the context of program design and delivery addressed in this text.

This text uses a systematic approach to program design and delivery. The content of therapeutic recreation services is provided by the Leisure Ability Model in the components of functional intervention, leisure education, and recreation participation. The process of program conceptualization, documentation, and evaluation is represented in the largest sense by the Therapeutic Recreation Accountability Model. These two models intersect to deliver the foundational concepts of program delivery in therapeutic recreation services. These models provide the basis for systematic, logical, and needs-driven programming that produces predictable, effective, and necessary client outcomes. One major intention of the text is to draw the reader to understanding the connections among each task carried out through the design, implementation, and evaluation of therapeutic recreation programs.

Format and Organization of the Fourth Edition

Significant changes have been included in this edition, strengthening the relationships between theory, evidence-based practice, and client outcomes. Each chapter contains updated information reflecting the latest trends and nuances in health care and human services. The twelve chapters in this book follow a logical sequence from theoretical foundations to a challenge for the future.

Chapter 1 has been reorganized and discusses literature pertinent to understanding the basis for delivering therapeutic recreation services to clients. Concepts such as health, quality of life, self-efficacy, intrinsic motivation, internal locus of control, and personal choice are presented as they relate to individuals' leisure lifestyles. Chapter 2 is devoted to the Leisure Ability Model and includes an update of pertinent literature to support the model. Chapter 3 details the Therapeutic Recreation Accountability Model, which provides the basis for the remaining chapters of the text; new information about evidence-based practice and client outcomes has been added.

Chapter 4 presents information and procedures related to comprehensive program planning of total unit or agency therapeutic recreation programs, and Chapter 5 addresses the structure and requirements of specific programs. Theory-based programming, a tremendous asset to our accountability, is discussed. Chapters 6 and 7 include even more examples of applying activity analysis and selection to client situations. New information on clinical guidelines and clinical pathways is included in Chapter 8 on intervention and diagnostic protocols.

Information about client assessment, the method by which to gather baseline information about clients in order to place them into programs designed to meet their needs, is upgraded in Chapter 9. New and more in-depth information is included in Chapter 10 on client documentation and Chapter 11 on program and client evaluation. Information about accreditation and regulatory agencies such as the Joint Commission and the Rehabilitation Accreditation Commission have been updated. Resources have been updated and added in Chapter 12. Some will find the addition of a social skills program in Appendix B, assessment instruments in Appendix C, common medical abbreviations and symbols in Appendix D, and the Glossary to be welcome extensions and additions.

Like its predecessors, the purpose of this book is to provide comprehensive and progressive program development information for the field of therapeutic recreation. The text carries a dual focus on program content and the process used to design, deliver, and evaluate intervention programs.

Acknowledgments

The fourth edition of this text in many ways represents a group effort. Over the years, students, colleagues, and clients have taught us many things, most of which we have tried to organize and include between these covers. Thanks to all who have taken time to teach us, debate issues and methods, and provide feedback on ideas.

As with the third edition, I would first and foremost like to thank Carol Peterson for her friendship, trust in my abilities, and professional wisdom. I have gained much. I would also like to thank: Drs. Nancy Navar, Department of Recreation Management and Therapeutic Recreation, University of Wisconsin—LaCrosse; Patricia Malik, RPMalik, Inc.; and Cynny Carruthers, University of Nevada—Las Vegas, for unwavering support and large doses of reality. Thanks to Patricia Thomas, University of Wisconsin—Milwaukee, who provided timely and helpful information about the Joint Commission, and Mary E. Hess, who wrote the new system on social behaviors. Thanks also to the five reviewers who helped us see other possibilities and opportunities for improvement: Marcia Jean Carter—University of Northern Colorado; Dr. Suzi Lane—Oklahoma State University; Jeff Witman—York College of Pennsylvania; Nancy Navar—University of Wisconsin—La Crosse; and Peggy Holmes-Layman—Eastern Illinois University. Special appreciation is extended to the hundreds of therapeutic recreation students who have graduated from Illinois State University for their continual questioning. Better teaching stems from students who want to know more. And many, many thanks to the Aussies and Kiwis for turning my world upside down! (Please send Tim Tams.)

Special thanks to Randy Duncan for his unbelievable patience, empathy skills, e-hugs, and sense of humor (not necessarily in that order!). My love and appreciation extends to my sisters, Barbara Busch and Nancy Lockett, and my father, Francis Stumbo, for years of encouragement, laughs, and hugs. Love you guys! I would also like to thank Christine Howe posthumously for always encouraging my writing spirit and believing that I would make a difference. She is still missed.

CHAPTER 1

Theoretical Foundations: The Basis for Service Development and Delivery

In order to be competent and successful, and to provide clients with necessary and meaningful intervention services, therapeutic recreation specialists must possess a comprehensive understanding of:

- The *theoretical basis for services* (including, but not limited to, internal locus of control, intrinsic motivation, personal causation, freedom of choice, and flow)
- *Therapeutic recreation content* (functional intervention, leisure education, and recreation participation)
- Aspects of *quality therapeutic recreation service delivery* such as analysis, planning, implementation, and evaluation of efficacious services
- A broad range of *typical client characteristics,* including needs and deficits

The intent of the first chapter of this text is to review pertinent theories and understandings about leisure, health, wellness, and quality of life as these concepts relate to the provision of therapeutic recreation services for individuals with disabilities and/or illnesses. The second chapter focuses on the Leisure Ability Model, which addresses therapeutic recreation content, sometimes referred to as therapeutic recreation's scope of practice. The components of the Leisure Ability Model (functional intervention, leisure education, and recreation participation) are used throughout this text as the content of programs that may address client needs. The third chapter presents the Therapeutic Recreation Accountability Model (TRAM) as a way to visualize the process of therapeutic recreation service program design and delivery. The remaining nine chapters each explain a specific part of the TRAM to help students and professionals understand how each component is connected and relates to the other components. As a therapeutic recreation programming text, this book does not attempt to focus on the specific and in-depth characteristics and needs of client populations. Readers are encouraged to refer to Mobily and MacNeil (2002) for an excellent and recent text that serves this latter purpose. However, the present text repeatedly requires the reader to apply specific information about conditions, diseases, illnesses, and disabilities to therapeutic recreation concepts and decisions.

Each of the four bulleted areas above is essential to conceptualizing and creating therapeutic recreation intervention programs that address certain client deficits and produce expected, valued, and meaningful client outcomes. So that the reader may better understand the content and process of therapeutic recreation services, a theoretical foundation focusing on the importance of leisure involvement to individuals' health, wellness, and quality of life is discussed.

Health, Wellness, and Quality of Life

The medical model of health care focuses almost exclusively on physical health and has been (and in some places continues to be) prevalent among physicians (Larson, 1997). It views health as being at the opposite end of the continuum from disease, illness, and/or disability, and focuses on functional ability, morbidity, and mortality (Larson, 1991). In this view, if an individual had a disease, disability, and/or illness, he or she was not capable of being healthy. The converse also was true—anyone without disease, disability, and/or illness was viewed as being healthy.

Disease is the failure of an organism's adaptive mechanisms to counteract adequately the stimuli and stresses to it, resulting in functional or structural disturbances at the cellular, tissue, and organ level (Edelman & Mandle, 1994; Emami, Benner, Lipson, & Ekman, 2000). **Disability** is a physical or mental impairment that substantially limits (past, present, or future; real or perceived) one or more major life activities, having a record of such impairment, or being regarded as having such an impairment (Americans with Disabilities Act [ADA], 1990). **Illness** is defined as when a person's resources are imbalanced with the needed responses, and results in decreased ability to survive and to create higher standards for the quality of life. Illness is a state of being; it is the person's subjective experience of the disorder, either with or without objective physical and biochemical evidence of the disorder; and it is the human experience of dysfunction and loss of well-being (Edelman & Mandle, 1994; Emami, Benner, Lipson, & Ekman, 2000). Stokols (2000) argued that when health was seen as mutually exclusive of disability, disease, and/or illness, potentially positive states of well-being for individuals with these conditions are negated.

The World Health Organization (WHO) took a different approach to defining health in 1947. The WHO defined **health** as the state of complete physical, mental, and social well-being, and not merely the absence of disease. "Healthfulness is a multifaceted phenomenon, encompassing physical health, emotional well-being, and social cohesion" (Stokols, 2000, p. 136). This approach looked at human health from a broader perspective and challenged health care providers to look not only for indications of the frequency and severity of disease, illness, and disability, but also to look toward the individual's overall level of well-being and quality of life.

In recent years, there has been a major change in the conception of health from a disease model to a health model. Human health is heavily influenced by lifestyle habits and environmental conditions. This enables people to exercise some measures of control over their health status. Indeed, through self-management of health habits people reduce major health risks and live healthier and more productive lives (Bandura, 1997). If the huge health benefits of these few lifestyle habits were put into a pill, it would be declared a spectacular breakthrough in the field of medicine. (Bandura, 2001, p. 10)

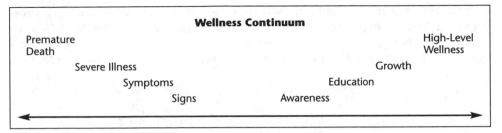

Figure 1.1 Wellness Continuum. The key is not so much where you *stand* on the Wellness Continuum as the *direction* you are facing. (adapted from Travis & Ryan, 1988, p. xvi)

The World Health Assembly (2001), part of the overall World Health Organization, recently reinforced that the terms impairment, disease, and handicap refer to dysfunction rather than the person's ability to enjoy well-being and participate in life activities. The Assembly also recognized that any two individuals with the same disease can experience different levels of functioning and two persons experiencing the same level of functioning may not have the same disease; that is, health, disease, disability, and illness are experiences unique to each individual and are extremely difficult to categorize into discrete and exclusive pigeonholes.

Wellness is an approach to personal health that emphasizes individual responsibility for well-being through the practice of health-promoting lifestyle behaviors (Hurley & Schlaadt, 1992). Wellness is a positive, proactive approach. It requires a coordinated, preventive, and integrated lifestyle. It is unique to each person (Ardell, 1979). "Wellness is not static; it is a dynamic process that takes into account all of the decisions we make daily, such as foods we eat, the amount of exercise we get, and whether we drink alcohol before driving, wear safety belts, or smoke cigarettes. Every choice we make potentially affects our health and wellness" (Edlin, Golanty, & McCormack Brown, 1999, p. 6).

Wellness is conceptualized as dynamic, a condition of change in which the individual moves forward, climbing toward a higher potential of functioning (Larson, 1997). High-level wellness for the individual is an integrated method of functioning that is oriented toward maximizing the individual's potential within the environment in which she or he is functioning. This definition does not imply that there is an optimum level of wellness but rather that wellness is a progression toward a satisfactory level of functioning. High-level wellness, therefore, involves (a) the progression forward and upward toward a higher potential of functioning, (b) an open-ended and ever-expanding tomorrow with its challenge of fuller potential, and (c) the integration of the whole being. The challenge posed by the concept of high-level wellness is how it can be achieved within everyday living and for humankind as a whole (Edelman & Mandel, 1994, p. 14). Figure 1.1 displays a continuum of wellness.

A third concept, **quality of life,** has gained impetus, especially since the mid-1980s. During this time, two initiatives influenced medical care to include a more comprehensive view of health. First, health care providers began to search for answers about which cancer treatments led to increased survival rates as well as improved well-being (Mendlowicz & Stein, 2000). These questions then spread to other health concerns beyond cancer. Second, health care outcomes and their measurement became important as payers, providers, and patients wanted additional information about results of quality medical care (Lehman, 1995). The new focus on quality of life extends far beyond immediate recovery to lifestyle factors and a sense of well-being.

The World Health Organization (2001) defined quality of life as

> *individuals' perception of their position in life in the context of the culture and value system where they live, and in relation to their goals, expectations, standards and concerns. It is a broad-ranging concept, incorporating in a complex way a person's physical health, psychological state, level of independence, social relationships, personal beliefs and relationship to salient features of the environment.*

Lehman (1995) noted that quality of life encompasses "what a person is capable of doing (functional status), access to resources and opportunities to use these abilities to pursue interests, and sense of well-being" (p. 94). He noted that the former two dimensions (functional status and access to resources) often are called *objective quality of life* and the latter (opportunities and well-being) are called *subjective quality of life.* "Within these overarching dimensions, life domains have been identified (for example, health, family, social relations, work, financial status, and living situation). Quality of life thus is a complex notion" (p. 94).

Mendlowicz and Stein (2000) also noted this multiplicity. "Quality of life refers to complex aspects of life that cannot be expressed by using only quantifiable indicators, it describes an ultimately subjective evaluation of life in general. It encompasses, though, not only the subjective sense of well-being but also objective indicators such as health status and external life situations" (p. 670). As they explained, objective health indicators, such as mortality and severity of illness, must be combined with more subjective individualized evaluations of health, such as personal preferences, satisfaction, and overall sense of well-being.

Tubesing and Tubesing (1991) also noted the complexity and interrelatedness of different aspects of health and well-being:

> *In reality, sickness is a disruption in whatever form it occurs, and healing is a return to wholeness by whatever means. . . . We struggle for wholeness and personal unity against whatever forces tend to wound us, and we heal naturally, by grace, through the process of living:*
> - *Our bodies self-correct through internal regulation (homeostasis).*
> - *Our emotions seek peace and acceptance in the face of worry.*
> - *Our intellect uses logic and memory to counteract confusion.*
> - *We respond to our social environment by making up, giving in, speaking up, or fighting back.*
> - *In the face of despair our spirits seek hope, faith, and meaning. (p. 15)*

Godbey (1999) wrote that **homeostasis,** the process of seeking equilibrium, is a natural occurrence and involves the constant ebb and flow of health and illness throughout the life cycle. He also noted that many factors contribute to illness, such as stress, diet, lack of physical activity, and other lifestyle factors.

One of the most written about lifestyle factors that negatively influences health is stress (Iso-Ahola, 1997). **Stress** is a state that results from an actual or perceived imbalance between the demand and the capability of the individual to cope with and/or adapt to that demand, that upsets the individual's short- or long-term homeostasis (Hood & Carruthers, 2002; Iso-Ahola, 1997; Iwasaki & Mannell, 2000; Mikhail, 1985). Monat and Lazarus (1985) noted that stress might lead directly to illness in three ways: (a) because of the powerful chemical alterations in body chemistry, (b) due to the individual's reactions, such as alcohol consumption or working harder, and (c) ignoring various bodily symptoms that signal serious health problems, such as migraine headaches. Mikhail (1985) reported that individuals differ in their reactivity to stress (what stresses one person may not stress another), that stress is determined by an individual's perception of the stressful situation instead of the situation itself, and that the extent to which the individual experiences stress depends on his or her appraisal of coping ability.

Coping with stress refers to any effort to master conditions of harm, threat, or challenge and bring the person back into equilibrium (Iwasaki & Mannell, 2000; Monat & Lazarus, 1985). How well individuals cope with stress often determines their health and quality of life (Godbey, 1999; Hood & Carruthers, 2002; Iwasaki & Mannell, 2000). In addition, Wheeler and Frank (1988) documented four "buffers" that consistently helped manage against stress: (a) sense of competence, (b) nature and extent of exercise, (c) sense of purpose, and (d) leisure activity. Hood and Carruthers (2002) presented two broad categories of coping strategies: reducing negative demands and improving positive resources. The authors categorized positive resources into physical (e.g., fitness and energy level), psychological (e.g., perceptions of self-efficacy and competence), social (e.g., social support), and lifestyle resources (e.g., ability to relax, self-responsibility, leisure patterns). The ability to cope adequately with stress affects an individual's sense of health, wellness, and quality of life.

Aaronson, Bullinger, and Ahmedzai (1988) presented four domains of health related quality of life: (a) disease- and treatment-related physical symptoms (such as side effects of medication), (b) physical functional status, (c) psychological functioning, and (d) social functioning. The latter three domains relating to health, wellness, and quality of life will be examined in the next section. In addition, because leisure is an important component of health, wellness, and quality of life (Siegenthaler, 1997), recent research on leisure in relation to these domains of function will be presented.

Benefits of Leisure

Leisure is defined by the main variables of perceived autonomy, or freedom of choice, and intrinsic motivation, which reflects behaviors that are enjoyable in themselves (Cassidy, 1996; Iwasaki & Mannell, 2000; Mannell & Kleiber, 1997). Health, wellness, and quality of life are fluid concepts, dependent on a number of lifestyle and functioning factors. "Both leisure and health vary on a continuum. Some leisure experiences are better than others. Similarly, even in the absence of illness, some people are healthier than others" (Iso-Ahola, 1997, p. 131). Leisure may contribute significantly to improved physical, social, and emotional or psychological aspects of health and well-being. Wankel (1994) stated the strong connection between leisure and health:

To a large degree, to experience leisure with the characteristics of perceived freedom, competence, self-determination, satisfaction, and perceived quality of life is to experience a subjective state of health. In this sense, the development of a broad repertoire of leisure skills to facilitate rich, meaningful experiences provides the foundation for extending such holistic quality experiences to all of life. Personal initiative, choice, meaningful involvement, and enjoyable, supportive social networks—key aspects for leisure—also have important implications for well-being. In the more extreme subjective view, distinctions between leisure and health disappear. (p. 28)

Clearly, leisure, health, and well-being become mutually beneficial. According to Iso-Ahola (1997), leisure may contribute significantly to a person's health in two ways:

Leisure can influence health in two principal ways. First, in and of itself, leisure is conducive to health. The mere existence of leisure in a person's everyday life has consequences for health. The fact that an individual acknowledges, values, and engages in leisure for its own sake, for its inherent characteristics, is one way in which leisure contributes to health. Another way is where leisure is used as a tool to achieve certain health outcomes. An example of this is a person who takes time to exercise regularly: leisure provides time for him or her to exercise. (p. 132)

Several benefits of leisure participation that have been documented recently in the research literature, and that relate to health and well-being, will be highlighted. These benefits, although largely overlapping and interrelated, can be separated into the following major categories of human functioning: (a) physical, (b) psychological, and (c) social. The selected research findings are not meant as an exhaustive review, but rather as an introduction to several outcomes of leisure involvement that contribute directly to the overall goals promoted and valued by health, human service, and rehabilitation service providers.

Physical Health and Leisure

The National Center for Chronic Disease Prevention and Health Promotion (2002) documented that physical activity has numerous physiologic effects on the cardiovascular, musculoskeletal, metabolic, endocrine, and immune systems.

The body responds to physical activity in ways that have important positive effects on the cardiovascular, respiratory, and endocrine systems. These changes are consistent with a number of health benefits, including a reduced risk of premature mortality and reduced risks of coronary heart disease, hypertension, colon cancer, and diabetes mellitus. Regular participation in physical activity also appears to reduce depression and anxiety, improve mood, and enhance ability to perform daily tasks throughout the life span. . . . In summary, physical activity contributes to health-related quality of life by enhancing psychological well-being and by improving physical functioning in persons compromised by poor health.

Physical activity during leisure plays an important role in maintaining the physical health and well-being of children and adults. In the US, only 15 percent of adults and 50 percent of children regularly participate in physical activity. About 25 percent of adults and children report not participating in any vigorous activity. The most popular leisure-time physical activities among adults are walking for pleasure and gardening or yard work (National Center for Chronic Disease Prevention and Health Promotion, 2002). According to research by the National Center for Chronic Disease Prevention and Health Promotion (2002), "consistent influences on physical activity patterns among adults and young people include confidence in one's ability to engage in regular physical activity (e.g., self-efficacy), enjoyment of physical activity, support from others, positive beliefs concerning the benefits of physical activity, and lack of perceived barriers to being physically active." Elsewhere the investigators stated that research on the most effective interventions and approaches to promoting positive physical activity continues, and that "schools, community agencies, parks, recreational facilities, and health clubs are available in most communities and can be more effectively used in these efforts." They concluded that "special efforts will also be required to meet the needs of special populations, such as people with disabilities, racial and ethnic minorities, people with low income, and the elderly. Much more information about these important groups will be necessary to develop a truly comprehensive national initiative for better health through physical activity."

Paffenbarger, Hyde, and Dow (1991, p. 56) "accept[ed] outright the recognition that physical activity is beneficial and *indeed essential* to health and survival." The authors indicated that physical activity was directly related to good health, well-being, and quality of life, and could, in certain situations, counteract the adverse health effects of other lifestyle elements, including obesity, cigarette smoking, and excess alcohol consumption. They called for more specific research in this area of physical activity counteracting adverse influences of negative lifestyles.

Froelicher and Froelicher (1991) advocated the preventive benefits of physical activity. "Recent studies of primary prevention support the lifestyle of regular physical activity" (p. 70). Some of the direct benefits they noted included decreased risk of coronary heart disease, decreased fatigue, increased physical performance, improved attention to health, and improved lifestyle modifications toward better health. Lakka (1995) authored one such study that showed a preventive link between leisure-time physical activity and cardiorespiratory fitness, with reduced risk of acute myocardial infarction.

Sternfeld, Ainsworth, and Quesenberry (1999) found, in a sample of 5,000 women, that women with the highest level of participation in sports and exercise who had pursued active-living behaviors were more likely to be younger, white, college-educated, without young children at home, and leaner. They also found that such women had high self-efficacy and social support for exercise, did not suffer from lack of motivation, and did not perceive external obstacles such as lack of facilities or equipment to be barriers.

Iso-Ahola and Park (1996), in a study of 252 individuals who practiced Tae Kwon Do, found that physical health problems were positively related to life stress; that is, as ratings of life stress rose so did ratings of physical health problems and perceived lack of health. Lack of perceived freedom and intrinsic motivation (two key factors in defining leisure) also were associated with poor health.

Physical activity has been shown to increase survival rate for individuals with spinal injuries who participated in physical activity (Krause & Crewe, 1987). In addition, for many individuals with disabilities, physical activity has been shown to decrease secondary complications, such as decubiti and urinary tract infections (Stotts, 1986), loss of flexibility (Adriaenssens, Eggermont, Pyck, Boeckx, & Gilles, 1988), and problems associated with recovery from surgery (Wolfer, Gaynard, Goldberger, Laidley, & Thompson, 1988). For some individuals, secondary disabilities are more limiting than the original condition, again showing the importance of leisure activity involvement.

Other studies report on physical benefits from specific recreational activities. Depending on the nature of the activity and the sample group, results cover a wide range of physical improvements. Among these studies are Brock (1988), who reported improved physical arm and leg coordination from a horseback riding program; Yoder, Nelson, and Smith (1989), who found improved range of motion for older adults through a cooking group; Rothe, Kohl, and Mansfield (1990), who documented increased work tolerance and decreased heart rate following a running and swimming program for children who were asthmatic; and Cutler Riddick (1985), who demonstrated that an in-home aquarium program reduced the diastolic blood pressure of elderly individuals. Better health ratings are predicted by a more positive leisure mood, more engagement in leisure, less negative attitude to leisure, and higher educational status (Cassidy, 1996).

The physiological benefits associated with leisure participation, particularly in more physically engaging activities, are many. Among those reported in the literature are:

- Reduction of numerous health problems such as high blood pressure, heart disease, and premature morbidity
- Improved physical health indicators, such as bone density, heart rate, and joint mobility
- Potential counteragent to lifestyle choices, such as smoking and obesity
- Reduction of secondary disabilities, such as decubiti and urinary tract infections
- Higher levels of reported self-efficacy, social support, perceived freedom, and intrinsic motivation
- Improved general health as a factor in perceived quality of life and life satisfaction

Emotional and Psychological Health and Leisure

Emotional well-being is an important component of overall quality of life and well-being, and is not simply at the other end of the continuum from mental illness. Keyes (2002) defined mental health as "positive functioning [that] consists of six dimensions of psychological well-being: self-acceptance, positive relations with others, personal growth, purpose in life, environmental mastery, and autonomy" (p. 209). Keyes indicated that mentally healthy individuals are seen as "flourishing" while those with mental illnesses seem to "languish in life," and that an individual's personal perception and evaluation of his or her own life in terms of affective states and psychological and social functioning determined a person's level of mental health (Keyes, 2002). An individual flourishes when the individual feels high levels of well-being, is filled with positive emotion, and functions well emotionally and socially (Keyes, 2002).

Fredrickson and Joiner (2002) noted that positive emotions (their term for flourishing) created an upward spiral of future positive emotions and heightened the individual's sense of **stress-coping.** They noted that the opposite effect (languishing) also was demonstrated, that depressive affect and narrowed, pessimistic thinking affect each other reciprocally, leading to ever-worsening negative emotions, eventually leading to depression.

> *Although an isolated experience of positive emotion is unlikely to increase emotional well-being or longevity, the broaden-and-build theory predicts that positive emotions accumulate and compound. The psychological broadening sparked by one positive emotion increases the odds that an individual will find positive in subsequent events and experience additional positive emotions. The upward spiral can, over time, build psychological resources and optimize people's lives. (p. 175)*

Leisure can provide both the context and experiences necessary to improve psychological and emotional well-being. Leisure can be an important mediator in improving self-definitions and understanding, as well as serve a crucial function for stress release and anxiety reduction. Individuals often participate in leisure for its psychological benefits more than for its physical or social benefits.

"The relationship between leisure and psychological well-being or mental health has generally concluded that a positive correlation exists. . . . The suggestion is that constructive use of leisure time, regardless of the type of activity pursued, may help to cope with stress in other life domains" (Cassidy, 1996, p. 78). In addition, Cassidy noted that another interpretation may be that constructive use of leisure time may reflect a style of cognitive appraisal and coping that is also effective in dealing with stress in other areas of life. "The beneficial effect would appear to depend on having a positive attitude towards what one defines as leisure time, to tend to engage in some form of enjoyable behaviors during that time and to gain some positive affect from that engagement" (Cassidy, 1996, p. 78). Those who experience positive affect during leisure feel healthier, less distressed, less depressed, less anxious, less hostile, and generally happier.

Interestingly enough, it has also been found that the opposite is true. People may actually feel unwell away from work (sometimes called the "weekend headache"), a phenomenon in which the individual does not feel positively about his or her leisure time, tends to not use it very well, and feels depressed or anxious as a result (Cassidy, 1996). Those who experience a negative mood during leisure, who engage in fewer leisure activities, and who have a strong negative attitude toward leisure experience the greatest levels of distress.

Iwasaki and Mannell (2000) found that beliefs that leisure contributes to empowerment and friendships directly contributed to the reduction of mental illness symptoms and promoted psychological well-being. In addition, stronger leisure friendship beliefs indirectly reduced mental illness symptoms and promoted psychological well-being by suppressing the level of stress experienced during the study period.

Iso-Ahola and Park (1996) found that leisure involvement also was related positively to mental health; as perceptions of perceived freedom and intrinsic motivation increased, perceived mental health also increased. As discussed in the next section, these researchers also found that having leisure friendships and companionship buffered against life stress and the adverse effects of stress on physical and mental health. In other words, if two people shared common life stressors, the one with more meaningful leisure companionships would be better able to cope with and adapt to life stress.

One of the psychological benefits described by Csikszentmihalyi and Kleiber (1991) is that leisure is a context in which to self-actualize, a term first coined by Maslow (1970). The authors felt that leisure provides ample opportunities for self-exploration of talents, capacities, and potential. Csikszentmihalyi and Kleiber (1991) felt that "leisure offers unique conditions for self-actualization that more constrained contexts do not, particularly as it allows an individual to broaden his or her experience while involved in culture-affirming practices . . . Involvement in an activity must be deep, sustained, and disciplined to contribute to an emerging sense of self" (p. 94).

Similarly, Haggard and Williams (1991) made a case for leisure impacting self-perceptions and self-affirmations. The concept of freedom of choice (to be discussed in more detail later in this chapter) is central to their assertions. Because leisure is associated with freedom of choice, the individual has ample opportunity to make choices and take responsibility for new identities and new experiences. In this sense, individuals can alter their perceptions of their abilities (either positively or negatively) through leisure, and can, in turn, control the experiences that help shape these self-perceptions. Haggard and Williams (1991, p. 112) explained: ". . . people strive to create identities for themselves. Leisure activities, primarily because they are unconstrained, may be particularly good vehicles for identity affirmation. People probably create given identities for themselves, partly by selecting themselves into given recreation activities which serve to bolster and/or furnish the identity images associated with that activity."

Self-determination is a closely related concept studied by Coleman and Iso-Ahola (1993). These authors maintained that an individual's sense of freedom, sense of control, and intrinsic motivation were instrumental in helping that person cope with stress. Leisure may be an ideal setting for such realizations, as most leisure experiences have similar attributes. As such, for many individuals leisure involvement serves as a "buffer" to stress and helps the individual cope better with daily life demands.

Searle, Mahon, Iso-Ahola, Sdrolias, and van Dyck (1995) found that a leisure education program was effective in increasing the perceived leisure control and leisure competence of a sample of elderly Canadians. Additionally, the program was effective in increasing life satisfaction and reducing leisure boredom. The authors concluded that the results showed that there was a positive improvement in psychological well-being as well as a potential positive impact on independent leisure behavior.

Cutler Riddick and Gonder Stewart (1994) found similar results in a study of older female retirees. They found that life satisfaction was directly affected by perceived health and leisure repertoire planning, and leisure activity involvement. In turn, leisure activity participation was affected by leisure repertoire planning, health, and income. In other words, leisure participation increased life satisfaction, an important aspect of psychological well-being.

In another vein, Kleiber, Hutchinson, and Williams (2002) noted that leisure involvement improved coping with and adjustment to negative life events. They suggested that leisure plays four important roles:

- Leisure activities, often offering immediate distraction and "distance," may buffer the impact of negative life events.

- Leisure activities, providing temporary relief and escape, buffer the impact of negative life events by generating optimism and hope about the future.

- Leisure activities buffer the impact of negative life events by aiding the reconstruction of a life story that is continuous with the past, providing "normalcy" in times of disruption.

- Leisure activities may be used in the wake of negative life events as vehicles of personal transformation to attain new goals and head in new directions.

Wankel and Berger (1990, 1991) reported on a number of studies that found that exercise and physical activity reduced anxiety. In studies of individuals in both non-psychiatric and psychiatric environments, the authors reported that exercise, such as noncompetitive, aerobic, individual, and rhythmic physical activity, was demonstrated repeatedly to lower both state and trait anxiety. Berger, Friedman, and Eaton (1988) reported research results that showed jogging and the relaxation response as more effective in reducing anxiety than group discussion and interaction. These authors also found that these activities were more effective for women than men.

Wankel and Berger (1991) also reported very similar research results for physical activity and depression reduction. Studies have shown that exercise reduces the occurrence, severity, and persistence of depression. Although the results are consistent, it is unknown whether the reduction is due to physiological, psychological, or cognitive mechanisms.

Driscoll (1976) found physical exertion and positive mental images effective in reducing anxiety. This author indicated "sufficient exertion can partially exhaust and inhibit the capacity for further anxiety arousal" (p. 88). Long (1984) reported that while aerobic conditioning and stress-inoculation programs were effective in reducing self-reported anxiety and increasing self-efficacy, activity participation had the additional benefit of producing cardiovascular fitness effects.

According to Cassidy (1996), leisure may be one way of helping people cope with stress and improve their perceived health. Teaching positive attitudes and encouraging engagement in a structured leisure program are important for the development of coping and health. Engagement in and attitude toward leisure may be a useful indicator of levels of both stress and health, and also of coping (Cassidy, 1996).

Ulrich, Dimberg, and Driver (1990, 1991) discussed the psychophysiological benefits of leisure, particularly those occurring in the natural environment. Paramount in this discussion was the contribution of natural environments (such as parks) to reduce stress. The authors stated that outdoor environments provide contexts that help individuals achieve greater control through active coping, experience temporary escape from daily problems and tribulations, exert physical energies, and become exposed to the therapeutic effects of nature.

In summary, the above research studies found evidence of the following psychological benefits of leisure participation:

- Improved self-exploration, self-identification, and self-actualization
- Improved opportunities for planning, making choices, and taking responsibility

- Improved opportunities for expression of freedom, control, and intrinsic motivation
- Improved ability to prevent, manage, and cope with stress
- Improved ability to adjust to and be less distressed by negative life events
- Decreased symptoms of anxiety and depression
- Improved quality of life, life satisfaction, and psychological well-being

Social Health and Leisure

Social well-being consists of at least two major concepts, **social adjustment** and **social support.** "Social adjustment is a combination of satisfaction with relationships (or problems), performance in social roles (including social participation and behavior), and adjustment to one's social environment. Social support is the number of contacts in one's social network, and overall satisfaction with those contacts" (Larson, 1997, p. 20).

Social behavior is the reciprocal exchange of responses between two or more individuals (Gaylord-Ross & Haring, 1987). Most of these interactions for children and adults happen during leisure time. Leisure is largely a social phenomenon (Kelly, 1983; Samdahl, 1992). As such, leisure plays an important role in the development of social skills and in the interplay of social exchanges. Leisure helps build social support networks and perceived social support (Iso-Ahola & Park, 1996). Connections or relationships between individuals may be strengthened and tested during leisure experiences. In fact, a great deal of relationship building occurs during leisure for most individuals. In addition, perceived social support, the level at which an individual feels cared for and attended to by significant others, often is displayed during leisure. Leisure, then, plays a vital role in the development, continuance, and enhancement of social relationships. And social support networks are vital to an individual's health, wellness, and quality of life.

Iso-Ahola and Park (1996) reported that a greater degree of leisure companionship reduced symptoms of depression, and improved mental and physical health. The overall relationships they found were clear: the higher the life stress, the lower the perceived health; the higher the leisure friendship, leisure companionship, intrinsic motivation, and perceived freedom, the higher the perceived health. They summarized that the buffering effects of social leisure are robust and important in order for individuals to maintain physical and mental health during times of life stress.

Coleman and Iso-Ahola (1993) stated that leisure-related social support and beliefs about self-determination act as buffers against stress and help individuals maintain health. For example, when individuals feel cared for and believe they have adequate support when needed (social support) and believe their actions are self-determined, freely chosen, or are autonomous (self-determination or self-efficacy), they handle stress better and have higher rates of perceived health. That is, participation in leisure that is highly social in nature promotes social support, which in turn reduces perceptions of stress.

Iwasaki and Mannell (2000) found that when individuals believe their leisure friendships lend social support, esteem support, tangible aid, and/or informational support from friends, they are better able to cope with stress. They also found that individuals often use leisure as a means to cope with stress by invoking companionship, palliative coping, and/or mood enhancement.

O'Hara, De Souza, and Ide (2002) analyzed the top priorities for self-care of individuals with multiple sclerosis in the United Kingdom. They found that for these individuals, social life/social networks (ranked number 3), exercise (number 8), and leisure (number 9), were among the highest priorities ⁀at individuals actually implemented in their own personal self-care.

Vandercook (1991) concluded from a research study on individuals with severe impairments that leisure activities may provide an ideal environment in which to learn, practice, and extend social skills, such as cooperation. This research study demonstrated that following instruction and mastery, individuals with disabilities generalized these social skills to leisure activity interactions with peers without disabilities.

Gaylord-Ross and Haring (1987) found that programs in which individuals with disabilities were taught to initiate with peers without disabilities were more successful than programs that taught individuals without disabilities to initiate. In addition, research showed that these programs increased independence, probability of successful interaction, frequency of interaction, and the social image of individuals with disabilities. In addition to finding that inclusionary settings (versus segregated settings) increased social contacts, the authors found that leisure provided more normalized and relaxed settings for social interactions to occur.

Orthner and Mancini's (1990, 1991) review of research literature suggested that leisure plays a significant role in the development and maintenance of family. For example, they documented research that showed that husbands and wives who shared leisure activities reported the highest marital satisfaction levels. They reported a similar relationship for families who spent time together through shared leisure experiences.

Leisure provides an ideal context for social exchanges. Thus, leisure provides an opportunity for a number of social benefits to be realized. Those documented in the above literature include:

- Development, practice, and application of social interaction skills
- Development, maintenance, and use of social support networks
- Improved ability to handle stress due to higher perceived levels of physical and mental health
- Creation and nurturing of relationships with significant others
- Improved interaction with and acceptance by individuals without disabilities
- Improved familial relationships

Leisure and Life Satisfaction

It is likely that reciprocal relations of causality exist, in that those who feel healthier and happier will be more likely to engage in leisure activities and feel positively toward leisure, and those who engage in and have positive attitudes toward leisure are likely to feel happier and healthier (Cassidy, 1996; Iso-Ahola, 1997) and report higher life satisfaction (Drummond, Parker, Gladman, & Logan, 2001; Edgington, Jordan, DeGraaf, & Edgington, 1998; Parker, Gladman, & Drummond, 1997).

"Leisure participation can affect and be affected by life satisfaction or well-being variables. Leisure, in fact, can be an important component contributing to the daily well-being of an individual" (Edgington, Jordan, DeGraaf, & Edgington, 1998, p. 8). Kinney and Coyle (1992) reported that for adults with physical disability, leisure satisfaction was the most significant predictor of overall life satisfaction, explaining 42 percent of the variance in life satisfaction scores.

Caldwell, Smith, and Weissinger (1992) found that college students with high levels of participation in a variety of leisure activities experienced higher rates of perceived physical, mental, and social health, and reported higher levels of leisure and life satisfaction. A curious finding of this study was that individuals who were involved in sports, entertainment, and adventure activities were more likely to report better perceived physical health, individuals involved in social activities and competitive sports perceived better mental health, and individuals involved in social, adventure, entertainment, nature, and competitive activities were higher in perceived social health. Conversely, Weissinger (1995) reported a distinct relationship between boredom in leisure and negative perceptions of physical and mental health.

Emami, Benner, Lipson, and Ekman (2000) conducted an interesting study of elderly Iranians and reported on their perceptions of health and life balance. The researchers presented five major themes from their personal interviews. First, health may be an overall goal in the lives of many individuals; its relationship to being able to function and carry out roles and responsibilities is important. Second, health is perceived as continuity and balance in life; continuity and balance occur when a person has a well-functioning social network in combination with mental strength that enables the person to relax and not be overly anxious. Third, health is experienced as peace between body and mind—health is a harmonic, holistic balance in which body and mind mutually respond to each other. Fourth, on the contrary, illness and disease are experienced as the discontinuity and imbalance of life forces. When balance and continuity are interrupted, a sense of dissatisfaction and unease often was accompanied by a sense of physical and mental distress. Fifth, these older adults assumed that disease was a natural part of growing older. In fact, they expressed a considerable degree of tolerance and acceptance of disease and pain, assuming that the person had sufficient inner strength (mental) and outer resources (well-functioning social life) to deal with them.

The researchers summarized the findings of their study thus:

Disease or physical illness is one reason, but not the only reason, for feeling ill. Most participants considered themselves healthy if they experienced unity within themselves and between themselves and others. Disease is just one component among many that may disrupt the experience of health. Health is perceived as a sense of well-being, can be achieved in spite of disease, and can be disrupted even in the absence of disease. Participants acknowledged the strong relationship between the mind and body within the environment, a holistic conception similar to various non-Western medical systems. . . . A holistic perspective takes into consideration [an] individual's physical conditions as well as their cultural, social, economic, and psychological situations. A holistic definition of health is based on a person's well-being which, for these Iranian elders, includes a sense of balance, coherence, social interactions, belonging, and continuity. (Emami, Benner, Lipson, & Ekman, 2000, p. 822)

Siegenthaler (1997) concluded that because leisure participation enhances physical, emotional and psychological, and social health, all individuals should have opportunities to experience meaningful leisure of their choice. She also noted that leisure professionals, including therapeutic recreation specialists, can promote leisure participation in three ways: (a) provide leisure education to help individuals discover leisure opportunities and options, (b) work to remove perceived and actual leisure constraints and barriers for all populations, and (c) seek to effectively communicate the benefits of leisure experiences and help individuals prioritize leisure within their lifestyles.

The next chapter will explore leisure education as one aspect of therapeutic recreation services. Box 1.1 lists several barriers to meaningful leisure that are experienced by adults. These examples will be used throughout the text to discuss the basis of therapeutic recreation programming. Box 1.2 provides examples of benefits or outcomes of therapeutic recreation services, also foundational information for therapeutic recreation service delivery.

Clearly, the relationships between health, wellness, and life functioning are important, and must take into consideration a person's cultural, social, and historical backgrounds. The benefits of leisure involvement are many and varied. In totality, the documented benefits point to the importance and impact of leisure on the lives of all individuals. The research in this area is rich and yet still developing. The discussion of benefits is included to highlight the concept that *leisure involvement is an important aspect of health, wellness, and quality of life.* Leisure participants as well as health and human service providers value these outcomes and many others.

Therapeutic recreation services have much to offer individuals in developing their leisure lifestyle and improving their psychological, physical, and social well-being. The focus on a satisfying and health-producing leisure pattern is exclusive to therapeutic recreation services, but it's vitally complementary to the overall health and rehabilitation mission of most health care and human service agencies. The next section expands on the notion of an independent leisure lifestyle, which forms the foundation for the Leisure Ability Model of therapeutic recreation service provision.

The Concept of Leisure Lifestyle

The Leisure Ability Model, as used in this text to explain therapeutic recreation services, is based upon several notions related to leisure behavior. One notion is that play, recreation, and leisure experiences are important aspects of human existence. Every individual has the right to fulfilling, meaningful, and satisfying leisure experiences. Leisure provides the context in which people may experience such things as challenge, social engagement, mastery, choice, individual expression, competence, and self-awareness. Leisure experiences provide opportunities to seek out numerous psychological, physical, and social benefits (some of which were discussed in the previous sections) that affect an individual's quality of life and life satisfaction. It is recognized that these benefits and methods of seeking them may change throughout the course of one's lifetime. "Because it is freely chosen, the leisure experience can contribute in a unique way to growth and development throughout one's life. Yet, during our lifetimes the activities we enjoy and participate in change. These changes are due in part to the development process that is part of the human experience" (Edgington

> **Box 1.1   Typical Leisure Barriers to Adult Leisure Behavior**
>
> Attitude that leisure is not important
>
> Lack of planning time or skills devoted to leisure
>
> Inability to make leisure-related decisions
>
> Fear of entering new situations or facilities
>
> Lack of leisure and recreation skills
>
> Lack of motivation to seek new alternatives
>
> Inappropriate social skills
>
> Lack of internal locus of control
>
> Concepts of "acceptable" age-related adult leisure behavior
>
> Lack of knowledge of recreation facilities and events
>
> Lack of experience in seeking leisure information
>
> Refusal to take responsibility for personal leisure
>
> Perceived inability to effect personal change
>
> Lack of financial means
>
> Limited knowledge of leisure opportunities
>
> Lack of reliable transportation
>
> Lack of ability to establish leisure as a priority
>
> Lack of lifelong leisure skills
>
> Negative feelings associated with playing instead of working
>
> Too tired to play
>
> Lack of a sense of competence in relation to leisure
>
> Lack of spontaneity; overplanning
>
> Decrease in time (real or perceived) available for leisure
>
> Limited physical ability
>
> Inability to control anger
>
> Fear of rejection
>
> Lack of personal hygiene skills
>
> Inability to appropriately manage emotions
>
> Inability to plan for leisure expenses
>
> Inability to manage time
>
> Lack of knowledge of transportation options
>
> Inability to attend to task
>
> Lack of physical coordination
>
> Decreased mobility due to disability or distance
>
> Lack of awareness of personal abilities and strengths
>
> Inability to plan for leisure events
>
> Lack of leisure partners
>
> Inability to manage stress

et al., 1998, p. 138). Parallel to their peers without disabilities, individuals with disabilities and/or illnesses are entitled to a meaningful life existence that includes satisfying recreation and leisure experiences. They also are entitled to modify their lifestyle, activities, and the meanings derived from involvement similarly to their peers without disabilities.

Individuals express a lifestyle through the daily and lifetime choices they make about clothes, activities, living arrangements and environments, religious or spiritual beliefs, health practices, social behaviors, etc. The totality of these decisions creates the individual's lifestyle (Edgington et al., 1998). Not surprisingly, leisure researchers

---

**Box 1.2   Typical Benefits or Outcomes
of Therapeutic Recreation Services**

Increased emotional control

Improved physical condition

Decreased disruptive behavior in group situations

Improved short- and long-term memory

Decreased confusion and disorientation

Decreased symptoms of anxiety and depression

Improved mobility in community environments and situations

Improved health indicators, such as bone density, heart rate, and joint mobility

Improved coping and adaptation skills

Increased awareness of barriers to leisure

Improved ability to prevent, manage, and cope with stress

Improved adjustment to disability and illness

Improved understanding of importance of leisure to balanced lifestyle

Improved communication among family members

Improved intrinsic motivation to participate in meaningful leisure activities

Increased ability to use assertiveness skills in a variety of social situations

Improved abilities for planning, making choices, and taking responsibility

Improved ability to locate leisure partners for activity involvement

Improved knowledge of agencies and facilities that provide recreation services

Greater belief in ability to produce positive outcomes in leisure

Improved knowledge of leisure opportunities in the community

Increased life and leisure satisfaction

Increased ability to develop and maintain social support networks

Adapted from Coyle, Kinney, Shank, & Riley, 1991 and Peterson & Stumbo, 2000.

---

and writers believe that an individual's "leisure lifestyle" is an important component of each person's overall lifestyle, not only in terms of its relative "slice of life" or *quantity* but also in its potential for improving the *quality* of a person's overall lifestyle (Mannell & Kleiber, 1997; Veal, 1989, 1993).

> *It is clear . . . that one cannot gain health benefits from leisure if one has not discovered leisure or uses it negatively, either by maintaining a sedentary lifestyle and/or by resorting to such health-damaging behaviours as drug use. Active leisure lifestyle, on the other hand, promotes health because participation in various leisure activities is geared towards seeking intrinsic rewards through use of one's cognitive, physical, and social skills. It is based on the principle of "use it or lose it." (Iso-Ahola, 1997, p. 135)*

Development, maintenance, and expression of an appropriate leisure lifestyle for individuals with disabilities and/or illnesses can be established as an area of human need and thus as an area for professional service. Therapeutic recreation has been established as the professional field of service that fulfills this need. Because many individuals with disabilities and/or illnesses may experience greater barriers to their leisure, therapeutic recreation is a necessary service to help reduce, eliminate, or overcome these barriers. The purpose of therapeutic recreation services is to help individuals with disabilities and/or illnesses develop, make choices about, and participate in a leisure lifestyle that may ultimately lead to a higher quality of life through increased physical health, emotional well-being, and social connections.

Central to this statement of purpose is the concept of leisure lifestyle. Within this conceptualization of therapeutic recreation, leisure lifestyle has a specific definition that provides understanding of the total approach as well as direction for program planning. Peterson (1981, p. 1) defined **leisure lifestyle** in the following way:

> *Leisure lifestyle [is] the day-to-day behavioral expression of one's leisure-related attitudes, awareness, and activities revealed within the context and composite of the total life experience.*

Leisure lifestyle implies that an individual has sufficient skills, knowledges, attitudes, and abilities to participate successfully in and be satisfied with leisure and recreation experiences that are incorporated into his or her individual life pattern. Box 1.3 gives a partial list of skills, knowledges, attitudes, and abilities that are necessary for leisure participation. An essential aspect of leisure lifestyle is the focus on day-to-day behavioral expression. This implies that leisure lifestyle is a routine engaged in as part of the individual's daily existence. "Leisure occurs in the minute-to-minute interactions of daily living" (Edgington et al., 1998, p. 120).

The quality and nature of one's leisure lifestyle may vary, but the fact remains that each person has one. Traditional and nontraditional leisure activities and expressions are an ongoing aspect of living. Daily actions thus can be used to describe and characterize the essence of an individual's unique leisure lifestyle. Additionally, the leisure lifestyle of a person cannot be viewed independently of all other actions. Other choices within the person's daily existence (for example, work, school, religion, family, friends) interface with the individual's leisure lifestyle. Likewise, the individual's leisure lifestyle is influenced by collective and accumulated life experiences. These participation and satisfaction levels ultimately speak to a person's quality of life and happiness.

Thus when the purpose of therapeutic recreation is stated as facilitating "the development, maintenance, and expression of an appropriate leisure lifestyle," it is implying a significant contribution. The improvement of the quality of an individual's life through a focus on the leisure component is much more complex than the provision of enjoyable activity or the delivery of some segmented therapy utilizing activity as the medium. Therapeutic recreation calls for a thorough understanding of the leisure lifestyle concept and the design of appropriate and comprehensive services that can be used to intervene in the lives of people in an influential and positive way.

The three areas of therapeutic recreation service delivery (functional intervention, leisure education, and recreation participation) that are implemented to accomplish these goals will be discussed more fully in the next chapter. First, it is necessary to present background concepts that provide a foundation for the Leisure Ability Model. These four concepts are: (a) perceived freedom and personal choice; (b) intrinsic motivation, (c) self-efficacy, internal locus of control, and causal attribution; and (d) optimal experiences.

Concepts Related to Leisure Behavior

While the Leisure Ability Model, through functional intervention, leisure education, and recreation participation services, provides specific information on service delivery content and outcomes, its underlying basis stems from these four areas so critical to leisure satisfaction and enjoyment, that is, a successful leisure lifestyle. Each of these four areas will be reviewed according to their relationship to the Leisure Ability Model approach to therapeutic recreation service delivery.

Perceived Freedom and Personal Choice

One of the foundational concepts of leisure behavior is perceived freedom (Iso-Ahola, 1997; Kelly, 1996; Mannell & Kleiber, 1997). This concept goes beyond a simplistic reduction or elimination of barriers to creating an environment in which the individual feels he or she has the opportunity to make and follow through on personal choices. **Perceived freedom** means that the activity or setting is more likely to be viewed as leisure when individuals attribute their reasons for participation to themselves (i.e., actions are freely chosen) rather than determined externally by someone else or by circumstances (Mannell & Kleiber, 1997). "Freedom is not the absence of limit or constraint, but involves some element of self-determination" (Kelly, 1996, p. 23).

> *Freedom implies that individuals have choice or perceive they have choice in the pursuit of leisure experiences. Freedom also suggests that an individual is free of the obligations that might arise from family, work, or home activities or of the constraints that may inhibit participation or involvement. Freedom is an abstraction. . . . To be free means to be able to act without the interference or control of another, to choose or to act in accordance with one's own will. Freedom also often implies the absence of external constraints or compulsions on an individual to act in a prescribed manner (Edgington et al., 1998, pp. 33–34).*

The Leisure Ability Model for therapeutic recreation services relies heavily on the concepts of perceived freedom and of personal choice. Inherent to and parallel with the concepts of intrinsic motivation, internal locus of control, and personal causality, freedom and choice imply that the individual has sufficient skills, knowledges, and attitudes to be able to have options from which to choose, as well as the skills and desires to make appropriate choices. Lee and Mobily (1988) stated that therapeutic recreation services should build skills and provide participants with options for participation. The Leisure Ability Model emphasizes content areas that help clients build skills in a variety of areas that, in turn, will allow them options for future independent leisure functioning.

Lee and Mobily (1988) extended the idea of choice when examining the notions of "freedom from" and "freedom to." Earlier in this chapter it was stated that many individuals without disabilities face barriers to their leisure experiences. Sometimes this becomes an "if only" scenario. The individual feels that he or she would have more fun "if only" he or she had more money, more time, fewer constraints, etc. These individuals express the need for more "freedom from" obligations and responsibilities. Individuals with disabilities, however, often have the opposite, but equally important, experience—needing "freedom to" participate. That is, having the requisite skills to participate, knowing where and with whom to participate, being able to get to a recreation facility at one's own convenience, etc. Leisure choices are only valid when the individual has the knowledges, skills, abilities, and resources to consider, make, and implement decisions freely. The role of therapeutic recreation services is clear in assisting the individual in expanding personal choice. "Freedom from" constraints and "freedom to" exercise options provide further basis for the need for therapeutic recreation services to be provided to individuals with disabilities and/or illnesses.

Intrinsic Motivation

A second cornerstone to leisure behavior is intrinsic motivation (Iso-Ahola, 1997; Iwasaki & Mannell, 2000; Mannell & Kleiber, 1997). Deci (1975) and Deci and Ryan (1985) first presented the notion of intrinsic motivation. Mannell and Kleiber (1997) applied the theory of intrinsic motivation to leisure behavior and noted its relationship to freedom of choice and self-determination.

> *Activities, settings, and experiences construed as leisure are likely to be perceived as providing opportunities for the development of competence, self-expression, self-development, or self-realization. When people engage in activities and settings that provide these opportunities, they are said to be intrinsically motivated. This attribute is clearly not completely independent of the freedom of choice attribute; self-determination is theorized to be an essential ingredient of intrinsic motivation. (Mannell & Kleiber, 1997, pp. 109–110)*

All individuals are intrinsically motivated toward behavior in which they can experience competence and self-determination. Thus, individuals seek experiences of incongruity (that is, slightly above their perceived skill level) or challenges in which they can master the situation, reduce the incongruity, and show competence. This process is continual, and through skill acquisition and mastery, produces feelings of satisfaction, competence, and control. "[I]nvolvement in leisure pursuits often occurs because participants are moved from within and not because they are influenced by external factors. This results in personal feelings of satisfaction, enjoyment, and gratification" (Edgington et al., 1998, p. 34).

> *The power and influence of intrinsic motivation has been demonstrated in many areas of human behavior, and it is an important feature of meaningful and beneficial leisure. Creating our own leisure or helping others experience meaningful leisure through program and service delivery or counseling and education is in large part dependent on fostering intrinsic motivation. If we are to facilitate intrinsic motivation in leisure pursuits, we must be sensitive to the social situation in which participation occurs and individual differences in how people react to those social circumstances. Attention to what participants are perceiving and feeling is also necessary. (Iwasaki & Mannell, 2000, p. 303)*

Iso-Ahola (1997) reported that intrinsic motivation correlates positively with both psychological and physical health. In addition, those individuals who "seek" intrinsic rewards through their leisure are healthier than those who choose to "escape" through passive and unrewarding leisure.

> *Escapism through passive leisure is psychologically troublesome because it leads to bore-dom, which in turn feeds into apathy and depression. It has been found that lack of awareness of leisure and its potential in one's life is the single most important factor con-tributing to boredom in leisure (Iso-Ahola & Weissinger, 1987). In other words, failure cognitively to realize or personally discover leisure is a significant antecedent to leisure boredom. Other factors significantly contributing to it are: poor leisure attitude or ethic, high work ethic, lack of leisure skills, barriers to leisure participation, and poor self-motivation in general (as a personality trait). These findings are important for two rea-sons. First, they demonstrate that leisure in itself is a negative thing for many people, because it (or, at least, a failure to discover leisure) leads to boredom and subsequently to depression. Second, the fact that lack of awareness, concurrently coupled with poor leisure attitude and a high work ethic, is the most significant contributor to leisure boredom reflects the extent to which leisure's influence on health is psychological. (pp. 134–135)*

For therapeutic recreation services, the notion of **intrinsic motivation** is impor-tant. As people seek meaning, enjoyment, and personal fulfillment from their leisure, the chances of doing so are increased when motivation comes from within and they are not forced or compelled to participate. Helping individuals find and seek such experiences is an important function of the therapeutic recreation specialist. In some cases individuals may need to experience several types of opportunities and activities before they find ones that "speak" to them as individuals and promote a sense of com-petence and self-efficacy.

Self-Efficacy, Locus of Control, and Causal Attribution

Self-efficacy or **self-determination** or **competence** is the central or pervasive per-sonal belief that an individual can exercise some control over his or her own func-tioning and over environmental events to reach some desired end (Bandura, 1997, 2001; Warr, 1993). Efficacy beliefs are foundational to the individual's sense of com-petence and control. Individuals with higher self-efficacy believe their choices and actions will affect the outcome of a situation; those with lower self-efficacy believe their choices and actions have little relationship to the outcome.

> *[E]fficacy beliefs affect adaptation and change not only in their own right, but through their impact on other determinants. . . . Such beliefs influence whether people think pes-simistically or optimistically and in ways that are self-enhancing or self-hindering. Effi-cacy beliefs play a central role in the self-regulation of motivation through goal challenges and outcome challenges to undertake, how much effort to expend in the endeavor, how long to persevere in the face of obstacles and failures, and whether failures are motivating or demoralizing. . . . A strong sense of coping efficacy reduces vulnerability to stress and depression in taxing situations and strengthens resiliency to adversity. . . . Efficacy beliefs also play a key role in shaping the courses lives take by influencing the types of activities*

and environments people choose to get into. Any factor that influences choice behavior can profoundly affect the direction of personal development. This is because the social influences operating in selected environments continue to promote certain competencies, values, and interests long after the decisional determinant has rendered its inaugurating effect. Thus, by choosing and shaping their environments, people can have a hand in what they become. (Bandura, 2001, p. 9)

Bandura (1997) explained that information sources for self-efficacy include: (a) vicarious experience (i.e., observing someone else perform the same or a similar task), (b) performance accomplishments (i.e., succeeding at the same or a similar task), (c) verbal persuasion (e.g., "you were successful at x, you can be successful at y"), and (d) physiological arousal (i.e., indications that the body is ready and able to accomplish the task).

Bandura (1997) suggested that self-efficacy best generalizes or translates to other tasks when (a) the second task requires subskills similar to those of the original task (e.g., learning tennis after being successful at Ping-Pong), (b) coping skills are learned or improved (e.g., learning to persevere in the face of failure), (c) two tasks are seen as similar (e.g., asking for help from staff and from a stranger), (d) two tasks are learned simultaneously (e.g., chair transfers and bathtub transfers), and (e) the performance accomplishment is so great that it spreads to other tasks (e.g., learning to ride a bicycle for the first time).

Haworth (1997) noted that Iso-Ahola (1992) argues that leisure participation is an important contributor and developer of a sense of self-determination through providing opportunities to exercise personal control. Leisure experience, he contends, encourages the development, maintenance, and enhancement of people's beliefs that they have capacities to initiate actions, persist in them, and achieve successful outcomes, and that by providing opportunities for exercising personal control, leisure helps buffer against stressful life events. Edgington et al. (1998) expressed a similar notion: "Perceived competence refers to skills an individual believes he or she possesses that, in turn, relate to satisfying participation in leisure experiences. In other words, the perception of having skills and abilities necessary to successful participation leads to a satisfying leisure experience" (p. 34).

However, Bandura (2001) countered that not all individuals want control in that their perceptions of self-efficacy are such that they believe they might not be successful at a certain task or group of tasks.

The exercise of personal control often carries heavy responsibilities, stressors, and risks. People are not especially eager to shoulder the burdens of responsibility. All too often, they surrender control to their intermediaries in activities over which they can command direct influence. They do so to free themselves of the performance demands and onerous responsibilities that personal control entails. [Handing over control] can be used in ways that promote self-development or impede the cultivation of personal competencies. In the latter case, part of the price [of handing over control] is a vulnerable security that rests on the competence, power, and favors of others. (p. 12)

An **internal locus of control** implies that the individual has the orientation that he or she is responsible for the behavior and outcomes he or she produces, and an **external locus of control** means the person believes that luck or chance or others are responsible for the outcomes (Iso-Ahola, 1980; Mannell & Kleiber, 1997). Typically, individuals with an internal locus of control take responsibility for their decisions and the consequences of their decisions. A typical statement might be "I am responsible for my leisure choices." An individual with an external locus of control may make the statement "It's your fault I didn't do this right" and place responsibility, credit, or blame on other individuals. Obviously, an internal locus of control is important for the individual to feel self-directed or responsible, be motivated to continue to seek challenges, and develop a sense of self-efficacy or self-competence. Mannell and Kleiber (1997) noted that opportunities for choice and the person's desire for choice need to coincide.

> [T]o understand leisure behavior not only do the actual opportunities for choice *available in the leisure setting need to be considered, but also* individual differences in how much control and freedom *people typically feel they have in their lives. These individual differences may influence how people perceive the actual choice available to them, and consequently, it may modify their leisure experience. (p. 168)*

Personal causality or attribution implies that an individual believes he or she can affect a particular outcome (Iso-Ahola, 1980; Mannell & Kleiber, 1997). For instance, when an individual experiences success, he or she can attribute that success either to personal effort (personal causality), or to luck or chance (situational causality). An important aspect of the sense of accomplishment, competence, and control is the individual's interpretation of his or her personal contribution to the outcome. Without a sense of personal causation, the likelihood of the individual developing an internal locus of control is reduced. Haworth (1997) characterized leisure as an important contributor to internal locus of control, and believed that it may lead to enhanced mental health and well-being.

These three concepts relate to therapeutic recreation in that the ultimate goal of an individual's satisfying and independent leisure lifestyle entails being self-efficacious, having an internal locus of control, and feeling a sense of personal causality. To facilitate these perceptions, therapeutic recreation specialists must be able to design, implement, and evaluate a variety of activities that increase the person's individual competence and sense of control. In relation to leisure behavior, Peterson (1989) argued that this includes improving functional abilities, improving leisure-related attitudes, skills, knowledges, and abilities, and voluntarily engaging in self-directed leisure behavior (see Box 1.3). Thus, the three service areas of functional intervention, leisure education, and recreation participation are designed to teach specific skills to improve personal competence and a sense of accomplishment.

Optimal Experiences

A fourth, closely related, concept is that of optimal experiences or "flow" researched and popularized by Csikszentmihalyi (1990). For a person to get into "flow" or to achieve "optimal experiences," a number of elements must be present (Godbey, 1999). **Optimal experiences** include feelings of

- Intense involvement
- Clarity of goals and feedback

Box 1.3   Typical Attitudes, Knowledges, and Skills Necessary for Leisure Participation

Physical abilities that allow leisure participation

Appropriate emotional control and expression

Social abilities for interaction with self and others

Cognitive abilities for naming, reasoning, recalling, strategizing, associating

Valuing leisure as an important aspect of life

Decision-making, planning, problem-solving, and prioritizing abilities

Financial planning in relation to leisure

Communication and relationship-building skills

Health and hygiene skills

Awareness of personal abilities and attitudes

Access to leisure resources in the home and community

Typical and nontypical leisure activity skills

Social support for leisure participation and trying new experiences

Balance between being able to plan for and spontaneously participate in activities

Ability to try new experiences and activities

Taking personal responsibility for leisure

Seeking and utilizing information about leisure opportunities

Locating and securing transportation to leisure experiences

- Deep concentration
- Transcendence of self
- Lack of self-consciousness
- Loss of a sense of time
- Intrinsic rewarding experience
- A balance between challenge and skill (Csikszentmihalyi, 1990; Edgington et al., 1998; Haworth, 1997; Mannell & Kleiber, 1997)

Among the strongest of these are the match between the challenge presented by the activity and the skill level of the participant. When skill level is high and activity challenge is low, the individual is quite likely to be bored. When the skill level is low and the activity challenge is high, the individual is most likely to be anxious. When the skill level and activity challenge are identical or nearly identical (both low or both high), the individual is most able to achieve a state of concentration and energy expenditure that Csikszentmihalyi (1990) has labeled "flow." "In order for a success-ful leisure experience to occur, individuals must perceive themselves to have a degree

Lifestyle Report

Keep a journal for three to six days with your daily activities, including school, work, self-care, and leisure. With whom is your lifestyle most similar and dissimilar? How satisfied are you with the leisure portion of your lifestyle?

REFERENCES

Aaronson, N. K., Bullinger, M., & Ahmedzai, S. (1988). A modular approach to quality-of-life assessment in cancer clinical trials. *Recent Results in Cancer Research, 111,* 231–249.

Adriaenssens, P., Eggermont, E., Pyck, K., Boeckx, W., & Gilles, B. (1988). The video invasion of rehabilitation. *Burns, 14,* 417–419.

Americans with Disabilities Act. (1990). Located at *http://www.eeoc.gov/laws/ada.html.*

Ardell, D. B. (1979). *High level wellness.* New York: Bantam.

Bandura, A. (1997). *Self-efficacy: The exercise of control.* New York: Freeman.

Bandura, A. (2001). Social cognitive theory: An agentic perspective. *Annual Review of Psychology, 52,* 1–26.

Berger, B. G., Friedman, E., & Eaton, M. (1988). Comparison of jogging, the relaxation response, and group interaction for stress reduction. *Journal of Sport and Exercise Psychology, 10*(4), 431–447.

Brock, B. J. (1988). Effect of therapeutic horseback riding on physically disabled adults. *Therapeutic Recreation Journal,* (3), 34–43.

Caldwell, L. L., Smith, E. A., & Weissinger, E. (1992). The relationship of leisure activities and perceived health of college students. *Society and Leisure, 15,* 545–556.

Cassidy, T. (1996). All work and no play: A focus on leisure time as a means for promoting health. *Counseling Psychology Quarterly, 9*(1), 77–90.

Coleman, D., & Iso-Ahola, S. E. (1993). Leisure and health: The role of social support and self-determination. *Journal of Leisure Research, 25,* 111–128.

Coyle, C. P., Kinney, W. B., Riley, B., & Shank, J. W. (1991). *Benefits of therapeutic recreation: A consensus view.* Philadelphia, PA: Temple University.

Csikszentmihalyi, M. (1990). *Flow: The psychology of optimal experience.* New York: Harper & Row.

Csikszentmihalyi, M., & Kleiber, D. A. (1991). Leisure and self-actualization. In Driver, B. L., Brown, P. J., & Peterson, G. L. *Benefits of leisure* (pp. 91–102). State College, PA: Venture Publishing Company.

Cutler Riddick, C. (1985). Health, aquariums, and the non-institutionalized elderly. In M. Sussman (Ed.), *Pets and the family* (pp. 63–173). New York: Haworth Press.

Cutler Riddick, C., & Gonder Stewart, D. (1994). An examination of the life satisfaction and importance of leisure in the lives of older female retirees: A comparison of blacks to whites. *Journal of Leisure Research, 26*(1), 75–88.

Deci, E. L. (1975). *Intrinsic motivation.* New York: Plenum Press.

Deci, E. L., & Ryan, R. M. (1985). *Intrinsic motivation and self-determination in human behavior.* New York: Plenum Press.

Driscoll, R. (1976). Anxiety reduction using physical exertion and positive images. *The Psychological Record, 26*(1), 87–94.

Drummond, A. E. R, Parker, C. J., Gladman, J. R. F., & Logan, P. A. (2001). Development and validation of the Nottingham Leisure Questionnaire (NLQ). *Clinical Rehabilitation, 15,* 647–656.

Edelman, C. L., & Mandle, C. L. (1994). *Health promotion throughout the life span.* St. Louis, MO: Mosby-Year Books.

Edgington, C. R., Jordan, D. J., DeGraaf, D. G., & Edgington, S. R. (1998). *Leisure and life satisfaction: Foundational perspectives* (2nd ed.). Boston: McGraw-Hill.

Edlin, G., Golanty, E., & McCormack Brown, K. (1999). *Health and wellness.* Sudbury, MA: Jones and Bartlett.

Emami, A., Benner, P. E., Lipson, J. G., & Ekman, S. (2000). Health and continuity and balance in life. *Western Journal of Nursing Research, 22*(7), 812–825.

Fredrickson, B. L., & Joiner, T. (2002). Positive emotions trigger upward spirals toward emotional well-being. *Psychological Science, 13*(2), 172–175.

Froelicher, V. F., & Froelicher, E. S. (1991). Cardiovascular benefits of physical activity. In Driver, B. L., Brown, P. J., & Peterson, G. L. *Benefits of leisure* (pp. 59–72). State College, PA: Venture Publishing Company.

Gaylord-Ross, R., & Haring, T. (1987). Social interaction research for adolescents with severe handicaps. *Behavioral Disorders, 12*(4), 264–275.

Godbey, G. (1999). *Leisure in your life: An exploration* (5th ed.). State College, PA: Venture Publishing Company.

Haggard, L. M., & Williams, D. R. (1991). Self-identity benefits of leisure activities. In Driver, B. L., Brown, P. J., & Peterson, G. L. *Benefits of leisure* (pp. 103–120). State College, PA: Venture Publishing Company.

Haworth, J. T. (1997). *Work, leisure and well-being.* New York: Routledge.

Hood, C. D., & Carruthers, C. P. (2002). Coping skills theory as an underlying framework for therapeutic recreation services. *Therapeutic Recreation Journal, 36*(2), 137–153.

Hurley, J. S. & Schlaadt, R. G. (1992). *The wellness lifestyle.* Guilford, CT: Dushkin Publishing Group.

Iso-Ahola, S. E. (1980). *The social psychology of leisure and recreation.* Dubuque, IA: Wm C. Brown Company Publishers.

Iso-Ahola, S. E. (1992). On the theoretical and empirical relationship between leisure and health. Paper presented at the International Conference on Leisure and Mental Health, Salt Lake City, UT.

Iso-Ahola, S. E. (1997). A psychological analysis of leisure and health. In J. T. Haworth (Ed.), *Work, leisure and well-being* (pp. 131–144). New York: Routledge.

Iso-Ahola, S. E., & Park, C. J. (1996). Leisure-related social support and self-determination as buffers of stress-illness relationship. *Journal of Leisure Research, 28*(3), 169–187.

Iso-Ahola, S.E., & Weissinger, E. (1987). Leisure and boredom. *Journal of Social and Clinical Psychology, 5,* 356–364.

Iwasaki, Y., & Mannell, R. C. (2000). Hierarchical dimensions of leisure stress coping. *Leisure Sciences, 22,* 163–181.

Kelly, J. R. (1983). *Leisure identities and interactions.* London: Allen & Unwin.

Illness and disability most often are referred to by given medical or psychiatric terms. These terms frequently result in stereotypic interpretations of abilities and limitations. In order to avoid inappropriate stereotyping, it appears beneficial to look at specific conditions relative to the actual limitation that the condition imposes on the individual in terms of physical, mental, social, or emotional functioning. These actual limitations then need to be analyzed for their impact on leisure functioning. It is this analysis and assessment that provides the rationale as well as the content for therapeutic recreation service.

At the current time, individuals with medical and psychiatric conditions are the primary clients involved in therapeutic recreation. However, there appear to be substantial and logical reasons for expansion of populations in the future. As leisure becomes more significant to society and claims a more central role in the lives of people, then leisure dysfunction may well appear as a major condition of importance. When and if that occurs, then any individual with problems or conditions that negatively impact leisure functioning may seek and receive specialized therapeutic recreation services. These services would be most likely delivered through existing recreation and leisure service agencies, community mental health centers, and various public and private counseling practices.

Therapeutic Recreation Service Settings

Any agency or center that serves individuals with limitations can be considered an appropriate setting for the inclusion of therapeutic recreation services. Therapeutic recreation is just one component of comprehensive services provided at a diversity of clinical, residential, and community facilities. Traditional examples of such settings would include:

- Mental health facilities, including outpatient day care, community mental health centers, and public and private psychiatric facilities or units
- Addiction treatment facilities, such as those for substance abuse or eating disorders
- Residential settings, such as group homes, half-way houses, assisted living, and shelters
- Centers and private and public facilities for people with developmental disabilities
- Physical rehabilitation centers or units, or subacute units
- General hospitals, with a variety of units such as pediatrics, cardiac care, burn units, or oncology
- Extended-care and long-term care health care facilities
- Public, not-for-profit recreation and leisure agencies
- Private, for-profit rehabilitation and vocational centers
- Special residential schools and centers serving such groups as individuals with visual impairments, hearing impairments, emotional and behavioral disorders, or severe multiple impairments
- Correctional centers and facilities, including adult and youth detention centers

---

Box 2.1   Therapeutic Recreation Services

Purpose: To facilitate the development, maintenance, and expression of an appropriate leisure lifestyle

Populations: Individuals with physical, mental, social, or emotional limitations

Process: Selection, development, implementation, and evaluation of goal-oriented services
>   Functional Intervention
>   Leisure Education
>   Recreation Participation

Settings: Treatment, residential, and community-based health and human service centers and recreation agencies

---

- Community-based recreation and special education facilities
- Year-round residential camps, such as those for individuals with emotional disturbances

In some settings, therapeutic recreation is only one aspect of a larger service offering. In others, therapeutic recreation is the only service offered.

Identifying all of the settings where therapeutic recreation takes place is difficult. One acknowledged problem is differentiation of the terms: setting, agency, and sponsorship. The purpose of this section is merely to identify the variety and diversity of settings that provide therapeutic recreation services. Box 2.1 outlines the purpose, populations, process, and settings within therapeutic recreation. The remaining sections of this chapter will describe in detail the Leisure Ability Model of therapeutic recreation service delivery.

The Leisure Ability Model

The Leisure Ability approach to therapeutic recreation defines and gives direction to the development and delivery of service to clients. The approach requires expansion and interpretation to enable operation. The Leisure Ability Model contains three major categories of service: (a) functional intervention, (b) leisure education, and (c) recreation participation. Each of these three service areas is based on distinct client needs and has specific purposes, expected behavior of clients, roles of the specialist, and targeted client outcomes. The model (Figure 2.2) is a graphic representation of the various therapeutic recreation services. Service purposes, roles of the therapeutic recreation specialist, and the concept of autonomy or choice for clients are portrayed. The model also attempts to illustrate the notion of a continuum, implying, at times, movement through the various service components. The model itself only represents those services that would be designed and implemented under the auspices of various agencies involved in the delivery of therapeutic recreation services. The ultimate goal of independent leisure involvement and lifestyle is beyond the parameters of the model. The overall anticipated outcome of therapeutic recreation service delivery is a

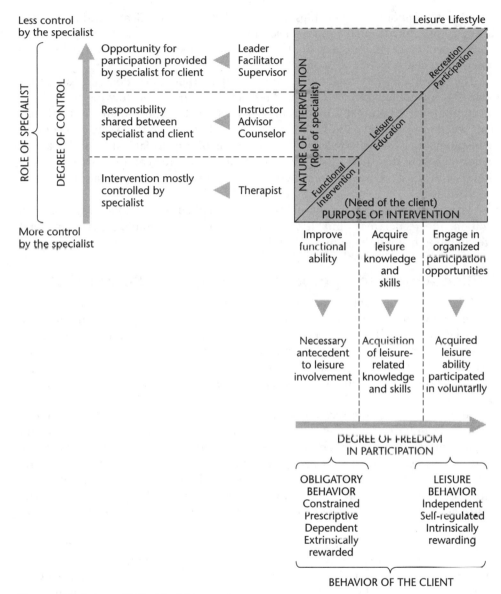

Figure 2.2 Leisure Ability Model.

satisfying leisure lifestyle—the independent functioning of the client in leisure experiences and activities of his or her choice. This, then, may lead to other psychological, physical, and social benefits that contribute to a person's overall quality of life, well-being, and life satisfaction.

Both advantages and difficulties are inherent in presenting a graphic representation or model of a multifaceted phenomenon. Very often a picture of a phenomenon or concept will make comprehension easier and more meaningful than will lengthy narrative descriptions. Relationships may be understood more clearly and movement through a process may make more sense. However, the difficulties of a programmatic model need to be mentioned so that the reader does not limit it to the two-dimensional characteristics of a page in a book.

The words chosen for a model are crucial in that space does not allow for extended explanations. Exact degrees of relationships on a static drawing are difficult to comprehend. Additionally, models may be presumed to encapsulate the total concept, when in reality models can, at best, offer a visual clue to the basics of a concept or phenomenon. We acknowledge the limitations of a pictorial model and ask that readers be aware that the various domains of therapeutic recreation services are very often not distinctly separate units of service, but, in fact, overlap or are conducted simultaneously.

Aspects of the model will be defined and described on the following pages. In addition, the reader may find that the model stimulates thought, discussion, and interpretation beyond the graphic illustration or the descriptions presented here.

A Client-Oriented Approach to Therapeutic Recreation

The Leisure Ability Model is based on the concept of identified client needs related to leisure involvement. Each of the three categories of service (functional intervention, leisure education, and recreation participation) addresses a specific and different need that clients with disabling conditions may have. Programs are developed based on the analysis of clients served by a specific agency. The nature of the agency and its mandate for service is also a consideration. A given agency usually will provide services in more than one category. For example, most public recreation departments will provide leisure education and recreation participation programs for individuals with disabilities and/or illnesses. Those who work in an inpatient, short-term psychiatric unit may find the most pressing client needs fall within functional intervention and leisure education. Those who work in a long-term health care facility will most likely find that their clients have leisure-related needs in all three categories of services. The principle remains: *the needs of the clients determine the nature of programs provided.* The nature of programs directs the content selected and the role of the therapeutic recreation specialist in that program.

A general analysis of clients served by a specific agency identifies the predominant areas of leisure-related client needs. This information provides the overall direction for the development of programs to be delivered. This basic program delivery structure then is developed and implemented. Individual client assessment techniques are selected and/or developed and used. Individual clients then can be placed in, or referred to, the specific programs that focus on their individual areas of need. This overall approach utilizes the concept that within a given agency, client needs usually cluster. Thus, programs can be developed related to these common areas. However, clients are assessed individually and appropriately placed within those programs that relate to their unique problems, areas for development, or needs for participation. This process represents the current state of the art, where therapeutic recreation services are most often delivered through group-oriented programs. Consequently, the ability to address client needs must be conceptualized within the constraints of high-client/low-staff ratios and group structures. It is, however, possible to identify common leisure-related areas of need, design programs to meet these needs, and individualize within this situation. Even agencies with high-staff/low-client ratios find that group programs are an appropriate and highly beneficial way to address certain areas of behavioral change and leisure development. Most recreation participation programs by intent are group oriented. Where one-on-one programming is possible, the same general principles and procedures of planning and implementation would be appropriate.

This approach addresses the need for individualized programming, which is a requirement within many agencies. The development of individual treatment plans, resident care plans, or education plans (or whatever individualized procedure is within a given agency) is simplified utilizing this approach. The initial conceptualization of client needs and the design of the basic service structure is the critical phase of the program development and delivery system.

A Word About the Term "Treatment"

Starting with the 2000 version of the Leisure Ability Model, the term "functional intervention" for the first component replaced the term "treatment." The major reason for this replacement was the changing nature of health and human services (including therapeutic recreation services). Treatment indicates any service that is: (a) based on client deficits, (b) designed and implemented to improve, reduce, or eliminate those deficits, and (c) targeted toward specific client outcomes as the result of participation in those programs. Thus, "treatment" means any one of a variety of services designed to bring about change in client behavior. This implies that functional intervention programs, leisure education programs, and, sometimes, recreation participation programs are "treatment" in that they are goal-oriented and implemented for the specific purpose of producing client outcomes. Thus, the name of the first component was changed to functional intervention, which focuses on the improvement of functional behaviors that are prerequisite to future leisure participation, and treatment now is used to encompass a wider range of services that focus on goal-oriented programs and client outcomes.

Depending on the setting, the terms *treatment, therapy, intervention,* or *rehabilitation* sometimes are used interchangeably to denote a specifically planned process to bring about desired positive change in behavior. The therapeutic recreation specialist should use these terms in the same ways as do other health and medical personnel. For the most part, health and human service professionals agree that the terms imply a process. This process involves: (a) an assessment of need; (b) a statement of the problem; (c) formulation of treatment goal(s); (d) design of a treatment plan; (e) implementation, monitoring, and progress reporting; and (f) designation of criteria for decision making regarding termination, continuation, or change. This procedure is a necessary aspect of the planning and conducting of therapeutic recreation functional intervention services as well.

Within most clinical settings, therapeutic recreation services are established in order to contribute to the treatment and rehabilitation mission of the agency. Within these settings, therapeutic recreation services must be compatible with the central focus of treatment as well as make a unique contribution related to the leisure needs of clients. The Leisure Ability Model provides an overall purpose for therapeutic recreation as well as specific definitions for the various categories of service. This information transferred to operational programs provides a strong rationale for, and understanding of, therapeutic recreation in any of the diverse clinical or community settings. Although the need for programs and the nature of the content and intervention may vary depending on the specific population served, the overall purpose of facilitating the development, maintenance, and expression of a successful leisure lifestyle appears to be appropriate for all populations served.

Functional Intervention as a Component of Therapeutic Recreation Service

The Leisure Ability philosophy provides a foundation from which functional intervention therapeutic recreation services can derive a logical and appropriate purpose. Simply stated, if independent leisure functioning is the overall purpose of therapeutic recreation services, then the functional intervention component can and should address functional behavioral areas that are prerequisite to, or a necessary part of, leisure involvement and lifestyle. Behavioral areas can be identified by using the commonly acknowledged domains of physical, mental/cognitive, emotional/affective, and social functioning. Each of these areas has obvious significance for leisure involvement. Deficits in these areas prevent the client from participating fully in recreation and leisure activities. Competence in each of these areas is prerequisite to the client's successful, daily involvement in leisure. In addition, these areas cut across all illnesses and disability classifications and thus are useful to a profession such as therapeutic recreation, which works with diverse populations in a variety of settings.

Functional abilities should be considered baseline abilities that are prerequisite to typical leisure behavior that most individuals without disabilities would possess. For example, a child with behavior disorders may have social skills deficits (hitting, kicking, scratching) to the degree that he or she cannot participate with others in a socially acceptable manner. Until these disruptive behaviors are minimized or replaced by appropriate social behaviors, the child will not be very successful in learning about or experiencing leisure. These deficits need to be reduced, at least to an acceptable minimal level, prior to the client's involvement with others. Another example might be seen in a physical medicine unit with an individual with a traumatic or acquired brain injury. This individual may have severe limitations in attention span. Until this person's attention span can be increased, it will be difficult for the person to learn or relearn recreation activities, especially those that involve rules, strategies, and specific modes of play. **Functional intervention services** help reduce functional limitations that prevent the individual from increasing leisure-related awareness, knowledge, skills, abilities, and involvement.

Examples of physical **functional abilities** include coordination, endurance, mobility, strength, hand-eye coordination, and other basic functions that are prerequisite to participation in leisure activities. Most individuals without impairments possess physical abilities to the degree that their participation in typical leisure is not hindered; the same may not always be true of individuals with disabilities and/or illnesses. Cognitive examples of functional abilities include memory, orientation, attention span, reading ability, ability to follow directions, and other mental functions that are prerequisite to leisure behavior. Again, most individuals of a certain age are expected to have basic cognitive abilities that would allow them to participate in most leisure activities; some client groups need to learn cognitive abilities or compensate for their absence. Examples of emotional or affective functional abilities include such things as anger management, emotional control, and emotional expression. The majority of individuals without disabilities are able to control and manage their emotions well enough to function in everyday life; some individuals with disabilities experience difficulty in this area. Social functional abilities include such targets as those fundamental behaviors that meet minimal social expectations. Society, in general, expects that people refrain from biting, kicking, and hitting others, and from screaming, spitting on others, and caressing strangers. Deficits in social functional abilities are represented by behaviors that are inappropriate for any individual under any circumstance. Baseline social skills may need to be taught to some client groups of therapeutic recreation services prior to attempting higher level social skills, such as relationship building.

The designation of these four behavioral domains as the target area of concern in the functional intervention component of therapeutic recreation serves another important role. Assessing clients using these four areas of functional ability gives a clearer and more objective picture of individuals and their capabilities and limitations. A given illness or disability affects different people in different ways. The client assessment should be able to measure functional limitations of each individual, without globally placing all clients into all programs. The assessment should be targeted toward specific functional limitations and capabilities, and assess each person individually yet accurately.

In the medical model, the major concern is with the presenting pathology. Despite the references to concern for the total person, more often than not the major treatment is focused on the illness or disability itself, and not on how the condition affects the total person and the day-to-day living situation. There is little value in being overly critical of the medical or psychiatric professions. Perhaps the role of the allied health professions and ancillary services is to keep a focus on the total person. Therapeutic recreation is one of those professions that by definition is concerned with individuals and how they cope with, adjust to, and compensate for an illness or disability. Facilitating the development and expression of an appropriate leisure lifestyle is a purpose that goes beyond the disability itself and seeks to assist the individual in establishing a meaningful and satisfying existence. Thus, in the provision of functional intervention services, the assessment of and focus on, the actual behavioral and functional limitations imposed on the individual by the condition becomes a critical factor. In most cases, therapeutic recreation is treating not the pathology itself, but the functional deficiency or limitation imposed by the pathology. The selection of the four areas of physical, mental, emotional, and social functioning enables an understanding of the actual results of an illness or disability and how these limitations may affect the living situation of the client. The therapeutic recreation specialist is particularly concerned with how these limitations relate to and influence leisure functioning.

An understanding of the physical, mental, emotional, and social behavioral areas as they relate to leisure involvement and lifestyle gives the therapeutic recreation specialist a rationale and purpose for the development and implementation of functional intervention services. Clients are assessed for their functional abilities in these four areas as part of a comprehensive assessment related to all areas of leisure ability. If the analysis of assessment data indicates problems in the behavioral functioning areas, then these problematic areas should be targeted for program intervention. This determination is made after careful consideration of the client's needs in all leisure-related areas. It is important to prioritize the client's needs. Functional problems may not be the client's major area of service need. A given client may have a greater need in the area of developing an awareness of leisure and acquiring some appropriate leisure skills. Some functional problems cannot be improved or changed (e.g., sight, hearing, ambulation). In these cases, a continued focus on the behavioral area would be short-sighted and not in the best interest of the client's eventual leisure lifestyle.

Many clients in clinical settings do have functional problems that relate to leisure involvement. Most of these problems can be addressed through functional intervention programs. Examples of functional problems include:

Cerebral Vascular Accident

- Lack of ability to control agitation and irritability
- Low frustration tolerance
- Lack of ability to incorporate disability into current lifestyle

Depression

- Decreased energy level
- Inability to express emotions appropriately to situation
- Decreased frequency of contact with others

Dementia

- Minimal orientation to time, place, and people
- Deficits in both short-term and long-term memory skills
- Deficits in attention span and on-task time

This list is not meant to be comprehensive. Each of the foregoing is merely an example of possible limitations that a given individual may display. Each of the limitations identified is a result of or directly related to the disability itself. Often a primary disability imposes other limitations on the individual. These are frequently referred to as **secondary disabilities.** An example of this might be an individual with a stroke who becomes withdrawn and begins to display symptoms of depression. Isolation and regressive social behavior also are common with many illnesses and disabilities. It is important to note that secondary disabilities are highly individualistic. They reflect a given client's response or reaction to the presenting primary disabling condition. The area of secondary disabilities is very significant to the therapeutic recreation specialist. As mentioned in the first chapter, secondary conditions often become the focus of therapeutic recreation services, as they are as important to future leisure functioning as are primary disabilities or illnesses.

It is important to note that in the examples found above as well as the examples related to secondary disabilities, there is a direct relationship of each of the problem areas to leisure functioning. Within the Leisure Ability approach to therapeutic recreation, this is the significant criterion as to whether the problem should be addressed through a functional intervention program.

When developing the functional intervention therapeutic recreation program, a group of related problem areas is usually clustered. For example, clients who are frail often display similar functional deficits, such as decreased range of motion, decreased social networks and social support, and decreased energy levels. Clients who are classified as at-risk youth may have decreased impulse control and risk assessment, decreased empathy and perspective-taking skills, and inattention to consequences. Programs then can be developed, with objectives, outcome measures, appropriate activities, and staff interventions. Each program, by addressing similar areas of functional ability and limitations, enables the referral and placement of clients by actual need. These needs then can be treated through a more thorough and focused group approach. In such programs, the activities are selected for their ability to contribute to the treatment goals and program objectives. Activity analysis (presented in Chapter 6) is a process that assists the therapeutic recreation specialist in the selection and modification of activities for treatment or intervention purposes. Activities selected and utilized in this way can be a viable and dynamic treatment modality. The process involves a well-planned intervention to bring about specific behavioral change or improvement. Activities are used not for their recreational or leisure potential, but rather for their specific inherent contribution to behavioral change. The ultimate outcome of functional intervention services is to eliminate, to significantly improve, or to teach the client to adapt to existing functional limitations that hamper efforts to engage fully in leisure pursuits. Often these functional deficits are such that the client has difficulty learning, developing his or her full potential, interacting with others, or being independent. The aim of functional intervention services is to reduce these barriers so that further learning and involvement by the client can take place.

Role of the Therapeutic Recreation Specialist

Figure 2.3, which displays only the first component of the total Leisure Ability Model, indicates two other important concepts related to functional intervention services. These are the role of the therapeutic recreation specialist and the autonomy or choice on the part of the client. These concepts, along with the purpose of this service category, are vital to the understanding of the development and delivery of these services.

The primary role of the therapeutic recreation specialist while engaged in the design and delivery of functional intervention services is that of therapist. This term is not used merely to designate a role; rather, it implies the acquisition and appropriate utilization of a variety of therapeutic facilitation techniques and strategies. The techniques needed depend on the population being served and also on the tradition or approach of the agency. For example, when working as a therapist with individuals with developmental disabilities, the therapeutic recreation specialist may be expected to utilize physical or environmental manipulation, positive reinforcement, shaping, or behavior modification. In a psychiatric setting, therapeutic techniques, such as reality therapy, reflective listening, cognitive therapy, or a vast number of other verbal and

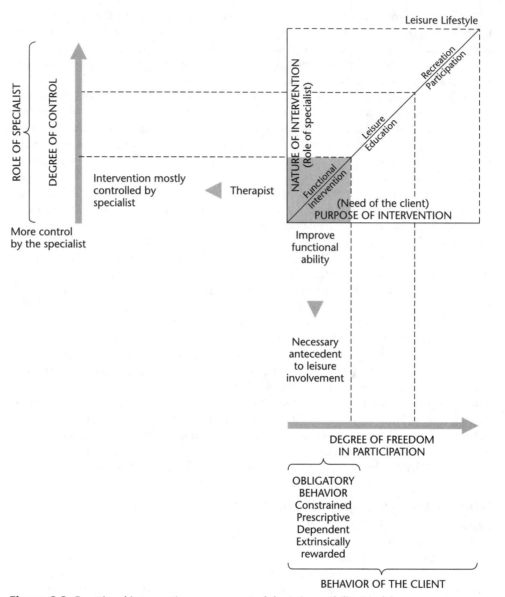

Figure 2.3 Functional intervention component of the Leisure Ability Model.

psychotherapy approaches, may be employed by the treatment team and thus are expected to be utilized by the therapeutic recreation specialist as well.

The specialist typically designates the client's level and type of involvement, while considering input from the client. In order to successfully produce client outcomes, the specialist must be able to assess accurately the client's functional deficits; create and implement specific interventions to improve these deficits; and evaluate the client outcomes achieved from functional intervention programs.

The role of therapist implies a carefully selected and appropriately implemented facilitation technique that is used to bring about some specific behavioral change or improvement in clients. When a functional intervention therapeutic recreation program is being designed, obvious consideration is given to the development of specific objectives that delineate the desired behavioral improvement. Careful consideration also is given to the selection of appropriate activities as the content that contributes to the attainment of the objectives. Equally important, however, is the selection and specification of the therapeutic facilitation technique(s) to be used by the staff. The facilitation technique(s) used must be appropriate for the clients in the program, must be compatible with the program objectives, and must be feasible given the program content (activities). In addition, the staff member must be competent in the use of the technique(s), which must be within the designated authority of the therapeutic recreation staff member.

The selection of an appropriate therapeutic facilitation technique should be based on the nature of clients and the purpose of the program. This implies that a skilled therapeutic recreation specialist needs a variety of facilitation skills and techniques. It is inappropriate to assume that one technique will be appropriate for all clients or in all functional intervention programs. Similarly, the adoption of one therapeutic facilitation approach based solely on the staff members' preference may be naive or self-serving.

Thus, in functional intervention services, the role of the specialist is that of therapist. The interactions and interventions within these programs are carefully designed to bring about predetermined client behavioral improvement or change. The role of therapist has inherent responsibilities and requires the acquisition of various therapeutic techniques and approaches. Different therapeutic strategies are used with different populations. Designing programs for a given population requires specific knowledge of appropriate, feasible, and effective therapeutic facilitation techniques.

Client Autonomy and Control

Engaging in an independent and meaningful leisure lifestyle implies freedom of choice on the part of the individual. Many of the definitions of leisure use the concept of freedom as a primary descriptor of the experience and phenomenon. The concept of freedom is part of the ultimate goal within the Leisure Ability approach to therapeutic recreation as well. Within functional intervention programs, client autonomy and choice are maximized to the fullest extent possible. Although some services in this area are quite prescriptive, the client, whenever possible, is still accorded as much autonomy to determine the outcome of services as possible. The client is ultimately responsible for his or her own success or achievement of goals at the completion of the program and beyond. While the therapist may be primarily responsible for the content and process of functional intervention programs, the client shares responsibility for his or her involvement and end behavior, to the fullest extent possible. As mentioned in the first chapter, self-determination, freedom, and choice are concepts important to leisure functioning. Clients who are actively involved in their own treatment process are more likely to see significant results than those who remain passive, uninvolved, or resistive.

Interdisciplinary Treatment

The information presented previously addresses specific functional intervention services as they relate to functional limitations as prerequisites to, or as a necessary aspect of, leisure involvement. Indeed, this is the unique contribution of functional intervention services. Many clinical settings, however, utilize an interdisciplinary treatment approach. In an interdisciplinary approach, treatment goals are arrived at by the entire professional staff. Some goals then are addressed in specific programs by a specific discipline. Other goals are targeted by all members of the team. When therapeutic recreation is part of an interdisciplinary team approach, its focus of service would have a dual responsibility. One aspect of programming would be the implementation of programs and interactions addressing the general treatment goals determined by the team. The second area is more complex and difficult. It involves integrating the significance of leisure into the total rehabilitation concept and approach, so that specific treatment goals related to leisure functioning can be a part of the total treatment plan. Thus, when client cases are presented and discussed, the team will have a basis for setting up treatment goals that take this area of client need into consideration. The therapeutic recreation specialist must take the responsibility for interpreting and educating the entire team regarding the leisure area of rehabilitation and treatment. Much of the information on the previous pages and in the sections that follow can be used to present explanations and rationales for the inclusion of therapeutic recreation as a significant area of client need and treatment focus. In an interdisciplinary-team approach, it is essential that client treatment goals related to leisure functioning be a part of the overall assessment and treatment plan. The absence of involvement at the critical client assessment and treatment planning stage would reduce therapeutic recreation to a role of insignificance, with little or no impact. Once treatment goals related to leisure functioning are understood and accepted by the team, specific programs can be delineated and implemented to address those specific goals. Therapeutic recreation then becomes a legitimate part of the interdisciplinary team and treatment approach, both contributing to general treatment goals and addressing specific leisure-related goals.

Leisure Education as a Component of Therapeutic Recreation Service

Leisure education is a broad category of services that focuses on the development and acquisition of various leisure-related skills, attitudes, and knowledge. The establishment and expression of an appropriate leisure lifestyle appears to be dependent on the acquisition of diverse knowledge and skills. Many clients of therapeutic recreation services do not have these knowledges and skills, have not been able to use them in their leisure time, or need to relearn them, incorporating the effects of their illness and/or disability. A repertoire of activity skills is not the only requirement. A cognitive understanding of leisure, a positive attitude toward leisure experiences, and various participatory and decision-making skills, as well as knowledge of and the ability to utilize resources, appear to be significant aspects of satisfying leisure involvement. These leisure education content areas can be utilized in programs that have as their purpose the acquisition of appropriate leisure-related skills, knowledge, and attitudes.

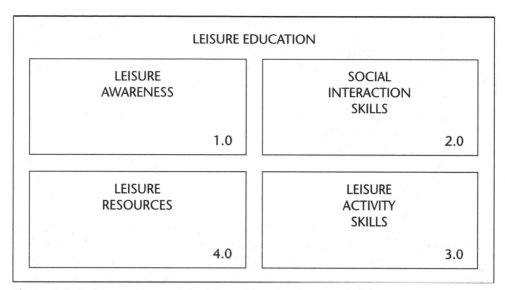

Figure 2.4 Basic components of the Leisure Education Content Model.

Figure 2.4 displays a model that organizes this conceptualization of leisure education content. The four components—leisure awareness, social interaction skills, leisure activity skills, and leisure resources—will be elaborated on later in this section.

Play can be considered a basic behavior. This implies that play behavior is inherent, or a natural part of human existence and expression. The role and form of play behavior, however, are directed by societal influence and sanction. The play behavior of very young infants is similar throughout the world and throughout history. The role, content, and structure of play for children, youth, and adults varies considerably based on the given culture. In postindustrial America, play has a significant role for individuals of all ages. The term *play* is not commonly used past the infant and childhood stages. Replacing *play* most often are the terms *recreation* and *leisure*. **Recreation** connotes to most people a vast variety of structured activities commonly sanctioned by the society and most frequently engaged in through some organized delivery system. **Leisure** seems to have a broader meaning and generally is accepted as activities, behaviors, and experiences that are voluntarily engaged in by the individual for intrinsic and self-rewarding outcomes. Several related concepts (internal locus of control, intrinsic motivation, personal causality, and freedom) were discussed in Chapter 1. It is not the intent of this text to explicitly define, defend, or differentiate between various terms used within the leisure arena. The terms are introduced here only to assist in an understanding of the leisure education and Leisure Ability concepts.

Play is most often understood as a behavior. It is a behavior that is identifiable, observable, and different from other forms of human behavior. It is content-free, implying that the behavior is displayed in many contexts. An individual can "play" within a structured, traditional recreation activity such as tennis or backgammon or within the unstructured form of daydreaming or watching television. An individual also can display play behavior within other human contexts. Many social interactions are adult forms of play behavior. Likewise, one can have playful moments within the work situation. Play, then, is viewed as behavior rather than as a specific activity. The term *leisure behavior* is more commonly used within our contemporary society to identify this human behavior. This term will be used within this text to designate the wide range of human expressions that are engaged in voluntarily, possess the element of freedom of choice, are intrinsically motivated, and display the characteristics of being enjoyable and meaningful to the individual.

Although play and leisure behavior are considered basic behaviors and are viewed as a right and need of individuals, many people require some assistance in developing an appropriate and satisfying leisure lifestyle. As noted in the first chapter, there are many barriers or constraints to leisure expression. The Protestant work ethic and its resulting impact related to idleness, self-enjoyment, and nonproductive activity still exert a strong influence on the lives of many people. In many ways, individuals with conditions of illness or disability are most often victimized by this influence. The disabling condition often removes individuals from socially defined productive activities (work) and leaves them without identifiable contributory roles. Unfortunately, a lingering view of leisure involvement is that leisure is earned as a reward for work, and thus, individuals are not entitled to leisure benefits or enjoyment if they are not contributing to society in some recognized manner. Within our contemporary society, and with the influence of more humanistic theories, this previous attitude has largely been rejected. The individual is seen as valuable and significant because he or she exists. The individual has rights and responsibilities like anyone else. Our human service system structure and legislative mandates support and reinforce this philosophy. However, the fact remains that many individuals with illnesses and disabilities are negatively impacted by previous attitudes and values of the society.

Because leisure is a significant component of contemporary life, it also must be viewed as an important and necessary aspect of existence for individuals with conditions of illness and disability. As argued in Chapter 1, the concept of quality of life is very much related to the opportunities available for leisure involvement and expression. Individuals with disabilities, however, may need assistance in the development and expression of an independent leisure lifestyle. The leisure education component of therapeutic recreation services addresses this need in a direct and comprehensive manner.

The leisure lifestyle of most people in our society evolves and develops throughout the life span of the individual. Early childhood and family experiences and social interactions in the neighborhood and schools shape the foundation of attitudes and values related to leisure. The teen and young adult years provide the opportunity for breaking away from family traditions and expectations and allow the individual to experiment with, and engage in, more self-initiated and self-directed forms of leisure. It is during the young adult stage of life that leisure routines and lifestyle appear to become more stable and set for most people. Likewise, if conscious awareness of leisure and a valuing of the phenomenon occurs, it most likely takes place at this stage of human development.

Individuals with congenital illnesses and disabilities (or ones that occur very early in life) often are inhibited in normal play and socialization opportunities. Thus, the formulation of play and leisure attitudes and behaviors are frequently developmentally or experientially limited. Individuals who acquire a disability or illness later in life frequently have difficulties in the expression of previous leisure involvements and interests. Their condition itself may appear to inhibit or prohibit leisure involvement through imposed, real, or perceived limitations. In other cases, the individual may just dismiss leisure as an insignificant and impossible component of living, since the focus of others and themselves shifts to the care and treatment of the condition itself. Individuals with congenital as well as acquired conditions of illness and disability appear to have difficulty with leisure involvement and expression.

Since the development and expression of an appropriate leisure lifestyle is an important aspect of the human condition, there appears to be substantial reason for therapeutic recreation specialists to intervene. Even if the individual is not concerned about leisure, and even in the absence of widespread concern by other medical and health professionals, the profession of therapeutic recreation has a role to play in the preparation or rehabilitation of the client relative to leisure.

Nature of Leisure Education Services

Leisure education services utilize an educational model, as opposed to the medical model. The educational model operates on the assumption that behavior can change and improve as the individual acquires new knowledge, skills, attitudes, and abilities. These changes occur through a learning process. The client is an active participant in the process, sharing responsibility for the change or growth that is targeted. Although illness or disability must be considered both in the content to be learned and the process through which learning takes place, the illness or disability is not the primary concern at this point. Behavioral growth and change are sought independent of the condition. In leisure education, the focus of learning (or desired area of behavioral change) is leisure ability.

Leisure education services, as presented in this text, were first conceptualized through an analysis of factors involved in successful leisure participation and utilization. Individuals without disabilities were studied to determine components of successful leisure involvement. Thus the model is based on a normalization or inclusionary concept. Observations and interviews were used as the primary methods of study. The information gained was analyzed and discussed with various professionals in the field. Results then were conceptualized and organized into areas related to general program content. Four general categories of leisure-related skills emerged. Each of these was further conceptualized and developed. Figure 2.5 presents this expanded Leisure Education Content Model.

All models have conceptual weaknesses. This is particularly true of a model that attempts to describe a phenomenon as complex as leisure. The Leisure Education Content Model is thus subject to inherent and acknowledged limitations. Nonetheless, its conceptualization and the resulting components and content have proven to be useful in the design of leisure education programs for diverse populations in a variety of settings. The model provides both students and practitioners with identified areas of possible client need (and therefore program content) related to the development of various leisure-related skills, knowledge, attitudes, and abilities.

The Leisure Education Content Model presented in this text is generic in nature. It is not designed for one specific illness or disability. It crosses disability lines to identify common aspects of leisure involvement and lifestyle development. Likewise, it is

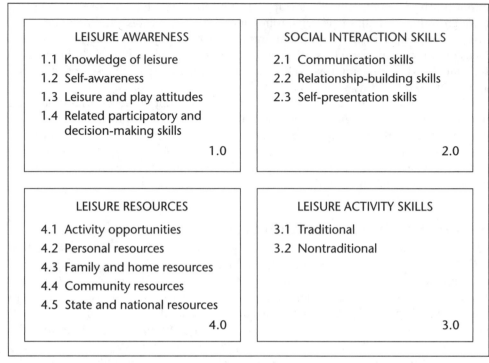

Figure 2.5 Leisure Education Content Model.

not specific for any given agency. Its content areas appear to be just as useful in community settings as in clinical settings. It has been used to design programs for individuals without disabilities as well as individuals with disabilities. Selection of content and the design of specific intervention techniques obviously will vary depending on the population and setting.

Content of Leisure Education Services

Four components have been conceptualized to identify the major aspects of leisure education content. Each of the four components will be described separately on the following pages. Figure 2.6 displays the first component of the total leisure education model previously presented.

Leisure Awareness.   An important aspect of leisure lifestyle and involvement appears to be a cognitive awareness of leisure and its benefits, a valuing of the leisure phenomenon, and a conscious decision-making process to activate involvement. These cognitive aspects seem to be what was missing in so much of past recreation and therapeutic recreation programming. The historical assumption seemed to be that individuals only needed to acquire recreation activity skills, and from there, they would apply those skills in some meaningful pattern of leisure involvement. That approach did not seem to influence positively the leisure involvement of most clients beyond the actual participation in the segmented agency-sponsored programs. The

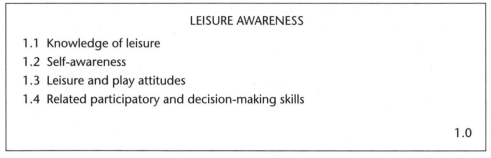

Figure 2.6 Leisure awareness component of the Leisure Education Content Model.

more contemporary approach, which focuses on some understanding of leisure, appears to have a better chance of facilitating the development and expression of an appropriate leisure lifestyle. For example, the client may need assistance in identifying his or her strengths that can be used for leisure, or need instruction in making decisions and taking responsibility for his or her leisure involvement. The relationship between this area and the prior chapter's discussion on self-efficacy, locus of control, perceived freedom, and personal choice is obvious. Regardless of whether the individual immediately responds to the content of leisure education programs, he or she is still exposed to knowledge and information that may be useful at some later point.

Within the component of leisure awareness, at least four content areas can be identified that appear essential in facilitating the development and expression of an appropriate leisure lifestyle. The first of these is *knowledge of leisure*. This content area can address a variety of topics. The following topics are ones that have been found to be useful with many populations. Many other topics could be added.

- The concept of leisure and its relation to quality of life
- The difference between leisure behaviors and other behaviors
- Benefits and possible outcomes of leisure involvement
- Barriers to leisure involvement
- Forms of leisure involvement
- Leisure as a context in which to learn new skills, meet new people, experience new events
- The concept of leisure lifestyle
- The balance between leisure, work, and other obligations
- The concept of personal responsibility for leisure lifestyle

A second area is that of *self-awareness*. This area focuses on a more personal understanding of leisure and the individual. The following are possible topic areas for inclusion in this content area:

- Actual and perceived abilities and skills that impact leisure involvement
- Actual and perceived limitations that impact leisure involvement
- Effects of a disability or illness on leisure behavior

- Past leisure and play patterns and activities
- Current leisure involvement and satisfaction
- Areas for future discovery and involvement
- Personal resources for leisure involvement
- Goal areas for development through leisure
- Effects of family and friends on personal leisure development

This list could easily be extended to include many other related topics.

Leisure and play attitudes is the third content area of the first leisure education component. Because attitudes and values are so important to the acceptance, development, and expression of a leisure lifestyle, this content area is separated from the previous two. Within this area, existing attitudes about play and leisure can be explored. This is often a critical point in terms of redirecting, or moving toward change in, leisure lifestyle development. Typical topics might include:

- Past, current, and future societal attitudes related to leisure
- Origin of one's personal beliefs and values about leisure
- Relationship between attitudes and behavior
- Appropriateness of former leisure attitudes with regard to current life situation
- Relationship between leisure attitudes and values, and life satisfaction
- Impact of leisure attitudes on current and future leisure lifestyle
- Evolution of attitudes about leisure throughout the life span

The fourth content area of the first component is entitled *related leisure participatory and decision-making skills*. Again, a variety of topics and processes can be identified for content inclusion in this area. Commonly identified areas include:

- Decision-making skills with regard to leisure involvement
- Leisure-planning skills
- Problem-solving techniques for daily use
- Long-term coping and adaptation strategies
- Creating and evaluating options for leisure participation
- Reducing and managing stress through conscious planning and decision making

Many of the above topics are "generic" in that there are several decision-making and problem-solving models that emphasize a general step-by-step approach. These models can be presented with a focus on application to leisure participation. All of these areas are processes that may require substantial time for learning. However, these skills appear essential if meaningful changes are to take place in the individual's leisure lifestyle and involvement.

This fourth area of related participatory and decision-making skills also includes topics that may vary considerably, depending on the specific population being served by the program. Examples of this may be such topics as the following:

Rehabilitation Center for Individuals with Spinal Cord Injuries

- Asking appropriate questions about physical accessibility of recreation facilities
- Asking for assistance when necessary
- Locating information about resources available to individuals with spinal injuries
- Interacting with nondisabled people in leisure participation (friends, staff, strangers)
- Deciding in which activity opportunities to participate
- Making long-term adjustments to a personal leisure lifestyle

Inpatient Unit for Individuals with Psychiatric Disorders

- Planning for leisure involvement post-discharge
- Using leisure to counter the effects of living with stressful situations
- Making appropriate decisions with regard to leisure involvement
- Making daily choices for leisure on the unit
- Deciding which leisure skills the individual would like to learn
- Planning for leisure participation, considering fatigue levels, interest, availability, etc.

Residential Facility for Individuals with Developmental Disabilities

- Reviewing options for leisure involvement
- Planning for involvement in leisure events
- Examining consequences of participation or nonparticipation
- Making choices about leisure involvement and participation
- Deciding which leisure activities are most enjoyable
- Reducing problems or barriers to leisure involvement

These examples are for illustration only. Obviously, none of the lists of possible related participatory skills or topics is complete. In addition, many other populations and settings were not included at all. However, the reader can develop such topic areas as needed.

This section has identified content related to the first component of the presented leisure education model. The identified content areas need to be conceptualized and developed into appropriate program structures prior to implementation. A few comments about program development will conclude this section.

The four content areas of the first component are rarely separated into different programs. Aspects of all four areas are generally combined into one leisure education program structure. The selection of topics is based on the specific population and their leisure-related information needs. In most cases, however, the information and skills found in the first component are not part of previously acquired knowledge. Thus, the conceptualization of the actual content for programs related to this component is at the discretion of the therapeutic recreation specialist designing the program.

The content or topic areas of this first component of leisure education are usually developed into programs that use a variety of cognitive and affective facilitation techniques. Group discussion, paper-pencil leisure and self-awareness activities, individual and group verbal exercises, leisure information discovery or investigation games, mini-lectures, presentations, and use of various audiovisual aids are all common techniques utilized to facilitate an understanding and acquisition of the content. In the development of any therapeutic recreation program, it is important to select appropriate facilitation techniques. Again, the techniques utilized should be compatible with the content of the program and appropriate for the clients being served. Since the content of this first component of leisure education is primarily cognitive and affective, the interventions most often utilized are instructional strategies or counseling techniques.

Because of the use of counseling techniques, programs in this first component have frequently been called *leisure counseling* programs. These writers object to the use of this title. It seems inappropriate to title a program by the type of facilitation technique used. The content of the programs most often focuses on leisure and self-awareness, leisure attitudes and values, participatory problems, and decision making. Thus, it would be more consistent to label the program by its content; for instance, leisure awareness or even leisure education. A variety of facilitation techniques are indeed used, and aspects of various counseling techniques are very useful and appropriate. However, the use of a given counseling technique is not sufficient reason to include leisure counseling in the title.

There is a legitimate service area that can be called leisure counseling. It is, however, quite different and distinct from the leisure education programs presented here. Leisure education has a specific and predetermined content, which is operationalized into programs. This section of this chapter has delineated leisure education content and will continue to do so. Leisure counseling, as well as other forms of counseling, does not start usually with predetermined content. Rather, the problem or focus of counseling originates from the individual client. This major distinction between counseling and education is an important one. It is, however, common for counselors to use educational techniques within the counseling process. Likewise, educators often use counseling techniques within the educational process. Leisure counseling also has some significant differences when it comes to the issue of qualifications and credentials. In general, it is reasonable to assume that most therapeutic recreation specialists are qualified to use some basic counseling techniques. It is not appropriate to assume that they have sufficient training to utilize the title "counselor."

When developing and implementing programs related to the first component of the leisure education model, it is important to take into consideration the other leisure education needs that will be presented in the following sections. Likewise, client needs related to the functional intervention and recreation participation aspects of service also must be analyzed. This consideration, it is hoped, will enable the development of programs that will be complementary and, in some cases, will need to be sequential. This very issue is a good reason to engage in comprehensive program planning at the onset. Master planning enables appropriate identification of client needs and selection of program components from all levels of the Leisure Ability Model to meet the identified needs. Client needs can be addressed within a compre-

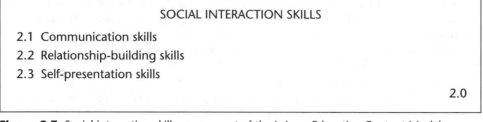

Figure 2.7 Social interaction skills component of the Leisure Education Content Model.

hensive program structure. Specific programs then are developed with prior knowledge of resource (time, budget, staff, equipment, facility) availability. Such planning eliminates the all-too-often segmented approach found in the past.

Social Interaction Skills.

The leisure education model presented in this book has three other components. The second component focuses on social interaction skills. Figure 2.7 presents this segment of the larger model.

Social interaction is a major aspect of leisure lifestyle. This is particularly true of adult leisure involvement. In many situations, the social interaction is more significant and important to the participants than the activity itself. The activity may be the reason to be together, but it is the social interaction that has real meaning for the people involved. Social dancing (ballroom, disco, rock, line dancing, and so forth) is an example of this point. In other situations, the activity has significant meaning to the participants, but interaction abilities are essential for successful involvement. Playing bridge, which requires interaction between partners as well as bidding against others, illustrates this point. Most team sports also require interaction between and among team members for successful participation. A third situation involving social interaction skills can be identified. Some group-oriented leisure activities require little social interaction, but the participation and enjoyment seem to be heightened by social interaction. Square dancing or bowling are examples of this point. Within the comprehensive concept of leisure lifestyle, there are many leisure participation situations that do not involve traditional activities at all. In such a conceptualization, a social encounter that is exclusively a verbal interaction could be considered a leisure experience depending on the motivation, content, and outcomes. When we realize how often this type of social interaction takes place for most individuals without disabilities, it becomes a very important consideration. Simply stated, social interaction among adults may be the most frequent form of leisure participation. In all four of the foregoing situations, adequate and appropriate social interaction skills are necessary for satisfactory participation.

Many individuals with conditions of illness or disability have less than adequate social interaction abilities. This may be the result of the primary pathology itself or a reaction to the major problem, which then becomes a secondary disability. With children with disabilities, parents often protect or shelter a child, which frequently results in few early and normal socialization opportunities. With adults, social isolation often is a defense or form of self-protection. In some cases, there are simply limited opportunities for social interaction. Regardless of the cause, the resulting inadequate social interaction skills interfere with, or create barriers to, leisure participation.

Since social interaction appears to be such a significant aspect of leisure participation and lifestyle, it is included as a component of leisure education. The skills and abilities involved in social interaction can be learned. They can be conceptualized into program structures. What is more important, they can be learned through involvement in various recreation and leisure activities and thus take on a more dynamic, action-oriented dimension. Acquiring social interaction skills in the context of activities allows for more realistic learning and application. Generally, learning interaction skills through activity involvement is enjoyable for the client as well. Fortunately, traditional recreation activities have within their structures all the various and basic interaction patterns normally required within our society. Careful assessment of the client's existing social interaction skill level and the analysis of additional interaction skills needed can be conducted. Activities then can be selected that have the appropriate inherent interactional requirements to facilitate the acquisition of the designated social interaction skills. Activity analysis (presented in Chapter 6) provides valuable information related to the process of activity selection for the development of social interaction skills.

The acquisition of social interaction skills, like any other skill acquisition, requires the planning of specific programs designed to facilitate the learning of the designated behavior. If social interaction skills are identified as a major area of need, then specific programs addressing these skills need to be developed. Depending on the population and setting, social interaction skill development may be a significant aspect of the comprehensive leisure education and therapeutic recreation mission. An example of this point may provide some clarification. Individuals with autism may need specific programs to develop appropriate social interaction skills. Individuals in substance abuse programs or in short-term psychiatric facilities may need only to have appropriate social interaction skills reinforced through other types of therapeutic recreation programming.

When developing and implementing programs that focus on the acquisition of interaction skills, the therapeutic recreation specialist functions in the role of educator. The interventions and facilitation techniques are selected from various instructional strategies. Although a therapeutic recreation specialist can counsel a client regarding the need for interaction skills, the actual acquisition of those skills involves a learning process. Thus, instructional techniques are the most frequently used facilitation techniques with social interaction skill development programs.

There are many ways to conceptualize social interaction skills. Models have been developed to characterize the various aspects and areas of interaction. Social development schemes have been provided by various disciplines. Applications of these have been made for some categories of disability, such as individuals with developmental disabilities. It is not the intent of this section to focus on social interaction in depth or comprehensively. A brief conceptual scheme is presented as part of the social interaction skills component. This scheme is general and is intended to cut across all disability categories. It is very limited, however, when applied to a specific disability group or to a given individual. The scheme is described here to provide just one brief view of some considerations within the social interaction area. This presents the second major area of change from the former Leisure Ability Model.

Communication Skills.   This set of skills enables an individual to communicate with others. It is felt that clear and honest communication is a necessity in everyday life, and since so much of leisure is social by nature, communication becomes important in this area as well. Many client groups have needs in this area, and an improvement in skills would enable them to participate more appropriately with others in a variety of leisure pursuits. A host of skills may be taught in this area, but some typical topics might include:

- Assertiveness skills
- Skills involving negotiation, disagreement, conflict, and compromise
- Conversational skills
- Active listening skills and responsive behavior
- Expressing feelings and thoughts
- Information-seeking and information-giving skills
- Empathy and perspective-taking skills

Relationship-Building Skills.   Relationship-building skills address those areas that assist an individual in locating, maintaining, and developing friendships and other relationships. Significant others play important roles in most people's lives and many skills are needed to maintain and sustain healthy relationships. As seen in Chapter 1, social networks and social support are important aspects to most individuals, and leisure pursuits provide many opportunities to develop these. Some client groups will need more work in the social skills area than others. Most individuals, however, find that relationships are an important contributor to their quality of life. Some typical skills that might be taught in this area include:

- Greeting and initiation skills, such as locating leisure partners
- Friendship development skills
- Self-disclosure and privacy issues
- Cooperative and competitive skills
- Developing and maintaining social networks
- Reciprocal social support (expressing care and concern for others and vice versa)

Self-Presentation Skills.   In order for communication skills and relationship-building skills to be utilized, the individual also must maintain some basic social etiquette rules. Some client groups will need more training in this area than others, but all will need to exhibit fundamental baseline skills. Often, the lack of these skills prevents an individual from being accepted and becoming friends with or meeting other individuals. Examples of these skills include:

- Skills involving politeness, etiquette, and manners, such as taking turns, sharing, etc.
- Hygiene, health, and grooming skills

- Appropriate attire and dressing
- Responsibility for self-care

Social interaction ability is an essential aspect of successful leisure involvement and lifestyle. Since the behaviors and skills involved can be learned and are, for the most part, independent of illness or disability itself, it is included as a component of leisure education. If the development of interaction skills is a need of clients, then appropriate programs need to be conceptualized and implemented that focus on this area. The absence of adequate interaction ability can be as much a barrier to leisure involvement as the absence of activity skills or knowledge of leisure and its significance.

This section does not intend to discount or ignore those leisure activities and experiences that the individual engages in and enjoys while alone. Indeed, there is a great need to assist individuals in developing a repertoire of activities and interests that can be done alone. Likewise, helping them to understand the need for and develop a positive attitude toward solitary leisure appears to be a significant aspect of an overall leisure lifestyle. This section, however, focuses on interaction skills that are not utilized within solitary leisure experiences.

Leisure Activity Skills. Expressing a satisfying leisure lifestyle implies that the individual has a sense of freedom and choice in leisure involvement. Choice involves having options and alternatives. Consequently, it appears logical that a repertoire of leisure activities and related interests is necessary for meaningful experiences. The issue is not simply one of acquiring as many leisure skills as possible. It seems more important to assist the individual in selecting and developing adequate skills in a number of activities that potentially will be a source of enjoyment and personal satisfaction for the individual across the life span.

The concept of developing an appropriate leisure lifestyle implies a shifting of responsibility to the individual for his or her ongoing leisure expressions. Once leisure skills are acquired, it is expected that they will become a meaningful aspect of the individual's leisure lifestyle. Some of the activities may be participated in through an organized delivery program, such as a bowling league, ceramics program, or photography club, but many of the skills will be utilized independent of any agency. These skills will be engaged in through commercial leisure opportunities, at home (or in the facility) alone, or with others in a social situation.

The role of the therapeutic recreation specialist is thus twofold relative to the leisure skills development component. One role is that of educator. Teaching a specific skill or group of skills requires the use of various instructional strategies and techniques. The major criterion is the appropriateness of the selected instructional technique to the skill being taught and to the learning style of the client. This obviously requires that effective therapeutic recreation specialists have at their command a repertoire of instructional strategies appropriate for use with the types of clients being served. The second role related to leisure skill development is more difficult to characterize. It involves assisting the client in the selection of appropriate leisure skills to be acquired. In that sense, the role requires that therapeutic recreation specialists have a knowledge of and the ability to use some counseling techniques and skills. It also requires a thorough understanding of the concept of leisure lifestyle and its various

---

LEISURE ACTIVITY SKILLS

3.1 Traditional leisure skills

3.2 Nontraditional leisure skills

3.0

Figure 2.8 Leisure activity skills component of the Leisure Education Content Model.

dimensions, which are significantly different from traditional activity programming. This point, it is hoped, will become clearer through the remainder of this section as specific skills are addressed in more depth. Figure 2.8 highlights both traditional and nontraditional leisure skills.

In the past, most activity skill development programs have focused on traditional recreation activities. These activities are ones commonly identified as recreational and sanctioned by the society. They have been promoted and programmed by the leisure and recreation profession. Countless classification and categorical systems have been developed to identify them. The following list is an example of the types of activities frequently referred to within the traditional recreation category.

Traditional Categories or Commonly Identified Forms of Recreation

- Sports
- Dance
- Aquatics and water-related activities
- Drama
- Outdoor
- Music
- Arts and crafts
- Other expressive arts
- Mental games and activities
- Hobbies

There is nothing inherently wrong with or inappropriate about activities that fall under the label of traditional recreation. Indeed, individuals with disabling conditions may need and want activity skills from the traditional categories. The problem, however, is the assumption that these activities, and only these activities, are important or appropriate. When we accept the concept of leisure lifestyle, we recognize that there is a multitude of leisure experiences and interests that extend far beyond traditional recreation activities. Observing what adults actually do with their leisure results in a very different list of activities and events. The following list attempts to identify the types of adult leisure pursuits and involvements that are common in our culture. These are in addition to the traditional activities previously identified.

Involvement in these leisure activities more adequately represents the content and nature of adult leisure lifestyles. Many of the actions are engaged in alone or with significant others as opposed to organized activity-centered groups. Many of the activities are less structured with fewer exact procedures or rules. Most often the environment for participation is the home or some general environment as opposed to a specific recreation activity or facility. The dimension of time is also different for many of the activities. Nontraditional activities are less likely to require a specific amount of time or time scheduled by someone else. An immediately obvious difference between these activities and traditional recreation activities is the absence of a program structure by a leisure service delivery agency.

Nontraditional Categories of Adult Leisure Involvement

- Social interaction
- Spectating and appreciating
- Leadership and community service
- Fitness
- Relaxation and meditation
- Cognitive and mental activities
- Eating
- Food preparation
- Fantasy and daydreaming
- Intimacy and sexually related activity
- Substance use—alcohol, drugs, tobacco
- Nothing

- Shopping
- Home improvement
- Living things maintenance—pets and plants
- Self-development
- Education
- Computer and Internet activities
- Travel
- Home maintenance
- Interaction with family and friends
- Telephone/e-mail conversations
- Watching television

It is important to note that the leisure involvements and activities identified as nontraditional do require various skills, knowledge, and participatory abilities. Many people evolve into and engage in these leisure pursuits without specific programmed instruction. However, it is possible to analyze these activities and develop programs that systematically address the acquisition of the various skills. Individuals with disabilities and/or illnesses may need this specific form of leisure skill development. If leisure lifestyle development and expression are the concern of therapeutic recreation services, then the understanding, selection, and programming of skills related to these leisure pursuits may take precedence over the traditional forms of recreation. The intention of differentiating between traditional and nontraditional categories, rather than other categorizations of activities (e.g., passive, outdoor, cultural, etc.), is that it brings to the forefront the concept of a repertoire of diverse leisure skills, in the largest sense. In order for a person to enjoy leisure fully, the individual should possess a wide range of activity skills—from organized and competitive skills to relaxing and contemplative skills—in alignment with his or her age, cultural preferences, lifestyle, and the like. This means that traditional skills (e.g., bowling and badminton) are taught simultaneously with nontraditional skills (e.g., computer games and pet care), so that the individual can experience choice, freedom, and diversity in selecting leisure involvement opportunities.

Assisting the client in the development of appropriate leisure skills takes on new dimensions when using this leisure lifestyle approach. The concern shifts from focus on the skills of a specific traditional activity to broader participatory abilities that include knowledge of leisure possibilities, selecting and learning appropriate leisure activities, and integrating leisure involvement within the total life situation. This does not mean that specific leisure skills are not part of the total programming focus. It merely means that specific activity skills must be viewed and selected within a broader context. Far more attention must be paid to the individual and the development of leisure skills and related participatory abilities for a unique lifestyle and situation.

In clinical and community settings, there is a need for leisure skills development programs for individuals with disabilities and/or illnesses. Indeed, many clients lack specific and general leisure activity skills appropriate for a meaningful ongoing leisure lifestyle. The task of the therapeutic recreation specialist is the selection of appropriate content for these leisure skills development programs. The concept of leisure lifestyle and the previously identified lists of activity categories may be useful in the selection process. The list below presents some of the criteria for selecting leisure skills to be taught to clients.

Additional Criteria for Selecting Leisure Skills

- Choice by the individual (selected from a range of options)
- Within functional ability and interests of the clients (evaluated through activity analysis)
- Feasible for clients' resources (money, equipment, access to facilities, etc.)
- Respect for the individual's cultural and ethnic preferences
- Compatible with the overall life situation of the individual
- Compatible with leisure interests of those with whom the individual may live
- Age-appropriate but also providing opportunity for continued development and involvement at later life stages
- Other considerations (e.g., place of residence, socioeconomic status, educational level, and religion)
- Opportunity for continuing leisure involvement rather than short-term focus
- Transfer of responsibility for leisure involvement to clients and helping them define and prepare for a leisure lifestyle independent of the current agency program structure
- Nature and mandate of the agency delivering the services

It is obviously difficult to determine how many and what kinds of leisure activity skills an individual needs. There are no absolutes or established standards that can be applied. Indeed, the absence of such global absolutes should be respected. The concept of an individualized and unique leisure lifestyle and activity repertoire deserves to be protected. Professional knowledge and judgment of the therapeutic recreation specialist, with input from the client, becomes the basis for decision making related to the development of a leisure skill repertoire of a given client. A well-developed comprehensive scheme or model of leisure lifestyle that includes leisure skills can be very useful in the assessment and programming efforts related to this component of leisure education.

Within community and clinical settings, the conceptualization, selection, development, and implementation of actual leisure skills development programs will be dependent on the nature of clients served. In general, however, it is quite clear that leisure skills development is a primary need of most clients and well within the mandate of the majority of agencies offering therapeutic recreation services. The amount of programming conducted in the leisure skills development component, however, must be carefully balanced with other client program needs identified within the Leisure Ability Model.

The designing of leisure skills development programs, like all other programs in therapeutic recreation, requires the specification of goals and objectives, and the delineation of task-analyzed activity content to assist in the learning of the material. The predominant facilitation style is instructional. This requires that the program designer and program implementers have a good command of a variety of instructional techniques, so that facilitation techniques can be selected that are compatible with the activity being learned and appropriate for the individual clients in the program. The learning of any activity skills can be facilitated greatly by good instructional techniques. Most therapeutic recreation specialists could increase their impact substantially by acquiring greater expertise in the understanding, selection, and use of instructional strategies.

In some ways, the design of good leisure skills development programs is easier than other kinds of therapeutic recreation programs. The desired outcomes are specific leisure skills. These skill behaviors are concrete, they are observable, and in most situations they can be adequately described and thus accurately measured. A high degree of accountability is achievable in such programs.

Leisure skills development programs are usually designed to be implemented independently of other leisure education programs. This means that the focus of the program is the specific leisure skill or cluster of related leisure skills. It is possible, however, to include objectives and content related to leisure resources, social interaction skills, and other content from the leisure awareness component. When these additions are included, they need to be related to the specific leisure skill being presented. A program of this nature can help clients to integrate the concepts, knowledge, and skills.

Leisure Resources.   The leisure resources component adds another important dimension to the leisure education category of program content. Knowledge of leisure resources and the ability to utilize these resources appears to be a significantly important factor in the establishment and expression of a leisure lifestyle. All too often, it is assumed that clients have a basic knowledge of information acquisition and utilization. In other cases, therapeutic recreation specialists have not understood the importance of identifying resources and assisting the client in acquiring the ability to be independent through the use of such resources. The concept of an independent leisure lifestyle requires that the client be able to seek out information and use it appropriately. Leisure resources information is an important link to enable the client to connect with activities and opportunities in his or her home, neighborhood, community, state, and, potentially, the nation.

Leisure is not a well-understood phenomenon in our society. Thus, it is not unusual that many people, both those with and without disabilities and/or illnesses, are at a loss when it comes to an awareness of leisure resources and how to use them. Individuals with some disabilities may be at an even greater disadvantage in that they may have been protected or isolated from resource information utilization in general. A well-planned, comprehensive leisure education program must include information

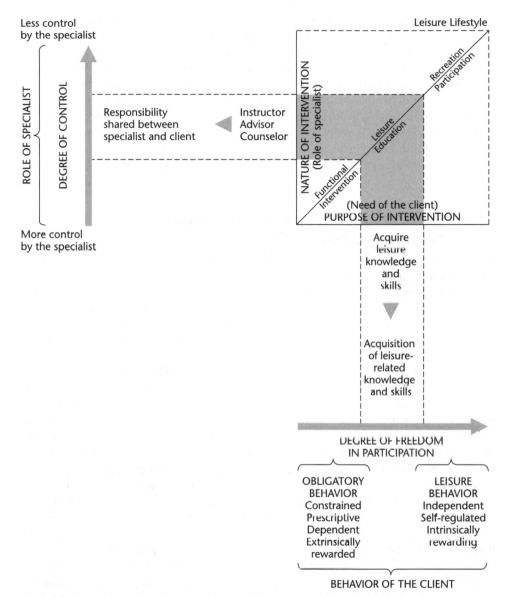

Figure 2.10 Leisure education component of the Leisure Ability Model.

client begins to take an even more participatory and involved role during leisure education programs, with a stronger personal responsibility for the outcome and future application of skills and knowledge. The role of the specialist during leisure education programs varies depending on the needs of the clients. The specialist generally teaches clients new knowledge or skills, and aids them in discovering personal attitudes and values. The client is then responsible for applying this information for the improvement of his or her own lifestyle. This component contains the essential knowledge and skills necessary to develop an appropriate and meaningful leisure lifestyle. Regardless of the disability and the limitations or barriers it presents, the individual has the right to experience leisure involvement and satisfaction. This opportunity, however, is dependent upon sufficient leisure-related attitudes, knowledge, and skills. Programs emerging from the leisure education concept and models provide for an understanding of leisure and the acquisition of participatory abilities and skills. The overall outcome sought through leisure education services is a client who has enough knowledge and skills that an informed and independent choice can be made for his or her future leisure participation. Leisure education includes increased freedom of choice, locus of control, intrinsic motivation, and independence for the client.

Recreation Participation as a Component of Therapeutic Recreation Service

The third major component of the Leisure Ability Model is entitled recreation participation. It encompasses a specific type of programming that is distinctly different from the previous two components. However, its contribution to the overall goal of Leisure Ability is equally significant. Functional intervention and leisure education programs can be viewed as prerequisite or developmental in relation to the leisure lifestyle concept. Recreation participation programs, on the other hand, may be part of the expression of leisure lifestyle.

Recreation participation delineates a type of structured and delivered program. The purpose of such a program is to provide opportunities for fun, enjoyment, and self-expression within an organized delivery system. Like recreation participation programs provided for individuals without disabilities, the motivation to participate and the outcomes of involvement are determined primarily by the individual. The agency basically provides the opportunity for participation by organizing diverse programs and participation exercises that are of interest to the clients. For example, after teaching clients the card game bridge in a leisure activity skills/leisure education program, the specialist may organize a holiday bridge tournament in which clients can choose to participate, may practice bridge skills, and may interact socially with others.

Recreation participation programs are an essential part of the total Leisure Ability Model and the Leisure Ability philosophy. One aspect of independent leisure involvement is the opportunity to select and engage in organized activities and leisure opportunities with others through a structured delivery system. Although these programs represent a small percentage of leisure involvement for most people, they do contribute a unique opportunity to participate. These programs can be described by the following activity or participatory characteristics:

Categories of Typical Recreation Participation Programs

- Activities that require many participants and an administrative structure. Leagues and tournaments are examples of these types of activities.
- Activities that are enjoyed in groups and are facilitated by an administrative structure. Activities such as dramatics, arts and crafts, and music often are provided through a group or club format.

- Activities that require a specific facility or type of equipment not usually owned by the individual. Fitness and exercise programs, ceramics, and square dancing are illustrations of such recreation participation programs.

- The provision of a specific facility, place, or equipment to be used by the participant for self-initiated and self-directed involvement. A park, playground, swimming pool, or drop-in center or program illustrate this point.

All four of these characteristics have one common dimension. The program or service is provided with the assumption that the participant has the activity skills and participatory ability necessary for satisfying or enjoyable involvement. Unlike the functional intervention component, which has a specific predetermined outcome—improved functional ability—or the leisure education component, which has predetermined outcomes in terms of the acquisition of various leisure-related knowledge, skills, and abilities, the recreation participation component more likely is aimed at broader outcomes, such as the display of decision-making abilities and improved ability to take responsibility for personal leisure. Often leisure education outcomes are displayed during recreation participation programs.

Programs in the recreation participation component do need to be designed carefully, just like programs in any other component of the Leisure Ability Model. Specific activities are described. The nature of the facilitation techniques to be used is specified. Other aspects of implementation and program operation are delineated. These aspects of design are necessary in order for the program to be evaluated appropriately and thus be accountable. The only aspect of the full systems design approach that may be absent in these programs is the specific objectives and corresponding client outcomes. Often, outcomes from leisure education programs are displayed through involvement in recreation participation programs. However, because many agencies require outcomes to be specified in order for programs to be offered, goals or outcomes can be determined. Client outcomes of involvement in recreation participation programs are highly individualistic, but may include such areas as: (a) increased ability to assume responsibility for personal leisure participation; (b) increased ability to make and follow through on decisions regarding leisure involvement; (c) increased competence in leisure skills through practice and involvement; and (d) an increased sense of mastery through attainment and performance of skills.

Although the nature and content of recreation participation programs are extremely diverse, there are two aspects that are constant. First is the issue of control by the individual. Individuals are more likely to voluntarily choose to participate. The client's role in recreation participation programs includes greater decision making and increased self-regulated behavior. The client has increased freedom of choice and intrinsic motivation. Clients may select the activity or program in which to engage. They also control the nature and intensity of their involvement. Thus, there is a high degree of freedom and participant control in these programs.

The second aspect focuses on the role of the therapeutic recreation specialist or staff member. In recreation participation programs, the staff member facilitates the involvement of the individuals. The specialist is generally no longer teaching or "in charge" per se. The client becomes largely responsible for his or her own experience and outcome, with the specialist moving to a different role. The role can be that of leader or supervisor, depending on the type of program. In the leadership role, the staff member directly interacts with the individuals or group to heighten, encourage, support, reinforce, or expand their participation. A variety of leadership techniques and strategies can be used. The specific technique employed should be appropriate for the individuals involved and compatible with the activity or nature of the program. Leadership is thus seen, not as one type of intervention, but as a variety of strategies to be acquired and utilized in a suitable way. The role of supervisor is quite different from the role of leader. The supervisor interacts with the participants only in a regulatory way, for safety of the individuals or protection of the facility or equipment. A staff member lifeguarding in a swimming program illustrates this point in the purest sense. Verbal or nonverbal interactions are strictly for safety or protection. A staff member may supervise a crafts area or a gym or a multipurpose area. In each of these situations, the staff person's presence is needed for legal as well as regulatory purposes. This person is, however, facilitating involvement through this important role. Indeed, participation in the chosen activity or experience would not be possible without the supervisory function. In many programs, the roles of supervisor and leader are combined. The staff member is supervising in a regulatory sense but also may enhance participation through verbal and nonverbal leadership interactions.

In recreation participation programs and services, the roles of leadership and supervision can greatly enhance the quality of the experience for the individuals involved. Thus, the acquisition and appropriate utilization of good leadership and supervisory techniques are a vital part of the therapeutic recreation specialist's total repertoire of facilitation skills.

Figure 2.11 displays the recreation participation component within the context of the total Leisure Ability Model. The major points presented in this first section are summarized with the dimensions of the model.

Recreation participation programs need to be further expanded within the context of community and clinical settings. The rationale for their provision, as well as the nature of content, varies considerably because of the uniqueness of these two very different settings.

Recreation Participation in a Variety of Roles

Recreation participation services may play a variety of roles, depending on the needs of clients and the settings in which services are provided. At least six roles can be delineated: (a) practice and application of skills, (b) inclusion into community services, (c) normalization of institutional routines, (d) focus on "well" aspects, (e) expression of a leisure lifestyle, and (f) diversion or palliative care. Each of these will be briefly reviewed as the reader is reminded of the position of recreation participation services within the total Leisure Ability Model (see Figure 2.11).

Practice and Application of Skills   Recreation participation programs provide ample opportunity for clients to practice and apply skills learned in functional intervention and leisure education programs, within a structured environment. Perhaps a leisure education program presented scrapbooking skills and the individual comes to the crafts room during open time to finish a project. Or chess was taught during a specific leisure skills session and the individual plays with another client to sharpen skills

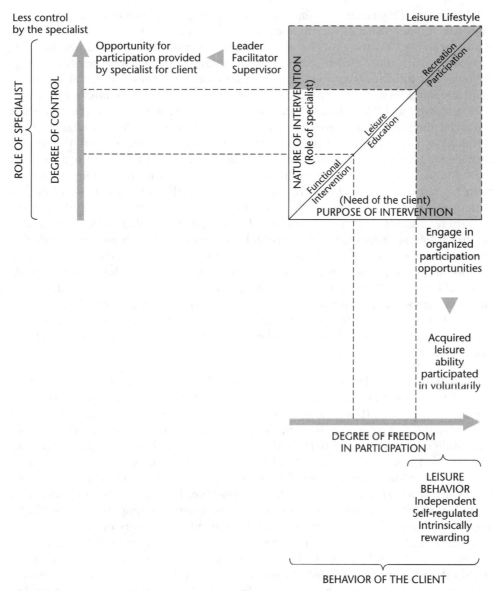

Figure 2.11 Recreation participation component of the Leisure Ability Model.

and strategy. A third example may be a dining skills and etiquette class that the client extends by practicing these skills with family in the facility's cafeteria. At this point the specialist has introduced the clients to the basic activity skills and now provides space, equipment, and the facility in order for the clients to be able to independently choose and participate in the activity. At this end of the spectrum the client has considerable choice, freedom, and autonomy to participate as he or she wishes, while the specialist minimizes his or her role.

Inclusionary Programs   In some instances participation in community-based programs is initiated through specific inclusion practices or programs. Often these programs are based on the entry-level skills that the individual has learned in prior program participation, either in a treatment setting or within a segregated setting. Involvement in inclusionary programs may be eased when the individual has some fundamental skills that can be practiced and improved within the community program.

Successful and full inclusion is dependent on several factors. First, the individual with the disability must have the activity skills, as well as the interaction skills, required to function within that program, even at a basic level. Second, the service providers of recreation programs in the public, voluntary, and private sectors must view the involvement of all individuals, including those with limitations, as part of their basic service responsibility. The Americans with Disabilities Act has had significant impact on the acceptance of the rights and abilities of individuals with disabilities.

There are responsibilities inherent in the adoption of a totally integrated approach for the individual with a disability or illness as well. Individuals with disabilities need to view the existing service structure as legitimately their domain. Clients' acceptance of personal responsibility for their own leisure lifestyle, the acquisition of leisure skills and interests, and the ability to function in an inclusionary setting are important considerations. Obviously, much of the responsibility for this approach also lies with professionals within health and human service fields such as special education, early childhood development, rehabilitation, social work, and therapeutic recreation.

Normalization of Institutional Routine   It has been previously stated that being in treatment does not remove the individual from the need for, or right to, leisure involvement. However, the individual in treatment might require assistance with leisure involvement, because the daily treatment facility routine is different from the home environment and many familiar resources may have been removed from use. In most situations, the individual leisure lifestyle of the client will be severely interrupted by the hospitalization. The nature of the illness or disability may make involvement in previous leisure patterns impossible. In other cases, hospitalization and treatment may render the previous leisure lifestyle unimportant. The clients themselves may or may not view leisure involvement as necessary or of any concern. Nonetheless, clients still have a need for leisure involvement, even if its nature and intent have changed. Ongoing leisure participation enables some normalization within the atypical environment of constant treatment focus. In most cases, involvement in leisure activities can help the individual adjust to the institutional routine and can introduce a degree of normalcy in an unnatural environment.

Focus on "Well" Aspects of Client   Another function of recreation participation may be to focus on the "well" aspects of the client. It has been suggested previously that therapeutic recreation may differ from other treatment disciplines in its focus on the abilities rather than the pathology of the individual. This focus on the "well" or holistic aspects of the individual is an important contribution to the individual's overall well-being. Recreation participation programs may focus on social interaction, fun, enjoyment, choice, and novelty. In addition, they may facilitate adjustment to illness or disability by focusing on what the client can do, and by providing "distance" or a "perspective" of the situation. Emotional equilibrium or balance is frequently cited as a benefit or outcome of leisure participation.

Expression of Leisure Lifestyle   Recreation participation programs in long-term settings take on a different dimension. In these settings, the provision of opportunity for self-directed leisure and recreation participation assumes a greater significance, owing to the length of time involved in treatment or care. In these situations, the recreation participation programs must reflect the concept of leisure lifestyle. In these cases, the therapeutic recreation program may be the only opportunities for leisure involvement the individual has; that is, the recreation participation program *is* the individual's leisure lifestyle.

For the patient or resident, these programs provide the opportunity for ongoing leisure participation and expression within the hospital or care setting. The therapeutic recreation specialist must carefully plan a full range of program and service offerings that adequately address the specific interests, preferences, and skills of the clients. It would appear that in the long-term setting, recreation participation programs should provide a great deal of variety and remain focused on the individual needs and interests of clients. Ideally, the nature and content of programs should be individualized and normalized to reflect appropriate adult and youth programs conducted for same-age groups living within the community.

In long-term and permanent-care settings in which the therapeutic recreation program utilizes a comprehensive approach incorporating functional intervention, leisure education, and recreation participation, the recreation participation program can and should include another aspect of program focus. As new leisure skills are learned, logically there needs to be an opportunity for engaging in those skills for enjoyment and self-expression. Thus, ongoing programs must parallel and provide the opportunity for personal choice within the leisure lifestyle that is being developed by the individual.

Some of the settings where therapeutic recreation is offered are those in which the clients will live their entire lives. Leisure lifestyle for these individuals must be viewed within the limitations of the disability and the long-term setting. Nonetheless, personal responsibility for one's own leisure lifestyle can be developed that culminates in the individual's choice and expression within many of the recreation participation programs.

Diversion or Palliative Purposes   Distraction, alleviation from boredom, release of emotions, and an opportunity to engage in action other than conversation and watching television often are cited by clients as reasons for desiring recreation participation programs while in treatment. These reasons in and of themselves can easily justify the establishment and operation of recreation participation programs.

Examples of the Leisure Ability Model in Practice

Briefly, two case studies will be outlined here to illustrate the utility and flexibility of the model, as well as typical clients and settings. The first is of adults on a physical medicine and rehabilitation unit, who have experienced traumatic spinal injuries as a result of automobile accidents, diving injuries, and gunshot wounds. The therapeutic recreation specialist has likely designed a program based on generic client needs as well as knowledge about the basic requirements for a satisfying leisure lifestyle. For example, functional intervention programs might include activities that increase endurance, sitting or standing tolerance, and strength, as these skills are prerequisite to many leisure and recreation activities, and are typical deficits of individuals with new spinal injuries. Leisure education programs may focus on self-awareness in relation to their new status; learning social skills such as assertiveness, coping, and friendship development; relearning or adapting premorbid leisure skills; and locating leisure resources appropriate to new interests and that are accessible. Recreation participation programs may involve practicing a variety of new leisure and social skills in a safe, structured environment. In designing and implementing these programs, the specialist builds in opportunities for the individual to exercise control, mastery, intrinsic motivation, and choice. The ultimate outcome would be for each individual to be able to adapt to and cope with his or her disability to the extent that he or she will experience a satisfying and independent leisure lifestyle, and be able to master skills usable in a variety of settings.

A second example is individuals diagnosed with depression in an outpatient clinic. The therapeutic recreation specialist, understanding the typical characteristics of individuals with depression and the features of a successful leisure lifestyle, conceptualizes, creates, implements, and evaluates a program of activities that aid the clients in developing satisfying leisure pursuits. For example, functional intervention programs may include working on the ability to make decisions as needed, and an exercise program to address loss of energy and frequent fatigue. Leisure education programs may focus on the identification of leisure barriers stopping individuals from enjoyable leisure; learning social skills such as initiation and assertiveness; learning new leisure skills that include physical exercise, leisure partners, and stress release; and learning about local recreation facilities of interest to individual clients. Recreation participation programs (if provided on an outpatient basis) may include involvement in a variety of activities that provide meaningful, healthy opportunities that provide a sense of competence, mastery, control, and choice. The targeted outcome would be for each individual to become competent in making decisions that result in healthy, satisfying leisure pursuits, both as an individual and with others.

The flexibility and utility of the Leisure Ability Model is one of its major strengths in service delivery. It provides a great deal of structure but also allows enormous creativity on the part of therapeutic recreation specialists in developing programs for various client groups in numerous settings.

Leisure Ability as a Holistic Approach

The Leisure Ability Model is an appropriate service delivery approach in any setting in which therapeutic recreation services are delivered. The three components (functional intervention, leisure education, and recreation participation) indicate areas of client need related to leisure. Within this conceptualization of three specific types of services, it is acknowledged that a given client or participant may require or need services in one, two, or all three areas. The nature of the setting and its mandate for service will determine which areas of program services are appropriate and justified for clients.

Although a continuum may be implied, in that improved functional ability may precede the acquisition of leisure-related skills, knowledge, and awareness, in many cases these two service areas may be addressed simultaneously. In other cases, the functional problem may be identified, but not acknowledged as an area in which improvement can be accomplished (e.g., sight or hearing). Such an individual may thus benefit from leisure education services that compensate for the functional problem and focus on the acquisition of leisure skills and knowledge within the constraints of the illness or disability. Regardless of the problems requiring functional intervention as a service area, or lack of knowledge or skills that would warrant the provision of leisure education services, it is most likely that all clients would benefit from, or enjoy, recreation participation services.

Services may vary, depending on the focus of the setting. Some short-term clinical settings, because of time and length of stay, may choose to deliver only functional intervention and/or leisure education services while still recognizing and endorsing the total Leisure Ability Model. Likewise some settings, such as public recreation, may view their mandate for service as being leisure education and recreation participation, though they easily can endorse the total approach, recognizing that functional intervention is a service component that is addressed in other settings.

Comprehensive programming necessitates a willingness on the part of the therapeutic recreation specialist to look at all areas of clients' leisure-related needs simultaneously and then appropriately prioritize service delivery based on client need and the availability of resources. Likewise, a given client may only need therapeutic recreation services in one area and should not be submitted to a full range of programs if they are not warranted.

The Leisure Ability Model provides a conceptual scheme to assist in the identification of clients' needs relative to their preferred leisure lifestyles. It also provides a solid and logical foundation for the movement of clients between various settings. Discharge of a client from a clinical setting to a community living situation is facilitated when both clinical and community agencies hold a common position regarding the nature of therapeutic recreation services. A continuity of therapeutic recreation service focus thus can be maintained regardless of the agency delivering services to the client at any given moment. The focus remains on the development, expression, and maintenance of a satisfying and freely chosen leisure lifestyle as the outcome of therapeutic recreation services.

Leisure Ability as an Outcome

The concept of a leisure lifestyle is very complex. It includes much more than a handful of activity skills and informational brochures. As noted by Iso-Ahola (1980), simply learning leisure activity skills does not create a satisfying, intrinsically motivating, or enjoyable leisure lifestyle. Leisure lifestyle means that the client:

- Has reduced major functional limitations that prohibit or significantly limit leisure involvement (or at least has learned ways to overcome these barriers)
- Understands and values the importance of leisure in the totality of life experiences
- Incorporates leisure into his or her daily life

- Has adequate social skills for involvement with others
- Is able to choose between several leisure activity options on a daily basis, and make decisions for leisure participation
- Is able to locate and use leisure resources as necessary
- Has increased perceptions of choice, motivation, freedom, responsibility, causality, and independence with regard to his or her leisure

These outcomes are targeted through the identification of client need, provision of programs to meet those needs, and the evaluation of outcomes during and after program delivery. A therapeutic recreation specialist designs, implements, and evaluates services aimed at those outcomes.

Summary

The Leisure Ability Model was developed to provide a descriptive and conceptual scheme for understanding the Leisure Ability philosophy. Each component (functional intervention, leisure education, and recreation participation) has been presented in depth within this chapter. The purpose, nature, and content of each of the three components has been explored in order to provide a rationale for programming as well as to give direction for program selection and development. The next section of this book will present information on the programming process used to incorporate these content areas.

STUDENT EXERCISES

Discussion Questions

1. Discuss why client need should drive program development and implementation, rather than other factors such as ease of delivery or interests of the specialist.
2. Explain, in your own words, the rationale for therapeutic recreation services.
3. Explain "intervention" or "treatment." Explain how functional intervention, leisure education, and recreation participation may all be considered intervention under the right circumstances.
4. What is the purpose of functional intervention? Give four or five examples of possible functional intervention activities for a group of clients with which you are most familiar. Compare your answers to those of other students in class.
5. What is the purpose of leisure education? Give four or five examples of possible leisure education activities for a group of clients with which you are most familiar. Compare your answers to those of other students in class.
6. What is the purpose of recreation participation? Give four or five examples of possible recreation participation activities for a group of clients with which you are most familiar. Compare your answers to those of other students in class.
7. Explain why leisure lifestyle is outside or beyond the reaches of the Leisure Ability Model. How does the focus on leisure lifestyle help the therapeutic recreation

specialist design and implement programs? How does it help define the scope of practice for therapeutic recreation?

8. How do the roles of the specialist and the roles of the client evolve throughout the Leisure Ability Model? How does this compare with the concepts of internal locus of control, self-efficacy, personal causality, and control, as introduced in the first chapter?

9. Review each component of the Leisure Education Content Model. Explain how each area contributes to a more meaningful leisure lifestyle of clients. What other areas might be important for inclusion within leisure education services?

10. Think about your own leisure lifestyle. How does it add to or detract from your quality of life or overall life satisfaction? How does your leisure lifestyle compare to that of other students in class?

Practice Test

1. Which of the following is the purpose of therapeutic recreation, according to the Leisure Ability Model?
   a. to provide activities to individuals with illnesses and disabilities
   b. to assess clients and analyze purposeful activities
   c. to make sure people with disabilities have fun
   d. to help individuals with disabilities develop a meaningful leisure lifestyle

2. Which of the following is included within the leisure resources component of the Leisure Ability Model?
   a. knowledge of activity opportunities
   b. understanding leisure attitudes
   c. social skills involving two or more people
   d. nontraditional leisure skills

3. What is the purpose of recreation participation?
   a. to facilitate an independent leisure lifestyle that involves self-efficacy, satisfaction, and external locus of control
   b. to provide diversion so people can have fun
   c. to provide an organized structure so people can practice skills and become independent
   d. to teach people social skills they will need later when they return to the community

4. Which of the following is an example of a goal that targets improving physical functional abilities?
   a. to increase orientation to reality
   b. to improve short-term memory
   c. to increase understanding of the role of leisure in life
   d. to improve fine motor skills

5. Which of the following is an appropriate goal for an individual who lacks interaction skills?
   a. to increase ability to control emotions
   b. to improve awareness of family resources

    c. to increase ability to converse with others

    d. to provide opportunities to interact with others

6. Which of the following is an appropriate goal for an individual who lacks ability to use leisure resources?

    a. to learn how to register for Park District programs

    b. to improve understanding of leisure as a state of mind

    c. to improve ability to join a group in progress

    d. to increase skills in programs that can be used outdoors

7. Which of the following best matches the overall purpose of therapeutic recreation?

    a. Activities are provided to allow the clients to have fun in their leisure.

    b. Activities are used to remediate functional limitations through treatment.

    c. Activities are designed to allow the person eventually to participate as independently as possible in leisure.

    d. Activities that teach leisure skills are used to reduce leisure barriers.

8. All programs in therapeutic recreation should be based on:

    a. community resources.

    b. client need.

    c. utilization reviews.

    d. specialist skill.

9. A leisure lifestyle is:

    a. the acquisition and utilization of leisure skills, knowledges, and abilities.

    b. having adequate social and physical skills to participate in a variety of leisure activities on a weekly basis.

    c. the daily incorporation of leisure-related attitudes, awareness, and activities within the total life experience.

    d. participating independently in various leisure activities with a variety of leisure partners.

10. The four components of leisure education include:

    a. functional intervention, leisure education, social skills, and leisure partners.

    b. leisure lifestyle, leisure awareness, leisure attitudes, and leisure partners.

    c. knowledge of leisure, self-awareness, leisure and play attitudes, and related participatory and decision-making skills.

    d. leisure awareness, leisure skills, social skills, and leisure resources.

Answers: 1. d, 2. a, 3. c, 4. d, 5. c, 6. a, 7. c, 8. b, 9. c, 10. d

Chapter Activities

Research Results

Use the *Therapeutic Recreation Journal,* the *Annual in Therapeutic Recreation,* the *American Journal of Recreational Therapy,* and any other health-related journals to locate studies that report research results for outcomes in the areas of functional intervention, leisure education, and/or recreation participation. How do the results help contribute to what specialists know about therapeutic recreation practice?

Activity Resources

Locate a variety of activity resources, such as books, periodicals, Internet sites, etc., for activities that can be used to provide functional intervention, leisure education, and recreation participation services. Start a file for future professional reference. Bring the resources to class and share them with other students.

Therapeutic Recreation Specialist Interview

Ask a local therapeutic recreation specialist about his or her functional intervention, leisure education, and recreation participation programs. What is the percentage of direct contact with clients in each type of service? Which types of services or programs are offered most often? What client needs do those programs meet? How are programming decisions made?

Therapeutic Recreation Specialist Shadowing

Shadow a local therapeutic recreation specialist for a day (or more) to see how functional intervention, leisure education, and recreation participation programs are offered to clients. What content is presented? What outcomes are achieved? How do therapeutic recreation services compare with other services within the agency?

REFERENCES

Iso-Ahola, S. E. (1980). *The social psychology of leisure and recreation.* Dubuque, IA: Wm C. Brown Company Publishers.

Kelly, J. R. (1996). *Leisure* (3rd ed.). Needham Heights, MA: Allyn and Bacon.

CHAPTER 3

Therapeutic Recreation Accountability Model

Accountability for the delivery of services to clients is of paramount importance to contemporary health care and human services for a number of professional disciplines, including therapeutic recreation. In addition to concepts related to the **scope of care** (for therapeutic recreation, that includes functional intervention, leisure education, and recreation participation) discussed in the last chapter, therapeutic recreation specialists also need to be concerned about *how* these services are delivered to clients. In other words, therapeutic recreation specialists are accountable not only for the content of the profession but also for the process of service delivery in a timely, efficient, and effective manner. Therapeutic recreation professionals are accountable for helping the client make a consistent and predictable change as a result of involvement in therapeutic recreation programs.

The first two chapters focused on the content of therapeutic recreation program delivery; this chapter begins the discussion about the process and procedures of delivering intervention programs to clients. The major way that professionals demonstrate accountability is through the documentation created or maintained at each step in the analysis, planning, implementation, and evaluation processes. The Therapeutic Recreation Accountability Model is one way of depicting the documentation used by therapeutic recreation specialists in demonstrating accountability for services. Accountability for services begins with initial program design and continues throughout the entire process of service delivery and evaluation.

Accountability for Therapeutic Recreation Service Provision

Accountability means being held responsible for the production and delivery of therapeutic recreation services that best meet client needs and move clients toward predetermined outcomes in the most timely, efficient, and effective manner possible. Increased accountability for service provision is being mandated by such groups as:

- Joint Commission on Accreditation of Healthcare Organizations (JCAHO)
- Commission on Accreditation of Rehabilitation Facilities (CARF)
- Centers for Medicare and Medicaid Services (CMS, formerly the Health Care Financing Administration, HCFA)

- National Therapeutic Recreation Society (NTRS)
- American Therapeutic Recreation Association (ATRA)

These groups want to know that services provided to clients are appropriate and of high quality. This usually is established through proof of adherence to specific standards that represent some benchmarks for quality of care. Navar (1991) explained this as "providing the right patient with the right service [at] the right time in the right setting at the right intensity and for the right duration" (p. 5). Several systems or procedures must be in place before accountable services can be delivered to clients dependably.

Systems Design and Therapeutic Recreation Intervention

The beauty of using a systems approach for designing therapeutic recreation programs is that the designer must specify the intended outcome as well as the process to get there *prior* to the implementation of the program. That is, systems design assumes that there is a well-defined, goal-oriented *purpose* to the activity or program being provided. Objectives, goals, and outcome measures help define where the program is going and how it is going to get there. There is a well-defined plan for getting the participant from point A to point B, through his or her participation in a program that has been specifically designed for that purpose. This is a major factor that helps system-designed programs to become intervention.

A program that is designed and implemented to be intervention has as its outcome some degree of client behavioral change (that is, behavioral change is the purpose of the program). This may mean an increase in knowledge, an increase in skill, a decrease in some behavior, and so on. To be considered intervention, a program has to be well designed and implemented according to a plan that specifically addresses participant change. On the other hand, *diversional* activities are provided for fun, enjoyment, or relaxation (that is, fun, enjoyment, and relaxation are the purpose of the programs).

Obviously, these two types of programs require different planning, implementation, and evaluation skills. A systems approach is a useful tool for intervention designers. But even if the total process suggested in this text is not completely followed, any designer receives benefits from being exposed to a systematic and logical program design and evaluation process. In order to see how this relates to program evaluation on a variety of levels, a more comprehensive way to view service design and delivery is needed.

Intervention as a Means for Creating and Measuring Client Change

What is suggested throughout these chapters is that programming start with a comprehensive program design that includes such actions as analyzing the "input" factors that may influence a program's operation, documenting a clear purpose of both the comprehensive and specific programs, and reviewing and selecting specific programs

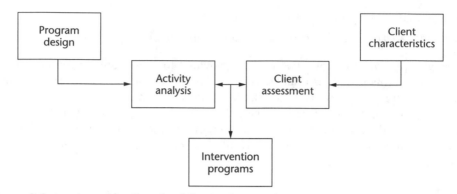

Figure 3.1 Input considerations for delivering intervention programs.

that meet the intended purpose. Obviously, one of the major input factors of comprehensive program design is client need. All programs are created to address some area of client need or deficit.

This is a good, logical start to ensure that programs will be purposeful, rather than provided "cafeteria-style" based solely on the specialist's interests and expertise. In Figure 3.1, this effort is labeled program design and represents all the decisions and end results that come from the comprehensive and specific program design.

To make sure that the participation requirements of each planned activity are understood fully, an **activity analysis** is conducted. This helps planners understand, for example, that crafts, movies, and bingo are *not* primarily social activities; that there is little in the rules of these activities that teaches and/or requires social interaction and, therefore, social interaction skills. Again, an activity analysis helps the programmer provide activities that are more likely to be designed as intervention than as diversion, simply because the specialist has had to look at the activity's requirements systematically through this process. Because the requirements of the activity are known and planned for (or modified) prior to the provision of the activity, activity analysis also can help in designing the evaluation. Figure 3.1 shows the relationship of activity analysis to program design.

On the other side of the model is the client group. While it is recognized that each client will have individual characteristics, a disability and/or disease process provides for some commonalities between and among people. For example, people with clinical depression may act in certain, somewhat predictable, patterns, just as individuals with acquired brain injury have some similar reactions, depending on the location of the injury. In therapeutic recreation programming, professionals depend on the ability to group participants in programs based on their disability and/or illness characteristics (it is *within* the program that individuals are treated uniquely). Planning for intervention programs relies heavily on the programmer's knowledge of the disability and/or illness characteristics of the participant group. This is represented on the right-hand side of Figure 3.1 as client characteristics.

The process of client assessment is used to place clients individually into programs. Without a valid and reliable assessment, a program has little chance of being interven-

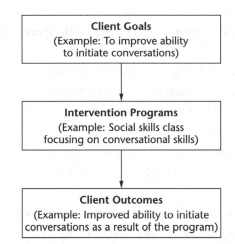

Figure 3.2 Relationship between goals, intervention programs, and outcomes.

tion. That is, when clients are not assessed individually for their strengths, weaknesses, and program needs, and all participants are encouraged or invited to come to all programs, this is a definite signal of nonintervention programming. Client assessment, conducted in a systematic and meaningful manner, is a major factor in providing intervention, as it helps to determine what types of behavioral change(s) are needed by the participant. Client assessment is just to the left of client characteristics in Figure 3.1.

Activity analysis helps to determine the participation requirements of individual programs or activities, increasing their potential to be intervention. Client assessment helps to determine the strengths, weaknesses, and programming needs of individual clients, thus increasing the potential to meet client needs through well-planned and -analyzed programs. It is the powerful combination of these two forces that almost ensures that the program will change the behavior of the client, and thus produce client outcomes. If the therapeutic recreation specialist neglects to perform meaningful activity analysis and/or client assessment, programs will have little chance of meeting the targeted goals of client behavioral change. In later chapters, the importance of the content of the program matching the content of the client assessment will be discussed at length. This match is vital to being able to place clients into the right programs that meet their needs and produce predictable client outcomes.

Client Outcomes

"**Outcomes** are the observed changes in a client's status as a result of our interventions and interactions. Outcomes can be attributed to the process of providing care, and this should enable us to determine if we are doing for our clients that which we purport to do" (Shank & Kinney, 1991, p. 76). Being accountable means being able to design and deliver programs that will bring about some predetermined outcome or behavioral change in the client. This implies that each service, such as nursing, social work, or therapeutic recreation, must be able to target specific behavioral change in the client that will occur as a result of the client's participation in that discipline's service. Figure 3.2 shows the relationship between goals, the programs, and outcomes.

Box 3.1   Typical Outcomes of Therapeutic Recreation Services

Functional Intervention

      Increased ability to manage anger appropriately

      Increased emotional control and healthy expression

      Increased physical endurance

      Increased ability to remain on task

      Improved adjustment to disability and/or illness

      Improved orientation to people, place, and time

Leisure Education

      Increased ability to make decisions related to leisure participation

      Increased knowledge of the importance of leisure in one's life

      Improved ability to initiate and maintain conversations

      Improved ability to compromise and negotiate a solution

      Increased ability to display acceptable hygiene practices

      Increased skill in an individual leisure activity

      Increased ability to locate and utilize a community leisure resource

      Increased knowledge of leisure resources within the home

Recreation Participation

      Improved ability to express self within leisure context

      Improved ability to select and participate in an activity of choice

---

Let's use nursing as an example. The anticipated outcome of a patient education program for those with diabetes may be that "the individual can self-inject the correct dosage of insulin in a sterile manner and with proper technique." The nurse, then, is responsible for providing the patient with sufficient education and practice until the outcome occurs and the client can demonstrate competence in that behavior. An example of an outcome in therapeutic recreation services may be that "the individual can identify and utilize community leisure resources of his or her choice within the community." That is, by the end of the program, the client will demonstrate competence in the target behavior—locating and using community leisure services of his or her choice. The therapeutic recreation professional is accountable for designing, delivering, and evaluating programs that will bring about this end for the client or group of clients. The outcome, or change in the client's knowledge, skills, and/or abilities, is the direct consequence of participation. Box 3.1 provides some examples of typical outcomes of therapeutic recreation services, although they are not yet written in measurable terms.

Important Characteristics of Outcomes   In essence, targets for behavioral change must be identified *before* programs can be designed and delivered to create that change. There must be a direct link between the process or delivery of care, and the outcomes expected from it (Riley, 1987a, 1991a). The desired outcomes drive how the program is designed and delivered, as Figure 3.2 shows. The ability to produce client outcomes is contingent on well-designed and systematic programs into which clients are placed based on the needs shown from assessment results. The relationship or causal link is a strong one (Riley, 1987a, 1991a; Stumbo, 2000, 2003b, 2003c; Stumbo & Hess, 2001a).

Dunn, Sneegas, and Carruthers (1991) noted that within the profession of therapeutic recreation a variety of terms (e.g., objectives, behavioral objectives, performance measures) have been used to define what is currently termed outcome measures (see Chapter 10). What outcomes are relevant? What outcomes carry the greatest importance to clients, given their demographic, ethnic, and cultural characteristics? What outcomes are attainable during (especially brief) intervention? The answers to these questions may be unique for each individual agency.

Stumbo (2000) documented six characteristics of outcomes that are valued and have utility for measurement purposes. These six characteristics are as follows.

- Outcomes must be *identified*. This task is of primary importance and must be done before other measurement tasks are undertaken (Johnson & Ashton-Shaeffer, 2000; Stumbo, 2000; Stumbo & Hess, 2001a). What outcomes from the therapeutic recreation service are important to the clients seen at this facility? What target outcomes fit within the scope of therapeutic recreation practice that will benefit these clients and fall within the intent of this facility and its other health care disciplines?

- Outcomes must be *measurable* (Buettner, 2000; Hodges & Luken, 2000; Peterson & Stumbo, 2000). While most health care providers believe their services contribute to the overall, global health and well-being of their clients, these "measures" often are deemed too broad and to lack meaning in today's health care environment. There is greater interest in defining outcomes more specifically and in smaller terms. Therapeutic recreation specialists need to locate and document outcomes in five areas: clinical status, functional status, well-being or quality of life, satisfaction with care, and cost/resource utilization (see Stumbo, 2003c). What categories of outcomes or outcome indicators are produced by therapeutic recreation services? What important outcomes of therapeutic recreation services are measurable, and how and when will they be measured? Will these measurements be sensitive to change within a short time period?

- Outcomes must be *achievable* (Hodges & Luken, 2000; Johnson & Ashton-Shaeffer, 2000). Shortened lengths of stay have complicated the accomplishments of most health care professionals. With fewer days of inpatient or even outpatient care, it is difficult and sometimes impossible to achieve the outcomes that may have been identified five or ten years ago. What can be accomplished within a patient's two-day or five-day stay? What is important in this person's treatment, and how can it be achieved? It has been a difficult task for most therapeutic recreation professionals to narrow their scope of measurement (and programming) to fit the patient's length of stay.

- Outcomes must be *demonstrable* or *documented* (Buettner, 2000; Peterson & Stumbo, 2000). For example, if a stress management program is to produce measurable changes in the clients' behavior, attitude, or level of stress, the therapeutic recreation specialist must be able to document that change. Often, this means having valid and reliable instruments or tools that measure the level of behavior, attitude, or knowledge that is targeted, and how that changed as the result of care. It also means having a body of research that supports these outcomes (Seibert, 1991).

- Outcomes must be **predictable** or **causal** (Riley, 1991b). That is, there must be a direct relationship between the intervention and the outcome. Using the example of a stress management program, it would be unwise to measure differences in leisure attitudes as an outcome, since a change in leisure attitudes is unlikely to be directly attributable to a stress management program.

- Outcomes must be *meaningful* (Buettner, 2000; Devine & Wilhite, 1999; Johnson & Ashton-Shaeffer, 2000; Lee & Yang, 2000; McCormick & Funderburk, 2000; Shank, Coyle, Kinney, & Lay, 1995). With all the constraints above, client outcomes must still be meaningful to the client and his or her recovery or health status, as well as valuable to third-party payers. What important contribution does therapeutic recreation make to the client's success? What unique contribution does therapeutic recreation make to other services provided by the health care team? What outcome changes in the client would make the most difference in his or her life?

A great deal of effort on the part of the specialist should be spent considering which client behaviors, skills, or attitudes can be changed, given the goals and design of the program. For example, if clients' average length of stay is seven days, it would seem difficult to change attitudes that took a lifetime to develop. Instead, the specialist might choose to help the client increase his or her knowledge of community leisure resources, an outcome that typically can be expected within seven days of intervention. The outcome has relevance, importance, and is attainable. Smaller, more measurable client outcomes may be preferable to larger, less measurable outcomes.

Several authors have provided guidelines for selecting and developing client outcome statements (Anderson, Ball, & Murphy, 1975, as cited in Dunn, Sneegas, & Carruthers, 1991; Shank & Kinney, 1991). These authors suggested that the specialist create and implement client outcome statements that consider:

- The efficiency and effectiveness of demonstrating client change
- A reasonable relationship between the services provided and the expected outcome
- The connection between occurrence of the outcome and the timing of data collection
- The relevance to the client and society
- The goals and intent of the program
- An appropriate level of specification, but not reduced to trivial detail
- Individual client variation within any given program

- Both long-term and short-term goals and objectives
- The social and home environment to which the client will return
- Behaviors that are generalizable and transferable to a variety of settings and situations

Factors Affecting Service Accountability

Although accountability often is equated with program evaluation, it starts with program conceptualization, design, and implementation and involves several decision points in this process. These decision points contribute to the specialist's ability to be accountable for services and affect client outcomes. The Therapeutic Recreation Accountability Model depicts the major decision points in the total programming process. As an introduction to this model, these factors are grouped into four categories: (1) program design, (2) client assessment, (3) client documentation, and (4) program evaluation.

Program Design. "Determining what is effective therapeutic recreation intervention depends upon examining the relationships between various program/treatment protocols for a specific illness/diagnostic category and the associated outcomes of those treatments" (Riley, 1991a, p. 54). This speaks to the direct connection or match between the services provided and the expected client outcomes (Carruthers, 2003; Dunn, Sneegas, & Carruthers, 1991; Navar, 1991; Shank & Kinney, 1991). In other words, the "right services" must be delivered to produce the "right outcomes" (Navar, 1991, p. 5).

According to Connolly (1984):

the bottom line of designing a program is to put together a strategy, intervention, or approach that will aid those who participate in the program to accomplish behavioral change in the form of improved functional abilities and/or acquisition of new knowledge and skills. One measure of the effectiveness of a program, therefore, is documenting the outcomes clients attain as a consequence of participating in the program. (p. 159)

Riley (1991a) draws attention to the concepts of "measurable change" and "relationship" (p. 59). "The causal relationship between the process of care (intervention) and the outcomes of care (change in patient behavior) is critical" (Riley, 1991a, p. 59). Several authors advocate that there must be a direct and proven link between the goals of the program, the type of program being delivered, and the client outcomes expected from participation in the program. It is this link that is central to the concept of intervention and accountability for services (Carruthers, 2003; Ross & Ashton-Shaeffer, 2003).

Intervention or outcome-oriented programs have unique characteristics that are distinguishable from nonintervention programs. In order for therapeutic recreation programs to be considered intervention, they must possess the following characteristics:

- Be systematically designed, prior to their implementation, with outcomes in mind
- Be part of a larger systematic collection of quality programs
- Be designed based on client characteristics and needs

- Have identified client outcomes that are relevant, important, and timely
- Be able to produce desired results or outcomes

The therapeutic recreation process begins with systematic program design. A systems approach for designing comprehensive and specific therapeutic recreation programs (discussed in depth in Chapters 4 and 5) implies that the designer must specify the intended outcomes as well as the process to accomplish the outcomes *prior* to the implementation of the program. Systems design assumes a well-defined, goal-oriented *purpose* to the activity or program being provided. There is a well-thought-out plan for getting the participant from point A to point B, through his or her participation in a program or programs that are specifically designed for that purpose (Carruthers, 2003; Ross & Ashton-Shaeffer, 2003). These direct linkages are among the major factors that help systems-designed programs produce client change.

A program that is designed and implemented to be **intervention** has, as its outcome, some degree of client behavioral change (that is, behavioral change is the purpose of the program) (Shank & Kinney, 1991; Stumbo, 2000, 2003a, 2003b; Stumbo & Hess, 2001a). This may mean an increase in knowledge, an increase in skill, a decrease in some behavior, an increase in functional ability, and so forth. The targeted outcomes must be applicable to the client upon discharge or exit from the program. It is part of the specialist's responsibility to identify relevant, meaningful, and timely outcomes that will affect the individual's future leisure lifestyle. To be accountable for producing client change, a program has to be well designed and implemented according to a plan that addresses the desired, specific participant change. On the other hand, programs that are not accountable often lack forethought into the content and process of delivery or the intended outcomes.

Specific or individual programs are designed and provided as part of the larger whole intended to meet the diverse needs of clients. This applies to the comprehensive series of therapeutic recreation programs as well as to the agency's overall system of services. Each specific program should complement other programs offered within the therapeutic recreation department or unit and within the larger agency's slate of services. Each discipline, through its provision of services to clients, contributes to the agency's overall service mission.

Typical Questions That Address Accountable Program Design

- What are the typical characteristics of the client group to be served?
- What is the mission of the agency and of the therapeutic recreation department?
- What knowledges and skills are important for the client to experience future success?
- What are the best ways to design and deliver programs to attain client outcomes?
- How will program success (outcomes) be determined?

Client Assessment.   A comprehensive set of programs designed and available to meet the range of incoming client needs is required so that each client may be placed into programs based on individual need (Carruthers, 2003; Ross & Ashton-Shaeffer, 2003). In addition to quality programs, this depends on an assessment procedure that produces valid and reliable results that are used for client placement. (This is discussed more fully in Chapter 9.)

A major requirement to establish validity and reliability is the alignment between the content of the programs offered and the content of the client assessment (Stumbo, 1997, 2002, 2003c). This match is important to the provision of intervention programs. When a match between programs and the assessment exists, the potential for the right clients to receive the right services is maximized; when a match does not exist, the potential for clients to receive the wrong or unnecessary services is maximized. The right client cannot be placed into the right program unless the assessment contains the right information (valid and relevant) and is refined to the point that placement is accurate (reliable) (Stumbo, 1991, 1994/1995, 1997, 2002, 2003c). Quality client assessment procedures typically have the following general characteristics:

- Content of the assessment matches the content of the programs into which clients are placed.
- Assessment results are consistent and repeatable.
- Testing and field studies have strengthened the confidence placed in the results.
- To the fullest extent possible, the assessment procedure is easy to understand, use, analyze, and interpret into practical results.
- Assessment results lead to client placement into programs with minimal error.

In this way, client assessment provides the bridge between the programs that are offered and the client's involvement in the programs. It is crucial that decisions surrounding client placement be made with a high degree of confidence so that the client may receive the fullest benefit.

Typical Questions That Address Accountable Client Assessments

- To what extent does the content of the assessment match the content of the programs offered?
- How accurate are the results of the assessment, from one administration to another, from one client to another, from one specialist to another?
- What research has been completed improving the qualities of the assessment?
- How will the results of the assessment be used to place clients into programs?

Client Documentation.   An important part of being accountable is documenting what happens to the client as a result of involvement in programs. A typical motto of many agencies is: "If it is not written down, it did not happen." This stresses the importance of accurate and timely written documentation about services provided to clients and their reactions to it. Because most client documentation has legal implications for accountability, great care must be taken to ensure that it is objective and descriptive. Examples of individual client documentation include assessment summaries, treatment or program plans, progress notes, and discharge/referral summaries. These forms document the connections between program goals, client goals, client program involvement, and client outcomes. Quality client documentation has several common characteristics:

- It is parallel in intent to the mission of the therapeutic recreation department's programs.
- It is focused on the anticipated outcomes of client involvement.
- It contains objective, accurate descriptions of client behaviors.
- The format is usually dictated by the overall agency's policies and procedures.
- It is usually performed in conjunction with other disciplines' documentation.

These pieces of documentation help to record the needs of the clients, services provided to them, and their behavioral change as a result of involvement in the program. They form the permanent record upon which many decisions are made.

Typical Questions That Address Accountable Client Documentation

- To what extent does the documentation objectively and accurately describe the planned and actual services received by the client?
- How well does the documentation reflect the goals of the comprehensive program and of the individual client?
- How well does the documentation measure and describe the outcomes achieved by the client?
- How well does the documentation convey important information about the client's movement through services?

Program Evaluation.   A key piece in the accountability process is program evaluation. Program evaluation helps determine whether both program and client outcomes were achieved. Whether conducted as a **formative evaluation** (one that takes place during the program) or a **summative evaluation** (one that takes place at the end of the program), information collected during evaluation helps determine whether a program helped clients achieve their outcomes and whether the program should continue as originally implemented, be modified in same way, or be terminated and replaced with another program deemed more likely to be effective (Widmer, 2001; Widmer, Zabriskie, & Wells, 2003).

Two processes are linked closely to program evaluation: continuous quality improvement and efficacy research. Continuous quality improvement, performance improvement, or quality assurance is a process, usually mandated by external agencies such as the JCAHO or CARF. Continuous quality improvement involves all disciplines, including therapeutic recreation, examining their services to determine the ways in which services can be improved (McCormick, 2003).

Efficacy research is designed specifically to scrutinize how effective programs are or were in attaining client outcomes. Program evaluation information may be obtained in a variety of ways, including client interviews, reviews of client and/or program documentation, and aftercare surveys of client satisfaction. Quality program evaluation that aids the specialist in maintaining accountability has several characteristics:

- It is often planned as the program is being designed.
- It measures the attainment of program and/or client goals.

- It follows accepted methods of data collection, analysis, and interpretation.
- It is systematic, objective, and thorough.
- It is used for improvement of services to clients.

Program evaluation is important to the overall improvement of programs. Without evaluation, specialists are much less likely to be accountable for service provision and outcomes, and they will have a more difficult time justifying the need for their services. As such, program evaluation is one of the most important tasks of the professional.

Typical Questions That Address Accountable Program Evaluation

- To what extent does the program evaluation measure the impact of the program on clients?
- How will the specialist ensure that the evaluation process is collecting the most important information?
- From whom and how will the data be gathered?
- How systematic, reliable, and objective are both the tool(s) and the data collection procedures?
- How will the results of the program evaluation be used, and by whom?
- How will the results of the program evaluation be used for improvement of future programs?

Each piece plays an important role in the overall scheme of creating an accountable system of service delivery. Each action has a distinct function in contributing to the overall accountability of service delivery to clients. Research has shown that therapeutic recreation departments that fail to perform even a single function outlined in the Therapeutic Recreation Accountability Model have much greater difficulty in delivering programs that produce predictable results and that change the behaviors of clients (Stumbo & Hess, 2001b). Only departments that design, deliver, and evaluate systematic intervention programs will survive in the future. The Therapeutic Recreation Accountability Model was created to help therapeutic recreation specialists view the overall picture of producing and delivering quality intervention programs to clients.

The Therapeutic Recreation Accountability Model

The **Therapeutic Recreation Accountability Model (TRAM)** was designed to help therapeutic recreation specialists conceptualize the connections between different tasks in the delivery of services to clients. These conceptual connections are important. Research has shown that if each job task in the model is handled separately and without regard to how it affects and is affected by other parts of the model, services are likely to be fragmented and without consistent purpose (Stumbo & Hess, 2001b). However, when various parts of the model are seen as interrelated and interdependent, services are more likely to be of high quality and oriented toward producing beneficial client outcomes. This, in turn, allows the specialist to be more accountable for program delivery and to justify inclusion on the health care treatment team.

The TRAM highlights the various accountability and documentation procedures used by the therapeutic recreation specialist to monitor and make decisions about the delivery of services for producing beneficial client outcomes. The model synthesizes several concepts (that later become separate chapters in this text, e.g., program planning, client assessment, or quality improvement) into a comprehensive *system* of accountable service provision. The TRAM depicts interrelationships between various decision or documentation points used by the specialist to provide and monitor appropriate, quality services. These logical linkages are crucial to providing clients with goal-oriented, outcome-based interventions.

Advantages

One of the major contributions of the TRAM is that it represents the first depiction of the relationship between various functions of the therapeutic recreation specialist described singly elsewhere in the literature. The components found in the model are not new; they each have been presented individually in prior literature. However, their individual presentations have allowed specialists to view the functions separately, when in fact, the *connections* and *relationships* between the tasks are of paramount importance. A well-designed program is of little use if an assessment fails to correlate with the program and therefore fails to place the right clients in the intended program. Likewise, if client objectives for participation in a program are not well matched with the program's goals, then involvement in the program is not likely to help the client reach his or her intended objectives/outcomes. The *relationship* between components of the TRAM is important if the specialist is to be accountable for program and client outcomes (Stumbo & Hess, 2001b).

The second major advantage of the TRAM is the focus on accountability that starts with initial program design rather than with summative program evaluation. Although program evaluation is important in collecting information for accountability purposes, the process of being able to justify programs and how they are offered to clients begins much earlier in the process. Accountability starts with considering and selecting the best programs to meet client needs. The selection and design of programs that move clients toward their targeted outcomes is one of the first and most important steps of accountability. The next section briefly outlines the key components of the TRAM that provide the basis for the remaining chapters in this text.

Components

The TRAM was created to help specialists visualize the interactive nature of documentation and decision points involved in the delivery, implementation, and evaluation of accountable programs. Expanding on the models and concepts documented by Peterson and Gunn (1984) and Carter, Van Andel, and Robb (1995), the TRAM attempts to depict the relationship between program input factors (such as activity analysis and assessment) and output factors (such as program outcomes and client outcomes).

The TRAM is presented in Figure 3.3. Each component of the model will be discussed separately, beginning with comprehensive program design. In practice, these

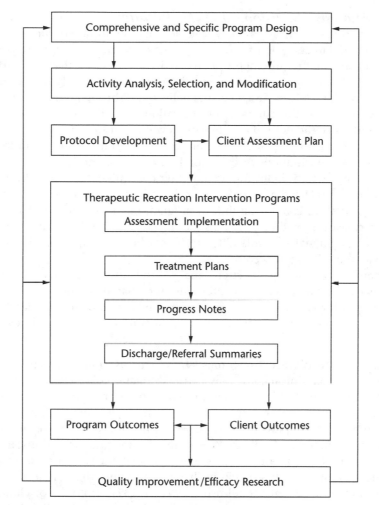

Figure 3.3 Therapeutic Recreation Accountability Model.

elements are highly interactive. Interactive arrows virtually could be drawn between all components of the TRAM; those with the strongest relationships are provided.

Comprehensive and Specific Program Design. Program design involves establishing the direction of the therapeutic recreation department, unit, or agency (Carruthers, 2003; Ross & Ashton-Shaeffer, 2003). This process entails gathering data about those factors (such as the community, agency and/or department, clients, and profession) that impact the program and its clients, and prioritizing and selecting those programs that best meet client needs. Implementation and evaluation plans are created to ensure that the right programs will be delivered and reviewed systematically. The direction taken by the therapeutic recreation department at this point is crucial to the success of its remaining operations. Chapters 4 and 5 discuss comprehensive and specific program design in more detail.

Activity Analysis, Selection, and Modification.   Activity analysis is the process used to systematically review specific activities to determine whether they have the potential to help clients achieve targeted outcomes. Activity analysis reviews the characteristics and requirements of an activity for client participation, so that the best activity—that is, one that can most efficiently and effectively help clients reach their goals—can be selected, designed, and delivered. "Through the processes of activity and task analyses, the [therapeutic recreation specialist] selects and sequences potential content so the desired client changes will result from participation" (Carter, Van Andel, & Robb, 1995, p. 127). The professional should "understand the activity and its potential contributions to behavioral outcomes" (Peterson & Gunn, 1984, p. 180). An activity analysis helps the programmer determine if any modifications need to be made to the selected activity in order that clients will benefit most fully. Thorough activity analysis is a critical link to program planning because it helps ensure that the specialist is providing programs that meet client needs and abilities. Activity analysis is an additional accountability factor that helps the specialist know that the "right services" are being delivered.

A system for completing an activity analysis and determining what modifications might be needed is presented in Chapter 6. Factors that affect the selection of appropriate activities for client involvement are outlined in Chapter 7. Clearly, activity analysis and selection are closely related to program design, protocol development, and client assessment.

Protocols.   **Protocols** are sometimes referred to as clinical practice guidelines. Hood (2001) defined clinical guidelines as "the distillation of the best collective thinking from the literature, from practicing clinicians, and from academics on how to treat a particular medical situation" (p. 193). As such, they provide practitioners with information about "best practices" to use with individuals who have specific needs, problems, or conditions. They are "a group of strategies or actions initiated in response to a problem, an issue, or a symptom of a client. They are not programs or program descriptions . . . but are approaches or techniques that will lead to expected treatment outcomes" (Knight & Johnson, 1991, p. 137). Protocols or clinical guidelines are meant to provide a blueprint of treatment for a specific diagnosis or client problem, and when validated through professional use and consensus, allow for program benchmarks to be set. There are two kinds of protocols, diagnostic (based on client deficits) and treatment (based on specific programs). Both kinds are useful for increasing the standardization of intervention programs within various service delivery agencies and departments across the country, primarily because they help define the input, process, and projected outcomes of well-designed intervention procedures (Ferguson, 1992). Connolly and Keogh-Hoss (1991) and Knight and Johnson (1991) asserted that protocols are a link between standards of practice and both efficacy research and quality improvement activities.

Both professional organizations are making progress on creating and publishing clinical guidelines. Some of the most recent efforts include Hood and Carruthers (2002), Carruthers and Hood (2002), Buettner (2001), and Buettner and Fitzsimmons (2003). More information about protocols and their usefulness to practice is presented in Chapter 8.

Assessment Plan.   Client assessment is the process used to place clients into therapeutic recreation programs based on their individual needs, strengths, and limitations. Without a valid and reliable assessment, a program has little chance of being intervention and a client has little chance of attaining outcomes. That is, when clients are not assessed individually for their strengths, weaknesses, and program needs, and all participants are encouraged or invited to come to all programs, this is a major indication that client outcomes will not be attained.

In this phase of the model, a plan for developing or selecting and implementing an assessment procedure is formed. Decisions about assessment content and implementation procedures are made. At least four major concepts are important to understanding how these decisions are made:

- The content of the assessment must reflect the content of the programs that have been selected for delivery to clients.

- The match between the assessment content and the program content implies that the assessment must be valid for its intended use, primarily for placing clients into the most appropriate programs to address their needs.

- In addition, the assessment process must be able to deliver reliable results, indicating that specialists need to have standardized procedures and tools.

- Client assessments play an important role in determining the baseline of client needs, abilities, and limitations, and this baseline is crucial to proving outcomes during or after the process of intervention (Stumbo, 2002, 2003a).

Client assessment, conducted in a systematic and meaningful manner, is a major foundation for providing outcome-based programs, as it helps determine what types of behavioral change(s) are needed by the participant. Client assessment is the topic of Chapter 9.

Intervention Programs and Client Documentation.   Therapeutic recreation intervention programs are provided to clients based on need. It is common practice to group participants in programs based on their disability and/or illness characteristics that imply similar needs. For example, individuals with traumatic brain injury may demonstrate similar needs to develop impulse control. Planning for intervention programs relies heavily on the programmer's knowledge of the disability and/or illness characteristics or expressed leisure-related needs of the participant group.

Shank and Kinney (1987) implied that the intervention process is one that requires careful and directed planning. "The clinical or therapeutic use of activity implies a careful selection and manipulation of the activities in a prescriptive sense" (Shank & Kinney, 1987, p. 70). This means that intervention programs must have the specific intention of modifying client behavior and be presented in a manner most likely to systematically produce these changes.

The likelihood of program success is improved by forethought during planning. As mentioned above, well-designed and systematic programs that include processes such as activity analysis and client assessment are much more likely to be planned as intervention and produce client behavioral changes.

The baseline for intervention is documented in a client assessment. Problems, strengths, and limitations are documented in order to determine the client's needs for services. As services are delivered, additional client documentation includes the client's individualized treatment plan, a periodic progress note(s), and a discharge/referral summary of services (Navar, 1984). The treatment plan outlines the goals and specific plan of action to be taken with a client (sometimes co-planned by the client). Progress notes are used to monitor progression toward or regression from the goals established in the treatment plan and to modify, if necessary, the original plan of action. Discharge and referral summaries are a compilation of the services received by the client, his or her reaction to the plan of action, and any future recommendations for leisure service involvement.

The focus of these action plans and summaries is on the expected or planned behavioral change (outcomes) within the client as a result of receiving appropriate and quality services. These pieces of documentation flow from the efforts taken within the program design, protocol development, assessment, and activity analysis phases. As a result of quality documentation, the specialist is better able to prove client outcomes and program effectiveness.

Guidelines for producing quality client documentation and some examples are provided in Chapter 10. These guidelines and examples can help the specialist improve the quality of his or her written documentation and ensure alignment with other professional accountability activities.

Program Evaluation/Program Outcomes.   In specific **program evaluation,** the specialist must gather and analyze selected data in a systematic and logical manner, for the purpose of determining the quality, effectiveness, and/or outcomes of a program. It makes sense that the plan for program evaluation closely follows the plan for program implementation (Caldwell, 2001, 2003; Widmer, 2001, Widmer, Zabriskie, & Wells, 2003). For example, program factors such as facilities, equipment, staff, budget, and advertisement/promotion can be evaluated as a function separately from individual client outcomes. Although they are undoubtedly interrelated, program documentation/evaluation focuses on program outcomes and client documentation/evaluation focuses on client outcomes.

Program evaluation questions might include the following: Were there adequate staff to implement the program and supervise clients? Was the facility adequate for the purpose of the program—enough space? accessible? Was the equipment functioning properly? How effective and efficient was the program format in assisting the clients in achieving their outcomes? Evaluation is helpful in refining the focus of intervention programs and in measuring client outcomes (Caldwell, 2001, 2003; Widmer, 2001; Widmer, Zabriskie, & Wells, 2003).

Client Evaluation/Client Outcomes.   Client evaluation implies that the focus will be on whether the client goals or outcomes targeted in the initial treatment plan have been accomplished. The focus will be on the end result of the intervention designed on behalf of the client, and it is one part of *patient care monitoring* (Sheehan, 1992). For the most part, client evaluations will be conducted on an individual basis (for example, as progress notes or discharge/referral summaries), although these individual evaluations may be synthesized later into grouped data that addresses larger program evaluation concerns. Again, the achievement of client outcomes may be highly interrelated to the achievement of program outcomes.

The targeted client outcomes will vary based on the different client needs and varied purposes of the programs. In non-outcome-based programs, the focus of client evaluation may be the number of times the client attended a program or the level of client enjoyment. While these are sometimes important, when therapeutic recreation services are delivered as planned interventions, different client outcomes usually are expected. In intervention programs, the focus of service provision is client behavior or functional change as a direct, proven result of the program, and the focus of client evaluations becomes one of measuring and documenting those changes. "Outcome measurements become especially important if we view TR as an agent of change, as a means to modify behavior, attitudes or skills. This is important because the outcome measurements that we specify . . . will indicate what the client is expected to achieve during treatment" (Sheehan, 1992, p. 178). That is, specialists must target goals for client change that are expected to come about as a result of a well-planned and well-designed program. Typical questions concerning client outcomes include: Did the client achieve the targeted outcome within the planned program? If not, what prevented the client from achieving this end? Did the client learn a skill? gain new knowledge? change a behavior? change an attitude? Other specific questions may exist according to the treatment plan established for/with the client.

Client outcomes depend on well-designed programs in which clients are placed systematically, and in which interventions are delivered for a specific purpose. In essence, client outcomes, like program outcomes, rely on all previous parts of the Accountability Model being in place and being conceptually cohesive. Chapter 11 addresses some of these concerns.

Quality Improvement and Efficacy Research.   The most common method of evaluating therapeutic recreation services at the comprehensive program level is through **quality improvement** (also called quality assurance, continuous quality improvement, and **performance improvement**) efforts that are mandated by external accreditation agencies, such as the Joint Commission or the Rehabilitation Accreditation Commission (McCormick, 2003). A parallel activity, which may or may not be a separate function, is efficacy research (McCormick & Lee, 2001; Shank, Kinney, & Coyle, 1993; Stumbo, 2000, 2003; Widmer, 2001; Widmer, Zabriskie, & Wells, 2003). Both of these activities are intended to provide useful data to document and improve the standard of care delivered to clients.

Quality improvement is defined as a "wide spectrum of activities ranging from determining an appropriate definition of care to establishment of actual standards of practice, that, if implemented, will result in acceptable levels of service" (Riley, 1991a, p. 54). The aim is to provide mechanisms for health care agencies to continually improve the services delivered to clients through self-inspection and on-site visitations by surveyors.

The new term performance improvement intends to focus the comprehensive evaluation on the organization's performance in providing the best care possible (McCormick, 2003). According to JCAHO (2002), "performance measurement in healthcare represents what is done and how well it is done. The goal is to accurately understand the basis for current performance so that better results can be achieved through focused improvement actions." Chapter 11 in this text provides more details about the current requirements of the (a) Joint Commission on Accreditation of Healthcare Organizations (JCAHO) [www.jcaho.org], (b) Rehabilitation Accreditation Commission (CARF) [www.carf.org], (c) National Committee for Quality Assurance (NCQA) [www.ncqa.org], and (d) Center for Medicare and Medicaid Services (CMS) [www.cms.hhs.gov].

In a similar vein, **efficacy research** also focuses on the outcomes, benefits, or results of service delivery (Shank, Kinney, & Coyle, 1993; Stumbo, 2001, 2003). It involves systematic data collection and analysis, with an aim of documenting service effectiveness, specifically client-based outcomes, for a particular group or groups of clients. While it does have distinct purposes and actions separate from quality improvement, it also shares some similar goals and professional benefits. In addition, it can be accomplished only through a careful and systematic analysis of program delivery factors. Useful resources about efficacy research in therapeutic recreation include Caldwell (2001, 2003), McCormick and Lee (2001), Shank, Kinney, and Coyle (1993), and Widmer, Zabriskie, and Wells (2003). Chapter 11 reviews both continuous quality improvement and efficacy research in the measurement of program and client outcomes.

Key Points

The purpose of the Therapeutic Recreation Accountability Model is to show the interrelationships between different tasks of providing intervention programs to clients (Stumbo, 1996). As such, several concepts are worth mentioning.

- In order to provide intervention, therapeutic recreation specialists must be aware of and competent in each task or type of documentation depicted in the Therapeutic Recreation Accountability Model.

It is the responsibility of every therapeutic recreation professional to become well-versed in the various aspects of providing therapeutic recreation intervention. This means increasing competencies in all accountability activities, such as protocols, client assessments, and performance improvement activities. The therapeutic recreation literature and conference offerings are becoming richer with resources to help specialists increase understanding of and competencies in improving program accountability. It is each specialist's responsibility to make sure he or she understands and can apply these concepts to practice.

- In order to produce client outcomes, therapeutic recreation specialists must conceptualize the interrelationships among program design, delivery, and evaluation.

In the past, it was acceptable to be satisfied with providing general programs targeted solely at client enjoyment. In the vast majority of health care settings, this is no longer the case. Providing quality programs is not enough; like other service providers, therapeutic recreation specialists must be able to produce client outcomes —especially those that make a difference in the lives of clients and are valued by other health care providers. Therapeutic recreation can address this change in service provision only through recognizing that all parts of program delivery and documentation must align with one another. It is no longer acceptable for example, to have a client assessment that gathers useless information (and dust!). It is now acknowledged that all parts of the accountability system must match and follow a logical, interconnected pattern.

- The connection between components must be clear and logical.

Again, the purpose of this model is to provide a visual context that allows the specialist to view the entirety of service provision. Descriptors, such as systematic, interrelated, alignment, connections, are crucial to ensuring that service provision be outcome based. Literally every component box on the model could be connected with every other box, because one action or decision affects all other actions or decisions. If one part of the model—for example, client assessment—is not in alignment with other components, then being able to produce valued and meaningful client outcomes is highly unlikely. The connections must be clear and logical.

- The guesswork needs to be taken out of "providing the right patient with the right service [at] the right time in the right setting at the right intensity and for the right duration" (Navar, 1991, p. 5).

One aim of the model is to help specialists become more systematic in delivering programs to clients. Therapeutic recreation specialists need to determine and document what works and what does not. Better, more comprehensive "systems" for service provision are needed. Each piece of the model plays a vital part in conceptualizing and improving the accountability of therapeutic recreation programs. Systematic research and data collection will improve the ability to predict and deliver consistent client outcomes.

Summary

The Therapeutic Recreation Accountability Model provides information on the process used to design an accountable system of services. It is useful for showing the different decision points of service delivery as well as the connections between each decision point. These relationships help increase accountability for client outcomes, as mandated by external accreditation bodies, health insurance companies, and other professions. The model can be used by practicing professionals as a diagnostic tool in evaluating their program operations, and by students as a conceptual learning aid. The proper documentation that aligns with the model may serve as an indication to the agency that the therapeutic recreation program design and documentation is of high quality and accountable. The remainder of this book outlines the steps in the Therapeutic Recreation Accountability Model.

STUDENT EXERCISES

Discussion Questions

1. Describe an example of a professional being accountable. To whom are therapeutic recreation specialists accountable?

2. What are the advantages of a "systems" approach to comprehensive program design? How does this relate to service accountability?

3. What is the purpose of Figure 3.1? What important relationships is it demonstrating?

4. Explain client outcomes. What client outcomes are desirable from therapeutic recreation programs (you might think back to Chapter 1)? What has to happen in order for clients to achieve outcomes as a result of participation in therapeutic recreation programs?

5. Explain how the outcome areas listed in Box 3.1 relate to the three components of the Leisure Ability Model.

6. Explain why each of the six characteristics of an outcome (identifiable, measurable, achievable, demonstrable, predictable or causal, and meaningful) are important to professional accountability.

7. Why are the client's characteristics (such as age, cultural background, education, home environment, lifestyle, relationships, etc.) important in targeting outcomes? How do they affect program delivery?

8. Three words are consistently used throughout this chapter and the rest of the text: systematic, relationships, consistency. How do each of these three concepts relate to accountability and the Therapeutic Recreation Accountability Model?

9. In your own words, summarize the four key points at the end of the chapter.

10. What are the advantages of using models or "pictures" of practice?

Practice Test

1. All of the following are examples of client outcome areas EXCEPT:
   a. increased ability to program appropriately.
   b. increased ability to plan for personal leisure.
   c. improved conversational skills with peers.
   d. improved utilization of home leisure resources.

2. What does a *causal* relationship between programs and outcomes mean?
   a. client can dress as they want on Fridays
   b. participation in a program should result in specific outcomes
   c. every client will reach every objective
   d. the assessment can predict what the client outcomes will be

3. Systematic program planning based on client need is important for all of the following reasons EXCEPT:
   a. to better understand the purpose, direction, and outcome of the intervention.
   b. to improve the client's understanding of what is to be expected during intervention.
   c. to improve the accountability of the therapeutic recreation specialist.
   d. to improve the activity analysis process.

4. According to this chapter, the two most important features that can make therapeutic recreation an intervention are:
   a. professional standards and treatment goals.
   b. written plans of operation and performance improvement mechanisms.

  c. philosophy and program evaluation.

  d. client assessment and activity analysis.

5. The purpose of client assessment is to:
 a. document the client's past leisure behavior.
 b. adequately modify activities for individual clients.
 c. place the client into appropriate programs.
 d. evaluate the client's performance in programs.

6. Which of the following is a typical outcome area for *leisure education* services within therapeutic recreation?
 a. increase awareness of self in relation to leisure
 b. increase social functioning
 c. provide opportunities for social interaction
 d. provide opportunities for enjoyment and self-expression

7. Activity analysis is the process of:
 a. examining clients' characteristics to best place them into programs.
 b. examining the activity components to check if they meet the intended purpose.
 c. evaluating the effects of the activities/programs on the client's outcomes.
 d. evaluating the resources/equipment needed to implement the activities.

8. Which is the BEST reason to select a specific activity for client participation?
 a. The TR specialist knows how to do the activity.
 b. The client likes to do the activity.
 c. The TR specialist saw it at a conference.
 d. It moves the client from need to outcome.

9. What is likely to happen if the client is placed into programs that are NOT specifically designed to meet her needs?
 a. She will not reach the intended outcomes of participation.
 b. She will be placed in groups with people who have similar needs.
 c. She will learn leisure skills that she can use after she is discharged.
 d. Her attitudes toward leisure participation will improve.

10. Cleo enters a substance abuse facility in San Diego and Clara enters a substance abuse facility in the Bronx. They receive standardized care from the TR specialists at these facilities to meet their needs. It is likely that the TR specialists use:
 a. step-by-step program design.
 b. protocols or clinical practice guidelines.
 c. client objectives.
 d. outcome plans.

Answers: 1. a, 2. b, 3. d, 4. d, 5. c, 6. a, 7. b, 8. d, 9. a, 10. b

Chapter Activities

Client Outcomes List

Add 15 to 20 additional outcomes to the list given in Box 3.1 (not yet written in measurable terms). Hint: Chapters 1 and 2 of this text should help tremendously in creating this list! Compile a list from all students, separating the outcomes into functional intervention, leisure education, and recreation participation goals.

Goals, Interventions, and Outcomes

Review Figure 3.2. Create 3 to 5 of your own examples of the connections between goals, intervention programs, and client outcomes. Have two other students review your work to make sure it is consistent, logical, and systematic. Have the class share their examples.

Interview a Therapeutic Recreation Specialist

Interview a local therapeutic recreation specialist about his or her practice. Use the Therapeutic Recreation Accountability Model to take notes about the specialist's practice at each step. How well does the practice adhere to the model? How well is the specialist able to produce measurable and meaningful client outcomes as a direct result of his or her practice?

REFERENCES

Anderson, S. B., Ball, S., & Murphy, R. T., and Associates. (1975). *Encyclopedia of educational evaluation.* San Francisco: Jossey-Bass.

Buettner, L. L. (2000). Gerontological recreation therapy: Examining the trends and making a forecast. *Annual in Therapeutic Recreation, 9,* 35–46.

Buettner, L. L. (2001). *A research monograph: Efficacy of prescribed therapeutic recreation protocols on falls and injuries in nursing home residents with dementia.* Alexandria, VA: American Therapeutic Recreation Association.

Buettner, L. L. & Fitzsimmons, S. (2003). *American therapeutic recreation association practice guidelines for treating disturbing behaviors.* Alexandria, VA: American Therapeutic Recreation Association.

Caldwell, L. L. (2001). The role of theory in therapeutic recreation: A practical approach. In N. J. Stumbo (Ed.), *Professional issues in the therapeutic recreation: On competencies and outcomes* (pp. 349–364). Champaign, IL: Sagamore Publishing Company.

Carruthers, C. (2003). Objectives-based approach to evaluating the effectiveness of therapeutic recreation services. In N. J. Stumbo (Ed.), *Client outcomes in therapeutic recreation services* (pp. 187–202). State College, PA: Venture Publishing Company.

Carruthers, C. & Hood, C. D. (2002). Coping skills program for individuals with alcoholism. *Therapeutic Recreation Journal, 36*(2), 154–171.

Carter, M. J., Van Andel, G. E., & Robb, G. M. (1995). *Therapeutic recreation: A practical approach.* (2nd ed.). Prospect Heights, IL: Waveland Press.

Connolly, P. (1981). *Analysis of a formative program evaluation procedure for therapeutic recreation services.* Unpublished doctoral dissertation, University of Illinois at Urbana-Champaign.

Connolly, P. (1984). Program evaluation. In C. A. Peterson and S. L. Gunn, *Therapeutic recreation program design: Principles and procedures* (2nd ed.) (pp. 136–179). Englewood Cliffs, NJ: Prentice-Hall.

Connolly, P., & Keogh-Hoss, M. A. (1991). The development and use of intervention protocols in therapeutic recreation: Documenting field-based practices. In B. Riley (Ed.), *Quality management: Applications for therapeutic recreation* (pp. 117–136). State College, PA: Venture Publishing Company.

Devine, M. A., & Wilhite, B. (1999). Theory application in therapeutic recreation practice and research. *Therapeutic Recreation Journal, 33*(1), 29–45.

Dunn, J. K., Sneegas, J. J., & Carruthers, C. A. (1991). Outcome measures: Monitoring patient progress. In B. Riley (Ed.), *Quality management: Applications for therapeutic recreation* (pp. 107–115). State College, PA: Venture Publishing Company.

Ferguson, D. (1992, July). *Recreation therapy protocols.* International Conference on Leisure and Mental Health, Salt Lake City, UT.

Hodges, J. S., & Luken, K. (2000). Services and support as a means to meaningful outcomes for persons with developmental disabilities. *Annual in Therapeutic Recreation, 9,* 47–56.

Hood, C. D. (2001). Clinical practice guidelines—A decision-making tool for best practice? In N. J. Stumbo (Ed.), *Professional issues in therapeutic recreation: On competence and outcomes* (pp. 189–214). Champaign, IL: Sagamore Publishing Company.

Hood, C. D. (2003). Standardizing practice and outcomes through clinical practice guidelines: Recommendations for therapeutic recreation. In N. J. Stumbo (Ed.), *Client outcomes in therapeutic recreation services* (pp. 151–166). State College, PA: Venture Publishing Company.

Hood, C. D., & Carruthers, C. P. (2002). Coping skills theory as an underlying framework for therapeutic recreation services. *Therapeutic Recreation Journal, 36*(2), 137–153.

Johnson, D. E., & Ashton-Shaeffer, C. (2000). A framework for TR outcomes in school-based settings. *Annual in Therapeutic Recreation, 9,* 57–70.

Joint Commission on Accreditation of Healthcare Organizations. (2002) Shared visions—New pathways. *Perspectives: The Official Joint Commission Newsletter, 22*(10), pp. 1, 3.

Knight, L., & Johnson, A. (1991). Therapeutic recreation protocols: Client problem-centered approach. In B. Riley (Ed.), *Quality management: Applications for therapeutic recreation* (pp. 137–147). State College, PA: Venture Publishing Company.

Lee, Y., & Yang, H. (2000). A review of therapeutic recreation outcomes in physical medicine and rehabilitation between 1991–2000. *Annual in Therapeutic Recreation, 9,* 21–34.

McCormick, B. P. (2003). Outcome measurement as a tool for performance improvement. In N. J. Stumbo (Ed.), *Client outcomes in therapeutic recreation services* (pp. 221–223). State College, PA: Venture Publishing Company.

McCormick, B. P., & Funderburk, J. (2000). Therapeutic recreation outcomes in mental health practice. *Annual in Therapeutic Recreation, 9,* 9–20.

McCormick, B. P., & Lee, Y. (2001). Research into practice: Building knowledge through empirical practice. In N. J. Stumbo (Ed.), *Professional issues in therapeutic recreation: On competence and outcomes* (pp. 383–400). Champaign, IL: Sagamore Publishing Company.

Navar, N. (1984). Documentation in therapeutic recreation. In C. A. Peterson & S. L. Gunn, *Therapeutic recreation program design: Principles and procedures* (pp. 212–266). Englewood Cliffs, NJ: Prentice-Hall.

Navar, N. (1991). Advancing therapeutic recreation through quality assurance: A perspective on the changing nature of quality in therapeutic recreation. In B. Riley (Ed.), *Quality management: Applications for therapeutic recreation* (pp. 3–20). State College, PA: Venture Publishing Company.

Peterson, C. A., & Gunn, S. L. (1984). *Therapeutic recreation program design: Principles and procedures* (2nd ed.). Englewood Cliffs, NJ: Prentice-Hall.

Peterson, C. A., & Stumbo, N. J. (2000). *Therapeutic recreation program design: Principles and procedures* (3rd ed.). Needham Heights, MA: Allyn and Bacon.

Riley, B. (1987a). Conceptual basis of quality assurance: Application to therapeutic recreation service. In B. Riley (Ed.), *Evaluation of therapeutic recreation through quality assurance* (pp. 7–24). State College, PA: Venture Publishing Company.

Riley, B. (1987b). (Ed.). *Evaluation of therapeutic recreation through quality assurance.* State College, PA: Venture Publishing Company.

Riley, B. (1991a). Quality assessment: The use of outcome indicators. In B. Riley (Ed.), *Quality management: Applications for therapeutic recreation* (pp. 53–67). State College, PA: Venture Publishing Company.

Riley, B. (1991b). *Quality management: Applications for therapeutic recreation.* State College, PA: Venture Publishing Company.

Ross, J. E., & Ashton-Shaeffer, C. (2003). Selecting and designing intervention programs for outcomes. In N. J. Stumbo (Ed.), *Client outcomes in therapeutic recreation services* (pp. 129–150). State College, PA: Venture Publishing Company.

Seibert, M. L. (1991). Keynote. In C. P. Coyle, W. B. Kinney, B. Riley, & J. W. Shank (Eds.), *Benefits of therapeutic recreation: A consensus view* (pp. 5–15). Philadelphia: Temple University.

Shank, J., & Kinney, W. B. (1987). On the neglect of clinical practice. In C. Sylvester, J. L. Hemingway, R. Howe-Murphy, K. Mobily, & P. A. Shank, (Eds.). *Philosophy of therapeutic recreation: Ideas and issues* (pp. 65–75). Alexandria, VA: National Recreation and Park Association.

Shank, J. W., & Kinney, W. B. (1991). Monitoring and measuring outcomes in therapeutic recreation. In B. Riley (Ed.), *Quality management: Applications for therapeutic recreation* (pp. 69–82). State College, PA: Venture Publishing Company.

Shank, J. W., Kinney, W. B., & Coyle, C. P. (1993). Efficacy studies in therapeutic recreation research: The need, the state of the art, and future implication. In M. J. Malkin & C. Z. Howe, (Eds.), *Research in therapeutic recreation: Concepts and methods* (pp. 301–335). State College, PA: Venture Publishing Company.

Shank, J. W., Coyle, C. P., Kinney, W. B., & Lay, C. (1994/95). Using existing data to examine therapeutic recreation services. *Annual in Therapeutic Recreation, 5,* 5–12.

Sheehan, T. (1992). Outcome measurements in therapeutic recreation. In G. Hitzhusen, L. Jackson, & M. Birdsong (Eds.), *Expanding Horizons in Therapeutic Recreation XIV,* (pp. 17–22). Columbia, MO: Curators University of Missouri.

Stumbo, N. J. (1991). Selected assessment resources: A review of instruments and references. *Annual in Therapeutic Recreation, 2,* 8–24.

Stumbo, N. J. (1994/1995). Assessment of social skills for therapeutic recreation intervention. *Annual in Therapeutic Recreation, 5,* 68–82.

Stumbo, N. J. (1996). A proposed accountability model for therapeutic recreation services. *Therapeutic Recreation Journal, 30*(4), 246–259.

Stumbo, N. J. (1997). Issues and concerns in therapeutic recreation assessment. In D. Compton (Ed.), *Issues in therapeutic recreation: Toward the new millenium* (pp. 347–372) (2nd ed.). Champaign, IL: Sagamore Publishing Company.

Stumbo, N. J. (2000). Outcome measurement in health care: Implications for therapeutic recreation. *Annual in Therapeutic Recreation, 9,* 1–8.

Stumbo, N. J. (2002). *Client assessment in therapeutic recreation.* State College, PA: Venture Publishing Company.

Stumbo, N. J. (2003a). Assessment: The key to outcomes and evidence-based practice. In N. J. Stumbo (Ed.), *Client outcomes in therapeutic recreation services* (pp. 167–186). State College, PA: Venture Publishing Company.

Stumbo, N. J. (2003b). The importance of evidence-based practice in therapeutic recreation. In N. J. Stumbo (Ed.), *Client outcomes in therapeutic recreation services* (pp. 25–48). State College, PA: Venture Publishing Company.

Stumbo, N. J. (2003c). Outcomes, accountability, and therapeutic recreation. In N. J. Stumbo (Ed.), *Client outcomes in therapeutic recreation services* (pp. 1–24). State College, PA: Venture Publishing Company.

Stumbo, N. J., & Hess, M. E. (2001a). On competencies and outcomes in therapeutic recreation. In N. J. Stumbo (Ed.), *Professional issues in therapeutic recreation: On competence and outcomes* (pp. 3–20). Champaign, IL: Sagamore Publishing Company.

Stumbo, N. J., & Hess, M. E. (2001b). The status of client outcomes in selected programs as measured by adherence to the therapeutic recreation accountability model. *Annual in Therapeutic Recreation, 10,* 45–56.

Widmer, M. A. (2001). Methods for outcome research in therapeutic recreation. In N. J. Stumbo (Ed.), *Professional issues in therapeutic recreation: On competence and outcomes* (pp. 365–382). Champaign, IL: Sagamore Publishing Company.

Widmer, M. A., Zabriskie, R., & Wells, M. A. (2003). Program evaluation: Collecting data to measure outcomes. In N. J. Stumbo (Ed.), *Client outcomes in therapeutic recreation services* (pp. 203–220). State College, PA: Venture Publishing Company.

CHAPTER 4

Comprehensive Program Design

One of the most important tasks for the therapeutic recreation specialist initially is to conceptualize the overall or comprehensive program for a unit, agency, or department. (Hereafter, the term *agency* will be used to imply any one of these three entities.) This task is extremely vital. Without a systematic method of determining client needs and converting these needs into a comprehensive program scheme, the staff often finds itself with segmented programs that reflect tradition, individual staff interests, and other nonjustifiable program offerings. A systematic approach provides a sequential and logical method of conceptualizing and developing the comprehensive program.

Figure 4.1 displays the Therapeutic Recreation Accountability Model (TRAM) and shows that comprehensive and specific program design is the first step to creating accountable programs that have the potential to deliver client outcomes. One of the primary considerations of this step is client needs. Client needs drive all program development. That is, therapeutic recreation programs are developed to address client needs usually by modifying, reducing, or eliminating the need through the client's involvement in the program.

Client Needs and Outcomes

Client needs are at the very heart of program development. The reason most clients participate or are involved in therapeutic recreation programs is to change some aspect of their attitude, knowledge, and/or behavior. Not surprisingly, therapeutic recreation specialists focus on clients needs that are within the scope of care of the profession. According to the Leisure Ability Model addressed in Chapter 2, these needs come under the broad headings of functional intervention, leisure education, and recreation participation. Client needs within these areas might include:

Functional Intervention

Physical functional deficits

Emotional functional deficits

Mental functional deficits

Social functional deficits

Leisure Education

Lack of leisure awareness

Lack of social skills

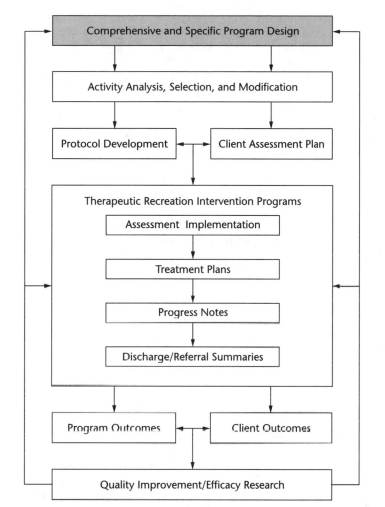

Figure 4.1 Program design component of the Therapeutic Recreation Accountability Model.

Lack of leisure activity skills

Lack of ability to utilize leisure resources

Recreation Participation

Lack of ability to self-regulate leisure behavior

Lack of ability to assume responsibility for own personal leisure lifestyle

In terms of program development, then, the specialist designs and implements programs based on needs within the areas of functional intervention, leisure education, and recreation participation that are identified for the population served by the agency. Program evaluation helps determine whether these client needs were met; that is, whether the planned change in client attitude, knowledge, or behavior was achieved through involvement in the program. Program evaluation helps determine whether client outcomes were produced by the client's participation in the program.

Client Outcomes: Evidence and Theory in Program Design

Two new trends are affecting therapeutic recreation program design: (a) evidence-based practice and (b) theory-based programming. Although this book cannot cover these two topics in depth, a brief introduction is given so that the reader may be aware of these trends and become part of the exciting new connections between research and practice.

The first trend is **evidence-based practice.** "Evidence-based practice can be described as the selection of treatments for which there is some evidence of efficacy" (Denton, Walsh, & Daniel, 2002, p. 40). This evidence must be gathered through well-designed and meaningful research efforts with client groups and be applicable to daily practice. It means that programs are created and designed using the best available information from effectiveness or efficacy research (Stumbo, 2003). For example, if research shows that meditation practices are more effective than aerobic exercise at inducing relaxation for older individuals, then therapeutic recreation program designs and their delivery should reflect the "evidence" from these research studies. In the literature, evidence-based practice also is termed *empirically validated treatment, empirically supported treatment, empirically evaluated treatment, empirical practice, research-based practice, research utilization, evidence-based treatment,* and *evidence-based health care* (Chambless & Ollendick, 2001; Denton, Walsh, & Daniel, 2002; Evidence-based Medicine Working Group, 1992; Kendall, 1998; Lee & McCormick, 2002).

Regardless of what it is called, it provides a strong connection between research results (the greater the quantity and quality of studies, the better) and programs and services delivered to clients. Using the best research information possible in addressing client needs and getting to client outcomes is the overall aim of evidence-based practice. Therapeutic recreation research in the United States is now available in three specific professional journals (*Annual in Therapeutic Recreation* [ATRA], *Therapeutic Recreation Journal* [NTRS], and the *American Journal of Recreational Therapy*). Additional research related to therapeutic recreation can be found in thousands of refereed health care and human service journals, published both in the United States and abroad. Every university library now has on-line access to the majority of these journals. In addition, newer textbooks, such as Mobily and MacNeil's *Therapeutic Recreation and the Nature of Disabilities,* are a strong attempt to integrate research information into programming processes. An example of using research to create a social skills program plan is found in Appendix B.

A second trend in therapeutic recreation service provision is **theory-based programming.** Led by several scholars in the field, theory-based programming is an idea whose time has come.

Becoming skilled in using theories to develop therapeutic recreation (TR) assessments, programs, and evaluations can lead to many important outcomes, such as increased programmatic efficacy and ability to better communication with colleagues. . . . Theories provide the foundation for understanding TR programming, and as a result, can become one of the most important tools a TRS can use. . . . All competent TRSs provide some reasoning behind what they do. Answers such as "I want to improve self-efficacy" or "The patient needs to increase anger-management skills" explains in general what the TRS's treatment goals might be. A good theory, however, will provide the tool to specify beforehand what might happen, and even more important, why it might happen. (Caldwell, 2001, p. 349)

Caldwell (2001, 2003) and Widmer, Zabriskie, and Wells (2003) provided numerous examples of theories that might be used in therapeutic recreation programming, many of which were discussed in the first chapter of this text. Some of these examples are: (a) self-efficacy, (b) perceived freedom, and (c) stress-coping.

An example of the extensive use of theory in program development is work done by Hood and Carruthers (Carruthers & Hood, 2002; Hood & Carruthers, 2002). Believing that "[t]heory is an extremely useful tool for understanding, predicting, and/or changing human behavior" (Hood & Carruthers, 2002, p. 138), these researchers studied stress-coping theory and applied it to individuals with alcoholism. Their research led them to two broad programming strategies for stress-coping: (a) reducing negative demands and (b) increasing positive resources. Each of these strategies included a number of substrategies (such as using social networks for support). Based on this accumulated information, they then built and tested a program of stress-coping skills for individuals with alcoholism. Theirs is but one example of the growing interest and efforts directed toward theory-based programming.

Why do evidence-based practice and theory-based programming matter to therapeutic recreation? The answers are many. First, they improve the chances of getting to client outcomes more quickly by focusing programming efforts on sound and proven information. Second, they improve the justification or rationale for services that are based on specific evidence and theory, rather than on happenstance or whim. Third, both efforts becoming more accepted and universally applied will improve the standardization of practice and create common ground among therapeutic recreation professionals and with their colleagues from other disciplines. Clearly, evidence-based practice and theory-based programming can greatly aid comprehensive and specific program designs' rationale and effectiveness.

Benefits of Comprehensive and Specific Program Design

The benefits of creating and delivering programs to clients that have been conceptualized using the systems-designed approach are many and varied. One of the most beneficial aspects of comprehensive program design is its *stability*. When grounded in client need and professional logic, therapeutic recreation specialists have the ability to produce powerful, life-changing programs that effect behavioral change in clients. The program conceptualization remains stable, having a foundation in therapeutic recreation philosophy, while other portions—for example, specific programs and activities—may evolve more dynamically. A second benefit is that of *flexibility*. The strong conceptualization effort provides the springboard for creativity in specific program and activity design. An innovative and creative programmer has few limits, within given resources, in designing programs that are directly beneficial to clients. Beyond the characteristics of both stability and flexibility, comprehensively designed programs offer a high degree of *accountability*. Because programs are grounded in professional philosophy and design is driven by a logical process of meeting client needs,

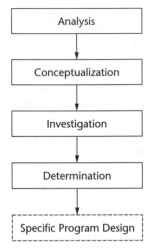

Figure 4.2 Therapeutic Recreation Comprehensive Program Planning Model.

the end result is one of being able to justify service provision and produce desired, predictable client outcomes. Systematic design processes start with strong conceptualizations and end with program and client evaluations. Professionals become more accountable for services provided and outcomes attained. The ability to produce *client outcomes,* of course, is what drives the entire system. Gone are the days of haphazard program design or selection. Today's professional must be prepared to think about what client outcomes are important and create and deliver programs that will affect those outcomes.

One of the added bonuses is that therapeutic recreation specialists, through this systematic process, may design and implement programs that *complement other disciplines,* regardless of the setting or client group served. In any number of facilities, comprehensive and specific program design can be used to target areas of concern in concert with the treatment team's overall mission. Valued contributions to the efforts of the treatment team are vital to the continued survival and success of therapeutic recreation professionals.

Therapeutic Recreation Comprehensive Program Planning Model

The Therapeutic Recreation Comprehensive Program Planning Model provides the basis for sound and logical program development. It helps the specialist to examine the factors that most affect program development and to develop programs, based on client need, in a systematic fashion. Figure 4.2 displays the Therapeutic Recreation Comprehensive Program Planning Model. Each of the steps outlined in this model will be discussed.

Analysis

A well-planned comprehensive program, which can be executed appropriately to address clients' leisure-related needs, must have a clear picture of its reason to exist. A statement of purpose and a set of goals provide this direction and definition. Prior to developing the statement of purpose and goals, a stage of analysis is required. The purpose of this analysis is to investigate thoroughly the clients and their leisure-related needs. In addition, it is necessary to study the various factors that influence the selection of the program direction, and, eventually, the operation of the total program. In essence, these areas are examined in the analysis stage to provide the background information necessary to write the mission statement and program goals in the conceptualization stage.

Five areas of analysis have been identified. These are:

- The community
- The agency
- The clients
- The therapeutic recreation department
- The therapeutic recreation profession

Within these five areas, there may be an overlap of some concerns and issues. However, if each of the five is addressed seriously and carefully, the program planner should have sufficient information for solid decision making in the program development stages that come later.

Community. Most contemporary clinical therapeutic recreation programs have a futuristic focus, which implies programming for where the client will be after discharge or termination. Whether the client currently lives in or will return to the community, a thorough understanding of the community is needed. It is the job of the therapeutic recreation specialist to provide services to the client so that he or she may effectively participate in the community to the fullest extent possible. Thus, an understanding of the predominant leisure lifestyles within a specific community is important. Clients should be able to move comfortably into leisure interests within the community after being involved in therapeutic recreation programs. It is acknowledged that there is no singular community leisure lifestyle. There are, however, identifiable leisure lifestyle subgroups based on geographic and seasonal variables, age groups, ethnic and religious orientations, and availability of various resources and services.

The location and characteristics of a community may affect greatly the programs offered at a particular agency. Consider three agencies in Illinois: one in Chicago, a metropolis of about 4 million; one in Bloomington/Normal, a town of about 120,000; and one in LeRoy, a town of about 1,000. The diversity, facilities, resources, opportunities, and drawbacks differ for each community and may affect how the therapeutic recreation specialist conceives and designs the overall therapeutic recreation program for clients.

A specialist who knows the community well, and perhaps a larger catchment area depending on the client base of the agency, will be able to deliver better programs that meet client needs. Factors that might be considered include climate and weather, demographics and economic conditions of the community, other agencies that provide similar or transition services, available community resources, including both public and commercial options, and transportation services. Other factors that are unique to the community, such as predominant businesses, religions, and/or ethnicities, also might be considered for their impact on the facility and program.

Agency.   The nature and type of the agency directly affects the mission of the agency, its clientele, and its programs. Each agency has a mandate for the kind of services it provides, based on the type of agency and, in some cases, legislation and regulation. A mental health facility has a different mission, type of client served, and set of services than does a physical medicine and rehabilitation facility or a community-based recreation agency. Most agencies stay within their mandates, although they often can extend their services and do more than their primary functions might indicate. And of course some agencies, such as general hospitals, serve multiple functions, with each unit or ward serving a distinctly different group of clients. Analysis and thorough understanding of the agency's mission and function is vital to comprehensive therapeutic recreation program planning.

One of the primary factors that influence the therapeutic recreation program is the agency's mission and/or vision statements. A vision statement includes a future-oriented description of the purpose and direction of the agency in general, value-laden, and sometimes emotional terms. A mission statement or statement of purpose usually is a more concrete explanation of the services provided to clients and general, intended outcomes of these services. Both of these are helpful in that they identify for the staff and clients the agency's intended uniqueness or niche in service delivery. This uniqueness may play a large role in how programs are to be developed.

In addition, reviewing the history and background of a given agency may provide useful information to the program designer. Often this information helps identify which programs are in sync with the current mission statement and which are not. Contemporary ideas and new directions for therapeutic recreation services should reflect the agency's statement of purpose.

A major factor that must be analyzed related to clinical agencies is the presence and type of regulatory bodies that accredit the facility. Most health-related facilities must comply with a set of standards established by a recognized accrediting group. The most common regulatory bodies are the Joint Commission on Accreditation of Healthcare Organizations (JCAHO) and the Rehabilitation Accreditation Commission (CARF). Each of these accreditation bodies has standards that have direct implications for therapeutic recreation services. Agencies accredited by the Joint Commission on Accreditation of Healthcare Organizations (JCAHO) must show proof of adhering to one of the following standards manuals:

- *Comprehensive Accreditation Manual for Ambulatory Care (CAMAC)*
- *Accreditation Manual for Assisted Living (AMAL)*
- *Comprehensive Accreditation Manual for Behavioral Health Care (CAMBHC)*
- *Comprehensive Accreditation Manual for Health Care Networks (CAMHCN)*
- *Comprehensive Accreditation Manual for Managed Behavioral Health Care (CAMMBHC)*
- *Accreditation Manual for Preferred Provider Organizations (AMPPO)*
- *Comprehensive Accreditation Manual for Home Care (CAMHC)*
- *Comprehensive Accreditation Manual for Hospitals (CAMH)*

- *Accreditation Manual for Critical Access Hospitals (AMCAH)*
- *Comprehensive Accreditation Manual for Long-Term Care (CAMLTC)*
- *Accreditation Manual for Office-Based Surgery Practices*
- *Comprehensive Accreditation Manual for Pathology and Clinical Laboratory Services (CAMPCLS)*

Similarly, CARF, the Rehabilitation Accreditation Commission, publishes eight standard manuals useful to individuals working in a wide variety of rehabilitation services:

- *Adult Day Service Standards Manual*
- *Assisted Living Standards Manual*
- *Behavioral Health Standards Manual*
- *Comprehensive Blind Rehabilitation Services Standards Manual*
- *Employment and Community Services Standards Manual*
- *Medical Rehabilitation Standards Manual*
- *Network Administration and Access Center Standards Manual*
- *Opioid Treatment Program Accreditation Standards Manual*

Knowledge of the appropriate standards and the agency's implementation of them will have an immediate impact on the type of comprehensive therapeutic recreation programming that is required or needed in a given agency. To date, similar external accreditation procedures do not exist for community-based recreation departments serving special populations.

Some agencies may be impacted directly by various forms of federal, state, or local legislation. Legislation may have implications for programming requirements. For example, the Americans with Disabilities Act (ADA) of 1990 has made a tremendous impact on the accessibility of public facilities and programs. The astute program designer becomes aware of such existing legalities prior to formulating the comprehensive program direction.

Analysis of the organizational and administrative structure of the sponsoring agency also is important. Although this analysis may not give immediate direction to the content of the program, it is vital to design a program that can be implemented within the given structure. The overall agency may have diverse roles and functions. A conscientious therapeutic recreation specialist will recognize the value in understanding the total agency prior to narrowing his or her concerns to the specifics of the therapeutic recreation program. The therapeutic recreation specialist should become familiar with the organizational chart within the agency, from the Board of Directors to the Therapeutic Recreation Department.

Agency resources are another important concern. Before developing a statement of purpose and goals and prior to conceptualizing operational programs, the therapeutic recreation specialist needs a full understanding of available and potential resources. Understanding resources at this level enables the designer to make program choices at a later time with these constraints in mind. Likewise, he or she makes initial conceptual decisions based on this important knowledge. At the analysis stage, the designer attempts to identify all available resources. In addition, one tries to identify potential resources so that the conceptualization and development of the program are not too narrowly defined. The following questions relate to various resources that may be of concern to the therapeutic recreation program designer:

Staff
Agency

- What other disciplines are represented in the agency?
- Which of these disciplines may be available for co-treatments?
- How is the distribution of each discipline likely to change in the near future?
- Are volunteers available to assist with programs?

Therapeutic Recreation Department

- How many therapeutic recreation staff members are there?
- What are their skills, abilities, and credentials?
- What is the likelihood of increasing the therapeutic recreation staff?
- How are volunteers incorporated into the department?
- How are student interns incorporated into the department?

Facilities
Agency

- What facilities within the agency are available for use in the therapeutic recreation program?
- What equipment and supplies within the agency are available for use in the therapeutic recreation program?
- What access to community facilities is allowed by agency policy?

Therapeutic Recreation Department

- What facilities are available for exclusive use by the therapeutic recreation department?
- What other areas can be used or converted for use?
- What equipment and supplies are available for exclusive use by the therapeutic recreation department?

Budget
Agency

- From where does the agency receive its current budget? What percentage of the budget comes from third-party reimbursement?
- What is the process for annually reviewing the budget? What individual or entity makes these decisions?
- What are the resources for external funding (grants, foundation support, contributions)?
- Is fund-raising permissible?

Therapeutic Recreation Department

- From where does the therapeutic recreation department receive its current budget? What percentage of the therapeutic recreation department budget comes from third-party reimbursement?
- How is the therapeutic recreation department budget reviewed?
- What is the level of funding for the therapeutic recreation department relative to other departments in the agency?
- What are additional ways to supplement the therapeutic recreation department budget, allowable by the agency?

Clients.   The comprehensive program is developed to address the leisure-related needs of the clients. In today's pluralistic and culturally diverse society, the therapeutic recreation specialist needs to consider the ethnic, cultural, age, and lifestyle preferences of clients. Thus, as much information as possible must be gathered about the clients to be served. This is a general analysis of the client population, not an assessment of specific individuals (development of the individual assessment occurs at a later stage). It is assumed that the agency, unit, or department serves an identifiable clientele and that the individuals served will have many of the representative characteristics of the overall target population. This means that client problems will "cluster." For example, individuals being admitted into a drug and alcohol rehabilitation unit will have a set of common characteristics or needs, based on their diagnosis. Individuals being admitted into a traumatic brain injury unit may have similar needs, due to their injury. Individuals being admitted to a long-term care facility often may have similar needs, also based on their reason for admission. These needs clusters are important for programming purposes.

A thorough analysis of the general clientele can and should produce information that will allow an appropriate statement of purpose and goals to be derived. Specific programs then can be selected and developed to address the goals. Individual clients will be assessed and referred to specific programs that are already identified and developed. Given the procedure, it is easy to see the importance of a thorough initial analysis of clients.

Analysis of the clients is undertaken with the knowledge that the eventual outcome will be the determination of leisure-related needs. This concept is important so that demographic, illness, and disability information is gathered and viewed from the onset with a specific purpose in mind. At each phase of the analysis, the programmer asks "What does this tell me about clients' leisure-related needs and, eventually, program considerations?" The following questions provide direction for the client analysis:

- Who are the clients to be served?
- How many clients are to be served per day, per week, and per year?
- What are their ages and age characteristics?
- What common disabilities, illnesses, or special conditions do they share?
- What is the level(s) of severity of disability, illness, or condition?
- What are the secondary disabilities?
- What is the usual percentage of males and females?

- What are their socioeconomic, occupational, cultural, ethnic, and educational characteristics?
- What are the predominant religious and/or ethnic groups served?
- Is the target population in transition? (For example, increasing severity or chronic conditions.)
- Where will the clients be living after discharge, and to what types of agencies will they be referred? Or will clients live in the facility until their death?
- Where do the clients currently live, and will those residential situations change?

After the initial demographic, disability, and general characteristics information has been gathered, the designer analyzes the target population relative to its leisure-related needs. A series of questions such as the following can help with this type of analysis:

- What functional problems do the clients have that would inhibit or prohibit leisure involvement?
- Can these functional problems be addressed and improved through functional intervention therapeutic recreation services?
- What secondary disabilities do the clients have that would inhibit or prohibit leisure involvement?
- Can these secondary disability problems be addressed and improved through functional intervention therapeutic recreation services?
- Do the clients have an awareness of leisure, an understanding of their responsibility for leisure, and an understanding of their potential in leisure?
- Do the clients have adequate leisure skills?
- Do the clients have knowledge of leisure resources and their utilization?
- Do clients have adequate social interaction skills for leisure involvement?
- Do clients have the ability to plan for and make decisions relative to leisure?
- What additional barriers to leisure exist for these clients (e.g., architectural barriers, stigma, financial resources, attitudes, lack of social networks, lack of stress-coping abilities)?
- What strengths and abilities do these clients have relative to leisure involvement?
- What would an appropriate leisure lifestyle look like for these clients?

Other questions about the clientele can be raised and investigated in addition to those mentioned. The purpose of all questions is to uncover as much information as possible about the targeted population. It is important to note that the nature of, and answers to, these questions will vary, depending on the type and size of the agency. For example, a public recreation department may have virtually all individuals with disabilities of a given community as its potential target clientele, whereas an inpatient children's psychiatric unit has a relatively small and easily identifiable target group. The fact remains that the program designer must have a clear understanding of the clients to be served, their characteristics, and their leisure needs in order to complete a comprehensive program planning process.

Therapeutic Recreation Profession. The therapeutic recreation staff is wise to determine the impact of certain professional actions and resources on the operation of the department. Several areas of the profession have direct bearing on program decisions. For example, the philosophy chosen by the department has a tremendous impact on how programs will be developed. Therapeutic recreation specialists who uphold the Leisure Ability concepts will program to address the clients' future leisure lifestyle. Professional standards and codes of ethics, especially those developed and published by the American Therapeutic Recreation Association (ATRA) and the National Therapeutic Recreation Society (NTRS), dictate the minimal actions and quality expected of departments across the country. Every therapeutic recreation specialist should be familiar with the latest editions of standards and codes.

Credentialing standards, such as those enforced by the National Council for Therapeutic Recreation Certification (NCTRC), impact the basic qualifications and competence of professionals entering and practicing in the field. Information on educational programs and standards, such as those that affect student internships, is important to the well-being of most quality departments. Professional resources, such as books and publications, and opportunities for continuing professional development, such as workshops and conferences, are important to the continued development of staff. Most of these resources, as well as many others, are easily accessible to members of the two national professional organizations (ATRA and NTRS). Additionally, most specialists find a wealth of information by networking with professionals from across the country in person, by telephone, or through Internet resources. Selected professional resources are highlighted in Chapter 12.

Typical questions to be asked about the impact of the therapeutic recreation profession on the individual therapeutic recreation department are:

- To what philosophy of therapeutic recreation service provision does the department adhere?
- How do the standards of practice impact the delivery of services in the therapeutic recreation department?
- What impact do the codes of ethics have on the design and delivery of programs for clients?
- What credentials do the therapeutic recreation staff possess? Need?
- What professional memberships are held by the therapeutic recreation staff? Needed?
- What conferences, workshops, or in-services are needed by the therapeutic recreation specialist staff to remain current in the field?
- What other professional resources are needed by the therapeutic recreation staff?
- If the department offers a student internship program, does it meet all professional standards?

Conceptualization

The first major task of the conceptualization stage is to develop and write a statement of purpose. The statement of purpose is generally a one-sentence statement that concisely indicates the purpose of the comprehensive therapeutic recreation program.

Once written, this statement becomes the core from which the entire comprehensive program evolves.

Content for the Statement of Purpose.   Once the essential factors related to the community, agency, clients, therapeutic recreation department, and therapeutic recreation profession have been identified and studied, the designer is ready to develop the statement of purpose. Chapter 2 presented the comprehensive Leisure Ability Model. Briefly summarized, this model indicates that program direction can be categorized by looking at three areas of therapeutic recreation service. These areas are:

- **Functional Intervention.** Programs with this intent focus on the improvement of clients' physical, social, mental, and/or emotional behaviors.
- **Leisure Education.** Programs of this nature focus on assisting clients in learning new leisure skills, acquiring social skills, establishing an awareness of self and leisure, and acquiring knowledge related to leisure resource utilization.
- **Recreation Participation.** Programs in this category provide individuals with the opportunity to engage in organized leisure activities and programs of their choice.

The model can be used for conceptualizing the basic content for the statement of purpose. Program direction can focus directly on any of the three areas or can reflect components or combinations of all three. The areas of service selected depend largely on the type of agency and the types of clients served. Programs are selected based on client need and the agency's mandate for service delivery.

Selecting the exact content for a statement of purpose for a given agency, unit, or department is dependent on the nature of the agency, the type of clients served, and the nature of their leisure needs. The information acquired in the previous analysis stage gives the designer the necessary background to make the appropriate decisions regarding the clients' leisure needs within the context of the agency's mandate.

Writing the Statement of Purpose.   The statement of purpose should be comprehensive yet brief. It should explain the reason for the program's existence without going into detail. The words selected should give a concise and clear message. Several examples are provided.

Example 1. Chemical Dependency Facility (McGowen, 1997).   To provide comprehensive therapeutic recreation services and programs that are designed to improve functional abilities related to leisure; promote the acquisition and application of leisure-related skills, knowledge, and attitudes; and provide opportunities to utilize their leisure interests in activities both in the facility and in the community.

Example 2. Physical Medicine and Rehabilitation Center (Hess, 1997).   To provide comprehensive therapeutic recreation services that focus on the development and improvement of needed physical, cognitive, social, and emotional functional abilities, and leisure-related skills, attitudes, and knowledge as they relate to maintaining a healthy, independent, and successful leisure lifestyle.

Example 3. Behavioral Health Facility.   To provide clients with high-quality, progressive, and innovative therapeutic recreation services that result in clients being able to function independently in their leisure upon discharge. These services include a wide range of programs that promote improvement in functional abilities and improvement in leisure-related skills and abilities.

Statements of purpose will vary somewhat in their content, format, and wording. Usually, they are one sentence long. They do not indicate *how* the service will be delivered. They focus on purpose or intent of the comprehensive program. Statements of purpose are the backbone of the planning process. Each successive stage of program development will reflect the direction of the statement. Therefore, careful consideration should be given to the content of the statement of purpose.

Comprehensive Program Goals.

Once a statement of purpose has been derived for a unit or agency, the next step is to develop comprehensive goals. Comprehensive program goals describe aspects of the statement of purpose in greater detail. They develop the comprehensive program's purpose. Usually goals are idealistic, yet they are capable of being put into operation through program components. Goals are not directly measurable; they are statements of intent.

Writing Goals.

Because goals play a major role in determining program content and direction, they should be developed carefully and with much attention to alternatives, resources, and desired interpretation of the statement of purpose. Content is of vital significance. Equally important are the format and wording of the statement. The following steps should be useful in deriving and stating goals:

Process for Deriving and Stating Goals

1. Review the statement of purpose.
2. Review the characteristics and needs of the population.
3. Review the nature and purpose of the agency, resources, and constraints.
4. Brainstorm possible goal areas.
5. Determine the appropriateness of goal areas for the specific population.
6. Develop goal statements.
7. Analyze goal statements.

This process will help make better goals, and this in turn will help develop better, more targeted programs. A criteria list follows that may be used for this final check of goal appropriateness and technical quality.

Criteria for Judging Goal Statements

1. The statement clearly delineates the goal area:
   a. The statement focuses directly on the key concept words.
   b. The surrounding wording does not change possible interpretations of the goal statement.
2. The statement has an appropriate level of generality and specificity:
   a. The statement excludes material that describes actual implementation concerns and strategies.
   b. The statement avoids levels of generality that are too broad to direct the reader to specific content.

3. Statements are parallel in style and general level of content:

   a. Statements are consistent in wording and format.

   b. Statements are consistent in nature of content presented.

4. Statements are both appropriate and feasible for population and agency:

   a. Goals can be substantiated through professional knowledge as appropriate for development or performance expectations.

   b. Goals reflect the philosophy and nature of the agency and are feasible within time, budget, and staffing constraints.

5. Statements reflect the nature and intent of the statement of purpose.

6. Goals are program goals that focus on program intention, not client goals or client outcomes.

Each agency or unit should develop its own goal statements, reflecting the unique needs of its population, the nature of its setting, and the philosophy of its staff. Generally, however, the content for goal statements reflects the three functions of therapeutic recreation service (functional intervention, leisure education, and recreation participation) or subcomponents of them (e.g., leisure awareness, social skills, leisure activity skills, and leisure resources).

The following suggestions for goal content are offered merely as a stimulus to the program developer. The areas are generic and not related to any specific illness, disabilities, or settings. *Each is presented as a content area and is not a fully developed program goal statement.* Note that the focus is on the program and what it intends to deliver to clients.

Functional Intervention Goals

- To provide services that improve physical fitness
- To provide activities that improve fine motor coordination
- To assist clients in maintaining current levels of memory
- To improve clients' cognitive functioning
- To provide stimulation to improve clients' orientation to reality
- To provide services that increase clients' endurance levels
- To help clients maintain current levels of task concentration
- To provide activities that improve clients' ability to use strategy in a game situation
- To assist clients in expressing emotions appropriately
- To provide services that increase clients' abilities to minimize disruptions

Leisure Education Program Goals

- To provide services that improve clients' awareness of leisure and its significance
- To help clients increase self-awareness in relation to recreation and leisure
- To provide activities that help clients identify personal barriers to leisure
- To assist clients in exploring and developing leisure attitudes and values

- To help clients develop and utilize problem-solving abilities in relation to leisure
- To increase clients' knowledge of leisure resources in their homes and neighborhoods
- To increase clients' knowledge of local leisure opportunities
- To provide direction for clients to develop a personal leisure philosophy
- To provide activities that increase clients' social interaction skills
- To improve clients' comfort level in social situations
- To improve clients' cooperative and competitive skills in leisure situations
- To provide a variety of activities that help clients develop nontraditional leisure skills
- To improve clients' personal repertoire of leisure skills
- To provide clients with exposure to new leisure skill areas
- To provide instruction in advanced leisure skills development

Recreation Participation Program Goals

- To facilitate clients' participation in previously acquired leisure skills
- To facilitate client's self-expression in leisure
- To provide clients with structured opportunities for social interaction
- To encourage clients to maintain ongoing conditions of health and fitness
- To provide an environment for the integration of diverse physical, mental, social, and emotional skills
- To provide opportunities for the reinforcement and support of other treatment programs
- To provide opportunities for creative and self-directed leisure involvement
- To provide opportunities for experiencing enjoyment and contentment

These suggested goal areas can be made more precise and appropriate once a specific population and setting are identified. For example, if a population is composed of children with developmental disabilities, a general physical goal might become more definitive—for example, "to provide a series of activities that develop physical coordination and basic body movements." The program planner is urged to make these refinements when selecting and developing goal statements. A vast number of goal areas related to therapeutic recreation programs are not mentioned here because of their uniqueness to a given setting, population, or approach. For example, a goal area for a long-term health care facility might deal with the reduction of disoriented behaviors. The planner can be concerned with the uniqueness of a particular population and, at the same time, refer to general lists such as the ones provided.

Goals clearly delineate an area of behavioral improvement, acquisition, or expression. They do not indicate *how* this will be accomplished. The next stage of comprehensive program development will address this issue. Goals identify major areas of intended program focus. They are brief, concise statements written to define and further clarify the intent of the statement of purpose. Generally, there will be from five to ten goals for a comprehensive therapeutic recreation program.

Three sets of examples of comprehensive goal statements are provided. They correspond with the programs used in the sample statement of purposes. The content areas provided within the brackets are there for clarification purposes only; normally these would not be included in a department's comprehensive program goals listing.

Example 1. Chemical Dependency Facility (McGowen, 1997).

1.0   To provide programs that increase clients' functional abilities in the physical, emotional, social, and cognitive areas. [functional intervention focus]

2.0   To provide programs that assist clients in utilizing previously acquired leisure skills or acquire new leisure skills appropriate to their limitations and future lifestyles. [leisure skills focus]

3.0   To provide programs to increase clients' knowledge of leisure resources for current and future sober utilization. [leisure resources focus]

4.0   To promote and foster the development of a personal awareness of leisure and its value. [leisure awareness focus]

5.0   To provide programs that increase clients' ability to interact with peers in an appropriate manner, in sober environments. [social interaction skills focus]

6.0   To provide opportunities for the client to participate in recreation activities in order to maintain and expand existing skills and interests. [recreation participation focus]

Example 2. Physical Medicine and Rehabilitation Center (Hess, 1997).

1.0   To provide programs that improve clients' deficits in the areas of physical, emotional, cognitive, and social functional abilities. [functional intervention focus]

2.0   To provide services that promote an awareness of the importance of a successful leisure lifestyle. [leisure awareness focus]

3.0   To provide programs that promote knowledge and utilization of leisure resources within the home and community. [leisure resources focus]

4.0   To provide programs that improve social skills necessary to function successfully in a variety of leisure environments. [social interaction skills focus]

5.0   To provide information and resources pertaining to physical and architectural barriers commonly found in the environment. [leisure barriers focus]

6.0   To provide services in which clients are actively involved in the community in order to promote independence when returning to the home community. [community reintegration focus]

7.0   To provide programs in a variety of leisure skill development areas. [leisure activity skill focus]

Example 3. Behavioral Health Facility.

1.0   To provide services targeted at improving the physical, social, emotional, and cognitive deficits of clients that hinder their leisure involvement. [functional intervention focus]

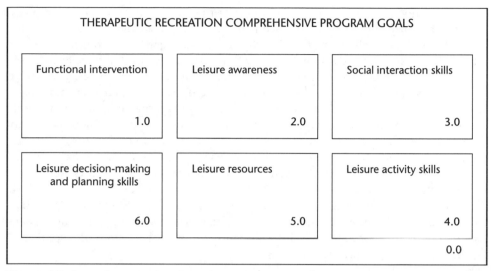

Figure 4.3 Example comprehensive program component chart.

2.0   To provide programs that improve clients' awareness of the need for leisure and its value in maintaining a healthy balance. [leisure awareness focus]

3.0   To provide services and programs that assist clients in improving their social interaction skills for use in a variety of settings and with a variety of people. [social interaction skills focus]

4.0   To provide skill improvement programs in both traditional and nontraditional leisure skills. [leisure activity skills focus]

5.0   To provide programs that teach clients about community leisure resources and how to use them as part of their overall leisure lifestyle. [leisure resources focus]

6.0   To provide programs that teach clients decision-making and planning skills in regard to utilizing their leisure time. [leisure decision-making and planning skills focus]

   Sometimes it is convenient to display these goals visually. Figure 4.3 displays the program goals outlined above for the behavioral health facility. This type of display can convey quite quickly the overall direction of the program and can help designers visualize in the next several steps how programs interrelate and connect to one another. It should be remembered that this is the comprehensive program level that gives direction but does not yet specify the specific programs and activities that are to be used to accomplish these overall goal areas.

Investigation

After a statement of purpose and the comprehensive program goals are written, the next stage in comprehensive program planning is to select program components. Program components are the operational unit for implementation of the program. Each program component carries out some aspect of the statement of purpose and goals. The number of components depends on the resources available to the therapeutic recreation staff, as well as on the scope of the goals. Regardless of the number and type of components, it is essential that they flow from the goals that have been determined. Each component selected later will be refined and designed in detail. The term "specific program" is used to identify program components when they have been selected and are in the development process. The general term "program component" is used at the conceptualization, investigation, and determination stages to identify the programmatic idea that will be used to translate goals into operational units. The terms can be used interchangeably, if desired. Each component can be distinguished by its intended purpose, area of content, and interaction process. Each component is implemented and evaluated separately from the other components.

The process of converting goals into program components is a difficult and challenging one. It calls for experience, expertise, and creativity. A wide range of possibilities exists for transforming goals into program components. Among the sources of inspiration for specific program ideas are:

- Published research results
- Related theories of human behavior, intervention, and leisure
- Published clinical practice guidelines or protocols
- Similar programs at other facilities
- Specific client-based interventions (e.g., Alcoholics Anonymous)

Several important concerns must be kept in mind when investigating and selecting program components. These seven concerns include:

- Translating goals into programs
- Ensuring that goals address the statement of purpose
- Resources available for programming
- Knowledge of possible program structures
- Prioritizing goals according to client need
- Considering multiple ways of achieving a goal
- Serious consideration of all goals

First, *the intent of every goal must be translated into some aspect of operationalized program components.* The very essence of all program components evolves from the goals. This direct relationship of programs to goals is what has often been missing in the past. Many staff have written goals and filed them in a drawer. Programs are created and implemented at the whim of staff. In a systems-designed comprehensive planning approach, this is not the case. Each program component is selected for its direct relationship between the operationalized programs and the agency's therapeutic recreation statement of purpose and goals.

The second concern is that the *goals state the intent of the comprehensive program.* Operationalizing that intent can be complex. Six goals do not translate necessarily into six program components. That may be an oversimplification. A given goal may require several program components to address it appropriately. Likewise, the intent of two or more goals may be combined into one program component. If a large and diverse population is served by the agency, one goal may need a different program component for each identified population subgroup or functional level. In other cases, one goal may be written to address the needs of one subgroup, and, thus, one program component for that one goal may be sufficient. The issue remains: Selection of program components to address adequately the intent of the goals is complex and difficult.

A third concern to consider is that of *resources.* Analyzing goals statements and selecting program components must be undertaken with a constant awareness of the available resources (staff, facilities, time, and budget). Without this reality in mind, it would be easy to select far more program components than could be feasibly implemented. Thus, the constraint of resources becomes a critical factor in the conceptualization and eventual selection of program components. It is important to keep in mind that, in the future, other program components can be added or existing ones expanded if and when additional resources become available or can be justified. These additional program components also will emerge from the existing goals, maintaining the integrity and interrelatedness of the systems approach. The statement of purpose and goals are written initially from an analysis of clients' leisure-related needs. Thus, these goals are sound, whether or not they can be operationally addressed as thoroughly as the designer would want at the beginning of the total program implementation.

The fourth concern related to transforming goals into program components focuses on the *knowledge of possible program structures.* Program structure implies the nature of the format or organization of the program component. Typical program formats include (Edgington, Hanson, Edgington, & Hudson, 1998):

- One-to-one: individually tailored
- Small group class: structured and focused on specific activity
- Drop-in or open formats: nonstructured, scheduled open use of facilities
- Competition: individual or team; leagues, tournaments, contests, meets
- Club: long-term, focused on common interest among participants
- Special events or mass activity: unusual activity or event
- Workshop or conference format: concentrated learning in short timeframe
- Interest group: shorter term, focused on common interest
- Outreach format: programming extending beyond agency facilities

Each of these structures has identifiable dimensions and characteristics. The appropriate structure needs to be selected to facilitate the desired outcome of a given program component. For example, a functional intervention program component might use the small group or one-to-one structure; trying to provide the same content in a league or open-facility structure would not likely be compatible with the desired behavioral change. Likewise, a leisure education program component would most likely use an instructional class or small group structure. Various structures are by definition more compatible with various categories of the Leisure Ability Model. The initial conceptualization and investigation of possible program components uses this

	Functional Intervention	Leisure Education	Recreation Participation
One-to-one	X	X	
Small group class	X	X	X
Drop-in or open format		X	X
Competition		X	X
Club		X	X
Special events or mass activity			X
Workshop or conference format		X	X
Interest group		X	X
Outreach format	X	X	X

Figure 4.4 Matrix of Leisure Ability Model components and potential program formats.

concept of structure to help give it definition and direction. However, the selection of structure must be followed by further explanation, specification, and description in order to be operational. At the current level of planning, it is helpful to explore and identify program components by indicating the basic structure that could be used.

Figure 4.4 shows a matrix that provides a generic comparison between components of the Leisure Ability Model and program formats. In many cases, program formats may or may not be appropriate depending on the content covered and the clients served. However, the matrix provides a sweeping overview and indicates that not all program formats are appropriate for all therapeutic recreation program content. One skill that the therapeutic recreation specialist needs to develop is the ability to select the best program format for the delivery of the program content to clients. This assumes that the therapeutic recreation specialist understands program formats and their potential for client learning.

The fifth concern in translating goals into program components is the *issue of priority of goals.* Although six or so goals may have been identified and stated for a comprehensive therapeutic recreation program, quite often some goals are conceptualized and viewed as being more important than others. When this is the case, it is logical to assume that those priority goals will most likely be operationalized through more program components or through more substantial or intensive program components. Identifying priority goals should be undertaken prior to investigating alternative program components.

The concept of *multiple ways to operationalize a given goal* is the sixth area of concern. The intent of any goal can be accomplished programmatically in many ways. The astute designer will brainstorm and investigate many possible program structures before arriving at a decision. Experience is important in this task, but creativity is of equal value. Brainstorming helps in clearing the mind of traditional or assumed ways of doing things. Often, creative workable ideas emerge when a group of planners feels the freedom to really explore alternative ways of addressing the intent of a given goal. Ideas that result from this process often are more efficient and may still be effective. When many goals are a part of a comprehensive therapeutic recreation program, multiple methods must be identified and considered prior to making the final program component selection.

The last concern when converting goals into program components is the issue of *thorough consideration of all goals.* When the designers initially derived and stated goals, they were, in essence, saying all goals are important and represent significant aspects of the clients' leisure-related needs. An important responsibility of the designer at the investigation stage is to address each goal thoroughly. This is best done by brainstorming and investigating program components for all goals before making any decisions. By using this holistic approach, the goals at the end of the list will have a chance of receiving equal attention and consideration. The result of this action may be that some goals receive a higher priority than other goals in the specific program design stages.

Procedural Steps in the Investigation Stage.   The following specific procedural steps are presented to assist the reader in understanding the investigation stage:

1. Review all goals with the purpose of understanding their intent.
2. Identify priority goals if desirable.
3. Brainstorm each goal for possible program components (including identification of possible program structure).
4. Review the goals for possible areas of combination.
5. Brainstorm possible combinations of program components.
6. Investigate each brainstormed idea for feasibility, practicality, and usefulness.
7. Discard ideas that are determined to be of no value, not feasible, impractical, or not useful.

An Example of Investigation of Program Components.   Using the third example of comprehensive program goals from a behavioral health facility, some program component ideas are brainstormed for possible inclusion as specific program areas.

Example 3. Behavioral Health Facility.
1.0 To provide services targeted at improving the physical, social, emotional, and cognitive deficits of clients that hinder their leisure involvement. [functional intervention focus]
Possible program components:

Physical fitness	*Concentration*	*Emotional control*	*Orientation*
Coordination	*Social tolerance*	*Anger expression*	

2.0 To provide programs that improve the clients' awareness of the need for leisure and its value in maintaining a healthy balance. [leisure awareness focus]
Possible program components:

Importance of leisure	*Leisure barriers*	*Leisure attitudes*
Leisure values	*Personal responsibility*	*Current leisure lifestyle*
Leisure satisfaction	*Balancing leisure*	*Family leisure*

3.0 To provide services and programs that assist clients in improving their social interaction skills for use in a variety of settings and with a variety of people. [social interaction skills focus]
Possible program components:

Assertiveness skills	*Conversational skills*	*Empathy expression*
Friendship development	*Developing social networks*	*Hygiene*
Grooming and dressing	*Etiquette and manners*	*Listening skills*

4.0 To provide skill improvement programs in both traditional and nontraditional leisure skills. [leisure activity skills focus]
Possible program components:

Expressive activities	*Physical leisure activities*	*Passive involvement*
Activities at home	*Solo or dual activities*	*Community leadership*
Pets and plant care	*Travel options*	*Relaxation*
Low-cost leisure activities	*Volunteer opportunities*	

5.0 To provide programs that teach clients about community leisure resources and how to use them as part of their overall leisure lifestyle. [leisure resources focus]
Possible program components:

Home resources	*Facility resources*	*Neighborhood resources*
Community resources	*Leisure equipment*	*State resources*
Financial aspects of leisure	*Leisure activities*	*Personal abilities*
Family and friends resources	*Internet resources*	

6.0 To provide programs that teach clients decision-making and planning skills in regard to utilizing their leisure time. [leisure decision-making and planning skills focus]
Possible program components:

Decision-making process	*Leisure planning skills*	*Overcoming leisure barriers*
Long-term coping strategies	*Leisure options*	*Stress reduction*
Information seeking	*Self-determination*	*Responsibility for choices*

These are just some of the options that may be available for program components to meet the intent of the intended comprehensive program goals. Selection of program components, again, depends on the nature of the agency, the clients, and the therapeutic recreation department. Note that the program components focus on the content of the goals and address the seven concerns for meeting the intent of program goals. The next step is to determine which of the brainstormed program components are most likely to meet the most important needs of the clients.

Determination

The next stage in the comprehensive program planning process is the actual selection of program components that will achieve the intent of the statement of purpose and goals. Many ideas and alternative program components were generated in the investigation stage. This information becomes the source for the determination process. The process starts by reviewing the possible program components and ascertaining their relationship to the established goals. Each alternative program component is studied for its strengths and weaknesses, its demands on resources, and its compatibility with other goals and program components. Eventually, after careful consideration, the specialist selects the most appropriate and desirable program components. A final check is made to ensure that all goals are adequately addressed through the selected program components. The specialist then moves on to the actual development and specification of each program component.

Obviously, the determination stage uses the human decision-making process. If each of the previous stages has been completed carefully, the decisions required in the determination stage will be made utilizing good information and will allow the specialist to be as objective and logical as possible. The program components that are selected will be related directly to the statement of purpose and goals. These goals and purpose statements should represent adequately the leisure-related needs of clients. The end result is a systematically derived comprehensive program plan that is both internally consistent and externally justifiable.

An Example of Determination of Program Components. The behavioral health facility example illustrated in the conceptualization and investigation stages is used to show that not all brainstormed program components are selected for client participation. One of the major functions of the determination stage is to filter program components to determine the best ones to meet the intent of the statement of purpose and the comprehensive program goals. Social interaction skills, leisure resources, and decision-making and planning skills were designated as being the most important areas for this group of clients, and therefore, have the greatest emphasis. The program components will be translated later into specific program goals and specific programs.

Example 3. Behavioral Health Facility.

1.0 To provide services targeted at improving the physical, social, emotional, and cognitive deficits of clients that hinder their leisure involvement. [functional intervention focus]
Selected program components:

Physical fitness	*Emotional control*	*Orientation*
Social tolerance	*Anger expression*	

2.0 To provide programs that improve the clients' awareness of the need for leisure and its value in maintaining a healthy balance. [leisure awareness focus]
Selected program components:

Importance of leisure	*Leisure barriers*	*Current leisure lifestyle*
Leisure values	*Personal responsibility*	

3.0 To provide services and programs that assist clients in improving their social interaction skills for use in a variety of settings and with a variety of people. [social interaction skills focus]
Selected program components:

Assertiveness skills	*Conversational skills*	*Hygiene*
Friendship development	*Developing social networks*	*Listening skills*
Grooming and dressing	*Etiquette and manners*	

4.0 To provide skill improvement programs in both traditional and nontraditional leisure skills. [leisure activity skills focus]
Selected program components:

Expressive activities	*Physical leisure activities*	*Relaxation*
Activities at home	*Solo or dual activities*	*Low-cost leisure activities*

5.0 To provide programs that teach clients about community leisure resources and how to use them as part of their overall leisure lifestyle. [leisure resources focus]
Selected program components:

Home resources	*Facility resources*	*Family and friends resources*
Community resources	*Leisure equipment*	*State resources*
Financial aspects of leisure	*Leisure activities*	*Personal abilities*

6.0 To provide programs that teach clients decision-making and planning skills in regard to utilizing their leisure time. [leisure decision-making and planning skills focus]
Selected program components:

Decision-making process	*Leisure planning skills*	*Overcoming leisure barriers*
Long-term coping strategies	*Leisure options*	*Stress reduction*
Information seeking	*Self-determination*	*Responsibility for choices*

These first four steps of comprehensive program design are essential to set the stage for selecting and designing specific programs. Analysis, conceptualization, investigation, and determination all play a vital role in establishing a logical, defensible, and accountable system of programs. In the next chapter, these first four steps are used as the foundation to develop specific programs using a systems-designed approach. The result of such an approach is the increased likelihood of producing client outcomes that are of importance to the client and the agency.

The purpose of this book is to provide a comprehensive and systematic process for therapeutic recreation program design. It is not the intent of this book to cover in depth such areas as documentation related to overall department or staff management. (See O'Morrow and Carter, 1997, for comprehensive coverage of these issues.) However, a brief introduction of such subjects as they relate to program design is necessary.

Other Comprehensive Program Documentation Issues

Beyond program design and the documentation that accompanies it, there are several other forms that concern the therapeutic recreation specialist. Among these are the policy and procedures manual and the written plan of operation.

Policy and Procedure Manual

Most therapeutic recreation departments in clinical, residential, or community settings have a policy and procedure manual. Included in such a manual are agency policies and departmental procedures that are of concern to employees. Examples include the following:

Personnel Policies

- Position descriptions
- Position qualifications and selection procedures
- Vacation, sick leave, and overtime policies
- Insurance and benefit information
- Salary information
- Employee rights and responsibilities
- Interns (recruitment, application, duties and evaluation)
- Volunteers (policies, training, evaluation)
- Personnel evaluation procedures
- Continuing education policies
- Family Medical Leave Act information
- Retirement benefits, qualifications, and procedures

Facility/Equipment/Supplies

- Vehicle use
- Use of buildings, rooms, and so on
- Purchasing procedures
- Repair and maintenance procedures
- Safety and sanitation procedures
- Off-grounds or overnight policies
- Housekeeping services

Administration/Supervision

- Organizational structure
- Professional and staff development
- Supervision methods and procedures
- Communication mechanisms (written and external to department and/or agency)
- Fiscal management
- Procedures related to in-service training, continuing education
- Contractual services and in-kind services procedures
- Evaluation, reward, and disciplinary procedures

Such a general policy and procedure manual is important to the administrative operation and efficiency of both the overall agency and the therapeutic recreation department. Administrative efficiency is improved when policies and procedures are regularly reviewed and updated.

Written Plan of Operation

In community settings, the written plan of operation may be the same document as the policy and procedure manual. In many clinical settings, additional information beyond that included in the policy and procedure manual is required.

In clinical settings, a comprehensive written plan of operation is imperative for each therapeutic recreation department. In relation to this written plan, two issues should concern the therapeutic recreation specialist: therapeutic recreation's involvement in the overall agency's written plan of operation and the specific therapeutic recreation department's written plan of operation.

Agency Plan. Therapeutic recreation services should be included in the overall agency's written plan of operation (**agency plan**). Each agency is responsible for formulating and specifying a written plan for professional services, including its goals, objectives, policies, and programs, so that performance can be measured. This plan describes the services offered by the agency and describes how the various services interact and interrelate.

Many therapeutic recreation professionals who are making efforts to be involved in the agency's accreditation process are disappointed if the accreditation surveyor fails to review the therapeutic recreation department. Frequently, accreditation surveyors will review or evaluate only those professional services that are reflected in the documentation of the overall agency's philosophy, goals, or major professional services. If therapeutic recreation is not documented adequately or described in the agency's written plan of operation, it may not be viewed as a major professional service. In these instances, the accreditation surveyor may choose not to review the therapeutic recreation department.

The therapeutic recreation administrator has a responsibility to attempt to integrate therapeutic recreation into the agency's overall written plan of operation. Without such a documented integration, therapeutic recreation will be seen as less important than those professional disciplines that are documented in the agency's written plan of operation.

Very often, therapeutic recreation specialists in clinical settings are involved directly in *patient management concerns* (that is, client assessment, treatment plans, progress notes, treatment plan reviews, and discharge summaries). To qualify for inclusion in the agency's written plan of operation, an agency also may expect involvement in *program management concerns.* Several program management concerns are described briefly below. Although terminology may vary among agencies, involvement in the following program management functions is typical when a service such as therapeutic recreation is viewed as a major professional service.

Quality or Performance Improvement Process. In general, **quality** or **performance improvement** may be interpreted broadly to mean the provision of continuously improved patient care. Quality or performance improvement implies that there are formal, documented mechanisms that will ensure accountability in the provision of quality patient services. These formal administrative procedures typically involve the review and evaluation of an agency's functioning. Quality or performance improvement is often an umbrella term that includes more specific administrative functions, such as patient care monitoring, utilization reviews, program evaluation, and performance evaluations.

Accreditation standards, such as JCAHO and CARF, are reviewed and revised on a regular basis. All accreditation standards can, in a general sense, be considered part of a quality or performance improvement mechanism. The therapeutic recreation specialist should be familiar with the entire accreditation manual or manuals that concern his or her particular agency. Regardless of the specific accreditation organization of concern, each accreditation manual will provide specific guidelines for documentation that will be useful in quality or performance improvement programs.

In addition, it is the responsibility of every therapeutic recreation specialist to keep informed of the evolving nature of external accreditation standards. As health care evolves, so too will the role that accreditation organizations play in improving quality services.

Utilization Reviews.   A **utilization review** program in a clinical agency attempts to demonstrate or document how effective the agency is at appropriately allocating its resources. Typically, the utilization review program will address underutilization, overutilization, and inefficient scheduling of the agency's resources. A therapeutic recreation department that is well integrated into the overall agency's functioning will be involved frequently in the utilization review program.

Patient Care Monitoring.   Patient care monitoring procedures typically will be specified in the agency's written plan of operation. These procedures help ensure that the treatment planned and provided for patients is evaluated and updated according to the needs of the patients. When therapeutic recreation services are an integral function in the client's treatment plan, they will be included in the facility's patient care monitoring program.

Quality or performance improvement, utilization reviews, and patient care monitoring are three of many possible program management functions that will concern therapeutic recreation specialists in clinical facilities. Therapeutic recreation administrators should become both knowledgeable and skilled in selective program management functions in their agency. Such involvement typically requires that the therapeutic recreation administrator investigate and initiate the necessary corresponding documentation mechanisms.

Therapeutic Recreation Written Plan of Operation

Regardless of the extent to which therapeutic recreation is included in the agency's written plan of operation, each clinical therapeutic recreation department should have its own written plan of operation. It is almost futile to expect that any clinical therapeutic recreation department could attempt to continue functioning in the "age of accountability" without such documentation.

There exists no universal format for a therapeutic recreation department's written plan of operation. The intent of such a plan should be to guide the therapeutic recreation specialist to design a format that is both comprehensive and useful. The major purpose of designing a therapeutic recreation written plan of operation is to ensure high-quality client care. The assumption here is that the delivery of high-quality client care is facilitated greatly when administrative goals and procedures assist specialists in implementing high-quality client services. A written plan of operation documents these concerns.

The following are suggestions for inclusion in the therapeutic recreation department's written plan of operation. Each therapeutic recreation department ultimately will include those items that are relevant to its particular therapeutic recreation service program.

- What is the philosophy of therapeutic recreation within the agency?
- What are the goals of the comprehensive therapeutic recreation program?
- What are the components of the comprehensive therapeutic recreation program (functional intervention, leisure education, recreation participation)?
- How are clients involved in each program component (by referral, requirement, voluntary participation, or based on client goals)?
- What are the goals of each program component?
- What specific programs are provided?
- How are specific programs and the comprehensive therapeutic recreation program evaluated? How often?
- What type of client assessment process is used? How is it used? When is it used? Who is qualified to perform client assessments? How are his or her qualifications reviewed?
- What policies and procedures are used by therapeutic recreation personnel? (The policy and procedure manual usually is included as part of the written plan of operation.)
- How does the therapeutic recreation department or therapeutic recreation services interact with other professional services?
- What is the role of therapeutic recreation in relation to patient management functions (intake, assessment, treatment plans, progress notes, treatment plan reviews, discharge summaries, and aftercare)?
- What is the role of therapeutic recreation in relation to program management functions (professional staff organization, quality improvement, utilization reviews, patient care monitoring, staff growth and development, research, patient rights, etc.)?

It is obvious that the documentation of a thorough written plan of operation is a lengthy process. Some therapeutic recreation departments simply will need to revise or improve on a policy and procedure manual, which can be expanded into a more comprehensive written plan of operation. Other therapeutic recreation departments, especially those that are just beginning to document their services, will have a lengthy, challenging task to undertake. Very few therapeutic recreation programs or departments will be expected to design or document a comprehensive, usable written plan of operation quickly. The wise therapeutic recreation administrator first will comprehensively conceptualize both the content and format of the therapeutic recreation written plan of operation. This "master plan" then can be included in the beginning written plan of operation. As long as a realistic time line for the completion of the comprehensive plan is included, those on the therapeutic recreation staff will have the confidence that they are on their way to completing a quality written plan of operation.

Summary

Comprehensive program design is crucial to the delivery of quality therapeutic recreation programs. At the comprehensive program design level, the steps of analysis, conceptualization, investigation, and determination each play a crucial role in determining overall client needs and the department's ability to meet those needs. These four steps lay the foundation upon which specific programs that meet client needs and produce client outcomes can be designed, delivered, and implemented. The next chapter provides the continuation of the systems-designed process for specific programs.

Several other documentation functions are of concern to a high-quality therapeutic recreation department. Among these documentation functions are the department's written plan of operation, quality or performance improvement, patient care monitoring, and utilization reviews. The importance of each of these functions is explained briefly.

STUDENT EXERCISES

Discussion Questions

1. What is the relationship between client needs and client outcomes? What steps does a therapeutic recreation specialist take to ensure that there is a relationship between client needs and client outcomes?

2. What are the advantages of evidence-based practice? What steps or actions have to be taken to implement evidence-based practice? What would happen in the field of therapeutic recreation if every professional implemented evidence-based practice?

3. What are the advantages of theory-based programming? What steps or actions have to be taken to implement theory-based programming? What would happen in the field of therapeutic recreation if every professional implemented theory-based programming?

4. Discuss the advantages of comprehensive and specific program design versus haphazard or "cafeteria-style" programming.

5. Outline the actions taken by the therapeutic recreation specialist at each of the four stages of comprehensive program design.

6. Discuss why therapeutic recreation programs in Chicago, Bloomington, and LeRoy, Illinois, may be different (as would programs in any other towns and cities across the nation). How is this reconciled with the need and push for standardized programming in therapeutic recreation services?

7. Go to the Web sites of the Joint Commission on Accreditation of Healthcare Organizations (*www.jcaho.org*), CARF (the Rehabilitation Accreditation Commission) (*www.carf.org*), and the Center for Medicaid and Medicare Services (*cms.hhs.gov*), and search them for their influence on health and human services, including therapeutic recreation. Bring this information to class and share it with other students.

8. For the analysis stage of comprehensive program design, explain each of the five areas that must be analyzed and what a therapeutic recreation specialist would need to know about each area.

9. In the conceptualization stage of comprehensive program design, what is the relationship between the statement of purpose and the comprehensive program goals?

10. What is the purpose of the investigation stage of comprehensive program design? Why is it important? What is likely to happen if it is not completed prior to program development?

11. What is the purpose of the determination stage of comprehensive program design? Why is it important?

12. Explain the purpose of policy and procedures manuals, written plans of operation, quality or performance improvement documentation, utilization reviews, and patient care monitoring.

Practice Test

1. Comprehensive program planning is important because it increases all of the following EXCEPT:
   a. understanding of the purpose, direction, and outcome of the intervention.
   b. clients' understanding of what is expected of them within the therapeutic recreation program.
   c. the ability to gain an overall view of outcomes prior to designing programs.
   d. the amount of time spent in client assessment.

2. The NTRS and ATRA professional *Standards of Practice* documents provide therapeutic recreation specialists with:
   a. specific details for designing, implementing, and evaluating programs.
   b. recommendations for meeting external accreditation standards, such as JCAHO and CARF.
   c. sample policies and procedures for personnel management.
   d. a comprehensive framework for service delivery.

3. Comprehensive program goals are developed with all of the following sources in mind EXCEPT:
   a. generic client characteristics and needs.
   b. community resources and facilities.
   c. professional philosophies, standards, and codes.
   d. individual client characteristics and needs.

4. The purpose of the analysis stage of the Stumbo and Peterson Program Planning Model is to:
   a. evaluate the effects of the community, agency, and client on the types of programs to be offered.
   b. write a comprehensive statement of purpose, goals, and objectives.
   c. analyze what types of programs are best suited to client needs.
   d. brainstorm and explore a variety of program ideas for their suitability to client needs and interests.

5. The purpose of the conceptualization stage of the Stumbo and Peterson Planning Model is to:
   a. evaluate the effects of the community, agency, and client on the types of programs to be offered.
   b. document the purpose and overall direction of the program.
   c. analyze what types of programs are best suited to client needs.
   d. develop a client assessment procedure to gather important information for programming purposes.

6. The purpose of the investigation stage of the Stumbo and Peterson Planning Model is to:
   a. write a comprehensive statement of purpose, goals, and objectives.
   b. analyze what types of programs are best suited to client needs.
   c. brainstorm and explore a variety of program ideas for their suitability to client needs and interests.
   d. develop a client assessment procedure to gather important information for programming purposes.

7. The purpose of the determination stage of the Stumbo and Peterson Program Planning Model is to:
   a. evaluate how the community, agency, and client affect the TR department and the program it offers.
   b. standardize practice through the development of protocols.
   c. analyze what types of programs are best suited to client needs.
   d. develop a client assessment procedure to gather important information for programming purposes.

8. Why is a statement of purpose important to comprehensive program planning?
   a. It gives direction to the development and implementation of the program.
   b. It allows specialists to design treatment plans and progress notes.
   c. It makes the therapeutic recreation department more credible.
   d. It justifies the addition of TR staff for programming purposes.

9. Specific programs are selected, designed, and implemented based on the:
   a. intent of the comprehensive statement of purpose and goals.
   b. staff's areas of expertise.
   c. NTRS standards of practice.
   d. results of the activity analysis.

10. Documentation is necessary in order to:
    a. comply with NTRS, ATRA, JCAHO, CARF, CMS, etc., standards.

  b. create a client assessment.

  c. complete an activity analysis.

  d. provide theory-based programming.

Answers: 1. d, 2. d, 3. d, 4. a, 5. b, 6. c, 7. c, 8. a, 9. a, 10. a

Chapter Activities

Therapeutic Recreation On-Site Visit

Arrange an appointment with a therapeutic recreation specialist at his or her facility. Ask to see the documentation that is created for both program and client purposes. What requirements does the agency place on the documentation? What requirements do JCAHO, CARF, CMS, ATRA, NTRS, etc., place on the documentation? Does the agency have adequate documentation for each step of the Therapeutic Recreation Accountability Model?

Comprehensive Program Design

Either in cooperation with a practicing therapeutic recreation specialist or from your experience, select a target population and agency, and create a comprehensive program design, as shown in the three examples in the text. Follow the four steps of comprehensive program design to do so. As much as possible, make your programs and ideas the result of research results or potential theories that fit your population and agency. (We'll use this beginning to create specific programs in Chapter 5.)

Theory-Based Programming Comparisons

Read Hood and Carruthers (2002), Carruthers and Hood (2002), Caldwell (2001, 2003), Widmer (2001), and Widmer, Zabriskie, and Wells (2003). What are the common themes of applying theory to service delivery? What steps did they take? How did they find out about the theories? How did they choose the best ones? How does this help them improve their programming? How does this help them evaluate client outcomes?

Research Journals

Select four or five (or more) issues of therapeutic recreation-related research journals. Read the articles in the journals and create a list of theories or results that would help you design therapeutic recreation programs for a specific population. If you do not find enough articles within these, do an on-line library database search (e.g., using MedLine, PsychInfo, ERIC, etc.) to locate information about the type of population you are interested in (e.g., at-risk youth) and the type of intervention you are interested in (e.g., leisure education). Make a list of theories, results, or ideas that would improve your therapeutic recreation services for this group of clients.

Research Efficacy Synopsis

Complete the same steps as in the previous assignment. Write a one- or two-page synopsis of the findings, and share this information with other students, making sure to include the full reference list of the sources of the information. What are the implications for therapeutic recreation programming?

REFERENCES

American Therapeutic Recreation Association. (2000). *Standards of practice*. Alexandria, VA: Author.

Caldwell, L. L. (2001). The role of theory in therapeutic recreation: A practical approach. In N. J. Stumbo (Ed.), *Professional issues in therapeutic recreation: On competencies and outcomes* (pp. 349–364). Champaign, IL: Sagamore Publishing Company.

Caldwell, L. L. (2003). Basing outcomes on theory: Theories of intervention and explanation. In N. J. Stumbo (Ed.), *Client outcomes in therapeutic recreation services* (pp. 67–86). State College, PA: Venture Publishing Company.

Carruthers, C. P., & Hood, C. D. (2002). Coping skills program for individuals with alcoholism. *Therapeutic Recreation Journal, 36*(2), 154–171.

Chambless, D. L., & Ollendick, T. H. (2001). Empirically supported psychological interventions: Controversies and evidence. *Annual Review of Psychology, 52*, 685–716.

Denton, W. H., Walsh, S. R., & Daniel, S. S. (2002). Evidence-based practice in family therapy: Adolescent depression as an example. *Journal of Marital and Family Therapy, 29*(1), 39–45.

Edgington, C. R., Hanson, C. J., Edgington, S. R., & Hudson, S. D. (1998). *Leisure programming: A service-oriented and benefits approach* (3rd ed.). St. Louis, MO: Brown and Benchmark.

Evidence-based Medicine Working Group. (1992) Evidence-based medicine: A new approach to teaching the practice of medicine. *Journal of the American Medical Association, 268*, 2420–2425.

Hess, M. E. (1997). *Comprehensive program package*. Unpublished paper. Normal, IL: Illinois State University.

Hood, C. D., & Carruthers, C. P. (2002). Coping skills theory as an underlying framework for therapeutic recreation services. *Therapeutic Recreation Journal, 36*(2), 137–153.

Kendall, P. C. (1998). Empirically supported psychological therapies. *Journal of Consulting and Clinical Psychology, 66*, 36.

Lee, Y., & McCormick, B. P. (2002). Toward evidence-based therapeutic recreation practice. In D. R. Austin, J. Dattilo, & B. P. McCormick (Eds.), *Conceptual foundations for therapeutic recreation* (pp. 165–184). State College, PA: Venture Publishing Company.

McGowen, A. L. (1997). *Comprehensive program package*. Unpublished paper. Normal, IL: Illinois State University.

Mobily, K., & MacNeil, R. (2002). *Therapeutic recreation and the nature of disabilities*. State College, PA: Venture Publishing Company.

National Therapeutic Recreation Society, (1995). *Standards of practice*. Arlington, VA: National Recreation and Park Association.

Stumbo, N. J. (2003). The importance of evidence-based practice in therapeutic recreation. In N. J. Stumbo (Ed.), *Client outcomes in therapeutic recreation services* (pp. 25–48). State College, PA: Venture Publishing Company.

Widmer, M. A. (2001). Methods for outcome research in therapeutic recreation. In N.J. Stumbo (Ed.), *Professional issues in therapeutic recreation: On competence and outcomes* (pp. 365–382). Champaign, IL: Sagamore Publishing Company.

Widmer, M. A., Zabriskie, R., & Wells, M. A. (2003). Program evaluation: Collecting data to measure outcomes. In N. J. Stumbo (Ed.), *Client outcomes in therapeutic recreation services* (pp. 203–220). State College, PA: Venture Publishing Company.

CHAPTER 5

Specific Program Design

After a comprehensive statement of purpose and goal statements are determined for a therapeutic recreation unit or agency, the specialist is faced with the task of developing specific programs. Specific programs are the operational units that put the comprehensive goals and purpose into motion. As discussed in the previous chapter, agency or unit goals must be translated and transformed into actual operational programs. These specific programs need to be developed and described in a very specific manner, so that desired outcomes are related directly to planned interventions and activities. Figure 5.1 displays the placement of specific program design in the Therapeutic Recreation Accountability Model. The reader will note that both comprehensive and specific program design are in a single box to indicate their mutual, symbiotic relationship.

Importance of Evidence and Theory to Specific Program Development

As discussed in the beginning of Chapter 4, research evidence and theories of intervention are important to program development, not only at the comprehensive design level but also at the specific program level (Caldwell, 2001, 2003; Stumbo, 2003; Widmer, Zabriskie, & Wells, 2003). Using research evidence and theories of intervention can aid the therapeutic recreation specialist in many ways, including:

- Reducing the amount of time and effort in creating "from-scratch" program designs by providing an overall framework and implementation strategies
- Improving the connection between clients' needs, program design and implementation, and client outcomes
- Improving standardization of and consensus about programs for specific client groups
- Improving the ability to evaluate program effectiveness for individual clients, for groups of clients, and for therapeutic recreation as a service

As discussed in Chapter 4, Hood and Carruthers (2002) researched models of stress-coping and examined their application to individuals with alcoholism. Two major intervention strategies emerged: (a) decreasing negative demands and (b) increasing positive resources.

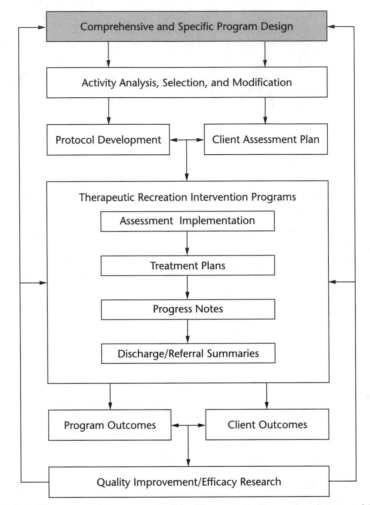

Figure 5.1 Specific program component of the Therapeutic Recreation Accountability Model.

After this thorough review of the literature, they designed a seven-session coping skills program, with goals, implementation details, and an evaluation strategy (Carruthers & Hood, 2002). After implementing the stress-coping program at three different hospitals, they reported that clients perceived the goals of the coping skills intervention program as very important, clients believed their own improvement on the goals as a result of the program was approximately 75 percent, and clients actually achieved the goals behaviorally approximately 80 to 95 percent of the time. The specialists who implemented the program at the three different hospitals felt the intervention was brief but more effective than previous attempts in this area.

This is but one example of evidence-based practice and theory-based programming in the therapeutic recreation literature. Readers are encouraged to seek out this and other examples as they build their program designs so that interventions are more powerful in the lives of clients. This also frees the specialist from spending significant amounts of time and energy "reinventing the wheel" when numerous examples of successful specific programs are available.

A **specific program** can be defined as a set of activities and their corresponding interactions that are designed to achieve predetermined goals selected for a given group of clients. The specific program is implemented and evaluated independently of all other specific programs.

Aspects of this definition require further exploration. Implied in the definition is the concept that each specific program identifies and addresses some major aspect of functional intervention, leisure education, or recreation participation. One specific program usually cannot focus adequately on all of these areas of client need. Thus, specific programs are selected and developed that relate to different categories of client need. Some programs will address various functional intervention concerns; others will be developed to focus on the diverse aspects of leisure education; still others will center on recreation and leisure participation opportunities.

Once the general topic of a specific program is selected, objectives will be derived and stated. These objectives will be delineated for a given group of clients (usually a subgroup of the total population served by the agency). Activities then will be developed that relate directly to the identified objectives and are appropriate for the designated clients. The term *activities* in this context does not mean just traditional recreation or leisure activities. It implies a broader category of actions or program content, which can include such areas as discussions, lectures, and written or cognitive exercises as well as traditional or nontraditional recreation activities. Thus, the term **activity** refers to the action, content, or media presented to the clients to address the objectives and, it is hoped, to achieve the desired outcomes.

Similarly, specific interactions will be designed to be used with those activities for that particular set of clients. The program is designed to be implemented independently of other programs. Its objectives, activities, and interventions have their own timelines, staff, resource allocations, and designated evaluation mechanism. A given client is placed or referred to one or more specific programs based on the client's need and the program's designed ability to address that need. This method of programming enables the individual leisure-related needs of clients to be met. It also allows for specific programs to be added, deleted, or changed as clients' needs dictate. Because each specific program has its own focus (purpose and objectives), it can be evaluated based on its contribution to the overall mission of the therapeutic recreation unit, agency, or department. Likewise, the progress of an individual client can be carefully monitored, based on achievement and participation within each assigned or designated program.

Specific programs must be developed and described so that they can be implemented by the specialist in a consistent manner. This description also allows the program to be repeated by the same person, or implemented by someone else. The thorough written description is also of value for the purpose of evaluation. Additionally, it allows the agency to maintain a high level of accountability in that all programs are documented before, during, and after implementation.

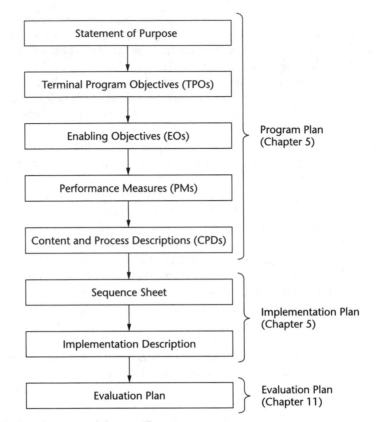

Figure 5.2 Development of the specific program.

The total development of the specific program requires three stages of design:

- The program plan
- The implementation plan
- The evaluation plan

Each of these stages has sequential procedures and tasks. Figure 5.2 presents an overview of the entire process.

This chapter presents the information necessary to complete the program plan and the implementation plan. Program evaluation is one of the topics in Chapter 11. The program plan consists of five major parts:

- Statement of purpose
- Terminal performance objectives (TPOs)
- Enabling objectives (EOs)
- Performance measures (PMs)
- Content and process descriptions (CPDs)

The implementation plan consists of:

- Sequence sheet or session format description
- Performance sheet
- Implementation description

Each of these pieces is developed for each specific program in the therapeutic recreation department. Briefly, the **statement of purpose** is a one-sentence description of the program's intended focus. The **terminal program objectives (TPOs)** are general outcome statements that the client is expected to achieve. The **enabling objectives (EOs)** are smaller behavioral units that specify the content to be covered within the larger terminal program objectives. The **performance measures (PMs)** are behavioral objectives that clients are expected to achieve by participating in the program. The **content and process descriptions (CPDs)** provide a clearer picture of the "what" and "how" of the program design. Within the implementation plan, the **sequence sheet or session format description** provides a session-by-session description of how the program will be offered to clients. The **performance sheet** helps record clients' attainment of the enabling objectives. The **implementation description** provides background information about the factors affecting the total program. Each of these steps builds on the previous material, so that the entire program is developed to accomplish its purpose through the use of systematic and interrelated parts. Box 5.1 provides a quick overview of these specific program parts.

Though it is quite possible to develop quality specific programs without completing each of these forms exactly as they have been designed, the steps used to create accountable programs are universal. The therapeutic recreation specialist must, for every program designed, understand what content is important, how it will be facilitated, what steps must be taken, what activities will be offered, what resources are needed, and what outcomes are expected. The steps, as outlined in this chapter, assist the specialist in determining the answers in a systematic, logical way. Again, the ability to produce predictable, reproducible client outcomes is enhanced when the procedure used to create and implement the programs is well thought out, connected, and systematic.

Appendix A contains a complete example of a program plan for relaxation and Appendix B contains one for social skills. As the remainder of this chapter is read, it may be helpful to refer to these appendices.

The Program Plan

Specific programs represent the major areas of content derived from the comprehensive program design. Specific program planning includes developing a statement of purpose, terminal program objectives, enabling objectives, performance measures, and content and process descriptions.

Statement of Purpose

The design of every program starts with a clear understanding of the program's intended purpose. The most appropriate way to ensure this understanding from the onset is to determine and write a brief statement of purpose for the specific program.

Box 5.1   Parts of the Specific Program Design

Program Plan

Statement of Purpose

> Concise, one-sentence explanations of the program's focus and purpose

Terminal Performance Objectives (TPOs)

> General outcome statements that reflect the intent of the statement of purpose and give direction to the rest of the program plan

Enabling Objectives (EOs)

> Smaller behavioral units of the terminal performance objective that target actual performance or knowledge to be gained by the client

Performance Measures (PMs)

> Statement of exact behavior that will be taken as evidence that the enabling objective has been achieved; normally called behavioral objectives, containing condition, behavior, and criteria for performance; also called client outcomes

Content and Process Descriptions (CPDs)

> Specification of the material and activities presented to clients to attain the performance measures, along with the facilitation techniques (instructional, leadership, or counseling techniques) the specialist will use during the sessions

Implementation Plan

Sequence Sheet or Session Format Description

> An estimation of how much time will be spent on each part of the session addressing the terminal performance objectives and the enabling objectives

Performance Sheet

> A coding sheet for marking client attainment of enabling objectives

Implementation Description

> Brief description of population; number, length, and frequency of sessions; staff requirements; and facilities, equipment, and supplies

---

Normally, this statement is a concise, one-sentence explanation of the program's focus. It delineates whether the program is oriented toward functional intervention, leisure education, or recreation participation. The purpose, however, goes beyond the general category of service. It is as precise as possible in its description. Consider the following example purpose statements for various programs:

- To provide activities and services to improve clients' physical fitness.
- To provide activities in which clients acquire, improve, and utilize social interaction skills that can be used within a variety of leisure contexts.

- To facilitate clients' personal understanding of leisure and its potential utilization.

- To provide services that help clients acquire knowledge of leisure, awareness of personal attitudes and values related to leisure, and knowledge of resources that would facilitate leisure involvement.

- To provide learning and practice situations for clients to acquire basic water readiness and safety skills necessary for advancement into a beginner-level swimming program.

- To provide services that assist clients in acquiring wheelchair maneuvering skills and basic basketball skills required for playing competitive wheelchair basketball.

Each of these examples pinpoints the intent of the program in clear and concise language. The statement of purpose is just that—a statement of intent. It is written from the point of view of the sponsoring agency or unit. The language used states what the program is intended to provide. Note also that the statement of purpose does not state how the program will accomplish this. The remainder of the program system will delineate the "how." Nor does the statement of purpose need to describe for whom the program is designed. That information, although vital to the program specification, is presented in the implementation description.

In order to address the diverse goals delineated by the therapeutic recreation agency, unit, or department, a variety of specific programs is generally selected. Each of these specific programs will require a statement of purpose. These combined statements provide the overall operational definition of the previously delineated agency's or unit's goals. Checking back this way is also an important monitoring step. At this point, the specialist can verify that the more generalized intent of the comprehensive goals has been reflected in actual programming efforts.

Program Titles.   Most programs are given a title, which is used in presenting the program to clients and other interested staff members, families, or outside groups. Often, the title given does not directly identify the purpose of the program—nor does it need to. The title is simply a code for communication and identification purposes. For example, a program may be entitled "Jogging." This title does not describe whether the program is teaching jogging, providing jogging for clients who want to jog for enjoyment or fitness, or whether it is oriented toward functional intervention used in the rehabilitation of patients with cardiac complications. Often, agencies use even more indirect program titles, such as "The Clang Gang," "Early Riser," or "Staying Alive." These examples illustrate that the title often gives little indication of the purpose or nature of a given program. Thus, the statement of purpose becomes even more important, at least to the designer, implementer, and administrator. Whenever possible, it appears appropriate to title a program so that it does imply the purpose. This simple act can do much to help clients and others understand the program, its purpose, and the reason for their involvement. Titles such as "Instructional Jogging," "Leisure Awareness," and "Conversational Skills" imply purpose and assist clients and the staff in understanding the role and nature of the various specific programs.

Terminal Program Objectives

After the specific program component has been identified and the statement of purpose has been written, the designer develops the terminal program objectives (frequently referred to as TPOs). TPOs are best described as general outcome statements. They are written in language that specifies anticipated outcomes related to the client. Thus, the phrase "to demonstrate" will always characterize the TPO.

Terminal program objectives are not complete behavioral objectives, since they do not identify conditions, specific behaviors, or criteria, which are all necessary parts of a measurable objective. This aspect of further development and specification will come later. Terminal program objectives identify more global behavioral outcomes. Their role is to break down the intent of the statement of purpose into separate identifiable and general outcome behaviors. Normally, each TPO can stand somewhat independently of the other TPOs. However, each TPO is needed to address adequately the overall concern or intent of the program. TPOs are the first-level behavioral outcome statements of the specific program. As such, they are not immediately measurable.

Several examples of TPOs are provided to illustrate their role, content, and language. Note the global nature of their content, the concept of independence between and among them, and yet the element of interrelatedness.

Statement of Purpose: To provide activities in which clients acquire, improve, and utilize social interaction skills that can be used within a variety of leisure contexts.

TPO1: To demonstrate ability to initiate, maintain, and end conversations with peers.

TPO2: To demonstrate ability to select clothing appropriate for a variety of situations.

TPO3: To demonstrate information-seeking and information-giving skills.

TPO4: To demonstrate ability to be assertive in selected situations.

Statement of Purpose: To facilitate clients' personal understanding of leisure and its potential utilization.

TPO1: To demonstrate knowledge of leisure and its potential contribution to life satisfaction.

TPO2: To demonstrate ability to make decisions regarding leisure involvement.

TPO3: To demonstrate ability to develop a plan for future leisure participation.

Statement of Purpose: To provide services that help clients acquire knowledge of leisure, awareness of personal attitudes and values related to leisure, and knowledge of resources that would facilitate leisure involvement.

TPO1: To demonstrate ability to distinguish between leisure and other behaviors.

TPO2: To demonstrate ability to articulate benefits and potential outcomes of leisure participation.

TPO3: To demonstrate knowledge of various barriers affecting personal leisure involvement.

TPO4: To demonstrate awareness of past, current, and future personal attitudes toward leisure.

TPO5: To demonstrate ability to locate and utilize community resources for future leisure involvement.

In all of these illustrations, the terminal program objectives state the general terminal or outcome behaviors expected of the client in the program. The combination of the TPOs for a given program is a further explanation or definition of the program's purpose.

Deciding on an appropriate level for the TPOs is often a problem for the beginning systems designer. Obviously, there are many ways in which the TPO could be written. The appropriate level for the TPOs is dependent on the population, its functional ability, and the nature of the program. For example, TPOs for a program developed for individuals with autism spectrum disorder may delineate smaller units of outcome behavior, whereas total activities or groups of related behaviors may be appropriate for other populations. Generally, a specific program has a minimum of two TPOs. A program with more than five TPOs will become very lengthy and may need to be separated into two different programs—a beginners' level and an advanced level. *A basic guideline is to conceptualize the intent of the statement of purpose in two to five terminal program objectives.*

Each TPO requires further breakdown. A TPO as written is not specific enough, nor is it measurable. The designer must analyze each TPO to derive enabling objectives and performance measures. Terminal program objectives serve as general outcome behavior statements, indicating a broad category of knowledge, skills, or ability that a client will be expected to acquire.

To assist in the description and organization of a systems-designed program, several forms have been developed. Figure 5.3 presents a blank objectives and performance measures (OPM) sheet. This form provides a space for the terminal program objective, and the next level of breakdown into enabling objectives and performance measures. It also identifies the name of the program and can be modified to include other additional information. One objectives and performance measures sheet is used for each TPO. Figure 5.4 presents a sample OPM form filled in for one TPO from a specific program on social skills to illustrate the positioning and nature of the various items that are found on this useful form.

Enabling Objectives

Each TPO needs to be broken down into smaller behavior units. These units, called enabling objectives (EOs), are the specific targeted behaviors around which the rest of the program system is designed. The selection of content and process is focused on these units. In addition, EOs are specific enough to be used for measurement purposes. In many ways, they are the most important and essential aspect of a systems-designed program.

EOs are conceptualized and selected through analysis of the TPO. The designer studies the intent of the TPO to arrive at necessary or desired units of behavior, skill, or knowledge that are appropriate for that topic and appropriate for the nature of the given population. During this process of analysis, the designer attempts not only to

Objectives and Performance Measures

PROGRAM: _____

TERMINAL PROGRAM OBJECTIVE: _____

ENABLING OBJECTIVE	PERFORMANCE MEASURE

Figure 5.3 Objectives and Performance Measures form.

Objectives and Performance Measures

PROGRAM: Social Skills

TERMINAL PROGRAM OBJECTIVE: 1. To demonstrate knowledge of manners

ENABLING OBJECTIVE	PERFORMANCE MEASURE
1. To demonstrate ability to perform table manners	Upon completion of the Manners Program, the client will display table manners as evidenced by the following: a. Eating with mouth closed b. Keeping hands to self c. Passing food and condiments when asked d. Using eating utensils e. Talking at a reasonable volume, as judged by the therapeutic recreation specialist
2. To demonstrate ability to perform appropriate greeting	Upon completion of the Manners Program, the client will greet peers by: a. Using appropriate greeting (hello, hi) and the person's name b. Using an appropriate voice volume for the setting c. Keeping hands to self d. Maintaining a minimum distance of one foot, as judged by the therapeutic recreation specialist

Figure 5.4 Example of Objectives and Performance Measures form for social skills program.

identify desired or necessary behavioral units, but also to arrive at units that are somewhat parallel in their content and level.

Some TPOs break down easily into logical areas of behavior. These are *concrete TPOs,* and they usually result in very concrete EO behavioral units. Here is an example of a concrete TPO and its resulting concrete EO behaviors. Assume the TPO states, "to demonstrate the ability to play table tennis." An analysis of this TPO produces the following EO content units:

1. Serving

2. Forehand

3. Backhand

4. Drop shot

5. Smash

6. Lob

7. Rules

8. Scoring

9. Etiquette

10. Strategy

Although there could be some disagreement over the possible number and types of behaviors, skills, and knowledge that could be included in the program, most people would agree that these ten areas comprise the essential aspects of playing table tennis. What is important is to identify the actual areas necessary for the game. Because this deals with a specific game and accepted procedures and rules, the areas of behavior are relatively concrete and direct. Many leisure activities and skills fall into this category of *concrete TPOs and EOs.* However, most functional intervention and leisure education (excluding traditional activity skills) programs are more difficult to conceptualize, since they fall under the category of *abstract TPOs and EOs.*

When programs have abstract or indirect TPOs and EOs, the designer must conceptualize and define the meaning of the TPO, because the content is subject to multiple meanings and interpretations. Take, for example, the TPO "to demonstrate ability to select clothing appropriate for a variety of situations." In this case, the developer must determine the content areas that represent the intent of the TPO for the specific population. Analysis is still part of the process. It is used to arrive at the specific content areas that define the meaning or intent of the TPO. Below are two examples of TPOs and their corresponding EOs. Notice how the EOs collectively define the content of the TPO.

TPO1: To demonstrate ability to select clothing appropriate for a variety of situations.

EO1: To demonstrate knowledge of a variety of clothing styles.

EO2: To demonstrate knowledge of the purposes of clothing (fashion, warmth, etc.).

EO3: To demonstrate ability to match different clothing with different situations.

EO4: To demonstrate ability to select own clothing depending on leisure activity.

TPO2: To demonstrate ability to make decisions regarding leisure involvement.

EO1: To demonstrate knowledge of personal responsibility for leisure-related decisions.

EO2: To demonstrate ability to review alternatives.

EO3: To demonstrate ability to weigh benefits and consequences of alternatives.

EO4: To demonstrate ability to select an alternative and make a decision.

EO5: To demonstrate ability to follow through with a leisure decision.

When analyzing abstract TPOs, the designer must carefully conceptualize the EO content areas. The EO content areas should be logical and, when added together, represent an adequate definition of the intent of the TPO. The EOs each should be related to the topic of the TPO and provide an appropriate coverage of the TPO's meaning.

Whether the designer is dealing with an abstract TPO or a concrete TPO, the process of analysis is essential. The EO behavioral areas that result from analysis are the designer's interpretation of the meaning or intentions of the TPO. It is critical that the EOs be logical and appropriate for the population being served. For example, the number, nature, and level of EO content areas would be quite different for a social interaction program designed for individuals with developmental disabilities and one designed for at-risk youth. The EO content areas operationally define the TPO for the group under consideration. Those who disagree with the breakdown still cannot refute the fact that the TPO has been operationally defined.

A final word about developing and stating enabling objectives. The EOs represent the core of the systems-designed program. The content and process of the program are developed to bring into existence the behaviors that are identified in the EOs. The measurement of the clients' achievement is focused on the intent of the EO. Thus, when developing the EOs, the designer is determining and specifying what the program intends to achieve. Although they are not yet measurable, EOs represent the client outcomes that will be targeted by the program.

And though EOs should be comprehensive enough to cover the topic appropriately or address desired or necessary behaviors, it is advisable to keep the number of EOs to a minimum. Additional or supplemental information, skills, and activities can always be added to the content of the program. This does not mean that additional EOs must, or should, be added. Rather, the EOs should address only the essential aspects of the program. EOs indicate the behavioral areas for which the program will be held accountable. Each EO specified and stated will be measured in terms of client gains and outcomes. Specific interactions and activities will be designed to achieve the intent of the EO. Thus, careful consideration must be given to the selection and specification of each EO. Once an EO is included in the program, the designer makes a commitment to the importance of that EO and to facilitating the clients' accomplishment of that behavior.

The EOs for a given TPO define and specify the meaning of the TPO. When a client has achieved all EOs for a given TPO, the implication is that the TPO has been mastered. When all EOs of all TPOs have been achieved, then it can be inferred that the client has accomplished the intent of the program's statement of purpose. In a systems-designed program, this concept of levels or hierarchy is central. A program starts with a statement of purpose. TPOs are then derived to target the overall outcomes of the program. TPOs then are further specified through enabling objectives. Behaviors, skills, or knowledge at the EO stage are an appropriate and feasible level for accurate observation and evaluation. In addition, they are at a level that allows for the comprehensive identification and selection of program content (activities) and processes (interactions).

Performance Measures

Enabling objectives identify the selected and desired outcome behaviors of the program. These behaviors are the skills, knowledge, or abilities that the program specifies as the targeted areas for behavioral change, improvement, or acquisition. After the EOs have been selected, all remaining developments and specifications of the program focus on them.

The first task after the determination of the EOs is the development of the performance measures (PMs). The performance measure is a statement of the exact behavior that will be taken as evidence that the intent of the EO has been achieved or accomplished. Whereas the EO delineates an area of behavioral concern, such as a specific skill or category of knowledge or unit of behavioral improvement, the performance measure identifies an exact definition of a behavior that is observable and measurable and can be taken as appropriate representation of the EO.

A performance measure is a complete behavioral objective, which includes three specific parts—the desired behavior, the conditions under which the desired behavior will occur, and the criteria or standards for judging the behavior. As a behavioral objective, its role is different from that of an enabling objective. The performance measure indicates and specifies the nature and type of measurement for the purpose of evaluating. There are several reasons for separating EOs from the performance measures. First, the EOs identify the targeted behavioral areas of concern for the program. All EOs are conceptualized and written prior to developing the performance measures. Thus, the identification and specification of EOs is a conceptual stage. When the EOs are written, they can be reviewed, and revised if necessary, to ensure that all of the essential or desired elements are included. Then the designer moves on to the next stage, developing the performance measures. The second reason is simply an issue of clarity in reading. Often, a performance measure becomes very lengthy, especially when many criteria are used as part of the measure. Interested readers can easily identify the focus of a program by scanning the enabling objectives. They then can go on to read the performance measures if they are interested in the measurement aspect of the program. In short, the technical nature of the format and language of a performance measure makes it difficult to identify easily the behavioral component, which is frequently the area in which an administrator or staff member is most interested. The third reason is probably the most important. The EO is the vital element of concern in the program. The actual activities and interventions of the program are selected to address the full intent of the EO. EOs are quite broad in their concern for a given skill, knowledge, or ability. The performance measure, by definition, can only select and define a representative task, behavior, or action for observation and measurement. Rarely can the full intent of an EO be incorporated into a PM. The performance measure cannot, and should not, be expected to be as comprehensive as the EO.

Each enabling objective will have at least one corresponding performance measure. Since EOs identify the desired target behavior for improvement or acquisition, it is only logical that each of the behavioral areas be evaluated. Thus, at least one performance measure must be developed for each EO. Below is an example of an EO and corresponding PM.

EO: To demonstrate ability to weigh benefits and consequences of alternatives.

PM: Upon completion of the Leisure Decisions program, the client will weigh benefits and consequences by:

a. Listing at least three leisure options

b. Brainstorming at least two benefits of each option

c. Brainstorming at least two consequences of each option

d. Deciding which option has the most benefit and the fewest consequences as judged by the therapeutic recreation specialist

The form in Figure 5.3 has been developed as a tool for organizing and displaying the terminal program objectives, the enabling objectives, and their corresponding performance measures. Figure 5.4 displays a developed objectives and performance measures sheet. Additional examples are found in Appendix A and Appendix B. Note the positioning of the performance measures relative to their corresponding enabling objectives.

Earlier, it was stated that enabling objectives provide the operational definition of the terminal program objective. That concept can be further refined with the addition of performance measures. Each enabling objective has a corresponding performance measure that defines the standards of behavior that are reasonable representations of the desired outcome. Thus, when a client has achieved or obtained all of the EOs, as evidenced by his or her ability to demonstrate the actions or behaviors specified in the performance measures, the client has in essence achieved the terminal program objective. A simple way of stating this is, "The sum of the EOs and their performance measures equals the terminal program objective." This is a useful concept, but it also means that the enabling objectives and corresponding performance measures must be complete and logically derived and specified.

Writing Performance Measures.   The therapeutic recreation specialist works primarily with clients and helps bring about desired and meaningful behavioral changes and improved skills for leisure expression. The program designer needs to be especially sensitive to these concerns while writing performance measures. Performance measures that require too much time to evaluate or are too demanding in terms of the level or amount of behavior to be observed, measured, and recorded will be neglected or totally rejected by the program implementer. Thus, the designer must develop appropriate and reasonable performance measures. *A basic guideline is to look* *for and select the least amount of behavior that is representative of the intent of the enabling objective.* For example, if the EO states, "To demonstrate ability to utilize community resources," then the designer will attempt to write a performance measure that selects a good representation of utilizing community resources, but with the least amount of behavior display possible. Likewise, if the program is teaching specific computer skills and the EO states, "To demonstrate the ability to utilize the computer as a leisure resource," then the designer selects the smallest amount of demonstrated computer skill that is representative and appropriate for the clients in question. Thus, the criterion might state the ability to log on and find one piece of information, rather than specifying competence in a variety of software packages.

Another principle is to observe and measure behavior in the most natural environment or situation possible. Evaluation of performance measures should be as unobtrusive as possible. Thus, good performance measures attempt to evaluate the behavior in the context of an activity itself, rather than in an obvious testing situation. In therapeutic recreation, this calls for the creative design of performance measures that provide for necessary measurement while allowing the action and nature of the program to continue.

These two principles (least amount of behavior and the most natural measurement situation possible) are critical to good program design and evaluation as well as vital to the acceptance of systems programs by implementers.

Three Aspects of a Performance Measure.

A performance measure is a complete behavioral objective, and as such has three distinct parts: the condition, the behavior, and the criteria. A performance measure for specific programs is very similar to a client objective used in treatment planning. That is, they both focus on very specific conditions, behaviors, and criteria that are expected of the client as a result of participation in the program. In this text, they are included in both places to remind the reader that the connection between clients and programs is the outcomes expected.

Although more complete information is included in Chapter 10 on Client Documentation, it is important at this juncture to note that the condition(s), behavior, and criteria are written in very specific format, so that outcomes can be adequately determined and measured.

Conditions.   A condition is the circumstance under which the desired behavior will occur and be observed. Sample conditions include:

- At the end of the Leisure Skills program . . .
- Under supervision of the therapeutic recreation specialist . . .
- When addressed by an authority figure . . .
- Given two options for participation . . .

Behavior.   The behavior is what evidence the client will provide to demonstrate completion or competence in the desired knowledge, skill, or ability. Sample behaviors include:

- . . . the client will verbally state a preference . . .

- . . . the client will select a leisure activity . . .
- . . . the client will converse with a peer . . .
- . . . the client will score her own game of bowling . . .
- . . . the client will choose clothing . . .

Criteria. The criteria indicate how well the client must perform the behavior in order for it to be considered "accomplished" or "achieved." Sample criteria include:

- . . . within one foot of the putting green, as judged by the therapeutic recreation specialist.
- . . . two out of three attempts, as judged by the therapeutic recreation specialist.
- . . . fifty percent of the time, as judged by the therapeutic recreation specialist.
- . . . using the correct form, as indicated in the tennis manual, as judged by the therapeutic recreation specialist.
- . . . for a minimum of three minutes, as judged by the therapeutic recreation specialist.

In combination, the condition, behavior, and criteria identify very specifically the outcome intended from the clients' participation in the program. When outcomes are specified to this degree during the program planning stage, it becomes evident that the remaining tasks of program planning and implementation are likely to address these outcomes. Performance measures become the focus of all remaining tasks. When performance measures are not indicated at the outset, outcomes are less clear and programs can stray from their intended purpose.

Multiple Performance Measures. Sometimes the area of concern identified in the enabling objective is too complex to be evaluated adequately by one performance measure. In other cases, the EO may require measurement of some knowledge, as well as the ability to perform some task. Often, the behavior is very abstract, with one or two testing situations needed to verify that the behavior in the EO has really been acquired or internalized. In these situations, it is appropriate to use multiple performance measures. This basically means writing two or more PMs for one EO.

For illustration, we will take an EO from a tennis instructional program. Assume that one of the EOs states: "To demonstrate knowledge of the rules and scoring." The program designer decides that he or she wants evidence that the client knows the rules and can utilize them in the regulation and scoring of tennis. Two performance measures are used to address these two concerns:

> *PM1: While playing a set of tennis, the client will score the game by determining the winner of each point and calling out the correct score before each point and each game, as judged by the therapeutic recreation specialist.*
> *PM2: On a written test, the client will score at least 80 percent or higher, as judged by the instructor.*

In this case, the second performance measure is used because it is unlikely that all of the issues or situations related to the rules and scoring would arise during a game.

By giving a written exam in addition to the actual playing, the instructor can include situations that are unique or problematic related to the rules and scoring. Thus, the instructor can more effectively test the client's knowledge of the rules and ability to keep score and utilize the rules in the actual playing situation.

Although multiple performance measures are discussed here, it is not meant to imply that they are always needed and should be used. Quite the opposite is true. One good PM for each EO would be most desirable.

Additional Comments About Performance Measures.

Performance measures are written for individuals. Although the kinds of programs described in this text are designed primarily to take place in a group context, the PM always focuses on one individual. The phrase "the client will . . .," "the patient will . . .," or "the participant will . . ." implies this focus on the individual. Also implied is that each person within the group program will be individually evaluated by the stated performance measure.

The purpose of the performance measure is to provide specific observable and measurable evidence that the intent of the EO has been achieved or accomplished by the client. Thus, the issue of when the PM is used within the implementation of the program becomes important to the development of the PM and how it is written. Most EOs address a behavior that is to be improved or increased, or a skill or knowledge that is to be acquired. These kinds of behavioral changes do not occur easily or quickly. They take time to evolve. Once the program is implemented, it is expected that each enabling objective will be addressed on a regular basis—meaning in more than one session. This allows the desired behaviors to be addressed, practiced, and, it is hoped, internalized. Stated another way, the intent of the program is to produce a permanent behavioral change that will remain after the program is completed. However, the PM is utilized within the program itself. The evaluation of the clients' progress or gains is part of the program process.

The PM is written to be used within the program after the EO has been addressed in a sufficient number of sessions. This does not mean that the last session of every program should be devoted to the evaluation of clients utilizing the PMs, nor does it mean that the PM can or should be used on the same day a particular EO is introduced. The PM should be used when there has been adequate time to acquire and practice the given behavior. It is, therefore, a "test" situation to see if the client has achieved the intent of the EO.

There are basically two ways to set up the evaluation of the PMs within a program. One is to designate time within a certain session of the program to evaluate selected PMs. For example, if EO3 of some program is introduced in session 2 and reviewed and practiced in sessions 3, 4, and 5, then the sequence sheet for session 6 may contain a comment in the description column that states, "Evaluate EO3." (A complete description of the role and nature of the sequence sheet is presented later in this chapter. The reader may also want to review the systems programs in Appendix A and Appendix B for an illustration of how the PMs are incorporated into the sequence sheet.) In other programs, there is not a singular designated session for the evaluation of the performance measures. The evaluation is described as being ongoing. This implies that the program implementer continuously is observing the designated behaviors as specified in the PM and documents the achievement of the PM when it occurs. This approach does imply, however, that the various behaviors of the EOs are being addressed and practiced throughout various sessions, so that the implementer has many opportunities to observe the behavior as it is being demonstrated. The latter approach does have the advantage of allowing for more variance in the individual's ability to acquire or improve some behavior within the timeline of the program.

The purpose of the performance measure is to specify the exact behavior that will provide evidence that the intent of the objective has been met. Thus, the conditions under which the behavior is expected to be performed, the representative behavior, and the criteria for judging whether the behavior has occurred are all extremely important.

A final word about performance measures is warranted. Performance measures are a vital aspect of the systems-designed program. They are, however, no more important than the other parts of the system. For many beginning program designers, the performance measures are initially the most difficult part of the system to develop, in terms of both content and technical correctness. Like any other programming skills, the development of good performance measures takes time to acquire. The initial inability to derive great performance measures does not imply that the whole systems approach is not valuable. Effective programs can be developed using this approach, since the steps that come before the PMs and the steps that come afterward are of equal importance. Over time, most programmers find that their skills in writing PMs improve substantially. Often, development of the rest of the program and the implementation and evaluation processes help the designer to see ways to improve the PMs as well as other aspects of the program.

Content and Process Descriptions

After terminal program objectives, enabling objectives, and performance measures have been derived and stated, the program designer moves on to the development of the content and process of the program. Within a systems-designed program, there is a very defined way of developing and stating the content and process. Each enabling objective is analyzed for its unique contribution to the program. Content and process descriptions then are developed to address each enabling objective as a separate unit. By developing a program this way, the specialist can be confident that each important aspect (EO) of the program is translated into designated activities and interventions.

Content.   To begin this stage of systems development, the EO and its corresponding PM are analyzed to determine what needs to be done to accomplish or establish the designated behavior. This step starts with task analysis. The EO is broken down into concrete tasks, behaviors, and activities that the designer feels are necessary to accomplish the intent of the EO. This breakdown produces the content for that EO. Content is the substance or material upon which the program focuses to achieve the intent of the EO.

Several factors must be considered in the development and specification of content. The designer must be aware continuously of the type of clients for whom the program is intended. For example, designing content for individuals with dementia may require more attention to the detailed breakdown and specification of a given skill or knowledge than for individuals with typical cognitive abilities. Age characteristics, the size of the intended group, the availability of resources (supplies, equipment, facilities), and the length of the program all play an important role in determining the level and amount of content that is appropriate for a given EO.

Task analysis of the EO itself is a primary concern. The designer needs to study carefully the intent of the EO and select the content that appropriately covers all necessary or desired aspects of the specified behavior. This procedure varies with the type of EO under consideration. A concrete EO, such as "to demonstrate a legal serve (Ping-Pong)" is relatively easy, since the parts of serving will be basically the same—grip, stance, hitting action, and definition of legal serve in terms of where it lands in the opponent's court. The designer can decide to add elements to this basic content, such as serving strategy and types of serves. However, the basic elements are relatively determined and apparent in a concrete EO. An example of an indirect EO is, "To demonstrate knowledge of the potential benefits of leisure involvement." An indirect EO requires that the designer literally determine what is meant or intended in the EO. The design of content for an indirect EO requires the specification of the operational definition of the EO. Once the operational definition is determined, then that information becomes the information to be task-analyzed. A task analysis is completed to determine what activities, discussion topics, and the like must be presented to cover the topic adequately.

Indirect EOs do give direction to the designer. Note the implied general content of the following EOs from different systems:

- To demonstrate knowledge of leisure resources in the community
- To demonstrate the ability to use a leisure-planning technique
- To demonstrate dyad conversational skills
- To demonstrate knowledge of personal leisure resources
- To demonstrate awareness of personal abilities and skills that impact leisure involvement
- To demonstrate awareness of disability on leisure behavior
- To demonstrate ability to disagree, negotiate, and compromise

For any of these EOs, it is possible to define their meaning operationally for a given population, setting, and leisure context. Once they have been defined, that definition or understanding can be task-analyzed to determine the actual content that needs to be developed for the EO within the program.

In program systems in which the EO calls for the selection of traditional or non-traditional leisure activities, a procedure called activity analysis can be very useful. Chapter 6 presents a comprehensive explanation of activity analysis. The material presented in that chapter enables the thorough examination of individual activities. Information gained through activity analysis can be used to determine if the selected activities will be helpful in accomplishing the intent of the EO. Activity analysis is a valuable tool for use in the selection of content for functional intervention and leisure education programs.

Designing content for a given EO, whether it is a concrete or an indirect one, is a technical as well as creative procedure. Determining and selecting actual activities, skills, knowledge, or topics that must be covered to relate logically to the EOs is the more technical aspect of the design. However, most EOs can be addressed in several ways, and thus, the creative aspect of design comes into existence. A good programmer thinks about the target population, the EO, and the many possible ways that content could be designed. Then he or she selects and specifies the content to be incorporated into that program. The amount of creativity and variety found in any given system is the product of the designer's ability. Systems can be designed to be very simple, basic, or even rigid, or they can be exciting, fun, unique, or complex, depending on the designer's ability, experience, and originality. It is the content selection and description that is the critical aspect of design in systems-developed programs. Although the TPOs and EOs determine the intent and outcome behaviors of a program, it is the content that delineates how the program will actually be presented.

Many beginning systems program designers ask the question, "How much content should be included in the specification of a program?" As obvious answer would be, "The more content and detail related to content, the better." Comprehensive specification enables more thorough evaluation of the total program process. However, most program designers have limited time for the writing of programs, thus efficiency is a factor. *One guideline to follow is to determine a level of content information and be consistent with that level for all EOs throughout the system.* The program systems in Appendix A and Appendix B display this concept of consistency of amount and level of detail for all of the EOs. The level chosen appears to be adequate to give the implementer sufficient information about program content for each EO. Regardless of the level of detail selected, the system is enhanced by consistency throughout, as opposed to having some EOs with high levels of content specified and other EOs with little detail presented.

Throughout this chapter, it has been mentioned that the EOs provide the real focus of the system. The PMs are merely the selected representative behaviors that can be used as evidence that the intent of the EO has been demonstrated in an observable, measurable form. Consequently, when task-analyzing to determine and select content for the program, the focus should be on the EO, not the PM. The EO by definition will always encompass a broader concern than the PM can measure. This concept is vital in the development of the content section of the system. By focusing on the EO, the designer is likely to develop a more complete and appropriate program. A thorough analysis of the EO enables a more comprehensive approach to the intent of the EO. The content sections of the system will deal frequently with information, skills, or behaviors that are beyond the scope of the one representative slice of behavior found in the PM. A well-developed system always will expand the content section to deal with the full intent of the EO. Additional, ancillary, or supportive information is appropriate to include in the content section. *Thus, another procedural guideline in systems development is to focus the content description on the full intent of the EO, not merely the PM.*

Specifying the content for an EO is organizationally made easier by the use of a form. Figure 5.5 displays a blank content and process description (CPD) sheet. Note that this form identifies the TPO number, the EO number, and the complete statement of the EO. The left-hand section is designed for the description of the content,

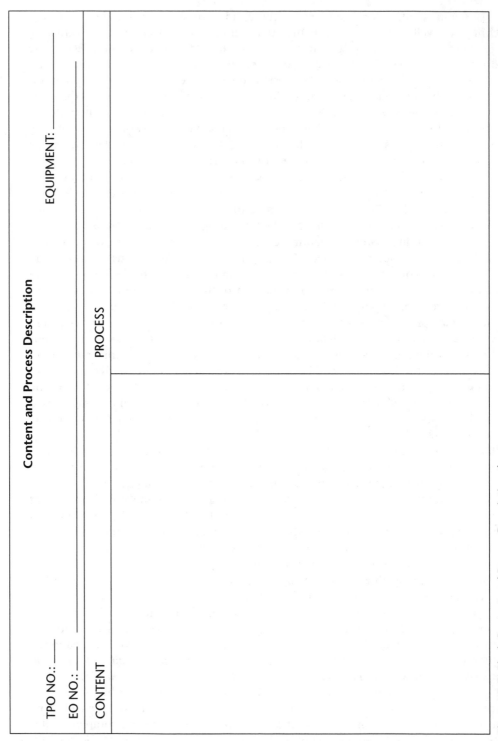

Figure 5.5 Blank Content and Process Description sheet.

which has been task-analyzed and selected for specification. Figure 5.6 displays a completed content and process description sheet that shows the positioning of the content relative to its corresponding process information on the CPD sheet. Also, review Appendices A and B for other illustrations of this use of the CPD sheet.

Process.   After the content has been specified for an EO, the designer develops the process for that content. Process refers to the way the content is presented to the clients. The process information, which appears on the right-hand side of the content and process description sheet, is a detailed breakdown of what the therapeutic recreation specialist will do with the content of that particular EO. The content is broken down, expanded, and explained in the content column. Paralleling each part of the content will be statements delineating how that content is to be handled by the specialist.

By the time a program has been developed to the current stage, it has already been determined whether it is oriented toward functional intervention, leisure education, or recreation participation programs. Previously it was discussed how different facilitation techniques (instructional, counseling, and/or leadership techniques) related to these three areas of service. Clearly, within each of these three areas of service, each category of techniques is broad and encompassing. Within the systems-designed program, very specific information is needed regarding the particular facilitation strategy or strategies that are to be used. It is the process section of the content and process description sheet that allows for this type of written description of the facilitation strategies that are selected for use.

In addition, specific parts of the content may require different facilitation techniques. Delineating the specific process or facilitation strategies for each part of the EO's content breakdown is essential. For example, assume the content of one EO relates to teaching a specific aspect of a leisure skill. The information in the content column breaks down the skill to its component parts. In the process column, a detailed description of how the skill will be taught appears. Several different instructional strategies may be incorporated. For some aspect of the skill, group instruction may be designated. For another aspect of the skill, one-to-one instruction may be desirable. Practice time requires a different form of facilitation. Perhaps a game situation is used to practice the skill further. The game situation may require additional forms of facilitation, including leadership and supervision. All of the information is described in the process section of the CPD sheet related to a given EO and its content.

The process section enables the designer to describe fully the overall facilitation strategy to be used, as well as the specific processes as they relate to the different aspects of the EO. Breaking down process statements so that they parallel the content enables the designer and implementer to have a much better explanation of "how" the program is intended to be presented. Figure 5.6 illustrates this concept of process paralleling content. Appendices A and B also can be reviewed to see the expanded use of this approach.

The concept of diverse facilitation techniques and the need to specify them is important to the systems-developed program. Knowing what to do and how to do it is vital to the implementation of the program. The more detail that it specifies related to content and process, the greater the likelihood that the program can and will be

Content and Process Description

TPO NO.: __2__

EO NO.: __2__   Demonstrate basic physical warm-ups and relaxation activities

EQUIPMENT: Mats or blankets

CONTENT	PROCESS
1. The purpose of warming up	Have participants stand in a circle at arm's length from one another.
a. The warm-up serves as a transition into a session of relaxation activities.	Introduce the warm-ups by reviewing the purposes of warming up. Tell participants that the beginning of each session will be spent doing warm-ups and that you will be starting with some simple movements or stretches.
b. The warm-up functions as a physical preparation by helping to prevent injuries by easing muscles into physical activity, helping to identify points of physical tension and initiating the process of releasing it, encouraging body awareness.	Explain that most of the warm-ups include breathing with the movements. Tell them it is important in getting full benefit from the warm-up to pay careful attention to the breathing instructions.
c. The warm-up aids in mental preparation for a session of relaxation by providing an activity that is relatively easy to concentrate on and is therefore useful in clearing the mind of daily stress.	
2. The processes of warm-up activities	Introduce the total body stretch by asking the participants to stretch as if they had just awakened from a night's sleep. The leader may want to demonstrate if the group is slow in getting started.
Total Body Stretch—Warm-up activity A	
a. Make your body as long as possible, stretching your hands over your head.	Discuss: Ask, "Why do you think we want to stretch in the morning?" (Focus: It helps to get blood back into muscles that haven't been working all night. That is how we get started in the morning, so it is a logical place to begin with warming up.)
b. Stretch the right side, making it as long as possible, leaving the left side relaxed.	Take participants through steps verbally and with demonstrations. Repeat 2–3 times.
c. Repeat above for left side, leaving right side relaxed.	
d. Make your body as wide as possible, stretching your arms out to the side, and standing in a straddle.	

Figure 5.6 Completed Content and Process Description sheet.

implemented appropriately. When a program is implemented as designed, more accurate information can be acquired through the evaluation process. This evaluation information then can be used to indicate areas of program improvement. Specifically, content and process can be reviewed thoroughly for their contributions to the program. Changes can be made to improve the content or process or both. However, if detailed information is not included at the time of design, the implementer may not be able to follow exact content or process procedures, and thus the evaluation process becomes vague as well.

Factors in Selecting Process.   For any content specified for a given EO, there are many alternative ways in which that content could be presented. Diverse facilitation techniques exist because there are countless instructional strategies, counseling techniques, and styles of leadership. The therapeutic recreation specialist needs to review alternative facilitation techniques or teaching–learning processes, and make the choice of which one(s) best suits the content and purpose of the program.

Several considerations for selecting the best process to "fit" the content exist. These include:

- Efficiency of technique to help clients reach outcomes
- Effectiveness of technique to help clients reach outcomes
- Appropriateness for client group
- Alignment with program content

First, program time is a scarce commodity for most agencies. This means that most programs must be designed and implemented efficiently. *Efficiency* refers to producing results with the least amount of energy, time, and/or resources. A specialist, when selecting the facilitation technique(s) to be used for a given program, should consider this issue. What technique or techniques will produce the desired outcomes with the least expenditure of time, energy, or resources? An example of this might be using a standard "explain, demonstrate, practice" group instructional technique as opposed to one-to-one instruction with the use of videotape equipment for feedback. Many would agree that the latter technique may be more effective; however, the number of clients, number of staff, and available time and resources may make the group instructional situation the most efficient.

The second principle is *effectiveness,* which refers to results and the ability to achieve the desired outcomes. Although there are usually multiple facilitation techniques that can be used with any given content, some techniques may be more effective with certain kinds of content. Selection of an appropriate facilitation technique should consider the issue of effectiveness. One of the major pitfalls to avoid in therapeutic recreation programming is becoming overly committed to a given facilitation technique without seriously looking at its ability to contribute to the desired outcomes. Inappropriate techniques reduce the effectiveness of delivering the content of the program.

A third principle to follow in the selection of facilitation techniques is that of careful consideration of the *targeted client population*. Specific facilitation techniques have been developed for use with certain populations. These techniques may not be effective or efficient with other populations. For example, backward chaining often is used to teach skills to individuals with developmental disabilities. This same technique would be unnecessary and even boring to individuals with typical cognitive abilities. Likewise, basic techniques used with individuals without disabilities may be totally inappropriate for a given special population. For example, a very cognitively oriented technique, such as cognitive behavioral therapy, may be beyond the mental functioning of an older person who is disoriented. Thus, knowledge of diverse facilitation strategies as they relate to different populations is vital for the appropriate selection of any technique. In addition to information related to a given disability group, the designer also must consider the age of individuals involved and the number of individuals to be included in the program. Facilitation techniques appropriate for young children could be totally inappropriate for use with adults. Likewise, a technique that is effective for a group of three or four will most likely be useless in a group of twenty.

The last principle to consider in the selection of facilitation techniques is the *program content*. The intervention strategies and processes selected must be appropriate for the clients; they also must match the content of the program. Ease of use and skills of the implementer are considerations. The strategies eventually included are selected for this ability to contribute to the attainment of the program's desired outcomes. They should, therefore, "fit" or match with all of the previously mentioned concerns. Common sense, logic, and experience all contribute to this selection process.

Many beginning program designers run into some debate over what is content and what is process when developing a systems program. This confusion is understandable when we look at common use of the two words, content and process. Many programs are a teaching process: the process of decision making, the process of leisure planning, the process of relaxation, the process of making or constructing something. Redefining the terms content and process for use in systems design may help. Content is the breakdown of the skills, knowledge, or behavior related to the program and the client. The content description includes the activities and substance of the program focus. Therefore, if the program content is addressing a process or procedure such as a relaxation technique, the description of that relaxation technique would be found in the content section of the CPD sheet. Process, on the other hand, is what the therapeutic recreation specialist will do with the content to present it to the clients. Thus, process statements will always focus on the facilitation by the specialist. In the case of the relaxation technique, the technique itself is content; how the therapeutic recreation specialist is to teach the technique will appear in the process section. Reviewing Appendices A and B with careful note of the division of content and process should help in understanding the role of these two sections and what material appears in each. *The description and breakdown of information about the EO's intent is content. The description of what the specialist does with that content is process.*

When the concept of content and process is understood, the designer proceeds to develop the written content and process descriptions for each EO in the program. In other words, each EO and its corresponding PM will have at least one content and process description sheet (depending on the level of detail that is selected for use in the program). The content and process description sheet describes in detail what is to be done and how it will be presented to the clients. If the program is designed well, the activities or actions should produce the desired results. If not, through the evaluation process, the designer has a more reasonable and systematic way of determining what worked and what did not. This information then can be used to revise and improve the system.

Sample Program Systems.   Throughout this chapter, reference has been made to the sample program system "Relaxation," in Appendix A, and "Social Skills," in Appendix B. These references were made to help illustrate a specific stage or aspect of the systems design procedure. At this point, the reader may wish to review again the sample systems in order to see the various parts as they interrelate with one another. The holistic reading of the systems should help in understanding the separate parts in context. It is acknowledged that the program content areas are only appropriate for specific populations in certain situations.

Recreation Participation Programs.   The development of specific programs as presented in this chapter is appropriate for programs oriented toward functional intervention and leisure education. These types of programs are designed to bring about some kind of predetermined behavioral change (improvement, establishment, or acquisition). Thus, specific objectives and performance measures are necessary to identify desired areas of behavioral change and to evaluate progress in the acquisition of the targeted behaviors. Recreation participation programs are designed to facilitate individuals' expression of leisure interests. It would be less appropriate to predetermine specific outcomes in such programs. This does not mean that recreation participation programs should not be well developed and specified. It does mean that specific behavioral objectives and performance measures would be less appropriate. Many aspects of systems design can be used to develop the recreation participation programs. A modified form of session content and process descriptions, sequence sheets, and implementation plan are all valuable ways to specify and describe the recreation participation program.

The Implementation Plan

A systems-designed program specifies terminal program objectives (TPOs), which are then broken down into enabling objectives (EOs), with corresponding performance measures (PMs). Each EO and PM then is task-analyzed to produce the content and process necessary for bringing the desired behaviors into existence. Although the specialist designs a program with general implementation considerations in mind, up to this point the implementation strategy has not yet been determined. This step, however, is vitally necessary and must be specified in detail as part of the overall program plan.

   In a systems approach, the specialist is saying that a particular program, implemented in a particular manner, should produce the desired results. If the desired results are not achieved, then a variety of factors can be analyzed and changed, if necessary, to improve the likelihood of success the next time the program is offered. The program, its implementation plan, and the evaluation plan are closely interrelated. Many times programs do not work, not because of their content, process, or objectives, but because the implementation strategy was deficient. Obviously, it is easier to revise the implementation plan than it is to rewrite the entire program system.

The implementation plan is composed of two separate but important and interrelated parts. One part is the sequence sheet. This is a form that specifies what is to be included in each session of the program. The second part is the implementation description. This is a written description of the general implementation strategy for the overall program.

The Sequence Sheet

In previous sections of this chapter, descriptions of enabling objectives (EOs), performance measures (PMs), and content and process descriptions (CPDs) were presented. Each EO and its corresponding PM contains a thorough description of the aims of the program. The content and process description sheet presents information about the activities (content) and procedures (process), which are designed to facilitate the accomplishment of the objective. While the content and process description presents information about the implementation of that particular objective, it does not indicate how that objective is interrelated with the rest of the program. This is the role and function of the sequence sheet.

The sequence sheet is a session-by-session description of how the total program is to be implemented. It includes which enabling objectives will be addressed in each session, what aspects of the content and process description are to be implemented, and time estimates for each of these activities. The content and process description sheet does not indicate the time allowed for any given objective or activity. It merely delineates the process designed to address that objective. The sequence sheet is the only place in the system where time allocations are specified. Figure 5.7 presents a blank sequence sheet. Appendices A and B include examples of completed sequence sheets.

Programs that are designed utilizing a systems approach can be of two different types: the set-number-of-sessions program, or the continuous-session program. The program with a set number of sessions implies that it is developed and will be implemented with a predetermined number of sessions. Many community-based recreation programs for individuals with disabilities are of this type. The program is usually set up on a seasonal schedule of eight, ten, or twelve weeks. Some programs in treatment or residential settings also use this approach. With this type of program, the designer knows from the beginning how many sessions will be held and the length of each session. The design of the content sequence of the program must take into account the number of sessions available. A later section of this chapter deals with the continuous-session program. The following pages focus on the set-number-of-sessions type of program.

The sequence sheet does several other things that are not indicated on the content and process description sheets. It indicates practice time and review opportunities. Many objectives are complicated and cannot be acquired in a given session. The sequence sheet allows the specialist to specify the session in which a given objective is to be reviewed or practiced. Most specific leisure skills require this type of reinforcement through practice if they are to be mastered. Likewise, in a program oriented toward functional intervention, a given targeted behavior for improvement would need time allocated over several sessions if permanent change in that behavior is to be

TPO	EO	DESCRIPTION	SESSION NO.	TIME (MIN)

Figure 5.7 Sequence Sheet.*

* Evaluation should take place on an ongoing basis. Performance measures should be reviewed prior to each session, and clients' progress should be recorded during or directly after groups.

expected. The sequence sheet carefully lays out this kind of information so that the program staff can address objectives in a systematic manner over the various sessions. An example of the specification of objectives to be addressed and the concept of review and practice is found in Figure 5.8.

The sequence sheet serves another important function. It indicates when and how the observation and recording of achievement of objectives is to be carried out. Time is actually scheduled on the sequence sheet for this kind of evaluation of the clients' progress toward accomplishing the objectives. This kind of observation time may be indicated on the sequence sheet. A tournament near the end of a leisure-skill program may be the specified evaluation time for checking various skills. The sequence sheet would include this information for a given session. An example is given in Figure 5.9.

The performance measure indicates how a given objective is evaluated. When scheduling time on the sequence sheet, it is important to note how the PM is written,

TPO	EO	DESCRIPTION	SESSION NO.	TIME (MIN)
		Warm up	2	5
1	2	Introduce backhand shot grip, position, swing, follow-through	2	10
		Practice exercise		15
1	1	Review forehand	2	10
		Practice		10
1	5	Rules and scoring	2	15

Figure 5.8 Section of a Sequence Sheet for a racquetball skills program.*

* Evaluation should take place on an ongoing basis. Performance measures should be reviewed prior to each session, and clients' progress should be recorded during or directly after groups.

TPO	EO	DESCRIPTION	SESSION NO.	TIME (MIN)
1	1,2,3,4,5	Singles tournament (staff evaluates designated EOs)	6	50
2	1	Review of racquetball facilities in the community	6	10

Figure 5.9 Section of a Sequence Sheet for a racquetball skills program.

so that the appropriate activity, time, or structure is set up for the evaluation process. Equally important is the manner in which the evaluation of objectives takes place. In therapeutic recreation, it would appear desirable to have the evaluation of objectives be as unobtrusive as possible. The utilization of free play, tournaments, practice sessions, or some program activity itself as the context for the evaluation of objectives keeps the focus on program participation and not on testing.

In some programs, the evaluation of the accomplishment of the objectives occurs continuously, throughout the program. As the program staff members observe the achievement of objectives, they record the information on the *performance sheet.* In these kinds of programs, the explanation of how objectives are to be evaluated should appear somewhere in the program materials. This information can be in the introductory implementation description or appear as a note in the sequence sheet.

A performance sheet is a simple form used to record the attainment of objectives. Clients' names are placed in a numbered left-hand column. All of the enabling objectives of the program are placed across the top of the form, on the diagonal lines. This is usually done by indicating the TPO number, the EO number, and an abbreviation of the EO content. A blank performance sheet appears in Figure 5.10. Completed performance sheets can be found in Appendices A and B.

The attainment of objectives can be recorded in various ways. A simple check can be used to indicate achievement. Some programmers have devised other recording methods, such as placing the date in the appropriate box when the objective has been achieved. If pretesting is used, a code can be created to indicate if the client has the skills or knowledge of the objectives in the beginning of the program. Another variation of coding is some numerical system indicating degree of attainment; for instance, 3 = can do with difficulty; 2 = can do with occasional difficulty; 1 = can do consistently and correctly. The performance sheet enables the programmer to keep an easy record of the accomplishment of objectives. Later, in the evaluation stage, this form provides quick access to information about individual achievement as well as information about problematic objectives.

The sequence sheet is the tool that is used to assist the designer in achieving a well-balanced and interesting program. At each session, the characteristics of the clients, their ages, their abilities and limitations, and their number should be taken into consideration. Attention span, learning style, and participation concerns also are important. Rarely would the staff address only one objective in a given session. Variety and balance are an issue when designing a program. The sequence sheet is the place in the systems-designed program where these considerations are addressed. Each session should be designed with attention not only to covering the important aspects of the objectives, but also to the design of an interesting and balanced session.

The sequence sheet has one additional function and feature. The EOs and PMs of a program indicate the minimal material to be covered in the program. They indicate the basic areas of a program that the staff members have delineated for accountability purposes. The total program can address other areas in addition to the specified EOs and PMs. This additional material will be indicated on the sequence sheet. For example, in the racquetball skill program illustrated in Figures 5.8 and 5.9, the designer may wish to include a brief history of racquetball, provide information about doubles play, and perhaps describe some advanced shots. However, the designer decides that this is not essential material and thus does not have enabling objectives, performance measures, or content and process descriptions related to these three areas. In other words, the clients are not being evaluated on this material, nor is the instructor being held accountable for the learning of the material. The material will be presented, however. Thus, it will appear on the sequence sheet in some appropriate session(s). Essential material, or the basic material for which the program is intended to be accountable, will always be included as enabling objectives. EOs are always evaluated and a PM is written for each EO. Additional or supplemental material appears only on the sequence sheet. This indicates its inclusion in the program, although acquisition of the knowledge or skills is not essential and thus is not evaluated by a performance measure.

The inclusion of additional information or material on the sequence sheet also enables the design of more creative and balanced sessions and of the total program as well. Introductory material can be added to any session. A party or presentation to parents could be scheduled for a concluding session. The sequence sheet maps out in advance the entire program as it is designed to be implemented.

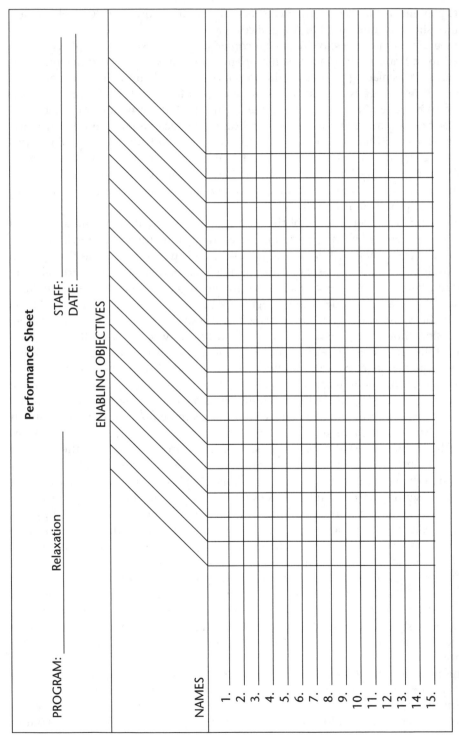

Figure 5.10 Performance Sheet.

The sequence sheet is a guideline or map to the implementation of a program. Since it is developed in the design stage of program planning, its content and time estimates are coming from a program designer's experience and best professional judgment. Obviously, errors in judgment may exist regarding the length of time that it takes to learn a given skill or acquire certain behaviors. Likewise, the sequence of activities in a given session or throughout the total program could be less than desirable. This information, however, will be discovered and documented as the program is implemented and evaluation information is recorded after each session (or at designated times). The existence of the sequence sheet, however, gives the program staff direction for implementation. The documentation and recording of information about the program's adequacy and usefulness give concrete information for program revision. The reader is encouraged to review the sequence sheets that appear in Appendices A and B for a more thorough understanding of the content and design of this important aspect of program development.

Sequence Sheet and Session Format Description for a Continuous-Session Program.   The sequence sheet as described in the previous pages has obvious advantages for programs that have a set number of sessions. Many public recreation programs for individuals with disabilities fit this model of programming; for example, a ten-week program with one-and-a-half hour sessions once a week. Some clinical or treatment facilities utilize this type of program structure as well. Many programs, however, especially in the clinical setting, are continuous. Clients are admitted and discharged from the facility at various times. Thus, the systems-designed therapeutic recreation programs must operate with a different structure than the carefully designed sequence plan for a program with a set number of sessions.

One method of scheduling continuous programs is to set up a definite number of sessions for the program. The number of sessions (and number of weeks) would be less than the average stay of clients. The EOs, PMs, and content and process descriptions would remain as before. The sequence sheet, however, would be designed so that there is no real beginning or end to the program, although each session would be designed to be as complete as possible in addressing a given objective. Clients then are referred to the program at any point in the sequence. They would stay in the program until they had participated in all of the sessions through one complete cycle. At that point, they would be referred to another program, remain in the targeted program for another cycle, or be terminated from the program. The sequence sheet is used in such a program primarily as a guide for the implementation of each session. Evaluation of objectives, as well as the evaluation of the entire program, is still very appropriate with this variation of the program structure.

This method of scheduling the continuous program has worked very well with many functional intervention programs as well as with leisure education programs. The program staff needs to be aware of the need to orient new clients individually as they enter a given program and to introduce newcomers to the rest of the group. In programs of this type, some review and practice time can be built in for the objectives of previous sessions. Such practice or review time, however, should be individualized for the members of the program, based on how long they have been in the program and how many objectives they have been presented previously.

Another method of scheduling the continuous program is to do away with the sequence sheet altogether and replace it with a session format description. In this alternative method of sequencing, the program still has EOs, PMs, and CPDs. The program staff looks at the clients in the program and selects EOs, PMs, and CPDs for each session on a day-to-day basis. The staff selects the objectives to be addressed based on the composition of the group currently in attendance and according to common needs within the content of the program. This method of scheduling also allows for objectives to be selected and implemented based on the progress of individuals within the group. New objectives are selected only when the group is ready to move on.

When a continuous program uses this method of scheduling, the sequence sheet is not needed or appropriate. It is desirable to replace it with a session format description. The session format description describes the content of a basic session. It indicates the length and structure of the session but leaves the specific content open to selection by the staff. An example of an implementation plan using the session format description is presented below. Additional information about the system is included to assist in the understanding of the total program.

Aspects of an Implementation Plan for an Ongoing Program

Wellness Program for Individuals with Substance Addictions

Agency and Population Description.   This program is designed for short-term inpatient and outpatient treatment for adolescents with substance addictions.

Program Purpose.   To increase clients' understanding and utilization of wellness concepts in their daily lives.

System.   The wellness program is an ongoing program that meets every day for one hour each time. The program helps clients learn wellness concepts, as well as adapt those concepts to their lives. Client census ranges from four to twenty, as individuals are admitted and discharged from the facility.

Program Referral and Basic Structure.   Wellness is considered a vital topic for these adolescents. Clients are assessed about their basic knowledge and use of wellness concepts in their own lives. The program rotates among five topics: Stress Management and Relaxation (Monday), Fitness and Exercise (Tuesday), Nutrition and Self-Care (Wednesday), Self-Responsibility (Thursday), and Leisure Involvement (Friday). These topics support other programs offered by the Therapeutic Recreation Department, as well as other therapies. The content and process within these topics each day depend on the needs of specific clients attending the program on any given day.

Terminal Program Objectives and Enabling Objectives.
TPO1: To demonstrate ability to recognize and manage stress.

EO1: To demonstrate knowledge of personal stress inducers.

EO2: To demonstrate knowledge of personal perspectives of stressful events.

EO3: To demonstrate ability to utilize stress management techniques.

EO4: To demonstrate ability to utilize relaxation techniques.

TPO2: To demonstrate ability to utilize fitness and exercise within a daily routine.

   EO1: To demonstrate understanding of fitness concepts.

   EO2: To demonstrate ability to incorporate fitness into personal lifestyle.

   EO3: To demonstrate understanding of impact of fitness on lifestyle issues.

TPO3: To demonstrate knowledge of nutritional and self-care responsibilities.

   EO1: To demonstrate understanding of nutritional concepts.

   EO2: To demonstrate ability to select pattern of healthy eating.

   EO3: To demonstrate ability to care for self.

TPO4: To demonstrate ability to take responsibility for self and actions.

   EO1: To demonstrate acknowledgment of personal responsibility.

   EO2: To demonstrate ability to make decisions regarding personal wellness.

   EO3: To demonstrate ability to follow through with personal well-being decisions.

TPO5: To demonstrate ability to make leisure decisions.

   EO1: To demonstrate understanding of sober leisure involvement.

   EO2: To demonstrate ability to explore alternative leisure opportunities.

   EO3: To demonstrate ability to make leisure-related decisions.

   EO4: To demonstrate ability to seek out leisure partners who support sobriety.

   Sample Session Format:
   1. Ten minutes of introduction of topic and group members.
   2. Thirty minutes of "activity" related to daily topic.
   3. Ten minutes of group discussion for closure.
   4. Ten minutes for setting personal goals related to topic.

Program Materials.   The therapeutic recreation specialist selects appropriate enabling objectives and corresponding content and process description sheets from the program materials, based on the assessed needs of the group. A full description of techniques for working on the EO is found in the process column of the CPD. Details about the five topics (stress, fitness, nutrition, self-responsibility, and decisions) and the content of the 20 one-hour sessions are located in the plan's appendices. Each one-hour session uses different activities to target the content intended for the day's topic.

   Whether a program has a set number of sessions or is ongoing, a description of its implementation by session is needed. The sequence sheet or the session format description provides this information. This information not only allows the program to be implemented correctly, but later allows for the utilization of evaluation information regarding the appropriateness of the sequencing and time allocations for various activities in relation to the achievement of objectives.

The Implementation Description

In addition to the sequence sheet or session format description, a systems-designed program requires a specified implementation description. This description is general in nature and refers to the overall strategy for implementing the entire program. In systems-designed programs, the given objectives and their corresponding content and process descriptions are to be implemented in a specific way for a designated population and with other specific identifiable inputs. When the program is implemented as planned, it should achieve the performance measures and accomplish the program's purpose. Although no system is perfect by design, this procedure does enable the collection of evaluation information, which can be used to make objective decisions regarding program revision. Thus, general implementation information is vital to the operation of the system. In a package of systems-designed program materials, the implementation description contains information on the following areas: description of the clients for whom the program is designed, description of the staffing requirements, description of the required equipment and facilities, and a description of the number, length, and frequency of the program sessions. Additional or explanatory information can be added to the implementation plan as needed.

Description of the Population.   A systems-designed program is developed for a specific population. The characteristics of that population are taken into account as enabling objectives and performance measures are written. Likewise, the content and process descriptions are developed based on the characteristics of the selected population. The sequence sheet or session format description takes into consideration the nature of the targeted population. Given this information, one would not expect the system to work with another population. Consequently, at the beginning, it is necessary to specify the intended population and the characteristics that are important relative to the specific program. Merely delineating that clients have developmental disabilities or are dual-diagnosed is not sufficient. The designer describes the actual limitations or abilities that are important. In some cases, prerequisite skills also may be described if they are important to the given program. An example of this would be basic swimming skills as a prerequisite for a canoeing class. Part of the population description is the identification of the age range and number of clients for whom the program is designed.

All of this information is important for the appropriate selection of clients for actual program involvement. Equally significant is the use of this information in the evaluation process. If a given client had difficulty with the achievement of objectives, the staff would check first to see if the client had the characteristics indicated for that program. Obviously, the program staff members would not revise a total program because of one client who was not within the intended target group; rather, they could individualize for that client within the program or refer the client to a more appropriate program.

An example of a description of population is found in the sample program systems in Appendices A and B.

Number, Length, and Frequency of Sessions.   At the beginning of the implementation description, some basic aspects of the program's structure are identified. The number of sessions, the length of sessions (for instance, one hour, forty minutes, one-and-a-half hours), and the frequency of sessions (number of sessions per week) are delineated. Although the number of sessions and length of sessions appear as part of the sequence sheet, it is useful to have this general information appear at the beginning of the program materials as well.

The determination of the number, length, and frequency of sessions is also an important aspect of decision making in program development. Client characteristics as well as program content are important factors to consider when making these decisions. For example, shorter sessions several times a week may be better for individuals with acquired brain injuries. Often constraints of the agency or unit must be considered in making these decisions. The ideal implementation for a given program might be every day; however, consideration of other therapies may make this type of schedule impossible. The program must be compatible in its environment as well as appropriate for its objectives and clients. In other settings, such as community-based recreation programs for individuals with disabilities, transportation may be an important issue. Thus, we often find such programs meeting once a week. Number, length, and frequency of sessions are determined after considering the population, the program content, and the constraints of the agency or unit. A description of number, length, and frequency of sessions is found in Appendices A and B.

When a designer decides to run a program for ten weeks for one-and-a-half hours each week, the designer is indicating that the objectives and performance measures should be possible to achieve within that time. In evaluating such a program, the amount of time spent on each EO is compared to the results achieved. Discrepancies or program failures then can be realistically analyzed relative to the amount of time needed to accomplish the program content. Revisions based on data then can be made. For example, a program may require more sessions or longer sessions to produce the desired outcomes. In other cases, the content of the program may need to be reduced to allow for the achievement of the objectives within the time available.

Description of Staff.   Systems-designed programs are planned with certain constraints and resources in mind. The implementation plan must identify these factors. Staffing requirements are central to the effective implementation and outcomes of the designed program. The implementation description identifies the number of staff members needed as well as the qualifications required. Here is an example of such a description for a bowling instruction program for individuals with physical disabilities.

> Staff. *One therapeutic recreation specialist with knowledge of physical disabilities, bowling, methods of adapting and modifying bowling equipment and procedures, and ability to use appropriate teaching techniques and physical assistive techniques. One adult volunteer or staff assistant for each alley used.*

The failure or less-than-satisfactory results of a program often can be attributed to the absence of the appropriately trained staff or numbers of staff as described in the implementation description. Two decisions can be made: Revise the program materials so a nontrained staff member or volunteer or fewer staff can operate the program, or implement the program again with trained staff to determine the value or adequacy of the program.

There is one additional consideration in the category of staff description. Staff descriptions should be based on what the program really requires for implementation. To designate a position title—such as "therapeutic recreation specialist"—is not sufficient. The exact skills and knowledge needed by the staff to implement the program are the issue.

Facilities, Equipment, and Supplies.   Systems-designed programs may require specific facilities, equipment, and/or supplies. Part of the implementation description delineates the necessary facilities and objects. Although equipment and supplies for a given EO are identified on each corresponding content and process description sheet, it is of value to have a master list of all needed items at the beginning of the program materials. Examples of facility, equipment, and supply descriptions are found in Appendices A and B.

Summary

Producing client outcomes as the result of clients' participation in programs requires that the therapeutic recreation specialist design the program quite specifically to achieve those intended outcomes. The process of specific program design, as found in this chapter, includes the program plan and the implementation plan. (Program evaluation is discussed in Chapter 11.) The program plan consists of five major parts: (1) statement of purpose, (2) terminal performance objectives (TPOs), (3) enabling objectives (EOs), (4) performance measures (PMs), and (5) content and process descriptions (CPDs). These five parts provide a comprehensive view of the targeted client outcomes and a general description of the program operation. The two parts of the implementation plan (sequence sheet and implementation description) provide a much more detailed account of how the program will be implemented for clients.

Completion of these actions and forms requires the therapeutic recreation specialist to truly contemplate the intended client outcomes and design specifically to attain those outcomes. A systems-designed program, because of all this scrutiny and contemplation, is much more likely to produce predictable client outcomes than are programs designed haphazardly or with little thought. Though there are many methods of designing programs, the systems-designed format used in this text ensures that the process is systematic, logical, and relevant to clients' needs.

STUDENT EXERCISES

Discussion Questions

1. Research evidence and theory are presented again in this section on specific program design. Why are they a favorable trend in therapeutic recreation programming?

2. How is program evaluation aided by the systematic design of programs? How are client outcomes aided?

3. What are the advantages of systems-designed programs—those that start from a broad perspective and move to a narrower and deeper specification—over programs that are presented to clients without this level of forethought and detail?

4. What is the relationship between the statement of purpose, terminal performance objectives, enabling objectives, and performance measures?

5. What are the advantages of specifying performance measures or client outcomes *prior* to delivering the specific program?

6. Discuss three reasons why an implementation plan is important.

7. The program plan, along with activity and task analysis, helps select the best programs to meet client needs. Is this important or is it superfluous to intervention programs?

8. Discuss the differences and relationship between program content and process.

Practice Test

1. A specific program is defined as a:
   a. way to determine whether activities are social in nature.
   b. set of activities that have a specific set of goals for a specific group of clients.
   c. method of evaluating clients' needs and determining which programs are best suited to address those needs.
   d. performance improvement activity that is required by the Joint Commission on Accreditation of Healthcare Organizations.

2. Research evidence and theories can help in determining all of the following aspects of a program EXCEPT the:
   a. content.
   b. process.
   c. facilitation technique or strategy.
   d. specialist's qualifications.

3. Which of the following are the general outcome statements that the program is designed for?
   a. terminal performance objectives
   b. enabling objectives
   c. performance measures
   d. content statements

4. Which of the following are the smaller, more specific behavioral units that are expected to be addressed within the program?
   a. terminal performance objectives
   b. enabling objectives
   c. performance measures
   d. content statements

5. Which of the following contain the behavior expected to be shown by the client as evidence that the outcomes have been achieved?
   a. terminal performance objectives

    b. enabling objectives

    c. performance measures

    d. content statements

6. Which is the best written terminal performance objective?
   a. To provide activities and services related to health and wellness
   b. To provide social skills programs
   c. To demonstrate active listening skills
   d. To demonstrate ability to plan a leisure event

7. Which of the following is the best enabling objective?
   a. To provide activities and services related to health and wellness
   b. To provide social skills programs
   c. To demonstrate active listening skills
   d. To demonstrate ability to plan a leisure event

8. An outcome statement that includes the client's end behavior and the conditions and criteria for judging it is called a(n):
   a. terminal performance objective.
   b. enabling objective.
   c. performance measure.
   d. evidence of performance.

9. Which of the following is NOT a principle of writing performance measures?
   a. Keep it as close to the original activity as possible.
   b. Specify the least amount of behavior needed to show the outcome.
   c. Observe and evaluate the behavior in as natural a setting as possible.
   d. Use only those behaviors that the specialist is able to observe.

10. If a systematic program design is created based on research evidence and theory, it will likely:
    a. help clients achieve their goals more efficiently and effectively.
    b. result in a higher staff-to-client ratio.
    c. deter the specialist from developing other outcomes-based programs.
    d. result in higher rates of client recidivism.

Answers: 1. *b*, 2. *d*, 3. *a*, 4. *b*, 5. *c*, 6. *c*, 7. *d*, 8. *c*, 9. *a*, 10. *a*

Chapter Activities

Therapeutic Recreation On-Site Visit

Arrange an appointment with a therapeutic recreation specialist at his or her facility. Ask to see the documentation that is created for specific programs. How does the specialist know what information to present and how to present it to clients? Is there research evidence or theory to support it?

Specific Program Design

Starting with the comprehensive program design you created at the end of Chapter 4, now extend the design with specific programs, preferably ones that are based on research evidence and/or theory. Follow each of the steps in the program plan and implementation plan. Bring it to class and share it with other students.

Theory-Based Programming Comparisons

Reread Hood and Carruthers (2002), Carruthers and Hood (2002), Caldwell (2001, 2003), and Widmer, Zabriskie, and Wells (2003). Now that you understand specific program design, what additional benefits do research evidence and theory have for "grounding" activities or experiences presented to clients? How do you think they affect client outcomes?

Information from Research Journals

Using the list of theories, results, and ideas you found in research journals from the sample assignments in Chapter 4, create terminal performance objectives, enabling objectives, and performance measures for a specific program of your choice. How does the research information help in specifying TPOs, EOs, and PMs? What effect would it have on the remainder of the program design?

Research Efficacy Synopsis

Complete the same steps as in the previous assignment for the research synopses you did for Chapter 4. As above, create terminal performance objectives, enabling objectives, and performance measures for a specific program of your choice. How does the research information help in specifying TPOs, EOs, and PMs? What effect would it have on the remainder of the program design?

REFERENCES

Caldwell, L. L. (2001). The role of theory in therapeutic recreation: A practical approach. In N.J. Stumbo (Ed.), *Professional issues in therapeutic recreation: On competencies and outcomes* (pp. 349–364). Champaign, IL: Sagamore Publishing Company.

Caldwell, L. L. (2003). Basing outcomes on theory: Theories of intervention and explanation. In N.J. Stumbo (Ed.), *Client outcomes in therapeutic recreation*. State College, PA: Venture Publishing Company.

Carruthers, C. P., & Hood, C. D. (2002). Coping skills program for individuals with alcoholism. *Therapeutic Recreation Journal, 36*(2), 154–171.

Hood, C. D., & Carruthers, C. P. (2002). Coping skills theory as an underlying framework for therapeutic recreation services. *Therapeutic Recreation Journal, 36*(2), 137–153.

Stumbo, N. J. (2003). The importance of evidence-based practice in therapeutic recreation. In N. J. Stumbo (Ed.), *Client outcomes in therapeutic recreation*. State College, PA: Venture Publishing Company.

Widmer, M. A., Zabriskie, R., & Wells, M. A. (2003). Program evaluation: Collecting data to measure outcomes. In N. J. Stumbo (Ed.), *Client outcomes in therapeutic recreation*. State College, PA: Venture Publishing Company.

CHAPTER 6

Activity Analysis

After the comprehensive and specific programs have been designed, the next task of the therapeutic recreation specialist is to analyze and select activities appropriate for client involvement. That is, the specialist at this stage selects the content (activities) to be delivered for clients and makes sure that the activities are the best possible choices to help clients achieve their intended goals. The placement of activity analysis is shown by the shaded area on the Therapeutic Recreation Accountability Model in Figure 6.1.

The activity analysis and selection process often is taken for granted and traditional activities are selected wrongly, based on staff skills or interests, available facilities, and limitations of budget. However, the analysis and selection of activities is crucial in the intervention process—it may mean the difference between a client achieving or not achieving his or her goals or, even worse, being harmed. Activities should be selected carefully according to the behavioral requirements of participants and their ability to contribute to the achievement of outcomes. This means that several activity options are reviewed, and only the best activities to meet the needs of clients are selected for implementation.

Sometimes the process is simple and quite logical. For example, if a client's outcome is to learn a certain set of skills—for example, learning to navigate the Internet—then the instructional program can be designed to teach this skill in sequential steps or tasks, with the outcome being that the client independently can negotiate the Internet to the point of locating needed information. Logically, the activities selected and delivered must relate to the skills being taught.

However, for other outcomes, such as those in functional intervention, the process requires more thought and knowledge of activity characteristics. For example, an outcome dealing with increasing social skills or increasing concentration does not directly indicate that a particular activity should be chosen. A variety of factors must be considered, such as age, gender, carry-over value, feasibility, budget, facility constraints, and staffing concerns. The competent professional, however, will select or design activities that have inherent characteristics that contribute to the objectives. The specialist is thus free to select from a wide range of possibilities. The specialist needs to know enough about a variety of activities that he or she can either select or modify an activity that will help teach this specific skill or set of skills. Activity analysis is the procedure that enables and facilitates this selection process. Thus, activity analysis is vital to the delivery of therapeutic recreation intervention programs that are intended to change client behavior. The ability to analyze, select, and modify

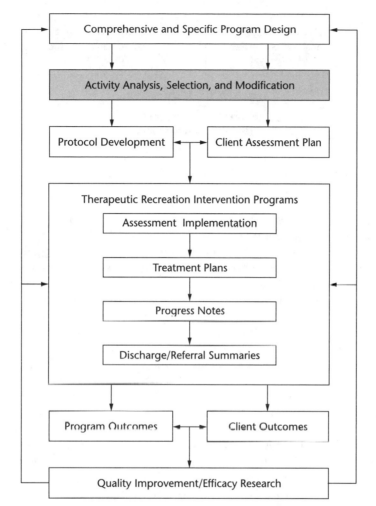

Figure 6.1 Activity analysis component of the Therapeutic Recreation Accountability Model.

activities that serve a specific purpose (to meet client needs) is unique to therapeutic recreation specialists.

Benefits of Activity Analysis

Activity analysis can be defined as *a process that involves the systematic application of selected sets of constructs and variables to break down and examine a given activity to determine the behavioral requirements inherent for successful participation and that may contribute to the achievement of client outcomes.*

It is a process that allows the therapeutic recreation specialist to understand an activity and its potential contributions to behavioral outcomes. Activity analysis provides a more exact method of selecting activities in that activity components are analyzed before utilization for their behavioral and interactional requirements. In activity

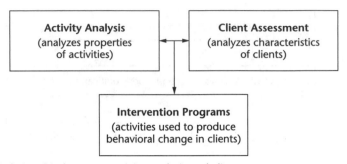

Figure 6.2 Relationship between activity analysis and client assessment.

analysis, different activities and their therapeutic or instructional value can be compared so that better programming decisions can be made.

Breaking down activities into their component parts allows the therapeutic recreation specialist to become aware of what participatory skills and abilities are needed by the client in order to engage in the activity. The specialist then can determine if the activity is appropriate for a group of clients or if modifications are needed.

Activity analysis evaluates the requirements of the activity, and client assessment evaluates the capabilities and limitations of the client(s). Being able to provide intervention—that is, programs that produce behavioral change in clients—depends on the correct matching of the right clients in the right programs. This intervention process depends on accurate and dependable activity analysis (selecting the right programs) and client assessment (placing the right clients in those programs) procedures. Figure 6.2 provides a display of this notion.

Activity analysis occurs independently of specific clients. The specialist can take an activity and analyze it for its basic requirements and demands in terms of actual participation factors. Of basic concern are the physical, cognitive, affective (emotional), and social components of the activity as it is traditionally engaged in. Such an analysis considers just the activity itself. The goal is simply to understand the activity and its typical characteristics. The process, however, has many applications in therapeutic recreation programming. If the program is instructional in nature, the process of activity analysis, combined with the functional assessment of a person with special needs, allows the specialist to know exactly what modifications of the activity are needed to accommodate that person. For example, an analysis of the physical requirements of the front crawl in swimming compared to the functional ability of an individual with cerebral palsy would indicate the exact areas needing adaptation; that is, the kick or the coordination of arms and breathing.

On the other hand, if the program is aimed at functional intervention, an analysis of a selected activity, compared with the stated treatment goal, would allow the specialist to ascertain whether that activity would contribute to the desired behavioral or functional improvement objective. Bingo, for example, has low social interaction requirements. The players listen for numbers, search their cards for those numbers, and cover them with tokens. In reviewing the rules of bingo, minimal social interaction is required. Through analysis, the activity that is commonly billed as a highly social activity is discovered to possess few of the essential components of human interaction. Therefore, it may not be an appropriate selection for a client goal of improving (teaching) social skills. It may, however, be a good activity for increasing concentration or letter/number recognition.

One consideration that must be remembered when conducting activity analysis is that the activity is scrutinized for its *inherent* characteristics, that is, when played by the rules under usual conditions. An activity sometimes can be modified later to suit a particular purpose or for particular clients, but activity analysis is concerned with determining which activities are best suited for producing particular client outcomes.

Admittedly, analysis is much more difficult for some activities than for others. Structured activities such as games and sports can, because of their exact rules and procedures, be more easily and more accurately analyzed and understood than unstructured activities such as crafts, camping, or free play. Unstructured activities vary in their analysis outcomes, based on the context, situation, and individual variation surrounding the participation experiences. Nonetheless, the attempt at systematic analysis of activity components is beneficial for comprehending participation requirements and possible outcome behaviors, regardless of the limitations imposed by the nature or structure of the activities.

Activities also vary considerably in their participation requirements and demands. A casual evaluation of an activity often can be misleading. The complexity of many activities is frequently hidden because of an assumed familiarity. Thus, an activity like checkers is considered simple because it is so well known, whereas in fact, the game requires advanced cognitive skills, including evaluation and decision making (strategy) as well as the recall of countless rules governing the play. It is this type of information that is gleaned from employing a systematic and comprehensive activity analysis.

Activity analysis leads to a more comprehensive and complete understanding of activity components and participation requirements. Activity analysis provides:

- A better comprehension of the expected outcomes of participation
- A greater understanding of the complexity of activity components, which then can be compared to the functional level of an individual or group to determine the appropriateness of the activity
- A basis for comparing and contrasting the relative contributions of several activity options to the desired participant outcomes
- Information about whether the activity will help the client achieve the intended outcomes
- Direction for the modification or adaptation of an activity for individuals with limitations or for a particular program outcome
- Useful information for selecting a facilitation, instructional, or leadership technique
- A rationale or explanation for the therapeutic benefits of activity involvement

Overview of Activity Analysis

When an individual engages in an activity, action is required in four behavioral areas, regardless of the type of activity: physical (psychomotor), cognitive (intellectual), social, and affective (emotional) behaviors. For example, when playing Ping-Pong, the physical actions are easily observed. The player must be able to grasp and hold a paddle and have sufficient elbow, shoulder, and wrist movement to hit the ball, enough mobility to move quickly, and hand-eye coordination. Cognitive skills also are required. There are rules to remember, there is continuous scoring, and there are strategies to plan. These cognitive or mental requirements add to the totality of the involvement. Social skills are required in the form of taking turns, playing fair, and the like. Affective requirements for controlling and expressing emotions also are part of the action. An activity analysis of Ping-Pong—or any activity, for that matter— examines each behavioral area in a systematic way.

A game, such as checkers, that is normally considered a mental game also makes demands in all four behavioral areas. Cognitive requirements include knowledge of rules and strategy and concentration. Physically, the game requires sight, as well as the ability to grasp and move pieces. Socially, the game requires turn taking, respect for another's need for quiet, and sitting still. Affectively, checkers demands control of emotions when pieces are jumped and removed, as well as when winning or losing.

The therapeutic recreation specialist must understand the demands in all four areas, realizing that they are complex and interrelated. Failure to be concerned with any one area could easily result in an inadequate activity analysis and may lead to inappropriate activity selection or modification. A systematic activity analysis is the best way to determine the potential of an activity to contribute to client outcomes.

Activity analysis should not be confused with *task analysis,* another term and proce-dure often used in therapeutic recreation. Task analysis is the breaking down of a skill into its sequential parts for the purpose of instruction. Activity analysis, which looks at the participation requirements in the various behavioral domains (physical, social, cognitive, and affective), will contribute to quality task analysis in that each sequen-tial part that needs to be taught will be better understood.

Principles of Activity Analysis

Figure 6.3 (page 203) contains the Activity Analysis Rating Form. It is one generic option for analyzing activities in the physical, cognitive, social, and affective domains. Additional factors can be identified for specific populations that have greater need in a particular area, such as individuals with Alzheimer's or with thermal burns. The attempt here is to provide general material that cuts across all groups. Therapeutic recreation specialists are encouraged to design their own activity analysis checklists, including items that are of specific concern to their clientele.

Regardless of whether the specialist chooses to use this generic form or create his or her own, there are a few general principles that apply to activity analysis. These must be considered before performing an activity analysis.

- *Analyze the activity as it is normally engaged in.* This means that the specialist should consider the activity as it is normally carried out, by the "rules." Any additional modifications to the activity come after the complete analysis, not before or dur-ing. Analyze the activity in its truest form.

- *When completing the Activity Analysis Rating Form, rate the activity as compared to all other activities.* For example, when rating the hand-eye coordination necessary for participation, the specialist should consider how much the activity in question requires hand-eye coordination in comparison to all other possible activities. This helps in deciding which activities best meet which client needs.

- *Analyze the activity without regard for any specific disability group per se.* For example, when analyzing bingo, the specialist should not consider modifications that may be made for individuals with reduced coordination. Bingo should be analyzed as it is played by the rules for a person without a disability. The disability or special need is considered during the activity modification stage, discussed later in this chapter.

- *Analyze the activity with regard to the minimal level of skills required for basic, successful participation.* For example, when analyzing golf, the specialist should consider the activity requirements needed for successful participation in golf as a recreational activity, not the level of skill needed for professional tournament participation. Since many therapeutic recreation clients are learning or relearning basic activity skills, this is the level of anticipated involvement that should be analyzed.

The Activity Analysis Rating Form

The Activity Analysis Rating Form was developed to help therapeutic recreation specialists analyze activities according to a standardized rating system. It is intended to help systematize the way in which activities are scrutinized for their potential to meet client needs, and thus produce predictable client outcomes. The Activity Analysis Rating Form has five sections: (1) physical, (2) social, (3) cognitive, (4) affective, and (5) administrative.

Physical Requirements

All recreational activity requires some physical action. Often it is difficult to distinguish what action is required to participate from what action may be associated with an activity. Some activities do not require specific actions. There are many ways to fly a kite, whereas other activities, such as square dancing, have definite ways of moving. The task is to identify the actual demands of the activity.

One can begin analyzing the physical requirements of an activity by noting the basic body position, then determining the body parts involved. Each involved body part must be identified separately, such as fingers, hand, wrist, and elbow, or by grouping parts into larger categories, such as arms or upper torso. The amount of detail needed usually relates to the population that is receiving the recreational services. For example, more detailed information may be required when analyzing activities for individuals with physical disabilities than when doing so for those with mental illnesses.

The types of movement also must be determined. Common body actions are bending, stretching, twisting, reaching, grasping, and rotating. These actions usually are part of a movement pattern that can be identified in broad terms such as catching, throwing, kicking, striking, or running. Pinpointing the fundamental movement patterns in an activity helps to determine the complexity of an activity and also what skills need to be taught. When more detail is needed, the therapeutic recreation specialist can isolate the exact motions involved for each body part.

It is also important to know the number and nature of the movements involved. For example, softball is extremely complex; it requires running, throwing, catching, and striking (batting), all with a high degree of accuracy. Bowling, on the other hand, has just one basic movement pattern. This type of information is crucial when it comes to the selection of activities for certain populations.

In a rehabilitation unit where the team consists of a physical therapist (PT), an occupational therapist (OT), and a recreation specialist (RS), the PT and OT may also use some form of activity analysis. These professions may analyze the physical requirements of a movement from a very detailed technical perspective, e.g., degree of hip rotation or identification of specific muscles used. The therapeutic recreation specialist should not attempt to replace or duplicate such rehabilitation analysis. The therapeutic recreation activity analysis has a different perspective. For our purpose, it is sufficient to break the activity down into the major parts of the body involved and the basic movements or movement patterns, such as grasping, throwing, or catching, that are needed in that specific activity.

The different senses also should be considered part of the physical requirements of activity participation. Sight is vital to successful participation in many activities, as is hearing. Rarely do we stop to analyze an activity for these two essential areas. The inability of a client to hear clearly in and of itself could make participation in many activities extremely frustrating, if not impossible. Smell and taste are not as often required for most activities, but touch is inherent in most sports, games, and expressive arts.

Coordination of body parts is another major factor to consider. Many activities require a high degree of coordination. Golf is a good example. It is a simple game by one standard, in that the entire game consists of one basic movement pattern, a swing of a golf club. However, coordination is critical, a fact to which any frustrated amateur duffer can attest. Activities that require using few body parts in coordination are easier to participate in—an insight that has obvious implications for special populations. Scheduling activities that continuously frustrate a client because too much coordination is needed certainly blocks the therapeutic intent or the enjoyment in participation. Many special populations, whether individuals with developmental disabilities, mental illness, emotional disturbances, or limitations related to aging, may (each for a different reason) have difficulty with activities requiring high levels of body part coordination.

Hand-eye coordination is another critical area. Many basic recreational activities require some form of hand-eye coordination, whether the activity is a sport, a craft, or a table game. Again the issue is determining how much coordination is required for successful participation. An awareness that the required level and amount of hand-eye coordination is extremely high in a certain activity may result in the selection of another activity to comply with the limitation of a person or group.

A variety of other physical factors can be analyzed. Among these are strength, speed, endurance, energy, and flexibility. Determining how much or how little of these elements are involved in a given activity is equally important when selecting and modifying program content.

Interaction and Social Requirements

Many recreation activities require some form of interaction, and thus require a certain degree of social skill. The nature of the interaction may be cooperative or competitive, and there may be any number of people involved. An analysis of these inherent interaction patterns within activities is significant in selecting activities appropriately and helping clients to develop social skills.

Interactional Patterns Inherent in Recreation Activities.   Elliott Avedon (1974) developed a classification system of interaction patterns found in recreation activities. It enables the therapeutic recreation specialist to understand quickly some of the dynamics of participation. Once an activity has been analyzed to determine which of the eight interaction patterns are inherent, the specialist can make a variety of judgments about the complexity, demands, or appropriateness of that activity for a specific individual or group. In addition, interaction analysis facilitates the selection and sequencing of activities for building social and interactional skills. Because many therapeutic recreation programs focus on social factors, it is advantageous to comprehend as much as possible about an activity's contribution in this area. The eight interaction patterns follow.

Intraindividual.   *Action taking place within the mind of a person or action involving the mind and a part of the body, but requiring no contact with another person or external object* (Avedon, 1974, p. 164).

Activities in this category are few and not frequently used in therapeutic recreation programming. Twiddling thumbs, daydreaming, meditation, and fantasizing fall into this category, although they have not been traditionally recognized as forms of leisure activity. Intraindividual actions are frequently engaged in by individuals, although they rarely are discussed in the professional literature. Needless to say, not all forms of intra-individual activities are likely to be offered to clients as formalized programs, but it should be recognized clearly that clients should and do participate in these opportunities.

Extraindividual.   *Action directed by a person toward an object in the environment, requiring no contact with another person* (Avedon, 1974, p. 164).

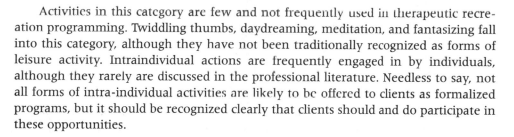

Countless activities fall into this category. Anything done alone that involves an object fits the requirements. Watching television, engaging in a craft project, working in the garden, playing solitaire or computer games, and reading—all can be considered extraindividual activities.

Most people engage in extraindividual activities. However, this category of activities is seldom directly addressed in therapeutic recreation programs. The reasons are usually time and resources. Because we are faced with providing programs for numbers of people, we tend to rely on group activities. Ironically, however, in the process of helping people prepare for independent leisure participation, we frequently overlook the fact that many individuals with disabilities and/or illnesses spend a large amount of time alone and thus need leisure skills that can be engaged in while alone. Extraindividual activities are therefore a must for program consideration. They are often a desirable starting place for teaching clients a progression of social skills. The ability to enjoy oneself while alone should be a basic concern of therapeutic recreation specialists who realistically confront the needs of individuals with illnesses and disabilities.

Extraindividual activities also can serve another major function: They can be used as the first phase of a carefully sequenced plan for developing social interaction abilities. It often is easier for a client to engage in a social experience when an activity is the focus, as opposed to an emphasis on interacting with others. Assisting clients to engage in individual activity is therefore an important step in acquiring interactional skills. When a person is comfortable engaging in an activity alone, it then may be possible for him or her to begin to interact comfortably with others.

Aggregate. *Action directed by a person toward an object in the environment while in the company of other persons who are also directing action toward objects in the environment. Action is not directed toward one another, and no interaction between participants is required or necessary* (Avedon, 1974, p. 165).

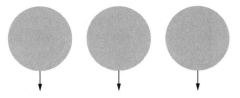

Many activities that can be done alone (extraindividual) also can be done in group settings. In therapeutic recreation, this is indeed common. Crafts programs, entertainment, and hobby groups are all examples of aggregate activities, as is the "infamous" game of bingo. Aggregate activities require no interaction between participants. This quality, however, has several inherent therapeutic characteristics and applications.

Physical proximity to others is one characteristic. When individuals are together, all engaging in their own projects or activity, they have the opportunity to warm up to one another without feeling any pressure to interact. Each individual focuses on his or her own activity, but spontaneous interaction stimulated by the action often results. Borrowing a piece of equipment, sharing a success, or asking a question are all social responses that are natural and easy to make. In a program designed to develop social and verbal interactional skills, aggregate activities are ideal in the early stages when nonthreatening interactions are essential. Aggregate activities are frequently used within a sequenced program of social interaction development.

Aggregate activities, as well as extraindividual activities, can be either competitive or cooperative. Solitaire, a crossword puzzle, a video game, or a pinball game can be competitive. The individual can learn competitive action without the reality or threat of another person as the opponent. Testing one's abilities against the game or task has a variety of therapeutic benefits. The ability to compete in many areas of life appears to be an essential ingredient of survival in our culture. Competitive aggregate activities provide a simulated experience for acquiring these skills in a safe and supervised situation.

Cooperative extraindividual and aggregate activities, such as crafts, woodworking, writing, reading, and gardening, allow the clients to gain internal motivation and stimulation without competitive demands. Increasing one's ability to enjoy an activity without feeling the pressures of competition can be an important experience. When actions are initiated by the individuals themselves, and conducted without external expectations or demands, a feeling of self-sufficiency and independence may result.

Aggregate activities provide opportunities for those involved to master activities independently of others. Because many people with disabilities and/or illnesses spend time alone, they should have a repertoire of activities in which they can engage without others. The aggregate pattern enables the therapeutic recreation specialist to facilitate the acquisition of such skills while still working in a group situation.

Interindividual.   *Action of a competitive nature directed by one person toward another* (Avedon, 1974, p. 166).

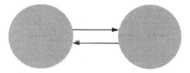

This interaction pattern is basic for many mental and physical activities. Chess, checkers, honeymoon bridge, singles tennis, horseshoes, and racquetball are examples. The pattern requires the ability to interact continuously with one's opponents and to apply the necessary skills with the intention of winning or at least enjoying the attempt. This competition simulates many interpersonal encounters in daily living in which individuals need to stand up for themselves in an interaction with another person.

Interindividual activities vary in the amount and degree of necessary interaction. A game of checkers requires very little, if any, verbal exchange; other games require calling out scores, requesting information, or responding verbally in other ways. Interindividual activities can be selected and sequenced to produce a progression of verbalization and other social responses.

Another therapeutic application of this pattern relates to the frequency of the interaction. A game like Ping-Pong requires continuous attention and response as the ball quickly moves from one side of the table to the other. Changes in frequency allow the specialist to provide a sequence of more and more challenging interactional activities.

Since the pattern is always competitive, it has the therapeutic quality of assisting people to deal with stress, pressure, and concepts of winning and losing. The therapeutic recreation specialist must attend to this aspect in order for it to be beneficial. Continuous losing can be destructive, as can be the overwhelming need to always win. Because interindividual activities are competitive, they always have rules. A characteristic of these activities is playing by the rules and regulating one's behavior according to the rules in order to participate successfully. The players agree to interact and behave in certain ways, to their mutual benefit. The value of such agreement extends beyond the game into many life situations. In interindividual activities, clients can experience appropriate role modeling for many other life interactions.

Unilateral.   *Action of a competitive nature among three or more persons, one of whom is an antagonist, or "it"* (Avedon, 1974, p. 167).

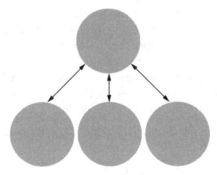

Many children's games have a unilateral pattern. Tag games, hide-and-seek games, and chase games are in this category. Fewer adult games are unilateral. Nonetheless, some characteristics of the unilateral pattern apply to the acquisition of interaction skills. Unilateral activities provide opportunities for role differentiation. In these kinds of games, all players except one have the same role. It is the beginning stage of the recognition that different players have different functions, a concept that is further developed in the complex roles found in games such as basketball or softball. When just one person is "it," the concept of different roles is quickly learned and understood.

Several other benefits occur from unilateral activities. When working with individuals with cognitive limitations, it often is easier to teach beginning concepts of competition with unilateral activities. With other populations, unilateral activities put one person in the limelight. The competitive pressure also shifts from one player to another, thus removing the continuous, competitive pressure in other types of activities. However, the specialist needs to be aware that individuals' skills must be fairly evenly matched or the player who is "it" often remains "it."

Multilateral.   *Action of a competitive nature among three or more persons, with no one person as an antagonist* (Avedon, 1974, p. 168).

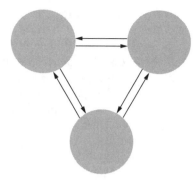

In multilateral activities, every player is against every other player. Games such as Scrabble, poker, and Monopoly are examples of activities that have this pattern. Multilateral activities have several characteristics that can be used for therapeutic outcomes.

Multilateral activities require each person to initiate competitive action with others. For the individual who cannot tolerate sustained, competitive action with just one person, activities of this type allow for a diffusion of effort. In multilateral activities, the individual often is pressured to perform by a number of people simultaneously. This simulated experience has value for other real-life situations when the individual has to face pressures that come from a variety of people at the same time.

Multilateral activities place the responsibility for control directly on each individual, since each is an independent agent within the game. Decision making, strategy, and action are not shared by team members. The result can be a feeling of self-sufficiency for the individual who is ready for it. Obviously, many clients need to work up to this type of interaction pattern, because it places high demands on internal initiative and independence.

Intragroup.   *Action of a cooperative nature by two or more persons intent upon reaching a mutual goal. Action requires positive verbal and nonverbal interaction* (Avedon, 1974, p. 169).

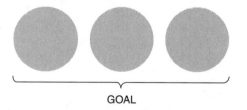

GOAL

Examples of activities requiring this pattern include such things as musical groups (bands and choirs), dramatic plays, service projects, and square or ballroom dancing. Learning how to cooperate and function successfully as a group member is a difficult task, but one that most clients need. Unfortunately, without the motivation of competition, it often is hard to build the concepts of cooperation. Although sometimes common group goals help participants stay on task and maintain motivation, recreational activities of the intragroup type do not inherently create cooperative action. Sensitive and astute leadership is needed to maximize the benefits of intragroup activities. Activities in this category are essential in helping establish social skills, since so many interactions in life require compromise and cooperation. Family life, most social situations, and work are everyday examples that require intragroup interactional abilities. Programming activities in this category is overwhelmingly important when we wish to assist clients in the development of positive and cooperative interactional skills.

Many professionals feel that competitive activities are overemphasized in therapeutic recreation programs. The concept that fun has to involve doing someone else in or beating the other person is indeed narrow. Enjoyment should be fostered through cooperative action as well. Certainly intragroup activities are in keeping with the current trend toward cooperative group initiatives such as team ropes courses and other adventure problem-solving games and activities.

Finding or creating good activities that utilize the intragroup pattern is a challenge for the therapeutic recreation specialist. It often is difficult to establish a mutual goal that is attractive enough to the participants to facilitate positive interactions. Nevertheless, the benefits resulting from successful participation in intragroup activities make the effort well worthwhile.

Intergroup.   *Action of a competitive nature between two or more intragroups* (Avedon, 1974, p. 170).

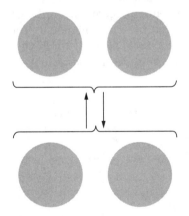

All team sports and games fall into this category. Softball, relays, doubles tennis, and bridge are examples. These activities are the most difficult to perform, because participants must cooperate with other team members as well as compete against their opponents. Far too often, clients are put into intergroup activities long before they are ready to handle the advanced interactional skills required. This often results in mass confusion, not to mention negative reactions. Therapeutic recreation specialists should avoid introducing intergroup activities until they are sure the participants are functionally and developmentally able to handle the diverse interactions involved. Unfortunately, many traditional and familiar activities are of this type; we overlook their complexity because of their popularity.

Intergroup activities have many pronounced therapeutic benefits. Learning to be a good team member is one. This interaction pattern represents many realistic life situations in which one group works against another group. The give and take needed to mount an effective attack can be experienced through games, with carryover to work, family, and other social situations.

An advantage of intergroup activities is that they often produce peer pressure among team members, which can effectively result in significant behavior changes in participants. This outcome, however, has both positive and negative implications. Good leadership is needed to influence the peer pressure desired. An understanding of group dynamics is needed to produce therapeutic peer pressure.

The fact that intergroup activities have the element of competition is another benefit, if handled wisely. The pressure to cooperate in order to win often brings a group together that otherwise could not or would not function as a unit. In essence, intergroup competition may foster intragroup cooperation. In this case, competition is a positive influence. Through the process, individuals frequently gain greater respect and liking for one another, which opens other avenues of positive interaction.

Another therapeutic benefit of the intergroup pattern is the concept of a support system. To be a member of a team, to have a sense of belonging, and to experience unity within a group are all important and positive experiences. Many times, these experiences are missing in the lives of individuals with disabilities. Intergroup activities may facilitate the feeling of belonging and give individuals a base from which to develop other group ties.

Understanding the inherent interaction patterns found in activities contributes a great deal to our comprehension of the dynamics of involvement as well as to the therapeutic possibilities in the selection and sequencing process. Analyzing activities with the use of interaction patterns provides a valuable tool for the development of social interaction skills by enabling us to focus on the critical issues surrounding activity participation. Some therapeutic recreation specialists have developed assessment procedures for social skills utilizing these eight interaction categories as the basis for client analysis.

Other Social Factors.   In addition to the interaction patterns inherent in activities, a variety of other social factors can be identified and used in analysis. Because the word "social" encompasses such broad categories of behavior in our culture, the list of factors could be extremely lengthy. Some of the more generic and useful factors for consideration include the number of individuals required for participation, physical proximity, physical contact, degree of communication required, appropriate clothing, and degree of noise generated. Each of these need to be considered carefully when analyzing activities for therapeutic purposes. They each play an important role in clients' successful participation in activities.

It has become imperative for the therapeutic recreation specialist to be knowledgeable in the social and interactional domain because few other professions concern themselves with this important area of client behavior. Being highly skilled in activity analysis of this domain greatly enhances the contribution that therapeutic recreation can make toward treatment and/or educational goals in this arena.

Cognitive Requirements

Cognition may be the most important requirement of activity participation, since the mind regulates body movement as well as other behavioral aspects of participation. Several aspects of cognition are important considerations in activity analysis.

The number and complexity of rules must be determined. Chess and bridge have many rules, whereas creative dramatics has no inherent rules. The leader may impose some, but the activity itself is rule-free. Not only must rules be remembered, but the players also must regulate their behavior according to them. Many individuals—such as those with mental retardation, emotional disturbances, traumatic brain injury, and cerebral vascular accidents—may have much difficulty in playing games that have complex rules.

Memory retention is another vital area of cognition. It pertains not only to rules but also to new information that needs to be processed, stored, and used continuously during the activity. Both the amount and nature of long- and short-term memory retention need to be analyzed before recommending the use of a certain activity.

Concentration needs also should be noted. Some activities require intense, continuous concentration. Ping-Pong is a good example. Bowling, however, requires intermittent concentration. The specialist must be aware of the level of concentration required to perform an activity, as well as its frequency.

Different activities require different levels of verbalization and command of the language. The act of speaking is actually physical, but generally language is considered a cognitive function. Activities have differing degrees of selecting, organizing, and using words. Bingo requires little verbalization, whereas planning and putting on a skit may require an extensive amount.

Strategy is another cognitive skill inherent in many recreation activities. It requires an ability to analyze alternatives and make decisions. There is a big difference between the amount of strategy required in Chinese checkers and a game of Old Maid, just as there is between tennis and horseshoes.

The requirements of intellectual skills versus chance also can be considered in activity analysis. Some activities involve some mental functioning, but the outcomes are pretty much chance related. For example, Parcheesi, poker, and blackjack depend more on luck of the deal or the roll of the dice than they do on intellectual skill. This means that participants' skill levels have little effect on the outcome of participation.

The academic skills of reading, writing, and math should be analyzed in relation to most activities. For example, countless activities require the ability to keep score, which is a mathematical calculation. Frequently, we take this ability for granted or overlook its complexity because an activity is primarily physical in nature.

Some activities also require recognition and use of forms, shapes, colors, sizes, numbers, and the like. An activity analysis should consider these areas important factors to evaluate, as many individuals with disabilities and/or illnesses may lack these important recognition skills.

The analysis of activities for an understanding of their cognitive demands is essential. More often than not, some cognitive inability makes a client's participation difficult, frustrating, or impossible. Cognitive requirements are as complex as physical or social requirements, but often are more difficult to detect and are thus more likely to be overlooked by the therapeutic recreation specialist.

Emotional (Affective) Factors

Of all the behavioral areas of functioning, the affective domain causes the greatest difficulty in activity analysis. One problem is that of definition. Affective behaviors can be difficult to understand and, as a result, often are just skipped over. They are, however, a vital part of activity involvement and therefore cannot be excluded from examination. Therapeutic recreation specialists are naturally concerned with how to recognize various emotional responses, since so much of therapeutic recreation programming focuses on developing, stimulating, and otherwise facilitating the appropriate expression of feelings.

Activities do not have set, inherent affective requirements that can be identified the way physical or cognitive requirements can be. Each client brings to the activity a lifetime of experience with a variety of ways of responding emotionally. An activity that causes excitement in one person fosters fear in someone else. Thus, there is no simple way to categorize the emotional responses or requirements of activities.

Emotions.   Six emotions are generally accepted as basic to the human experience. These six can therefore be generalized in relation to activity participation. The following descriptions are offered as guidelines for understanding possible emotional responses, but are in no way intended to be absolute. Individuals could be expected to vary in their responses. The therapeutic recreation specialist can, however, be aware of possible outcomes and thus become more prepared to cope with emotional reactions. Predominantly, we are concerned with whether the activity provides an opportunity or outlet to express a particular emotion or whether the client must control or inhibit the expression of the emotion during participation in the activity.

Joy.   We want people to feel good about themselves, to experience enjoyment, or at least to feel contentment. One thing that seems to produce this feeling in many cultures is winning. Any activity that involves competition and in which the participants have a fairly equal amount of skill should produce a sense of enjoyment for the winner. Unfortunately, the loser will probably sense a different emotional response. Very few people have really mastered the ability to feel good because of performing well even if they lose, or just feeling good for having participated. Our egos are too involved with being the best, and that is quickly determined in any competitive activity.

Normally, enjoyment results from a pleasurable interaction with another person. Activities, therefore, that have a high possibility of creating social interactions are likely to produce some emotional feeling like joy and contentment.

Completing a task is another event that seems to bring good feelings to many people. Note the frustration level when individuals cannot complete a craft project because the time is up, or when tennis players have to get off the court in the middle of a set because the court is reserved by someone else. Contentment seems to be tied to a sense of closure.

Guilt.   Guilt is a very powerful emotion. It is associated with a sense of shame and inadequacy, and often results in counterresponses of resentment and hostility. Individuals feel guilty when they let someone else down. This happens frequently in competitive team situations. Players feel they are not good enough, or other team members convince a player that this is true. Feeling inadequate at something and then being forced to play and to have the outcomes affect others can trigger a guilt response. People generally feel guilty when they hurt someone else. Any activity that has much combative contact has a high probability of producing guilt, whether the act of hurting was intentional or accidental.

Pain.   Pain or hurt can be experienced through physical, mental, or emotional occurrences. We feel pain when we lose a game or when we have to acknowledge that we are not as good as someone else. Competitive activities produce this response. There can only be one winner; someone always loses. We feel pain when we are rejected or eliminated. Activities that send an individual away to the sidelines or outside the circle can produce hurt. Musical chairs or a simple elimination dodgeball game selectively exclude more and more people as the activity continues.

Physical pain is easily understood. Lots of activities, such as those with a high degree of physical contact, have a high risk of physical pain and should be considered carefully. Emotional or social pain is harder to predict, since it is more concerned with an individual's personality and previous experience.

Anger.   Anger can be expected in a variety of situations. Any activity that requires physical restraint will normally produce anger in the person being held down or held back. King of the mountain and wrestling are good examples of this.

Being struck by a person or object also produces anger (as well as the possibility of physical pain). Many activities require striking, directly or indirectly, and thus have a high potential for this emotional response. Obvious activities are boxing and fencing, but other activities, such as tag, volleyball, floor hockey, and dodgeball, have the potential of producing this response.

If someone needs to express anger, the activity can be analyzed similarly. It often is useful to select activities in which striking is a requirement of the action. However, the striking is best done through an object and toward an object. Softball, tennis, golf, and bowling allow for appropriate hitting within the rules and without danger to others.

Anger also needs to be understood as well in terms of symbolic attacks. Capturing pieces on a chess or checkers board or sending a piece home in Parcheesi can produce the same response of anger as a direct physical blow.

Activities and situations that create a great deal of dependency on others also can result in anger and hostility. Although dependency is inherent in some activities, this condition more often is created by the therapeutic recreation specialist.

An individual can become angry over a vast array of events or circumstances that the therapeutic recreation specialist cannot know about and that are unrelated to an activity. Anger can result from defeat, frustration, or from not meeting one's own standards of performance. In these examples, the response obviously is not inherent in the nature of the activity, nor is it predictable unless the specialist is very familiar with the client.

Fear.   Fear is a strange emotion. In most cases, it is perceptual and usually unrealistic, but the felt response of the individual is real. Fear often results when individuals are insecure about their abilities to perform or when they are concerned about the judgments of others related to their abilities. People are afraid of failing or of not meeting expectations. These psychological fears often keep people from participating in order to protect themselves from perceived humiliation. Many people avoid activities where they lack skill for fear of looking foolish, while other people fear going to public places alone. Most often therapeutic recreation specialists do not initially know what fears people have relative to activity involvement and thus cannot make many judgments about them ahead of time.

Some fears are easier to identify and understand, such as the fear of physical injury or the fear of social rejection. An activity can be analyzed to anticipate fear reactions to some of its characteristics.

Frustration.   This emotional response is a common one and is expressed frequently during activity involvement. It is not inherent in activities, but is again a factor that the individual brings to a situation based on personality makeup and past experience. Frustration commonly occurs when one's abilities do not match the requirements of the task. A high-skill physical activity is likely to produce frustration because of the exact coordination of body parts required. Golf is a good example. Activities requiring a great deal of accuracy, such as archery and riflery, are likely to create frustration because the feedback is immediate. Other activities that do not have a well-defined outcome are less likely to be frustrating, such as crafts, or camping, or watching a television show.

Frustration is an expected response when two or more people are unequally matched in any competitive activity. It is also a common response when individuals are not performing at the level at which they know they are capable. Frustration is seen frequently when chance factors over which the individual has no control affect the outcome. It also occurs when individuals perceive that they are not meeting the expectations of others, particularly the leader.

Frustration levels vary a great deal. Some individuals are easygoing and are not easily frustrated. Others have high standards of performance and suffer a great deal of frustration in any activity. The therapeutic recreation specialist has the task, regardless of individual personality factors, of selecting activities that can be performed realistically by clients.

Much more needs to be known about affective behaviors before activity analysis in this area can claim any real sophistication or accuracy. For the moment, awareness, observation, and common sense appear to be essential when considering this aspect of activity selection. The limited material presented here perhaps raises more questions than it gives answers. We hope that we are moving in the direction of being more concerned about affective stimuli and responses related to activity involvement.

Predicting responses and being aware of possible outcomes appear to be important beginning points, as long as generalizations are not carried too far.

Administrative Aspects

When analyzing activities for client involvement, the therapeutic recreation specialist also needs to consider some administrative factors. For example, considerations such as required leadership style, type of equipment and facilities needed, duration of the activity, and number of required participants all are crucial for the smooth delivery of an activity. An activity such as basketball cannot be played by the rules without the proper equipment and facility. Similar to other aspects of the Activity Analysis Rating Form, reviewing the administrative aspects may direct the specialist to areas needing modifications for successful client participation.

Using the Activity Analysis Rating Form

The Activity Analysis Rating Form (Figure 6.3) provides an example of a variety of items that have proven useful for analyzing a given activity. It also demonstrates different ways of rating activities, such as the absence or presence of characteristics, frequency ratings, simple checklists, and the use of Likert scales. It is not absolute; many other items could be added, and others presented could be deleted.

The reader is encouraged to select an activity and analyze it with the use of the form. Focus on the activity and its inherent requirements as it is traditionally engaged in. While doing this, try to follow the principles outlined earlier in this chapter. Analyze just the activity itself, without consideration at this point of potential specific disability groups or possible activity modifications.

A therapeutic recreation specialist would not use a form such as this to analyze each activity under consideration for a program on a continuous basis. It serves as a learning tool. Most therapeutic recreation specialists find that they can conduct an activity analysis in their heads after they have learned the procedures and have become familiar with the various items.

Activity Selection Factors

The ability to analyze an activity thoroughly in all four behavioral and the administrative areas enables the therapeutic recreation specialist to more accurately select appropriate activities for predetermined therapeutic or instructional outcomes. Assessing client needs and specifying client objectives have been previously discussed. Once objectives have been stated, the task of selecting the most appropriate activities for a program is undertaken. It is obviously valuable to use activities that have inherent in their structure the qualities that relate most directly to the objectives. This information is ascertained only by activity analysis. The process also allows several activities to be compared, so that the best ones can be selected and used.

Some professionals have found that the process of activity analysis has expanded their repertoire of assessment categories as well. For example, by realizing the many aspects of cognitive action involved in activity participation, professionals have added

Activity: _____

PHYSICAL ASPECTS:

1. What is the primary body position required?

   _____ lying down   _____ sitting   _____ other: _____

   _____ kneeling   _____ standing

2. What body parts are required?

   _____ arms   _____ feet   _____ upper torso

   _____ hands   _____ neck   _____ lower torso

   _____ legs   _____ head

3. What types of movement does the activity require?

   _____ bending   _____ punching   _____ reaching

   _____ stretching   _____ catching   _____ grasping

   _____ standing   _____ throwing   _____ skipping/hopping

   _____ walking   _____ hitting   _____ running

4. What are the primary senses required for the activity?

   _____ touch   _____ sight   _____ smell

   _____ taste   _____ hearing

5. What is the amount of coordination and movement between body parts required by the activity?

   | Much | 1 | 2 | 3 | 4 | 5 | Little |

6. What is the degree of hand-eye coordination needed for the activity?

   | Much | 1 | 2 | 3 | 4 | 5 | Little |

7. What is the degree of strength needed for the activity?

   | Much | 1 | 2 | 3 | 4 | 5 | Little |

8. What is the degree of speed needed for the activity?

   | Much | 1 | 2 | 3 | 4 | 5 | Little |

9. What is the degree of endurance needed for the activity?

   | Much | 1 | 2 | 3 | 4 | 5 | Little |

10. What is the degree of energy needed for the activity?

    | Much | 1 | 2 | 3 | 4 | 5 | Little |

11. What is the degree of flexibility needed for the activity?

    | Much | 1 | 2 | 3 | 4 | 5 | Little |

SOCIAL ASPECTS

1. What is the primary social interaction pattern required in the activity?

   _____ Intraindividual (action taking place within the mind or action involving the mind and a part of the body; requires no contact with another person or external object)

(continued)

Figure 6.3 Activity Analysis Rating Form.

_____ Extraindividual (action directed by a person toward an object; requires no contact with another person)

_____ Aggregate (action directed by a person toward an object while in the company of other persons who also are directing actions toward objects; action is not directed toward each other; no interaction required among participants)

_____ Interindividual (action of a competitive nature directed by one person toward another)

_____ Unilateral (action of a competitive nature among three or more persons, one of whom is an antagonist; interaction is in simultaneous competitive relationship)

_____ Multilateral (action of a competitive nature among three or more persons with no one person as an antagonist)

_____ Intragroup (action of a cooperative nature by two or more persons intent upon reaching a mutual goal; action requires positive verbal or nonverbal interaction)

_____ Intergroup (action of a competitive nature between two or more intragroups)

2. What is the minimum (fewest) number or maximum (greatest) number of people required for the activity?

_____ minimum number _____ maximum number

3. What clothing is needed to be socially appropriate?

4. How much physical proximity is required by the activity?

Close   1   2   3   4   5   Distant

5. How much physical contact is required by the activity?

Much   1   2   3   4   5   Little

6. What degree of communication is required by the activity?

High   1   2   3   4   5   Low

7. What degree of noise is generated by the activity?

Much   1   2   3   4   5   Little

COGNITIVE ASPECTS

1. How many rules are required in the activity?

Many   1   2   3   4   5   Few

2. How complex are the rules to understand?

Complex   1   2   3   4   5   Simple

3. What degree of strategy is required in the activity?

Much   1   2   3   4   5   Little

4. What degree of complexity is involved in scoring?

Much   1   2   3   4   5   Little

5. What degree of long-term memory is required in the activity?

Much   1   2   3   4   5   Little

6. What degree of short-term memory or immediate recall is required in the activity?

Much   1   2   3   4   5   Little

Figure 6.3 (continued)

7. What degree of verbalization of thought process is required in the activity?

    Much   1   2   3   4   5   Little

8. What degree of concentration is required in the activity?

    Much   1   2   3   4   5   Little

9. What degree of concrete thinking is required by the activity?

    Much   1   2   3   4   5   Little

10. What degree of abstract thinking is required by the activity?

    Much   1   2   3   4   5   Little

11. To what degree are each of the following skills used in the activity?

Reading	Much	1	2	3	4	5	Little
Writing	Much	1	2	3	4	5	Little
Math	Much	1	2	3	4	5	Little
Spelling	Much	1	2	3	4	5	Little

12. To what degree does the participant need to identify or use the following?

Form and shape	Much	1	2	3	4	5	Little
Colors	Much	1	2	3	4	5	Little
Size	Much	1	2	3	4	5	Little
Numbers	Much	1	2	3	4	5	Little
Body parts	Much	1	2	3	4	5	Little
Directionality	Much	1	2	3	4	5	Little

AFFECTIVE ASPECTS

1. To what degree does the participant have the opportunity or outlet to express the following?

Joy	Much	1	2	3	4	5	Little
Guilt	Much	1	2	3	4	5	Little
Pain	Much	1	2	3	4	5	Little
Anger	Much	1	2	3	4	5	Little
Fear	Much	1	2	3	4	5	Little
Frustration	Much	1	2	3	4	5	Little

2. To what degree must the participant control or inhibit the expression of the following?

Joy	Much	1	2	3	4	5	Little
Guilt	Much	1	2	3	4	5	Little
Pain	Much	1	2	3	4	5	Little
Anger	Much	1	2	3	4	5	Little
Fear	Much	1	2	3	4	5	Little
Frustration	Much	1	2	3	4	5	Little

Figure 6.3 *(continued)*

ADMINISTRATIVE ASPECTS

1. What type of leadership style is required by the activity?

    _____ specific activity-skill expertise _____ supervisory

    _____ general activity-skill expertise _____ no specific leadership style needed

2. What type of equipment is needed for the activity?

    _____ specific commercial product (specify: _____)

    _____ can be made (specify: _____)

    _____ no equipment required

3. What type of facility is required by the activity?

    _____ specific natural environment (specify: _____)

    _____ specific created environment (specify: _____)

    _____ no specific environment required

4. What is the duration of the activity?

    _____ set time

    _____ natural end

    _____ continuous

5. What is the number of participants required for the activity?

    _____ any number can participate

    _____ fixed number or multiple (specify: _____)

Figure 6.3 (*continued*)

these dimensions to their assessment of client needs, and as a result, may end up with different or expanded objectives dealing with these areas.

Age

Although we cannot categorize activities specific to age, certain activities are more appropriate at different stages of life. A common violation of this factor occurs when we program children's activities for adults. This situation can be dehumanizing and humiliating. It occurs frequently, however, when working with adults with developmental disabilities and older adults in long-term care facilities. Occasionally, the opposite situation occurs. Children are asked to participate in activities that are above their physical, social, emotional, or mental development. For example, elementary school-aged children may be pushed into team competition or learning social dance skills too soon. Successful programming considers the appropriateness of the activity to age and developmental factors.

Number of Clients

The sheer number of people to be served influences the selection process. Square dancing cannot be successfully done with fewer than eight people; likewise, individual leisure skills are difficult to schedule when the client population is large.

Staff/client ratios, as well as budget considerations, enter into this critical area. However, program content should never be determined solely by expediency.

Facilities Available

A certain activity may be advantageous for an identified client need, but the absence of the required facility may render it impossible. Some activities require very specific facilities and areas, while other activities are less dependent on the environment.

Equipment and Supplies

Many activities require specific equipment or many supplies; limited budgets often hinder buying them. In this situation, the therapeutic recreation specialist must find a similar activity, one with the same characteristics and dynamics, but without the heavy emphasis on paraphernalia.

Staff Skills

Selecting an activity that the staff member does not have the skills to conduct is obviously inappropriate or even dangerous (for instance, an unqualified person taking clients swimming). However, program content does not need to be limited just to activities that the staff likes to do or can do. The staff should acquire skills through in-service training or professional development opportunities. In some situations, volunteers can supplement existing staff abilities. In either case, program content related to client needs should not be dictated by staff skills.

Carryover Skills

Whenever possible, activities should have the greatest possible amount of carryover value. Selection procedures can be based on knowledge of a client's future lifestyle and environment. The narrow focus on the immediate setting and its resources defeats the long-range goals of therapeutic recreation services.

The selection of activities for program inclusion requires attention to a vast number of variables. The nature of the program and its goals and objectives are of primary concern. The nature and abilities of clients also must be considered. Constraints and characteristics of the agency and its resources are equally important. Consideration of these factors along with the information acquired through activity analysis should, however, enable the process of activity selection to be much more precise and appropriate. These concepts are discussed more thoroughly in the next chapter.

Activity Modification

Activity analysis allows us to determine the appropriateness of selected activities for specific functional intervention, leisure education, and recreation participation objectives. It also serves a second basic function. It enables us to modify activities realistically and appropriately when needed to address client characteristics. Two major conditions require activity modification. Each of these is described as follows.

Modification for Individual Participation

The first condition occurs when working with individuals with disabilities in recreational participation, leisure activity skills development, or instructional programs. The analysis of the activity indicates the actual participation requirements for the physical, social, cognitive, and affective areas. The individual then is assessed relative to these standard requirements. When certain functional abilities are absent or impaired, this indicates where a modification needs to take place. Sometimes the regulation of the activity is modified; for example, a rule is eliminated or simplified. Sometimes a procedure is changed; for instance, rolling a bowling ball from a stationary position. Sometimes a change is made in the equipment or the way it is used, as in adapting an art brush so that it can be used with a person's mouth. Regardless of the type of modification, several factors should be considered:

1. *Keep the activity and action as close to the original or traditional activity as possible.* It is not much fun for an individual with a disability to engage in an activity when the new version is too far removed from the traditional one. A high degree of modification means that the skills learned by the client will be less transferable to inclusive settings.

2. *Modify only the aspects of the activity that need adapting.* An individual with a developmental disability may need the rules of the game to be simplified (cognitive aspects) but may be fully capable of performing the physical actions required. Therefore, there is need to modify the rules of the activity, but no need to modify the physical action in the activity. This keeps the modified activity close to the original and helps the individual learn as many aspects of the activity as he or she is capable of.

3. *Individualize the modification.* No two people with the same disability have exactly the same adaptation needs. By individualizing modifications, individual client needs are more likely to be considered and met, thereby assisting clients in reaching individualized goals/outcomes more successfully.

4. *The modification should be as temporary as possible.* In order for individuals to learn skills as close as possible to those of their peers without disabilities, whatever modifications are made within activities should be considered temporary. The specialist should help the individual build skills or knowledges toward participation in the regular activity to the fullest extent possible.

An example of these four rules of activity modification is wheelchair basketball. While many modifications could be made, few actual equipment and rule changes are required. For example, wheelchair basketball uses standard basketballs and standard basketball courts (including heights of hoops). If these were modified greatly, the individual would have a more difficult time playing on regulation courts and with regulation equipment. However, whatever rule changes needed to accommodate wheelchairs are made. For example, rule modifications are made for dribbling, shooting free throws, fouls, and traveling, among others. Only those rules that need to be changed are. When not in regulation play, an individual requiring more modifications could be accommodated through other adaptations, until he or she gained adequate skills.

Modification to Enhance the Therapeutic Benefit

The second major condition that requires activity modification occurs most often in treatment or rehabilitation programs in which client needs have been assessed and treatment objectives written. An activity analysis determines the appropriateness or contribution of an activity to the treatment goal. The activity is analyzed, based on a variety of factors previously described, and it is judged appropriate to the attainment of the goal. A quick second analysis is made concerning the group members who will engage in the activity. This analysis reveals that some individuals may have difficulty with certain aspects of the activity. Minor modifications then are made for those individuals or for the group, so that the therapeutic benefits can be obtained.

Here is an example of this process. The treatment goal for a group of individuals on a psychiatric unit is to increase the ability to concentrate. The game of Parcheesi is selected and analyzed. It meets all the physical, social, and mental requirements. It contributes to focusing attention and concentration. The individuals know how to play it and have the necessary control and skills. Therefore, Parcheesi is chosen as the activity.

A quick analysis of the actual clients on the unit who would be involved in the program reveals that one client cannot grasp and move the pieces or roll the dice because he has cut his wrists in a suicide attempt, resulting in restrained movements due to stitches and bandaging. The activity is modified for this person by assigning a partner to do the physical actions while the client makes all of the decisions. Because focusing attention and concentration are the goals, the game is modified by decreasing the pieces from four to two and also decreasing the length of the game, and thus increasing the possibility of all clients being able to stay focused throughout the game. Over several sessions, the other pieces would be reinstated as the ability to focus attention increases.

In this case, the modifications were made to enable the therapeutic outcome of the activity; often, these minor modifications are necessary and beneficial to the treatment concept. Whether modifications are made to enable participation by a person with a disability or for therapeutic purposes, activity analysis and functional assessment of the client are required. This process ensures that just the necessary adaptations are made.

The Activity Selection and Modification Model (Figure 6.4) serves as a helpful tool in learning activity modification procedures. It deals with administrative or operational concerns as well as with participation requirements. It can be used as a final check of an activity's appropriateness in the selection process or as a guide to areas in which modification needs to occur. It summarizes the many aspects of activity analysis, and thus initially should be used in conjunction with the Activity Analysis Rating Form. The Activity Selection and Modification Worksheet (Figure 6.5) provides the opportunity to examine the modified activity.

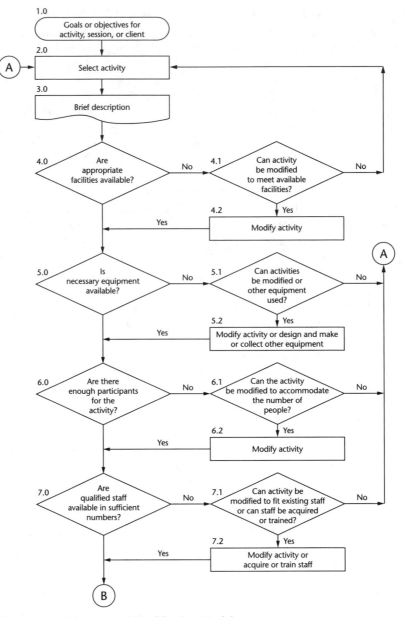

Figure 6.4 Activity Selection and Modification Model.

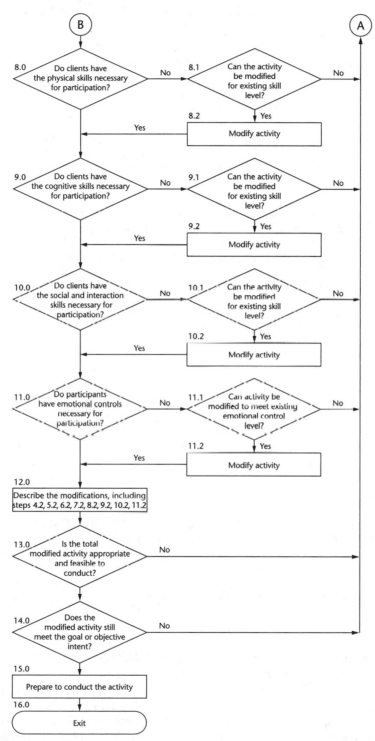

Figure 6.4 *(continued)*

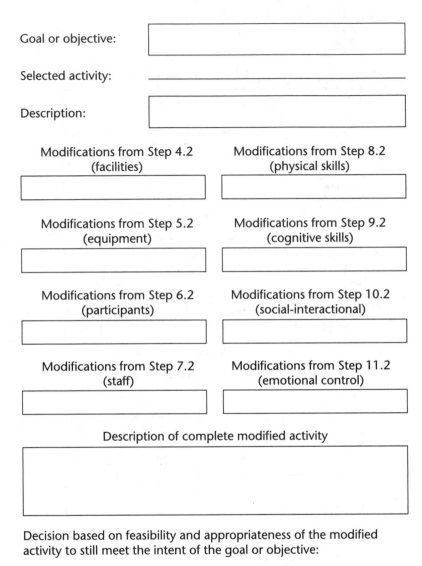

Goal or objective:

Selected activity:

Description:

Modifications from Step 4.2
(facilities)

Modifications from Step 8.2
(physical skills)

Modifications from Step 5.2
(equipment)

Modifications from Step 9.2
(cognitive skills)

Modifications from Step 6.2
(participants)

Modifications from Step 10.2
(social-interactional)

Modifications from Step 7.2
(staff)

Modifications from Step 11.2
(emotional control)

Description of complete modified activity

Decision based on feasibility and appropriateness of the modified
activity to still meet the intent of the goal or objective:

_____ Accept   _____ Reject

Figure 6.5 Activity Selection and Modification Worksheet.

Summary

Activity analysis is a practical and necessary tool of the therapeutic recreation specialist in the program planning stage. In its purest form, activity analysis focuses on determining the inherent characteristics of activities. It enables a greater comprehension of
participation requirements and gives insight into the dynamics of activity involvement. Practically applied, activity analysis makes it possible to select appropriate activities for therapeutic outcomes and facilitates sequencing and modification of instruc-

tional and recreation programs. Activity analysis gives more accuracy and accountability to program design efforts.

STUDENT EXERCISES

Discussion Questions

1. What is the purpose of activity analysis? What benefits does it provide to intervention programming? Why is a structured form useful?

2. How does activity analysis relate to client assessment? Why are they each important to achieve client outcomes?

3. What are the four domains examined by activity analysis and why is each important to activity participation?

4. Explain the four principles of activity analysis and why each is important.

5. What is likely to happen if the specialist does not properly analyze the activity in the physical domain? social domain? cognitive domain? emotional domain?

6. Often the social interaction patterns required in an activity are overlooked during an activity analysis. Why do you think this happens and what could be the consequences for clients?

7. Think about the recreation and leisure activities in which you participate. What are their dominant physical, social, cognitive, and emotional requirements?

Practice Test

1. The purpose of activity analysis is to:
    a. identify the key components or requirements of an activity.
    b. provide baseline information about the clients' characteristics.
    c. help determine the comprehensive goals of the program.
    d. modify the activity to meet the clients' needs.

2. In order for therapeutic recreation programs to have the potential to be intervention, what two key actions must the specialist complete?
    a. activity modification and program planning
    b. activity analysis and client assessment
    c. protocols and client assessment
    d. activity analysis and efficacy research

3. Activity analysis leads to a better determination of all EXCEPT:
    a. modifications for client participation.
    b. inherent characteristics of the activity.
    c. appropriateness of client participation in the activity.
    d. quality improvement of services.

4. In the Activity Analysis Rating Form used in this text, the items dual, small group, and large group interaction skills would best fit into which category?
    a. physical
    b. social

  c. emotional
  d. intellectual

5. Which of the following is NOT a rule for activity modification?
   a. Keep the activity as close as possible to the original.
   b. Plan only activities that the specialist is familiar with.
   c. Modify the activity as little as is feasible.
   d. Modify only the parts that need to be modified.

6. In activity analysis, the areas of memory and concentration are examples of what category of requirements?
   a. physical
   b. social
   c. intellectual
   d. emotional

7. An example of an activity that uses an "extraindividual" social interaction pattern is:
   a. daydreaming.
   b. watching television.
   c. bingo.
   d. chess.

Questions 8–10

Using the following social interaction patterns, choose the one that is appropriate for each example.

I. Aggregate
II. Interindividual
III. Unilateral
IV. Intragroup

8. Requires cooperation with other group members
   a. I
   b. II
   c. III
   d. IV

9. Does not require participants to interact with another individual
   a. I
   b. II
   c. III
   d. IV

10. Bingo is an example
    a. I
    b. II
    c. III
    d. IV

Answers: 1. a, 2. b, 3. d, 4. b, 5. b, 6. c, 7. b, 8. d, 9. a, 10. a

Chapter Activities

Activity Analysis

Form groups of two or three students. Choose a specific activity and analyze it using the form given in the text. Analyze the activity "by the rules" without modification. Compare your activity analysis with those of other groups of students.

Social Interaction Patterns

Create a list of five to ten recreation or leisure activities that involve each of the social interaction patterns. Compare your answers with those of other students in class and discuss any differences in your analyses.

Activity Modification

Think of a recreation or leisure activity. Conduct an activity analysis. Now select a specific client group and, using the form, note what modifications need to be made in that activity to be appropriate for that client group. Follow the principles of activity modification and list any changes you would make.

Recreation and Leisure Activity Diary

Keep a diary for five to ten days noting all the recreation and leisure activities in which you participate. Make notes about your participation patterns; are your activities primarily physical? social? What social interaction patterns are you most often engaged in? Share your summary with the class.

REFERENCES

Avedon, E. M. (1974). *Therapeutic recreation service: An applied behavioral science approach.* Englewood Cliffs, NJ: Prentice-Hall.

CHAPTER 7

Activity Selection and Implementation

Selecting the right activities for client participation is among the most crucial tasks for the therapeutic recreation specialist. If the ultimate mission of therapeutic recreation services is to change some aspects of client behavior, and this is done through the client's participation in specific, selected activities, then it becomes quickly apparent how important the process of activity selection is. However, this selection process is challenging and requires a tremendous amount of skill, flexibility, and creativity on the part of the therapeutic recreation specialist.

The purpose of this chapter is to provide a basis for discussion about the selection of activities for intervention purposes. Placement of activity selection within the Therapeutic Recreation Accountability Model is displayed in Figure 7.1. Again, it should be noted that comprehensive and specific program design, and activity analysis, selection, and modification are all closely linked and interrelated. Often, in practice, these functions occur simultaneously. However, they are separated in these discussions to aid in learning and comprehending the importance of each.

Before a discussion about factors and principles affecting activity selection begins, it is useful to review some of the basic assumptions about producing client outcomes and therapeutic recreation specialist competencies.

Client Outcomes

Much has been stated in the health care and therapeutic recreation literature about the pressing need for professionals to deliver client outcomes. As the call for accountability grows louder, more entities such as external accreditation organizations, third-party payers, consumer groups, and professional associations join the chorus. This has put tremendous pressure on all disciplines to re-envision their services and focus on the end product of changed client behavior. The survival and success of each profession will depend to a large extent on how well it answers this call.

Several words are associated with producing client outcomes. Among them are *relationship, causal, predictable,* and *replicable.* Selecting or designing programs and activities that produce client change implies a relationship between where the client enters the service at Point A, takes part in Program B, and comes out with changed behavior at Point C. This means there must be a strong, logical, and systematic *relationship* between each of the three points. For example, if a client enters a facility with a lack of knowledge of leisure resources (Point A) and participates actively in a well-

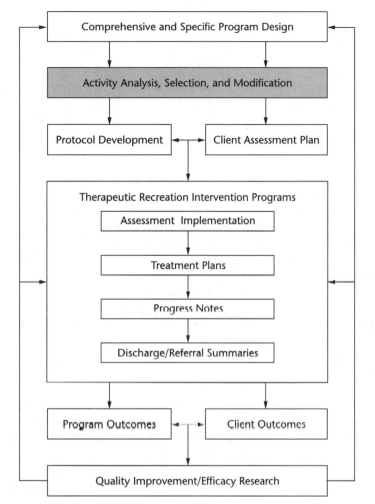

Figure 7.1 Activity selection component of the Therapeutic Recreation Accountability Model.

designed leisure resource program (Point B), it is logical that the client will exit with increased knowledge of leisure resources (Point C). Point A, Point B, and Point C all have a direct relationship. Figure 7.2 displays this relationship.

On the other hand, if a different client has the same need (Point A) and partici- pates in volleyball (Point D) instead of a leisure resource program (Point B), the client in this scenario is likely to exit at Point E, with volleyball skills, rather than leisure resource knowledge. Point A, Point D, and Point E do not have a direct relationship. The client is ending up with skills other than those that he or she needed at Point A.

The client in the first scenario is likely to exit with the targeted outcomes (increased knowledge of leisure resources), while the client in the second scenario is likely to exit with a second, different set of outcomes (volleyball skills). In other words, in order for the client to reach his or her targeted outcome, the need or goal, program, and outcome must have a strong, logical, and systematic relationship. These

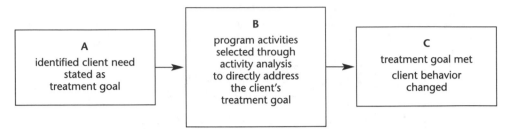

Figure 7.2 Client outcome and program activity relationship.

scenarios also address **causality** (participation in Program B is likely to cause outcome C), **predictability** (outcome C can be reasonably predicted from participation in Program B), and **replicability** (outcome C is likely to occur for all or nearly all clients in Program B).

This logical approach is the focus of selecting and designing programs that enable a client to change his or her behavior, knowledge, or skills. In addition, it needs to be stated that each intervention program focuses on this A-B-C sequence. In most clinical facilities, activities or programs must be geared toward intervention, that is, changing some aspect of client behavior, knowledge, or skills. In most facilities and for most clients, activities that are provided for pure enjoyment or entertainment are not seen as part of the treatment package, and are typically not funded by third-party payers. When offered, they often are implemented by paraprofessionals or volunteers.

Nonintervention activities, however, may be worthwhile in some settings and with some clients, but even then must have a clear-cut purpose and reason for implementation. For example, one legitimate purpose may be to observe clients when they have the opportunity for independent choices. The therapeutic recreation specialist might observe during recreational activities if clients have competence in decision making, problem solving, planning, social interaction skills, and so on. If the clients show difficulty in areas being targeted through treatment goals, this observational assessment opportunity leads to a prescription of new or revised intervention programs.

Therapeutic Recreation Specialist Competencies

The focus on outcomes presents several challenges to therapeutic recreation specialists in particular. First, it means that simple activity provision (often called cafeteria-style programming) is no longer viable. Therapeutic recreation specialists either will adapt to this call for accountability and complement other professions in the production of client outcomes or will be viewed as peripheral to the health and human service arena. Only those professions that move clients toward essential outcomes will remain viable.

Second, therapeutic recreation specialists will need to continue to learn new skills and face new directions. Not only does this include new activities and modalities, it means keeping abreast of new processes of accountability, such as critical pathways, protocols, clinical competencies, and performance measures. Part of being a professional means being responsible for keeping current with the latest professional developments. No one can afford to rest on his or her baccalaureate degree.

To be able to survive and thrive in the new century, the astute and professional therapeutic recreation specialist needs to have a great deal of knowledge concerning:

- **Philosophy.** How the therapeutic recreation specialist interprets therapeutic recreation impacts greatly the types of services he or she will deliver to clients. For example, if Leisure Ability is the preferred concept, the therapeutic recreation specialist will focus on the leisure-related attitudes, knowledge, and skills necessary for a healthy, satisfying, and meaningful leisure lifestyle. The concepts introduced in the first chapter of this text form the essential beginning for understanding leisure lifestyle and the impact it has on programs provided under the auspices of therapeutic recreation services. The Leisure Ability Model presented in Chapter 2 provides content for programs (functional intervention, leisure education, and recreation participation), as well as direction for future client outcomes, through the concept of leisure lifestyle.

- **Client Needs.** Because client needs drive all program development and implementation, the therapeutic recreation specialist must be aware of the characteristics of disabilities and illnesses, including the impact of secondary disabilities. Client "needs clusters" are important to consider as the therapeutic recreation specialist begins the program design process and they continue to be important as program implementation and evaluation occur. Each specialist must be knowledgeable about the implications of a range of diagnoses, prognoses, medical procedures and treatments, and medications. This often includes a working knowledge of medical terminology, anatomy, and pharmacology.

- **Activities.** It is a given that the therapeutic recreation specialist must be knowledgeable about a wide variety of activities, programs, and services in order to deliver the same to clients. This means knowing the rules to a variety of games, activities, and sports; understanding the requirements of nontraditional activities; and comprehending the reasons and motivations behind people's participation in activities. This also implies that the specialist be very familiar with different programming formats, from one-on-one sessions to small group discussions to round robin tournaments, in order to select the most appropriate format for client participation. All of the above implies a very strong understanding of the principles and uses of activity analysis and activity modification. The therapeutic recreation specialist must be able to design, deliver, and evaluate diverse programs, taking all these factors into consideration.

- **Facilitation Techniques.** The content of activities is important, but so too is the process by which the therapeutic recreation specialist delivers the activity. Facilitation (instructional, leadership, and counseling) techniques often are needed in order to deliver the program or activity in the most effective and efficient manner possible. The competent therapeutic recreation specialist is well versed in a variety of facilitation techniques. These include counseling techniques such as reality therapy, cognitive restructuring, reality orientation, remotivation, values clarification, milieu therapy, and active listening; instructional techniques such as demonstration, small group discussion, and hand-over-hand practice; and leadership techniques such as group correction, consensus building, and activity sequencing. Much like activity skills, the more competent the therapeutic recreation specialist is with a variety of facilitation techniques, the more likely the specialist will be able to rapidly and meaningfully facilitate change in client behavior. The therapeutic recreation specialist must be able to demonstrate extensive leadership skills while conducting various programs for diverse groups of clients.

Each of these four factors—activities, philosophy, client needs, and facilitation techniques—impacts which activities the specialist selects and how they are implemented for individuals or groups of clients. It is imperative that the therapeutic recreation specialist have a clear and thorough understanding and working knowledge of each of these four areas.

Factors Influencing Selection of Activities

Throughout this text, several ideas, concepts, and procedures for improving service delivery to clients have been explored. In fact, this text is singularly concerned with the improvement of therapeutic recreation services for the purposes of addressing client needs and producing client outcomes. However, because the process of activity selection is paramount to those two purposes, additional material is presented here to more clearly make the point.

The following discussion is divided among the three major factors that influence the selection and implementation of intervention activities: activity content and process, client characteristics, and resource factors. It should be noted that these factors overlap and all may affect an activity and its selection and implementation simultaneously. Examples are given to illuminate each concept.

Activity Content and Process

Activities are the method by which therapeutic recreation specialists help clients change their abilities, knowledge, and attitudes. Therefore, a clear understanding of their usefulness and purpose is needed. Nine factors concerning activity characteristics are presented.

Factor 1: *Activities must have a direct relationship to the client goal.* That is, activities must be able to contribute to the achievement of the goal. As mentioned early in this chapter, the A-B-C relationship must be logical, systematic, and reproducible. Specialists should select and implement only those activities that a thorough activity analysis demonstrates are useful in helping the client achieve his or her goals. Selecting an activity for client participation simply because it is known to the specialist, easy to implement, or currently popular is inadequate when the intention is to produce client outcomes. Each activity in which a client participates must be able to move the client in the desired direction.

For example, a client goal may be to improve leisure awareness. Having the client participate in activities such as cooperative games generally will not improve his or her leisure awareness, as this is not the intention of these trust-building activities. On the other hand, if the client goal is to improve trust with peers, then cooperative initiative games may be an excellent way for clients to achieve the stated goal. Intervention activities for client involvement should be selected based on the activity's ability to contribute to client behavior change.

Application

CLIENT GOAL: Improve leisure awareness

GOOD ACTIVITY SELECTION: A paper-and-pencil activity identifying personal leisure experiences and when they occur

POOR ACTIVITY SELECTION: Monopoly

Factor 2: *Functional intervention activities should focus on the ability of the activity to help the client reach his or her goals, rather than on the activity for activity's sake.* In other words, select activities with which the client is familiar or that are easily learned, so that the focus is on the attainment of outcomes rather than the participation requirements of the activity per se. At times clients may benefit from participating in known activities so that they do not have to learn new rules and strategies when that is not the designated purpose of their participation. For example, if clients are unfamiliar with computers, it may be detrimental to use logging on to the Internet as an activity to teach sequential skills. Too much time may be spent becoming familiar with the hardware and software, with little attention paid to learning and practicing sequencing skills. Similarly, the finished product of a birdhouse may not be as important as other functional intervention client outcomes such as the ability to follow sequential directions, improve fine motor control, or increase concentration. The role of the specialist is to help clients focus on the goals or purpose of the activities. At the same time, the specialist should consider the carryover value of the activity for the client's future lifestyle.

Application

CLIENT GOAL: Increased physical endurance

GOOD ACTIVITY SELECTION: Walking

POOR ACTIVITY SELECTION: Pilates

DISCUSSION: Using this factor, why is walking the better choice?

Factor 3: *Functional intervention and leisure education activities should have very predominant characteristics that are related to the problem, skill, or knowledge being addressed.* This speaks to the importance and power of activity analysis. Activities that have the strongest capability of producing outcomes are those that need to be selected for client participation. For example, if a client needs assistance with improving social skills, activities such as bingo, softball, and in-line skating are not likely to help this occur. A thorough activity analysis would find that interactional skills are not required to a great degree in these activities and that other activities that do have social skills as a primary component would serve as better selections for teaching clients social skills. Choosing activities that teach social skills directly (as with any other skill-improvement program) is the most direct and productive way to ensure skill attainment. Selecting activities that have a primary, rather than by-product, relationship will help ensure goal attainment. The therapeutic recreation specialist has a primary responsibility to conduct an activity analysis of several activities and select the one(s) that *best* address the client need.

Application

CLIENT GOAL: Increase dyad interaction

ACTIVITY SELECTION #1: Backgammon

ACTIVITY SELECTION #2: Video games

DISCUSSION: Which of the two selections best illustrates this factor and why?

Factor 4: *Activity characteristics are important considerations for the successful implementation of a program.* Several considerations must be reviewed carefully before final selection of an activity. Some important characteristics, such as social interaction patterns, are discovered through a complete and thorough activity analysis. Others, such as whether to provide an activity in a group or individual format, are less obvious but still important. The format of a program will depend on the staff/client ratio, available resources, intended outcomes, and so on. Often, however, it is easy to use one primary format to the exclusion of others, even when other formats may be more appropriate. Likewise, the content of the program is also crucial. The specialist's decision on whether to choose traditional versus nontraditional leisure activities is an important one. The specialist always must consider the factors that will help make the program the most successful and the most relevant to the client group to be served. For example, not every activity should be delivered in a small group discussion, paper-and-pencil exercise format. Most individuals process information at a higher level by being actively involved, rather than by simply listening. Children, especially those with behavior disorders, may benefit more from activities that actively engage them (e.g., scavenger hunts, board games, role plays) rather than those that constrain them to sit quietly and complete a worksheet.

Application

CLIENT TYPE: Adolescent, moderate developmental disability

CLIENT GOAL: To improve concentration

ACTIVITY SELECTION #1: Video game

ACTIVITY SELECTION #2: A square dance

ACTIVITY SELECTION #3: A crossword puzzle

DISCUSSION: Assume that each of the activities presented is related to the goal. Using the points raised in this factor, what concern or criticism might you have for each of the activity choices presented?

Factor 5: *Clients should be able to place an activity in some context in order for them to see it as useful and applicable to their overall rehabilitation or treatment outcomes.* While creativity and innovation are to be encouraged, activities that are extremely unfamiliar to the clients or are seen as outrageous by them may decrease in their value of participation. When clients see no purpose, meaning, or relevant outcome to an activity, their participation is hindered and their outcomes less likely. For example, teaching clients a rare Argentinean dance in order to promote flexibility and movement might be unique, intriguing, and fun. It is likely to be less successful in producing desired out-comes than other dances such as ballroom and line dancing, which are more familiar to more clients. Too often clients would focus on the uniqueness, intrigue, and fun, and not get to the real purpose of increasing flexibility and movement. This is not say-ing that Argentinean dance is unimportant. However, for most people, relevance is important to the learning process; a context in which to place the activity for future participation is necessary.

Application

CLIENT TYPE: 12-year-old male, spinal cord injury paraplegia

SETTING AND CONTEXT: Acute rehabilitation unit

CLIENT GOAL: To acquire new leisure skills

ACTIVITY SELECTION #1: Bridge

ACTIVITY SELECTION #2: Building remote-controlled model airplanes

ACTIVITY SELECTION #3: Designing and sewing clothes

DISCUSSION: Considering typical leisure patterns of adolescents, which activity choice is most likely to be appropriate? What is the rationale for not selecting the others?

Factor 6: *A single activity or session is not likely to produce a desired behavioral change.* Many of the skills, knowledge, and attitudes addressed by therapeutic recreation ser-vices are complex and are to replace deeply imbedded notions held by the client. Many long-held skill and knowledge deficits cannot be changed quickly. Thus, when selecting or designing activities the therapeutic recreation specialist needs to think about a sequence of activities within a session and over a series of sessions. This con-cept is discussed briefly in Chapter 5 and needs to be reiterated here. Skill building may need to occur over time, may need to be addressed through a variety of program formats, may need activities of progressing complexity and challenge, and may need a variety of media. Learning research shows that multimedia methods work best for most people. Seeing, hearing, touching, doing—all present different avenues that help clients learn more efficiently and effectively. Most people learn better through discovery and actual hands-on practice, including clients. For example, a client is more likely to become aware of his or her own leisure attitudes through a program series that uses visual cues, written or creative exercises, verbal discussion, and in-depth exploration than if any of these methods were used singularly in one individual activity. Likewise, a client is more likely to learn a new leisure skill when he or she can view a videotape of the skill, see and hear a personal demonstration by the instructor, and practice with the necessary equipment. Skill building, attitude change, and knowledge acquisition take time, practice, and mastery. The therapeutic recre-ation specialist needs to be familiar with teaching–learning concepts, such as learner readiness and repetition of content.

Application

CLIENT TYPE: Adult, single below-the-knee leg amputation with new prosthesis

CLIENT GOAL: To increase standing and walking endurance and balance

POSSIBLE ACTIVITIES: Darts, shuffleboard, Ping-Pong, ballroom dancing

DISCUSSION: How many sessions and of what length would you estimate it would take to achieve this goal? How would you sequence the activities to achieve this goal? Why use more than one activity?

Factor 7: *Consider the types of activities in which people will engage when they have choice.* Therapeutic recreation specialists should attempt to provide activities that are of interest and benefit to clients (rather than of interest to the therapeutic recreation specialist). This is especially true when working with leisure activity skills acquisition programs. Again, creativity in programming is prized but the end result must be a skill in which the client can gain proficiency and can engage in, in his or her own leisure time. Often this means looking to nontraditional leisure skill areas. In the past there was an overly heavy emphasis on sports skills, especially those for large competitive groups (using intergroup participation patterns). However, it is recognized that most clients, especially older adults, do not have opportunities or the desire to participate in large-group competitive sports. Whenever possible, client choice of activity should be taken into consideration, even in those activities in which functional intervention is the predominant goal. A primary consideration is a projection of the client's future lifestyle—in what activities will the person be involved in the future? The therapeutic recreation specialist should be familiar with nontraditional activities as well as more traditional activities.

Application

CLIENT TYPE: Female, age 73, cerebral vascular accident (CVA)

SETTING: Long-term care facility; permanent placement

CLIENT GOAL: To improve adjustment to disability and the facility

ACTIVITY SELECTION #1: Plant care

ACTIVITY SELECTION #2: Community folk dance club

DISCUSSION: Which of the two selections best illustrates this factor and why?

Factor 8: *Program to the client's outcomes and priorities.* In recent years, clients' length of stay in most health care and human service facilities has been shortened. In many agencies, this may mean that clients spend less than one week in treatment. This puts the emphasis of programs squarely on the outcomes and treatment priorities of the client, with little time to squander or waste in misdirected programs. Like all other disciplines, this means that therapeutic recreation specialists must focus very specifically on the targeted outcomes and maintain that focus throughout service provision. This, in turn, may mean some shifting in terms of the core priorities of the program. It may mean teaching clients about "processes" instead of specific content. As one example, the specialist may teach a client about a decision-making process of reviewing alternatives, weighing benefits and consequences, and selecting the option that has fewest costs and most benefits, rather than teaching the clients specifically how to make a leisure decision for next weekend. The former teaches a generic process that can be used for any decision; the latter focuses on one decision.

In another example, the therapeutic recreation specialist may function as a resource person and be the bridge to community programs that teach necessary skills.

Instead of teaching leisure skills within the facility, the specialist may help clients develop a cognitive understanding of the value of leisure participation and teach clients once they are discharged how to access community resources that teach leisure skills. The specialist's time is spent on teaching the client the *process* of finding community resources rather than teaching the *content* of finding one specific resource. Both of these examples show that the specialist must continue to focus on the actual needs of the clients, while considering all the constraints under which programs are implemented. With the reduction of staff-client contact hours comes the clear need to rethink and prioritize program direction.

Factor 9: *Client involvement in activities should be enjoyable (or at least not drudgery).* It is not possible or desirable for clients to be entertained, laughing, and frolicking every moment within therapeutic recreation programs. That is not the point. However, learning or behavior change best takes place under generally enjoyable conditions. The specialist has everything to gain if he or she can design programs that focus on outcomes while making the experience enjoyable for clients. This includes the environment in which activities take place, materials used for activities, and the general attitude of the staff. It also includes selecting activities that have the potential to be enjoyable. When rooms are dreary, materials old or worn, and staff sour or uninviting, the clients' motivation to participate fully will be decreased. Clients often reflect back what they see in staff and the surroundings. It is the responsibility of the therapeutic recreation specialist to ensure a proper environment for clients to participate fully in intervention activities.

Client Characteristics

Client characteristics are important in the selection of activities. As mentioned in the program design chapters, programs are designed or selected based on the unique mix of the community, agency, and client characteristics. Clients bring with them to the agency a background and history that is important to acknowledge, because it both affects them as individuals and affects the implementation of programs. Two principles apply.

Principle 1: *Clients' demographic characteristics such as gender, age, socioeconomic status, ethnicity, education level, religious orientation, and financial condition need to be considered while selecting or designing programs.* Consideration of these characteristics is important for several reasons. First, these characteristics will affect the background, history, and experiences of the clients. These in turn affect their preferences and future orientations, and of course, their leisure preferences and leisure orientations. As mentioned before, clients are more likely to participate willingly when they see relevance, importance, and timeliness in the services offered. Resistance to involvement or lack of motivation become less of a problem when services and programs are of interest and immediate value to the clients. The specialist who understands the demographic characteristics of clients entering the agency's services will be better prepared to design and implement more meaningful and targeted programs.

Application

Provide specific examples of how the following characteristics might influence activity selection:

    GENDER
    AGE

SOCIOECONOMIC STATUS
ETHNIC BACKGROUND
EDUCATIONAL LEVEL
RELIGIOUS ORIENTATION

Now combine several of these characteristics and come up with an activity that would be appropriate for the given treatment goal.

EXAMPLES:

Male, African American, age 27, electrical engineer

Treatment goal: increased ability to manage anger

Female, age 34, Hispanic, housewife and mother, Catholic

Treatment goal: increased ability to manage anger

Principle 2: *Clients should see obvious carryover value in activity participation.* Similar to the above, clients should be able to detect immediate relevance to their future in the programs that are offered. The therapeutic recreation specialist must be aware of future goals of the clients and focus on skills and knowledges that are both transferable and generalizable to the clients' future lifestyle. Skills that have limited applicability or limited use are of little value to most clients. This means that the specialist needs to know to what environment the client will be returning when he or she leaves the facility (if ever), and what that environment holds in terms of the individual's leisure lifestyle. Since the specialist would be hard pressed to be familiar with every community to which clients might return, one alternative is to teach clients about "processes" such as decision making, leisure planning, relaxation, stress management, and locating community leisure resources. This is more likely to help the client develop a satisfying leisure lifestyle than teaching isolated, individual skills, such as locating the zoo, planning for one weekend event, or making one leisure decision. If clients learn basic processes, then they are able to apply these processes in the future to any individual situation that they may encounter.

Application

CASE SITUATION: After one month of intensive rehabilitation in an acute rehabilitation facility, the client, a 72-year-old male who has received a total hip replacement, will be discharged to his condo in an active retirement community. He will be living alone and is expected to be ambulatory and independent in all activities of daily living (ADLs). What activities would you select for his leisure education program considering principle 2?

Resource Factors

Resources are also important considerations when selecting activities. Adequate staff and resources help keep the focus on productive, worthwhile programs. Three considerations for program selection center on resource factors.

Consideration 1: *The number of clients to be included in the activity and the number of staff conducting the session have implications for the degree of difficulty of the activity selected and the safety concerns.* This notion has immediate recognition for many "risk" activities, such as ropes courses, snowboarding, and kayaking. However, the principle is applicable to all activities regardless of "risk." Inadequate resources and staff result in several consequences: (1) degree of activity difficulty needs to be reduced, (2) less content will be covered or learned in the same amount of time, (3) more time is needed to reach the targeted goal(s), and (4) clients may be put at higher risk. The converse of each of these statements is true when adequate resources and staff are present. This means that the specialist has to take into account available resources before determining activities so that the program goes as planned, and the client reaches the intended destination safely. Inattention to these details will result in frustration for both the client and the staff. For example, the specialist cannot teach twenty clients to use a telephone book for locating community resources in a half hour when only one telephone book and one staff member is available. This is too much to ask from limited resources (telephone books and half-hour time limit) and staff (one specialist). If there were fewer clients, more telephone books, more staff, or more time, the targeted goal would likely be more easily reached. In planning the activity or program, the specialist must make an honest assessment of available resources and limitations. Often this is one of the reasons why selecting smaller goals that can be accomplished, given the client load and available resources, is a better choice than ambitious goals that are unattainable. The therapeutic recreation specialist is accountable for client outcomes, but usually has considerable latitude in selecting which goals to target.

Consideration 2: *For all programs, but especially for leisure education skill development programs, consider adequate time to learn, practice, and enjoy parts of the skill.* As mentioned earlier, most new learning, whether it is new knowledge, a new attitude, or a new skill, takes time. Clients who lack certain knowledge, have negative or unfocused attitudes, or lack specific skills will not master these skills quickly. This may depend to some degree on the clients' status. That is, if the client has little experience in learning new things, then the client will need more time, especially to learn the unfamiliar. Clients who have been active learners are more likely to pick up new knowledge, skills, and attitudes more quickly. In both cases though, the specialist needs to allow adequate time for learning, practice, and mastery. Clients who do not have some sense of mastery or competence will be less likely to follow up with the skill postdischarge. A client who is taught how to use a VCR, but who is not allowed to practice the skill until mastery, is less likely to be able to initiate this skill when in his or her home. If the goal is to change some aspect of the client's behavior, then therapeutic recreation specialists have to be able to teach them the skills to do so.

Consideration 3: *Too much equipment or lots of highly specialized equipment detracts from the focus on the treatment goal.* There is much to be said for adaptive equipment when it suits a purpose and fills a need. However, overuse of equipment can detract from the client's involvement and may not be available to the client in the future. A corollary is not overmodifying the rules of an activity. The further the activity or its equipment appears from the original, the less "normalized" the activity becomes. In some cases, such weight is given to the use of equipment for equipment's sake that the meaning and context of the activity are lost. In addition, equipment often needs repair, often has only a single purpose, gets lost or damaged, and is sometimes expensive.

Bowling ramps, used by individuals with physical limitations to head the bowling ball down the lane with momentum, can provide an example. First of all, not all bowling alleys have bowling ramps, which means the individual who was taught bowling only using the ramps would need to supply his or her own or not go bowling. To bowl, the individual then becomes responsible for purchasing the ramp and transporting the ramp to the alley. Second, there is no other logical purpose for a bowling ramp, so that while it can be used for bowling, it has no use for other leisure activities. For an individual to buy adaptive equipment for every leisure activity in which he or she participates, both money and storage space would be needed. Third, while the use of a bowling ramp may be essential for some, for others it may signal a certain degree of segregation and dependence. Reliance on adaptive aids when the person has the potential to develop the skill means unnecessary dependence on devices rather than skill development. While some adaptive equipment is required, it is in the best interest of most clients to develop skills as close as possible to those of their counterparts without disabilities. Full inclusion is more likely to occur when individuals with disabilities develop prerequisite skills.

Examples of Activity Selection

Two examples will be used to illustrate how the various factors mentioned in the earlier sections are implemented. These are generic examples and are not meant to represent any particular agency or group of individual clients.

Program A

In Program A, the therapeutic recreation specialist is not familiar with the concept of intervention to bring about client change. He understands how to implement individual activities and has adequate resources in the department. At this rehabilitation facility, the therapeutic recreation department offers a very diverse selection of activities. The therapeutic recreation specialist selects these activities as new ideas are discussed at conferences, through books checked out at the public library, or through a creative programming newsletter he receives. The activity calendar is filled with activities like card games, creative expression, community outings, exercise, entertainment groups, pet-facilitated therapy, and leisure skills groups. Most programs are designed so that all clients in the facility can attend all programs. The activities are well designed and run smoothly and successfully.

The client assessment consists mostly of an activity interest survey, identifying which leisure activities are of interest to the clients. The client group participates voluntarily in these activities, when clients have the energy or interest. Other staff members encourage the therapeutic recreation specialist to involve as many clients as possible in each activity. However, both the clients and treatment team members see the activities as nonessential, and often clients are taken from the therapeutic recreation programs to go to or rest for other more "essential" therapies.

Activity attendance and participation are recorded in the clients' charts, often with goals such as "improve attendance to three times per week" or "improve mobility." The specialist finds it difficult to write goals that are measurable, as well as to identify outcomes of client involvement in programs. The specialist also has difficulty in documenting quality improvement or effectiveness of services and makes statements such as "clients appear more mobile and involved" in his quarterly administrative report.

Although these are excellent recreation participation programs and may fill some purpose, they are not likely, *as designed,* to be intervention programs. That is, they are not likely to target some aspect of client behavior, knowledge, attitudes, or skills for change. And since they are not specifically designed to change specific client behavior, it is unlikely that they will. *Producing client outcomes begins with selecting the right activities that suit the purpose of changing a specific aspect of a client's behavior.* Unfortunately, the specialist, even though he produces quality programs, ignored the activity selection factors previously discussed in this chapter, and does not produce quality *intervention* programs.

Program B

In Program B, the therapeutic recreation specialist is familiar with the concept of intervention to bring about client change. She is an excellent programmer and has adequate resources in the therapeutic recreation department. At this rehabilitation facility, the programs include a very diverse selection of activities. The therapeutic recreation specialist selects these programs based on client needs. Since the clients are typically young adults with addictions, she knows they have certain characteristics and needs. For example, the group (in general) needs help with: (1) identifying and gaining skill in meaningful sober leisure activities; (2) finding leisure partners who will support sobriety (unlike many of their current friends); (3) locating resources in the community that offer sober leisure opportunities; (4) social and communication skills to interact with family and friends; and (5) fitness, exercise, and nutrition. *These needs are identified by reviewing the deficits common to individuals with addictions.*

Most programs are designed to address these needs. For example, typical program areas at this facility include: (1) leisure activity skills; (2) leisure partners; (3) leisure resources; (4) social and communication skills; and (5) fitness, exercise, and nutrition. The programs are well designed and run smoothly and successfully.

The client assessment consists of a series of questions that help identify which clients have which specific deficits. Clients then placed in those programs in which they have deficits or needs. Client involvement in all prescribed programs is expected. Other staff members understand the value of therapeutic recreation and its outcomes and see the service as essential to client success after discharge. Some of the above programs are co-led with therapists from other disciplines.

Client outcomes are the focus of client charting; some typical outcomes are: "client will name two community resources of interest for leisure participation post-discharge" and "client will locate two new sober leisure partners." The specialist does not have difficulty writing measurable goals, nor identifying outcomes of client involvement in programs. As a result, the specialist does not have difficulty documenting quality improvement or effectiveness of services and supplies quantitative research data for her quarterly administrative report.

These are excellent programs and may fill very specific purposes, that is, targeting a specific aspect of client behavior, knowledge, attitudes, or skills for change. And since they are specifically designed to change specific client behavior, it is likely that they will. *Producing client outcomes begins with selecting the right activities that suit the purpose of changing a specific aspect of a client's behavior.* Fortunately, the specialist produces quality programs selected based on the activity selection factors previously discussed in this chapter, and she produces quality *intervention* programs.

The stark contrast between Program A and Program B is meant to quickly illustrate the impact of activity selection. These factors cannot be ignored if the intent is to provide intervention programs. Intervention means not only quality programs, but also their ability to produce predictable, targeted outcomes. In Program A, activities are analyzed and selected based on their popularity, the specialist's expertise, or the ability of the activity to accommodate all clients in the facility. In Program B, activities are analyzed and selected based on their ability to contribute to valued and targeted client goals. Just as the overall programs are designed to meet two different types of goals (entertainment or enjoyment versus client needs or outcomes), activities also are selected for different reasons.

Selecting Activities Based on Client Goals

Let's look at the relationship between activities and client goals in two ways. First, start with a client goal (outcome) of "improve conversational abilities." The therapeutic recreation specialist determines there are three activity options that may be available for this purpose: (1) a small group discussion, with a one-to-one role play practicing telephone skills with the therapeutic recreation specialist; (2) an arts and crafts project in which clients are required to share supplies; and (3) a group trip to the mall to purchase personal toiletries that requires interaction between clients and salesclerks.

These activities likely will have varying degrees of success in helping clients "to improve conversational skills." An activity analysis conducted on each of the three activities would help the therapeutic recreation specialist determine that the role play is the most likely to address the client goal. This activity directly *teaches* the individuals in the small group the skills necessary to improve their conversational abilities using the telephone. During the role play, the specialist may use a variety of facilitation techniques, especially instructional techniques such as demonstration, repetition, and practice, to teach conversational skills.

The arts and crafts project was designed to force sharing by having a limited amount of supplies on hand, but this does not necessarily translate into improved conversational abilities of the clients. This may be a situation where clients can *practice* conversational skills, but only if they have been taught these skills prior to the arts and crafts activity. The activity itself probably will not *teach* them the necessary conversational skills. The role play is a better choice for teaching conversational abilities.

The value of the mall trip depends on how the leader designs the activity. If there is a large number of clients per an individual or few staff members, then likely these staff are more concerned about overall client safety than actual skill improvement. The smaller the number of clients per staff member, the more likely that instruction in conversational skills can take place, although to do this in public may not be in the best interests of the clients. A ratio of one client to one staff member may make the teaching–learning situation more appropriate, but will still require the staff member to be unobtrusive in the teaching of conversational skills. Therefore, the role play is the most natural choice, given the three choices, to *teach* conversational skills, although the design and delivery of an activity greatly affects its ability to address the client goal.

Selecting Client Goals Based on Activities

A second way to view activity selection is by looking directly at the actual activity first (versus the client goal). Let's look at three activities: volleyball, hand-held computer games, and hiking alone. A quick activity analysis of volleyball reveals that it is an intergroup activity that requires coordinated gross motor movements such as jumping and knowledge of rules and strategy. A quick analysis of hand-held computer games reveals that they are an extra-individual activity that requires fine motor control, vision, and quick hand-eye coordination. Hiking alone requires gross motor movements such as walking and minimal social, emotional, or intellectual skills.

Given the diversity and similarities, which of these activities might the specialist choose for the client goal of "to improve cooperation skills"? "To improve fine motor hand-eye coordination"? "To improve emotional control"? "To improve long-term memory"? "To improve physical endurance"?

Volleyball is the only one of the three activities mentioned that requires cooperation, with one team cooperating to compete against another team. Hand-held computer games is the activity most likely to improve fine motor hand-eye coordination. Hiking is probably the one to choose for endurance, in that it usually requires more continual activity from the participant than team sports like volleyball in which the action is shared among team members. Probably none of the above three activities should be chosen for goals of long-term memory or emotional control, as these are not basic elements of these activities. (An astute therapeutic recreation specialist skilled in activity modification could change these activities to meet other goals, but would need to be cautious that the original intent of the program and the client goal are both considered simultaneously.)

The point to be made is that nearly every activity can be designed and implemented to meet a client goal, but not every activity can meet every client goal. Specialists, through a thorough activity analysis and selection process, choose the best activity (usually in its most natural state) to meet the intended goal. All aspects of the activity as well as typical client characteristics must be examined.

For example, far too often clients have difficulty with an activity (or refuse to play) because the interactional skills required are too demanding or just not part of their current functional ability. For example, a client may know the activity skills necessary to play volleyball but avoids the game because he or she cannot handle the verbal interactions needed to be a team member. Another example might be expecting a child with behavioral disorders to bowl on a team, an activity that, in addition to complex physical skills, requires a delicate balance of cooperative and competitive skills, skills that he or she may not yet possess. A third example might be adolescents with developmental disability who have the physical and cognitive skills to eat at a restaurant but lack the social interaction skills expected in public places. The analysis of interactional requirements is, thus, critical for total comprehension of participation demands.

One of the most prominent skills of the therapeutic recreation specialist not held by individuals in other human service or health care disciplines is that of being able to analyze, select, and modify activities to meet specific client goals. Activity leadership can be learned by many. Selecting the right activity, based on a thorough analysis of the activity requirements and its potential to address client needs, is indeed an extraordinary skill. Providing intervention programs that bring about a desired change in client behavior is a skill unique to the therapeutic recreation professional.

Activity Resources

The therapeutic recreation specialist must be familiar with a wide range of activities, both nontraditional and traditional. There are three primary sources for locating information about activities: written materials, Internet sites, and professional conferences and workshops.

There are literally thousands of books containing activity ideas. Some are specific to therapeutic recreation intervention activities, such as those focused on leisure education activities, and some are more generalized materials, such as those on tennis or card games. University and public libraries have dozens of these resources. In addition, some publishing companies specifically focus on recreation, parks, and leisure literature, and often carry books on therapeutic recreation activities. Chapter 12 lists some of these companies.

More Internet sites on therapeutic recreation are being developed every day. Some represent certain organizations, some represent universities, and some represent commercial companies selling products. Many of them contain activity ideas and most are able to link professionals with common concerns through chat rooms or e-mail addresses. Chapter 12 lists some of the more popular sites.

Therapeutic recreation conferences and workshops are offered at the national, regional, state, and local levels. Very often several sessions on activity ideas and leadership are offered. The two professional organizations hold one or two major conferences per year, while some state or local groups offer several workshops annually. Automatic notices of upcoming meetings are sent to all paid members of an organization or to individuals on mailing lists (usually membership lists can be purchased). Information on the two professional organizations (National Therapeutic Recreation Society and American Therapeutic Recreation Association) is located in Chapter 12.

It is the responsibility of the professional to evaluate these resources for their particular use. It is appealing to "buy" the first flashy activity idea that comes along, hoping to put more spark into the therapeutic recreation program. However, the therapeutic recreation specialist must be a good consumer and be aware that not all products, services, or ideas are appropriate for all client groups. Having a solid understanding of intervention programming principles and client needs will guide the specialist in selecting and implementing sound program ideas.

Summary

The intent of this chapter is to help specialists understand that one of the most crucial decision-making points in the intervention process is the selection and implementation of appropriate activities. The therapeutic recreation specialist has to consider several factors to ensure that the right client is receiving the right service. The "right service" means that activities are selected or designed for a purpose (with the help of activity analysis), taking into consideration client needs and resource availability. The therapeutic recreation specialist must be aware of this complex mix in order to provide the best programs to meet client needs and produce client outcomes.

STUDENT EXERCISES

Discussion Questions

1. List five to ten reasons that proper selection of activities is important to therapeutic recreation. Bring your list and compare it with those of other students in class.

2. What is the relationship between activity selection and client outcomes?

3. Choose an activity and use Figure 7.2 to explain how it might be used as an intervention.

4. For each factor 1 through 9, provide an example of what might happen when the specialist pays attention to that factor and an example of what might happen when he or she does not.

5. Do the same for the client characteristics principles and the resource considerations.

Practice Test

1. Activities should be selected for client participation based on the activity's ability to:
   a. contribute to the achievement of client objectives.
   b. be led with minimal staff retraining.
   c. contribute to the development of social skills.
   d. be modified by the specialist.

2. What is the most important factor to consider in selecting activities for client intervention?
   a. They must meet the assessed needs of the clients.
   b. They are well-known by the specialist.
   c. They fit into the daily schedule.
   d. They are fun and enjoyable.

3. All of the following are rules for selecting activities for client involvement EXCEPT:
   a. has appropriate social interaction goals
   b. contributes to the achievement of objectives
   c. can be modified to meet client abilities
   d. staff has expertise or can get expertise to lead the activity

4. If activities are NOT selected based on their ability to help clients achieve their goals, what is likely to happen?
   a. Clients will report high satisfaction.
   b. Clients will improve their internal locus of control and perceived freedom.
   c. Clients will not attain their goals.
   d. Clients will not return to the facility.

5. Which of the following activities is most likely to help clients develop cooperative skills?
   a. bingo
   b. bird watching
   c. bowling
   d. cooking class

6. Given the goal statement below, which of the following is the most appropriate TR activity/program?

   Goal: To improve decision-making skills
   a. Leisure awareness discussion group
   b. Community out-trip planning session
   c. Social skills development group
   d. Backpacking skills course

7. Given the goal statement below, which of the following is the most appropriate TR activity/program?

   Goal: To increase social skills in dyad situations
   a. Friday night bingo club
   b. Big brother/big sister program
   c. Saturday night at the movies
   d. Annual soccer tournament

8. The activity of woodworking is most likely to address which of the following client goals?
   a. improve intergroup social interaction skills
   b. improve physical endurance
   c. improve stress-coping skills
   d. improve fine motor coordination

9. The activity of planning for weekend leisure involvement is most likely to address which of the following client goals?
   a. improve aggregate social skills
   b. improve problem-solving and decision-making skills
   c. improve short-term memory
   d. improve range of motion in upper extremities

10. The therapeutic recreation specialist needs to find an activity that improves the clients' short-term memory. Which activity would you suggest?
    a. "Vacation Memories"
    b. "Beatles Sing-Along"
    c. "Boogie Boards and You"
    d. "Concentration"

Answers: 1. a, 2. a, 3. a, 4. c, 5. d, 6. b, 7. b, 8. d, 9. b, 10. d

Chapter Activities

Activity Brainstorm

Have the class develop a list of 20 to 30 client goals. Each person is to select one goal and select or develop an intervention that directly addresses that goal for a specific group of clients. Compare activities with others who shared the same goal. How similar or dissimilar were your activities? Which is the best one to address that goal? Repeat at least once.

Activity Manuals I

Have the class develop a list of 20 to 30 client goals. Each person is to select one goal. Browse through available activity manuals (such as those available from Venture Publishing) and select one that directly addresses the goal for a specific group of clients. Compare activities with others who shared the same goal. How similar or dissimilar were your activities? What modifications were required? Which is the best one to address that goal? Repeat at least once.

Activity Manuals II

Use available activity manuals and have each person select one activity. If the activity description includes program or client goals, discard or cover them. Read through the activity description and get very familiar with the process and action of the activity. Write a client goal or outcome statement that would result from participation in this activity. Compare with others in class.

Activity Resources

Using your local community library, university library, publisher catalogs, the Internet, etc., create a list of at least 20 activity resources that would be used to develop ideas for activities with clients. Make one copy for each person in class and share your lists.

Professional Interview

Ask to shadow a therapeutic recreation specialist for a day when he or she will be implementing activities or programs with clients. Ahead of the sessions, ask what client goals will be addressed. Observe the activities and programs and note how the goals are addressed for each client. Discuss your observations with the specialist after the sessions are over.

CHAPTER 8

Treatment and Diagnostic Protocols

The preceding chapters of this text have presented various facets of therapeutic recreation program design including comprehensive program design (Chapter 4), specific program design (Chapter 5), activity analysis (Chapter 6), and activity selection (Chapter 7). Each of these tasks of program design requires that the specialist be systematic and logical, and use the best resources possible in order to improve the likelihood that the desired client outcomes will be reached. The next task in the Therapeutic Recreation Accountability Model, protocols, requires these same characteristics of each therapeutic recreation specialist. Figure 8.1 demonstrates the placement of protocols within the Therapeutic Recreation Accountability Model.

Before covering more detailed information, we would like to acknowledge that we have purposefully chosen to retain and use the term "protocols" although other terms are being introduced and used in the health care literature and in practice. Other terms that are gaining popularity are clinical guidelines, clinical pathways, critical pathways, and care maps, and like most new terms, there has not been deep consensus about their definitions. We will briefly define these terms for use in this chapter, introduce their centrality to standardization of practice, and then return to a fuller discussion of protocols within therapeutic recreation.

Protocols are documents that describe the "best practice" of a specific intervention as applied to a specific group of clients or client needs that have been standardized and result from recent research evidence, literature reviews, or professional consensus. Protocols document the purposeful procedures used to deliver intervention to clients, and provide a basis for evaluating the efficacy of those procedures. Once specific programs are in place, with proven strategies for planning and implementing intervention activities, protocols are developed that describe these programs. In essence, protocols describe the collective and proven strategies of specific interventions to bring about targeted behavioral change in clients.

In most cases, protocols address the intervention strategies of a single profession, such as therapeutic recreation. Protocols can be written either from the "program" side—treatment protocols—or from the "client" side—diagnostic protocols. Complete examples of each are presented later in this chapter. Two additional published therapeutic recreation protocols based on the best available research are available at the time of this writing: *Efficacy of Prescribed Therapeutic Recreation Protocols on Falls and Injuries in Nursing Home Residents with Dementia* (Buettner, 2001) and *American Thera-*

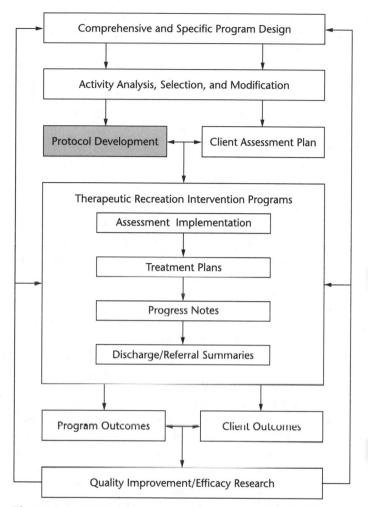

Figure 8.1 Protocol development component within the Therapeutic Recreation Accountability Model.

peutic Recreation Association Practice Guidelines for Treating Disturbing Behaviors (Buettner & Fitzsimmons, 2003).

The term clinical guideline often is used synonymously with protocol, and appears to be coming into favor in many health care arenas. Clinical practice guidelines are "systematically developed statements to assist practitioner and patient decisions about appropriate health care for specific clinical circumstances" (Institute of Medicine, 1990, as cited in National Guideline Clearinghouse, 2003). This definition is broad and covers a wide range of possibilities, from which screening and diagnostic tests physicians should order, to how to provide medical or surgical services, to how long patients should stay in the hospital based on the illnesses they have (Woolf, Grol, Hutchinson, Eccles, & Grimshaw, 1999). Rosoff (1994) noted that clinical practice guidelines are of two generic types: (a) quality enhancing, which call for more and better care, with higher levels of technology and competence, and (b) cost reducing, which represent an attempt to reduce the amount of care given to subsequently reduce health care costs. Two prominent Web sites for published clinical guidelines are the Agency for Healthcare Research and Quality (*www.ahrq.gov*) and the National Guideline Clearinghouse (*www.ngc.gov*). The majority of the time, clinical guidelines are identical to protocols (e.g., treatment of depression, diabetes, infertility, hypertension), but sometimes they are not (e.g., recommendations for annual breast examinations for certain groups of women). Hood (2001, 2003) expressed the tasks, concerns, and benefits of clinical practice guidelines in therapeutic recreation.

Clinical pathways, critical pathways, care maps, and **care tracks** are multidisciplinary plans of the best clinical practice for specified groups of clients with a particular diagnosis or within a diagnostic-related group (DRG) (e.g., mastectomy, acquired brain injury, total hip replacement, childbirth, postoperative pain management, decubitus ulcers) that aid in the coordination, delivery, and valuation of high-quality patient care. They are usually, but not always, agency specific. They are documents that contain information about the treatments that the client, based on his or her diagnostic-related group (DRG), receives from the multidisciplinary team, and usually contain a timeline from admission to discharge. Clinical pathways in many facilities are replacing individualized patient care plans because they document the typical patient's care requirements and expected outcomes that are consistent with the average length of stay for a particular DRG and are easily transferable to automated documentation systems (Springhouse Corporation, 2002).

Clinical pathways typically are set up in a grid, with the timeline across the top (i.e., admission, day 1, day 2, day 3, etc.) and the expected, customary interventions, events, and outcomes down the left-hand side. This form can then be used to document when a certain action is performed or a certain outcome reached in the client's treatment. For example, when an individual is admitted for a surgical removal of a cancerous tumor, certain actions are expected to happen to and be undertaken by the patient on certain days. The person will have certain diagnostic tests (e.g., blood analysis) upon admission, go NPO within 12 hours prior to surgery, receive anesthetic within a specified timeframe before and during surgery, be expected to ambulate a certain number of hours or days after surgery, etc. All of the actions are accepted as the normal routine of care for a patient with this condition, being treated by a multidisciplinary team. These events then become the grid upon which an individual's actions or reactions are recorded (Iyer & Camp, 1999). Clinical pathways set the standard for patient progress and provide a format to track this progress on an hourly and daily basis (Springhouse Corporation, 2002). In that way clinical pathways not only represent the best possible care but also immediately signal variances or unexpected events that need swift medical care (e.g., a spike in body temperature or pain while ambulating) (Iyer & Camp, 1999; Springhouse Corporation, 2002). There is some concern that clinical pathways do not lend themselves to individualized patient care (Meiner, 1999). Not all professionals agree that clinical pathways have this drawback (Coty, Davis, & Angell, 2000), and some project that clinical pathways can standardize care for 60 to 70 percent of patients (St. Vincent's Hospital, 2003). Clinical pathways have become a central part of case management (Springhouse Corporation, 2002).

Need for Standardization of Practice

Protocols or clinical guidelines provide a prime example of the connections among the components of the TRAM as well as emphasize the need for standardization within the field. In fact, they are a major factor in being able to standardize and produce predictable client outcomes. Protocols, when properly researched and validated, may provide the common basis for therapeutic recreation treatment procedures used across the country (Hood, 2001, 2003). They have the potential for standardizing practice procedures so that intervention received by clients in one part of the country is more similar to than different from treatment received in a different part of the country. These standardized frameworks provide the opportunity for specialists to use the "best practices" known to be effective with a certain diagnosis or group of diagnoses, and to use these best practices consistently.

Protocols are documents that specify the framework of treatment that is designed to meet a special purpose, be repeatable, and provide predictable outcomes. There are two kinds of protocols: treatment and diagnostic. Treatment protocols (also called intervention or program protocols) provide a framework for designing, delivering, and evaluating programs based on one area of care. Diagnostic or problem-based protocols provide a framework for how a specific group of individuals with a common "diagnosis" or "problem" is served by the therapeutic recreation program. Both kinds of protocols will be discussed more fully in a later section.

Examples of Potential Treatment or Intervention Protocols for Therapeutic Recreation:
Stress-coping, social skills, leisure awareness, community reintegration, leisure skills, community leisure resources, leisure planning skills, etc.

Examples of Potential Diagnostic or Problem-Based Protocols for Therapeutic Recreation:
Acquired brain injury, schizophrenia, Alzheimer's, substance abuse, post-traumatic stress disorder, at-risk youth, spinal cord injury, etc.

The purpose of protocols is to provide a defensible and consistent way of treating or serving client needs. They help improve the quality of care by specifying ahead of time the way in which clients can expect to be treated, given a certain condition or deficit. This improves the ability to select programs based on client need, deliver them in a dependable manner, and obtain reasonably consistent results from clients time after time. The benefits of predictable programming designed to correct or help some client deficit and that can deliver these outcomes repeatedly are wide ranging. Below are some of the professional benefits of protocols. They:

- Provide a reasonable guarantee to clients and others that programs are designed and delivered for a specific purpose
- Help specialists focus on meeting client needs rather than providing programs without purpose

- Ensure relative consistency of treatment from client to client, day to day, and specialist to specialist
- Group clients into programs based on need rather than convenience
- Help determine content of client assessments
- Provide direction for content of client documentation
- Aid in producing predictable client results from programs
- Allow better data collection about program efficacy in meeting the needs of clients
- Increase communication between therapeutic recreation specialists throughout the country, as well as with other disciplines
- Provide explanation of therapeutic recreation services to auditing groups such as third-party payers, accrediting bodies, and administrative policy makers

These benefits can be divided into areas regarding the program, the clients, therapeutic recreation specialists, and external (to therapeutic recreation) audiences. Benefits to the overall therapeutic recreation program result as close attention is paid to the planning, selecting, and designing of programs to meet a specific purpose or area of client need. This requires systematic forethought and diligence on the part of the therapeutic recreation specialist as well as a reasonable knowledge of research evidence and theories related to intervention. At present, some specialists select programs based on ease of delivery, a popular fad, or personal interest. As a result, client needs are not met and the desired outcomes are not obtained.

Benefits to clients stem from the systematic and purposeful planning that must take place with protocols. Clients can be reasonably assured that there is a specific purpose, implementation plan, and predicted outcomes that remain the focus of the program. Clients are more guaranteed that there is a desirable end result of participation in the program. For many clients this assurance results in increased motivation to participate actively in the programs described in the protocol.

Benefits to therapeutic recreation specialists are many. Knowing that programs have a defined purpose and targeted outcomes helps the specialist implement and evaluate them with more confidence and uniformity. Program delivery becomes standardized rather than haphazard. Protocols also are very useful for standardizing the terminology used. For example, standardized treatment protocols allow a specialist in New York to communicate with a specialist in Texas or Wisconsin about similar programs. And of course the benefits from that are tremendous—from improved opportunities to network, to better efficacy research opportunities, to national standards of care.

Another benefit then becomes the ability to better communicate and market therapeutic recreation services to outside constituents. These may include other disciplines, health care administrators, external accrediting bodies, and insurance companies. The ability to provide consistent, high-quality, and predictable client care is essential in this era of accountability. Shorter lengths of client stay support more predictable timelines for interventions and protocols allow therapeutic recreation specialists to be more responsive in this area. Protocols provide the documentation of common practices that moves the profession toward greater accountability.

Intervention/Treatment Protocols

Program protocols document the way in which specific services are delivered to clients. To date, the profession has yet to determine a singular method of documenting protocols, although Hood (2001) outlined the requirements of the U.S. National Library of Medicine and the American Psychiatric Association. More work, with a focus on research-based outcomes and professional consensus, is needed (Stumbo, 2003a, 2003b). Hood and Corruthers (2002) and Carruthers and Hood (2002) are notable efforts in this direction.

The National Therapeutic Recreation Society collected a number of diagnostic and treatment protocols from its membership in the late 1980s (NTRS, 1989). Sample diagnoses included in this document are spinal injury, head injury, arthritis, stroke, and Alzheimer's. Among the program protocols are detoxification, residential, and aftercare. Connolly and Keogh-Hoss (1991) and Knight and Johnson (1991) discussed protocols and provided examples in an ATRA publication, edited by Riley (1991). Kelland (1995) provided program protocols for approximately 25 therapeutic recreation programs as delivered by the staff at Alberta Hospital Edmonton in Canada. Examples of program titles included: community living, fitness, leisure education, planned group activity, and community social program.

Ferguson (1992) reported on the work of the American Therapeutic Recreation Association's Protocol Committee. Over the years, this committee developed a format for establishing both intervention and diagnostic protocols.

Format of Therapeutic Recreation Intervention Protocols

Ferguson (1992) provided a listing of components to be covered in intervention protocols. This listing includes:

- Program title
- General statement of purpose
- Description of program
- Appropriate presenting of client problems that may be addressed
- Referral criteria
- Contraindicated criteria
- Therapeutic recreation intervention activities or techniques employed
- Staff training/certification requirements
- Risk management considerations
- Outcomes expected
- Program evaluation
- Approval signature and date

The *program title* should reflect the content of the program, such as social skills training, stress management, leisure awareness, and leisure resources. The program's **statement of purpose** identifies the intent of the program. A sample statement of purpose for a social skills training protocol is: "To provide programs that improve the ability of the clients to interact with significant others, peers, and authority figures in a variety of settings and situations." The *program description* includes a brief overview of how the program will be offered to clients. An example might be: "Social skills are taught and practiced within a small group format, using the teach-demonstrate-practice format. Real-life scenarios selected by the participants are used for role-playing. Positive feedback and group correction strategies are used throughout the training." *Appropriate presenting problems* help identify which groups of clients are most likely to benefit from participation. Clients with greatest need are identified typically through an assessment or screening process. Following the social skills training example above, a typical statement for describing clients who may benefit from the program might include: "Clients who are aggressive, withdrawn, or otherwise lack expected adult social skills."

Referral criteria spell out how clients are referred into the program, whether that results from a physician's orders or from the case manager's general assessment. *Contraindicated criteria* are those that identify which groups of clients are known to not benefit from participation. For social skills training, for example, some individuals with extreme social inadequacies or hostilities may benefit from one-to-one training for a significant period of time before entering a small group program like the one mentioned above.

Therapeutic recreation activities and interventions are defined so that anyone reading the protocol can understand the basics of how the intervention will be implemented. This section would include more detailed descriptions about the programs being offered, and the ways in which they are to be implemented. Information might include the order in which material is presented, the major topics to be covered, and how the specialist will interact with the clients. *Staff training and certification* may be required for some programs, depending on the qualifications of the staff. The most widely known certifications are first aid and life saving, which are required for aquatic programs. Other training may be needed in specific facilitation techniques, such as reality therapy, biofeedback, or sensory stimulation. *Risk management* considerations are any actions that the specialist might take to reduce the potential liability in the delivery of a program. Examples of risk management might include counting number of supplies, such as scissors, before and at the end of a program, using safety devices in the transport of clients, and specifying staff/client ratios.

Expected outcomes are the end products of the service being delivered. These typically include the expected changes in the clients' behavior that relate back to the problems being addressed. Following the social skills example, typical outcomes may be improved initiation of conversations with peers, improved monitoring of nonverbal behavior, improved ability to assert oneself appropriately, and increased ability to control impulsive behaviors. The description of the *program evaluation* may include what and how evaluation of the attainment of outcomes is to be accomplished. It may include what data is to be collected and how it is to be monitored and fed back into the program planning process. The requirement of a *signature and date* is typical for most agency policies.

In combination, these descriptions provide an overview of how the program is to function for a specific category of client need and what results are to be expected for clients. These help define the standardization of care and establish the connections between purpose, process, and outcomes.

**Box 8.1   Sample Treatment/Intervention Protocol
for Therapeutic Recreation**

Protocol Outline for Recreation Therapy—Aftercare Services

I. Philosophy
   A. Statement of Services
      To provide opportunities for reorientation and adjustment to community environment for facilitating positive leisure time experiences and enhance activity in community lifestyle.

II. Program Content
   A. Special Events—Monthly
      Large group activities are organized to encourage social development, peer relationships, and a sense of trust and safety. Example: holiday events, such as Christmas dance, St. Patrick's Day party, or movies, field trips, guest speakers.
   B. Leisure Education Group
      This group meets monthly and facilitates individual needs around their leisure time. Problems or barriers are processed. Peer support occurs and linkage of similar interests. Continuation of individuals' awareness of the internal and external world and its relationship to their sobriety and leisure time needs.

III. Leisure Counseling
   A. Individual
      An individual can be referred to our staff for individual leisure counseling around specific issues to be worked on around their leisure time.

IV. Evaluation
   A. Follow-up Testing
      Every six months an individual will be contacted to come back in for a follow-up evaluation. This will give data on how this individual is doing and our effectiveness within Recreation Therapy Services.

Adapted from NTRS, 1989.

Box 8.1 provides an example from NTRS (1989) for aftercare services and Box 8.2 provides an example from Kelland (1995) for a leisure education program. Though these treatment protocols do not match the above criteria identically, they are valuable for initially outlining the structure of programs for patient involvement.

Diagnostic Protocols

Diagnostic protocols are of two types: one that focuses on specific diagnoses and one that focuses on related problem clusters. An example of a specific diagnosis protocol may be one for acquired brain injury. A client would have to have this diagnosis in

Box 8.2   Sample Treatment/Intervention Protocol for Therapeutic Recreation

Leisure Education Program

General Program Purpose: To develop the leisure-related skills, knowledge, and attitudes of clients to better meet their needs for leisure involvement.

Program Description: A small group or individual program that uses a multifaceted approach to examine the leisure interests, needs, barriers, and resources of clients and that, ultimately, assists clients to plan their leisure lifestyles.

Deficits the Program Might Address:
(a) Lack of knowledge and/or awareness of personal resources
(b) Lack of knowledge of or limited ability to use community resources
(c) Unsatisfied with use of free time
(d) Limited actual or perceived activity skills
(e) Limited leisure partners
(f) Barriers to leisure involvement

Facilitation Techniques:
(a) Individual intervention
(b) Discussion groups
(c) Experiential learning
(d) Lectures and other educational methods
(e) Pen-and-paper exercises
(f) Audiovisual aids
(g) Discussion/interpretation of assessment tools
(h) Guest speakers
(i) Values clarification exercises
(j) Personal contracting

Staff Responsibilities/Requirements:
(1) Recreation Therapist
    (a) Program Protocol
    (b) Program Plan
    (c) Risk Management Considerations
    (d) Program Evaluation
    (e) Program Observations
    (f) Program Delivery
(2) Recreation Therapy Assistant
    (a) Assist with program delivery

Expected Program Outcomes:
(a) Increase understanding and acceptance of leisure
(b) Increase awareness of attitudes toward leisure
(c) Increase awareness of barriers to leisure involvement
(d) Increase knowledge of methods to overcome barriers
(e) Increase awareness and use of personal leisure resources
(f) Increase awareness and use of community leisure resources
(g) Increase use of leisure time in a personal and rewarding manner

From Kelland, J. (Ed.). (1995). *Protocols for recreation therapy programs.* State College, PA: Venture Publishing, Inc., pp. 35–36. Reprinted with permission from Venture Publishing.

order to be considered for involvement in the protocol. A problem cluster protocol does not depend on diagnoses per se, but rather on major categories of symptoms or problems. An example of a problem cluster is confusion and disorientation, which many persons with various disabilities and illnesses may experience. Individuals with recent strokes, Alzheimer's disease, or other cognitive injuries would be included because of the commonality of the symptoms of confusion or disorientation.

While both intervention and diagnostic protocols focus on client problems, diagnostic protocols focus first and foremost on client deficits. A therapeutic recreation department may develop a wide range of diagnostic protocols based on the diversity of client disabilities and illnesses served by the department. Services provided to each client group would be known and planned based on client needs. Clients with specific diagnoses then would know what services they will receive from the therapeutic recreation department. For example, a woman with advanced metastatic breast cancer may expect a different protocol of treatment from that of a child with leukemia, due to their differing needs, even though they both have experienced cancer.

Format for Therapeutic Recreation Diagnostic Protocols

Ferguson (1992) reported a format for establishing diagnostic protocols, again as the result of work from the ATRA Protocol Committee, now called the Clinical Practice Guidelines Committee. Although in some areas the information to be included is similar to treatment protocols, diagnostic protocols serve a different purpose and have a different focus.

According to Ferguson (1992), the following are representative of information that needs to be included:

- Diagnostic grouping
- Specific diagnosis
- Identified problems
- Defining characteristics
- Related factors or etiologies
- Process criteria
- Outcome criteria

Diagnostic grouping includes information about the category in which the diagnosis falls. For example, the *Diagnostic and Statistical Manual IV-Revised (DSM-IV-R)* categorizes mental illnesses, such as depression or bipolar disorders, by category. *Specific diagnosis* further describes the illness, such as major depressive episode, within the category. *Identified problems* are those symptoms or results of the illness that are treatable by therapeutic recreation services. Symptoms for depression might include loss of appetite, inability to make decisions, scattered thoughts, low energy, or fatigue. *Defining characteristics* include those criteria that help identify the presence of the illness, either through objective or subjective means. Often these characteristics are determined by test scores or behavioral observations.

Related factors or etiologies include other diagnostic groupings that may be associated with the specific illness. For example, individuals with other diagnoses, such as Alzheimer's and substance abuse, may be likely to exhibit symptoms in this category, similar to depression, and need intervention within this protocol. *Process criteria* include those activities or techniques that will be used by the specialist within the intervention protocol. Examples may include naming specific programs, such as stress management or physical fitness, or may include naming techniques such as reality therapy, empowerment, or values clarification.

Outcome criteria identify the changes that can be expected within the client as a result of participation in the outlined intervention. Related quite closely to the *identified problems* (see above examples), outcome criteria include statements such as improved appetite, increased ability to make decisions, increased concentration on task at hand, and improved energy level. These outcomes are identified for the client group as a whole, and not individual clients per se.

Box 8.3 provides an example of a diagnostic protocol written by Connolly and Keogh-Hoss (1991) for dementia. Box 8.4 displays a problem-based protocol (NTRS, 1989), while Box 8.5 outlines a slightly different structure used by Knight and Johnson (1991). All three examples of diagnostic or problem-based protocols differ from the exact format by Ferguson (1992), but all contain the same basic elements. The protocols illustrate a framework from which to provide therapeutic recreation services to individuals with specific diagnoses or problems.

It is not important to memorize the content outline of either type of protocol. It is important to understand the rationale behind creation of the document and the benefits it affords both clients and professionals. A significant amount of effort must be expended by therapeutic recreation professionals in the very near future to create and validate evidence-based clinical practice guidelines.

Relationship of Protocols to Program Design, Client Assessment, and Client Outcomes

Protocols are among the most powerful and the most needed tools in the therapeutic recreation profession. Only in the last decade or so have therapeutic recreation specialists become active in developing protocols for intervention purposes; a significant amount of work remains to be done in this area. With growing understanding about this useful piece of the accountability system, professionals are working on developing standardized, predictable frameworks for program delivery.

What is now understood is that protocols provide the bridge between program design and specific client outcomes that result from client involvement in those programs. The placement of protocols on the Therapeutic Recreation Accountability Model between program design and client intervention is quite purposeful. This is to show that the link between these functions (program design, protocols, and outcomes) is a strong one.

Likewise, the placement of protocols adjacent to client assessment planning also is quite purposeful. Protocols identify general client deficits and general program content to address those deficits. Client assessments identify deficits of specific clients

---

Box 8.3   Sample Diagnostic Protocol for Therapeutic Recreation

Dementia/Alzheimer Type

1. *Diagnostic Grouping:* Dementia

2. *Specific Diagnosis:* Alzheimer Type

3. *Specific Problems* (Relevant to therapeutic recreation):
   (a) Loss of recent memory
   (b) Confusion/disorientation/forgetfulness
   (c) Loss of judgment and ability to abstract
   (d) Possible loss of skills in any life area

4. *Assessment Criteria:* Assess fine and gross motor skills, receptive and expressive communication skills, cognitive and social skills. Request results of SPECT & PET scans (look at brain activity) [can be done at any hospital with a radiology department] for confirmation of diagnosis.

5. *Overall Objectives:* To provide an assessment that allows for the development and implementation of an individualized treatment plan, provide information to others working with the individual, identify intact skills, identify lost skills, and focus on tasks that provide positive experiences.

6. *Etiology/Specific:* Progressive brain disorder with no known cure. Rate of progression unique to individual. Seven causes under investigation:
   (1) Genetic
   (2) Abnormal protein
   (3) Infectious agent-virus
   (4) Toxin-salts of aluminum
   (5) Blood flow reduction
   (6) Acetylcholine-biochemical disturbance
   (7) Elephant combination of above

7. *Process Criteria (Interventions):*
   (a) Communicate the need for activities and a consistent structured environment to all persons involved with care.
   (b) Review background information and assessments.
   (c) Conduct an assessment.
   (d) Develop an activity calendar listing time, place, and activity. Have calendars promptly posted and available for all.
   (e) Provide points of orientation in the environment (i.e., clocks, calendars, current magazines and newspapers). Reality Orientation classroom techniques not recommended.
   (f) Provide range of activities for physical, mental, and social stimulation. Activities for mental stimulation should focus on reminiscence, remote memory, and matching skills. Where possible incorporate discussion sessions on common past experiences. Mandatory to provide many opportunities and encourage verbalization.
   (g) Limit the size of a group on mental stimulation to no more than six persons. Ensure that other groups are of a manageable size. Four is the ideal number.
   (h) Provide a structured environment for activities (free of distraction with comfortable furniture and pleasant surroundings).

   (continued)

Box 8.3   *(continued)*

   (i) Monitor responses to activities at least weekly using the Activity Observation Checklist.

   (j) Should an individual exhibit inactivity, request an evaluation of the medication regimen with the prescribing physician, pharmacist, and other professionals.

   (k) Follow any behavior program developed for the individual. Institute behavior programs with the team if needed.

   (l) Follow established bowel and bladder routines.

  (m) Eliminate the use of restraints where possible.

   (n) Use cue-response-consequence when providing instruction for the extremely confused.

   (o) Provide opportunities for nutritious snacks with activities keeping special diets in mind.

8. *Outcome Criteria:*

   (a) Maintenance of skills in as many life skill areas as possible.

   (b) Responses to different types of activities measured with the Activity Observation Checklist.

   (c) Identification of the activities the individual can do.

   (d) Demonstration of a reduction in identified behavior problems.

   (e) Demonstration of a reduction in signs and symptoms of agitation and wandering, if present.

   (f) Identification of medications that sedate individuals and promote confusion, disorientation, and falling.

9. *Resources* (list bibliography for finding information)

10. *Cross-References*

11. *Signature and Titles of Committee Members*

From Riley, B. (Ed.). *Quality management: Applications for therapeutic recreation* (pp. 129–131). State College, PA: Venture Publishing. Reprinted with permission from Venture Publishing.

who would benefit from specific programs. In the assessment planning stage, the content of the assessment is matched with the content of the programs. In this way, similar purposes and content are linked between program design, protocols, and client assessment. Not surprisingly, when these processes align, client outcomes are more likely to be produced.

For example, in the protocol on Leisure Education (Kelland, 1995), the following client deficits were mentioned: (1) lack of knowledge and/or awareness of personal resources, (2) lack of knowledge of or limited ability to use community resources, (3) unsatisfied with use of free time, (4) limited actual or perceived activity skills, (5) limited leisure partners, and (6) barriers to leisure involvement. It is assumed that the client assessment would focus on measurement of these deficits for specific clients in order to place them into specific programs within the Leisure Education framework. When this is true, program design, protocols, client assessment, and outcomes are parallel, logical, and consistent.

Box 8.4   Sample Diagnostic Protocol for Therapeutic Recreation
Santa Clara Valley Medical Center
Recreation Therapy Department
Protocol for Head Injury and General Rehabilitation Services

I. Purpose

To provide therapeutic recreation intervention to inpatients on the Head Injury and General Rehabilitation Services Units. Structured programs will be used to maximize an individual's potential as it relates to his or her leisure lifestyle.

II. Evaluation

An initial therapeutic recreation assessment will be completed within five (5) working days of a patient's admission. If a patient is unable to give input on his or her current and premorbid leisure interests, the recreation therapist will seek input from the patient's family and/or friends. Based upon the patient's needs, interests, functional skills, and cognitive status, the recreation therapist will develop goals and objectives for an appropriate treatment plan.

III. Programming Levels Used by Recreation Therapy

(Levels were developed by Rancho Los Amigos Hospital in Downey, California, and revised by SCVMC to meet the needs of recreation therapy programming)

Level I: (Nonresponsive)

Goal: Prevent sensory deprivation

Recreation intervention will consist of bedside activities involving sensory stimulation. Patients at this stage need maximum assistance. Evaluation is ongoing.

Level II: (Generalized Response)

Goal: Attempt to heighten these responses and eventually channel them into meaningful activity

Recreation intervention will be individual therapy. Treatment time will need maximum to moderate assistance. Work on reality orientation. Evaluation is ongoing.

Level III: (Localized Response)

Goal: Abilities should be channeled into basic activity, to accomplish a task, to work on prefunctional skills

Recreation intervention will be individual and/or small group treatment. Quick, stimulating activities are best for this level. Modalities such as ball throwing and batting at balloons are good. Work on reality orientation. Simple, one-step commands that are verbal and/or demonstrated are good for this level. Introduce simple games that involve choice or matching. Evaluation is ongoing.

(continued)

Box 8.4   *(continued)*

Level IV: (Confused—Agitated)

Goal: To decrease agitation to enable the patient to begin to process external input, increase attention to the environment

Recreation intervention consists of individual and/or group treatment. Activities should be held in a structured environment. Focus on patient choice and simple gross motor activities. Modalities such as ball throwing that are automatic are best with patients at this level. Do not expect total participation at this level due to energy level and patient agitation. Work on relaxing techniques; use music. Evaluation is ongoing.

Level V: (Confused—Inappropriate)

Goal: Successful participation in tasks with assistance

Recreation intervention consists of individual and group activities. Focus on working on reality orientation, memory, and sequencing. The activities should be structured by decreasing the rate, complexity, or duration of the activity. Keep instructions minimal and consistent. Modalities such as games are beneficial (e.g., Fish, War, puzzles with few parts, ball games, memory games, and category tasks). Pet-assisted therapy and basic sports, such as swimming, can be introduced along with some special events. Evaluation is ongoing.

Level VI: (Confused—Appropriate)

Goal: Decreasing structure gradually toward minimal supervision in tasks

Recreation intervention consists of individual and group activities. Structure the activities to focus on increasing complexity and responsibility. Modalities should include higher-level table games, pet-assisted therapy, swimming, leisure education, community reorientation, special events, and social interaction skills. Evaluation is ongoing.

Level VII: (Automatic—Appropriate)

Goal: Development of skills for functioning in the home and in the community

Recreation intervention consists of individual and group activities. Activities should focus on time management, improving judgment, and increasing responsibility. Activities should involve opportunities for the patient to work on improving residual deficits including developing higher cognitive skills, such as insight, abstract reasoning, and memory. Patients should begin to assist with planning their program, setting goals, and learning how to use leisure time constructively. Family involvement is very important.

Modalities could include community reorientation outings, video games and programs, special events, swimming, simple sports, leisure education, and higher-level table games. Encourage patient to recognize his or her deficits. Evaluation is ongoing.

(continued)

Box 8.4   *(continued)*

Level VIII: (Purposeful—Appropriate)

Goal: Maximum involvement in home community setting within physical or cognitive deficits

Recreation intervention consists of individual and group activities. Focus on patient-initiated activities and developing aids to structure time. Work on decision-making skills. Involve in activity-planning process. Assist patient with developing community resource information. Modalities should include community integration, leisure education, swimming, special events, and social interaction skills. Patient and family involvement in planning for discharge is important. Referrals to community programs should be made. Discharge note completed.

Note 1: Due to the uniqueness of head trauma, it should be noted that the various levels of cognitive functioning will vary and therefore each patient's progression through the levels is unpredictable. Some levels will overlap or in some cases one level or more may be skipped. The patient's treatment plan is reviewed by the entire head injury treatment team. Goals and objectives are developed by the recreation therapist(s) in accordance with the rest of the team goals. Decisions involving recreation therapy intervention are the responsibility of the primary recreation therapist on the HI/GR service.

Note 2: Patient medical status may indicate that recreation therapy intervention may be inappropriate at a given time or level of cognitive functioning. The recreation therapist will note that the patient is "off program" and will reevaluate the patient's program potential every two weeks.

Adapted from NTRS, 1989, p. 43–45.

Trends in TR Protocol Development

The late 1980s and early 1990s brought therapeutic recreation into the era of protocol development. In the beginning, there was little consistency in format and little data-based substantiation of the protocols. Both of these are moving forward. Knight and Johnson (1991) and Ferguson (1992) were among the first credited with the development of a standardized format for both treatment protocols and diagnostic protocols. In the mid-1990s, three publications, Kelland (1995), Grote, Hasl, Krider, and Mortensen (1995), and Hood and Krinsky (1998) became available. More recent efforts include Buettner (2001) and Buettner and Fitzsimmons (2003). Other protocols or clinical guidelines are currently in development at the time of this writing.

The other welcome change is that the information contained in the protocols is more likely to be the result of considerable research. Some protocols are based on thorough literature reviews, receive considerable peer reviews from experts in the field, and are subjected to data-based research for evaluation purposes. It is expected that this level of scrutiny will improve greatly the quality and usability of the developed protocols. There is continued need for research- or data-based protocols in the field of therapeutic recreation.

A third change that is interesting to note is that more individuals, students and professionals alike, are involved in protocol development. In the last few years, more individuals have understood the need for and benefit from protocols and have

---

Box 8.5   Sample Diagnostic Protocol for Therapeutic Recreation

Therapeutic Recreation Protocol

1. Problem
   Impaired physical mobility of upper extremities

2. Defining Characteristics

   Subjective Data:
   - Client complains of fatigue, loss of sensation, or weakness in one or both upper extremities

   Objective Data:
   - Inability to move one or both upper extremities
   - Impaired grasp
   - Limited range of motion (ROM) of one or both extremities
   - Mechanical devices preventing full ROM
   - Inability to perform self-care activities
   - Neglect of one or both upper extremities
   - Partial or total loss of one or both upper extremities
   - Impaired coordination of upper limbs

3. Outcome Criteria (Client will . . .)
   - Maintain or increase mobility, strength, and endurance of upper limbs
   - Demonstrate skills necessary for participation in desired leisure activities
   - Demonstrate improved quality of purposeful movement of upper extremity

4. Process Criteria (TRS will . . .)
   Increase upper extremity mobility, strength, and endurance if possible by:
   - Using activities that assist prescribed ROM exercises
   - Emphasizing use of the affected side to reinforce use of affected arm
   - Placing objects to affected side to reinforce use of affected arm
   - Instructing use of unaffected arm to exercise affected arm

   Teach adaptive skills necessary for participation in activities of desired
       leisure lifestyle
   Teach safety precautions re: heat, cold, and sharp objects
   Provide reinforcement of collaborative team efforts in treatment

5. Related Factors/Etiologies:
   Trauma (e.g., fractures, crushing injuries, lacerations, amputation)
   Surgical procedures (e.g., joint replacement, reduction of fractions, removal
       of tumors, mastectomy)
   Systemic disease (e.g., multiple sclerosis, CVA, Guillain-Barré, rheumatoid
       arthritis, Parkinson's, lupus)

   From Riley, B. (1991). *Quality management: Application of therapeutic recreation* (pp. 146–147). State College, PA: Venture Publishing, Inc. Reprinted with permission from Venture Publishing.

---

worked on their development. It is likely that this work will continue and will provide the field with numerous protocols that will provide clients with more defined services. Again, it is hoped that these documents will result from sound research techniques and professional consensus.

Summary

Protocols play an important role in the standardization of therapeutic recreation practice. Both treatment protocols and diagnostic or problem-based protocols help provide the framework of what services benefit a specific group of clients. Protocols help provide consistency and predictability of service delivery. Although therapeutic recreation has come a long way in protocol development, much work in this area remains.

STUDENT EXERCISES

Discussion Questions

1. Why is standardization of practice important? How is this reconciled with individualization of patient care?

2. What are the similarities and differences between protocols, clinical guidelines, and clinical pathways? What is the purpose of each, and how does it help practice?

3. Why should protocols, clinical guidelines, and clinical pathways be based on "best practice" or the best available research evidence? Why does this strengthen or increase the confidence placed in the document?

4. Give two reasons why protocols, clinical guidelines, or clinical pathways might be seen as assets by third-party payers, clients, regulatory agencies, or other professionals.

5. Describe why protocols or clinical guidelines might be considered a "bridge" between program designs and client outcomes. What is their relationship to client assessment?

6. Describe at least two similarities and two differences between intervention protocols and diagnostic protocols.

7. List two areas of priority (from your experience) for therapeutic recreation intervention protocols and two areas of priority for diagnostic protocols.

8. How would your own education change if therapeutic recreation had research-based protocols or clinical guidelines for each area of service?

Practice Test

1. Which of the following statements about protocols is FALSE?
   a. Protocols and specific program designs are the same documents.
   b. Protocols are an important step in standardizing care for clients.
   c. Protocols should be based on research evidence that demonstrates the effectiveness and efficiency of select intervention strategies.
   d. Protocols can be based on either a set of interventions or a specific client group or problem.

2. Clinical pathways are documents that:
   a. diagnose the client's problems, needs, and deficits.
   b. track the progress of a particular client on a "map" of typical care.

    c. show clients and family members how to navigate the hospital corridors.

    d. analyze the contributions of each activity to help the client reach his or her goals.

3. Which of the following might be a topic for an intervention-based protocol in therapeutic recreation?

    a. dementia, Alzheimer's disease, and related cognitive disorders

    b. ambulation with assistive devices

    c. depression

    d. social interaction skills

4. Which of the following is a likely result of a profession having and adhering to protocols?

    a. More people are likely to enter the field.

    b. The specialist can provide better services that are more similar to others provided around the country.

    c. Clients will need to stay in treatment facilities longer to receive the full benefits of the protocol.

    d. Insurance companies are likely to deny payment for services in the protocol.

5. The best and most useful protocols are based on:

    a. research evidence.

    b. specialist opinion.

    c. tradition.

    d. program evaluation.

6. When a physician or case manager creates a master list of client deficits and develops a timeline of action focused on these deficits, this is called a:

    a. problem-oriented medical record.

    b. treatment protocol.

    c. case load of the physician on staff.

    d. critical pathway of client care.

7. What is the relationship between program protocols and client assessment?

    a. They both focus on similar content and impact client outcomes.

    b. They both must be tested through test-retest procedures.

    c. They both focus on the results of the activity analysis.

    d. There is no relationship between program protocols and client assessment.

8. Which of the following statements about therapeutic recreation protocols is TRUE?

    a. Protocols have been developed and validated for every area of service.

    b. There is no interest in developing protocols in the field.

    c. It is not possible to develop protocols for a profession such as therapeutic recreation.

    d. Much has been accomplished but much work remains.

9. Diagnostic protocols are based on client problems that:

    a. can only be helped through clinical pathways.

    b. the intervention will target.

    c. are likely not to present barriers in the future lifestyle of the individual.

    d. are secondary to the primary diagnosis.

10. Even if protocols are not available for specific therapeutic recreation interventions or client groups, each professional can improve his or her service delivery through:
    a. using research evidence and theory to develop programs.
    b. borrowing heavily from other disciplines' protocols.
    c. focusing on the leisure interests of clients.
    d. using a small group process.

Answers: 1. a, 2. b, 3. d, 4. b, 5. a, 6. d, 7. a, 8. d, 9. c, 10. a

Chapter Activities

Retrieving Clinical Practice Guidelines

Using the Internet, go to *www.ahrq.gov* and *www.ngc.gov.* Locate and print two clinical guidelines for populations or conditions in which you have interest. Bring them to class and share them with other students.

Therapeutic Recreation Clinical Guidelines

Locate copies of the newer clinical guidelines in therapeutic recreation (check *www.atra-tr.org* or *www.nrpa.org* and bring them to class. In what ways are they similar to and different from the protocols that are given as examples within this chapter?

Research-Based Programming

Using your library's electronic database or hard copies of journals, locate at least five research articles on a specific client group (e.g., at-risk youth, attention deficit disorder) and/or a specific intervention (e.g., social skills instruction, leisure education). List five findings that would guide program development and/or delivery in therapeutic recreation. Discuss in class how research evidence would aid intervention programs to achieve client outcomes.

REFERENCES

Buettner, L. L. (2001). *A research monograph: Efficacy of prescribed therapeutic recreation protocols on falls and injuries in nursing home residents with dementia.* Alexandria, VA: American Therapeutic Recreation Association.

Buettner, L., & Fitzsimmons, S. (2003). *American therapeutic recreation association practice guidelines for treating disturbing behaviors.* Alexandria, VA: American Therapeutic Recreation Association.

Carruthers, C., & Hood, C. D. (2002). Coping skills for individuals with alcoholism. *Therapeutic Recreation Journal, 36,* 154–171.

Connolly, P., & Keogh-Hoss, M. A. (1991). The development and use of intervention protocols in therapeutic recreation: Documenting field-based practices. In B. Riley (Ed.), *Quality management: Applications for therapeutic recreation* (pp. 117–136). State College, PA: Venture Publishing Company.

Coty, E. L., Davis, J. L., & Angell, L. (2000). *Documentation: The language of nursing.* Upper Saddle River, NJ: Prentice-Hall Health.

Ferguson, D. D. (1992). Problem identification and protocol usage in therapeutic recreation. In G. L. Hitzhusen, L. T. Jackson, and M. A. Birdsong (Eds.), *Global therapeutic recreation II.* Columbia, MO: Curators University of Missouri.

Grote, K., Hasl, M., Krider, R., & Mortensen, D. M. (1995). *Behavioral health protocols for recreational therapy.* Ravensdale, WA: Idyll Arbor.

Hood, C.D. (2001). Clinical practice guidelines—A decision-making tool for best practice? In N. J. Stumbo (Ed.), *Professional issues in therapeutic recreation: On competence and outcomes* (pp. 189–214). Champaign, IL: Sagamore Publishing Company.

Hood, C. D. (2003). Standardizing practice and outcomes through clinical practice guidelines: Recommendations for therapeutic recreation. In N. J. Stumbo (Ed.), *Client outcomes in therapeutic recreation* (pp. 151–166). State College, PA: Venture Publishing Company.

Hood, C. D., & Krinsky, A. (1998). *A protocol for therapeutic recreation services designed to address poor coping skills for clients in treatment for chemical dependency.* Monograph prepared for the American Therapeutic Recreation Association.

Hood, C. D., & Carruthers, C. (2002). The use of coping skills theory in therapeutic recreation services. *Therapeutic Recreation Journal, 36,* 137–153.

Institute of Medicine. (1990). *Clinical practice guidelines: Directions for a new program.* Washington, D.C.: National Academy Press.

Kelland, J. (Ed.). (1995). *Protocols for recreation therapy programs.* State College, PA: Venture Publishing Company.

Knight, L., & Johnson, D. (1991). Therapeutic recreation protocols: Client problem-centered approach. In B. Riley (Ed.), *Quality management: Applications for therapeutic recreation.* (pp. 137–150). State College, PA: Venture Publishing Company.

Meiner, S. E. (1999). Current approaches in charting. In S. E. Meiner (Ed.), *Nursing documentation: Legal focus across practice settings* (pp. 15–28). Thousand Oaks, CA: Sage Publications.

National Guideline Clearinghouse. (2003). *Inclusion criteria.* Retrieved January 5, 2003, from: *http://guideline.gov/STATIC/about.inclusion.asp?view=about.inclusion.*

National Therapeutic Recreation Society. (1989). *Protocols in therapeutic recreation.* Arlington, VA: National Recreation and Park Association.

Riley, B. (1991). *Quality management: Applications for therapeutic recreation.* State College, PA: Venture Publishing Company.

Rosoff, A. J. (1994). The role of clinical practice guidelines in health care reform. *Issue Brief, 1*(2). Retrieved January 5, 2003, from: *http://www.upenn.edu/ldi/issuebrief1_2.html.*

Springhouse Corporation. (2002). *Chart smart: The a-to-z guide to better nursing documentation.* Springhouse, PA: Author.

Stumbo, N. J. (2003a). The importance of evidence-based practice in therapeutic recreation. In N. J. Stumbo (Ed.), *Client outcomes in therapeutic recreation* (pp. 25–48). State College, PA: Venture Publishing Company.

Stumbo, N. J. (2003b). Outcomes, accountability, and therapeutic recreation. In N. J. Stumbo (Ed.), *Client outcomes in therapeutic recreation* (pp. 1–24). State College, PA: Venture Publishing Company.

St. Vincent's Hospital. (2003). What are clinical pathways? Retrieved January 5, 2003, from: *http://wwwsvh.stvincents.com.au/qi/Clin_pathways/cp_what.htm.*

Woolf, S. H., Grol, R., Hutchinson, A., Eccles, M., & Grimshaw, J. (1999). Clinical guidelines: Potential benefits, limitations, and harms of clinical guidelines. *British Medical Journal, 318,* 527–530.

CHAPTER 9

Client Assessment

Client assessment plays an important role in being able to provide therapeutic recreation intervention programs to individuals with disabilities and/or illnesses. One of assessment's major functions is to determine the needs, deficits, and strengths of individual clients in order to place them into the most appropriate programs that will, in turn, change the behavior that has been targeted as needing modification. Client assessment results provide the baseline from which to measure client change from participation or involvement in therapeutic recreation programs. The numerous interrelationships between programs, assessment, documentation, and outcomes are noted in the Therapeutic Recreation Accountability Model in Chapter 3. Figure 9.1 outlines two separate tasks related to client assessment. First is the assessment plan, which addresses the need to make sure that client assessment aligns with the programs to be offered to clients. Second is the assessment implementation task, which focuses on the actual delivery of the assessment to clients. This chapter will expand on both of these functions and will discuss systematic decisions to deliver the best possible assessments and intervention programs.

Purposes and Uses of Assessment

In this therapeutic recreation program text, the focus is on client assessment as a tool to gather baseline information for program placement, monitoring progress, and evaluating involvement. The remaining sections of this chapter will adhere to this focus. However, it should be noted that client assessment may serve other functions (Stumbo, 2002).

- Individual client information
  - Initial baseline assessment (treatment planning/program placement)
  - Monitoring progress (formative information)
  - Summarizing progress (summative information)
- Research on program efficacy and effectiveness
- Communication within and among disciplines
- Administrative requirements

Assessment also can be used for research purposes to determine the most effective and efficient interventions for clients or groups of clients. By comparing scores at the beginning and end of interventions, specialists can determine what outcomes were produced and for whom. Communication between and among disciplines is also

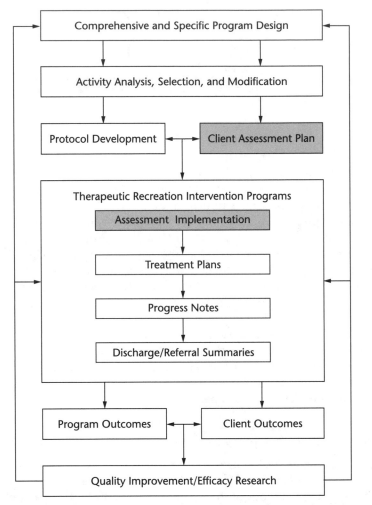

Figure 9.1 Assessment plan and assessment implementation components within the Therapeutic Recreation Accountability Model.

important. Just as measures of blood pressure and flexion communicate treatment goals and direction, so too should therapeutic recreation assessment measures. In addition, client assessment fulfills various administrative requirements, such as those by JCAHO, CARF, and CMS. In all, a high-quality assessment procedure is the cornerstone of many job functions of the therapeutic recreation specialist, not the least of which is program placement, monitoring, and evaluation.

Definition of Client Assessment

Client assessment is *the systematic process of gathering and analyzing selected information about an individual client and using the results for placement into a program(s) that is designed to reduce or eliminate the individual's problems or deficits with his or her leisure, and that* *enhances the individual's ability to independently function in leisure pursuits.* This definition has several key concepts. Assessment involves:

- Gathering selected pieces of data
- About an individual, involving a
- Systematic process of collecting, analyzing, and reporting that
- Results in the ability to make decisions for placement into therapeutic recreation programs that
- Have been designed to reduce or eliminate problems so that the
- Individual can independently function in his or her leisure

The above list implies that the specialist needs to make numerous decisions during the assessment planning and implementation process. For example, the specialist needs to decide *what information* is important for program placement; what *data collection technique(s)* (e.g., observations, interviews, etc.) is best to gather the information; how the *data will be interpreted* for decisions about program placement; and how the assessment and program placement *relate to the individual's future lifestyle.* Obviously, assessment decisions are closely parallel to programming decisions. The importance of these key concepts will be discussed more fully throughout the remainder of the chapter.

Principles of Therapeutic Recreation Client Assessment

Client assessment provides a strong link between clients and programs. Like activity analysis that provides a breakdown of *program* characteristics and capabilities, assessment provides a breakdown of *client* characteristics and capabilities. The interaction between these two types of analyses is vital if the intention is to deliver intervention programs that change some aspect of client behavior. Before more technical aspects of assessment are discussed, some basic principles of client assessment might be helpful so that a clearer rationale and understanding of the purpose of assessment is gained.

Principle 1: Client assessment is not just a piece of paper, but a systematic process of deciding what information is important to gather, how to collect the information, how to analyze the results, and what kinds of decisions are appropriate from the data gathered.

Client assessment really involves a series of decisions on the part of the specialist. What are the outcomes expected of programs? What are the typical needs of the clients? What is the best way to gather information from or about clients? How can results be analyzed for their fullest benefit? What types of program placement decisions should be and can be made from the results? How systematic are the processes used to make these decisions?

Client assessment is an ever-evolving process that allows clients to receive the maximum benefit from their involvement in therapeutic recreation programs. The decisions mentioned above are most likely to have positive impacts on the clients' outcomes when they are made systematically, logically, and with great care. One of the intents of this chapter is to discuss assessment as a systematic and deliberate process that requires a great deal of attention from the specialist. The difference between a good and a poor assessment could mean the difference between a client achieving or not achieving intended outcomes. Thus, valid and reliable assessment results are essential to the intervention delivery process.

Principle 2: There must be a logical connection between the assessment and programs delivered to clients.

One basic principle that provides the foundation for all assessment development and implementation is that *the content of the assessment must match the content of the program.* First of all, the program is built upon the need of the generic characteristics of clients. For example, individuals with depression as a group have these common characteristics: low energy, poor eating patterns, poor concentration, difficulty making decisions, sense of hopelessness, and loss of interest in daily events. Program offerings match these characteristics with areas of need, and specific programs are designed to meet these needs; for example, Fitness and Exercise, Nutrition and Foods, Decision Making and Planning, Concentration Skills, etc. The client assessment is then used to identify *specific, individual* client needs and must align with these specific program offerings. The client assessment would cover content related to fitness and exercise, nutrition and foods, decision making and planning, ability to concentrate, and the like.

If, on the other hand, the programs provided include Fitness and Exercise, Nutrition and Foods, Decision Making and Planning, and Concentration Skills, and the assessment content focuses on past leisure involvement, leisure interests, and family history, the assessment results will not provide adequate information to place clients into appropriate programs. The content of the assessment would not match the content of the programs. This principle is explored throughout the remainder of this chapter.

Box 9.1 shows examples of matched and mismatched assessment and program content. In the top example, the assessment content does not match the program content. In this case, it will be highly unlikely that the results of the assessment can be used systematically and logically for client placement into programs. The results will not lend themselves to making dependable, worthwhile decisions. In the bottom example, the assessment content does match the program content. Although there are other factors to consider, the results of an assessment that contain content matching that of programs is much more likely to help place clients into the programs they need. The match between assessment and program content is a basic element or building block to produce valid and reliable assessment results. This is true both for assessments that are "agency-specific" and assessments purchased from a commercial vendor. If the content of the assessment and that of the overall program do not match, the likelihood of correct placement into programs is minimized.

Principle 3: The assessment process must yield dependable and consistent results in order to be useful.

The assessment procedure must be standardized enough to be able to yield dependable and accurate results between specialists, between clients, between administrations, and over time. The tool and procedure need to be developed and tested to the point that all specialists administer the assessment in the same way—for example, using the same questions, the same phrasing, and the same probes, etc. If this is not

---

**Box 9.1   Examples of Assessment Content Matching
and Not Matching Program Content**

Poor Example: The content of the assessment does not match the content of the program.

Program Content	Assessment Content
Leisure Awareness	Personal history
Leisure attitudes	Leisure activity preferences
Self-awareness	Functional abilities
Leisure barriers	
Social Skills	
Conversational skills	
Assertiveness skills	
Problem-solving skills	
Leisure Resources	
Community resources	
Community Reintegration	

Better Example. The content of the assessment does match the content of the program.

Program Content	Assessment Content
Leisure Awareness	Leisure Awareness
Leisure attitudes	Leisure attitudes
Self-awareness	Self-awareness
Leisure barriers	Leisure barriers
Social Skills	Social Skills
Conversational skills	Conversational skills
Assertiveness skills	Assertiveness skills
Problem-solving skills	Problem-solving skills
Leisure Resources	Leisure Resources
Community resources	Community resources
Community Reintegration	Community Reintegration

From Stumbo, N. J. (1997). Issues and concerns in therapeutic recreation assessment. In D. Compton (Ed.), *Issues in therapeutic recreation: Toward the new millennium* (2nd ed., pp. 347–372). Champaign, IL: Sagamore Publishing, Inc. Reprinted with permission.

---

true, then differences in the clients' scores or results are likely due to the specialists and not the clients. In addition, each specialist also needs to be consistent when he or she administers the tool or procedure to clients. For example, if a specialist takes twenty minutes for one client's assessment and two hours for another, the differences in results may be a result of the administrations and not the clients. Last, we need to know that if the same assessment were given twice to the same client in a relatively short period of time, the results would be very similar.

Two concerns here are the actual tool (for example, the content, the number and types of questions, and the length) as well as the procedure used to administer the tool (for example, environment, interviewing, or observation skills). Both will be discussed more fully in the sections on validity and reliability, as well as the development of assessment protocols.

Principle 4: Client placement into programs should be based on assessment results, not just opinions or judgments of the specialist.

When client assessment is done poorly, the specialist is left with problematic, sketchy, or misleading results that tell very little about the clients' need for programs. Typically, then, the specialist has little choice but to "make it up as he or she goes" and place clients into programs without the benefit of systematic data and results. This total reliance on judgment is a concern because of the high likelihood of mistakes and inaccurate program placements. Errors of this nature almost guarantee that client outcomes will not be achieved, because clients are most likely placed in the wrong programs, ones that do not meet their needs. The next section provides a clear graphic depicting the possible effects of the client needs and program placement relationship.

Principle 5: The assessment process should provide baseline information from which a client's progression or regression as the result of participation in programs can be judged.

This principle, again, addresses the need for the assessment results to be valid and reliable for the intended purpose. The results of the assessment should offer enough precision about important client characteristics and needs that it not only directs decisions for appropriate program placement, but also for the evaluation of client outcome attainment at the end of program involvement. If the assessment results are specific enough about the areas deemed to be important, then they also can be used later to determine the effects of the program on the client. Where did the client start and what changes have occurred as the result of his or her involvement in the program?

These principles are similar to those that provide the basis for the Accountability Model (see Chapter 3). Each decision is connected to all other decisions. Each area of accountability is connected to all other areas of accountability. Each decision about client assessment is affected by and affects decisions about program delivery. These relationships are important because they highlight the interconnectedness of quality program delivery. No decision or action occurs without considering its impact on other decisions or actions. These concepts and others will be discussed throughout this chapter.

Relationship Between Client Assessment and Program Placement

A major requirement to establish validity and reliability is the alignment between the content of the programs offered and the content of the assessment. The importance of this match cannot be overstated. When the match exists, the potential for the right clients to receive the right services is maximized; when the match does not exist, the potential for clients to receive the wrong or unnecessary services is maximized. Paraphrasing a statement from Navar (1991), appropriate programs are provided when we can assure that the client is receiving the right program (including timing of delivery, the setting in which it occurs, and with the proper frequency, duration, and intensity) to meet his or her needs. One way to know that this happens is by properly

---

Box 9.2   Relationship Between Client Placement into Programs and Client Needs

	Client Placed into Program	Client Not Placed into Program
Client Needs Program	I. **Correct Decision** Client receives necessary services—likely to be intervention	II. **Incorrect Decision** Client does not receive necessary services—no or unnecessary program involvement
Client Does Not Need Program	III. **Incorrect Decision** Client receives unnecessary services—not likely to be intervention	IV. **Correct Decision** Client does not receive services—program involvement not necessary

From Stumbo, N. J. (1997). Issues and concerns in therapeutic recreation assessment. In D. Compton (Ed.), *Issues in therapeutic recreation: Toward the new millennium* (2nd ed., pp. 347–372). Champaign, IL: Sagamore Publishing, Inc. Reprinted with permission.

---

assessing clients' needs and placing them in the programs specifically designed to meet those needs. However, clients cannot be placed into the right programs unless the assessment contains the right information and is refined to the level that placement is accurate.

Box 9.2 explains the relationship between program placement and client needs (Stumbo, 1997). Down the left side are two decisions about whether the client does or does not need the program (based on assessment results). Across the top are the two decisions of whether a client is actually placed in the program or not (matching client needs with the potential of the program to meet those needs). The four quadrants provide a quick view of the potential results of assessment and placement decisions.

Quadrants I and IV indicate correct decisions—the match between the client needs (from assessment results) and their placement into programs is correct. Clients who need programs receive services, while clients with no need do not. In Quadrant II the assessment results indicate needed program involvement that is not realized—an incorrect decision. The end result is that clients involved with erroneous Quadrant II decisions do not receive the necessary services. Quadrant III also indicates faulty matches or decisions. In these cases, clients receive services that do not match their needs. Programs provided in Quadrant III are likely to be misdirected in that clients without need are involved in programs without clearly defined outcomes. Whether this is due to agency mandates, high staff/client ratios, client diversity or other reasons, the specialist often resorts to "smorgasbord" programming, often with the intent of keeping clients busy, without concrete goals for improving behavior. Or worse, the specialist creates misdirected goals and outcome statements that are not likely for a certain program, for example, stating that participation in bingo or volleyball will improve social skills (an activity analysis would show that although these programs require social skills, they do not teach social skills). Producing meaningful and reliable client outcomes is less likely in situations where clients with widely varying characteristics and needs are placed into one program or clients are placed into programs that have not been analyzed correctly for their potential to address client needs.

Let's use the example of surgery to make the utility of the quadrants apparent. In Quadrant I, the client needs and receives the right surgery (good decision!). In Quadrant IV, the client does not need surgery (based on assessment results) and therefore does not have it (also a good decision!). In these two cases, both the patient and the surgeon should be satisfied that the correct decisions were made. The client "placement," as a result of the systematic assessment decision, matched the client needs. Both the client and the surgeon would be less happy with decisions falling into Quadrants II and III. In Quadrant II, the patient needed surgery and did not receive it. Obviously, depending on the condition, this could be life-threatening. In Quadrant III, the patient did not need surgery but received it anyway (probably to keep the patient busy!). Few of us would tolerate medical services that did not meet a specific need or were performed without a clear need for services.

Similar parallels can be drawn for therapeutic recreation services. Part of being accountable for outcomes means providing the appropriate services to affect client behavior. Clearly, Quadrant I contains the "right" programs in which the "right" clients are placed. Therefore, it has the greatest likelihood to be outcome-based intervention—that is, produce measurable, predetermined client outcomes. It requires the mix of an appropriate assessment procedure that is able to produce valid and reliable assessment results and appropriate programs that are designed based on common client needs. This match is essential for correct client placement decisions.

A Second Approach

Figure 9.2 offers a convenient yet relatively simplistic view of the relationship between client needs and program placement. Figure 9.2 illustrates the decisions involved in assessment at a more in-depth level. To demonstrate how this relates to practice, an example of a person on an oncology unit is provided.

In Scenario A, the therapeutic recreation specialist focuses the client into correct programs that have been specifically designed to meet these needs. Since these areas are typical for persons with cancer, it is likely that several individuals at this facility also need these services, so they are likely to be group programs.

In Scenario B, the specialist did not link the person's program involvement with her needs. Although the institution might have fine programs, the client's assessment results do not indicate she needs work in these areas. This mismatch likely will result in no predictable or meaningful outcomes.

In Scenario C, the person was not placed into any programs, and this is also a placement error. When clients do not receive necessary therapeutic recreation services, they will not achieve outcomes in the needed areas.

This "real-life" example demonstrates, for the client, the importance of correct placement decisions and the consequences if they are not correct. It illustrates, in a different graphic, similar information to that in Box. 9.2.

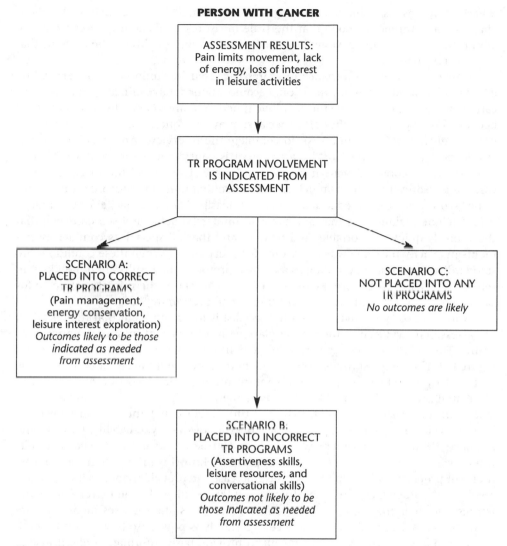

Figure 9.2 Examples of program placement decisions.

Assessment as a Measurement Tool

The job of the specialist is to select the best, most appropriate, and most useful assessment instruments and procedures to fit the purposes of the program and the needs of the client (Stumbo & Thompson, 1988). In order to select a commercial assessment or develop an agency-specific assessment, the specialist must be familiar with the measurement properties of validity, reliability, fairness, and practicality and usability. These properties revolve around two concepts of **error** and **confidence.**

Every score, including those received from therapeutic recreation assessments, has error in it. No score will be perfectly 100 percent valid and reliable. Scores vary for a variety of reasons, sometimes for logical, "intentional" reasons, such as the client changing an attitude or mood that the scale measures. The client's scores from one administration to another would be expected to change roughly in the amount that the attitude changes.

However, sometimes variance in scores is caused by "unintentional" error. The client may misunderstand the question, become fatigued, have difficulty in communicating an answer, or not have the cognitive function to answer validly. The room may become hot, noisy, or stuffy. The specialist may ask questions in different ways, become distracted, or be in a rush to complete the interview. Any condition that is "irrelevant" to the purpose of the assessment is considered error variance. That is, error causes a score to deviate from its "true" score. The goal of the specialist, in all cases, is to reduce the error as much as possible so that more of the score is the client's "true" score, and error is reduced as much as is feasible. For example, efforts to reduce error include making sure that questions are understandable and standardized; that the room is quiet, comfortable, and private; and that all specialists conduct assessments in exactly the same way every time for every client. When these conditions are standardized and tested according to a defined protocol, the results are more likely to reflect the client's true score. Reduction of error, in fact, is the primary rationale for assessment protocols and periodic staff training and retraining.

Another closely related goal of the specialist is to be confident that the results of the assessment will lead to the correct placement of the client into intervention programs. This relates to making correct placement decisions as shown in Box 9.2 and Figure 9.2. The specialist needs to be confident that the client's needs or deficits will be best met by placement into a certain intervention program(s). Confidence in this placement process is increased by using assessments that produce results as valid, reliable, fair, and usable as possible. This, in turn, means that the specialist needs to become well versed in the measurement properties of validity, reliability, fairness, and usability. While no assessment will produce 100 percent valid and reliable results (there will always be some degree of error present), knowing information about measurement properties will help the specialist increase the probability of producing better results and reducing chance error. In addition, knowledge of validity, reliability, and fairness will help the professional become a better consumer of assessments that are marketed for sale. In this case, knowledge certainly is power (to buy or not to buy).

The following discussions are meant to provide basic information about assessment instruments as measurement tools. Statistics and measurement books provide more in-depth information about testing and measurement properties, and interested readers should consult them for more advanced study.

Validity

Validity *of an assessment refers to the extent to which it meets its intended purpose. It concerns what the test measures and how well it does so.* Validity describes how well the assessment results match their intended purpose; that is, whether the assessment is measuring what the user thinks it is measuring. For example, the relationship between program content and assessment content has been noted earlier. This direct relationship is one basis for determining validity. The ability to produce valid results for the purpose of placing the right clients into the right programs is a concern for every client assessment process.

It should be noted, however, that an assessment does not possess "validity" for all purposes or all populations or all conditions. Each assessment has to be tested for a particular use and for a particular population. The more evidence is collected about the tool's results, the greater degree of validity the scores may represent. For example, to say the Leisure Diagnostic Battery (Witt & Ellis, 1989) is a "valid" tool because of its significant research history is incorrect. The Leisure Diagnostic Battery, as any other assessment or measurement tool, is likely to produce results that have some degree of validity for some uses and some populations (those purposes, conditions, and populations for which it has been tested and proven to perform well). If the Leisure Diagnostic Battery were to be used for a different purpose or for a different sample from which it was tested, it may produce results that may have a low or no degree of validity. Therefore, it is crucial for the specialist to become fully aware of the purpose, population, and testing procedures used in commercial assessments so that intelligent judgments about appropriateness can be made.

Another important factor is that there is no such entity as a universally valid assessment. Validity cannot be expressed in such absolutes; it is always the degree to which a tool produces valid results that is of concern to the professional. Sometimes a lower degree of validity would be acceptable, depending on the difficulty of measuring certain content or with certain people (such as decision-making skills with clients with brain injuries). Other times, only a very high degree of validity is warranted. Much depends on the significance of the decisions stemming from the assessment scores.

Types of Evidence of Validity.   "Describing validity as a unitary concept is a basic change in how validity is viewed. The former types of validity (content, criterion-related, and construct) are now simply considered to be convenient categories for accumulating evidence to support the validity of an interpretation" (Gronlund, 1993, p. 161). Three types of evidence of validity exist: content, criterion-related, and construct validity. Each has its own purpose and method of determining to what degree assessment results are valid.

Evidence of Content Validity *is the degree to which the assessment content covers a representative sample of the content in question.* Evidence of content validity asks the question of how representative the assessment is to the overall concept (e.g., leisure lifestyle) it is supposed to be measuring. Evidence of content validity of client assessment often is measured by the extent to which the content of the assessment matches the content of programs delivered. Content validity addresses the question "Would experts agree that the content of the assessment is representative of the content of the programs?" Box 9.1 is a demonstration of preliminary evidence of content validity of client assessments and intervention programs. Content validity is a concern for all client assessments in therapeutic recreation. It tends to be nonstatistical in nature and relies on the judgments of experts in the field to evaluate the representativeness of the assessment's content to the use for which it is intended.

Evidence of Criterion-Related Validity *concerns the inferences or predictions made from a person's assessment results in relation to some other variable called an independent* *criterion*. Most individuals have experience with tests such as the ACT or the SAT (predictor) to predict success in college (criterion).

There are two types of evidence of criterion-related validity: *concurrent* and *predictive* validity. Both concern the use of the term "prediction" to examine the relationship of two sets of scores; the difference lies in the amount of time elapsing between the two test occurrences and how many variables are in question. In **concurrent validity,** the desire is to predict one set of scores from another set of scores that are taken at the same or nearly the same time measuring the same variable. For example, a professional might want to be able to predict a client's score from one assessment covering social skills (Social Skills Assessment A) by knowing that person's results on a second assessment on social skills (Social Skills Assessment B). Testing could be completed with a sample or samples of clients to establish the concurrent validity of these two sets of assessment results from two different assessments covering approximately the same content or variable, taken at approximately the same time (concurrently).

Predictive validity is concerned with how accurately one set of scores measuring one variable predicts a second set of criterion scores measuring a second variable taken at some point in the future. For example, a specialist may want to know the degree to which future leisure satisfaction (criterion score—Leisure Satisfaction Test B) can be predicted from an assessment of leisure awareness immediately prior to discharge (predictor score—Leisure Awareness Test A). In this case, two variables are measured at different times to test their predictive relationship. Measuring the predictive validity of these variables assumes many things, such as the reliabilities of the predictor score results and the criterion score results, time elapsed between tests, and value of the criterion. Usually evidence of predictive validity of any two sets of scores will be low because of all the possible sources of error likely to be present. Most assessments used in therapeutic recreation do not report criterion-related validity because of the difficulties involved in tracking clients after discharge, as well as the measurement difficulties involved.

Measuring criterion-related validity involves calculating the relationship between the scores on a test (assessment) and the criterion measure, using a correlation coefficient (r). A correlation coefficient expresses the degree of relationship between two sets of scores. There is a perfect, positive relationship if the person who scores the highest on the first set of scores also scores highest on the criterion set, the person who scores second-best on the first set also scores second-highest on the criterion set, and so on throughout the sample. The correlation between the test scores would have a value of +1.00. If the person who scores highest on the first set scores lowest on the criterion set, and the person who scores second-highest on the first set scores second-lowest on the criterion set, and on throughout the sample, this is said to have a perfect, negative relationship. The correlation between the test scores would have a value of −1.00. A zero correlation indicates a complete absence of a systematic relationship (that is, a random relationship) and is indicated by a 0.

In most cases for therapeutic recreation, a positive relationship between two sets of scores is desired (as a person's performance on one set of scores goes up, it also goes up on another set of scores). Depending on the purpose and the tests, correlations between $r = +.40$ to $+.70$ are within the acceptable range. (Conversely, if negative correlations are sought—as one set of scores goes up, the other set goes down—r values of $-.40$ to $-.70$ are acceptable.)

Although there are different correlation coefficients that can be selected depending on the nature of the variables, the most frequently used correlation coefficient is the Pearson Product-Moment Correlation Coefficient. Most statistics books provide steps on how to calculate the correlation coefficient for a given set of data.

Evidence of Construct Validity *is important when an unobservable "trait" is being measured to assure that it is being measured adequately.* Psychological constructs that are familiar are anxiety, extroversion, depression, and intelligence. Constructs in therapeutic recreation may include leisure satisfaction, perceived freedom, leisure motivation, and quality of life. It is believed that these constructs exist, but they exist only to the degree that they can be described, organized, and tested.

The purpose of gathering evidence of construct validity is to accumulate support that the measurement tool truly is measuring the construct in question. Evidence of construct validity cannot be established with a single study on a single population; it is accomplished through statistical and rational means. For example, evidence for construct validity can be built through calculations of correlations with other tests, factor analysis (a statistical procedure), convergent and discriminant validity, and expert panel reviews of the test content. While it is not impossible, few therapeutic recreation assessments will utilize construct validity because the content is more focused on "behavior" (for example, leisure participation patterns, acquiring leisure partners, or social interaction skills) rather than "constructs" (such as leisure satisfaction or leisure motivation). Similarly, most therapeutic recreation programs focus on teaching behaviors rather than teaching constructs.

Gronlund (1993) noted that collecting various points of evidence about content, criterion-related, and construct validity is no longer considered a mutually exclusive set of tasks. Because validity is a unitary concept, all three types of evidence may help in inferring a greater degree of validity.

> *For some interpretations of test scores only one or two types of evidence may be critical, but an* ideal *validation would include evidence from all three categories. We are most likely to draw valid inferences from test scores when we have a full understanding of (1) the nature of the test content and the specifications that are used in developing the test, (2) the relation of the test scores to significant criterion measures, and (3) the nature of the psychological characteristic(s) or construct(s) being measured by the test. Although in many practical situations, the evidence falls short of this ideal, we should gather as much relevant evidence as is feasible within the constraints of the situation. (p. 161)*

Box 9.3 provides typical questions that are to be answered by the different types of validity evidence. Notice that in combination the answers would yield useful information about the degree to which the evidence supports that the test measures what it is intended to measure.

```
┌─────────────────────────────────────────────────────────────────────────┐
│                                                                           │
│  Box 9.3    Questions Answered by Approaches to Validation                │
│                                                                           │
│  Type of Evidence           Question to Be Addressed                      │
│                                                                           │
│  Content-related evidence   How adequately does the sample of assessment  │
│                             items represent the domain (totality) of the  │
│                             content to be measured?                       │
│                                                                           │
│  Criterion-related evidence How accurately does performance on the        │
│                             assessment predict future performance         │
│                             (predictive evidence) or estimate present     │
│                             performance (concurrent evidence) on some     │
│                             other valued measure called a criterion?      │
│                                                                           │
│  Construct-related evidence How well can performance on the assessment    │
│                             be explained in terms of psychological        │
│                             characteristics or constructs?                │
│  ─────────                                                                │
│  Adapted from Gronlund, 1993.                                             │
└─────────────────────────────────────────────────────────────────────────┘
```

Reliability

Reliability *refers to the estimate of the consistency of the assessment results.* Reliability of test results means that a sample of persons would receive relatively the same scores when reexamined on different occasions, with a different set of equal items, or under specific conditions. The concept of true and error scores plays prominently in reliability. The goal is to increase the measurement of true test score and reduce the amount of error score as much as is possible.

Since a person's absolute true score is difficult to determine, reliability actually represents an estimate of the effects of changing conditions on the person's score. Reliability of test scores can be estimated in three ways: *stability* measures (how stable is the instrument over time?); *equivalency* measures (how closely correlated are two or more forms of the same assessment?); and *internal consistency* measures (how closely are items on the assessment related?) The type(s) of reliability tested on an assessment depends upon the nature of the information needed and the purpose and intended use of the instrument.

Stability of test results is estimated through the use of test-retest correlation coefficients. Test-retest statistics calculate the relationship between scores obtained by a group of people on one administration of a test with their scores on a second administration of the same test. Obviously, time lapsing between administrations is important; too long a period (months, years) and the change in scores may fluctuate due to error, too short a period (hours, days) and the first administration is likely to affect the second administration. The time period between testings should always be reported in test manuals and protocols and should note any significant events that may have occurred to the sample group between administrations (such as other interventions or developmental growth).

Equivalent-form (also called parallel-form or alternative-form) reliability is used to estimate the consistency between two forms of a test that have similar but not the same items. This condition attempts to reduce some of the time-based errors

---

Box 9.4   Questions Addressed by Reliability Estimates

Type of Evidence	Question(s) to Be Addressed
Test-retest (Stability)	How stable is the instrument over a given period of time? To what degree are the two sets of scores alike?
Equivalent forms (Equivalency)	How closely related are scores from two or more forms of the same assessment? How consistent are scores from different forms of the assessment (i.e., different samples of items)?
Internal consistency	How closely related are items on a single assessment? How consistent are scores over different parts of the assessment?

Adapted from Stumbo, 2002.

---

inherent in the test-retest situation. One group is given one form during one administration and the second form during a subsequent administration. The reliability coefficient is calculated between scores of the two forms.

Most therapeutic recreation assessments do not have "identical" equivalent forms. Some assessments have short forms (say with 30 items) and long forms (with 60 items), but these are not truly equivalent forms. All things being equal, a test with more items will have a higher reliability, simply because it has more items to measure the content in question, and will show higher reliability coefficients.

Internal consistency is important for tests that only have one form and are intended to be given only one time. Internal consistency measures view each test as two halves that measure the same thing and can be compared with one another. Similar to the above situation, test length or number of assessment items has an effect on internal consistency coefficient results. Since the two halves contain fewer items than the entire test, reliability coefficients for internal consistency are typically smaller.

There are a number of statistical calculations devised to calculate internal consistency: (1) split-half reliability, (2) Kuder-Richardson's formula, and (3) Cronbach's alpha. Each method has advantages and disadvantages and is best used for certain types of tests. Those readers interested in more in-depth information are guided to psychological testing and statistics books.

Box 9.4 provides typical questions that address the three estimates of reliability: (a) stability, (b) equivalence, and (c) internal consistency. The answers to these questions would yield useful information about the particular type of consistency that each process yields.

A Special Case of Reliability

The above discussion of validity and reliability focuses mostly on paper-and-pencil assessments that are either conducted through interviews or are self-administered. Another method of gathering assessment information is through observations. One of the major sources of error in observations is the individual performing the observation. In these cases, the specialist becomes a source of error because observations require the judgment of the specialist on whether the behavior occurred or to what degree the behavior occurred. Obviously, the more concise and descriptive the behavioral observation tool, the less opportunity for rater error.

When using different observational rating systems, it should be noted that there is a difference between agreement and accuracy (Stumbo, 2002). Although two or more scorers (observers) may agree, their observations may not be accurate concerning what actually occurred. Agreement is the extent to which observers agree on their scores of behavior. Accuracy is the extent to which observations scored by an observer match those of a predetermined standard for the same data.

Salvia and Ysseldyke (1998) suggested four different calculations to determine **inter-rater reliability:** (a) simple agreement, (b) point-to-point agreement, (c) percentage of agreement for the occurrence of target behaviors, and (d) kappa index. Stumbo (2002) discussed the calculations of these four methods and noted that the progression of the four formulas attempts to take into account the difference between agreement and accuracy.

Manuals for observational assessments should always report inter-rater reliabilities, which method was used to calculate the reliabilities, and describe the circumstances under which they were obtained.

Fairness

Fairness in assessments is the reduction or elimination of undue bias or stereotypes (Kubiszyn & Borich, 1993). The intent is to reduce or eliminate any introduction of bias or stereotyping that might artificially lower an individual's or a subgroup's scores because of inflammatory, biased, or specialized information. For example, assessments that refer to all individuals as "he" or that contain stereotypes for specific age, racial, ethnic, or gender groups, may be seen detrimentally by individuals of these groups and others. Such negative or emotional reactions may introduce error into the person's or subgroup's scores.

Both assessment developers and users must be vigilant about screening for potential bias and unfair items and content. For assessment developers, these considerations should occur during the assessment development process (not after it is completed). Assessment documentation should include the process used to reduce or eliminate bias and increase fairness, such as using expert panels or searching for particular inflammatory words. For assessment users, these considerations should be one of the screens used to evaluate potential assessments before purchase. Assessments that contain biased items will produce error in the results.

Practicality and Usability

Practicality and usability *is a nonstatistical concept that is concerned with the practicality of the assessment.* Ward and Murray-Ward (1999) indicated that practicality involves two aspects: whether the assessment is "do-able" and whether it serves the purpose for which it was intended in ways better than other available assessments. Typical usability concerns include availability, cost, time for administration, scoring and interpretation, and amount of staff expertise needed. These are very real factors for many specialists to consider when deciding on whether to purchase a commercial assessment and/or to develop an agency-specific assessment. An assessment procedure that produces reasonably valid and reliable results is of little value if it is too expensive or time consuming, or requires inaccessible computer scoring.

Client assessments in therapeutic recreation must possess the ability to produce results that are valid for their intended purpose and that are consistent and usable. Confidence in the results increases and likelihood of error decreases with adequate research and documentation. In addition, the entire procedure, including cost and time resources, must fit the needs of both the client group and the therapeutic recreation department. Validity, reliability, fairness, and usability factors are equally important in determining how the assessment fits into the entire intervention process. Assessment plays a vital role in the ability of the specialist to produce client outcomes, and it must possess a reasonable degree of validity, reliability, fairness, and practicality to do so. Box 9.5 provides a list of questions pertinent to measurement concerns.

Client Assessment as a Systematic Process

Client assessment involves measurement of client needs, limitations, and abilities in order to place that client in the most logical programs that are designed to address those needs, limitations, and abilities. The fact that assessment involves measurement means that the assessment:

- Must be selected or developed based on a specific purpose
- Must be able to gather necessary information in a logical and straightforward way
- Must meet the needs of the clients and intent of the agency
- Must produce results that are valid and reliable to the greatest degree possible

Therefore, therapeutic recreation specialists must have an extensive understanding of measurement characteristics and the ability to apply those to the therapeutic recreation assessment process. Because there are so many decisions to be made surrounding client assessment, two models are introduced so that a greater level of detail can be presented. Both follow the Therapeutic Recreation Accountability Model presented in Chapter 3.

The first model discusses the assessment plan. This phase is important because decisions made here affect the type of assessment selected or developed, as well as how it will be implemented for clients. Figure 9.3 outlines the steps of the Assessment Plan Model. The Assessment Implementation Model addresses how the specialist interacts with the client while administering the assessment, as well as how results are used for decisions about client placement into programs. The Assessment Implementation Model is demonstrated in a later figure. In other past models (cf. Dunn, 1984), these two have been combined. They are separated here to underscore their importance to the entire intervention process.

Box 9.5   Questions Concerning Therapeutic Recreation Client Assessments

	Yes	No
Validity		
Does the content of the programs focus on the intended outcomes of participation?	____	____
Does the content of the assessment closely and equally match the content of the programs?	____	____
Do the assessment results integrate into other assessments completed by other therapists on staff?	____	____
Do the results or scores from the assessment determine placement into program (vs. best guess)?	____	____
Was the assessment built specifically to relate to the programs that are offered in TR?	____	____
Was the assessment built specifically for the type(s) of population served by the program?	____	____
Have other TR specialists been asked to review the content of the program vs. the assessment?	____	____
If criterion-referenced, is there an adequate relationship between the predictor and the criterion?	____	____
If construct, has there been sufficient evidence of measuring the construct of interest?	____	____
Did someone review a number of available assessments to select or develop the one used?	____	____
Are the directions clear, either to the client (self-administered) or to the specialist (other types)?	____	____
Is the vocabulary and level of difficulty appropriate for the clients?	____	____
Is the assessment administered when the client is calm, relaxed, and rested, able to do his or her best?	____	____
Reliability		
Is the assessment administered exactly the same way to every client? (e.g., prompts, time, etc.)?	____	____
Does the assessment have enough questions to cover the important parts of what is being measured?	____	____
Do clients who differ from one another (e.g., experience, knowledge) receive different scores?	____	____
Do the clients who receive similar scores get placed in the same programs as each other?	____	____
Have test-retest studies been conducted to see if the client receives the same score a second time?	____	____
Has the assessment been reviewed for possible bias against some groups (e.g., gender, culture)?	____	____
Is there a written and standardized protocol for administering the assessment to clients?	____	____

(continued)

Box 9.5   *(continued)*

	Yes	No
Is there a written and standardized protocol for scoring the assessment?	_____	_____
Is there a written and standardized protocol for interpreting the results or scores of the assessment?	_____	_____
Does the department have periodic training to ensure that all staff administer, score, and interpret the assessment in the same way?	_____	_____
Does the department have systematic training for interns to learn to conduct, score, and interpret assessments used within the department?	_____	_____
If the assessment is done by interview, are periodic checks for similar phrasing and probes conducted?	_____	_____
If the assessment is done by observation, are periodic checks for inter-rater reliability conducted?	_____	_____
Are all clients given the assessment when free from fatigue, health problems, and emotional strain?	_____	_____
Is the assessment environment free from noise and other distractions?	_____	_____

Fairness

	Yes	No
Does the assessment treat both genders equally?	_____	_____
Does the assessment treat all ages equally?	_____	_____
Does the assessment treat all cultural, racial, and ethnic groups equally?	_____	_____
Is the assessment free of stereotypical and biased language?	_____	_____
Is the assessment free of stereotypical and biased situations?	_____	_____

Usability

	Yes	No
Has the assessment been changed (and revalidated) if there has been a recent change in programs or clients?	_____	_____
Can the assessment be administered, scored, and interpreted in an efficient and effective manner?	_____	_____
Is the cost of the assessment (both purchase and staff time) sufficiently low?	_____	_____
Does the assessment meet JCAHO, CARF, or other external standards?	_____	_____
Does the assessment meet NTRS or ATRA professional standards of practice?	_____	_____
Does the assessment meet the agency's level of care and standards?	_____	_____

Adapted from Stumbo & Rickards, 1986.

The Assessment Planning Process

From the very first considerations weighed by the specialist, client assessment decisions must be systematic and logical. Because assessment is interrelated to program design, documentation, and client outcomes, the assessment planning process must consider the closely related decisions in these areas.

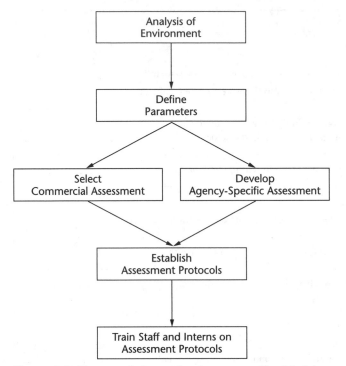

Figure 9.3 Therapeutic Recreation Assessment Plan Model.

The assessment planning process takes place during the initial conceptualization of a department or comprehensive program and is evaluated and updated periodically as the agency, clients, programs, or specialists change direction. The assessment planning process should provide a stable base of information from which decisions about the assessment implementation and client documentation phases are made (Stumbo & Rickards, 1986). Figure 9.3 outlines the five basic steps to the assessment planning process.

Analyze Environment

Agency Considerations.   Similar to the analysis stage used in program design, the specialist must consider agency characteristics as the first step in assessment planning. Since each agency is unique in its mission, services delivered, and clients served, these factors, among others, must be considered in order to select or develop and implement an assessment. Some sample questions about the agency that affect the client assessment choice might include:

- What is the mission of the agency? What are new areas of program focus?
- What are the unique features or characteristics of the agency?
- What standards impact the delivery of services at this agency?
- What client groups are served, and is this changing? What about length of stay?

- What types of assessments are used by other disciplines in the agency?
- What types of resources are available for the purposes of client assessment?

The answers to these questions should assist the therapeutic recreation specialist in viewing the impact of the agency's characteristics on client assessment. For example, several agencies might serve individuals with substance abuse problems. However, they may differ greatly in whether they primarily deliver inpatient, outpatient, or day treatment programs; whether their intent is detoxification, individual counseling, or group peer counseling; or whether they are accredited by the Joint Commission, as just a few examples. The agency's characteristics will impact greatly the assessment chosen by the therapeutic recreation specialist and other disciplines. The specialist must have a clear understanding of the nature, purpose, and operation of the sponsoring agency.

Client Considerations.   Similar to agency characteristics, the specialist must review the typical characteristics of clients or participants served by the agency. Reviewing the client characteristics helps the specialist to know the level of content appropriate for the assessment, as well as how to implement the assessment procedure. Below are some sample questions that the professional should answer in beginning to plan the client assessment:

- What are the typical client needs of this population group? Why are they being admitted or seen at this agency? How do their needs cluster?
- What are the typical limitations of this population group that would impact the assessment process? Describe their reading ability and comprehension level, their ability to make decisions regarding their treatment and their future, their level of independence, conversation ability, honesty, and so on.
- Where will the clients be going after discharge or leaving the agency? How will their future impact the current services received, and, in turn, how will this affect the assessment?

These types of questions point to the need for the specialist to know his or her clients' characteristics well. Certainly, whether clients can read, respond to questions, be honest, value their treatment process, and the like all impact the decisions made by the specialist regarding the content and process of the assessment. If clients cannot read, then self-administered assessments are not likely to be used. If clients cannot focus for sufficient periods of time, then assessments must be shortened or administered in parts. The professional must have a firm understanding of generic client abilities and limitations, and their impact on the assessment process.

Therapeutic Recreation Program Considerations.   One of the most important preliminary considerations is the types of programs offered within the therapeutic recreation department or agency. The specialist needs to consider both the content of the program (functional intervention, leisure education, or recreation participation), the level of program (beginner, intermediate, advanced), as well as the purpose of the program (functional improvement, skill building, creative expression, etc.). These are important because they affect the types and depth of questions asked in the assessment. If, for example, the program involves a sensory stimulation component for individuals with advanced Alzheimer's disease, the types and depth of information required on the assessment reflect this. For this example, due to the nature of the program, the assessment might involve observation (instead of interview) and several in-depth questions leading to the best sensory technique for each individual (response to touch, smell, sight, hearing, taste). Because programs and assessment are so intimately linked, considerable attention must be paid to this area.

Sample questions regarding the therapeutic recreation program might include the following:

- Which areas of the Leisure Ability Model are represented by the therapeutic recreation programs?
- What specific content is covered within the programs?
- At what level are the programs delivered? What is the intent of the program(s)?
- What client outcomes are expected as the result of participation in each of the therapeutic recreation programs?
- What type(s) of information are needed to determine whether a client could benefit from participation in the program?
- What standards affect therapeutic recreation programs that also may influence the client assessment tool or procedure?

As demonstrated in Box 9.1, the content of the assessment must match the content of the program. This means that the intent and delivery of the programs must be carefully outlined and considered so that this match may occur. This can be accomplished only when the programs and services to be provided to clients are specified in a significant degree of detail during comprehensive and specific program planning.

Staff and Resource Considerations.   Realistically, the availability of staff and other resources plays a large part in the selection and implementation of client assessments. Staff become a consideration in that their talents, strengths, and weaknesses affect how well they conduct client assessments. How well they understand related concepts, such as validity, reliability, data collection, interpretation of scores, and documentation impacts how they make assessment decisions. Continuing education and training focused on new developments in client assessment are important for staff on a regular basis, but their basic skill level does impact client assessment. Likewise, the amount and type of resources that the department or agency can devote to client assessment affects its quality and delivery. Questions that address some of these resource concerns include:

- What talents, strengths, and weaknesses do staff bring to the assessment process?
- In what areas are additional staff education and training necessary to improve the overall process of client assessment?
- What is the department or agency budget for assessment, especially if commercial assessments are to be purchased?
- How much time can be allotted per assessment, per specialist, per client?

- In what environments can the assessment be conducted? Is a quiet, safe, private space available to administer client assessments?

- How will assessment protocols be developed, and who will be responsible for ensuring that staff adhere to the protocols?

All of these factors point to the need for an honest appraisal of department and agency resources that can be devoted to the assessment process. If few resources are available, then the assessment must be tailored for this; if many resources are available, then a more comprehensive assessment might be appropriate. When making this appraisal, the decision makers will want to consider the importance of client assessment to proper program placement and the achievement of client outcomes.

Define Parameters

After the agency, client, therapeutic recreation program, and staff and resource considerations have been examined, the next step is to define more closely what the assessment is expected to do. Three basic areas need to be examined: function, content, and implementation strategy.

Determining the Function of the Assessment.   First, the specialist needs to decide what *function* the assessment will serve, from one of four options. Client assessments may focus on (1) basic screening, (2) identifying the problem(s), (3) narrowing the problem(s), and/or (4) reassessing or monitoring client progress (Dunn, 1984). To describe these four functions, let's use the example of social skills. In *initial screening*, the specialist may ask very basic questions, such as "Does the client have adequate social skills?" The answer (either yes or no) then primarily divides clients into two options—yes, the person has adequate skills and does not need social skills training, or no, the person lacks adequate skills and does need social skills training. The yes response means that the client is not placed into social skills programs, and the no response means that the client may receive more intensive social skills evaluation and programs.

When *identifying problems*, the assessment may be used to determine a more detailed level of information about the client's abilities. For example, a question used to identify problems may be "Does the client have adequate conversational skills with peers?" If the answer is yes, then the client does not receive further training in that area. If the answer is no, then the client receives further training on conversational skills with peers.

In a similar vein, when further *defining problems*, more specific information is gathered. Using the same social skills situation, a "narrowing" question may be "If the client has difficulty with conversing with peers, where does the difficulty lie?" Answer options here might include (1) approaching peers, (2) initiating the conversation, (3) responding to others' conversation, or (4) using appropriate body language, gestures, and proximity. The specialist observes the client, and places him or her into programs that address the deficiencies as noted in the assessment. It is easy to "diagnose" any difficulties when they have been adequately defined ahead of time—with

---

Box 9.6   Examples of Client Assessment Functions and Related Items

Assessment Function	Purpose	Example of Items for Social Skills Training Programs
Basic Screening	Need for services?	Does the client have adequate social skills?
Identifying Problem	Which services?	Does the client have adequate conversational skills with peers?
Defining Problem	Specific training needed?	If the client has difficulty conversing with peers, where does the difficulty lie?
Reassessing or Monitoring	Progress made toward outcome?	What difficulties have been improved or remedied by participation in the social skills program?

---

the assurance that they match the program content of the social skills training program. The client with difficulties is placed into exact programs that address his or her needs or deficits.

The last function served by assessment includes *reassessing or monitoring client progress.* In this capacity, an assessment that produces valid and reliable results can be used to reassess the changes that may have occurred in the client as a result of participation in the programs. Using the conversational ability example above, a similar question focuses on the current status of the client. The question might read "What difficulties have been improved or remedied by participation in the social skills program?" Answers may include: (1) approaching peers; (2) initiating the conversation; (3) responding to others' conversation; (4) using appropriate body language, gestures, and proximity. When compared with the original, baseline assessment information, the reassessment information provides an analysis of the difference between preprogram and postprogram client skills. When adequately defined, reassessment should highlight which skills were improved as the result of program involvement and which skills were not. Box 9.6 provides a visual overview of these four functions.

Determining the Assessment Content.   There is probably no more important step in the assessment planning process than to review closely the content of the assessment. As seen in Box 9.1, the content of the assessment must align with the content of the programs offered. This is crucial because if the assessment content is not aligned with the programs, the assessment will contain questions that do not lead to program placement. However, this does require the specialist to conduct an in-depth analysis of therapeutic recreation program offerings. For example, if the major programs offered include functional intervention, leisure resources, and social skills, the assessment must ask the specific questions related to these content areas to know whether clients should or should not be placed in those programs. On the other hand, if these programs are offered and the assessment contains questions about leisure history, leisure interests, and leisure skills, then the information gained from the assessment will not be useful in placing the right clients in the right programs.

In addition, the specialist must determine at what level the assessment questions should be asked. Leisure resources provides a clear example. If the leisure resource program teaches utilization (teaching clients how to utilize resources instead of just basic knowledge) of community leisure resources, then the assessment also should focus on the utilization level of content (instead of knowledge). For example, a good leisure resource *utilization* question would be: "Describe how you would find out what time the art museum opens." The client is expected to explain the steps in finding out what time the art museum opens. (While asking the client to actually demonstrate the behavior would be even better, more time is involved.) A leisure resource *knowledge* question may be: "What time does the library open?" The knowledge question does not ask the client to explain or demonstrate the *skill of utilizing* the knowledge and does not align with the program that teaches at the utilization level. The content and level of each assessment question should relate directly to some aspect of the therapeutic recreation programs offered. Again, it is important to match the content and intent of the assessment questions with the content and intent of the therapeutic recreation services.

Determining an Implementation Strategy.   In addition to function and content, the third parameter that needs to be determined is the implementation strategy. There are four basic strategies for gaining client assessment information: interviews, observations, self-administered questionnaires, and records reviews. There is considerable interrelationship between the content of the assessment and the strategy for collecting the information. If the specialist desires in-depth information about the client's knowledge or perceptions, then interviews are appropriate. If the client's behavior is the focus, then observations are in order. If it may be necessary for the client to complete the assessment independently or at another time, a self-administered questionnaire may be appropriate. Records reviews are important when the information needed is already stored elsewhere (for example, in nursing's assessment), when the client is unavailable or incapable of completing an assessment interview, or as a confirmation of information gathered in an interview or observation.

In turn, the implementation strategy affects the way in which information is gathered and the types of questions asked. For example, one of the primary advantages to an interview is the ability to ask open-ended questions, probe for clarification, and interact with the client. Therefore, it is best to use open-ended questions ("Tell me about how you might spend a Saturday with no obligations"), use follow-up questions, and observe the client during the interview. The content and form of the questions should match the reason for selecting the implementation strategy.

Information gathered about the function and content of the assessment, as well as the implementation strategy, provides the basis for the remaining assessment selection decisions. Considerable attention needs to be paid to these three areas because they provide the foundation for decisions about whether to select a commercially available assessment or to develop an agency-specific assessment. The next two sections look at these two options.

Select a Commercial Assessment

After the assessment function, content, and implementation strategy have been determined, one option is to review and select a commercially available assessment for use. Appendix C contains a list of assessments sold to therapeutic recreation specialists. Several assessments have been developed and are available nationally for sale. Two examples are the Leisure Diagnostic Battery (Witt & Ellis, 1987) and the Leisure Competence Measure (Kloseck, Crilly, Ellis, & Lammers, 1996). These assessments are examples of highly developed and validated assessments that are available from commercial vendors. Portions of the two assessments are provided later in this chapter.

Caution is needed to make sure that the assessment selected for purchase fits the criteria mentioned previously. Though it may be tempting to purchase or use a commercial assessment because of its packaging, marketing, or availability, a systematic evaluation must occur to make sure that it fits the intended purpose and can produce reliable results for the clients on whom it will be used. The above questions related to agency, clients, program, and resource considerations also apply to commercial assessments. These should be answered to the satisfaction of the therapeutic recreation specialist. Below are some additional questions to determine whether a commercial assessment is appropriate for use in a specific agency (see Dunn, 1989). These are important factors to consider *prior* to purchase.

- Is the population on which it was validated or tested the same as the clientele within the agency?
- Was the assessment developed upon a solid foundation of therapeutic recreation content that would match the programs within the specific agency intended for use?
- How closely does the content of the assessment match the content of the programs offered at the specific agency?
- What evidence is given for validity (content, criterion-related, and/or construct) depending on the purpose of the test?
- What testing was done to make sure the assessment produces reliable results over time, between clients, and/or between administrations?
- How extensive is the protocol for administration of the assessment?
- How extensive is the protocol for analysis and scoring of the assessment?
- How extensive is the protocol for interpretation of scores?
- How will the scores produced enable placement of clients into the programs of interest?
- How well does the assessment address cultural, racial, ethnic, and gender concerns of clients?
- To what degree is the assessment free of stereotypes and bias?
- Do the time, money, and resources required to conduct the assessment with individual clients match those available at the specific agency?

These questions and others need to be answered prior to the decision to purchase and use a commercial tool. Choosing a poorly developed tool or one that does not fit

---

Box 9.7   Dos and Don'ts of Using Commercial Client Assessments

Do use a commercial assessment that:

- is based on content matching that of the agency's therapeutic recreation programs.

- has been validated on a population similar to clients served by the agency.

- has had appropriate tests conducted for the type of assessment it is. (For example, if measuring a construct such as leisure satisfaction, has construct validity been tested? If conducted by observation, does it report inter-rater reliability?)

- has adequate protocols documented for administration, scoring, interpretation, and reporting.

Don't use a commercial assessment:

- simply because it is well-packaged, marketed, well-known, or presented at conferences.

- that does not match the clients' needs, therapeutic recreation programs, or mandates of the agency.

- that has minimal documentation about its development and validation procedures.

- that does not have administration, scoring, interpretation, and reporting protocols.

- that reports faulty information about its development and use.

- in partial form when the assessment was validated as a whole.

---

the agency's or clients' needs has no advantage over developing a quality agency-specific tool. The specialist needs to be very familiar with measurement characteristics in order to make a sound decision prior to purchase. Box 9.7 provides a list of dos and don'ts regarding purchase and use of commercial client assessments.

Develop an Agency-Specific Assessment

Similar to selecting an assessment that can be purchased, a client assessment can be developed by the therapeutic recreation specialist within a specific agency, given that adequate consideration and thought is given to its development. In actual practice, more therapeutic recreation specialists rely on agency-specific assessments than on nationally available tests. One major reason may in fact be that the content of commercial assessments rarely matches the content of the programs offered by specific agencies, and thus locally developed assessments, given adequate attention to development and testing, often are more closely aligned with the needs of the clients and types of programs delivered. This is similar to national standardized tests (again, such as the ACT or SAT) versus the classroom tests most often developed by the teacher. Although the standardized tool has received repeated and advanced testing for validation purposes, it still does not meet the needs of the average classroom teacher because the content, purpose, and intended outcomes differ. So it is with therapeutic recreation assessments. This may continue to be the case until national treatment protocols are researched and utilized in all similar programs across the country. When this becomes the case, assessments to align with those programs will be developed and made readily available. Until that time, many therapeutic recreation specialists will continue to create their own assessments to use within their agencies. This means, however, that in order to have confidence in the ability of the results to place clients in the right programs, the specialist becomes responsible for reducing inadvertent error whenever possible. Development of an agency-specific assessment does not excuse the specialist from similar measurement and testing requirements as expected for national tests.

There are three basic steps in developing an agency-specific assessment: planning the assessment, item writing, and item analysis and testing. In planning the assessment, several factors must be considered. Agency, client, program, and resource factors must be noted, along with the assessment function, content, and implementation strategy as outlined above.

Complete information on assessment item writing is not possible within the limited confines of this chapter, but can be located in Stumbo (2002). In all cases, assessment developers are urged to use common sense in developing assessment items. Sometimes because measurement implies statistics and advanced formulas, it is assumed that test development is more difficult than it needs to be.

There are several types of test items appropriate to therapeutic recreation assessments. The most popular types of closed-ended questions include the options of yes/no items, checklists, rating scales, and rankings. Typical open-ended questions include short answer (one or two words) or extended answer items.

Two primary and immediate concerns in item type selection is that the content of the assessment (and item) matches the content of the program(s), and that the item produce results that can be used for placement into programs. Below is an example of these two concepts.

Program: Stress Management
Program Content:

Cognitive Component	Physical Component
Teaching clients to:	Teaching clients:
assess situation	diaphragm breathing
review alternatives	relaxation techniques
choose best option for stress relief	exercise, fitness, and nutrition
act upon option	
Thought stopping or reframing	

Intended Program Outcome:

Clients' improved ability to manage stress to adequately function on the job and in the community

Sample Assessment Item:

When you are under a great deal of stress, what do you do?

Get angry, break things, withdraw, do nothing, eat/drink excessively, etc.   −1
Take a walk, take a deep breath, meditate, look at my options, think
positively, stop irrational thoughts, etc.   +1

The client does not necessarily see the answer options, as in the case of interviews. These options are provided for the ease of the specialist scoring the client's answer. If the client responds with any answer like the first set, the person receives a –1 and is placed into the stress management program. The person's responses indicate that he or she needs intervention in the stress management area. If the person responds with answers closer to the second set, the client receives a +1 score and does not receive stress management training. Notice that the content and outcomes of the program have to be specified in order to know the content of the question and acceptable classes of responses. These three areas (program content, outcomes, and assessment content) must align.

Box 9.8 provides a few examples of items that are likely to produce error-filled results. These items were taken directly from assessments currently used by therapeutic recreation departments. Box 9.9 provides examples of various item formats using the same content of leisure barriers. Notice that relatively the same content is used although the format changes, and that most of the items can be administered, scored, and interpreted relatively quickly.

Additional caution must be given to testing the assessment to make sure it meets quality measurement standards, including testing for validity and reliability. Dunn (1987) discussed some of the specifics of this process, and the reader is encouraged to review Stumbo (2002) for further information. Box 9.10 lists dos and don'ts regarding creating an agency-specific client assessment.

Establish Assessment Protocols

An **assessment protocol** is a document that provides clear information on the standardized procedures for preparing for, administering, scoring, interpreting, and reporting assessment information. This documentation is necessary whether the assessment is commercially available or agency-developed. The best commercial assessments provide very detailed protocols to improve the specialist's ability to implement the assessment as it has been planned and tested. In the case of agency-specific assessments, the therapeutic recreation staff is responsible for developing and testing the assessment protocol. Dunn (1989) provided excellent guidelines for using or creating the necessary documentation to accompany assessments.

A typical assessment protocol will include details and instructions concerning:

Preparation

- Environmental conditions under which the assessment is to take place
  (for example, quiet, private location, minimal distractions, proper lighting, furniture arrangements)
- Needed resources
  (for example, assessment kit, accessories, paper and pencil, score sheet, length of time required)

Administration

- Instructions for interviews
  (written script with introduction, transitions, explanations, acceptable probes, closing)

Box 9.8   Examples of Poorly Written Assessments/Items

Example #1

RECREATION THERAPY EVALUATION

DIAGNOSIS: _____ AGE: _____

COMMUNICATION: _____

Receptive Skills: e.g., Reading, Auditory Comprehension _____

_____

Swallowing _____

COGNITIVE FUNCTIONING: e.g., Attention Span/Distractability, Judgment/Problem Solving,

Memory _____

PHYSICAL FUNCTIONING RELATIVE TO ACTIVITY INVOLVEMENT: e.g., Upper

Extremity Use, Transfers, Vision, Hearing, Visual Perception/Left Neglect _____

_____

SOCIAL BACKGROUND: e.g., Transportation, Current Living Arrangements, Family

Relationships _____

_____

Example #2

ACTIVITY INTEREST SURVEY	FREQUENCY	COMMENTS

1. Creative Expression: _____

_____

2. Outdoor Recreation: _____

_____

3. Physical Activity: _____

_____

4. Passive Activity: _____

_____

5. Social Activity/Community Organizations: _____

_____

(*continued*)

Box 9.8   *(continued)*

Example #3

TIME MANAGEMENT   ☐ At Present   ☐ Prior to Disability

1. OBLIGATED TIME   ☐ Work   ☐ School   ☐ Therapy

   ☐ Self-care   ☐ Household activity   ☐ Other _____

2. UNOBLIGATED TIME/LEISURE-RECREATION PARTICIPATION

   A. With whom does patient spend most of his or her leisure time?

      ☐ Alone   ☐ Immediate family   ☐ Extended family

      ☐ Peers   ☐ Others _____

   B. During what time of day does patient usually engage in leisure/recreation activity?

      ☐ Morning   ☐ Afternoon   ☐ Evening   ☐ Weekdays   ☐ Weekends

   C. How does the patient describe his or her leisure/recreation experience?

      ☐ Active   ☐ Planned   ☐ Structured   ☐ Participant

      ☐ Spectator   ☐ Passive   ☐ Spontaneous   ☐ Unstructured

      ☐ Other _____

Example #4

Social Functioning

   Prefers being alone: _____

   Prefers being in groups/friends: _____

   Prefers one-to-one contact: _____

   Communication issues: _____

   Independent: _____

Emotional Functioning

   Makes needs known: _____

   Expresses emotion: _____

   Style of communication (i.e., aggressive/assertive): _____

   Attitude toward therapeutic recreation: _____

**Box 9.9   Examples of Item Formats
Using Leisure Barriers as the Content**

Program Content: Leisure Barriers
Assessment Content: Leisure Barriers

Item Formats:

Yes/No Checklist

Does the client have physical barriers to his or her leisure?	Yes	No	Don't Know
Does the client have cognitive barriers to his or her leisure?	Yes	No	Don't Know
Does the client have emotional barriers to his or her leisure?	Yes	No	Don't Know
Does the client have social barriers to his or her leisure?	Yes	No	Don't Know

Or

Which of the following physical barriers does the client have in his or her leisure?
Check all that apply.

_____ Lack of endurance   _____ Lack of coordination   _____ Lack of mobility

_____ Lack of flexibility   _____ Physical disability   _____ Other; explain _____

Rating Scales

How often do any of the following physical barriers negatively affect your leisure time?	Daily	Weekly	Monthly	Less than Monthly
Lack of endurance?	1	2	3	4
Lack of coordination?	1	2	3	4
Lack of mobility?	1	2	3	4
Lack of flexibility?	1	2	3	4
Physical disability? Explain _____	1	2	3	4
Other: Explain _____	1	2	3	4

Ranking

From 1 being the largest barrier to 6 being the least barrier, rank the following physical barriers that may negatively affect your leisure.

_____ Lack of endurance

_____ Lack of coordination

_____ Lack of mobility

_____ Lack of flexibility

_____ Physical disability

_____ Other; explain _____

Fill in the Blank

Finish this sentence:

The physical barrier that most prevents me from participating in leisure is _____.

Short/Extended Answer

Explain the physical barriers that most prevent you from participating in leisure.

Box 9.10   Dos and Don'ts of Using Agency-Specific Assessments

Do create an agency-specific assessment when:

- an appropriate commercial assessment cannot be located.

- therapeutic recreation programs and/or clients have unique characteristics.

- a comprehensive program design has been conducted and results in a clear view of program content that is to be matched by the client assessment.

- therapeutic recreation staff have enough time and expertise to devote to development and testing.

- adequate documentation can be refined about administration, scoring, interpretation, and reporting.

Don't create an agency-specific assessment when:

- a commercial assessment is readily available that suits the purpose and clients.

- the staff has limited expertise or interest in validation and testing procedures.

- program offerings are haphazard and not based on a comprehensive program design.

- Instructions for observations
  (written information on types of behaviors to be assessed, observation conditions, etc.)

- Exceptional conditions
  (for example, procedures for when a person refuses to complete the interview or observation, fatigues quickly, or becomes disruptive)

Scoring

- How the answers to each question or item are to be scored
  (for example, if a person responds to item 12 with "X" answer, how is this scored differently from the person who responds "Y" to the same item?)

- How the total assessment is scored
  (for example, calculating subscores or total test scores)

Analysis and Interpretation

- How the answers to each question or item are to be analyzed and interpreted for program placement
  (for example, in which program(s) does a person who scores a "5" belong?)

Reporting

- How the answers are to be recorded and reported to other disciplines, if appropriate
  (for example, what is the standardized format for reporting assessment scores or results? How is program placement recorded?)

- Considerations of informed consent
  (including clients' rights to confidentiality and privacy)

Train Staff and Interns on Assessment Protocol

Prior to implementation, each therapeutic recreation staff member and intern needs to receive complete training on the total assessment protocol, including preparing for, administering, scoring, interpreting, and reporting assessment information. The purpose of this step is to ensure that all specialists are fully able to complete and adhere to the protocol as written. This will increase the likelihood that specialists are delivering the assessment in a similar fashion and will likely increase the reliability of the assessment results through consistency of efforts. Adherence to the assessment protocol will reduce unwanted error and increase confidence that can be placed in the results. Periodic training and evaluating adherence to protocol is necessary to decrease discrepancies from specialist to specialist and likely will be a vital part in the quality improvement process.

The Assessment Implementation Process

The five-step assessment planning process outlined in the last section occurs during the initial stages of overall program development and is reviewed periodically as changing conditions may warrant. On the other hand, the assessment implementation process as reviewed in this section takes place daily in the life of a practicing professional. The assessment implementation process occurs when the specialist actually gathers the information from the client for assessment purposes, transforms the information into a usable format, makes decisions on the information gathered, and reports it to other concerned professionals. This entire process is described within seven steps, as outlined in the Assessment Implementation Model found in Figure 9.4. The seven steps include: (1) review the assessment protocol, (2) prepare for assessment, (3) administer assessment to the client, (4) analyze or score the assessment results, (5) interpret results for placement into programs, (6) document results of assessment, and (7) reassess client as necessary to monitor progress.

Review Assessment Protocol

In this step, the specialist is responsible for initial preparation before beginning to administer a client assessment. The specialist also is responsible for reviewing (perhaps even mentally) the standardized assessment protocol. When this is accomplished prior to assessment administration, the specialist is more likely to adhere to the protocol, which in turn is more likely to produce more valid and reliable results. It is important that each specialist administer the assessment, according to the standardized protocol, to each client in the same way every time. Deviations are likely to result in flawed results, translating into program placement errors and inability to produce and document client outcomes. Periodic staff training on this issue is beneficial to help specialists understand that adherence to assessment protocols is crucial to the entire process of placing clients into therapeutic recreation programs that will meet their needs.

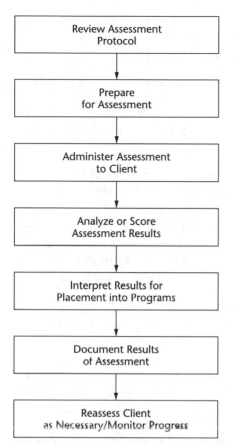

Figure 9.4 Therapeutic Recreation Assessment Implementation Model.

Prepare for the Assessment

This stage also is required prior to administration of an assessment to a client. In this phase, the specialist is responsible for adhering to the protocol on preparation. For example, the staff member needs to gather any supplies or equipment needed for the administration of the assessment. The environment or place in which the assessment will occur needs to be secured and checked for availability, privacy, noise level, adequate seating (if necessary), adequate lighting, ventilation, and temperature. Whenever possible, the specialist should ensure that the environment remains the same from administration to administration. When the environment changes (such as loud noise levels, interruptions, distractions, etc.), the results of the assessment may be affected negatively.

Administer the Assessment to the Client

In this step, the specialist implements the procedures for administration of the assessment results that were outlined and reviewed in the Establish Assessment Protocol stage. Assessments in therapeutic recreation tend to be of four kinds: interviews, observations, self-administered surveys, and records reviews. Each type collects unique information and has its own advantages and disadvantages. These four types may be used in combination to strengthen the validity of the results.

Interviews.   Interviews involve face-to-face contact with clients and/or their families. The primary reason for completing interviews is to allow the client to provide in-depth answers to open-ended questions, while the specialist observes the client's behavior in an interview setting (Ferguson, 1983). Several principles apply to client assessment interviews:

- **Be consistent.** The protocol for administering an interview should include the words to be stated by the specialist. This includes establishing rapport, the introduction, transitions, probes, and closure. Consistency increases reliability and reduces the chances for error in the assessment results due to the procedures used by the specialist.

- **Know the clients' characteristics.** Gathering information through client interviews may not be the most reasonable course of action for all client groups. Some individuals with cognitive deficits, such as acquired brain injury, cerebral vascular accident, or mental retardation, or younger clients, may not respond well to interview situations. The specialist often is responsible for gathering background information (perhaps from records reviews) about each client prior to interview situations.

- **Establish rapport/introduction.** It is important that the specialist establish rapport with the client (or family) by introducing him- or herself and the department, stating the purpose of the interview, explaining the basic structure of the interview and types of questions to be asked, and how the information will be used for programming purposes. Issues of patient rights, confidentiality, privacy, and informed consent may be part of the interview's introduction. It is assumed that the environment is comfortable, quiet, private, and conducive to the interview process.

- **Ask open-ended questions.** Because the purpose of the interview is to gather in-depth information, it is a prime opportunity to ask open-ended questions to which the client may have an extended answer. (Reserve closed-ended questions for self-administered surveys or observations.) Interview questions should contain content that is parallel to program content. Specialists should be aware that good open-ended questions are difficult to write, but worth the effort in terms of eliciting client responses. Notice that the questions below relate directly to an area of therapeutic recreation content, as opposed to questions that are much more general and lack focus on leisure ability. Examples of open-ended questions include:
  What actions do you take to manage stress on a daily basis?
  Explain how you would find out what time the city bus ran to downtown.
  What stops or prevents you from fully enjoying your leisure?
  Explain how you would introduce yourself to a stranger at a community center.
  What items or equipment do you have in your room/home that are available for leisure?

*Given that they take equal amounts of time and money, how do you decide between two
recreation activities in which you'd like to participate?*

If you had a Sunday afternoon with no obligations, what would you do?

How would you find information about a new park in town?

- **Use probes and restatements for clarification.** The specialist should have
specific questions ready for when clients are unclear or unsure of their answers.
For example:

What do you mean when you say . . .

Could you explain that in more detail?

What I understand you to say is . . .

How does _____ relate to _____?

What else would you like to add here before we move on?

To summarize your comments thus far . . .

- **Close the interview.** The purpose of the interview closure is to summarize the
interview and the information that has surfaced. The specialist may reemphasize
the results of the interview, how the results relate to program placement, and
what goals or outcomes are to be expected or worked on. The closure also is a
prime time to reiterate the services offered by the therapeutic recreation department, the schedule of programs, and how the specialist can be reached. The client
should be thanked for his or her time and cooperation.

Observations.   Observations involve the specialist viewing the client's behavior,
either directly or indirectly. In some cases, the client will know he or she is being
observed; in other cases, he or she may not. The specialist should be aware of client
autonomy and rights in conducting observations unknown to the client. The primary
reason for conducting observations is to record the client's behavior (not perceptions
of behavior as in interviews) in situations as close to real life as possible. The specialist
usually records observations of the client's behavior on score sheets that may include
systems such as checklists, rating systems, and open-ended narratives (Stumbo, 1983,
2002). Typically, the specialist chooses to create closed-ended rating systems to
shorten the length of time spent recording the observations and to increase comparability across clients.

Principles that apply to observations include:

- **Be consistent.** Similar to interviews, the specialist needs to be consistent across
observations. Protocols for administering observations should include the informed consent of the client, the environment or situation in which the client is
to be observed, the scoring mechanism(s) for recording observations, and how
scores result in program placement.

- **Determine which scoring system suits the purpose of the observation.**
There are four basic types of observational recording systems: tally, duration,
interval, and instantaneous time sampling. Tally systems record how *frequently* a
behavior occurs. Duration systems record *how long* a behavior occurs. Interval
recording systems measure *both frequency and duration.* Instantaneous time sampling is reserved for those instances when continuous observation is not possible

and *periodic checks* are used. Each system has its own benefits and drawbacks, and the choice will depend on the purpose of the observation and the expertise of the specialist (see Stumbo, 2002).

- **Select behaviors that are clearly defined and observable within the available time period.** Behavioral rating systems are more easily created when the behaviors of interest are easily observable and happen with enough regularity to occur within the observation timeframe. For example, "interacting with other clients" is too vague to be usable and consistently recorded. Better examples of observable behavior might include: "greets other clients," "initiates conversation with peers," or "maintains eye contact."

- **Understand the limitations of observations.** Observations are excellent for recording client behaviors. They do not, however, explain the reasons or motives for the behavior. A specialist may observe a client sitting alone in a corner, but cannot draw conclusions about why this behavior is occurring simply from the observation itself. The specialist should always separate the action or behavior from the interpretation of that action or behavior.

Self-Administered Surveys.   An option that is becoming more frequently used in therapeutic recreation assessments is self-administered surveys. Especially for individuals who are cognitively intact and can process information without the assistance of a specialist, self-administered surveys may provide a viable alternative. The primary purpose of survey assessment devices is to gather information in a very quick fashion for the specialist. The client completes the survey without assistance, and quite likely on his or her own time, so this option frees the specialist of time spent on individual assessment. The major drawback would be the lack of rapport-building opportunities available in interview or observation situations.

For the most part, the questions on the survey should be closed-ended (checklists, rating scales, or ranking) with open-ended response formats minimized. This reduces the burden on the client to provide lengthy, written responses whenever shorter, closed-ended responses are a logical option.

Principles that apply to self-administered surveys include:

- **Be consistent.** The protocol for administering the self-administered survey should be consistent between specialists and between clients. Inconsistent instructions from "Do whatever you can" to "Take this very seriously" will change the nature of the client's responses and will possibly add error to the results.

- **Provide complete written instructions.** Complete written instructions on the top of the survey help the client to finish the survey as accurately and as completely as possible. Written instructions at the end of the survey on how and to whom to return the survey are also important.

- **Ask only what is important for client placement into programs.** While this principle applies to all forms of assessment, it is especially important to note within this section to ask only what is important to client placement into programs. As the self-administered assessment requires minimal specialist time, there is a tendency to ask many questions that have some curiosity factor, but are irrelevant to program placement. Obviously, this can quickly become a privacy issue for clients.

Records Reviews.   A fourth way to gain information about clients for placement into therapeutic recreation programs is to review some form of documentation kept by other disciplines or institutions. For example, instead of asking a client about his diagnosis during an interview, the specialist would be well served to locate this information on the main client chart prior to the interview. There are several reasons for conducting records reviews. First, it can give the specialist background about the client prior to other assessment forms, so the specialist can be informed and establish rapport more quickly. Second, it can be very repetitious to most clients to be asked for the same information from a variety of disciplines within a one- to three-day admission or intake period. Unnecessary duplication of information implies that the disciplines lack coordination in their treatment efforts. (The exception to this rule is to verify that a client is consistent in responding to set questions.) Third, the data from records reviews can help confirm any information gathered in other ways. If the client states active involvement in social events during an interview and similar information does not appear in other records, there may be need for further clarification from the client.

Principles that apply to records reviews include:

- **Information is only as good as its source.** The specialist should establish that the record is a credible source for gaining information about clients.

- **Check available written records prior to other assessment forms.** In almost all cases, having background information on the client, assuming it is correct, is helpful to other assessment-gathering techniques.

- **Do not duplicate information that can be found in documented records.** As noted above, unless there is a specific reason, clients should not be asked to repeat information that is already known and available elsewhere.

In summary, regardless of information-gathering technique(s) used, assessments need to be administered consistently to the fullest extent possible. That means that each assessment technique needs a specific protocol that is consistent across: (1) departments (if programs are similar), (2) specialists, (3) administrations by an individual specialist, (4) clients, and (5) assessment environments. Deviations from these consistencies lower the confidence that can be placed in the results and program placement decisions.

Box 9.11 provides a comparison of the advantages and disadvantages of the different methods of information gathering for assessment purposes. These comparisons are for illustrative purposes only; any method for collecting data can be improved by knowing the advantages and limitations of various methods.

Analyze or Score Assessment Results

Regardless of how the assessment gathers information (interview, observation, survey, records review), a scoring mechanism needs to be in place. Following the established protocol for scoring the assessment, the specialist summarizes the information

---

Box 9.11   Comparison of Four Methods of Information Gathering for Assessment Purposes

Interviews

Advantages

Opportunity to establish rapport with the client.

Opportunity to explain department and programs to the client.

Target clients' knowledge or perceptions of behavior.

Disadvantages

Time consuming to administer for the specialist.

Time consuming to score and interpret.

Likely to be inconsistent between specialists, clients, and administrations.

Observations

Advantages

Targets real behavior of clients.

Can produce concrete data from which to compare clients' behaviors.

Increased likelihood of being able to compare preprogram and postprogram behavior of individual clients.

Disadvantages

Time consuming to develop and administer for the specialist.

Does not get at reasons or motives for behavior.

Difficult to view clients in similar, consistent situations.

Self-Administered Surveys

Advantages

Time efficient for the specialist.

May be time efficient for the client.

Client can answer at own pace.

Disadvantages

Client may not be the one completing the survey.

Does not allow opportunity to establish rapport with the client.

Limited opportunity to explain questions or meanings to the client.

Records Reviews

Advantages

Time efficient for the specialist.

In most settings, data is readily accessible.

Reduces redundancy for the client.

Disadvantages

Information only as good as the source.

Records may contain limited or dated information.

Reduces personal contact with the client.

---

collected through the assessment process in a clear and concise way. Also referred to as "data reduction," this summary condenses quantitative (numbers) and/or qualitative (words) data into an understandable and cohesive picture of the client.

Obviously, it is easier and quicker to summarize and score assessment results that stem from closed-ended or quantitative information. It usually takes longer to reduce and summarize qualitative data that results from open-ended questions. (However, it usually takes more effort and time to construct quality closed-ended questions than similar quality open-ended items.)

Unfortunately, the vast majority of therapeutic recreation assessments do not have adequate protocols for reliable scoring. In fact, many, because they rely on purely qualitative or open-ended data, are difficult to "score" due to the lack of an agreed-upon, congruent method of gathering and synthesizing information. For example, asking "How do you spend your leisure time?" as an open-ended question with no established categories for marking an answer is likely to result in a diversity of answers that are difficult to categorize after the fact.

Indeed, it is probably this step that has been one of the most problematic for therapeutic recreation specialists. Because standardized scoring procedures are all but nonexistent (especially for agency-specific assessments), the specialist often is forced to rely on personal judgment for summarizing the results (and this may fluctuate based on many superfluous reasons, such as mood, need to fill programs, or personal preference). That is, the specialist collects assessment data (perhaps largely because of external or agency mandates), but then ignores any systematic procedure to score the results and later places clients into programs based on personal preferences or the need to fill certain programs—or worse yet, every client is placed in every program. This inconsistent, unreliable "method" of program placement results in faulty decisions and the inability to produce client outcomes. Thus, it jeopardizes the entire programming process and threatens the quality of therapeutic recreation program delivery.

Clearly, procedures for scoring are needed in order to make sense from the information given by the client and to provide a consistent basis of program placement. The previous Stress Management example in the section on Developing Agency-Specific Assessments demonstrates how, when assessment content matches program content and when categories of answers are predetermined, the scoring system may be devised quite easily. Scoring can be simplified as long as it places the right clients into the right programs.

Interpret Results for Client Placement into Programs

After scores are calculated, the next step is to interpret what the "scores" mean for client placement into programs. The goal of this step is to make objective, consistent, and correct decisions for placing clients into therapeutic recreation programs. That is, the specialist wants to make correct Quadrant I and Quadrant IV decisions (see Box 9.2). These placements should be based on the results of the assessment process obtained in the fourth step. If the results were obtained through a valid and reliable process, the interpretation of the results and placement decisions also are more likely to be valid and reliable. If two clients have similar scores or results on the assessment and they are placed in similar programs, as indicated as necessary from the assessment, then these "right" individuals are likely to be receiving the "right" service. On the other hand, if two clients have similar scores or results on the assessment, and they are placed in different programs, then the process is probably not producing valid or reliable results and is resulting in faulty interpretation and placement decisions. Some scoring procedures, such as the previous example of Stress Management, link scoring and interpretation quite closely.

Because consistency is a major issue in assessment, one aim of specialists is to create standards from which to judge clients' scores for program placement. Scores either can be interpreted through *norm-referenced* or *criterion-referenced* means. **Norm-referenced scores** provide benchmarks against which scores are judged according to how the client's peers score. The social skills example will be used here. Let's say the range of scores on a social skills assessment ranges from –10 to +10. A client's score is

+5. One way to view this person's score is by *comparison with the scores of peers*. Where does a score of +5 stand in relative terms to all others admitted on the unit within the last 90 days? If everyone admitted in the last 90 days scored higher than this person, does that mean +5 is a low score, and the person should be placed in the Social Skills program? In norm-referenced situations like this one, how the group performs affects the interpretation of the individual's score and thus his or her placement into the program. For **criterion-referenced scoring** systems, *each person is measured against a set standard*. For example, if the standard is set so that anyone who scores below 0 is placed in the program, then a score of +5 means the person does not get placed into the Social Skills program. The individual's score is interpreted against the backdrop of a set, preestablished criterion. Whether the person qualifies depends on his or her individual score and does not rely on others' scores, only whether the criterion was met. Every person can qualify or not qualify; each person is only judged against his or her own score, not in comparison with others.

Assessment scores can be interpreted in the same two ways. Individual scores can be compared against their peers or against a certain measure or standard. The choice depends on what makes the most sense for program placement. Take the example of a Social Skills Training program. Using a norm-referenced system, the specialist collects information and concludes that the clients who have the five lowest scores are the least socially skilled without some intervention programming. These individuals then would be targeted for the social skills training program for this time period. In a criterion-referenced system, the specialist collects data and finds that individuals who score below a –5 (criterion) need corrective programming. A client receiving a score under –5 then would always be placed in the social skills training program, regardless of how other clients scored. Either method is effective depending on the intended outcome, and the selection decision should be based on the ability to improve the odds of correct program placement decisions.

It is clear that interpretation and use of assessment scores is closely related to how those scores are obtained and recorded. If data reduction or scoring is problematic, then interpretation of the data similarly will be problematic. Often specialists rely too heavily on personal judgment, and their placement of clients into programs is imprecise. This results in either clients not receiving necessary services (Quadrant II) or clients receiving unnecessary services (Quadrant III). The goal of quality client assessment is to make correct Quadrant I or Quadrant IV decisions the vast majority of the time.

Document Results of Assessment into Treatment or Program Plan

This step is a vital checkpoint for the utility of the assessment results. The true test of the entire assessment process is that the therapeutic recreation specialist is able to document unique, useful, and meaningful baseline information into the client's record. This information will help determine the action (course of treatment) taken with and for the client by the professionals involved in his or her care.

Whereas the format of client records often is decided at the agency level, the content that professionals enter into the record usually is decided by the department's staff, in consultation with other disciplines. The content to be reported from the results of the assessment is determined by the content of the programs and, in turn, the content of the assessment. Usually, each contributing department has distinct areas of interest, parallel to its accepted scope of care within the agency.

One frustration, if the previous five steps have been done incorrectly or incompletely, is that the therapeutic recreation specialist may have little valuable or unique information to report. When prior assessment steps have not followed a logical, consistent, and justifiable sequence or if programs are not based on a systematic analysis of client needs, the information provided by therapeutic recreation specialists may not differ greatly from other disciplines or may not contribute to the client's goals or treatment plan.

For example, a therapeutic recreation specialist may be providing valuable intervention programs with the *content* of: (1) leisure awareness, (2) social interaction skills, and (3) community leisure resources. These are well-designed, outcome-oriented intervention programs that appear to be successful and complement the treatment programs of the other disciplines. However, her assessment *content* includes: (1) personal history, (2) past leisure interests, and (3) future leisure interests. How well does the content of the assessment match the content of the program? What can she say about client placement into programs? How will the "right" clients be placed systematically into the "right" programs? How will the link be translated in the client record?

The answer is that client placement into the correct programs is unlikely and the specialist will have little of value to report in the client record or to the treatment team. As a beginning, the specialist needs the assessment to reflect the program content of: (1) leisure awareness, (2) social interaction skills, and (3) community leisure resources. Other information may have little value and be regarded poorly by other members of the treatment team.

Reassess Client as Necessary to Show Progression or Regression

The final phase of reassessment was mentioned previously. Whenever the status of a client needs to be examined, conducting a reassessment using the same tool as the initial assessment appears logical. This reassessment may be necessary to write progress notes or discharge/referral summaries. If the original assessment tool produces results that are valid and reliable, then no better tool exists to determine the progression or regression of a particular client.

This does mean that the original assessment must have the precision (reliability) to determine sometimes small increments of movement. For example, if it is determined from the original assessment that a client lacks social interaction skills (and therefore the client is placed into a social skills program), the assessment must measure these skills with enough consistency to determine if change has been made during or at the completion of the program. If the assessment provides rough or "crude" estimates of ability, then reassessment will be difficult, if not impossible. If this is the case, the specialist will have an extremely difficult time "proving" that the client achieved the intended outcomes of the therapeutic recreation program. This provides an additional reason that assessment items should be focused and provide concise results.

All seven steps point to the need for the assessment process and results to be both valid and reliable, and this requires a great deal of specialist expertise, competence, and effort. The above discussion shows that each step is intricately linked and that poor decisions in one phase result in mistakes or poor execution in other steps. As the key information source for further involvement with the client, assessment plays a critical role in providing intervention to clients that can produce dependable outcomes.

Issues Surrounding Client Assessment*

Like many other health-related professions, there is cause for concern about the state of the art of therapeutic recreation client assessment. Of all the professional tasks to be completed within the Therapeutic Recreation Accountability Model, client assessment remains the most problematic. There are a number of reasons why this is true; a few are presented below. They are presented within this chapter so that students, practitioners, and faculty can focus on areas of improvement rather than repeat past mistakes. For a more complete review, see Howe (1984, 1989), Stumbo (1991, 1994/1995, 1997, 2002), Sneegas (1989), and Witt, Connolly, and Compton (1980).

Availability of Assessments and Assessment Resources

- Fewer than 50 assessments available; few developed specifically for therapeutic recreation practice
- Few developed for specific population groups (e.g., at-risk youth, substance abuse)
- Difficult or costly to obtain some assessments
- Lack of TR specialists' knowledge of how to access assessment resources
- Lack of trainers with expertise

Conceptualization and Development of Assessment Procedures

- Inadequate conceptualization of assessment content
- Inadequate attention to desired results or programming outcomes
- Emphasis on functional abilities (not unique to therapeutic recreation purposes)
- Inappropriate use of statistics and measurement techniques
- Lack of psychometric testing on assessments in use
- Cannibalizing quality assessments into pieces that are inappropriate
- Lack of field-based research using targeted client groups
- Complexities of measuring human and leisure behavior

*This section is adapted from Stumbo, N. J. (1997). Issues and concerns in therapeutic recreation assessment. In D. Compton (Ed.), *Issues in therapeutic recreation: Toward the new millennium* (2nd ed.; pp. 347–372). Copyright 1997 Sagamore Publishing Company, Champaign, IL. All rights reserved.

Use of Assessment Procedures

- Overuse and inappropriate use of activity interest inventories
- Misuse of assessment for wrong type of agency
- Misuse of assessments for wrong population
- Using assessments intended for other disciplines
- Lack of consistency among TR specialists
- Lack of protocols for interviews and observations between specialists
- Lack of periodic testing for specialist "drift" or shifts over time
- Lack of systematic training for assistants and interns
- Lack of consistent procedures for scoring, interpreting, and reporting results

Peer Review of TR Assessments

- Lack of avenues to provide critiques of commercial assessments
- Lack of interest in reviewing assessments' properties

Professional Constraints

- Shortened length of stay for clients
- Integrated/interdisciplinary assessments (e.g., multidisciplinary assessments limited to one page)
- Workforce reduction/increased job duties
- Fewer opportunities for adequate training

Therapeutic Recreation Faculty Members

- Lack of knowledge about measurement, psychometrics, and testing principles
- Lack of understanding about relationship of assessment to client outcomes
- Lack of instructional materials available for classroom use

Therapeutic Recreation Specialists

- Lack of training about measurement, producing client outcomes through programs
- Lack of practice/skill about data collection (interviewing, observation, etc.)
- Lack of motivation/opportunities to receive updated, quality training
- Heavy reliance on familiar techniques

There is a need to evaluate honestly the state of the art of therapeutic recreation assessments. Lists of problem areas, such as the one above, are created to draw attention to areas in which improvement is needed. Awareness of difficulties appears to be the first step in creating better solutions. The status of client assessments will be only as good as the specialists who develop and use them. As with all areas of the Therapeutic Recreation Accountability Model, students, specialists, and faculty must each play a role in improving the state of affairs in therapeutic recreation assessment.

Thoughts About Activity Interest Inventories

One of the main types of client assessment used today is the activity interest inventory. In these inventories, clients are asked to respond whether they participate or are skilled in a variety of recreation and leisure activities. While this may be beneficial in some cases, specialists should use this approach with great caution.

This cautionary warning is due to the tie between assessments and programs (the content of the assessment must match the content of the programs). When this match is addressed, the results of the assessment are more likely to result in proper program placements. For an activity interest inventory to have high validity, it means that the programs in which clients are placed consist of primarily activity skill or participation programs. For example, the therapeutic recreation department would offer a diverse number of activities (both to increase skill and perhaps for general participation), and the assessment would be used to place the clients in the right programs according to their interests and skills. In this scenario the match is correct.

However, most therapeutic recreation programs do not rely solely on activity skill or participation programs. The majority of therapeutic recreation programs have functional intervention and/or leisure education programs as their primary focus. This would mean that the use of activity interest inventories would be an improper fit for these programs (the content of the assessment would not match the content of the programs). While there may be justification to use interest inventories in certain cases, in all situations they must be able to help place clients into the right programs. When the programs are not strictly activity based, this is probably not the case.

This problem is noted because a significant number of therapeutic recreation departments utilize activity interest inventories in lieu of other more results-oriented assessments. A more thorough discussion of the issues surrounding this can be found in Stumbo (1992, 1993/1994, 2002).

Examples of Commercial Therapeutic Recreation Assessments

There are approximately fifty therapeutic recreation assessments available, some more easily obtained than others. Appendix C contains a listing of the most well-known assessments and references to locate further information about each. Box 9.12 and Box 9.13 demonstrate examples of items of two assessments that vary quite significantly in their intent, content, and use. The first is the Leisure Diagnostic Battery (Witt & Ellis, 1989), one of the oldest and most widely researched assessments in therapeutic recreation. The Leisure Diagnostic Battery consists of two forms: Long Form and Short Form. Within the Long Form and Short Form, there are two versions, one for adolescents and one for adults. The Long Form generally consists of eight scales: A—Perceived Leisure Competence Scale; B—Perceived Leisure Control Scale; C—Leisure Needs Scale; D—Depth of Involvement in Leisure Scale; E—Playfulness Scale; F—Barriers to Leisure Involvement Scale; G—Leisure Preferences Inventory; and H—Knowledge of Leisure Opportunities Test. Sample questions shown in Box 9.12 are from the Perceived Leisure Competence Scale, Version A, for

Box 9.12   Sample Items from the Leisure Diagnostic Battery, Perceived Leisure Competence Scale, Version A

	Sounds Like Me	Sounds a Little Like Me	Doesn't Sound Like Me
1. I'm good at almost all the recreation activities I do.	A	B	C
2. If I try, I usually win.	A	B	C
3. I'm good enough to play sports.	A	B	C
4. In group activities, I'm a good leader.	A	B	C
5. I'm good at thinking of new things to do.	A	B	C
6. I learn new activities fast.	A	B	C
7. I'm good at playing games with other people.	A	B	C
8. I'm good at thinking of fun things to do.	A	B	C
9. I'm better than most people at doing my favorite recreation activity.	A	B	C
10. It's easy for me to pick a recreation activity to do.	A	B	C

From Witt, P. A., & Ellis, G. D. (1989). *The Leisure Diagnostic Battery Users' Manual.* State College, PA: Venture Publishing, Inc. Reprinted with permission from Venture Publishing.

adolescents. Information on validity and reliability of the LDB are found in Witt and Ellis (1989).

The Leisure Competence Measure (Kloseck, Crilly, Ellis, & Lammers, 1996; Kloseck & Crilly, 1997) is intended to measure functional skills, knowledge, and behavior related to leisure functioning. The seven scales used to measure leisure competence include: leisure awareness, leisure attitudes, leisure skills, social appropriateness, group interaction skills, social contact, and community-based participation. The scales were created to align with the Functional Independence Measure (Hamilton, Granger, Zielenzy, & Tashman, 1987), a tool widely used in physical medicine. The Community Re-Integration Skills scale is shown in Box 9.13. Data on validity and reliability as well as ordering information is located in Kloseck, Crilly, Ellis, & Lammers (1996; Kloseck & Crilly, 1997).

These two assessments represent a considerable effort to validate an assessment tool for the population for which it was intended. As such, they represent the best known researched tools in the field.

Summary

Assessment plays an important role in the intervention process. It is the key link between sound program development and client outcomes by providing information to place the right client into the right programs. Validity, reliability, fairness, and usability are important characteristics of all assessments, regardless of whether they are commercially available or agency-specific. A step-by-step process for planning and

---

Box 9.13   Sample Items from the Leisure Competence Measure, Community Re-Integration Skills Scale

Application of antecedent skills for successful involvement in community leisure activities.

NO HELPER

7. COMPLETE INDEPENDENCE: *Client initiates, plans, and follows through* with chosen community-based leisure activities.

6. MODIFIED INDEPENDENCE: With the *provision of necessary resources,* client *initiates, plans, and follows through* with chosen community-based leisure activities.

HELPER

5. MODIFIED DEPENDENCE: With *cueing and/or reassurance,* client initiates, plans, and follows through with chosen community-based leisure activities.

4. MODIFIED DEPENDENCE WITH MINIMAL ASSISTANCE: Client initiates and plans chosen community-based leisure activities. Client requires *assistance with follow-through.*

3. MODIFIED DEPENDENCE WITH MODERATE ASSISTANCE: Client initiates choosing community-based leisure activities. Client *requires assistance planning and following through* with chosen community-based leisure activities.

2. MODIFIED DEPENDENCE WITH MAXIMAL ASSISTANCE: Client *requires assistance initiating, planning, and following through* with community-based leisure activities. Even with assistance, involvement in community-based leisure activities is *not successful.*

1. TOTAL DEPENDENCE WITH TOTAL ASSISTANCE: Due to *cognitive and/or physical deficits* client is unable to *initiate, plan, or follow through* with community-based leisure activities.

Reprinted with permission, *Leisure Competence Measure,* copyright Kloseck and Lammers, 1989, in Kloseck, M., & Crilly, R. G. (1997). *Leisure Competence Measure: Professional Manual and Users' Guide (Adult Version).* London, Ontario, Canada: LCM Data Systems, 9 Mount Pleasant Avenue, (519) 679-1833.

---

implementing assessments is outlined so that assessments can be created and/or used with some degree of consistency and dependability. While this process discusses the ideal, there are several issues and concerns surrounding therapeutic recreation assessment. Each student and professional should take responsibility for increasing his or her knowledge of and competence in using assessments wisely.

STUDENT EXERCISES

Discussion Questions

1. What is the relationship between systematic program design, client assessment, and client outcomes?

2. Select any of the assessment principles and give two scenarios: (a) what happens when this principle is violated in therapeutic recreation assessment? and (b) what happens when this principle is upheld in therapeutic recreation assessment?

3. Explain the importance of Box 9.1 to the specialist's ability to place clients in the correct programs and produce meaningful and predictable client outcomes.

4. Box 9.2 and Figure 9.2 describe consequences of correct and incorrect placement decisions based on assessment results. What actions can therapeutic recreation specialists take to improve the percentage of their correct program placement decisions?

5. Explain how evidence for the three types of validity is gathered. Why is each important and what does it contribute to the total evidence of validity of the assessment results?

6. What "proof" would you look for in an assessment's documentation to determine if it is valid for a specific purpose? For a specific group of clients? For a specific type of agency?

7. Explain the ways in which estimates of reliability are gathered. When is each used and why would that evidence be important in therapeutic recreation assessments?

8. What "proof" would you look for in an assessment's documentation to determine if it was reliable for a specific purpose? For a specific group of clients?

9. When is inter-rater reliability important to calculate? Why does inter-rater reliability matter and how might it affect client assessment scores if it were low?

10. Why is fairness an important measurement concept and how might it relate to therapeutic recreation assessment?

11. Explain each step of the Assessment Planning Model. Why does assessment planning take place while the comprehensive program is still being developed?

12. Under what circumstances should a therapeutic recreation specialist select and use a commercial assessment? An agency-specific assessment?

13. Explain why the assessment items in Box 9.8 may present problematic results, in terms of validity, reliability, fairness, and usability.

14. Explain each step of the Assessment Implementation Model. Why do you think it is presented as a separate model from assessment planning?

15. For three of the assessment issues mentioned in the chapter, outline one or two ways to improve the current state of affairs in therapeutic recreation assessment.

16. Explain why activity interest inventories may not be appropriate for therapeutic recreation intervention programs. Under what conditions might they be appropriate?

Practice Test

1. The major purpose of therapeutic recreation client assessments is to:
   a. analyze the potential of activities to produce change in clients.
   b. group clients for programming purposes.
   c. place clients into programs based on their needs.
   d. communicate client needs to other disciplines.

2. The content of the client assessment should match the:
   a. content and process sheet of the specific program design.
   b. content of the therapeutic recreation program.
   c. clinical practice guidelines for therapeutic recreation.
   d. kinds of activities in which the clients usually participate.

3. Validity relates to which of the following questions?
   a. How stable is the assessment over time?
   b. Are two forms of the same test similar?
   c. What score does the client receive?
   d. How well does the assessment content match the program content?

4. Reliability relates to which of the following questions?
   a. How stable is the assessment over time?
   b. Is the assessment equally fair to all individuals or subgroups of individuals?
   c. How well does the assessment content match the program content?
   d. How much time, money, and staff effort must be dedicated for the assessment?

5. Inter-rater reliability is calculated for which type of assessment?
   a. Observations
   b. Interviews
   c. Records reviews
   d. Self-administered surveys

6. When does the assessment planning process take place?
   a. During comprehensive program development
   b. After treatment goals have been documented
   c. Before clinical practice guidelines are developed
   d. While client outcomes are being measured

7. A commercial therapeutic recreation assessment should be selected under all of the following conditions EXCEPT when it has:
   a. minimal documentation provided for administering, scoring, and interpretation.
   b. content related to the program content.
   c. been validated on similar services and clients.
   d. appropriate assessment protocols.

8. An agency-specific therapeutic recreation assessment should be developed under all of the following conditions EXCEPT when:
   a. an appropriate commercial assessment cannot be located.
   b. staff have expertise or interest in developing a quality assessment.
   c. programs are designed systematically and outcomes are specified.
   d. programs are haphazard and are based on staff preference.

9. Observations should be used as assessments when the specialist is interested in:
   a. the individual's perception of his or her behavior.
   b. the individual's actual behavior.
   c. catching the client off guard.
   d. the leisure interests of the client.

10. Assessments are administered and results are calculated so that the specialist can:
    a. adhere to standards of practice.
    b. have information to report during treatment meetings.
    c. develop treatment goals and objectives with the client.
    d. reassess the client after he or she is discharged.

Answers: 1. c, 2. b, 3. d, 4. a, 5. a, 6. a, 7. a, 8. d, 9. b, 10. c

Chapter Activities

Assessment Purposes

For each assessment purpose, write a short paragraph on how a therapeutic recreation assessment's results can be used. Explain how a high-quality or a low-quality assessment would affect each example.

Professional Interview

Interview a therapeutic recreation specialist about his or her assessment. How was it selected or developed? How well does it match the content of the programs offered? Is there a protocol or other documentation on how to administer, score, interpret, and report results? How are staff and interns trained and retrained on the assessment? How often is it updated? How well does it coincide with the assessments of other disciplines?

Assessment Decisions

Create examples of assessment and program placement decisions similar to those in Figure 9.2 for clients in substance abuse facilities, physical medicine and rehabilitation, pediatric units, adolescent mental health, hospice, community therapeutic recreation, etc.

Validity and Reliability Information

Make a list of 10–15 things necessary to know about a client assessment before purchasing it (validity, reliability, fairness, and practicality/usability). Review any commercial assessment and determine if all of these characteristics are present.

Assessment Scoring

For each of the examples of poor assessment items in Box 9.8, improve the items by providing a closed-ended scoring mechanism that would lead to easier program placement.

REFERENCES

Aiken, L. R. (1997). *Psychological testing and assessment.* (9th ed.). Boston: Allyn and Bacon.

Anastasi, A. (1988). *Psychological testing* (6th ed.). New York: Macmillan.

Dunn, J. (1984). Assessment. In C. A. Peterson & S. L. Gunn (Eds.), *Therapeutic recreation program design: Principles and procedures.* (2nd ed.; pp. 267–320). Englewood Cliffs, NJ: Prentice-Hall.

Dunn, J. K. (1987). Establishing reliability and validity of evaluation instruments. *Journal of Park and Recreation Administration, 5*(4), 61–70.

Dunn, J. K. (1989). Guidelines for using published assessment procedures. *Therapeutic Recreation Journal, 23*(2), 59–69.

Ferguson, D. (1983). Assessment interviewing techniques: A useful tool in developing individual program plans. *Therapeutic Recreation Journal, 17*(2), 16–22.

Graham, J. R., & Lilly, R. S. (1984). *Psychological testing.* Englewood Cliffs, NJ: Prentice-Hall.

Gronlund, N. E. (1993). *How to make achievement tests and assessments* (5th ed.). Boston: Allyn and Bacon.

Hamilton, B. B., Granger, F. S., Zielezny, M., & Tashman, J. S. (1987). A uniform national data system for medical rehabilitation. In M. J. Fuhrer (Ed.), *Rehabilitation outcomes: Analysis and measurement* (pp. 137–147). Baltimore: Paul H. Brookes.

Howe, C. (1984). Leisure assessment instrumentation in therapeutic recreation. *Therapeutic Recreation Journal, 18*(2), 14–24.

Howe, C. Z. (1989). Assessment instruments in therapeutic recreation: To what extent do they work? In D. Compton (Ed.), *Issues in therapeutic recreation: A profession in transition* (pp. 205–221). Champaign, IL: Sagamore Publishing Company.

Kloseck, M., and Crilly, R. (1997). *Leisure Competence Measure: Adult version, professional manual and users guide: An introduction to measuring outcomes in therapeutic recreation.* London, ON: Leisure Competence Measure Data System.

Kloseck, M., Crilly, R. G., Ellis, G. D., & Lammers, E. (1996). Leisure Competence Measure: Development and reliability testing of a scale to measure functional outcomes in therapeutic recreation. *Therapeutic Recreation Journal, 30*(1), 13–26.

Navar, N. (1991). Advancing therapeutic recreation through quality assurance: A perspective on the changing nature of quality in therapeutic recreation. In B. Riley (Ed.), *Quality management: Applications for therapeutic recreation* (pp. 3–20). State College, PA: Venture Publishing Company.

Salvia, J., and Ysseldyke, J. E. (1998). *Assessment* (7th ed.). Boston: Houghton-Mifflin.

Sneegas, J. J. (1989). Can we really measure leisure behavior of special populations and individuals with disabilities? In D. Compton (Ed.). *Issues in therapeutic recreation: A profession in transition* (pp. 223–236). Champaign, IL: Sagamore Publishing Company.

Stumbo, N. (1983). Systematic observation as a research tool for assessing client behavior. *Therapeutic Recreation Journal, 17*(4), 53–63.

Stumbo, N. J. (1991). Selected assessment resources: A review of instruments and references. *Annual in Therapeutic Recreation, 2*(2), 8–24.

Stumbo, N. J. (1992). Rethinking activity inventories. *Illinois Parks and Recreation Magazine, 23*(2) 17–21.

Stumbo, N. J. (1993/1994). The use of activity interest inventories in therapeutic recreation assessment. *Annual in Therapeutic Recreation, 4,* 11–20.

Stumbo, N. J. (1994/1995). Assessment of social skills for therapeutic recreation intervention. *Annual in Therapeutic Recreation, 5,* 68–82.

Stumbo, N. J. (1997). Issues and concerns in therapeutic recreation assessment. In D. Compton (Ed.), *Issues in therapeutic recreation: Toward the new millennium* (2nd ed.; pp. 347–372). Champaign, IL: Sagamore Publishing Company.

Stumbo, N. J. (2002). *Client assessment in therapeutic recreation services.* State College, PA: Venture Publishing Company.

Stumbo, N. J., & Rickards, W. H. (1986). Selecting assessment instruments: Theory into practice. *Journal of Expanding Horizons in Therapeutic Recreation, 1*(1), 1–6.

Stumbo, N. J., & Thompson, S. R. (1988). *Leisure education: A manual of activities and resources.* State College, PA: Venture Publishing Company.

Ward, A. W., and Murray-Ward, M. (1999). *Assessment in the classroom.* Belmont, CA: Wadsworth Publishing.

Witt, P., Connolly, P., & Compton, D. (1980). Assessment: A plea for sophistification. *Therapeutic Recreation Journal, 14*(4), 3–8.

Witt, P. A., & Ellis, G. D. (1989). *The Leisure Diagnostic Battery users' manual.* State College, PA: Venture Publishing Company.

CHAPTER 10

Client Documentation

Client documentation involves the written records that are kept regarding the actions taken for, with, and by the client. This paperwork often becomes the official and legal record of client service. Therefore, the importance of thorough and accurate record keeping in therapeutic recreation services is clearly evident. In an effort to describe documentation as a crucial function of professional services, some administrators have coined the phrase, "If it's not in writing, it didn't happen." Such an exaggerated statement exemplifies the increasing importance that professional records hold in clinical, residential, and sometimes community therapeutic recreation services. Every student and therapeutic recreation professional is responsible for learning quality documentation methods and updating this knowledge as necessary.

The Therapeutic Recreation Accountability Model (TRAM) emphasizes four components of client documentation: assessment implementation/results, treatment plans, progress notes, and discharge/referral summaries. In addition, this chapter also will discuss critical incident reports, although these are completed on an as-needed rather than an ongoing basis. Figure 10.1 provides an overview of where client documentation fits into the Accountability Model. Note that client documentation plays an important role of connecting the program plan and the assessment plan with measurement of program and client outcomes. Client documentation verifies the "process" that happens with and to clients in order to achieve measurable and predictable outcomes.

Types of Documentation

Documentation, or written records, can be categorized into two broad types: *client* management documentation and *program* management documentation. These two functions are highly interrelated, but serve different, distinct purposes.

Client management documentation includes all records that address individual client concerns. The following types of documentation are related to client management functions: (1) individual client assessments, (2) individualized treatment or program plans, (3) progress notes, (4) discharge/referral plan and summaries, and (5) follow-up or aftercare records.

Program management documentation includes all documentation that addresses groups of clients, administrative, supervisory, or programmatic records. Examples of program management documentation include the therapeutic recreation written plan of operation, the comprehensive and specific program plans, and policy and proce-

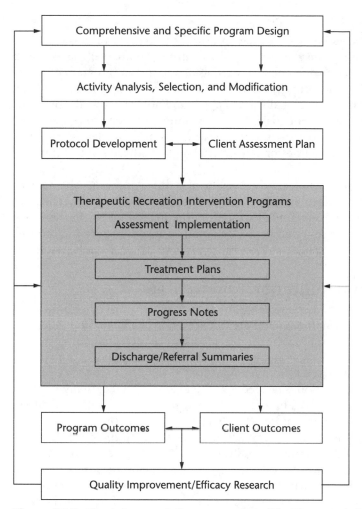

Figure 10.1 Client documentation component of the Therapeutic Recreation Accountability Model.

dure manuals. Many of these program documentation forms were discussed in Chapter 4.

This chapter will focus heavily on the client management functions of documentation and present examples of several types of documentation. Prior to discussing the individual types of records, an overview of the rationale for high-quality documentation is presented.

Rationale for Quality Documentation

Although each agency may provide its own rationale for records and documentation, the following reasons are appropriate and apply to most agencies providing therapeutic recreation services (Navar, 1984).

Assurance of Quality Services

Clients of therapeutic recreation services have the right to receive professional services that are of high quality. One way of assuring that programs are well planned and appropriate to client needs is to document the details of a particular program offering. The therapeutic recreation specialist, in essence, will be documenting what will happen in a particular program, what actually did happen, and how effective the program was in achieving program and client goals. Client documentation describes what services were provided, evidence that the services were necessary, the clients' response to said services, and any modifications or adjustments made to those services (Springhouse Corporation, 1999).

The National Therapeutic Recreation Society and the American Therapeutic Recreation Association both have Standards of Practice documents that establish the minimal guidelines for the delivery and evaluation of therapeutic recreation services. Both of these documents reference client documentation as a necessary indicator of quality service provision.

Facilitation of Communication Among Staff

Accurate records about a program or a client can serve as a method of communication among staff members. Other staff members are not always available for an immediate verbal conversation or consultation. The written record of client or program progress actually can be considered a time management technique that provides up-to-date information when personal contact is not feasible.

This avenue of communication is needed for several reasons. First, many facilities offer 24-hour service that is covered by staff in three or more shifts. Staff from different shifts must be able to communicate what happened during their shift to other staff. Second, health care and human service organizations, by their very nature, experience a high degree of staff changes and turnover. This may be due to attrition, reorganizations, promotions, layoffs, downsizing, leaves of absence, and illnesses. Nonetheless, the client deserves accurate documentation and communication of service provision. Third, several different disciplines may be involved in the service to clients. Communication must be strong to allow professionals to be consistent and supportive; to avoid duplication of services; and to facilitate multidisciplinary, transdisciplinary, and interdisciplinary team functioning. Client documentation must be of high quality, accurate, and meaningful to fulfill all these purposes.

Professional Accountability and Self-Regulation

A professional can be expected to be held accountable for services provided and outcomes achieved. Accurate records are written evidence that services were provided or that plans for providing service are a reality. Written evidence becomes a major responsibility of those who wish to be identified as professionals on the treatment or program team. In addition, reimbursement for services can never be expected without optimal record keeping (Springhouse Corporation, 1999).

Another indicator of professionalism is the practitioner's desire and willingness to engage in self-regulation. Therapeutic recreation specialists voluntarily can facilitate the documentation process and thus assist in the self-regulation of their own therapeutic recreation department by following the standards of practice and administrative guidelines established by their professional association(s). The National Therapeutic Recreation Society and the American Therapeutic Recreation Association both are sources for this information. In addition, the National Council for Therapeutic Recreation Certification verifies the importance of professional accountability through its certification standards and examination.

In many instances, documentation provides a legal record that can be used to protect the client, agency, or the professionals who provide services. Accurate, up-to-date records are critical to the concept of legal and professional accountability.

Compliance with Administrative Requirements

The content and methods of record keeping vary among settings. At times, both the content and format for record keeping will be determined by agency administration. In other instances, an administration may simply request particular types of data and the therapeutic recreation specialist will determine the method or format for collecting and recording the data. In still other situations, therapeutic recreation specialists voluntarily will initiate a particular type of record keeping because they feel it is important to collect and use the information, even if no one is requesting or requiring it.

Each therapeutic recreation specialist should become familiar with his or her agency's documentation requirements. In addition, it is useful to investigate and discover the source of a particular requirement.

Some documentation procedures are unchangeable. Others are simply procedures that have been adopted in the past yet could be altered if they are no longer efficient and appropriate. By finding the source of a documentation procedure, the therapeutic recreation specialist can determine which procedures are required and which procedures or record-keeping systems can be changed to better suit the needs of the therapeutic recreation staff.

Several sources of documentation procedures are commonly found. The type of documentation oversight is generally determined by the type of the facility and its ownership.

Agency Administration.   In some community recreation agencies, it is possible to identify the individual responsible for initiating or altering documentation procedures or record-keeping systems. This individual is typically the chief administrator or director. Changes in documentation procedures often may occur by obtaining approval from this individual.

In some clinical agencies, the approval of forms and records is the responsibility of the medical records committee, review board, or department. In these instances, alterations in documentation policies or procedures will entail a formal and thorough review of the proposed changes. In this situation, acceptance of new documentation procedures can be a very long and possibly tedious process. However, when there is staff consensus that records are redundant or outmoded, such a change process can be quite useful in streamlining documentation procedures.

Corporation and Multifacility Agencies.   Many health care facilities, such as long-term care, mental health facilities, substance abuse treatment agencies, and cancer treatment centers, belong to a larger corporation, legal entity, or "chain." Some public agencies, such as Veterans Affairs Medical Centers, also are part of a larger administrative structure. In these instances, a parent governing body may provide standardized policies and procedures that dictate record-keeping or documentation systems. The addition or alteration of record-keeping policies often will need the approval of corporate or administrative headquarters. Decisions are based typically on the applicability of documentation procedures for each member facility or agency.

Accreditation Agencies.   Many clinical and residential facilities must meet minimal standards determined by that agency's accreditation organization. An accreditation organization sets minimal standards for the purpose of providing quality services to consumers or clients. When an agency attempts to comply with accreditation standards, that agency may initiate corresponding documentation or record-keeping policies.

Accreditation standards may dictate the content of records but seldom will dictate the form that an agency must follow. Thus, the agency and, specifically, the therapeutic recreation department have much freedom in developing record-keeping policies and procedures that will comply with the intent of the accreditation standards.

Accreditation organizations that commonly affect agencies providing therapeutic recreation services include the Joint Commission on Accreditation of Healthcare Organizations (JCAHO), the Rehabilitation Accreditation Commission (CARF), the Accreditation Council for Services for Mentally Retarded and Other Developmentally Disabled Persons (AC-MR/DD), and the American Camping Association (ACA).

Each accreditation agency will have standards that directly influence the type of documentation records that are maintained by the therapeutic recreation department. For example, it is typical for accreditation agencies to require that each person's medical record contains an assessment, a plan of care, medical orders, progress notes, and a discharge summary (Springhouse Corporation, 1999). It is the professional responsibility of each therapeutic recreation specialist to become familiar with such standards and create or maintain the appropriate and meaningful corresponding documentation.

In addition to the previously mentioned voluntary accreditation agencies, some governmental agencies at the state and national level are involved in approving agencies or programs within agencies. During a survey of an agency, a great deal of time is spent in reviewing documentation.

For example, the Centers for Medicare and Medicaid Services (CMS) regularly is involved with long-term care facilities or nursing homes. This agency dictates the content of some forms of documentation such as resident assessments (called Minimal Data Sets or MDS). Not only do therapeutic recreation specialists within these facilities comply with such documentation requirements, but many also provide additional documentation when they want more thorough resident assessments than required by the MDS forms.

Third-Party Payers.   Third-party payers, such as Medicare reviewers and representatives from insurance companies, make decisions about reimbursement based on information found in the clients' records. These decisions can be influenced greatly by the quality and completeness of the treatment plans and progress notes. In addition, the credibility of the services provided is enhanced by the comprehensiveness of the therapeutic recreation department's program documentation (e.g., written plan of operation, comprehensive program design).

Though third-party payers will not dictate the form of the specific documentation, they often dictate the content that must be included. The informed therapeutic recreation specialist will stay current with documentation expectations of third-party payers without sacrificing the integrity of program offerings.

Provision of Data for Quality Improvement and Efficacy Research

One of the most important documents of every professional therapeutic recreation department is its therapeutic recreation written plan of operation. (This documentation was explained in greater detail in Chapter 4.) Unless the philosophy, purpose, goals, and objectives (all included in the written plan of operation) are documented, little meaningful program evaluation can occur.

In addition to departmental documentation, individual client treatment or program plans must be documented accurately when working in a clinical setting. Without complete records, it is almost impossible to judge whether the client's individualized program is meeting his or her needs. The success or failure of a client treatment plan or a program plan cannot be judged unless an objective review and evaluation of that written plan can be conducted.

Therapeutic recreation specialists must become more concerned about longitudinal program changes and effectiveness. A particular therapeutic recreation department may have had an excellent program for the clients it served last year. However, if the nature of the clients has changed (because of shorter stay, more multiple disabling conditions), the program also has to change. Documentation enables the specialist to record these program changes over time and, consequently, better judge the program's effectiveness.

Longitudinal studies are becoming more common as a means of program evaluation. In a longitudinal study, client functioning is investigated at various time intervals after discharge or termination from an agency's program. The therapeutic recreation department needs accurate and complete records of the type of therapeutic recreation services clients received before discharge in order to participate fully in these longitudinal studies. Most facilities have quality management committees that oversee client care and documentation. Therapeutic recreation specialists need to be aware that clinical outcomes are now a prime focus for quality management efforts (Springhouse Corporation, 1999).

Summary of Rationale for Documentation

One of the simplest methods of keeping the issue of documentation in perspective is to follow this advice: "Do what you say and say what you do." In other words, the operation of the therapeutic recreation program should correspond with its written statement of purpose and its written plan of operation. Written records that are accurate, detailed, and relevant are needed for each aspect of the therapeutic recreation program.

Although agencies vary in their method of record keeping, each therapeutic recreation department is concerned with accurate and complete documentation in order to (1) assure the delivery of quality services, (2) facilitate communication among staff, (3) provide for professional accountability, (4) comply with administrative requirements, and (5) provide data for quality improvement and efficacy research.

Basic Types of Client Documentation

Client documentation is a major concern in most clinical settings. In addition, some community therapeutic recreation specialists are concerned with individual client records, such as the Individualized Educational Plan (IEP) or other records based on specific care categories, such as home-based care. In most cases, however, individual client records are primarily a concern of therapeutic recreation specialists employed in clinical and residential agencies. In the past, most community-based therapeutic recreation departments did not use individual client records, although this is changing to some degree. Most terminology used in client documentation, therefore, is clinically oriented and often relies on the words "patient" or "client" rather than "participant" or "consumer."

Documentation related to the individual client usually is organized and stored in a main client record or chart. Because terminology varies among agencies, the terms "charting," "individual client documentation," and "client or patient records" are used interchangeably in this chapter.

Principles of Quality Client Documentation

Regardless of the type of client documentation and setting in which it is used, some basic principles apply that generalize across all settings, programs, and client groups. Springhouse Corporation (1999) called the principles the three Cs of good charting: consistency, conciseness, and clarity. Students and beginning professionals likely will need considerable practice prior to meeting the following quality guidelines.

Consistency and Accuracy of Information

All client documentation must be accurate, objective, and consistent. Three principles apply to the area of consistency and accuracy.

- **Objectivity.** Client documentation should contain only information that is factual and objective. The specialist should never record false information, exaggerated data, or information from third-party sources that cannot be confirmed. Accuracy also is needed in using correct spelling, grammar, and punctuation. A client's record is a permanent, legal document that must be as consistent and accurate as possible.

- **Behavioral Language.** In all cases, documentation and written records should focus on client behavior, rather than the specialist's perceptions or guesses. In each case, the specialist is responsible for selecting the most significant aspects of client behavior for documentation. Once the behavior is observed and deemed important, it is necessary to write about this behavior in *behavioral language*. That is, the reader should be able to reconstruct the scene from the descriptive action words, not vague references to perceptions of behavior. For example, compare the two descriptions below. Note that the second describes the client's behavior in more descriptive and meaningful language.

Lack of Behavioral Language

Pt. appeared depressed at the evening treatment program.

Better Use of Behavioral Language

Pt. came 15 minutes late to the evening treatment program. Pt. sat by self, slumped in chair, and did not initiate conversations with peers or therapist. Pt. looked at floor with hands in lap, and did not respond to questions or initiations from other clients.

- **Consistency in Information.** Consistency in charting and other forms of client documentation is very important. There are several considerations of consistency. One is from client to client. The specialist should be looking at approximately the same behaviors from all clients to indicate client need for intervention or achievement of goals. Many times, the behavior to be observed is indicated directly on the form that the specialist is using, say in the format of a checklist or rating scale, so the observations by the specialist are directed toward specific behaviors of the client.

Likewise, professionals in all disciplines usually agree, at least tacitly, to certain behaviors that indicate progress toward goals. However, often in therapeutic recreation, a client's behavior during a therapeutic recreation session may differ from that same client's behavior in other situations. Recording this behavior variance requires attention to detail and surrounding circumstances. It is important that the therapeutic recreation specialist not provide contradictory information about a client. In other words, the specialist should not contradict what another professional charted unless explanations are provided. The two notes below show an example of providing consistent information.

Inconsistent Information Without Explanation

Nursing Note: Pt. insists on using w/c rather than crutches.

TR Note: Pt. walked on crutches today.

More Complete Note

Pt. voluntarily walked to afternoon TR session on crutches. Smith (RN) indicated that pt. refused to use crutches earlier same day.

In addition to maintaining relative consistency between clients and specialists, the therapeutic recreation specialist must be careful to maintain consistency in documentation over time. The specialist should check back to what has been charted previously. The content of the writings should accurately describe the client's behavior at the time of writing, and note any significant changes in client behavior. The conscientious professional will maintain consistency in documentation. Such consistency is one indication of an organized and well-implemented approach or program plan.

Conciseness in Client Documentation

Information in a client's chart should be presented concisely. Short, succinct sentences are recommended. Some agencies permit the use of sentence fragments or an outline form. One agency may consider a progress note appropriately thorough while another might consider the same note too long. Whatever style is used, clarity and consistency in style should not be sacrificed for brevity.

> *Brief Progress Note*
>
> Pt. states that she is bored after 3 weeks at the center and that she misses her parents and friends.

> *Progress Note That's Too Long*
>
> On Wed. morning, pt. approached CTRS to announce her dissatisfaction with the program and her residence. After further inquiry, CTRS was able to discern that the pt. is homesick, probably missing both her parents, siblings, and other neighborhood acquaintances.

> *Progress Notes That's Too Short* (not clear, lacks context)
>
> Pt. is bored.

Clarity in Client Documentation

Clarity in documentation relies on several factors, and certainly relates to consistency and conciseness. Clarity in writing depends on using meaningful phrases and making sure the meaning is immediately clear to the reader. Again, considerable practice usually is necessary until this skill is mastered.

Meaningful Phrases.   This relates to documenting information, as much as is possible, in behavioral terms. The therapeutic recreation specialist should document only meaningful information. Vague phrases, such as "seems to be" or "appears to" have little meaning when recorded, and most agencies do not allow this type of phrase to be used in client records.

In the past, the trend was to use these phrases to help protect the staff from documentation errors. In reality, these phrases have been greatly overused and have made professionals look uncertain. Rather than writing, "Pt. seems to be enjoying herself," use descriptive, behavioral language, as in the following example: "Pt. smiled and laughed while conversing with peers. When asked if she was having a good time, pt. responded, 'You bet! This is a great activity!'"

Technical Guidelines.   Although some agencies are beginning to document progress notes with computers, most progress notes still are handwritten. It is essential that each entry be legible and written in ink. Only standard medical and agency-approved abbreviations may be used.

Correcting Errors.   If a documentation error is made, there will be a specific agency policy indicating how to correct it. A common method of correcting writing errors includes the following three procedures:

1. Draw a single line through the error. This avoids corrections, such as erasing and using correction fluid, which create the appearance of tampering.
2. Write the word "(error)" above the crossed portion. Some agencies suggest writing in the correct word.
3. Initial and date the correction. This procedure helps to authenticate the correction.

Sample Correction:

> (error) arrived RRD 3/17
>
> Pt. ~~invited~~ . . .

Signing Notes.   Every entry made into a client's record should be signed and dated. This legal signature should include professional credentialing initials (e.g., CTRS for those with professional NCTRC certification).

Abbreviations.   Abbreviations can be a time and space saver when documenting in a client's record. Most medical facilities have a list of approved abbreviations that are the only abbreviations that should be used in the client record in that particular facility. Appendix D lists some of the most common medical abbreviations and symbols used in charting.

Writing Style.   Often the writing style used in client documentation can affect its clarity. The following lists provide examples of commonly misused words and phrases:

Inappropriate in Professional Documentation	Possible Alternatives
kids	children
a lot (a lot of toys)	many, several, approximately ten toys
good	appropriate, feasible
bad	inappropriate
sort of, kind of	(omit these phrases!)
in order to	to
in regards to	in regard to, concerning
to have fun	provide enjoyable leisure/recreation experiences or activities
incompetent	lacks the skill, does not have the skill

Many times, the use of an absolute lessens the credibility of the written statement. Because there usually is an exception to each idea, the therapeutic recreation specialist would increase the clarity and credibility of the written word by using absolutes infrequently.

Commonly Used Absolute	Possible Alternatives
must/should/ought (Tom should swim)	could
all the time	frequently
all (all the clients)	most, many, the majority
everyone	most, many
never	seldom, infrequently
will (exercise will help)	may, could

Redundant words can greatly interfere with the clarity of written documents. Care should be taken to K. I. S. S. (keep it sweet and simple).

Commonly Used Redundant Phrases	Possible Alternatives
necessary requirements	requirements
cooperate together	cooperate
ask the question	ask
for a period of two weeks	for two weeks
all of	all
check up on	check
later on	later
during the time	while
come in contact with	meet
evaluate the value	evaluate
final outcome	outcome
as a general rule	as a rule

Too often, an accurate or important issue is overlooked or discounted if the documentation is not professionally written. It is the responsibility of each therapeutic recreation specialist to communicate effectively through written documents that adhere to a professional style.

Common Methods of Charting

There are four major methods of charting or client documentation: (a) narrative, (b) problem oriented, (c) focus charting, and (d) charting by exception. Each of these is described below in considerable detail. Some agencies use combinations of each and others modify one of these methods to meet the needs of that particular agency or corporation (Coty, Davis, & Angell, 2000). This section explains each of these methods using progress notes as the examples, but these same formats also can be used for initial treatment plans and discharge/referral summaries. In addition, four other forms of charting are discussed briefly so that therapeutic recreation students and professionals have a basic understanding of each. These four additional methods of charting are: (a) PIE, (b) FACT, (c) Core, and (d) Outcomes (Iyer & Camp, 1999; Springhouse Corporation, 1999).

Narrative Format

When client records are organized according to **narrative records,** each professional group or source typically keeps data separate from the other professional groups or sources. Sometimes this method is called **source-oriented** record keeping.

Few guidelines are provided for the format of the narrative. That is, the staff member may record events, activities, problems, or issues in any logical order. The page is basically unstructured. There is often space, in a narrative-style note, for a relatively detailed account of activities that were performed for and by the clients. There is also room to explain the client's behaviors, interactions, and other information relevant to therapeutic recreation services. Because of this wide latitude and handwritten requirement, many find the narrative format very cumbersome and time-consuming to use (Iyer & Camp, 1999).

In order to stay current on a client, a staff member needs to read all of the paragraphs written in each discipline. In large agencies or units or when the staff/client ratio is high, staff will be pressed to complete this task in a timely manner.

"Knowing when to document, what to document, and how to organize the data are the key elements of effective narrative notes" (Springhouse Corporation, 1999, p. 67). These authors suggest that the following be documented in narrative records: (a) change in patient's condition, (b) patient's response to treatment or medication, (c) lack of a change in condition, and (d) patient or family member's response to teaching. They suggest doing this by asking the following questions to add order to the narrative note:

- How did I first become aware of the problem?
- What has the patient said about the problem that is significant?
- What have I observed that is related to the problem?
- What is the plan for dealing with the problem?
- What steps have been taken to intervene?
- How has the patient responded to interventions? (Springhouse Corporation, 1999, p. 69)

Currently, fewer facilities rely on narrative documentation because of the time involved and instead typically combine some form of narrative with flow sheets or checklists (Iyer & Camp, 1999; Springhouse Corporation, 1999).

Advantages of source-oriented medical records are that they (a) are familiar to most staff, (b) are easily combined with other documentation methods (such as flow sheets or clinical pathways), (c) contain information on problems, interventions, and responses (although this may be inconsistently done), (d) provide the most flexibility, (e) help reduce training time, and (f) have utility in situations in which chronological events need to be documented (Iyer & Camp, 1999; Meiner, 1999; Springhouse Corporation, 1999). Disadvantages are that they (a) lack structure, (b) are time consuming, (c) are difficult to retrieve information (especially patient trends) easily and quickly, (d) lack consistency in documenting patient outcomes, (e) often contain too much irrelevant or vague information, and (f) do not always allow for evidence of underlying professional decision making (Iyer & Camp, 1999; Meiner, 1999; Springhouse Corporation, 1999).

Box 10.1   Sample Narrative Progress Note

Date	Time	Progress Notes
01/31	1900	Arrived early for leisure education decision-making session. Independently ambulated. Attentive, alert, responsive to verbal requests and comments. Contributed seven or eight comments or suggestions for exploring alternatives for leisure involvement. Stated he would like to attend similar discussion groups to get ideas about leisure opportunities after discharge. Expressed concern about effects of stroke and ability of family to maintain close contact.

(Signature)   *Elizabeth Torcan, CTRS*

Box 10.1 shows a sample progress note using the narrative style. Note the level of detail that can be included as well as the free-form style.

Problem-Oriented Medical Record

Since the late 1960s many agencies have used the **problem-oriented medical records (POMR)** system, instead of the narrative format, as a way to improve the organization of the client's chart and facilitate the retrieval of data from the charts. The POMR focuses on the *problems* of the patient rather than the source of information.

Included in the POMR format are these five components:

- Database or initial assessment results that help determine needs and plan of care
- Client problem list related to diagnosis (usually problems are numbered)
- Initial treatment plan, including interventions and outcomes expected
- Progress notes using SOAP, SOAPIE or SOAPIER formats
- Discharge summary noting problems and resolutions (if achieved) (Intermed Communications, Inc., 1981; Iyer & Camp, 1999; Springhouse Corporation, 1999)

The **SOAP** note format was introduced by Dr. Lawrence Weed as a part of the problem-oriented medical record. This SOAP format may be used for initial notes, progress notes, and discharge notes.

When a SOAP note is written, the following format is typically followed for each stated problem: subjective data, objective data, analysis, and plan.

S - Subjective data—what the client states about the problem; what client says he or she feels

O - Objective data—what behaviors, signs, or factual data the staff observes or measures

A - Analysis—conclusion staff comes to, based on the interpretation of the subjective and objective data about the patient's problem

P - Plan—what the specialist plans to do about the problem now or in the future

Because SOAP fails to address the intervention or evaluation aspects of care, two newer versions—**SOAPIE** and **SOAPIER**—have been developed (Iyer & Camp,

1999; Springhouse Corporation, 1999). In SOAPIE, **I** stands for **interventions** (specific interventions implemented) and **E** stands for **evaluation** (the patient's response to interventions). The additional **R** in SOAPIER stands for **Revision** (changes made from the original treatment plan) (Springhouse Corporation, 1999).

Advantages of the SOAP, SOAPIE, and SOAPIER formats are that they (a) have increased structure and organization, (b) reflect the entire process of care, (c) improve ability to track problems, (d) complement more traditional care plans, (e) foster communication among team members, and (f) promote continuity of care (Iyer & Camp, 1999; Meiner, 1999; Springhouse Corporation, 1999). Disadvantages include (a) their emphasis on chronology of problems rather than priority of problems, (b) the need for training on what specific information corresponds to each letter, (c) the possibility that the original goal of structure and logic may be bypassed when modifications are made at the local level, (d) possible redundancy between flow sheets, care plans, and SOAP(IER) notes, (e) time inefficiency if the problem list is lengthy, and (f) resistance in agencies where multidisciplinary treatment is not valued (Iyer & Camp, 1999; Meiner, 1999; Springhouse Corporation, 1999).

Box 10.2 provides a brief example of a SOAPIER note for therapeutic recreation services. Note the content that is addressed in each section.

Focus Charting

Focus charting is a method for organizing information in the narrative portion of the client's record to include data, action, and response for each identified concern. It is a client-centered approach to documentation using simple professional terminology to describe client status and services of care provided.

Focus charting uses a column format to separate topic words or phrases from the body of the progress notes. The column format helps the writer organize the information into groups of related data and helps the reader locate specific information quickly. The primary purpose of the focus column is to aid communication among members of the treatment or health care team (Lampe, 1992, 1997). Focus charting attempts to identify each member of the treatment team as a professional decision maker. There is room in the format for analysis and synthesis of information as well as documentation of client outcomes.

The word "focus" replaces "problem" used in SOAP(IER) notes (Iyer & Camp, 1999). Advocates of focus charting take pride in the fact that a *focus* in much more comprehensive than a *problem* as is used in POMR. A focus is the current concern or behavior, or a significant event in client status.

A focus can be any of the following conditions or events:

- Key word or diagnostic category or a collaborative client problem (e.g., self-care, eating, activity tolerance)

- Current client concern or behavior; the topic of the narrative note (e.g., pre-op teaching, discharge planning, aggressive social behavior)

- A sign or symptom of possible importance to the treatment plan (e.g., fever, poor personal hygiene, suicide threat)

- An acute change in client condition (e.g., seizure, expressed apathy, decreased appetite)

Box 10.2   Sample SOAP(IER) Note

Date	Time	Prob. No.	Problem	Progress Note
1/30	1400	3	Excessive fatigue	S: "I'm tired. I just want to sit in this chair and be left alone."
				O: Pt. minimizes energy expenditure. Does not get exercise of any kind.
				A. Pt.'s continued pattern of being sedentary contributes to fatigue. Progressive exercise would improve energy level and physical condition.
				P: 1. Continue to observe and encourage involvement in active movements.
				2. Schedule two 20-minute sessions with pt. to discuss need for stamina and energy postdischarge.
				3. Enroll pt. in exercise group 5×/wk. starting 2/1; focus on strength, flexibility, and endurance.
				I: Test and observe pt.'s strength, flexibility; work toward greater endurance during exercise group.
2/1	1500			E: Pt. showed limited strength and flexibility in arms and legs. Warm-up and cool-down stretches recommended and demonstrated.
2/6	900			R: Pt. complains of boredom with exercising; recommend substituting Tai Chi and yoga for exercise group starting 2/7.

(Signature)   _Janai Ehret, CTRS_

- Significant events in client care (e.g., community reentry, family visit, trial off ventilator, chemotherapy, surgery)

- Key word or phrase indicating compliance with a standard of care or with hospital policy (e.g., TR assessment, diabetic education, transfer techniques)

- Identify the discipline making the entry and the topic of the note (i.e., therapeutic recreation/discharge planning, physical therapy/bedside exercise tolerance)

As noted in the preceding list, the focus can include problems and also can include positive events or factual occurrences. The column format of the focus helps each member of the team locate relevant information on a particular client.

The narrative portion of the focus charting progress note typically, although not always, includes three categories: (a) data, (b) action, and (c) response. In addition, many times, the note ends with a plan section, describing the next progression of interventions.

- Data—subjective and/or objective information supporting the stated focus or describing observations at the time of significant events.

- Action—a description of the actions taken by the therapist in the form of interventions or programs.

- Response—a description of the client's response to the interventions, activities, or situation. It can include a statement that treatment plan goals have been attained. Client outcomes are included in this section.

- (Plan)—next interventions to be implemented.

Advantages of focus charting include (a) a structure similar to, but more streamlined and flexible than, SOAP(IER) notes, (b) its emphasis on patient response to interventions, (c) greater ease of locating information, which saves time, (d) its focus on concerns larger than just patient problems, and (e) promoting analytical thinking by analyzing data and drawing conclusions (Iyer & Camp, 1999; Meiner, 1999; Springhouse Corporation, 1999). Disadvantages include (a) the need for intensive training to ensure useful documentation, (b) the ease of leaving off patient response, which renders the note less useful, (c) the fact that focus charting requires additional time to sort information into appropriate categories, and (d) the need to ensure clear alignment between all parts of the note (Iyer & Camp, 1999; Meiner, 1999; Springhouse Corporation, 1999).

Box 10.3 outlines a typical progress note using the DAR (data, action, response) format. Note the differences and similarities between the SOAP and DAR formats.

Charting by Exception

Charting by exception (CBE) is the fourth method of client documentation. Created in 1983, the purpose of CBE is to make trends in patient status more obvious, reduce the amount of time spent in documentation, and make current information about the patient's status readily available (Iyer & Camp, 1999). Only findings that are significant, abnormal, or that deviate from professional standards or protocols are

Box 10.3   Sample Focus Note

Date	Time	Focus	D = Data A = Action R = Response
4/15	1100	Interaction	D: 44-yr.-old female has not participated in scheduled groups nor spoken with peers for the last 5 days, since leaving closed psych unit.
			A: TR gave in-depth therapeutic recreation assessment; prescribed 4 groups/wk. to focus on self-disclosure and listening skills.
			R: Pt. willingly attended and participated in this morning's assertiveness group. Pt. initiated self-disclosure 2× and successfully completed 2 listening exercises with peers. Pt. expressed desire to "try this again."
			P: Compliment pt. each time she appropriately self-discloses. Encourage pt. to comply with 4 therapeutic recreation tx. groups/wk.
		Therapeutic Recreation Assessment	D: Comprehensive therapeutic recreation assessment results: Leisure Barriers Inventory: below agency norms on Time, Money, Transportation; Leisure Partners; Understanding Leisure; Leisure Resources, Leisure Responsibility; Fun/Enjoyment; and Age, Illness, and Disability scales; above agency norms on Activity Skills scale. Leisure Competence Measure: below agency norms on Leisure Awareness, Leisure Attitude, Social Appropriateness, and Primary Group Interaction Skills. Above norms on Leisure Skills and Leisure Participation.
			A: TRS discussed assessment results with pt. Collaborative planning occurred.
			R: At first pt. resisted "taking paper assessments" but then cooperated while completing the Leisure Barriers Inventory and the Leisure Competence Measure. Pt. agreed she needs to acquire social skills and increase opportunities to meet new friends.
			P: Pt. will participate in social skills training classes 3×/wk.; will participate in leisure planning class 2×/wk.
		(Signature)	*Mary Vickyle, CTRS*

recorded, thus reducing repetitive charting (Springhouse Corporation, 1999). The entire CBE system contains several components: (a) flow sheets, (b) documentation referencing standards of practice, (c) protocols and incidental orders, (d) a database, (e) diagnosis-based care plans, (f) and SOAP(IER) progress notes (Iyer & Camp, 1999).

Flow sheets, briefly, have spaces for a physician's order (for example, "referral to therapeutic recreation stress management class 1x/day") and then a series of horizontal boxes in which the status of the individual is quickly marked on a per-event basis. A checkmark means that the action is completed, an asterisk means that significant abnormal findings are present, and a right-facing arrow means the person's status is unchanged from the previous entry. These marks then represent a quickly understandable "map" of the individual's condition over time. Nursing flow sheets, for example of the patient's blood pressure and temperature, often are kept bedside for their convenience.

Standards of practice, protocols, and incidental orders become requirements as adherence to them represents expected typical care, noted by checkmarks, while asterisks mean that not all standards were followed. Of course this means that standards of care must be defined ahead of time for specific client conditions, and that attention is paid more to atypical responses to interventions rather than documenting routine and normal care patterns. **Incidental orders** are one-time, miscellaneous orders that break routine patterns of care.

Likewise, another component of CBE charting is a **database** that contains the typical range of scores for assessment tools. For example, if a typical score is found, it is marked with a checkmark in the appropriate box, but an atypical score requires additional description. The database part of the system requires that typical assessment scores be known for the client population. **Treatment plans** and **progress notes** are similar to formats previously described and contain information on client problems or diagnosis, expected outcomes, and interventions. Because standards of practice and protocols also are required, treatment plans and progress notes are brief and focus on unusual circumstances and reactions rather than normal patterns of patient responses (Iyer & Camp, 1999; Springhouse Corporation, 1999).

Advantages of charting by exception include (a) readily available and readable information, (b) flow sheets that provide a convenient, predesigned form, which allows for minimal documentation, (c) guidelines on the back of the forms that provide immediately accessible directions, (d) easily determined trends in a patient's status, (e) the fact that normal findings are precisely identified, so agreement exists, (f) minimizing of repetitive charting, (g) decrease in charting time, and (h) easy adaptability to clinical pathways (Iyer & Camp, 1999; Meiner, 1999; Springhouse Corporation, 1999). Disadvantages are that (a) duplication of charting is reduced but not eliminated, (b) not all professions have clear-cut agreed upon standards of patient care, (c) the design in most facilities is specific to nursing so CBE must be adapted for other disciplines, (d) CBE requires a major change in an agency's documentation system, (e) major educational efforts are necessary for adoption, (f) CBE may have a negative impact on reimbursement until it is more widely accepted, and (g) debate still occurs about the legalities of CBE (Iyer & Camp, 1999; Meiner, 1999; Springhouse Corporation, 1999).

Four Additional Methods of Charting

The four additional charting methods were developed by nurses and aim to either focus attention in a specific direction or reduce the need for extensive documentation that distracts providers from patient care. The charting methods mentioned briefly include: (a) PIE, (b) FACT, (c) Core, and (d) Outcomes.

The **Problem-Intervention-Evaluation (PIE)** system involves flow sheets and allows care plans to be integrated within progress notes. PIE charting does not contain assessment data per se (Meiner, 1999). A problem list is created (usually from an accepted nursing diagnosis) and each problem is labeled P#x (where "x" is the number of the problem, for example, P#1). Corresponding interventions are noted with IP#1, and evaluations of the effects are noted with EP#1 (Iyer & Camp, 1999; Springhouse Corporation, 1999).

The **FACT** method of charting is named for its four key elements: (a) flow sheets individualized to specific services, (b) assessment with standardized baseline parameters, (c) concise, integrated progress notes and flow sheets documenting the patient's condition and responses, and (d) timely entries recorded when care is given (Springhouse Corporation, 1999). FACT closely resembles charting by exception.

The **Core** system focuses on the nursing process and consists of a database, plans of care, flow sheets, progress notes, and discharge summaries. Core charting requires nurses to assess and record a patient's functional and cognitive status within eight hours of admission (Springhouse Corporation, 1999).

The **Outcomes** documentation system focuses on the process of care, especially the patient's behaviors and reactions to interventions and teaching. The system features a database, a plan of care, and expected outcome statements. Criteria for outcome statements include specification of (a) specific behaviors which show that the patient has progressed toward or attained a goal, (b) standards for measuring the patient's behaviors, such as how much the patient does and for how long, (c) the conditions under which the behavior is expected to occur, and (d) a target date or time by which the behaviors should occur (including short-term and long-term goals) (Springhouse Corporation, 1999). Meiner (1999) noted that clinical pathways or care maps may be considered outcomes charting. (Chapter 8 in this text discusses clinical pathways).

Each type of client documentation has unique features, although in reality, many agencies use some combination or variation of these types. Each therapeutic recreation student and professional benefits from understanding the differences and similarities between charting methods as well as their advantages and disadvantages. Reviewing these basic types of documentation formats helps with the discussion of specific pieces of client documentation. The next sections will discuss client treatment plans, progress notes, and discharge/referral summaries.

Treatment Plans

Treatment plans are documents kept in a client's chart that outline the action to be taken with, for, or by the client who is receiving intervention services within the sponsoring agency. Other names for treatment plans, depending on the agency type, are habilitation plans, individualized education plans, individualized program plans, and resident care plans. The basic principles among all these plans are the same. They each attempt to specify goal-directed services designed to meet an individual client's needs. They each provide an accountable method of documenting the need and goals of the client and the type of services that will be provided. For ease and consistency in reading, the term "treatment plan" will be used to indicate all forms of client-oriented plans.

Treatment plans are perhaps the most important form of individual client documentation. More than one regulatory agency surveyor has stated, "If it is not documented in the treatment plan, there is no need to be providing the service." This implies several related concepts:

- Treatment plans must be compatible with the comprehensive program design and program offerings within the therapeutic recreation department.
- Content in treatment plans must be consistent with the aims of the agency's and therapeutic recreation department's mission and scope of service.
- Content in progress notes and all subsequent client documentation must be based on and align with the initial treatment plan.

Agency policy will determine both the format and the process for the development of a client's treatment plan. In some agencies, one individual (physician, psychiatrist, physiatrist, primary therapist) will have the major responsibility for the development of a client's treatment plan. In other instances, the treatment plan is developed by a treatment team. It is important that the therapeutic recreation specialist be considered a part of the treatment team and have input into the treatment planning process. Even when one individual is responsible for the development of the treatment plan, the therapeutic recreation specialist should have the same avenues for input to that plan as do other rehabilitation and professional services staff.

Agencies differ in the specificity of the treatment plan. Some agencies will have brief treatment plans and expect that each professional discipline will maintain a more detailed treatment plan for each client they serve. For example, some agencies may indicate briefly that social work, therapeutic recreation, and psychology each will be assisting the client in the social and emotional goal areas listed in the plan. Each of these disciplines then will separately specify the detailed methods for helping the client to accomplish these goals. When this method is used, the therapeutic recreation comprehensive and specific program plans are used as the basis for determining and documenting the client's individualized treatment plan.

In many agencies where the team approach is used in the actual development of the treatment plan, the plan itself may be quite detailed. In addition to the overall treatment goals that will be addressed by many disciplines, specific therapeutic recreation goals might also be listed in this general treatment plan. The therapeutic recreation specialist in this instance will still benefit by having a thoroughly documented comprehensive program plan, including specific program plans, that are the basis for specifying how individual client goals will be achieved.

Writing the Therapeutic Recreation Treatment Plan

Because of the great variation in agency treatment plans, specific treatment plan formats are difficult to discuss. For the sake of the text, sample content and format for therapeutic recreation treatment plans are presented, as opposed to an overall treatment plan with therapeutic recreation integrated into it.

The treatment plan or individual client program plan is a step-by-step outline of procedures to be followed in assisting the client to achieve individual goals. Treatment plans should be written with enough detail so that all staff members understand the procedures and can maintain consistency. As the client progresses, the plan is updated and changed through the use of progress notes.

Treatment Plan Components

In the truest sense, the client's treatment plan should be based on the assessed client needs in conjunction with the stated scope of services provided by the therapeutic recreation department at that particular agency. That means that the treatment plan designed by the therapeutic recreation specialist should focus on those problems that are addressed within the scope of services provided within the therapeutic recreation programs. When these programs are designed based on generic client needs (see Chapter 4 on comprehensive program design), the task of defining client problem areas and establishing client goals and outcomes becomes much easier.

Two areas may appear on the client's master treatment plan that likely are collected and/or documented by staff other than the therapeutic recreation specialist. These include demographic background and history and referrals. (Usually referrals to therapeutic recreation services are made by the physician or primary therapist; the therapeutic recreation specialist also may make referrals to other disciplines, although this occurs less frequently.) These two areas are discussed briefly prior to the introduction of information most likely to be gathered and recorded by the therapeutic recreation specialist.

Demographic Background and History.   A significant amount of background information may be included in the client's chart. An up-to-date chart will contain client assessments from several disciplines, including therapeutic recreation. There is no need to duplicate efforts by reassessing what another discipline already has assessed. Therefore, the therapeutic recreation specialist should utilize all available relevant information before collecting this generic background and history information from the client. Examples of background information may include such items as the client's age, address, educational level, marital or relationship status, family members, religion, current or former employment, and brief medical history. Every discipline needs this information, but it is beneficial to the client if the information is gathered only once, and all other disciplines rely on that source instead of asking the client again. Only in situations in which the veracity or cognitive status of the client may be in question should disciplines duplicate such background information on their assessments.

Occasionally, the treatment plan must be written before all the necessary client information can be gathered. In this situation, the treatment plan should specify what additional data is needed, who is responsible for obtaining this information, and a time schedule for documentation of the information.

Referrals to and from Therapeutic Recreation Services.   At times, specific referrals to therapeutic recreation will provide direction for the development of a treatment plan. The referral from a physician may indicate a specific physical condition or problem that needs to be addressed in the therapeutic recreation treatment plan. A referral from the psychologist or social worker may indicate a special social, family, or behavioral concern that must be considered. In general, referrals may be to specific programs, such as social skills, leisure awareness, or time management, or for a specific problem, such as "problem with decision making" or "problem with flexibility and endurance." Sometimes the specificity of the referral depends on how knowledgeable the referring professional is with the services offered by the therapeutic recreation department. Naturally, the therapeutic recreation specialist should take responsibility for educating referring professionals with specific information about the services he or she provides, as well as the anticipated outcomes. As mentioned in Chapter 8, clinical practice guidelines with program descriptions and client outcomes would be useful in this educational process.

Sometimes, the therapeutic recreation specialist will discover a client problem or condition that warrants a referral to another discipline. When it is in accord with agency policy, the therapeutic recreation specialist may include a referral suggestion in the client's treatment plan. Because agency policies vary, the therapeutic recreation specialist must first identify the approved process for referrals in that particular agency, and then follow that procedure in making a referral.

Besides the demographic information and referrals section of the treatment plan, other information of concern to the therapeutic recreation specialist includes:

- Assessment results/client problem areas or deficits
- Client goals and objectives
- Action plan for client involvement
- Facilitation styles and approaches
- Staff and client responsibilities
- Reevaluation schedule
- Signature and date

Each of these areas is discussed below, with therapeutic recreation examples provided. As each agency may differ in its information or format requirements, the reader should treat these as generic examples for illustration purposes and be aware that specific agency requirements may differ.

Assessment Results/Client Problem Areas or Deficits.   Chapter 9, on assessment, discussed the client assessment process that results in data that can be used to place clients into programs. The results of a client assessment should provide information on the client's deficits or needs that are targeted for intervention by the therapeutic recreation specialist. *When the content of the assessment matches the content of the programs, the assessment results are more likely to be able to place clients into programs that are* *useful for changing some aspect of the behavior—that is, the client's problem or need—and, as a result, be able to produce client outcomes. The connection between the programs, assessment, goals, and outcomes is a logical one, and one that cannot be overstated.*

Some agencies focus only on problems while others include both problems and strengths as the foundation of the treatment plan. The content of either the problem or strength list depends on the type of agency. For example, a client may have a hearing impairment and also be in a rehabilitation agency with a traumatic brain injury. Although the hearing impairment may affect the treatment process, it would probably not be listed as a "problem" since no treatment would be provided for the hearing impairment. Similarly, a person with paraplegia who uses a wheelchair may be admitted to a substance abuse unit. Although the spinal cord injury certainly is noticeable and must be considered in treatment (and may indirectly cause problems for the individual), it probably would not be on the problem list of the client's substance-abuse-focused treatment plan. As noted earlier in this chapter, the charting method at a particular agency also will determine the type and extent of the problem list. It is likely that most agencies will use a combination or variation of the charting methods discussed.

Problems and strengths are stated in measurable, observable, and behavioral terms. Typically, diagnostic terminology (e.g., schizophrenia) should not be used alone as a description of the client's problem. The therapeutic recreation professional should not be using diagnostic labels (e.g., depressed) in the formulation of problem statements. A more measurable, observable, and behavioral way of describing depression might be "interpersonal withdrawal from peers" or "without intervention by staff, patient sleeps all day."

When strengths are included, they too must be specific and descriptive of the client as an individual. Strengths can be attributes that the client could use to help resolve problems and reach goals. For example, "Patient has athletic skills and may be able to develop leisure skills and interests in this area" or "patient has good social support network."

Below is a list of generic problem/strength areas that could be used by a number of agencies serving individuals with illnesses and/or disabilities.

- Psychological functioning (thinking, feeling, perception, self-image)
- Physical functioning (mobility, balance, coordination, endurance, weight, senses, exercise patterns, speech and communication patterns)
- Behavioral and emotional functioning (aggression, abusive behaviors, emotional control, emotional expression)
- Social/interpersonal functioning (skills, support network, interpersonal relationships, social appropriateness)
- Intellectual functioning (ability to process, concentration, learning, memory, problem-solving and decision-making abilities)
- Leisure functioning (awareness, skills, interests, resources, motivation, planning skills, partners, barriers)
- Independent living skills (self-care, hygiene, home maintenance, transportation, education, employment, money management)
- Miscellaneous (religion, culture)

- Aftercare planning (problem that may delay discharge or require a special effort)

In addition, each type of agency (e.g., mental health, physical medicine and rehabilitation, long-term care) may have an additional list, depending on the characteristics of clients served. For example, in a substance abuse facility, the following problems/strengths may be considered in addition to those above.

- Substance abuse/use (alcohol, medications, illegal drugs, nicotine, caffeine, non-substance addictions)
- Legal status (criminal actions, guardianship, protective services)

Regardless of the type of agency or categories used to develop the problems/strengths list, the therapeutic recreation specialist should refer back to the therapeutic recreation philosophy and mission as well as the scope of services delineated in his or her comprehensive therapeutic recreation program plan. The client problems and strengths targeted by programs and reviewed in the client assessment are areas for goal development.

Questions to be asked include: What functional problems is the therapeutic recreation specialist able to address in programs (psychological, physical, mental, social, spiritual, or emotional problems)? What leisure-related problems will interfere with the client's successful discharge, treatment outcomes, and community reintegration (leisure decision making, leisure resource utilization, social skills, leisure skills, etc.)? The specification of the problems/strengths list will determine directly the formulation of the client goals that are included in the treatment plan.

Because the client assessment is the prime place to identify these problems and strengths, it plays a prime role in developing a workable and meaningful list of client deficits and abilities. If assessment results are vague or nonexistent, then this crucial link in the intervention chain is broken. The assessment must be able to produce a reasonable list of areas in which the client needs intervention. The two lists below give some indication of how difficult or easy it might be to create goals or action plans from assessment results.

Sample Assessment Results (inappropriate)

Poor social skills

Appears apathetic

Few leisure skills or interests

Watches excessive amount of television

Sample Assessment Results (appropriate)

Client scores low on stress management skills

Client received low score on ability to make leisure-related decisions

Client reports strong social network as evidenced by community involvement*

Client received low score on knowledge of community leisure resources

*Assessment results may reflect positive scores (behaviors) of clients as well as low scores.

Box 10.4 provides an overview of the content relationship between the Leisure Ability Model leisure education content areas (program areas), barriers the client may have in those areas, and client goals. It is worth noting that once program content is determined (from an analysis of several factors outlined in Chapter 4), the same content is reviewed for client problems. This helps the therapeutic recreation specialist stay within the boundaries of the profession and targets goals and outcomes related to therapeutic recreation's scope of practice. Client problems, to be targeted by therapeutic recreation, then coincide with those which the programs are designed to affect. It naturally follows then that the client goals flow from these program content areas and client problem areas. Notice that the content within all three columns is very similar—and is very focused on the problems that can be worked on within the programs as designed.

Client Goals and Objectives.   Treatment plans usually will include individual client goals, and sometimes client objectives. Each client goal or objective should be as measurable as possible. Although the format for documenting measurable client goals and objectives does vary among agencies, most agencies are now requiring that all professional staff record only measurable goals and objectives. Again, this process is easiest when programs have been well conceptualized, assessments have been well designed, and assessment results yield scores or information that leads to intervention programming. Note that performance measures, discussed in Chapter 5, look and function very similarly to client objectives, in that both focus on client outcomes. Performance measures, when written during the program design stages, relate to the outcomes expected of clients from participating in the specific program. Outcome statements written into the program plan then become easier to link with client objectives written in treatment plans.

Below are some examples of vague or inappropriate client goals and more measurable goals.

Sample Client Goals (inappropriate)

To improve self-concept

To improve socialization

To increase responsible use of leisure

Sample Client Goals (appropriate)

To give and receive constructive criticism

To give and receive compliments

To maintain eye contact

To verbalize personal responsibility for own actions

To initiate/sustain a conversation with a peer

To make a leisure decision when given a choice between two options

To identify leisure resources available in the community

The preceding goals can be measured, although they are not yet written in fully measurable terms. Note that one of the major differences is that the second set of

Box 10.4   Comparison of Leisure Education Content, Typical Client Barriers, and Typical Client Goals

Typical Content	Typical Barriers	Typical Goals
1.0 Leisure Awareness		
1.1 Knowledge of Leisure		
Benefits of Leisure	Unable to identify benefits of leisure	Identify 3 benefits of leisure involvement
Outcomes of Leisure Involvement	Unable to identify positive outcomes	Identify 3 positive outcomes of leisure
Personal Responsibility for Leisure	Inability to take personal responsibility	Verbalize responsibility for leisure
1.2 Self-Awareness		
Actual and Perceived Abilities	Unable to identify personal abilities	Identify 3 personal strengths for leisure
Past and Current Leisure Patterns	Unable to identify patterns of leisure	Relate past, present, and future involvement
Areas of Personal Achievement	Inability to realize accomplishments	Identify 3 accomplishments in leisure
1.3 Leisure and Play Attitudes		
Origin of Leisure Attitudes	Lack of awareness of family influences	Identify family influences on current behavior
Values Clarification of Attitudes	Inability to place value on leisure	Recognize importance of leisure in life
Relationship to Behavior	Inability to make time for leisure	Schedule time for leisure involvement
1.4 Related Participatory/ Decision-Making Skills		
Decision-Making Skills	Unable to make leisure decisions	Examine alternatives and make decisions
Leisure Planning Skills	Unable to plan for own leisure	Make and carry out plans for leisure
Problem-Solving Techniques	Inability to solve leisure-related problems	Identify and solve leisure-related problems
2.0 Social Interaction Skills		
2.1 Communication Skills		
Assertiveness Skills	Lack of assertion in appropriate situations	Assert one's needs without aggression
Conversational Skills	Lack of ability to initiate conversation	Initiate conversation with peer
Perspective Taking Skills	Lack of ability to take another's perspective	Verbalize another's perspective
2.2 Relationship-Building Skills		
Self-Disclosure Skills	Inability to determine appropriate disclosure	Determine appropriate disclosure
Social Networks	Inability to maintain close ties with peers	Contact peers to maintain closeness
Expression of Care and Concern	Inability to express concern for another	Express genuine concern for another
2.3 Self-Presentation Skills		
Manners and Etiquette	Lack of taking turns and sharing	Take turns and share with others
Attire and Dressing	Inability to determine appropriate attire	Select proper attire for occasion and season

(continued)

Box 10.4 *(continued)*

3.0 Leisure Activity Skills

Content Area	Deficits	Objectives
3.1 *Traditional Skills* Sports, Aquatics, Drama, Outdoor, Arts and Crafts, Hobbies, Music	Lack of physical skills done alone Lack of creative expression skills Lack of skills that can be done outdoors	Learn 1 physical skill that can done alone Learn 1 form of creative expression Learn 1 outdoor activity for each season
3.2 *Nontraditional Skills* Fitness, Relaxation, Meditation, Cooking, Home Improvement, Plant and Pet Care	Lack of skills that don't require other people Inability to identify leisure in the home	Learn 1 skill that can be done alone at any time Identify 3 activities that can be done in the home

4.0 Leisure Resources

Content Area	Deficits	Objectives
4.1 *Activity Opportunities* Identifying Possible Leisure Activities, Identifying Preferences	Inability to identify leisure opportunities Inability to determine leisure preferences	Identify 15 leisure opportunities List 10 favorite leisure activities
4.2 *Personal Resources* Finances, Educational Level, Past Leisure Experiences, Abilities and Limitations	Inability to budget for leisure experiences Inability to self-teach leisure skills	Budget for 2 leisure events per month Identify and learn one new leisure skill
4.3 *Family and Home Resources* Abilities and Interests of Families and Friends, Available Resources in the Home	Lack of common leisure skills with family Inability to identify home leisure resources	Identify 2 skills in common with family Identify 3 leisure resources in each room
4.4 *Community Resources* Identification and Utilization of Local Agencies and Facilities That Provide Leisure Opportunities	Lack of knowledge of community resources Lack of ability to utilize community resources Lack of ability to locate low-cost activities	Identify 10 community leisure resources Utilize 3 community leisure resources Identify 5 low-cost activities for summer
4.5 *State and National Resources* Identification and Utilization of State and National Agencies and Facilities for Leisure	Lack of knowledge of state/national resources Lack of ability to utilize state/national resources Lack of ability to identify transportation	Identify 5 state leisure resources Utilize 1 state leisure resource in next year Identify 2 means of transportation

---

Box 10.5   Sample Format: Client Goals and Objectives

Treatment Goals	Behavioral Objectives

1. To initiate conversation with new group of people	1. After two weeks of training, the client will:
	  a. identify when interruption is appropriate
	  b. stand within two feet of group
	  c. make eye contact
	  d. listen to conversation of group without immediate interruption
	  e. say hello to known person(s)
	  f. make eye contact
	  g. use appropriate gestures in greeting
	  h. add to topic, ask questions, offer to help or otherwise contribute to conversation, while using appropriate gestures, and maintaining body space, as judged by the TRS

2. To make a leisure-related decision	2. After completion of the Leisure Planning class, the client will:
	  a. name two leisure options for desired time frame
	  b. locate information about each option, including location, price, duration, transportation, accessibility, etc.
	  c. list strengths and weaknesses of each option
	  d. compare strengths and weaknesses with desires
	  e. make selection between the two options, as judged by the TRS

---

goals begins with an *action verb*. In that way, professionals and clients begin to *see* what action will be expected to prove that the client has achieved the goal. This helps with measurement. In addition, it becomes clearer what types of programs the client needs to be involved in to achieve the goal. Client **goals** and objectives, which result from proper client assessment, are the bridge between the program being offered and the client's participation in it. Again, increased specification helps keep the specialist and client focused on the outcomes that will be anticipated from involvement.

Box 10.5 provides an example of a treatment plan in which client goals are supplemented by more specific client objectives. Note that the goals are somewhat generic and that the objective more clearly defines the behaviors to be observed to confirm that the client has achieved this outcome. More information about writing goals and objectives will be discussed later in this section.

Some agencies will require the therapeutic recreation specialist to distinguish between long-range (long-term) and short-range (short-term) goals. There are no universal definitions for these terms. Long-range goals in one agency may imply four months, while another agency may consider long-range goals to imply one year. While long-range goals keep the ultimate goal of independent leisure functioning in mind, smaller short-term goals are necessary in many cases. Fewer, concrete achievable goals are preferable to many, vague long-term goals that are unattainable. This is

---

Box 10.6   Examples of Long-Term Goals and Short-Term Goals

Client: Frances Douroumes

Problem: Physical aggression

Short-Term Goal: Client will not hit staff or peers for 3 days

Long-Term Goal: Client will not act physically aggressive toward others for 1 month

Client: Caleb Barrett

Problem: Lacks peer support network

Short-Term Goals: Client will learn 2 leisure skills that foster social interaction
Client will utilize 1 community leisure resource
Client will initiate 1 independent social leisure activity

Long-Term Goals: Client will create leisure plan for postdischarge
Client will write in social leisure journal that documents friendship-related efforts and activities

---

especially true as therapeutic recreation specialists and other professionals are being challenged to produce and document client outcomes.

Box 10.6 provides examples of long-term goals and short-term goals. Again, note that the short-term goals are more measurable and can lead to a better specification of client outcomes.

Client Objectives.   Once again, the agency will dictate the format used for client objectives. However, the most common type of objective is the behavioral objective. Because behavioral objectives translate into client outcomes, some extended discussion is needed on their development and format. Behavioral **objectives** are usually very specific and contain condition, behavior, and criterion.

Conditions.   A **condition** is the circumstance under which the desired behavior will occur. Phrases that indicate common conditions include:

- On request . . .
- When given the necessary equipment . . .
- When given a choice of three activities . . .
- With an opponent of equal ability . . .
- With Level 4 minimal assistance . . .
- On a written examination . . .
- After completion of the program . . .
- After one week of active participation . . .

Sometimes conditions are unique to a situation, setting, population, or program. An example follows:

- While involved in a trip in the community with the therapeutic recreation specialist and after completing the program of assertiveness training, the client will . . .

Conditions of a behavioral objective primarily set the stage by identifying necessary equipment, activities, timelines, or other events that are essential to the performance of the desired behavior. Normally, the condition is the first phase of the behavioral objective. It starts with a preposition and is set off from the rest of the behavioral objective by a comma. Occasionally, the conditions are scattered throughout the behavioral objective. Conditions occur throughout the following behavioral objective and are italicized for identification:

- *On request,* the client will play a game of checkers *with an opponent of equal ability,* staying on task throughout the activity as evidenced by continuous attention to the game and completion of the game within a reasonable amount of time, as judged by the therapeutic recreation specialist.

In this example, some conditions are not mentioned but are implied. The checkers game itself is not specified. Often, when a condition is obvious, it can be eliminated to reduce the length of the complete behavioral objective.

Behavior.   The **behavior** identified in the behavioral objective is the central focus. It is the phrase that identifies what action the client will demonstrate to prove that he or she has achieved the desired knowledge, skills, or ability. The behavior must be observable and measurable in order to meet this requirement. Although measurement of the specific action is most often dealt with in the criteria section of the behavioral objective, the behavior focuses the attention of the reader on the behavior of concern. Some examples of the behavioral part of an objective are:

- . . . the client will name leisure resources in the home . . .
- . . . the client will walk . . .
- . . . the client will explain the difference between work and leisure . . .
- . . . the client will plan a weekend trip . . .
- . . . the client will serve an overhand tennis shot . . .
- . . . the client will converse . . .
- . . . the client will verbalize the actions needed to get from the center to downtown . . .

Note that the wording always includes the phrase "the client will," followed by an *action verb.* The challenge for the therapeutic recreation specialist is to select the most important, representative behavior that would indicate that the client has achieved the targeted outcome. One difficulty of writing good objectives is to stay focused on the important behavior, while making it specific enough to measure it well.

Some agencies also stress that the behavior should be stated in *positive terms,* rather than negative. For example, an objective might read "client will keep hands to self" rather than "client will not hit peer." Just like other aspects of the behavioral objective, this positive focus often requires practice in writing.

Criterion.   The **criterion** in the behavioral objective delineates the exact amounts and nature of the behavior that can be taken as evidence that the objective has been met. A criterion is a precise statement or standard that allows individuals to make judgments based on the observable, measurable behavior. Good criterion statements are so clear that two or more different evaluators have no problem making the same decision about whether the desired behavior occurred.

The criterion section defines more specifically the exact act or representation of the behavior stated, along with standards of form, frequency, or other behavioral descriptions. Writing criterion statements requires selection of representative behaviors and then description of the amounts and nature of those behaviors. Criteria can be written in many ways. Selecting the right or most appropriate kind of criterion is directly related to the nature of the knowledge or skill identified in the behavior portion. The following sections identify and describe the commonly used types of criteria.

1. *Number of Trials.* Some behaviors occur by chance, and thus the criteria need to be written in the standard format, "x out of y attempts." For example, hitting a target with darts, catching a ball, or executing a Ping-Pong serve can occur by chance if just one trial or attempt is called for. In situations such as these, the designer is wise to use a number of trials as the criterion. An example of this is:

On request, the client will make a legal Ping-Pong serve three out of five times, as judged by the instructor.

It is unlikely that the client can serve the ball three out of five times by chance. Note that the word "legal" designates a criterion. There is a standard definition of a legal serve, and thus the criterion does not need further definition.

When asked to groom himself for the afternoon activity group, the client will brush his teeth two out of three times, as judged by the instructor.

In this case, the number of trials may become important in knowing how the client progresses in remembering steps to self-grooming. For some clients in this situation, it may also be necessary to include whether the client completed the behavior with or without prompts from the staff.

2. *Level of Accuracy.* Certain behaviors require a criterion of accuracy to be useful. The ability to throw a baseball, putt in golf, or bowl usually is judged by a degree of accuracy in order to be credible. An example of the level of accuracy is:

After completion of the Community Reentry program, the client will estimate the cost of dinner and a movie, within three dollars.

Given a putting green with a circle one yard in radius drawn around the hole, and upon request, the client will putt six out of ten golf balls into the circle, as judged by the instructor.

Note that the latter behavioral objective combines accuracy and number of trials.

3. *Amount of Time.* Some behaviors are best judged by utilizing time as a criterion. Here is a sample of this type of criterion:

On request, the client will dress in appropriate clothing for a community outing within ten minutes.

On request, the client will run the 100-yard dash within twenty seconds, as judged by the instructor.

Note that this behavior may not need the number of trials. The client either can or cannot run that fast. The same can be said for such activities as bike riding or swimming. A client either can or cannot do the activity. In other words, it would be unlikely that the behavior could occur by chance alone. Thus, increasing the trials only increases the amount of evaluation time required.

4. *Percentages or Fractions.* Certain behaviors are valid only if they are maintained over time. The problem is that all activities are not consistent in terms of the amount of time required for action or number of opportunities available. A percentage criterion allows for such variation. A behavioral objective of this nature might read:

While engaged in a basketball game, the client will make 25 percent of the attempted field shots, as judged by the instructor.

By completion of the activity, the client will write down information about 25 percent of the resources in the "My Community Directory" notebook, as judged by the specialist.

5. *Form.* Some behavioral objectives require the specification of form in order to be appropriate. This is often the case when dealing with activity skills that include an aspect of physical performance, such as sports and dance. For example, form is important in executing a forehand shot in tennis, a specific stroke in swimming, or a golf swing. Likewise, form is vital to ballet, gymnastics, and many other motor skills activities or, in these cases, is highly related to success or accuracy within the activity. There are several ways this can be described:

a. Relate the behavioral objective to an existing, known standard that is generally respected and accepted. For example:

On request, the client will swim 25 yards using the side stroke as described in the Red Cross manual, as judged by the instructor.

At the restaurant, the client will use proper table manners, as outlined in the Manners and You program, as judged by the specialist.

b. Judgment of an expert. A good golf instructor knows and can judge form with consistency. In this case, the behavioral objective might read:

On request, the client will drive a golf ball a minimum of 100 yards with acceptable form, as judged by the instructor.

Note that this behavioral objective combines form and distance for a thorough criterion.

When given the choice of two pieces of leisure equipment, the client will select which product represents the best value for her dollar, as judged by the specialist.

Note that in this case, the answer of which product has the most value is not clear cut, and so the answer will need interpretation by the specialist.

6. *Procedures and Characteristics.* Many behavioral objectives for therapeutic recreation programs deal with content and behavior that are not adequately specified by criterion statements using form, number of trials, percentages, or accuracy. Countless situations exist in which the best criteria would be statements that are developed to describe the specific procedure or characteristics of the representative behavior itself. These characteristic statements are appropriate, valid, and reliable. They can be observed and measured. In most cases, they enhance the quality of the behavioral objective because of their specificity and direct application to the behavior being addressed in the particular behavioral objective. Behavioral objectives using the procedures and characteristics criteria use the phrase "as characterized by" immediately following the identified behavior and then list the selected statements in narrative form. The following behavioral objective illustrates this type of criteria use. Note that other types of criteria often are used in combination with this approach.

During the evening meal, the client will converse with another patient during the meal, as characterized by:

a. *initiating a conversation with another resident*
b. *listening to the other resident's response*
c. *continuing conversation on an appropriate topic*
d. *speaking in an acceptable tone and at an appropriate volume*
e. *maintaining appropriate eye contact and body positioning throughout*
f. *concluding the conversation in an appropriate manner, as judged by the therapeutic recreation specialist*

Most often, when these types of criteria are used, they also require the use of the phrase "as judged by" as a necessary aspect of the criteria. The phrase indicates that some knowledge and expertise are held by the person making the judgment. In the preceding behavioral objective, a variety of "appropriate" topics, tones, volumes, and completions of the conversation may fulfill the specified criteria. The specialist is expected to make these judgments based on experience, previously discussed acceptable behaviors, and common sense. The criteria in the example are a bit loose, but they serve as adequate guidelines for judging whether the client has acquired the desired behaviors.

Two other examples of behavioral objectives that use the procedure and characteristic criteria:

Upon request, the client will take own pulse rate as characterized by the following:

a. *placing second and third fingers on neck*
b. *finding pulse and maintaining finger position*
c. *counting number of beats for thirty seconds*
d. *doubling that number to get heart rate, as judged by the therapeutic recreation specialist*

Upon request, the client will name a personal preference for leisure activities as characterized by:

a. *completing an appropriate leisure education activity in writing*
b. *verbally describing a preferred leisure activity for each section depicted in the form, as judged appropriate by the therapeutic recreation specialist*

The use of procedures and characteristics criteria is very common in the writing of behavioral objectives for therapeutic recreation programs. The value of this type of criterion cannot be overemphasized. This approach allows the therapeutic recreation specialist to focus on the behavioral descriptions that capture the essence of the desired representative behavior in the most precise and meaningful way possible.

Almost all behavioral objectives contain the phrase "as judged by . . ." Regardless of the type of behavior and criteria used, all behavioral objectives must be viewed and judged by someone. Although it may appear tedious to place this phrase in all behavioral objectives, it is a necessary aspect of most behavioral objectives. In most of the examples given so far, the criteria are very explicit, and almost anyone could view the behavior and make the judgment based on the criteria. This is most often true of behavioral objectives that involve physical skills. However, there are many behavioral objectives for which this is not true; the judgment by an expert is an essential part of the criterion itself. Many of the programs in therapeutic recreation that deal with improved functional behavior and leisure awareness will require this judgment by an expert to make the behavioral objective credible. However, the specialist must be forewarned that professional judgment alone, without other stated criteria, defeats the purpose of behavioral objectives. Observable and measurable behavioral descriptions are by definition a necessary part of the behavioral objective. Several examples of poor behavioral objectives may help to illustrate how vague the behavioral objective is without criteria for the desired behavior. They also show how nebulous the behavioral objective is when only the judgment of the therapeutic recreation specialist is stipulated.

> *Upon request, the client will demonstrate increased endurance, as judged by the therapeutic recreation specialist.*

> *Upon request, the client will demonstrate awareness of leisure preferences and patterns, as judged by the therapeutic recreation specialist.*

> *At the end of the program, the client will have improved self-esteem, as judged by the therapeutic recreation specialist.*

> *By the time of discharge, the client will have improved social skills, as judged by the therapeutic recreation specialist.*

The absence of the representative behaviors and criteria for judgment in each of the foregoing examples makes these behavioral objectives useless.

The purpose of behavioral objectives is to specify the exact behavior that will provide evidence that the intent of the objective has been met. As such, the conditions under which the behavior is expected to be performed, the representative behavior, and the criteria for judging whether the behavior has occurred are all extremely important. One of the major reasons for writing and designing client involvement goals to achieve the objectives is to increase accountability and improve services. Client behavioral objectives help keep the client and specialist focused on the important aspects of behavior, and the intended outcomes of participation.

One method for evaluating behavioral objectives is to ask the following questions, which should be answered affirmatively:

- Can you readily identify the behavior that is to be demonstrated by the client to show that he or she has achieved the objective?
- Can you readily identify the conditions under which the behavior will be demonstrated?
- Can you readily identify the standard to which the client's behavior must conform?
- If two staff members looked at this behavioral objective and a client's performance, could they agree whether the standards and limits had been achieved?

Writing and reading behavioral objectives are enhanced by using a standard format. It is highly recommended that the sequence of the parts be the same for all behavioral objectives. The most common format arranges the parts in the following sequence: condition, behavior, and criterion. The phrase "as judged by" appears as the last line. The format allows all readers to identify the various parts easily.

Action Plan for Client Involvement.   A major focus of any treatment plan is the specification of programs in which the client will be involved. *These programs must be logically linked to helping resolve the problem, reaching the goals and objectives, and thereby achieving the intended outcomes.*

Assume that the therapeutic recreation department already has conceptualized its programs into categorizations that include functional intervention, leisure education, and recreation participation. Each of these program areas may be categorized further into specific programs, such as emotional control and expression (functional intervention), activity skill acquisition (leisure education focus), and so on. When this type of conceptualization has occurred, it is a relatively simple task to indicate or document these programs in the client's treatment plan.

The most difficult situation arises when the therapeutic recreation department has neither comprehensively conceptualized nor documented a detailed description of the therapeutic recreation programs. Although not impossible, it is at best difficult, in this instance, to indicate stable, ongoing program involvement in the client's treatment plan.

Therapeutic recreation specialists are strongly encouraged not to list specific activities (e.g., cross-stitch or bicycling) in the treatment plan. It is a wiser choice to list the specific program type (e.g, hobbies or physical activity) in the treatment plan. This way, if changes in the specific activity are made (e.g., because of client interest or skills, scheduling, or equipment issues), the treatment plan still remains accurate. The progress notes could name specific activities if that seems important to document.

In some instances, individual clients may have special needs that cannot be addressed adequately within an ongoing therapeutic recreation program. In these cases, the treatment plan should specify other mechanisms for dealing with individual clients. Frequently, one-to-one staff/client sessions and nontherapeutic recreation staff or volunteers are used to help meet the special or unique needs of individual clients.

Frequency and Duration of Participation.   The treatment plan should indicate both the frequency and duration of the client's proposed involvement in various specific programs. Without such specification, it is difficult to tell whether the treatment plan is being implemented as originally designed.

Many staff members, though including the starting date of a client's involvement in programs, fail to indicate a tentative termination date. When it is not possible to estimate a realistic termination date, this date can coincide with the projected treatment plan review date. The accuracy and possible credibility of the treatment plan are dependent on the specificity of the plan.

Facilitation Styles and Approaches.   To ensure consistent staff/client communication and interaction, it is important to suggest recommended facilitation styles or approaches for the staff to utilize. Such "hints for dealing with the client" will facilitate the treatment milieu or environment.

At times, the recommended interaction techniques are guidelines for the therapeutic recreation staff who are conducting the specific programs. In other instances, suggestions for interacting with clients during nonprogrammed times are useful. Consistency in staff/client interactions, both within a specific program and external to a specific therapeutic recreation program, can facilitate the treatment process.

Staff and Client Responsibilities.   It is important to delineate and document both staff and client responsibilities. Examples of staff responsibilities may include contact to be made with community agencies, ordering of special equipment, or other tasks completed on behalf of the client. Each agency will have its own policy concerning the documentation of staff names in a client's chart. When last names are not permitted, professional titles (e.g., Therapeutic Recreation Specialist) are usually included.

Whenever possible, the client should play an active role in his or her own treatment. For this reason, it is advisable to delineate and document specific responsibilities of the client. It also is advisable to document a plan for monitoring the implementation of these responsibilities. Examples of client responsibilities may include completing worksheets or projects outside of activity time, following up on calling community resources, maintaining a daily, personal exercise program, or recording leisure expenditures during the week.

Reevaluation Schedule.   Too often, staff members fail to indicate when the treatment plan will be reevaluated. The unfortunate result is that treatment plan reviews become a haphazard occurrence and not in the client's best interest. If a plan is not working, it should be changed. If the client has achieved all, or most, of the treatment plan goals, the plan should be updated and made relevant.

Signature and Date.   Most agencies require that the designer of the treatment plan sign and date the completed plan. Other agencies require that each staff member involved in the client's treatment indicate this involvement in writing.

In some agencies, such a routine loses its meaning and becomes a mere ritual. However, the rationale behind such a procedure is sound. Signatures imply a personal awareness of professional responsibility in relation to the client's treatment plan. They also can serve as a quality improvement mechanism, documenting professional accountability and timely communication.

Many agencies will include the client's signature on the treatment plan. This procedure documents the client's involvement and input into his or her own treatment process.

Box 10.7 provides an abbreviated version of a client treatment plan. Note that this plan follows the basic outline as discussed in the previous sections.

Decisions Made During the Treatment Planning Process.   Treatment plan design is a complex process. In the previous example, the therapeutic recreation specialist made several professional decisions.

- What data sources are available? What information do I have (if not all assessments or interviews are complete)?
- What are the patient's major problems?
- Which problems are priorities?
- Which problems are within the domain (scope) of therapeutic recreation?

Box 10.7   Sample Client Treatment Plan

Name: Barbara Lockett   **Education:** Bachelors
Age: 26   **Hometown:** Ames, Iowa
IQ: 124   **Occupation:** Estate Planner

Background/Demographic Information: Barbara has held a variety of jobs, currently employed as an estate planner. Completed bachelors degree at local university last year. Single, living with college friend in apartment. Relatives live in another state. Current diagnosis: Depression. Exhibits depressed mood, sleeps 12 hours per day, low energy level, low self-esteem, difficulty concentrating or thinking, not involved in pleasurable activities.

Note: Although the preceding background is incomplete, much preliminary information would be available in the client chart for the development of an initial treatment plan.

Referral to Therapeutic Recreation Services: Received referral for therapeutic recreation services from case manager.

Assessment Results:
Pt. received low scores on Knowledge of Community Resources, Social Support Network, and Decision-Making Skills. Expresses limited contact with family, feelings of boredom, and disinterest in leisure involvement. Expresses lack of initiative to follow through with making and keeping plans.

Client Goals and Objectives:

1. To identify leisure resources available in the community
   Upon completion of the Activity Exploration program, the client will name three leisure resources available in the community for her personal leisure involvement, as judged by the TRS.

2. To verbalize personal responsibility for leisure
   Upon completion of the Values Clarification program, the client will develop a daily leisure plan based on her identified priorities within the areas of work, leisure, and home involvement, as judged by the TRS.

3. To make a decision regarding personal leisure involvement
   Upon completion of the Decisions, Decisions program, the client will decide between two leisure options and follow through with her plan for involvement in one activity, as judged by the TRS.

Action Plan for Client Involvement:

1. Enroll pt. in Activity Exploration program (leisure resources focus) MWF 1:00 to 2:00 PM from 11/11 to 12/11. Focus on:
   a. Activity opportunities available within the community at low cost
   b. A variety of leisure resources that may hold present and future interest for the client
   c. Assisting the client in developing skills at locating leisure resources on own

2. Enroll pt. in Values Clarification program (values identification and planning focus) MWF 3:00 to 4:00 PM from 11/11 to 12/1. Focus on:
   a. Identifying life priorities of the client
   b. Verbalizing the place of leisure within her total life experience
   c. Developing a plan for daily involvement in leisure

(continued)

Box 10.7   *(continued)*

3. Enroll pt. in Decisions, Decisions program (leisure planning focus) TTh from 9:00 to 10:00 AM from 11/11 to 12/4. Focus on:
   a. Exploring options for leisure involvement
   b. Weighing the costs and benefits of each option
   c. Making a leisure choice based on reviewed costs and benefits
   d. Acting on planned option for leisure activity

4. Use Reality Therapy approach with client, focusing on personal responsibility and decision making.

5. Compliment pt. when successful at identifying leisure options, verbalizing priorities, and/or making decisions.

6. Redirect conversation when client complains of boredom or lack of skill.

7. Reevaluate 12/11.

Randi Ray, CTRS

- How can problems be converted into goals?
- Which goals are within the domain of therapeutic recreation services?
- Are goals potentially measurable?
- What specific programs will help the client achieve these goals?
- What facilitation styles or intervention techniques will be most effective?
- Does the patient have any unique needs or goals that cannot be addressed in ongoing programs?

When writing the treatment plan, care should be taken that the client's original problems and goals will be addressed through implementation of the plan. Continuity and consistency throughout the treatment plan are essential.

It is very possible that each client will present a challenge to the therapeutic recreation specialist, who may have to make new professional decisions for each client. Yet there are specific stable guidelines that the therapeutic recreation specialist can use when formulating client treatment plans. Such stability relies greatly on the existence of a well-conceptualized, comprehensive therapeutic recreation program.

One stable assumption that will facilitate treatment plan design is the concentration on the scope of therapeutic recreation practice. That is, the therapeutic recreation specialist should focus goals, treatment, and outcomes on those areas that are covered by the therapeutic recreation discipline. Questions such as: In which area(s) of the Leisure Ability Model does the client have the greatest needs? problems? deficits? potential goals? The driving force behind good treatment planning is the focus on areas of service or competence with functional intervention, leisure education, and recreation participation.

Functional Intervention Component of Therapeutic Recreation Services

Are there predominant physical, mental, emotional, or social behavioral areas that will greatly inhibit the client's leisure involvement and lifestyle?

Which of these areas can and should be improved?

Leisure Education Component of Therapeutic Recreation Services

Does the client have an adequate awareness and knowledge of the role of leisure and the ability to solve problems and make responsible leisure decisions?

Does the client have adequate social skills to initiate and participate in leisure pursuits?

Does the client have knowledge of the existence of, and the ability to use, available leisure resources?

Does the client have an appropriate repertoire of leisure activity skills?

Recreation Participation Component of Therapeutic Recreation Services

Does the client have a need to participate in supervised, organized activities prior to complete independence?

"Meeting individual needs" does not necessarily imply a totally different treatment plan for each individual client. A well-conceptualized and well-implemented comprehensive therapeutic recreation program should help meet the primary needs of the majority of clients served. As seen in the chapter on comprehensive program design, programs are designed and implemented based on the global needs of clients. That is, programs and activities are selected for their potential to contribute to the broad needs of the client group being served. The uniqueness of each client's treatment plan occurs when each client is assessed and professionally guided into the specific programs that will address individually determined needs. Uniqueness, or individualized client planning, also will occur through the type of staff/client interaction that occurs within each specific program area. Thus, while the content of treatment plans may be very similar for several clients, the treatment process still will be individually determined.

Improving Efficiency of Treatment Plans.

As stated earlier, each facility will provide its own format for treatment plans. The length of the therapeutic recreation treatment plan also will vary among agencies. The plan must contain a sufficient amount of detail to be useful yet not be so lengthy that it becomes impractical to document on a regular basis. In the instances when the therapeutic recreation department develops its own treatment plan, a usable, practical format should be chosen. There are at least two options for streamlining, but still ensuring that essential information is included in, the client outcome process.

The first option is to include more detailed information on behavioral objectives and client outcomes within the program documentation. Since writing behavioral objectives for every individual is time consuming (and lengths of stay have decreased so significantly), some departments include behavioral objectives for each specific program (performance measures) within the program documentation rather than the client documentation. In this way, clear outcomes can be delineated once, in the pro-

---

Box 10.8   Example of Goal Statements for At-Risk Youth

Example #1: Staff's handwritten goals for children taken directly from treatment plans.

Increase abilities to utilize leisure/recreation time
   Think of activities on his own to play
   Choose age-appropriate toys and activities during free time
   Utilize free time by playing independently
   Initiate activities in free time and decrease bothering adults to entertain him
   During leisure time, pick appropriate activities for age, interact more with peers, and pick
       activity other than watch TV
   Come up with ideas for special time on his own
   Choose free time activities on own and not bother peers
   Use free time by playing on own and using equipment in an appropriate manner
   Choose appropriate activities during quiet times, FTs, etc.
   Choose things to do for special time on own, rather than always telling staff he is bored
   Increase her ability to utilize free time by being a self-starter in activities and keeping on task
       during them

Example #2: Staff's new checklist for client objectives.

Increase abilities to utilize leisure/recreation time
   Within _____ days/weeks, the child will:
   _____   select one activity to play during free time, independently without prompts
   _____   make decisions for independent leisure participation without direction
             from peers or adults
   _____   select play toys or equipment by self, without disturbing others' use
             of toys or equipment
   _____   interact with peers appropriately, by taking turns, sharing, keeping hands to self
   _____   stay on task for _____ minutes during free play time

---

gram description or protocol, instead of once per client, in the client treatment plan. The success of this option is dependent entirely on the adequacy of the program documentation for enabling other individuals, such as those in other disciplines or insurance carriers, to track the information on outcomes to a specific client.

The second option requires considerable experience and creativity. For many specialists, goal writing becomes repetitive since many clients have similar problems and subsequent goals. In this case, when a specialist has become quite familiar with the majority of client needs, forms that require less time on a daily basis can be created. Box 10.8 provides an example from a residential treatment facility for at-risk youth. The first example includes direct excerpts from staff's handwritten notes in the children's individualized treatment plans concerning use of independent leisure and recreation time.

The second example takes these basic but repetitive ideas and creates a checklist of client objectives in this goal area. By using a checklist similar to this, specialists are using time more efficiently—saving time in repetitive documentation and potentially using it more wisely in client treatment. The list was created by analyzing the content of the treatment notes for a certain period (in this case, two years) and noting the typical goals used by staff in this area. Then a checklist was created, focusing on the most used goals, with blank lines to either fill in information or check when appropriate. In addition, a blank line is left at the end for any truly unique needs of an individual child that are not contained on the checklist. In this way, treatment goals can be personalized for each client, but time is saved when the form becomes a checklist. With shortened lengths of stay, specialists will have to think creatively on how they use their time in order to provide clients with the best services possible that can produce measurable outcomes.

In this section, examples and detailed information have been given about treatment plans. It is acknowledged that each agency will have its own policies and procedures related to the development and specification of treatment plans. Thus, examples and information provided here must be read for their contributions to general concepts and principles. As noted earlier, there is great value in having a thoroughly developed, comprehensive therapeutic recreation program with highly developed specific programs that can be immediately and directly included in the individual's treatment plan.

Progress Notes

Progress notes provide periodic information updates to the client's original treatment plan. The issues addressed in this section have applicability in both POMR and source-oriented record keeping, as well as other types of record-keeping systems. As mentioned in the earlier section on problem-oriented medical records, the typical format for progress notes is SOAP(IER).

Format of Progress Notes

S stands for subjective data that describes the statements a client makes about the problem or course of treatment. If the client is not able to communicate, statements from family and friends also may be considered appropriate. In some cases, even when a client is communicative, statements from families and friends are beneficial. Such statements should be attributed to the correct source. Below are a few examples of typical S comments in progress notes.

> S: "I want to stay in my room. Leave me alone."
>
> Client said, "I learned a new skill today."
>
> After the program, the client stated, "I feel like I'm making better decisions."
>
> Pt.'s mother stated, "Claudia is really responding your program. She seems to really enjoy being here with the other children."

O stands for objective data that is gathered through observation of the client's actions or behaviors. This information must be stated in specific behavioral terms that can be understood by everyone reading the chart. This does not include opinions, conclusions, or vague statements. Rather, the only observations included are those observable behaviors that relate to the client's problems or deficits, specifically those noted in the initial treatment plan. Below are some examples of behavior as noted in a progress note.

O: Pt. refused TRS's request to attend evening social. While remaining in her room, client smiled and laughed while engaged in 10-minute conversation with another 16-yr.-old pt. Pt. responded to questions from visiting pt. and initiated conversation related to favorite television shows.

Pt. asked questions about transportation to the activity, ticket prices, seating, food, length, and return time.

A stands for analysis or interpretation that the specialist makes from the combination of the client's statements (S) and behaviors (O). Analysis information can indicate progression, regression, or no change in the patient's condition relating to a specific problem. The conclusions or interpretations made should be based on the subjective and objective sections of the progress note. Examples of these conclusions are below.

A: Pt. has adequate social interaction abilities and can interact for sustained periods with peers.

Pt. asked appropriate questions about activity, indicating an understanding of the activity and its participation requirements.

P represents the plan that is designed in alignment with the specialist's interpretation of the client's statements and behaviors. The plan should relate directly to the client's problem(s). Vague references, such as "enroll pt. in therapeutic recreation group" or "get pt. involved in activities" are not acceptable. Thoroughness and specificity are essential when writing the plan. The plan should be based on the following guidelines:

- What additional information must be collected?
- Have any other progress notes provided further direction?
- Have any referrals been made for therapeutic recreation?
- In what specific programs will the client participate?
- What are the various staff and client responsibilities?
- What intervention techniques will be used?
- What is the planned frequency and duration of participation?
- When will the plan be reevaluated?

Below are some sample statements representing the P portion of the progress note.

P: Schedule two 1:1 sessions with pt. to reassess conversational skills and attitudes toward leisure involvement.

Enroll pt. in leisure planning class 5x/wk. starting 7/10, to increase planning and decision-making skills.

Focus on pt.'s social assets. Emphasize need for social network. Reevaluate pt. on 8/12.

I stands for interventions that are delivered to meet this client's needs and reach the expected outcomes. Interventions should directly relate to the client's diagnosis or problem areas, subjective state and information gathered, the interpretation, and the plan. As the patient's health status changes, interventions may need to be modified. This part of a client record is easy to document when protocols, clinical practice guidelines, or clinical pathways have been developed and tested ahead of time. If specific programs and interventions are well constructed and documented, the I part of the note can be brief.

I: Stress Management Program, co-led with nursing.

Leisure Awareness Program.

Community Skills Program, taxi to local restaurant and shopping area.

E stands for evaluation of the effectiveness of the interventions and includes the patient's response to the interventions. It is at this point that the specialist determines whether the goals and objectives were achieved by the client. If expected outcomes have not been reached, the evaluation process can be used as a basis for developing alternative interventions.

E: Patient satisfaction survey indicated high levels of satisfaction with social skills program outcomes; noting that skills gained make it easier to meet new friends.

Pt. did not meet exercise goal of three times a week due to complications from infection.

R stands for revisions to the plan. As the patient progresses through treatment, goals and objectives (outcomes) often are accomplished and new ones are established. Revisions may relate to adjustments in interventions, goals and objectives, outcomes, or target dates. The last part of a SOAPIER note contains these changes and documents what needs to be modified from the original plan of care.

R: Pt. met expected outcome of making a leisure plan for a weekend night with spouse and following through.

Increase program involvement as tolerated.

Move from intermediate to advanced leisure skills class.

Content of Progress Notes

Frequently, beginning professionals are unsure what to include in progress notes. What really is significant information? Although not exhaustive, the following list of guidelines can be used to determine the relevance of content to be included in progress notes:

- Progress toward attainment of client goal
- Regression from attainment of client goal
- New patterns of behavior

- Consistency of behavior
- Verbal information provided by the client
- Successful or unsuccessful attempts at a task
- Appropriate or inappropriate interactions with staff, peers, visitors
- Client responses to questions, instructions, requests
- Initiative with actions, ideas, problem solving, decision making
- Follow-through or lack of follow-through with commitment

Even with such guidelines, many professionals are unsure of the significance of some client behaviors. General behavior and participation patterns, specific behavioral cues, and environmental cues are all potentially significant information to be included in progress notes.

Attendance and Participation.   The significance of attendance and participation will vary greatly among clients. While it may be significant that patient A did not choose to attend the evening social, it also may be significant that patient B attended yet did not participate. Such observations become useful when they are documented and thus become available to all staff.

One error frequently made by many professionals is mistakenly documenting a client's attendance as evidence of participation. Although it is often important to indicate that an individual client attended a particular activity, the documentation of attendance is insufficient content for a progress note and certainly insufficient information in general.

The following questions will help the therapeutic recreation specialist decide whether a client's attendance or participation at a specific activity is truly a significant behavior:

- Did the client attend voluntarily?
- Did the client respond to staff or peer requests?
- Did the client merely observe the activity?
- Was the client actively participating in the session?
- Did the client assume a leadership role?

Note the difference in explanatory information and resulting clarity or lack of clarity in the following two sample progress notes:

Incomplete Progress Note

3/28   Pt. attended a cooking class.

More Complete Progress Note

3/28   Pt. voluntarily participated in Friday's cooking class. He offered three appropriate suggestions to help organize other pts. assigned to different tasks, completed his task, and willingly volunteered to help with cleanup.

Physical Cues.   In addition to general behavior and participation patterns such as those previously mentioned, there are specific behavioral cues that often need to be documented. Again, the significance of these cues depends on the client, the setting, and the purpose for documenting.

The following sample physical cues often are observable and can help describe accurately a client's behavior:

Dress: Sloppy, neat, formal, clashing colors, informal, disarrayed, soiled, filthy, stained, conservative, stylish, brightly colored, darkly colored

Hygiene and grooming: Clean, dirty, unbathed, uncut hair, well-scrubbed, unshaven, meticulously groomed, messy hair, body odor

Posture: Slouched, erect, arms crossed, rigid, slumped, legs crossed

Movement: Jerky, fast, slow, tapping foot, wringing hands, shuffling feet, awkward, clumsy, agile, graceful, excessive movement, hyperactivity, twitches

Social distancing: Touching, moving away from, ignoring, moving close to

Face: Lips quivering, jaws clenched, eyes red, maintaining eye contact, cheeks flushed

Mood and affect: Lively, neutral, normal, blunted, flat, stable, labile, defensive, calm, sad, hostile, guarded, distant, evasive, cooperative, open

Speech: Talkative, verbose, clear, slurred, monotonous, dull, slow, fast, even, jerky, halting, loud, soft, inaudible, whispering, silent

Orientation: Oriented/disoriented to person, place, time, event

Environmental Cues.   The following environmental cues are often significant, as they help to place a client's behavior in a realistic context:

Weather conditions

Temperature

Surrounding objects (cluttered room, open space)

Social patterns (quiet small group discussion versus loud, active competitive game)

Positioning (front of room, alone, behind table)

Setting (indoors, outdoors, familiar areas)

General behavior patterns, the circumstances surrounding attendance, and participation, physical cues, and environmental cues are all potentially significant information. The documentation of such information will help the therapeutic recreation specialist keep objective and accurate client records.

The following sample progress notes provide examples related to the use of physical and environmental cues:

Incomplete Progress Note

5/30   Pt. voluntarily participated in the holiday outing.

More Complete Progress Note

5/30   Pt. voluntarily participated in the holiday outing. Although the weather was cold and rainy, pt. arrived in his cut-offs and dirty T-shirt.

Assume that the previous client was working on grooming skills and appropriate dress. The second progress note, although brief, still provides more relevant information. The inclusion of physical and environmental cues can help place the client's behavior into a meaningful context.

When to Document Progress Notes.   The frequency with which progress notes are written by staff varies. Three factors relate to this timing: agency regulations and requirements, therapeutic recreation staff-time usage, and the delivery of quality services.

Agency Regulations.   Each agency will specify the required frequency of progress notes. For example, some general hospitals require daily charting; a psychiatric facility may require weekly progress notes; and the extended-care facility may require monthly or quarterly progress notes. Usually, this is determined by the accrediting agency, the clients' average length of stay, and how often the treatment team meets. If clients stay for a very short period, then progress notes will be written more frequently and likely record smaller increments of behavioral improvement. Likewise, the schedule of treatment team meetings often is based on client length of stay. In a short-term facility, the staff will meet quite regularly, sometimes perhaps daily. In a longer-term facility, when less immediate progress is expected of clients, progress notes will be documented less frequently and staff will meet less frequently on each individual client. The therapeutic recreation specialist should inquire about the agency's charting requirements and follow the same documentation schedule required of other team professionals.

Therapeutic Recreation Staff-Time Usage.   A common complaint among therapeutic recreation specialists, as well as other allied health professionals, is the lack of time for documentation. Time for documentation and charting should be regularly scheduled into the therapeutic recreation specialist's daily, weekly, or monthly schedule.

Many therapeutic recreation departments have paralleled their documentation time allotments with other professional disciplines in their facility. Although there is no national standard, some therapeutic recreation departments allocate 30 to 50 percent of staff time for administrative issues (documentation, charting, planning, conferences, committee work, in-service training, program evaluation, continuing education, etc.).

Delivery of Quality Services.   As discussed in the first part of this chapter, timely documentation helps to facilitate communication among staff members, thus enabling improved professional services. The therapeutic recreation specialist may choose to write in the client's chart more frequently than is required if more frequent documentation provides important information about an individual client.

Progress notes are a critical aspect of individual client record keeping. The professional therapeutic recreation specialist will be expected to provide client documentation and progress notes regularly and accurately.

Discharge and Referral Summaries

The **discharge summary** is usually the final component included in the client's record. Discharge and referral summaries present an interesting dilemma. On one hand, as health care in general focuses more on the functioning of the client post-discharge, the case could be made that the use of discharge summaries should increase. On the other hand, as lengths of stay for most clinical facilities decrease, there is less staff time per client to document information, especially for those clients who are leaving a facility. The move from inpatient care to outpatient care also affects whether discharge summaries are used in a facility.

As with other types of client documentation, each agency will provide its own guidelines for both the content and format of the discharge summary. Some agencies use the SOAP(IER) format for the discharge summary, while other agencies prefer a narrative summary or a standardized form combined with a narrative. A common slogan in many clinical agencies is, "Begin making plans for discharge the day the client is admitted." More clients would be better served if this motto were adhered to more frequently.

Therapeutic recreation departments adhere to this guideline best when they focus on the postdischarge leisure functioning of the client beginning with comprehensive program development, discussed in Chapter 4. This focus should be evident throughout the therapeutic recreation department's program goals, client goals and objectives, and corresponding client documentation. Within the discharge summary, the therapeutic recreation specialist usually summarizes the client's involvement and progress within the therapeutic recreation programs.

Given the diversity among agencies with regard to the discharge summary, there is no standard format or content appropriate for all therapeutic recreation departments. The following suggestions are presented as sample information that the therapeutic recreation specialist might include in a client's discharge summary.

Major Client Problems or Goals

This list or narrative typically will address what client problems or goals the client achieved while receiving services. Therapeutic recreation's input includes problems and goals directly or indirectly related to present or future leisure functioning of the client.

Services Received by the Client

A summary includes the type of therapeutic recreation services that the client received. Many discharge summaries also will include the frequency and duration of the client's involvement in such services.

Client's Responses to Functional Intervention, Leisure Education, and Recreation Participation Services

Client responses to various services might include a summary of sequential client assessment information and a summary of highlights from client progress notes. Although some agencies permit the addition of new information in a discharge summary, many agencies permit only a summary of previously documented client progress or status.

Remaining Problems or Concerns

Functional intervention and leisure education processes seldom are complete for a client at the time of discharge. Many clients will have remaining problems or potential problem areas after discharge. Many discharge summaries will enumerate and briefly explain problems and concerns related to the client's postdischarge leisure functioning.

Plan for Postdischarge Leisure Involvement

Too often clients are discharged from an agency without a clearly identifiable or clearly understood plan of action. Ideally, clients should be involved in the development of their postdischarge plan. When this is not feasible because of the client's functional level, a written plan still may be quite useful.

The content of the discharge plan certainly will depend on the individual client's needs and abilities. The client's future residence also should influence the content of the discharge plan. A client who is discharged from a hospital and referred to an extended-care facility will have very different social and leisure involvement than a client who will be discharged to live at home with family members. The discharge plan frequently accompanies the client when agency referrals are made. The discharge plan also could accompany the client who returns to a home environment. In each instance, client's responsibilities and agency's responsibilities should be delineated clearly.

Incident Reports

Each agency will have a special form for documenting accidents, incidents, and unusual occurrences. Federal, national, and state accrediting bodies require documentation and analysis of incidents as part of risk management efforts (Iyer & Camp, 1999). Examples of incidents that must be reported include:

- Client injury or death
- Broken equipment (such as a van lift)
- Runaway client
- Medication error
- Child abduction
- Patient falls

Incident reports are completed immediately following the incident and submitted to the appropriate person(s). This process allows full disclosure of liability and inefficiencies or flaws in the care system that must be corrected (such as need for training or visual alarms). Each agency will have very specific guidelines on the handling of incident reports and professionals should become familiar with these guidelines. Incident reports should not be included in the patient's medical record (Meiner,

1999). Agencies that require documentation of incident reports typically require the following information (Iyer & Camp, 1999; Springhouse Corporation, 1999):

- When and where the incident occurred
- Findings at the scene (facts: visual and material information)
- Care of client (preincident and postincident)
- Client's comments
- Who was notified
- What preventive steps are/were taken

Springhouse Corporation (1999) provided six guidelines for documenting incident reports. They are:

- Write objectively: record details of the event in factual terms, recording only what was seen or heard, as well as actions taken after the incident.
- Include only essential information: document the time and place of the incident and the name of physician who was notified.
- Avoid opinions: while opinions may be shared verbally with the staff member's supervisor or risk manager, opinions are not appropriate for inclusion in the incident report.
- Assign no blame: steer clear of placing blame on the patient or colleagues or agency policy.
- Avoid hearsay and assumptions: each staff member who witnessed or was involved in the incident should file an incident report, without collaborating with colleagues.
- File report properly: incident reports traditionally are not included within a patient's medical record, but are sent to an individual designated by agency policy (such as a risk manager).

Computer Use in Client Documentation

Most of the prior discussion about client documentation has focused on the traditional methods of writing, typing, and printing. At many facilities there is movement toward computer use in client documentation, in an effort to become more efficient with staff time (Springhouse Corporation, 1999). Forms used for documentation are electronic and specialists insert information for individual clients where appropriate. An effective computer system must have certain capabilities, such as recording and sending data to appropriate departments, adapting easily to the agency's needs, displaying highly selective information on demand, and providing easy access to storage and retrieval while maintaining client confidentiality (Springhouse Corporation, 1999).

One of the greatest benefits of computer use is the reduction of repetitive writing time for staff. Additional advantages include improved legibility, fewer errors, decreased recording time and costs, improved communication among staff members, and greater access to and manipulation of patient data for patient care, education, research, and quality improvement (Iyer & Camp, 1999; Springhouse Corporation, 1999). In addition, the ability to transmit data from remote facilities (such as in-home health care) or between care providers (such as a skilled nursing facility and a hospital) is a definite bonus of computerized records (Springhouse Corporation, 1999).

As more functions in everyday living become computerized, so too will the health care and human service industries. Therapeutic recreation specialists will benefit from training in computer applications such as word processing and spreadsheets, as well as gaining competence in areas such as Internet interfacing and electronic mail.

Summary

Client documentation serves an important function in recording the services provided on behalf of the client and his or her reaction to the services. Sometimes there are very specific guidelines that must be followed, and at other times, few guidelines are available. The therapeutic recreation specialist will benefit greatly from thorough knowledge of administrative guidelines, such as those found in individual agencies, as well as from organizations such as the American Therapeutic Recreation Association, the National Therapeutic Recreation Society, and the Joint Commission on Accreditation of Healthcare Organizations. As information from these sources changes and improves, so too must the documentation created by the therapeutic recreation specialist.

STUDENT EXERCISES

Discussion Questions

1. How does client documentation contribute to providing quality services to clients?

2. What additional rationales, other than the ones discussed in the text, may be given for ensuring high-quality client documentation?

3. Explain why consistency, conciseness, and clarity are important features of client documentation.

4. Explain the difference between source-oriented and problem-oriented medical records. What are the advantages and disadvantages of each?

5. With which method of charting do you have the most experience? From the descriptions and examples, are there others that are more streamlined, focused, and still able to meet patient documentation needs?

6. In the SOAP, SOAPIE, and SOAPIER progress notes formats, why is each section separated? How does that help or hinder the professional in performing quality documentation?

7. How are program documentation and client documentation aligned? Why does client documentation depend so heavily on quality program documentation?

8. What is the purpose of including Box 10.5? What does it demonstrate about the relationships between program content, typical client problems, and typical client goals?

9. Describe three or four examples of situations or occurrences within therapeutic recreation services that would trigger the filing of an incident report.

10. What would be the advantages and disadvantages of a facility moving to computerized client documentation?

Practice Test

1. SOAP notes are considered one type of:
   a. source-oriented record keeping.
   b. problem-oriented record keeping.
   c. focus charting.
   d. outcome charting.

2. All parts of a SOAP progress note should relate directly to the patient's:
   a. problem.
   b. treatment plan.
   c. future lifestyle.
   d. diagnostic-related grouping.

3. Interventions targeted for a specific client are described in a:
   a. clinical or critical pathway.
   b. written plan of operation.
   c. treatment protocol.
   d. treatment plan.

4. All of the following have an impact on the format of client documentation EXCEPT:
   a. external accreditation standards.
   b. legal requirements.
   c. agency guidelines and procedures.
   d. professional certification.

5. A treatment plan should be created in cooperation with all of the following EXCEPT:
   a. the patient.
   b. other professionals.
   c. peer groups.
   d. the case manager.

6. When a physician or case manager creates a numbered, master list of client deficits and develops a plan of action to eliminate or reduce these deficits, this is called a(n):
   a. problem-oriented medical record.
   b. incident report.
   c. case mix.
   d. source-oriented medical record.

7. Which of the following is an example of "subjective" data that may be recorded in a progress note?
   a. The client has a prominent odor late in the day.
   b. The client's sister said, "He doesn't really look forward to getting out."

   c. The client seems really happy during therapeutic recreation activities.

   d. The client appears depressed and withdrawn.

8. Which of the following is a TRUE statement about source-oriented record keeping (SOMR)?

   a. The client chart is organized around client problems.

   b. The client chart is organized around team disciplines.

   c. Components include database, problem list, initial plan, progress notes, and discharge summaries.

   d. SOMR makes it easier to track client progress on a particular problem.

9. The development of a treatment plan allows for:

   a. step-by-step procedures of treatment/intervention to be outlined.

   b. the inclusion of subjective data.

   c. treatment to be based on assessment data.

   d. all of the above.

10. A "good" progress note allows for:

    a. considerations of physical, social, intellectual, and emotional aspects.

    b. demonstration of a clear relationship between goals, objectives, and plan of action.

    c. an information update from the assessment and treatment plan.

    d. all of the above.

11. Which of the following is NOT a purpose of progress notes?

    a. to increase the quality of care given to a client

    b. to increase communication among treatment team members about the client's status

    c. to repeat information from the treatment plan

    d. to document the patient's interventions

Answers: 1. b, 2. a, 3. d, 4. d, 5. c, 6. a, 7. b, 8. b, 9. d, 10. d, 11. c

Chapter Activities

Interview a Therapeutic Recreation Professional

Ask to visit a local health care agency that has therapeutic recreation services and review the client documentation. Write a short summary of the types of documentation used, how disciplines communicate through the documentation, and whether it is required by an accreditation or payer agency.

Client Documentation

Ask local agencies for blank copies of their client documentation forms and bring these to class. Compare information and styles and see if the class has gathered at least one example of each method of client documentation. Discuss the advantages and disadvantages of each method.

Charting Methods Comparison

Make a graphic or table outlining the basics of each client documentation method, and its advantages and disadvantages. Use this graphic or table to compare the different methods for their utility in client documentation.

Case Study: Treatment Plan and Progress Note

Create a profile of a client (not using names) with whom you are familiar. Using the format provided in this text, create a treatment plan. Create at least two progress notes using two different formats. Bring this to class and discuss how easy or difficult it was to create a treatment plan and/or a progress note.

Case Study: Incident Report

Have two students role play in front of the class a therapeutic recreation situation that would require an incident report. Each student then is to write his or her account of the incident. What was seen or heard? After the "reports" are completed, compare answers and select the best representation of accurate yet objective reporting. Repeat until most students in the class can achieve this standard.

REFERENCES

Coty, E. L., Davis, J. L., and Angell, L. (2000). *Documentation: The language of nursing.* Upper Saddle River, NJ: Prentice-Hall Health.

Intermed Communications, Inc. (1981). *Documenting patient care responsibly.* Horsham, PA: Author.

Iyer, P. W., and Camp, N. H. (1999). *Nursing documentation: A nursing process approach* (3rd ed.). St. Louis, MO: Mosby.

Kettenbach, G. (1995). *Writing S.O.A.P. notes.* Salem, MA: F. A. Davis Company.

Lampe, S. (1992). (Ed.). *Focus charting, What we have learned: A collection of articles from primary nursing newsletters.* Minneapolis, MN: Creative Nursing Management.

Lampe, S. (1997). *Focus charting: Documentation for patient centered care* (7th ed.). Minneapolis, MN: Creative Nursing Management.

Meiner, S. E. (1999). *Nursing documentation: Legal focus across practice settings.* Thousand Oaks, CA: Sage.

Navar, N. (1984). Documentation. In C. A. Peterson & S. L. Gunn, *Therapeutic recreation program design: Principles and procedures* (2nd ed.; pp. 212–266). Englewood Cliffs, NJ: Prentice-Hall.

Springhouse Corporation. (1999). *Mastering documentation* (2nd ed.). Springhouse, PA: Author.

CHAPTER 11

Program and Client Evaluation

Evaluation is an integral part of program planning and implementation. A properly conducted evaluation can aid the specialist in making informed decisions about improving the quality of individual specific programs and the comprehensive program in total. The purpose of this chapter is to provide information to help design appropriate and meaningful evaluations in order to get usable information and feedback. Evaluation can be conducted on a variety of levels (individual client, specific activity, specific program, and comprehensive program) and using a variety of methods and techniques. Evaluation is represented on the Therapeutic Recreation Accountability Model by three separate boxes: Program Outcomes, Client Outcomes, and Quality Improvement/Efficacy Research (Figure 11.1).

Evaluation as a Management Tool

The mention of the word *evaluation* brings several related terms to mind. Lundegren and Farrell (1985) noted that three related terms often are associated with management functions and concerns. *Accountability* is when the specialist is held responsible for meeting predetermined goals or a predetermined course of action. It is usually through evaluation procedures that it is determined whether these goals have been met or whether the appropriate actions have been taken. One of the major ways in which professionals are held accountable is through evaluation of their efforts. *Cost effectiveness* implies that participants are receiving the maximal benefits at the lowest possible cost; a mix, perhaps, of striving for budget efficiency and program effectiveness at the same time. Evaluation can help determine both the benefits to participants as well as the operational costs. *Decision making* is an important end result of evaluation; that is, one of the prime reasons for conducting an evaluation is to provide information to make informed decisions for future actions. Decision making is also important throughout the evaluation process, in that the evaluation designer and implementer must make several decisions while conducting an evaluation (e.g., what information to collect, how to collect the information). It is easy to see that evaluation plays a large role in helping therapeutic recreation specialists become more accountable and cost effective, in part due to the professional's increased ability to make informed decisions.

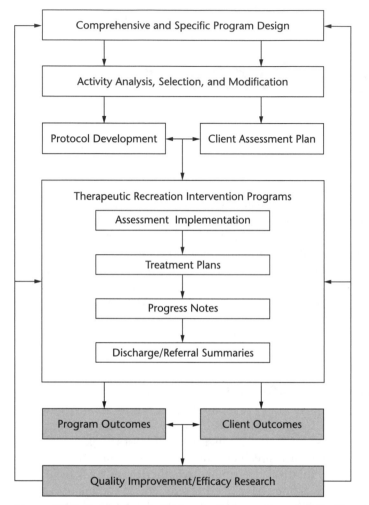

Figure 11.1 Program and client evaluation component of the Therapeutic Recreation Accountability Model.

Definition of Evaluation

Evaluation can be defined as *the systematic and logical process of gathering and analyzing selected information in order to make decisions about the quality, effectiveness, and/or outcomes of a program, function, or service.* This definition has some key concepts that are central to the understanding and implementation of program evaluation. In order for the results of the evaluation to have meaning and to be trusted, data collection must occur using *systematic* or *logical* procedures. One major purpose of this chapter is to provide information about systematic data collection, analysis, and reporting. *Selected information* means that, given the workload of most therapeutic recreation specialists, the evaluation process has to focus on the information deemed most important, as many specialists do not have time to collect data that is not likely to be used. One of

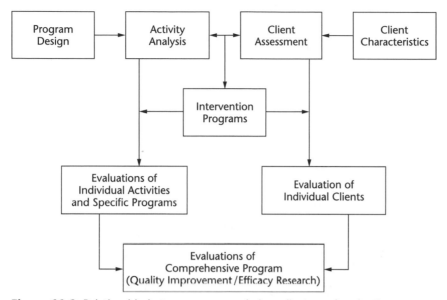

Figure 11.2 Relationship between program design, clients, and evaluation.

the first decisions in the evaluation process is to decide what information is important and usable in the decision-making process. *Quality, effectiveness, and/or outcomes* are prime concerns of any evaluation endeavor. They are likely to be the main focus of the evaluation and help in narrowing the selected information to be collected. It is also important to note that evaluations can be conducted on a variety of levels, from looking at individual clients, to specific activities, to specific programs, to comprehensive programs. Later in this chapter, a general decision-making evaluation model that provides the foundation to design and implement evaluations at any one of these levels will be discussed. But first, a few words about the logic behind systems design that makes evaluation a complementary function of program design.

In Chapter 3, a model was presented in Figure 3.1 that depicted the relationships between program design and activity analysis and client characteristics and client assessment. The end result of programs designed with these four factors in mind is often the ability to change client behavior through intervention programs. This model can be extended, as in Figure 11.2, to explain the role and implications of program and client evaluation. The reader will note that this model looks quite similar to the Therapeutic Recreation Accountability Model.

On the program side of the model, program design and activity analysis are primary factors in allowing specialists to design program evaluations (from individual activity, specific program, and comprehensive program evaluations). It is easier to conduct a program evaluation with a well-designed program than one that has no written plan. On the client side of the model, full understanding of the client group's characteristics and the assessment are prime concerns for creating client evaluations. Similar to program evaluations, a client assessment process that is soundly conceptualized greatly aids in the client evaluation process. Each component is key to providing intervention programs. Before each of these types of evaluations can be discussed

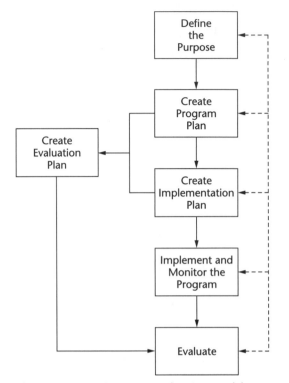

Figure 11.3 Basic program planning model.

individually, an evaluation planning model is presented to introduce a generic process for creating and implementing evaluations.

A Generic Evaluation Design Model

Since evaluation is a process, a model can be created to show what steps are to be taken, and what actions must occur at each step. As was stated in Chapter 4, the evaluation plan should and can be created during the program planning process. As Figure 11.3 shows, evaluation design may occur simultaneously with program design. An evaluation plan is easier to conceptualize while one is thinking about program goals and implementation strategies. These two processes, designing the program and designing the evaluation, should happen in tandem.

Prior to planning an evaluation, some basic questions about the evaluation will need to be considered. The answers may not be immediate, but may become clearer as further decisions are made. These basic questions relate to terms often associated with program evaluation.

The first two terms are *internal* and *external* evaluation. *Internal* evaluation means that someone from within the agency is responsible for collecting and analyzing the data. The advantages are that internal evaluation can be less costly and happen more quickly. Also, depending on the agency, staff may be more willing to help collect data and to use the results. On the other hand, *external* evaluation, one conducted by someone outside of the agency, can imply greater objectivity and use a broader per-spective in comparing programs. External evaluations can prove to be more costly when an outside consultant is employed; however, peer reviews would also come under the heading of external evaluation.

The second set of terms includes *formative* and *summative* evaluation. *Formative* evaluation means that data collection is ongoing and occurs while the activity or program is in progress. Information is collected along the way, and this information is used to modify the program as it is implemented. For example, when unit staff meet at the end of the programming day to make recommendations for changes in the next day's program, that is considered formative evaluation. It involves daily or weekly fine tuning to improve the program while it is being implemented. It also may take place *during* the actual implementation of a program. For example, if four clients come to a group that was designed for eight, the specialist automatically begins to review the situation and make program changes based on events *as they occur.* This does not mean that the program and programmers career wildly out of control, changing program content or format on a whim, but it does imply that skilled special-ists are able to adapt to the variable needs of any given client mix. This is easier to accomplish when a systems design approach to program documentation and planning is taken.

Summative evaluation is conducted at the end of the program and provides data that can be used to (1) compare programs with one another or (2) provide informa-tion for the next "season" of programming. Summative evaluations have advantages for cost-benefit analyses, when an agency may be trying to decide which programs are most worthwhile and should be offered again. The clear disadvantage is that the program in question is completely finished by the time data is collected. If client satis-faction is low for some reason that could have been changed or client behavior was not changed as planned, summative evaluation provides little help. Program partici-pants have already exited the program by the time summative data is collected, ana-lyzed, and reported.

Figure 11.4 displays a generic evaluation model that contains five basic steps: (1) planning, (2) designing, (3) implementing, (4) analyzing, and (5) applying results. This model is an adapted version of one introduced by Lundegren and Farrell (1985). This generic evaluation model can be used as an overlay for collecting all evaluation data, including information on clients, specific programs, and comprehensive pro-grams. The remainder of the chapter will focus on its use in these three areas.

Planning the Evaluation

The first step in systematic evaluation is planning. In the planning stage, the informa-tion to be targeted in the evaluation is decided upon. Much like actual program plan-ning, systematic evaluation planning requires that the purpose or intended outcome of the evaluation be specified. The purpose statement should give the evaluation a general direction and target the general area of concern for the remaining evaluation steps. Below are some examples of evaluation purposes for different types of evalua-tion projects:

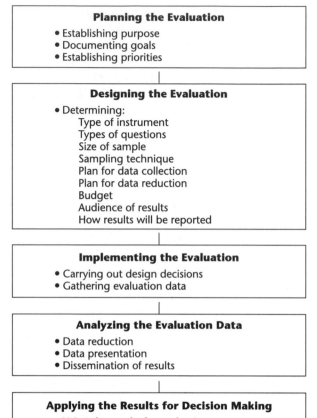

Planning the Evaluation
- Establishing purpose
- Documenting goals
- Establishing priorities

Designing the Evaluation
- Determining:
    Type of instrument
    Types of questions
    Size of sample
    Sampling technique
    Plan for data collection
    Plan for data reduction
    Budget
    Audience of results
    How results will be reported

Implementing the Evaluation
- Carrying out design decisions
- Gathering evaluation data

Analyzing the Evaluation Data
- Data reduction
- Data presentation
- Dissemination of results

Applying the Results for Decision Making
- Using the results for evaluation purposes

Figure 11.4 Generic evaluation model.

- To determine the effectiveness of the Leisure Awareness program.
- To determine the differences between the planned (intended) and actual implementation of the Family Education and Support Group programs.
- To determine patient satisfaction with the Community Inclusion program.
- To determine to what degree clients increase their social skills as a result of the Social Skills Instruction training program.

The written purpose statement should help in narrowing the intent and establishing priorities for the evaluation. It should define at what level (client, specific program, comprehensive program) the evaluation will occur and with what specificity.

Once the purpose has been determined, it is helpful to write evaluation goals that are logical extensions of the purpose statement and specify the content that becomes the focus of the evaluation. These content evaluation goals will be used in later steps to help make many decisions, such as what types of questions will be asked, how the data will be collected, and so on. For example, let's take the evaluation purpose "To

---

Box 11.1   Types of Evaluation Instruments or Techniques

Questionnaires	Interviews	Observations	Record Documentation
On-site surveys	Personal, face-to-face	Direct	Program evaluation forms
Mailed surveys	Telephone	Indirect	Client records
Internet surveys		Unobtrusive	

---

determine patient satisfaction with the Community Inclusion program." The following evaluation goals are six examples that may be used to reach this purpose:

Evaluation Goal 1: To determine patient satisfaction with the program's purpose.

Evaluation Goal 2: To determine patient satisfaction with the program's format.

Evaluation Goal 3: To determine patient satisfaction with the specialist's leadership abilities.

Evaluation Goal 4: To determine patient satisfaction with the transportation provided.

Evaluation Goal 5: To determine patient satisfaction with the amount of skills gained from the program.

Evaluation Goal 6: To determine patient satisfaction with the transferability of skills gained to situations outside of the agency.

The creation of a purpose statement and several evaluation goals is helpful in determining where the evaluation is headed and in keeping the evaluation designer focused on the task at hand. Both the purpose statement and evaluation goals may be revised and refined as the process continues.

Designing the Evaluation

The second step is to design the evaluation, that is, to decide how it is to be carried out. The step involves making several decisions about the evaluation process. Regardless of the type of evaluation to be conducted, several factors must be determined before any further action can be taken. These factors are highly interrelated but will be separated here for ease of presentation.

Type of Instrument or Technique.   There are several choices for the types of instrument or data collection technique to be used in an evaluation (see Box 11.1). The first category is *surveys* or *questionnaires*. These are probably the first that come to mind when most people think of evaluation instruments. There are three basic types of questionnaires: *on-site, mailed,* and *Internet.* On-site questionnaires are those that are handed to individuals to be completed immediately, often while the evaluator waits for them to be returned. Mailed questionnaires obviously go through the mail and are used less frequently because of the need for accurate mailing addresses and the cost and time involved. Some agencies have Web-based surveys that clients can complete once they leave the facility.

As mentioned earlier, the timing of an evaluation is important. For example, patient satisfaction surveys may be most relevant after the client has returned to his or her home community and has experienced leisure within that context. Mailed or Internet questionnaires might be useful in this instance. On-site surveys may be most relevant at the end of a specific program when an immediate reaction is warranted.

Interviews come in two types: *personal face-to-face* or *telephone*. Both require a great deal of skill in order to get the respondent to answer questions both fully and honestly. Interviews have the capability to gather in-depth information by using open-ended questions and allowing for probing and clarification. Personal interviews give the evaluator a chance to establish rapport and notice nonverbal messages, while telephone interviews have been made more difficult with today's frequent telemarketing campaigns. Again, timing, purpose and clients' communication skills are important considerations.

There are three types of observations that can be used for evaluation purposes: *direct, indirect,* and *unobtrusive*. Observation allows the specialist to gather information about the client's *behavior,* rather than the client's perception of his or her behavior. Direct observations are those that the client knows are occurring, such as when the specialist is supervising an activity. Indirect observations are those when the actions of the specialist are not known, such as when clients are observed behind a one-way mirror. Unobtrusive observations do not involve the client directly as do the other two forms of observation, because they focus on the artifacts left behind by the client. For example, a specialist might be able to tell which "free time" activities are most popular by which pieces of equipment or types of supplies are checked out of the activity closet most often.

Another type of technique that is often useful is *record documentation*. Often, in any given department, there are several forms that are completed daily, weekly, monthly, and annually by the therapeutic recreation staff. These forms might include client participation records or number of hours spent in direct client contact, for example. The synthesis and analysis of the data on these forms is one way to conduct an evaluation. Evaluation activities often rely on documentation forms for collection of data.

The decision about which of these ten kinds of data collection instruments or techniques to use depends on the purpose and goals of the evaluation. Some evaluations require that data be gathered directly from the patient, so a questionnaire or interview might be appropriate (e.g., patient satisfaction, barriers to leisure participation), while others dictate that natural behaviors (e.g., conversational skills) be recorded through observations. For example, say that the purpose of the evaluation is to determine patient satisfaction. There are several options, including on-site, Internet, and mailed surveys and face-to-face and telephone interviews. Observations of any kind to determine patient satisfaction are probably not appropriate for most client groups. An exception may be individuals with cognitive deficits, who may show "satisfaction" through overt behaviors, such as smiling or clapping.

The point is to make a decision about which type of instrument will collect the best and most meaningful information for the evaluation, given such constraints as time, money, and staff availability. The chapters on client assessment and documentation provide further details on some of these data collection techniques.

Types of Questions.   Highly related to the type of data collection instrument or technique is the type(s) of questions to be asked. Both the purpose and type of data collection selected make a difference as to the types of questions to be asked. In general, there are two types of questions: *closed-ended* and *open-ended*. Types of closed-ended questions include rating scales, forced choice (such as yes/no or true/false), and ranking. Types of open-ended questions include short-answer/fill-in-the-blank and long-answer/essay. Closed-ended questions, which produce categorical or numerical data, are usually easier to analyze but provide limited information and do not allow for expansion of answers. Open-ended questions, which produce descriptive data, while more difficult to analyze systematically, allow for fuller answers, such as those desired in personal, face-to-face interviews. More information on types and formats of questions was given in Chapter 9.

Size of Sample.   Because this discussion covers a wide variety of types of evaluations, talking about the sample size is a bit tricky, because the sample in each type of evaluation will differ. For example, in individual client evaluation, the sample might be the specific behaviors that are to occur by the conclusion of the program (e.g., client will name three leisure resources). In this case, the size of the sample means how many times the specialist will observe the client in order to determine if she has the ability to name three leisure resources. Will the client be given two attempts? five attempts? twenty?

In program evaluation, the sample might be the number of sessions observed, number of goals that are measured, and so on. If a leisure education program runs for ten sessions, how many sessions will be evaluated? Will each goal of each session be examined or will only two goals of each session be sampled? In quality assurance/quality improvement activities, the sample might be the number of former clients who will be surveyed postdischarge concerning their skill acquisition during the therapeutic recreation program.

Type of Sampling Technique.   **Sampling technique** refers to the method used to select the sample to be evaluated. There are two basic types of sampling techniques: **probability** and **nonprobability** or **purposive sampling.** The selection of the sampling technique is highly related to the sample size. Probability sampling for evaluation means that every entity (i.e., person, goal statement, etc.) has an equal chance of being selected. Nonprobability sampling means just the opposite—that not every entity has an equal chance of being selected, that is, the selection is purposeful, based on some preestablished criteria. Patient satisfaction surveys provide an illustrative example of sampling techniques.

In conducting a postdischarge patient satisfaction survey, the specialist has two broad sampling technique options: probability, in which all discharged patients have an equal chance of being selected for the evaluation, and nonprobability, in which some patients are selected for the evaluation based on specified criteria. It is easy to see that nonprobability sampling has a greater chance for bias, in that the specialist may choose predetermined criteria, such as success while in treatment, to select the sample. When the sample is selected for some purpose, it is less likely to resemble or represent the total population or group from which it was taken. More information about sampling techniques and sampling theory can be found in measurement and research texts, and readers seeking additional information are directed to these sources.

Resources.   Availability of resources is another factor in planning and conducting evaluations. A major question is whether the evaluation can be conducted within the financial, time, and personnel limitations of the department or unit. These factors may play an important part in the decision-making process, in that they impact the way in which the evaluation will be conducted. For example, there may not be enough departmental resources to devote the staff time to evaluate every individual program that is offered in the department. Other alternatives, such as a sampling of a representative number of programs, need to be explored.

Plan for Data Collection.   Another decision during the design stage is how the data of interest will be collected. Such decisions center around how the data will be collected, from who will be responsible for certain actions to when and where the data will be gathered. The plan for data collection is tied quite closely with previous decisions made concerning the type of instrument and questions, the size of the sample and type of sampling technique, and availability of resources. The plan for data collection draws all these decisions together in an outline for action or an implementation strategy. In a multiperson department, the data collection plan needs to be well documented so that all professionals know their responsibilities in helping carry out the plan.

Plan for Data Reduction.   The plan for data reduction is similar to the one for data collection. Data reduction means analysis—how will the information be analyzed so that it can be put to use for decision making? Most evaluations can produce a large amount of information in a relatively short time, and the focus should be on the information that is the most important and how it will be used in the future. Data reduction relies heavily on the purpose statement and goals established at the beginning of the evaluation process as guideposts for analysis.

Data analysis often involves some use of statistics, especially for evaluation instruments that use closed-ended questions. The statistics need not be overly complicated as long as the data is analyzed using accepted procedures, and the information targeted in the goals is provided. Even elementary statistics, such as mean (arithmetic average) and range (from high to low), can be used meaningfully to answer a broad array of program evaluation questions. Open-ended questions, which produce qualitative data, can be analyzed using a technique called content analysis. The reader is encouraged to learn more about these techniques from books aimed at these subjects.

Audience.   Another factor in designing evaluations is to whom the information will be reported after it is collected and synthesized. It is generally known from the beginning whether the audience will be clients and their families, agency administrators, professional peers, external accreditation reviewers, or the larger public. Because each audience has a different level of knowledge about and investment in the department's operations, the data collected and the method for reporting it also will differ.

For example, a report that will be distributed to a resident council may be designed and worded differently from one to a CARF or JCAHO reviewer. Obviously, levels of sophistication will differ.

Report Format.   Closely related to the audience is the format in which the final results will be reported. Will the results be presented in a brief report, a lengthy report, a verbal presentation, a slide presentation? What level of detail will be necessary in this format? Will there be a need for graphics or comparisons with other departments? What types of information will the audience need and how sophisticated is the audience in understanding the information? Are there either agency or external standards that define the report format?

All these factors are important in the designing stage of evaluation. It is easy to understand that although they are presented separately above, these factors are highly related and making a change in one area often impacts another area. Once a workable plan has been created, the next step is implementation.

Implementing the Evaluation

The design stage involves many decisions that need to be made before the evaluation is conducted. The next stage, implementation, involves putting those decisions into practice. It is when the actual data is collected (e.g., through interviews, observations, etc.) according to the plan previously created.

Much like program planning, some things may need to change during the implementation stage if clients are discharged unexpectedly, clients cannot be located for aftercare evaluations, or when programs were not implemented due to a staff member's resignation. These situations do not create unnecessarily large problems if the staff person knows other evaluation alternatives and is at least somewhat prepared to change course.

Analyzing the Data

The plan for analyzing data was created in the designing stage. It involves knowing how one will reduce a large quantity of information into grouped data that can be easily understood. Generally, statistics are the tools used to understand large amounts of data. Remember that even averages (means), ranges, and standard deviations are statistics. The specialist does not have to be a statistician to analyze evaluation data, but he or she does have to know at least some elementary statistics. For example, is it helpful to know basic math concepts, such as fractions and percentages; measures of central tendency, such as mean (average), median, and mode; as well as measures of dispersion, such as range and standard deviation. Analysis also involves common sense in trying to answer the questions established in the planning stage of the evaluation.

Utilizing the Evaluation Results

The last stage of the model is utilizing the evaluation results. After the data has been reduced and documented in some format, there also must be a conscious decision to use the evaluation results. One of the major purposes of conducting an evaluation is to aid in program revision and improvement, and it would be a waste of effort to collect data that is not put to good use. Typically, data stemming from a well-designed evaluation is fairly straightforward about the improvements or changes needed. In a client evaluation, if the person did not meet his or her goals, it may be relatively clear why this did not occur. In specific program evaluation, if the program did not go as planned and did not meet its intended purpose, it may be obvious to the specialist why this did not occur. In comprehensive program evaluation when indicators or thresholds are not met, there is usually a quick response as to the problem areas.

This information about remaining deficiencies or problem areas can be used not only for program improvement, but also for improvement in the next round of designing evaluations. It also may indicate that evaluation is needed at another level. For example, if client evaluation shows that several clients are not meeting their treatment objectives, specific program evaluation or comprehensive evaluation may need to occur.

Summary of Basic Evaluation Model

The basic evaluation model discussed here has five steps: planning, designing, implementing, analyzing results, and utilizing results. Each of these steps is important in creating and conducting a systematic evaluation that will produce dependable and usable data. The end result should be information that can be used to improve the direct delivery of services to clients.

The next section of this chapter will examine evaluation at three levels: client evaluation, specific program evaluation, and comprehensive program evaluation. Each discussion will generally follow the outline of the generic evaluation model. Note that each type of evaluation starts with a clear direction and proceeds until data is analyzed and reported. The generic evaluation process presented is applicable to decision making at any level. In each section the unique features of each level of evaluation, such as the unique concerns of measuring client outcomes at the client evaluation level, are presented.

Client Evaluation

Client evaluation, one aspect of patient care monitoring, implies that the focus will be on whether the client outcomes targeted in the initial treatment plan have been accomplished. The focus will be on the end result of the intervention designed on behalf of the client (Carruthers, 2003; Dunn, Sneegas, & Carruthers, 1991; Sheehan, 1993). For the most part, client evaluations will be conducted on an individual basis, although these individual evaluations may be synthesized later into grouped data that addresses larger program evaluation concerns.

> . . . [T]he bottom line of designing a program is to put together a strategy, intervention, or approach that will aid those who participate in the program to accomplish behavioral change in the form of improved functional abilities and/or acquisition of new knowledge and skills. One measure of the effectiveness of a program, therefore, is documenting the outcomes clients attain as a consequence of participating in the program. (Connolly, 1984, p. 159)

**Box 11.2   Sample Client Outcome Areas
of Therapeutic Recreation Intervention**

Increased ability to stay on task

Increased sitting tolerance in wheelchair

Decreased disruptive behavior in group situations

Improved mobility in community environments and situations

Increased knowledge of leisure activity opportunities in the community

Increased awareness of barriers to leisure

Improved understanding of importance of leisure in a balanced lifestyle

Improved ability to explore alternatives and make decisions in regard to leisure

Increased ability to utilize informational sources for leisure participation

Improved knowledge of agencies and facilities that provide recreation services

Improved ability to identify leisure resources available in the home and
neighborhood

Improved ability to take self-responsibility for decisions and actions

Increased ability to initiate and maintain a conversation with peers or family
members

Improved ability to locate leisure partners for activity involvement

Increased ability to use assertiveness skills in a variety of social situations

Increased knowledge of rules and regulations in a specific team sport

Improved skills in a recreation activity that can be done in the winter months

---

The targeted client outcomes will vary based on the different purposes of the programs. In nonintervention programs, the focus of client evaluation may be the number of times the client participated in a program or the level of client enjoyment. When therapeutic recreation services are delivered as planned interventions, different client outcomes are expected. In intervention programs, the focus of service provision is client behavior change as a direct, proven result of the program, and the focus of client evaluations becomes one of measuring and documenting those changes. Box 11.2 provides some examples of client outcome areas typical of therapeutic recreation intervention programs. In the client's treatment or program plan, the outcomes must be stated in more specific, definable, and measurable terms, but this listing provides some overall areas for program consideration. These types of goal statements would help direct the evaluation and would impact decisions made at a later time, such as the types of questions to be asked and the plan for data collection.

One example of the difference between nonintervention and intervention programs is that in nonintervention programs, the most important data may be counting the number of times someone attended programs or how many people were at a certain program. That is, the focus of client evaluation is on attendance. In intervention programs, the focus is more likely to be on the outcome of participation—that is, what the client was doing, what knowledge or skills the client gained from being in the program, or how the client's behavior changed. It is important to design, implement, and evaluate intervention programs in order to be accountable to clients, the profession, and to the accrediting bodies.

Measuring Client Outcomes as a Result of Intervention Programs

"Outcome measurements become especially important if we view TR as an agent of change, as a means to modify behavior, attitudes, or skills. This is important because the outcome measurements that we specify . . . will indicate what the client is expected to achieve during treatment" (Sheehan, 1992, p. 178). That is, therapeutic recreation specialists must have targeted goals for client change that are expected to come about as a result of a well-planned and well-designed program (Stumbo, 2000, 2003).

Riley (1991a) noted that "measurable change" and "relationship" are important factors in this process. "The causal relationship between the process of care (intervention) and the outcomes of care (change in patient behavior) is critical" (Riley, 1991a, p. 59). There must be a direct and proven link between the goals of the program, the type of program being delivered, and the client outcomes expected from participation in the program (Patrick, 1997, 2001).

Timing of the data collection process is also important. If the goal is for the individual client to be independent in the community, the specialist is not likely to be able to determine success or failure until a considerable time postdischarge. Whereas the overall goal of independence is paramount to therapeutic recreation services, few professionals have the resources to conduct follow-up studies. Shank and Kinney (1991) encouraged the professional to choose goals wisely so that the data needed to support the idea can be collected and reported appropriately. Less ambitious, more measurable client outcomes may be preferable to larger, less measurable outcomes. This relates back to the accountability issues mentioned at the beginning of this chapter.

Let's take social skills training as an example. Little change in the client's behavior would be expected from an activity or program that does not focus directly on teaching specific social skills. However, it is not atypical for a therapeutic recreation specialist to claim that social skills are being improved through the client's attendance at a group activity, such as bingo, or in a well-populated environment, such as on a community out-trip. The relationship between the type of program and the client outcomes is a weak one, and measurable change is unlikely. A second example may be one in which the specialist task-analyzes a specific social skill, such as entering a group conversation, and teaches the client, step by step, the process of entering a group conversation. The relationship between the type of program and expected outcomes is more clear and causally linked—a degree of cause and effect can be established. It is more likely that the client will experience a behavior change in the latter program and that outcomes can be specified and measured as a direct result of the planned intervention. That is, the client is likely to gain social skills as a direct result of the social skills intervention.

Box 11.3   Example of Task Analysis of Making a Leisure Decision

Client Outcome Area/Client Goal: To improve ability to make a decision regarding leisure

Task Analysis of Leisure Decision Making	*Criterion*
1. Identifies time period for participation	Decides when he or she is available
2. Gathers information about options for participation during that time period	Uses newspaper to locate information
3. Identifies options for participation	Lists at least three options
4. Weighs the advantages and disadvantages of each option	Lists at least two advantages and two disadvantages of each option
5. Decides on one option for participation	Selects the option with the most advantages or fewest disadvantages

---

If the specialist wants to increase the client's social skills, then social skills instruction must occur. This emphasizes the "causal link" mentioned by Riley (1991a). One cannot assume that an individual will improve social skills in bingo, an activity in which a low level of social skill is required. This is why activity analysis and client assessment prove to be such important factors in designing intervention programs. One must know the requirements of the activity and the needs of the client in order to design intervention programs.

The relationship between the program or activity plan and the expected outcome must be direct. All prior parts (e.g., activity analysis, client assessment, client documentation, etc.) in the Therapeutic Recreation Accountability Model address the need for direct and causal relationships in order to produce logical, consistent outcomes.

An Example of Specifying Client Outcomes

Box 11.3 is an example of a task analysis of leisure decision making. The format, an abbreviated version of the systems design format advocated within this text, includes the behavior to be taught, as well as specification of the criterion level. Notice that the behaviors are defined in very clear terms, so that all specialists (and clients) would agree whether the behavior had occurred. The expected outcomes are easily recognized, and the format can be used as a teaching tool during a therapeutic recreation program.

When the intentions for client behavior are delineated within a task analysis such as this, the specialist will have little trouble indicating expected client outcomes in the form of a client objective. Box 11.4 is an example of a client objective that specifies the exact behavior expected of clients, as related to the task analysis found in Box 11.3.

While Box 11.4 is a detailed client outcome, it specifies important behaviors, contains a skill that is both important and relevant to most clients, and can be taught within a reasonable time period. It provides an evaluative measure for a complex client behavior for which most specialists could easily determine its attainment.

**Box 11.4   Example of Detailed Client Outcome
for Making a Leisure Decision**

Client Outcome/Client Objective:

At the end of the leisure decision-making program, the client will make a leisure decision as characterized by:

1. Identifying a time period for participation that he or she is available
2. Gathering information from the newspaper for options during that time period
3. Identifying at least three options for participation during that time period
4. Identifying at least two advantages and two disadvantages of each option
5. Selecting the most suitable option for participation

Astute readers will note that outcome measures are identical to performance measures as discussed in Chapter 5.

Application to the Generic Evaluation Model

The five-step evaluation model introduced earlier can be applied easily to client evaluation. In the planning stage, the specialist must understand the client outcomes to be specified that relate directly to the purpose and goals of the evaluation. This stage looks at targeted, not incidental, client outcomes. Which ones are important, relevant, timely? The designing phase includes the determination of the details for carrying out the evaluation, such as deciding how, when, and where data will be collected and analyzed. Implementation involves the actual data-gathering process, which may involve observations or interviews with clients or their families. The actual data collection process depends on the purpose or client outcomes that are targeted. Analysis involves making sense of the gathered data and preparing it for others to see. This may mean determining which client outcomes were achieved and which were not, perhaps tabulating how many objectives or performance measures were attained and to what degree. The application stage, then, is when the client's future course of action is noted. Here, the specialist applies the gathered information to the individual's treatment plan or future involvement elsewhere.

Client evaluation depends on the ability to determine precise specifications for the targeted outcomes of intervention. Their cumulative effect has a direct relationship on program evaluation. The next section explores specific program evaluation of therapeutic recreation services.

Specific Program Evaluation

Evaluation of individual activities or programs also is an important step in establishing accountability. Whether evaluating a two-hour activity or a ten-week program, the same five-step process of planning, designing, implementing, analyzing, and utilizing can be used. The evaluator must gather and analyze selected data in a systematic and logical manner, for the purpose of determining the quality, effectiveness, and/or outcomes of a program. Specific program evaluation procedures can be internal or external, formative or summative. It makes sense that the plan for program evaluation closely follows the plan for program implementation. One such procedure was developed by Connolly (1981).

An Example of a Specific Program Evaluation Procedure

The most comprehensive program evaluation model for therapeutic recreation services to date was developed by Connolly (1981). Named the "Formative Program Evaluation Procedure" (FPEP), the comprehensive procedure's purpose is to "collect evaluation information during the implementation of the program in order to identify program strengths and weaknesses to revise and improve the program" (Connolly, 1984, pp. 147–148). The procedure includes both specific program and client outcome information.

Among the forms used to support FPEP are the Post-Session Report Form, the Performance Progress Instrument, the Client Performance Sheet, the Client Profile Form, the Post-Analysis Form, and the Modifications Analysis Form. These forms are outlined in detail in Connolly (1984). For the purposes of this chapter, the Post-Session Report Form and the Post-Session Analysis Form will be highlighted.

The Post-Session Report Form contains nine areas of questions. Among these are (Connolly, 1984, p. 149):

1. Was the session implemented as designed? If not, what changes or modifications were made?
2. How appropriate were the activities (content) used in relation to program objectives addressed in this session?
3. How appropriate were staff interaction or intervention strategies (process) in this session?
4. Did the sequence of activities appear to be logical and appropriate?
5. Was a sufficient amount of time available for the objectives and activities planned for this session?
6. Were required materials, supplies, equipment, and facilities available for this session?
7. Was an adequate number of staff members, appropriately trained, involved in this session as planned?
8. What was the nature of client and staff involvement in this session?
9. What unanticipated events or outcomes occurred in this session that were not planned in the original design?

It is not difficult to understand that these questions stem from decision points made in the program planning process. Underlying each question is the assumption that the specialist considered these factors in designing the program and now the evaluation's intent is to review the level of success experienced during the implementation of these factors. For example, if a decision is made during the program planning process that three staff are needed for a specific program, the evaluation will expect an answer to the question of whether three staff members were adequate. The nine areas showcase considerations for program planning as well as evaluation planning.

Figure 11.5 contains the entire Post-Session Report Form as designed by Connolly (1984). One of its companion forms is the Post-Session Analysis Form, which allows the specialist to summarize data from several Post-Session Report Forms. It condenses the numerical data from up to ten program sessions and aids greatly in determining the overall strengths and weaknesses of a program. The Post-Session Analysis Form is located in Figure 11.6. Both forms are included here due to their immediate relevance to specific program evaluation.

Evaluation data gathered from these forms is used to improve the program in the future. Evaluation provides the systematic information from which specialists can improve both the program delivery and outcomes produced.

The Formative Program Evaluation Procedure, in its entirety, is a classic example of a thorough program evaluation procedure based on systems program design. It yields systematic and logical data that can be used to improve the program, both now and in the future. It demands that the user review basic program design and evaluate the utility of the program to meet its intended outcome.

Application to the Generic Evaluation Model

The generic evaluation model introduced in the beginning of the chapter has five steps of planning, designing, implementing, analyzing results, and utilizing results. Much like evaluating client outcomes, measuring specific program outcomes requires the specialist first to delineate goals and objectives for the evaluation. For example, a specific program evaluation goal might be to determine if enough resources were available for the implementation of the program. Connolly's (1984) Post-Session Report Form provides nine areas suitable for evaluation goal writing. These nine areas are:

- Implemented as planned
- Appropriateness of program content
- Appropriateness of program process
- Activity sequence
- Amount of time
- Materials, supplies, equipment, and facilities
- Adequate and appropriate staff
- Client/staff interactions
- Unanticipated events

The specialist needs to determine which of these are most important, relevant, and timely. The second step of designing includes the many decisions that need to be made for data collection. For example, how will data be gathered—observations? interviews? questionnaires? How many people need to be involved? At what point will they provide information?

DIRECTIONS: A POST-SESSION REPORT FORM is to be completed at the conclusion of each regularly scheduled program session. Please provide as much detailed information as possible for each question below.

PROGRAM TITLE: _____

SESSION No: _____   SESSION DATE: _____

NUMBER OF CLIENTS PRESENT: _____

NUMBER ABSENT: _____   NAMES OF ABSENT CLIENTS: _____

1a. Was the session implemented as designed? (circle one)

> Yes (skip to question #2) 1
> No 2

1b. If no, please describe the changes or modifications made during implementation and the reasons for making changes:

CHANGES OR MODIFICATIONS	REASONS OR RATIONALE

1c. How effective do you feel these changes or modifications were in comparison to the original session design plan? (circle one)

1	2	3	4	5

very effective   very ineffective

1d. Are there any additional changes or modifications in the session design that would further improve this session? (circle one)

> Yes 1
> No (skip to question #2) 2

If yes, please explain the additional changes or modifications: _____

_____

_____

(continued)

Figure 11.5 Post-session report form.

2. How appropriate were the *activities* used for this session in relation to program objectives addressed in this session? (circle one)

1	2	3	4	5

very appropriate   very inappropriate

Please explain your answer: _____

_____

_____

3. How appropriate were *staff interaction or intervention strategies* used in this session in relation to session activities, nature of clients, and achievement of program objectives? (circle one)

1	2	3	4	5

very appropriate   very inappropriate

Please explain your answer: _____

_____

_____

4. Did the *sequence of activities* in this session appear to be logical and appropriate? (circle one)

Yes (skip to question #5) 1

No 2

If no, please identify changes that may be made to improve the sequence:

5. Was the *amount of time* allowed for client achievement of program objectives in this session sufficient? (circle one)

1	2	3	4	5

very sufficient   insufficient, more or less time needed

Please explain your answer: _____

_____

_____

6. Were planned resources (i.e., materials, supplies, equipment, and facilities) available for this session? (circle one)

Yes (skip to question #7) 1

No 2

If no, please explain: _____

_____

(continued)

Figure 11.5 *(continued)*

7. Were *adequate numbers and appropriately trained staff* involved in this session as planned? (circle one)

Yes (skip to question #8) 1

No 2

If no, please explain: _____

_____

_____

8. What was the *nature of client and staff involvement* in this session?

_____

_____

_____

_____

9. What unanticipated events or outcomes occurred in this session that were not planned in the original session design?

POSITIVE UNANTICIPATED EVENTS OR OUTCOMES: _____

_____

_____

_____

NEGATIVE UNANTICIPATED EVENTS OR OUTCOMES: _____

_____

_____

_____

10. Additional comments on this session: _____

_____

_____

_____

_____

Figure 11.5 (*continued*)

EVALUATION QUESTIONS	SESSIONS										AVERAGE OF RATINGS
	1	2	3	4	5	6	7	8	9	10	
Date											
No. present											
No. absent											
Implemented as designed											
Changes or modifications											
Effect of changes											
Other changes											
Activities appropriate											
Intervention appropriate											
Sequence of activities											
Amount of time											
Resources available											
Adequate no. of trained staff											
Client/staff interactions											
Unanticipated positive events/ outcomes											
Unanticipated negative events/ outcomes											

Additional comments

Evaluator notes

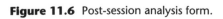
Figure 11.6 Post-session analysis form.

During the third step of implementation, the specialist collects the data as designed in the previous stage. The fourth stage of analysis involves data reduction of some sort. Often "raw" data, from interviews, observations, or the like, is combined and synthesized into "grouped" data that is more easily understood and digested by the audience. The final step of application is when the audience, in whatever form, uses the data to modify (hopefully improve) the program during its next implementation.

Using these five steps, the specialist can carry out a specific program evaluation on any type of program, although it is particularly useful for intervention programs. In some cases, specific program evaluations can be grouped to give a fuller picture of the overall program or can be used to compare and contrast various program offerings against one another. The next section reviews comprehensive program evaluation, speaking largely to quality improvement activities, as required by external accrediting bodies.

Comprehensive Program Evaluation

Evaluation at the comprehensive level is important yet sometimes can be overwhelming. The overall purpose of comprehensive program evaluation is to ensure that professionals, collectively, are performing their job tasks in such a manner as to provide a safe, comfortable, and supportive environment that allows the client to reach desired outcomes and expectations within the most efficient and effective course of care. It's no surprise that those programs designed from a systems approach are more easily evaluated than ones that are haphazard or not founded on a strong service delivery model.

For the most part, external accreditation agencies and insurance companies mandate some form of comprehensive program evaluation, usually at the agency level. As McCormick (2003) noted, terminology related to service evaluation changes frequently. He noted that the Joint Commission on Accreditation of Healthcare Organizations (JCAHO) started with "consistently optimal" in 1975 and moved to "quality assurance" in 1979, "continuous quality improvement" in the early 1990s, and "performance improvement" in 1996. Not all accreditation agencies used the same terminology, but all have the same intent: to provide mechanisms for health care agencies to continually improve the services delivered to clients through self-inspection and on-site visitations by surveyors. According to JCAHO (2003b), "performance measurement in healthcare represents what is done and how well it is done. The goal is to accurately understand the basis for current performance so that better results can be achieved through focused improvement actions."

This section will briefly describe the evaluation programs of four agencies, before proceeding with how comprehensive program evaluation aligns with the generic evaluation model previously discussed in this chapter. The four regulatory agencies that will be highlighted are the:

- Joint Commission on Accreditation of Healthcare Organizations (JCAHO) [www.jcaho.org]
- Rehabilitation Accreditation Commission (CARF) [www.carf.org]
- National Committee for Quality Assurance (NCQA) [www.ncqa.org]

■ Centers for Medicare and Medicaid Services (CMS) [www.cms.hhs.gov]

To the best of our knowledge this information is accurate at the time of this writing; the reader should confirm the currency of information on the respective Web sites.

Voluntary and Governmental Accreditation Agencies

Joint Commission on Accreditation of Healthcare Organizations   The JCAHO is a private, not-for-profit agency that monitors a wide variety of health care services. Because most health care organizations receive a majority of their revenues from sources other than inpatient care, such as ambulatory and ancillary services, JCAHO, in turn, has focused on more flexible modes of health care (Pawlson & O'Kane, 2002). Following is a list of standards manuals administered by JCAHO in 2003 (JCAHO, 2003d):

■ *Comprehensive Accreditation Manual for Ambulatory Care (CAMAC)*

■ *Accreditation Manual for Assisted Living (AMAL)*

■ *Comprehensive Accreditation Manual for Behavioral Health Care (CAMBHC)*

■ *Comprehensive Accreditation Manual for Health Care Networks (CAMHCN)*

■ *Comprehensive Accreditation Manual for Managed Behavioral Health Care (CAMMBHC)*

■ *Accreditation Manual for Preferred Provider Organizations (AMPPO)*

■ *Comprehensive Accreditation Manual for Home Care (CAMHC)*

■ *Comprehensive Accreditation Manual for Hospitals (CAMH)*

■ *Accreditation Manual for Critical Access Hospitals (AMCAH)*

■ *Comprehensive Accreditation Manual for Long-Term Care (CAMLTC)*

■ *Accreditation Manual for Office-Based Surgery Practices*

■ *Comprehensive Accreditation Manual for Pathology and Clinical Laboratory Services (CAMPCLS)*

JCAHO accreditation is based on agencies receiving a passing score on a set of standards that it creates (Pawlson & O'Kane, 2002). These standards also meet Medicare requirements (that is, if a facility meets JCAHO standards, the CMS waives it own accreditation process).

In 1999, hospitals and long-term care facilities seeking accreditation from the JCAHO (and nearly all did and do) were required to be active in quality improvement activities using measures from the Oryx® measurement set and were free to select any of the more than 200 measures. This left little comparability between hospitals on a large scale, although JCAHO reported each hospital's levels of accreditation status and scores of specific standards on its Web site (JCAHO, 2002a; Pawlson & O'Kane, 2002).

As of July 1, 2002, the Joint Commission began progressive implementation of its "Shared Visions—New Pathways" initiative, which changes how health care agencies perform and report quality and performance reviews (JCAHO, 2002a, 2003c). The new initiative will take full effect January 1, 2004, and consolidates the former Joint Commission standards, introduces a continual self-assessment process, requires data from multiple sources, uses an automated database to focus the on-site survey, and uses individual patients for evaluation of patient care (JCAHO, 2003a, 2003b, 2003c).

According to the Joint Commission, the benefits of the new "Shared Vision—New Pathways" initiative are:

- Continuous emphasis on performance improvement
- Focus on the quality and safety of direct care delivery systems
- Enhanced educational and interactive aspect of the survey
- Customized to the characteristics of individual health care organizations
- Reliant on new technologies to facilitate continuous flow of information between health care organizations and the Joint Commission
- Reduced accreditation-related costs

Because of widely publicized medical errors, "[I]n addition to revising a number of safety-related standards, JCAHO is also continuously evaluating the efficacy of all of its standards as they relate to providing a safe environment for patients, employees, and the community. The focus of this new approach is on proactively identifying and reducing the inherent risks in healthcare instead of reacting to near misses or actual events that cause injury to patients" (Cudney & Reinbold, 2002, p. 216). As it began in 2002 and 2003, the new process focused on five core areas: (a) acute myocardial infarction, (b) heart failure, (c) community-acquired pneumonia, (d) pregnancy and related conditions, and (e) surgical procedures and complications (the last in cooperation with CMS) (JCAHO, 2002a, 2003c). Focus is expected to expand to additional areas in coming years.

Rehabilitation Accreditation Commission   CARF, also a voluntary, not-for-profit accrediting agency, reviews a wide range of rehabilitation and human services programs in the United States, Canada, and Europe (CARF, 2003c). The stated mission of CARF is to "promote the quality, value, and optimal outcomes of services through accreditation that centers on enhancing the lives of the persons receiving services" (2003c). CARF accreditation is a well-defined continuous quality improvement process that helps agencies to achieve the highest possible standards of service excellence, performance, and customer satisfaction, and provides value-added benefits to consumers (CARF, 2003b).

As of 2003, CARF published accreditation standards manuals for the following types of services (CARF, 2003a):

- *Adult Day Service Standards Manual*
- *Assisted Living Standards Manual*
- *Behavioral Health Standards Manual*
- *Comprehensive Blind Rehabilitation Services Standards Manual*
- *Employment and Community Services Standards Manual*
- *Medical Rehabilitation Standards Manual*

- *Network Administration and Access Center Standards Manual*
- *Opioid Treatment Program Accreditation Standards Manual*

National Committee for Quality Assurance
The NCQA operates a voluntary accreditation plan for managed care plans (health maintenance organizations [HMOs]) and employs a set of quality indicators called the Health Plan Employer Data and Information Set (HEDIS). This program has become so successful that many employers are now using HEDIS information to select managed care plans for their employees (Scott, 1998). Approximately 80 percent of managed care plans report data to the NCQA and as a group represent more than 50 million individuals (Pawlson & O'Kane, 2002). Beginning in 1999, the NCQA started a "clinical measures of performance" initiative as the focus of an HMO's accreditation score. This and other information about accreditation decisions and performance are found on their Web site in a report card format, easily accessible to consumers (Pawlson & O'Kane, 2002).

Centers for Medicare and Medicaid Services
The CMS (formerly the Health Care Financing Administration [HCFA]) is a federal government body that is responsible for the regulatory review of hospitals that bill for Medicare and Medicaid recipients. Medicare is a federal health insurance program for individuals over the age of 65 and Medicaid is a combined program of state and federal insurance and medical assistance for qualified needy individuals of any age (Springhouse Corporation, 2002).

About 40 percent of all "bed-days" in hospitals across the country are paid through Medicare. If hospitals have a "deemed status" accreditation from a private accrediting body (such as JCAHO or CARF), that accreditation substitutes for a formal review by CMS (Pawlson & O'Kane, 2002).

As the nation's largest health care program, Medicare recently began to require a "quality assessment and performance improvement" (QAPI) process that currently goes beyond HEDIS. In the very near future a "quality improvement system for managed care" (QISMC) that reports comprehensive quality improvement efforts in both clinical and nonclinical arenas will be required (Pawlson & O'Kane, 2002; Scott, 1998).

Although each may have a unique meaning created by its sponsoring agency, for the most part, the terms **quality assurance, quality improvement, continuous quality improvement, clinical practice improvement,** and **performance improvement** are aimed at the same target: to document accountability for the improvement of health care services for all individuals. It is fortunate that the systems design method presented in this book parallels many concepts and practices found in the quality improvement literature. "While QA talks about 'outcomes,' systems [literature] uses 'terminal performance objectives' or 'performance measures.' When QA talks about 'processes,' the systems literature has incorporated 'teaching/learning activities' or 'content and process' as forms of documentation" (Navar, 1991, p. 7). The commonalities between systems design and quality improvement are many, and are based on the systematic application of valid and reliable methods of data collection and analysis. Both methods emphasize a goal orientation to guide the collection and utilization of information.

One of the most basic approaches to comprehensive service evaluation involves a ten-step process that focuses on (a) seeking out problematic areas that lower quality, (b) correcting those problems, and (c) evaluating how well those corrections are solv-

---

Box 11.5   Commonalities Between Evaluation Process Model and Ten-Step Model

Evaluation Design Model	Ten-Step Model

Planning the Evaluation
  Delineation of purpose or outcome
  Specify priorities
  Document evaluation goals
	1. Assign Responsibility
	2. Delineate Scope of Care

Designing the Evaluation
  Type of instrument or technique
  Types of questions
  Size of sample
  Sampling technique
  Resources
  Plan for data collection
  Plan for data reduction
  Audience
  Report format
	3. Identify Important Aspects/Elements of Care
	4. Identify Indicators
	5. Establish Criteria or Thresholds

Implementing the Evaluation	6. Collect and Organize Data
Analyzing the Data	7. Evaluate Care
Utilizing the Evaluation Results	8. Take Action 9. Assess the Effectiveness of Actions 10. Communicate Information

---

ing the problems. This ten-step process is easily comparable to the generic evaluation model introduced earlier in this chapter. See Box 11.5 for this comparison.

Application to the Generic Evaluation Model

Planning the Evaluation.   The first stage of the generic evaluation model, planning the evaluation, contains two of the ten steps: (1) assign responsibility and (2) delineate scope of care. In the planning step, the primary focus is on establishing the parameters for the evaluation, including its purpose, establishing priorities, and documenting evaluation goals. The actions parallel those taken in assigning responsibility and delineating scope of care for quality assurance. Responsibility is assigned to whomever is in charge of overseeing and carrying out the monitoring and evaluation activities. That person, and perhaps others in the department, then begin the process by establishing the scope of care or key functions of the department. This may include creation of a vision statement, mission statement, or statement of purpose that draws the line around the functions of the therapeutic recreation department. It focuses on the unique mission or purpose or contribution of therapeutic recreation services to the institution or agency (Russoniello, 1991).

Focusing on the clear purpose of service provision will aid the evaluator in focusing on the thrust of the evaluation. For example, if the department mission statement

---

**Box 11.6   Sample Elements of Care for Evaluating Quality
of Service Provision**

Client Assessment	Program Implementation
Treatment/Program Plans	Staff Professional Development
Progress Notes/Client Documentation	Community Reintegration Program
Discharge and Referral Summaries	Social Skills Training Program
Patient Safety/Risk Management	Patient Follow-up Services
Patient/Family Support Group	Special Events
Program Evaluation	Clinical Privileging
Co-Treatment Programs	Outpatient Program

---

implies a heavy dual emphasis on inpatient care and follow-up services, then it is likely that the evaluation also will center on these issues.

Designing the Evaluation.   It is in this stage that all the details of data collection are to be decided. This includes types of instruments or forms, types of questions, sampling technique, plan for data collection, and plan for data reduction. Three of the ten steps fall within this area: (3) identify important aspects/ elements of care, (4) identify indicators, and (5) establish criteria or thresholds. Because these three steps are so crucial to the process, each will be discussed separately.

Identify Important Aspects/Elements of Care.   Usually, three to seven important aspects of care are identified (Huston, 1987; Navar, 1987). Important aspects of care are those that are believed to be most closely linked to the quality of care in the organization and those that have been identified by the profession. Huston (1987) noted four questions crucial to documenting important aspects of care:

1. What are the important functions of TR services?
2. What are the necessary elements in the TR process?
3. What are the major responsibilities of a TR professional?
4. What indicates quality of TR services? (Huston, 1987, p. 70)

In addition, it has been suggested that important aspects of care are "events" or "decision points" when specialists make important professional service delivery decisions; for example, during assessment, treatment planning, patient care monitoring, and discharge follow-up (Wright, 1987). A parallel concept is to choose aspects of care that tend to be high volume (for example, client assessments), high risk (treatment plans present a high risk when not based on assessment results), and problem prone (programs in which clients are less likely to achieve intended outcomes) (Huston, 1987).

Box 11.6 lists some examples of important aspects of care for therapeutic recreation services. Individual departments select those that are most appropriate to their agency.

Identify Indicators.   The fourth step is to identify indicators. At this point, staff develop measurable indicators that will be used to monitor the important aspects of care outlined in the previous step. The relationship between the element of care and the indicator must be clear.

> *An indicator is defined as a measurable dimension of the quality or appropriateness with respect to an important aspect of patient care. Indicators describe measurable care processes, clinical events, complications, or outcomes for which data should be collected to allow comparison against an established threshold. . . . Valid and reliable data concerning expected/desired results and undesired/unexpected results (whether measured with reference to the occurrence of single "sentinel" events, rates of occurrence of clinical events, or changes in health status, quality of life, level of function or patient satisfaction) can play an important role in a comprehensive monitoring and evaluation system. (Scalenghe, 1991, p. 32)*

Although indicators can be structure, process, or outcome oriented, client outcomes have become the primary focus of all health care evaluation processes. Client assessment is used to illustrate the three views.

Important Aspect/Element of Care: Client Assessment

Structure: Staff are qualified to perform client assessments.

Staff have adequate time to conduct client assessments.

Process: Staff perform client assessments according to assessment protocol.

Client goals are derived directly from assessment results.

Outcome: Client is placed into appropriate programs, based on assessment results.

Client's functional limitations are improved based on client involvement in the program.

Establishing Criteria or Thresholds.   The fifth step is establishing criteria or thresholds for evaluation. Within this step several actions must occur. The first is to establish the criteria that will be used as the "cut-off." Let's use one of the above illustrations as an example: "Client is placed into appropriate programs, based on assessment results." The threshold for this outcome may be set at 95 percent—that is, at least 95 percent of the time, it must be found that clients are placed into programs as a direct result of the assessment data. (In the next two steps, evaluating care and taking action, any threshold that has not been met, say one at 94 percent, indicates a more intensive evaluation.) While establishing criteria, several related decisions need to be made, for example, how the data will be collected and analyzed. Decisions concern size of sample (how many cases will be examined), sampling technique (how cases will be selected for examination), data collection (how and when data will be gathered), and data analysis (how results will be analyzed). All these decisions follow from establishing the threshold at which the quality and appropriateness of the program will be evaluated further.

Implementing the Evaluation.   After the plan for the evaluation is established, the sixth step of the ten-step evaluation process involves the actual implementation or data collection phase of the evaluation. A variety of sources may be used for information gathering, including patient or participant records, the department's written plan of operation, program records (e.g., incident reports, participation records, etc.), and institution-wide data systems. Additionally, a variety of techniques may be used to collect the data, including client perception surveys, direct observation, client chart/ record review, utilization review, and the like. In this step the data is collected for the purpose of organizing the information in an understandable fashion.

Analyzing the Data.   The seventh step involves evaluating the care by performing further analysis. The collected data is now ready for further reduction and analysis. The evaluator is looking for potential problems, such as differences between intended and actual practice, particular patterns that may be occurring, difficulties that may have been encountered, and the like. Special attention is paid to those occurrences that conflict with the threshold established above. If difficulties or discrepancies are found, the results most likely reflect a need for further information gathering and closer scrutiny. A more intense review may need to take place.

In this stage, charts, graphs, and tables may become useful in displaying the data in usable form. The results should be presented in a way that is immediately apparent to the audience and helps to indicate the degree of adherence to the preestablished standards.

Utilizing the Evaluation Results.   The last stage in the evaluation model contains the final three steps of the ten-step model. The actions taken in these steps depend heavily on the results found throughout the evaluation process.

Take Action.   Now that the results indicate where, if any, problems lie, the next step is to take action toward their resolution. This step focuses on improving quality of care for clients as well as correcting, minimizing, or eliminating the problem areas or risks. The idea is to continue to review instances or areas where quality of client care can be improved and where chances for undue risk, harm, or problems for clients and staff can be lowered.

Assess the Effectiveness of Actions.   This step implies that quality improvement is a continuous, ongoing process in which data collection, analysis, and application are cyclical. This step evaluates whether client care has improved, and if it has not, whether further corrective actions are warranted. Thresholds may be increased, new problems investigated, and new methods of data collection may be utilized as the process for improving services to clients moves forward.

Communicate Information.   The final step involves reporting the results of the quality improvement activities to the appropriate audiences. The reporting may include a summary of actions taken throughout the ten-step process, the outcomes or results, any conclusions or recommendations that can be made from the results, and any further actions that were or will be taken to remedy areas of concern. Usually these reports, besides being presented to the therapeutic recreation staff, are directed to agency quality improvement monitors, clinical staff, and various administrative personnel. The distribution of the information will be unique to the agency setting.

Efficacy Research

Efficacy and effectiveness research play important roles in determining whether a certain intervention or interventions are successful in producing intended outcomes (Stumbo, 2003). Both terms of research focus on whether the program(s) are successful in changing some form of client behavior and ask questions such as: Is this program effective in producing x outcomes in y clients? Under which condition(s) is this intervention most effective? For which group of clients is this intervention most or least effective? Efficacy research questions how an intervention performs under ideal or more controlled circumstances; effectiveness research evaluates interventions as they are actually practiced with clients.

Efficacy and effectiveness research is thus complementary to both program evaluation and quality improvement activities. Both program evaluation and quality improvement can provide a foundation for further clinical research (Patrick, 1997, 2001).

Program evaluation information is gathered to make decisions usually about individual programs. Its focus is on whether the program serves its intended purpose of changing some aspect of client behavior. All professionals in all settings are required to conduct program evaluations in order to comply with professional standards of practice (e.g., NTRS Standards of Practice [2003] and ATRA Standards of Practice [2000]). Many quality improvement activities have moved from examining structure and process concerns to those showing outcomes of professional performance improvement. Focused primarily on clinical services, such mandates come from external accrediting agencies such as JCAHO and CARF. These agencies are focusing on better professional performance in the areas of efficient use of resources, reduction of risk, and increased patient/family satisfaction. These activities are not focused solely on specific program outcomes, but, depending on the problem on which the investigation is focused, can be more narrowly or broadly defined. For example, it might focus on the client assessment as the "problem" under investigation, and while assessment clearly influences program outcomes, it is not a "program" per se. On the other hand, when it focuses on a program, it can be very parallel to program evaluation.

Efficacy and effectiveness research produces results that can provide powerful information on the impact of therapeutic recreation interventions (Stumbo, 2000, 2003). Coyle, Kinney, and Shank (1993) and Patrick (1997) discussed practice-based research and provided excellent coverage of various research designs that could be used by practicing professionals to increase the scientific rigor of program evaluations and activities to the level necessary for research. Coyle, Kinney, and Shank (1993) stated that a research design "considers when, where, and under what conditions the research will be conducted. The primary purpose of the research design is to answer the research questions while controlling for sources of error that could invalidate the results of the research" (p. 207). Though it is not the intent of this text to cover the details of research design, it is worth mentioning that there are several research designs that are appropriate for efficacy research. Interested readers are referred to the Malkin and Howe's (1993) research text that contains the Coyle, Shank, and Kinney chapter, and Stumbo's (2001) professional issues text that include chapters by Patrick, Widmer, and McCormick and Lee.

Clearly, program evaluation, quality improvement, and efficacy research efforts can be connected. As the need for more outcome-based, scientifically driven information increases, so too will the logical extensions of these three functions. Students and professionals alike should learn all they can about evaluation, research design, statistics, and report writing to ensure future job success.

Summary

Evaluation processes can be established to determine the successes and areas of improvement for individual programs, individual clients, and comprehensive programs. Evaluation can be conducted only on well-designed and thought-out programs that have measurable goals and meaningful targets. Evaluation starts with identifying outcomes that are important and applicable, creating and implementing programs aimed at achieving those outcomes, and then measuring the success of delivering those outcomes. The link between goals, programs, and outcomes is a strong one.

This chapter provided information on how to design and conduct program evaluation using a generic five-step evaluation model. The model helps the specialist in making the numerous decisions involved in conducting program evaluation. Linkages to quality improvement and efficacy research are discussed.

STUDENT EXERCISES

Discussion Questions

1. Discuss the relationships between program evaluation, accountability, cost effectiveness, and decision making. What function does each serve? What are their contributions toward a higher quality comprehensive program?

2. What are the benefits of conducting systematic program evaluations? What are the consequences of not conducting systematic program evaluations?

3. Explain Figure 11.2 in your own words, using an example of a therapeutic recreation program with which you are familiar.

4. What are the actions a specialist takes during each stage of the generic evaluation model? (See Figure 11.4.) Explain the importance of designing the evaluation plan while designing the program plan. How do comprehensive evaluation goals relate to comprehensive program goals?

5. What are the differences between internal and external evaluation? Formative and summative evaluation? What are the benefits and drawbacks of each kind?

6. Review the techniques for collecting evaluation data, and note which ones you have experience with and which ones you do not. Which are most likely to be used in your future places of employment?

7. Why is attendance a weak indicator of outcomes for intervention programs? What evidence would be better to collect to demonstrate client outcomes?

8. Review Figures 11.5 and 11.6. How would collecting and analyzing this information assist a therapeutic recreation specialist in improving the program the next time it is offered? What other information do you think needs to be collected to demonstrate client outcomes and/or program success?

9. Discuss the similarities and differences among the Joint Commission on Accreditation of Healthcare Organizations, the Commission on Accreditation of Rehabilitation Facilities, the National Committee for Quality Assurance, and the Centers for Medicare and Medicaid Services. What is the role of each? What types of facilities and/or clients do they serve?

10. Discuss why third-party payers, consumers, and accrediting agencies are interested in efficacy or effectiveness research. What are the benefits for professions that have conducted efficacy or effectiveness research to show the impact of their services? What are the consequences for those professions that do not?

Practice Test

1. Quality assurance/continuous quality improvement is:
   a. a method of comprehensive program evaluation.
   b. a method for implementing in-service staff training.
   c. required in all clinical and community agencies.
   d. the first step in designing a comprehensive program.

2. Programming that involves individual client assessment, individual program planning, implementation of a program, and evaluation of the effect of the program is often called:
   a. intervention programming.
   b. recreation for special populations.
   c. special recreation.
   d. diversional recreation.

3. What is the major benefit of the Therapeutic Recreation Accountability Model (TRAM)?
   a. It explains to other disciplines how activities are selected for client involvement.
   b. It explains the process of selecting and implementing client assessments.
   c. It shows the connections between different actions or functions of the TR specialist.
   d. It demonstrates the need for therapeutic recreation services.

4. Which of following is/are necessary to produce client outcomes?
   I.   Well-designed programs that have a targeted purpose
   II. Client assessment that places clients into the right programs
   III. Documentation that focuses on client behavior
   IV. Quality improvement systems that focus on program effectiveness
   a. I and II
   b. I, II, and III

   c. II, III, and IV

   d. I, II, III, and IV

5. Which of the following is an action that takes place during the design phase of an evaluation?

   a. establishing the purpose

   b. gathering data

   c. using the results for future program improvement

   d. deciding on the type of instrument to collect data

6. Which of the following is a private, not-for-profit agency that accredits community employment services for people with disabilities?

   a. Joint Commission on Accreditation of Healthcare Organizations (JCAHO)

   b. Rehabilitation Accreditation Commission (CARF)

   c. National Committee for Quality Assurance (NCQA)

   d. Centers for Medicare and Medicaid Services (CMS)

7. An example of efficacy research is:

   a. For one month, clients who entered the therapeutic recreation program were given a standardized intervention, according to the research protocol.

   b. In a laboratory setting, clients were randomly assigned to a treatment group or control group, and their results were compared against one another.

   c. Newspaper ads solicited individuals to participate in an exercise program; 120 individuals enrolled in the program.

   d. The therapeutic recreation specialist gathered all her program evaluation data for 12 months and synthesized it into one annual report.

8. All of the following are important to providing intervention programs to clients EXCEPT a(n):

   a. sound comprehensive program design.

   b. activity inventory of past and future leisure interests.

   c. series of protocols that address basic client needs and outcomes.

   d. quality improvement program that feeds information back to improve the program.

Answers: 1. a, 2. a, 3. c, 4. d, 5. d, 6. b, 7. b, 8. b

Chapter Activities

TRAM Comparison

Ask a therapeutic recreation specialist to share his or her program and client documentation forms. Compare the forms and their content with the Therapeutic Recreation Accountability Model. What areas are present and which are absent? How does this affect the program's ability to help clients achieve outcomes?

Research Study

Use the *Therapeutic Recreation Journal,* the *Annual in Therapeutic Recreation,* the *American Journal of Recreational Therapy,* or another closely related journal and locate one or two articles that report either efficacy or effectiveness research in therapeutic recreation.

Describe the clients, the intervention, and the outcomes. What are the implications of this research for the field of therapeutic recreation?

Comprehensive Program Design Evaluation

Using the comprehensive program design you created in Chapters 4 and 5, design an evaluation plan that would help identify achieved client outcomes. When, where, and how would you collect data?

REFERENCES

Compton, D. M. (Ed.) (1997). *Issues in therapeutic recreation: Toward a new millennium* (2nd ed.). Champaign, IL: Sagamore Publishing Company.

Connolly, M. (1981). *Analysis of a formative program evaluation procedure for therapeutic recreation services.* Unpublished doctoral dissertation, University of Illinois at Urbana-Champaign.

Connolly, C. (1984). Program evaluation. In C. A. Peterson and S. L. Gunn, *Therapeutic recreation program design: Principles and procedures.* (2nd ed.) (pp. 136–179). Englewood Cliffs, NJ: Prentice-Hall.

Coyle, C. P., Kinney, W. B., & Shank, J. W. (1993). Trials and tribulations in field-based research in therapeutic recreation. In M. J. Malkin and C. Z. Howe, *Research in therapeutic recreation: Concepts and methods.* (pp. 207–232). State College, PA: Venture Publishing Company.

Cudney, A. E., & Reinbold, O. (2002). JCAHO: Responding to quality and safety imperatives. *Journal of Healthcare Management, 47*(4), 216–219.

Huston, A. D. (1987). Clinical application of quality assurance in the therapeutic recreation setting. In B. Riley (Ed.). *Evaluation of therapeutic recreation through quality assurance.* (pp. 67–96). State College, PA: Venture Publishing Company.

Joint Commission on Accreditation of Healthcare Organizations (2002a). Information on final specification for national implementation of hospital core measures. Retrieved January 6, 2003, from: *http://www.jcaho.org/pms/core+measures/information+on+final+specifications.htm*

Joint Commission on Accreditation of Healthcare Organizations (2002b). "Shared visions—New pathways." *Perspectives: The Official Joint Commission Newsletter, 22*(10), 1, 3.

Joint Commission on Accreditation of Healthcare Organizations (2003a). The accreditation process circa 2004. Retrieved January 6, 2003, from: *http://www.jcaho.org/accredited+organizations/svnp/accred_process+04.htm.*

Joint Commission on Accreditation of Healthcare Organizations (2003b). Performance measurement in health care. Retrieved January 6, 2003, from: *http://jcaho.org/pms/index.htm.*

Joint Commission on Accreditation of Healthcare Organizations (2003c). "Shared visions—New pathways." Retrieved January 6, 2003, from: *http://www.jcaho.org/accredited+organizations/svnp/svnp.htm.*

Joint Commission on Accreditation of Healthcare Organizations (2003d). Standards: Frequently asked questions. Retrieved January 6, 2003, from: *http://www.jcaho.org/accredited+organizations/standards=faqs.htm.*

Lundegren, H. M., & Farrell, P. (1985). *Evaluation for leisure service managers: A dynamic approach.* Philadelphia: Saunders College Publishing.

Malkin, M. J., & Howe, C. Z. (1993). *Research in therapeutic recreation: Concepts and methods.* State College, PA: Venture Publishing Company.

McCormick, B. P., & Lee, Y. (2001). Research into practice: Building knowledge through empirical practice. In N. J. Stumbo (Ed.), *Professional issues in therapeutic recreation: On competence and outcomes* (pp. 383–400). Champaign, IL: Sagamore Publishing Company.

McCormick, B. P. (2003). Outcome measurement as a tool for performance improvement. In N.J. Stumbo (Ed.), *Client outcomes in therapeutic recreation* (pp. 221–232). State College, PA: Venture Publishing Company.

Navar, N. (1987). Therapeutic recreation's written plan of operation: The step before quality assurance. In B. Riley (Ed.). *Evaluation of therapeutic recreation through quality assurance.* (pp. 43–54). State College, PA: Venture Publishing Company.

Navar, N. (1991). Advancing therapeutic recreation through quality assurance: A perspective on the changing nature of quality in therapeutic recreation. In B. Riley (Ed.), *Quality management: Applications for therapeutic recreation.* (pp. 3–20). State College, PA: Venture Publishing Company.

Patrick, G. (1997). Making clinical research happen. In D. M. Compton (Ed.), *Issues in therapeutic recreation: Toward the new millennium* (2nd ed.). (pp. 327–345) Champaign, IL: Sagamore Publishing Company.

Patrick, G. (2001). Perspective: Clinical research: Methods and mandates. In N. J. Stumbo (Ed.), *Professional issues in therapeutic recreation: On competence and outcomes* (pp. 401–418). Champaign, IL: Sagamore Publishing Company.

Pawlson, L. G., & O'Kane, M. E. (2002). Professionalism, regulation, and the market: Impact on accountability for quality of care. *Health Affairs, 21*(3), 200–207.

Riley, B. (1987). Conceptual basis of quality assurance: Application to therapeutic recreation service. In B. Riley (Ed.). *Evaluation of therapeutic recreation through quality assurance.* (pp. 7–24). State College, PA: Venture Publishing Company.

Riley, B. (1991a). Quality assessment: The use of outcome indicators. In B. Riley (Ed.), *Quality management: Applications for therapeutic recreation.* (pp. 53–68). State College, PA: Venture Publishing Company.

Riley, B. (1991b). *Quality management: Applications for therapeutic recreation.* State College, PA: Venture Publishing Company.

Russoniello, C. V. (1991). "Vision statements" and "mission statements": Macro indicators of quality performance. In B. Riley (Ed.), *Quality management: Applications for therapeutic recreation.* (pp. 21–28). State College, PA: Venture Publishing Company.

Scalenghe, R. (1991). The Joint Commission's agenda for change as related to the provision of therapeutic recreation services. In B. Riley (Ed.), *Quality management: Applications for therapeutic recreation.* (pp. 29–42). State College, PA: Venture Publishing Company.

Scott, J. S. (1998). Questing for quality: QISMC-ly cutting the QAPI. *Healthcare Financial Management, 52*(10), 32–33.

Shank, J. W., & Kinney, W. B. (1991). Monitoring and measuring outcomes in therapeutic recreation. In B. Riley (Ed.), *Quality management: Applications for therapeutic recreation.* (pp. 69–82). State College, PA: Venture Publishing Company.

Sheehan, T. (1992). Outcome measures and therapeutic recreation. In G. Hitzhusen and L. T. Jackson (Eds.), *Expanding Horizons in Therapeutic Recreation XIV* (pp. 177–192). Columbia, MO: Curators University of Missouri.

Sheehan, T. (1993). Outcome measures and therapeutic recreation II. In G. Hitzhusen and L. T. Jackson (Eds.), *Expanding Horizons in Therapeutic Recreation XV,* (pp. 129–142). Columbia, MO: Curators University of Missouri.

Springhouse Corporation. (2002). *Chart smart: The a-to-z guide to better nursing documentation.* Springhouse, PA: Author.

Stumbo, N. J. (2000). Outcome measurement in health care: Implications for therapeutic recreation. *Annual in Therapeutic Recreation, 9,* 1–8.

Stumbo, N. J. (2001). (Ed.) *Professional issues in therapeutic recreation: On competence and outcomes.* Champaign, IL: Sagamore Publishing Company.

Stumbo, N. J. (2003). Outcomes, accountability, and therapeutic recreation. In N. J. Stumbo (Ed.), *Client outcomes in therapeutic recreation* (pp. 1–24). State College, PA: Venture Publishing Company.

Widmer, M. A. (2001). Methods for outcome research in therapeutic recreation. In N. J. Stumbo (Ed.), *Professional issues in therapeutic recreation: On competence and outcomes* (pp. 365–382). Champaign, IL: Sagamore Publishing Company.

Wright, S. (1987). Quality assessment: Practical approaches in therapeutic recreation. In B. Riley (Ed.). *Evaluation of therapeutic recreation through quality assurance.* (pp. 55–66). State College, PA: Venture Publishing Company.

CHAPTER 12

Accountability:
Challenge for the Future

Therapeutic recreation is concerned with the direct delivery of services to clients with disabilities, illness, or special needs. The previous eleven chapters of this book cover the concepts and processes used to deliver those services in a systematic and predictable way. When services are planned, implemented, and evaluated with specific client needs in mind, the professional's accountability for outcomes increases significantly.

What does a professional have to know, do, or be involved in to develop or maintain professional accountability? First, each person entering or in the field needs to remain informed. Obtaining a degree and a first job only allows a person entry into the field, and diplomas and job contracts signify only the beginning of a lifelong commitment to keeping informed of professional advances and activities. Professional knowledge has a very short life span and to keep current, professionals must remain informed through reading, participating in conferences (notice we did not say just attending!), and networking with peers. Professionals who maintain a desire to stay abreast of current information have a greater likelihood of taking advantage of new information and technologies that make their professional life more meaningful, yet easier to accomplish. Clients deserve to interact with professionals who are excellent, well informed, and on the cutting edge. Here are some ways to get and keep informed:

- Get certified by the National Council for Therapeutic Recreation Certification as soon as you qualify.
- Read at least one therapeutic recreation book or article per month.
- Read at least one book or article on a subject related to therapeutic recreation services (e.g., wellness, stress management, health care outcomes, facilitation techniques) per month.
- Read at least one book or article per month on disability issues and settings issues (such as inclusion and managed care).
- Visit at least one Internet site related to therapeutic recreation per month (e.g., post questions, interact in a chat room, download usable information, join a listserv).
- Read professional newsletters (e.g., ATRA and NTRS) cover to cover.
- Read NCTRC's certification newsletter cover to cover.

- Contact local, state, and national organizations serving individuals with disabilities and illnesses to keep track of the latest research and service issues.

Second, each student, beginning specialist, and seasoned professional must understand the connections and direct relationships between each job function and task. It is no longer acceptable to conduct assessments that have little or nothing to do with program placement. It is no longer acceptable to document protocols that have no relationship to the overall program design or client needs. And it no longer justifiable to evaluate clients on how many activities they attended rather than what outcomes they gained from participation. Each individual must make sure that the relationships between each professional task, as viewed on the Therapeutic Recreation Accountability Model, are strong and logical. That means clearly understanding the purpose, role, and function of each of the components of the model and being able to conduct them well. If all professionals would share in this responsibility of making sure their day-to-day operations adhere to standards and produce predictable, desirable outcomes, the profession would be far ahead of where it is today. Here are some ways to make sure services provided to clients are the best they can be:

- Tour therapeutic recreation departments in similar facilities and compare notes on what does and does not work well with clients.
- Pilot intervention or problem-based protocols with neighboring facilities that have similar programs and/or clients.
- Start a networking system with professional peers in surrounding communities and share materials and resources.
- Form a peer-review system with the area or state to evaluate each others' services and accountability systems.
- Join or form a chapter affiliate group with ATRA or join the state organization related to NTRS/NRPA—in addition, of course, to joining the two national organizations.
- Participate in conferences at which there is ample opportunity to speak with professional colleagues in similar positions.
- Establish a schedule (monthly? quarterly? annually?) to review how the department is making the relationships between job tasks work.
- Hire a knowledgeable consultant and receive advice on how to improve the department's services.
- Understand external accreditation and professional standards and how they impact the delivery of therapeutic recreation services.

Third, lest professionals think they can sit back and just take in information that someone else creates, it is the responsibility of each specialist to get involved and help create new information and technologies to advance the field. There are numerous ways to serve the profession, and it takes each individual's commitment to make a profession work. Remember, the profession *is* the very professionals it serves. Each person's contribution counts. Ways to make this happen include:

- Offer to serve on or chair a committee on a specific topic of professional interest (e.g., legislation, protocols, inclusion, ethics, research, reimbursement, etc.).
- Run for office of a local, state, regional, or national therapeutic recreation organization.
- Contact faculty at a local university and conduct collaborative efficacy research on client outcomes.
- Volunteer to become an associate editor or a reviewer for the research journals in the field.
- Present a paper at a conference concerning the outcomes of therapeutic recreation services.
- Publish an article in a journal or newsletter that contributes to the knowledge base.

There is no limit to the responsibility to keep informed of the latest developments, and there is no limit to the potential for each individual to contribute to the future of the profession. Each individual is responsible for representing the profession in such a way that clients, other professionals, and the general public gain an appreciation of the need for and place of therapeutic recreation services in health care and human service arenas. The future of the profession is dependent on each individual's commitment to the field's advancement.

Useful Resources

Rather than include professional documents, such as the Standards of Practice or Codes of Ethics in appendices, it seemed more reasonable and timely if resource information concerning these documents were included instead. By contacting the professional organizations and resource centers below, the reader is guaranteed to get the most recent literature available.

The two major professional organizations, NTRS and ATRA, have extensive resources available, from research journals to newsletters, from smaller, single-topic publications to larger volumes. NCTRC, as the profession's credentialing group, has a newsletter for certified members, as well as candidate bulletins for those interested in becoming certified and taking the national examination.

American Therapeutic Recreation Association

URL: www.atra-tr.org

1414 Prince Street, Suite 204

Alexandria, Virginia 22314

Phone: (703) 683-9420

Fax: (703) 683-9431

E-mail: membership@atra-tr.org

National Therapeutic Recreation Society

URL: www.nrpa.org

22377 Belmont Ridge Road

Ashburn, Virginia 20148

Phone: (703) 858-0784

Fax: (703) 858-0794

E-mail: ntrsnrpa@aol.com

National Council for Therapeutic Recreation Certification

URL: www.nctrc.org

7 Elmwood Drive

New City, New York 10956

Phone: (845) 639-1439

Fax: (845) 639-1471

E-mail: nctrc@nctrc.org

Although there are others, two publishing companies focus exclusively on recreation and leisure literature and have a large selection of related books. ATRA and NRPA/NTRS (above) also have a lengthy list of related publications for sale.

Sagamore Publishing Company, L.L.C.

URL: www.sagamorepub.com

804 N. Neil St., Suite 100

Champaign, Illinois 61820

Phone: (800) 327-5557 or (217) 359-5940

Fax: (217) 359-5975

E-mail: books@sagamorepub.com

Venture Publishing Company

URL: www.venturepublish.com

1999 Cato Avenue

State College, Pennsylvania 16801-3238

Tele: (814) 234-4561

Fax: (814) 234-1651

E-mail: vpublish@venturepublish.com

Related Internet Sites

A list of related Internet sites virtually could be limitless. There are hundreds, covering everything from animal-assisted therapy to backpacking, adventure therapy to needlepoint. Readers are encouraged to explore the Internet, as well as the library, for resources of interest. Because they affect so greatly the daily operations of most therapeutic recreation professionals, the Joint Commission's and CARF's sites are listed below. In addition, two sites that link to other related sites also are given below. Both have as their primary interest to supply resource information and connect therapeutic recreation professionals with each other.

CARF—The Rehabilitation Accreditation Commission
URL: www.carf.org
4891 East Grant Road
Tucson, Arizona 85712
Phone: (520) 325-1044
Fax: (520) 318-1129

Centers for Medicare and Medicaid Services
URL: www.cms.hhs.gov
7500 Security Boulevard
Baltimore, MD 21244-1850
Phone: (877) 267-2323

Joint Commission on Accreditation of Healthcare Organizations
URL: www.jcaho.org
One Renaissance Boulevard
Oakbrook Terrace, Illinois 60181
Phone: (630) 792-5000
Fax: (630) 792-5541

National Committee for Quality Assurance
URL: www.ncqa.org
2000 L Street, NW, Suite 500
Washington, DC 20036
Phone: (202) 955-3500
E-mail: webmaster@ncqa.org

Therapeutic Recreation Directory
URL: www.recreationtherapy.com

Project TRAIN
URL: www.uwlax.edu/TRAIN/

Summary

Each individual entering or practicing in the profession of therapeutic recreation has the responsibility to keep abreast of the newest information and techniques, as well as contribute to moving the profession forward. The future of the profession depends on the success of the individual professionals to access resources and improve their practices.

Relaxation: A Program System
Carolyn Lemsky[1]

Introduction

The following pages contain a complete systems-designed program, utilizing the technology and methods presented in Chapters 4 and 5. Frequent reference is made in those chapters to this appendix for illustration and application of all parts in appropriate format and sequence.

---

[1] Materials used with the permission of the designer, Carolyn Lemsky.

PROGRAM: Relaxation

Purpose: To present basic concepts related to stress and relaxation and to teach relaxation techniques for self-control of tension.

Program Objectives

TPO 1. To demonstrate knowledge of the concept of relaxation

    EO 1. To demonstrate knowledge of the potential benefits of using relaxation techniques

    EO 2. To demonstrate an awareness of stress and its sources

    EO 3. To demonstrate the ability to identify physical manifestations of stress

TPO 2. To demonstrate the ability to perform relaxation techniques

    EO 1. To demonstrate relaxed diaphragmatic breathing

    EO 2. To demonstrate basic physical warm-ups and relaxation activities

    EO 3. To demonstrate progressive relaxation

    EO 4. To demonstrate the centering technique

IMPLEMENTATION DESCRIPTION

Population

This program is designed for a group of 5 to 10 individuals with emotional or psychiatric problems. It can be used with adolescents or adults. It is desirable to group participants by similar ages, so that discussions can be more relevant. Clients must have receptive and expressive language and be able to make verbal contributions to the group that are authentic and relevant in nature. Each participant must be able to concentrate for 20 minutes at a time on a task that is mainly cognitive. Individuals with physical limitations can be incorporated into the program with minor modifications based on their individual needs.

Program Length and Duration

This program is designed with 8 sessions, each lasting 50 minutes. The sessions are optimally scheduled twice a week for a period of 4 weeks. A period of less than 4 weeks does not allow adequate time for learning and practicing the techniques. A period lasting longer than 4 weeks may not provide enough contact with the group to motivate them or enable appropriate practice between sessions.

The program does require work outside the scheduled session times.

Program Context

This program can be implemented in any agency serving the described population. Thus, the program could be used with inpatient, outpatient, or partial-hospitalization clients. It could be utilized within clinical or community-based settings.

Staff

One professional staff member is needed for every 5 clients. The staff member must have a knowledge of and ability to teach relaxation techniques, the ability to lead group discussions, knowledge of the psychiatric and emotional conditions of the participating clients, and the ability to utilize facilitation and behavioral-management techniques.

Facility

A quiet room, free of distractions, where lights may be dimmed is essential to conduct this program. This room should have enough floor space for participants to lie down

Equipment

A mat or blanket for each participant
Tapes or records of semiclassical music
Record player or tape recorder
Paper and pencils
Handouts (described in text of system materials and presented in the attachments section)

ADDITIONAL IMPLEMENTATION INFORMATION

Session Content and Sequence

Information on the sequence of content to be presented is found on the *Sequence Sheet* within the text of the materials. The *Sequence Sheet* provides direction for the sequence within each session as well as the sequence of the total program.

Program Content and Process

The objectives, and the exact content and process related to each objective, are described in the Content and Process Sheets found within the text of the materials.

A Note on the Discussions

Much of the learning in this program is based on discussion. Leaders must, therefore, be capable of guiding discussions according to the needs and experiences of the group members. Stimulating discussion may require that the leaders contribute information and personal experiences; however, they should not dominate the session. Instead, they should build as much as possible on the responses of clients.

Evaluation of the Performance Measures

Evaluation of client performance should be conducted on an ongoing basis. Participants will be meeting most of the criteria stated in the performance measures during discussions. It is therefore necessary that leaders record progress made during or directly after conducting a session. Notes made during the session should be taken as unobtrusively as possible. Before each session, it is advisable for leaders to review the performance measures relevant to the content being covered.

A Note on the Use of Music

Tapes of semiclassical music and dimming the lights during warm-ups and relaxation exercises is advised. Participants should optimally be provided with information on, or assistance in, obtaining music for home practice.

A Note on Instructions

Instructions on the Content and Process Sheets are presented in a narrative style. This is to facilitate an understanding of how the material may be presented. Leaders are to note this style, but should not memorize or read the instructions while conducting group sessions. Instead, an attempt should be made to reproduce the relaxed, conversational tone when giving instructions to the group.

ORDER OF THE MATERIALS WITHIN THIS PROGRAM SYSTEM PACKAGE

Terminal Program Objectives Sheets

These sheets contain the Terminal Program Objectives (TPOs), the Enabling Objectives (EOs), and Performance Measures (PMs) that accompany each Enabling Objective.

Content and Process Sheets

These pages specify the exact content and process that will be presented within the program to address each Enabling Objective.

The Sequence Sheet

This is a session-by-session breakdown of content sequencing, with time estimates for material and activities within each session.

The Performance Sheet

This is a form that enables the monitoring of the accomplishment of objectives for each participant.

References

Attachments

Objectives and Performance Measures

PROGRAM: RELAXATION

TERMINAL PROGRAM OBJECTIVE: 1. To demonstrate knowledge of the concept of relaxation

ENABLING OBJECTIVE	PERFORMANCE MEASURE
1. To demonstrate knowledge of the potential benefits of using relaxation techniques.	1. Upon request, the client will state (verbally or in writing) one of the following potential benefits of using relaxation techniques: a. increase in a sense of control over behavior when tense b. decrease in physical tension, or alleviation of some symptom related to physical tension c. decrease in feelings of anxiety or some symptom of anxiety as judged appropriate by the therapeutic recreation specialist.
2. To demonstrate an awareness of stress and its sources.	2. Upon request, the client will state one personal source and one symptom of stress that he or she has experienced, as judged appropriate by the therapeutic recreation specialist.
3. To demonstrate the ability to identify physical manifestations of stress.	3. Upon request, the client will identify physical manifestations of stress by: a. locating a symptom of tension using another client or leader as a model, and b. verbally identifying muscle tension in his or her own body as judged appropriate by the therapeutic recreation specialist.

Objectives and Performance Measures

PROGRAM: RELAXATION

TERMINAL PROGRAM OBJECTIVE: 2. To demonstrate the ability to perform relaxation techniques

ENABLING OBJECTIVE	PERFORMANCE MEASURE
1. To demonstrate relaxed diaphragmatic breathing.	1. Upon request, the client will perform diaphragmatic breathing as characterized by: a. the abdomen (not the chest) rising with each breath b. breathing at a relaxed and natural pace (approximately 12–15 cycles/minute) for two minutes as judged appropriate by the therapeutic recreation specialist.
2. To demonstrate basic physical warm-ups and relaxation activities.	2. When given the names of 2 of the 9 regularly used physical warm-up and relaxation activities introduced in the program and upon request, the client will identify activities as characterized by the following: a. proper body positioning and movements as described on the C & P sheets, and b. proper breathing for 5 repetitions of the activity or 1 minute (depending on the activity), as judged appropriate by the therapeutic recreation specialist.

Objectives and Performance Measures

PROGRAM: RELAXATION

TERMINAL PROGRAM OBJECTIVE: 2. To demonstrate the ability to perform relaxation techniques *(continued)*

ENABLING OBJECTIVE	PERFORMANCE MEASURE
3. To demonstrate progressive relaxation.	3. Upon request, the client will demonstrate the progressive relaxation technique as characterized by: a. tensing and relaxing muscles as described in the progressive relaxation process b. achieving an average score of 3 for at least 2 out of 3 sessions of progressive relaxation as recorded on Form I, Relaxation Data Sheet as judged appropriate by the therapeutic recreation specialist.
4. To demonstrate the centering technique.	4. Upon request, the client will demonstrate the centering technique as characterized by: a. maintaining proper body position b. appropriate breathing throughout one complete presentation of the technique, as judged appropriate by the therapeutic recreation specialist.

Content and Process Description

TPO No.: 1

EO No.: 1   To demonstrate knowledge of the potential benefits of using relaxation techniques

EQUIPMENT: _____

CONTENT	PROCESS
1. The importance of practice	Review the content at the left for participants as an introduction to practice discussions.
a. In order for the techniques we will learn during our group sessions to be effective, they must be practiced. The relaxation response must become natural for it to work for you in times of stress.	It is important that these attitudes be reinforced throughout the course. Suggestions for doing so are found in the rationale and in the introductions of many of the activities.
b. Keep track of your independent practice using some kind of record sheet or diary.	
c. To start with, practice before you go to sleep at night or at a time when activity in the area where you will be relaxing is at a minimum.	
It is suggested that you do not try to practice after meals because this may interfere with and slow up the digestive process.	
2. Personal applications of relaxation techniques	Five minutes per session are set aside for discussion of practice as it is recorded by the participants.
	The leader gives a summary of the techniques learned in the group and asks participants to discuss their experiences with them both inside and outside of class. The leader should also practice techniques outside of class and be prepared to give personal input to stimulate discussions.

Content and Process Description

TPO No.:   1

EO No.:   1   To demonstrate knowledge of the potential benefits of using relaxation techniques *(continued)*

EQUIPMENT: _____

CONTENT	PROCESS
3. Applications of individual techniques	Suggestions for discussion are offered within the instructional process. The leader should think of the discussion questions provided as guidelines. The most appropriate way to present the material for discussion is dependent on the leader and participants. Sections labeled *Discuss* are intended only as a point of departure for leaders. It is therefore advisable that the leader prepare for each session by reviewing the content and thinking about discussion questions and other methods of presentation which she/he feels would be appropriate for the group.

4. Potential benefits of relaxation
  a. Increased sense of control over behavior when tense
  b. Decrease in physical tension or alleviation of some symptom related to physical tension
  c. Decrease in feelings of anxiety or some related symptom
	Review the content at the left for participants as an introduction to relaxation techniques.
	
	It is important that this content be reinforced throughout the course. Suggestions for this are found with the instructional processes. The leader should also remember to include this content where appropriate in practice discussions.

Content and Process Description

TPO No.: __1__

EO No.: __2__   To demonstrate an awareness of stress and its sources

EQUIPMENT: Blackboard and chalk or poster and marker

CONTENT	PROCESS
1. Stress defined	Present the content at the left very briefly.
Any aspect of the environment that requires the individual to make an adaptive change in behavior may be considered stress.	The leader should invite questions from the group and adapt the presentation to the participants.
Animals faced with an attacking predator must either run away or fight. The fear of death or injury experienced by the animal motivates this survival-oriented reaction.	
Predators, because they must eat, feel some stress, which motivates them to hunt. That stress may be identified as hunger. Stress motivates adaptive reactions.	
Stress is not always negative. Some stress is necessary to keep us active.	
Everyone has the ability to adapt to stress. However, when the amount of stress in the environment is too great, the individual may not react appropriately.	
2. Identifying stressful situations	The leader asks the group to list some common sources of stress on the blackboard or poster. Some examples of common sources of stress may be found at the left. As each source of stress is recorded, the group is asked to identify what appropriate adaptive behaviors are required.
a. Identifying sources of stress	
External stress	
Fear generated because of something in the environment—real physical danger.	
Internal stress	Once the group has recorded 5 to 10 sources of stress, the leader gives a brief explanation of the content at the left regarding internal and external sources of stress. The group
Anxiety that is self-generated and has no apparent cause in the environment.	

Content and Process Description

TPO No.: __1__

EO No.: __2__   To demonstrate an awareness of stress and its sources *(continued)*

EQUIPMENT: Blackboard and chalk or poster and marker

CONTENT	PROCESS

Some common sources of stress people experience
  Death of a relative or friend
  Marital problems
  Social obligations
  Disagreements with family or friends
  Financial problems
  Employment difficulties
b. Identifying the behaviors associated with stressful situations
c. Identifying feelings associated with stressful situations
 	
The source of stress depends partially on how a situation is experienced. External stress is determined by the extent to which the state of mind of the individual controls how the situation is experienced.
 	
3. Physiological reactions related to stress
Fear and anxiety cause some physical responses, which are the body's way of getting ready to handle danger. These physiological events are called the fight or flight response.
 	
This response occurs in three stages identified by Dr. Hans Selye.
a. Alarm: Danger is recognized in the environment, and a message is sent to a part of the brain called the hypothalamus, which is involved in producing feelings of fear and anger. The hypothalamus releases a
	should be able to differentiate between fear and anxiety at the end of the explanation. The leader then asks the group to go through the list of stressors that has been formulated and identify which are external stressors, which result in fear, and which are internal stressors, which are anxieties.
	
	During the above process, the leader should not encourage participants to discuss at length their individual difficulties. If the conversation is kept general, the attention of the participants may be maintained and the length of the discussion kept brief. The leader may want to emphasize issues relevant to the entire group.
	
	The information at the left is reviewed by the leader.
	The following are some questions intended to help the leader summarize the content at the left:
	"What is fear?"
	"What is anxiety?"
	"At a time when you remember feeling stressed, do you remember experiencing any of these physical reactions?"
	"When would these physical reactions be helpful?" (Focus: when there is a physical danger that must be avoided.)

hormone called adrenaline, which sets off the following reactions:

Lungs puff as in chest breathing, to increase the body's oxygen supply.

Skin becomes pale as blood moves to organs and muscles where it will be needed.

Perspiration begins to flush out wastes and cool body.

All functions not necessary for fight or flight shut down, and blood leaves the digestive tract, causing the sensation of the stomach dropping. Bowels and bladder relax.

b. Resistance: The individual responds to the danger with some action.

c. Exhaustion: Messages are sent to glands from the hypothalamus to stop the secretion of adrenaline. The individual feels weary and out of breath.

These reactions occur when we sense something which makes us afraid or anxious. These reactions occur unconsciously, whether they are necessary or not.

Some things we do unconsciously may cause a feeling of stress. Tense muscles and chest breathing, which are parts of the fight or flight response, may cause the individual to feel anxiety, which in turn may set off the fight or flight response.

Going through the stages of the fight or flight response is very taxing, both physically and emotionally. Prolonged or frequent periods of stress may lead to heart disease, ulcers, and other physical illnesses. It may also lead the individual to feel helpless or cause him or her to feel unable to handle stress.

"When would these reactions be harmful?" (Focus: when there is no physical danger to be avoided, and these reactions contribute to the individual's feelings of stress.)

"How can chest breathing contribute to feelings of anxiety?" (Focus: by triggering the fight or flight response, or by the individual unconsciously associating feelings of anxiety with chest breathing.)

"What are some of the possible consequences of prolonged periods of stress?" (Focus: physical damage, as in the case of heart disease and ulcers; emotional damage, which may cause the individual to feel he or she is incapable of handling stress effectively.)

Note: The leader should prepare for the presentation of this material by referring to sources as listed in the reference section. An understanding of this information on a more detailed level will facilitate the leader's ability to answer questions and lead discussions effectively.

Recommended reading: Tanner, *Stress*, pp. 15–29; Benson, *The Relaxation Response*, pp. 39–53 (see Suggested References).

Content and Process Description

TPO No.: ___1___

EO No.: ___3___   To demonstrate the ability to identify physical manifestations of stress

EQUIPMENT: Copies of Form II CTASS
Attachment A or blackboard/
poster, pencils, large box
or suitcase with heavy
removable objects inside

CONTENT	PROCESS
1. Identification of physical manifestations of stress. (See Attachment A for CTASS forms.)	Before clients arrive, leader places box at center of room.
	Have the participants sit in a formation conducive to informal communication (e.g., a circle with participants seated).
	The leader should use the following as an example of how this session might run. The leader should be prepared to communicate the content to participants on the basis of the group's responses and questions.
	Discuss: Ask, "What do you think relaxation is?" (Focus: to get participants to express their ideas about what relaxation is.)
	Ask, "What do you do to relax?" (Focus: some activities feel relaxing, rest is relaxing, etc. The intent of asking this question is to get participants to recognize that there are things we do specifically to relax.)
	Ask, "Has there ever been a time when you wanted to relax but couldn't? A time when you felt nervous or tense?" The leader might want to give examples to get the group going (e.g., going to the dentist, taking an exam).

Pick a situation that most of the participants indicate is familiar. Ask, "How did you feel? What physical sensations can you remember?" (Focus: any physical manifestations of stress; e.g., "butterflies in the stomach," feeling "tight," etc.)

The leader may want to begin with an example; e.g., the leader sits facing the group and says, "I am going to show you what I look like waiting in a dentist's office." The leader then tenses legs, arms, and perhaps taps foot or bites nails.

Ask, "How do you think I was feeling?" (Focus: nervous, anxious, stressed.)

Ask, "How could you tell I was feeling that way?" (Physical manifestations of stress.)

The leader gives a few more examples of how stress is manifested. These should include the obvious (e.g., nail-biting, foot-tapping) as well as the subtle (e.g., muscle tension) stress behaviors. Group members should be given the opportunity to act out their contributions themselves. Questions from the group should be answered by group members when possible.

Pass out CTASS (Form II in Attachment A).

Introduce the form by telling participants that it is a list of the things we have been talking about. The participants may keep it as a summary of the session. The leader may want to have pencils available so that she/he can read through the form aloud, answering questions to help participants fill it out.

An alternative to using this form is listing stress behaviors participants come up with on a blackboard or poster. However, the CTASS handout has an advantage, since it can be kept by the participants.

Content and Process Description

TPO No.:   1

EO No.:   3   To demonstrate the ability to identify physical manifestations of stress
(continued)

EQUIPMENT: Copies of Form II CTASS

Attachment A or blackboard/poster, pencils, large box or suitcase with heavy removable objects inside

CONTENT	PROCESS
2. Physical tension is the result of an unconscious reaction to stress.	Discuss: Ask, "We've been talking about some of the things we do when we're nervous. Can you think of any reasons why we do them?" (Focus: fright, anxiety, etc.)
	The leader begins the next exercise by telling a participant to move the heavy box to the center of the room. The leader then gives a false reason for asking that participant to leave the room (e.g., getting something from another room). While the participant is gone, the leader removes the heavy object from the box and places it out of sight. The leader asks the other participants not to tell the one who has left what she/he has done, and to watch while the participant picks up the box again. Upon reentering the room, the participant is asked again to pick up the box.
Explanation: The participant's muscles were ready for the heavier load. She/he didn't have to think about it. It just happened, as a result of his or her expectations.	Discuss: Ask, "Why do you think she/he reacted this way?" (Focus: because she/he expected the box to be heavier.)
Excess muscle tension, or other physical reactions, results from similar processes. These processes are set into motion by our expectations of the environment.	Ask, "Do you think she/he would have reacted differently if we had told him or her that the box is now light?" (Focus: our expectations of a situation can determine how we react to it.)
We can feel more relaxed by controlling physical tension. The relaxation techniques we will learn are to be used in controlling tension.	The leader presents closure in the form of an explanation.
	The leader asks if the participants have any questions or concerns regarding the material covered.

Content and Process Description

TPO No.: __2__

EO No.: __1__   To demonstrate relaxed diaphragmatic breathing

EQUIPMENT: <u>Mats or blankets</u>

CONTENT	PROCESS
1. Breathing from the diaphragm means taking deep breaths, which cause the abdomen (as opposed to the chest) to rise. Even though this is the most natural way to breathe (infants and most people breathe this way while they are sleeping), some of us get into the habit of chest breathing. Getting deep, full breaths increases the flow of oxygen to vital organs and, in this way, aids in relaxation.	Ask participants to lie on the floor in a complete supine position. Have them place their right hand on their stomach over the navel. Ask participants if their hand is rising when they breathe in. Leaders should watch to see that participants are in the correct position and whether their hands are rising. Because participants may begin to alter their natural breathing patterns when trying to concentrate, remind them to breathe slowly and naturally. Counting aloud to the group, as in the following example, may aid participants in breathing naturally. "Take a nice easy breath. Now, I–N–H–A–L–E and E–X–H–A–L–E." The words *inhale* and *exhale* should be stretched to sound for the duration of an average breathing cycle. The best way to time this is to stay with your own relaxed breathing pattern and watch those of participants. This is only necessary if participants are having trouble. Assure the participants that diaphragmatic breathing may not come naturally and with practice it will become easier. Review the content while allowing participants to continue to practice for a few minutes.
2. Diaphragmatic breathing allows the body to function in an integrated way. Quick, shallow breathing causes a generalized feeling of stress or arousal, which may not be warranted by the activity or the environment being experienced.	*Discuss:* Ask, "Do you feel relaxed after doing this kind of breathing? When do you breathe with quick shallow breaths (chest breathing)? How do you feel when you are breathing this way?" (Focus: chest breathing usually occurs with arousal of some kind and is not conducive to relaxation.)

Content and Process Description

TPO No.: __2__

EO No.: __2__   To demonstrate basic physical warm-ups and relaxation activities

EQUIPMENT: Mats or blankets

CONTENT	PROCESS
1. The purpose of warming up	Have participants stand in a circle at arm's length from one another.
a. The warm-up serves as a transition into a session of relaxation activities.	Introduce the warm-ups by reviewing the purposes of warming up. Tell participants that the beginning of each session will be spent doing warm-ups and that you will be starting with some simple movements or stretches.
b. The warm-up functions as a physical preparation by— helping to prevent injuries by easing muscles into physical activity helping to identify points of physical tension and initiating the process of releasing it encouraging body awareness	Explain that most of the warm-ups include breathing with the movements. Tell them it is important in getting full benefit from the warm-up to pay careful attention to the breathing instructions.
c. The warm-up aids in mental preparation for a session of relaxation by providing an activity which is relatively easy to concentrate on and is therefore useful in clearing the mind of daily stress.	
2. The processes of warm-up activities	Introduce the total body stretch by asking the participants to stretch as if they had just awakened from a night's sleep. The leader may want to demonstrate if the group is slow in getting started.
Total Body Stretch—Warm-up Activity A	
a. Make your body as long as possible, stretching your hands over your head.	*Discuss:* Ask, "Why do you think we want to stretch in the morning?" (Focus: it helps to get blood back into muscles that haven't been working all night. That is how we get started in the morning, so it is a logical place to begin with warming up.)
b. Stretch the right side, making it as long as possible, leaving the left side relaxed.	
c. Repeat above for left side, leaving right side relaxed.	Take participants through steps verbally and with demonstrations.
d. Make your body as wide as possible, stretching your arms out to the side, and standing in a straddle.	
(Repeat 2 or 3 times.)	

Rotating Joints—Warm-up Activity B

a. Move all of your fingers as if you were trying to get sticky crumbs off of them.

b. Rotate your wrists as if you were stirring thick batter with a spoon in each hand.

c. Rotate your elbows as if you were drawing large circles with your hands.

d. Rotate your shoulders as if your arms were the blades of a windmill moving slowly.

e. Rotate your neck by first trying to touch your right ear to your shoulder, then touching your chin to your chest—trying not to let your shoulders move.

f. Rotate your neck in the other direction, starting with your left ear to your left shoulder.

(Each step should be repeated 4 or 5 times.)

Take participants through steps verbally and with demonstrations.

Keep the movements of participants gentle and easy. If participants are moving too fast, help them out with an image—for example, trying to imagine that they are underwater, weightless, or in a pool filled with Jell-O.

Siren—Warm-up Activity C

a. Begin by bending over as if to touch your toes, allowing your knees to bend.

b. Take a deep diaphragmatic breath. (It is nearly impossible to breathe from the chest in this position.)

c. Start as soft and low pitched a tone as you can make, saying "Ah. . . ."

d. As you straighten up slowly, gradually make the sound louder and higher in pitch until you are standing up straight with your hands over your head, and the tone is as high and loud as you can make it.

e. Gradually reverse the process so that you end up in the bent-over position.

f. Repeat the siren 4 or 5 times, getting smoother and faster until you can feel your voice and body working together.

Tell the participants that this activity is intended to help integrate breathing with body movement.

Take participants through the steps verbally and with demonstrations.

Content and Process Description

TPO No.: __2__

EO No.: __2__   To demonstrate basic physical warm-ups and relaxation activities *(continued)*

EQUIPMENT: Mats or blankets

CONTENT	PROCESS
Seated Stretch—Warm-up Activity D* (Repeat 2 or 3 times)	Take participants through steps verbally and with demonstrations.
a. Sit comfortably with both of your legs stretched out in front of you, your arms over your head, until your palms come together.	Participants should be reminded to pay close attention to the breathing associated with the movements.
b. Look up at your hands, and as you begin to breathe out, bend slowly forward from the hips, keeping your legs flat. Stretch your arms out as far as they will go, and as you exhale all your air, reach forward and grasp your ankles or your feet, whichever you can reach.	
c. Pull gently, stretching your spine as far as it can go.	
d. Release your grip and come up slowly, breathing in deeply, bringing your hands back up over your head until the palms touch.	
Bridge—Warm-up Activity E†	Take participants through steps verbally and with demonstrations.
a. Lie on your back and relax until you are as flat on the floor as you can be.	
b. Draw your knees up until your feet are close to your buttocks. Relax arms at sides, palms down on floor.	

*From *The Centering Book* by Gay Hendricks and Russell Wills, p. 122. Copyright © 1975 by Prentice-Hall, Inc. Published by Prentice-Hall, Inc., Englewood Cliffs, NJ 07632.

†Ibid., p. 123.

c. As you inhale, raise your body gently off the floor by pressing down your feet. Keep your neck and shoulders relaxed as you arch your back into a bridge.

d. Exhale and lower yourself to the original position. Relax and let your body sink deeply into the floor.

(Repeat 3 or 4 times.)

Shoulder Stand—Warm-up Activity F*

a. Sit on the floor with your legs drawn up to your buttocks and your hands next to your buttocks.

b. Roll back, bringing your knees over your forehead and sliding your hands under your lower back to support you. Relax in this position, making sure that your back and neck are relaxed.

c. Begin to raise your legs gently until they are straight above you. Do not strain, but find a position that is straight but not uncomfortable.

d. Relax in this position and breathe deeply, letting all of the unnecessary tension leave your body.

e. When you're ready to come down, lower your knees slowly to your forehead, then roll your back down to the floor slowly and gently. When you are all the way down to the floor, relax your body completely, feeling yourself totally supported by the floor.

Cobra—Warm-up Activity G†

a. Lie on your stomach, stretching your feet out behind you and placing your palms down next to your armpits.

b. Rest your forehead gently on the floor.

Take the participants through steps verbally and with demonstrations.

It may be necessary to demonstrate the complete process before asking participants to perform the shoulder stand.

Have the participants hold this position for 10 seconds at first. This may be increased to a minute in later sessions.

Take participants through steps verbally and with demonstrations.

The Cobra should always be done after the shoulder stand, to stretch the spine in the opposite direction. This should be pointed out to participants.

*From *The Centering Book* by Gay Hendricks and Russell Wills, p. 122. Copyright © 1975 by Prentice-Hall, Inc. Published by Prentice-Hall, Inc., Englewood Cliffs, NJ 07632.

†Ibid., p. 126.

Content and Process Description

TPO No.: __2__

EO No.: __2__   To demonstrate basic physical warm-ups and relaxation activities *(continued)*

EQUIPMENT: Mats or blankets

CONTENT	PROCESS
c. Begin to breathe in smoothly, and as you do, begin raising your head, then your neck. d. As you breathe in more, continue to raise your neck and your spine, without lifting your hips and pelvis, until your chest is off the floor as far as it will go comfortably. e. When you get to the top, relax in that position, then exhale slowly and roll yourself back down until your forehead again touches the floor. f. Relax your shoulders, your neck, and your back . . . letting yourself sink into the floor. (Repeat 2 or 3 times.) *Corpse—Warm-up Activity H[‡]* a. Lie on your back on the floor and let your body sink down until it is completely supported by the floor. b. Close your eyes and sink back in total relaxation, letting your mind and your body recharge with pure, fresh energy.	Tell participants that the Corpse is used between and after exercises like the foregoing. *Discuss:* Ask, "Can you tell me why the Corpse might be useful in between exercises?" (Focus: to get ready for the deep relaxation necessary to do the warm-ups described previously.) Ask, "When else might we want to use the Corpse?" (Focus: any time we want to relax fully and have an appropriate place to lie down.)

[‡]Ibid., p. 128.

*Salute to the Sun—Warm-up Activity I**

a. Stand up comfortably straight. You should feel light and relaxed. Take a few deep breaths, feeling lighter and more relaxed with each one.

b. Inhale, bending back gently with your arms over your head and your back slightly arched.

c. As you exhale, bend over forward as if to touch your toes. Do this gently; don't strain.

d. Place your palms on the floor, letting your knees bend, and as you do, begin to inhale.

e. As you complete this inhalation, stretch your right foot out behind you, letting your left knee bend.

f. As you exhale, shift your weight to your palms, and bring your left foot behind you. This should leave you in a "push up" position.

g. As you begin to inhale, let your knees and legs drop gently to the floor. You are now in the position which begins the Cobra.

h. Sway your buttocks back toward your heels, and continuing to inhale, run your chin, then chest, then stomach against the floor and end in the arched position of the cobra.

i. Curl your toes under, getting ready to bear weight. As you exhale, swing your buttocks up until you are in a V position.

Demonstrate the complete process of Salute to the Sun, doing the correct breathing and not speaking. One leader may demonstrate while the other points out the inhale-exhale breathing pattern that goes with the movements. Explain that the breathing is as important as the movements. The hardest thing about the exercise is coordinating the breathing and the movements. Eventually this will become natural, but it will take practice.

Have one leader demonstrate while the other gives the directions and points out the breathing process.

Have the participants practice a few times at their own speed. Tell them to let their natural breathing determine the speed of the movements.

If any of the participants feel light-headed, tell them to watch until they feel better, and then try the salute again, paying careful attention to their natural pace of breathing.

Content and Process Description

TPO No.:   2

EO No.:   2

EQUIPMENT: Mats or blankets

To demonstrate basic physical warm-ups and relaxation activities *(continued)*

CONTENT	PROCESS
j. As you inhale, bring your right knee toward your hands.	*Discuss:* Ask, "How did that feel? Did you have trouble getting your breathing and the movements to work together? Was this exercise relaxing?" (Focus: this is a Yoga exercise used first thing in the morning. It aids in stretching out the body, and is good for gaining energy upon waking or before doing an unpleasant task. The effect of getting body and breathing together is somewhat like centering. After doing this exercise, many people feel energized and relaxed. This may take practice.)
k. As you exhale, bring your left knee in until you are in a squat with your palms on the floor.	
l. As you inhale, straighten your knees until you are in a bent-over position with your knees straight and your arms hanging down.	Ask, "When do you think we could use Salute to the Sun?" (Focus: any time we feel the need to become more in touch with our bodies and breathing—for example, before a session in relaxation, or any time we feel nervous and there is the time and a quiet, appropriate place to do it.)
m. Continue to inhale, straightening your back vertebra by vertebra, slowly and smoothly, ending with your arms over your head and your back slightly arched.	
n. As you exhale, bring your hands back to your sides and end in the comfortable position that you started in.	

Content and Process Description

TPO No.: __2__

EO No.: __3__   To demonstrate progressive relaxation

EQUIPMENT: Mats or blankets, copies of Form I, Relaxation Data Sheet, Attachment B

CONTENT

1. Rationale for progressive relaxation*

Introduction

a. The procedures are called progressive relaxation training.

b. Progressive relaxation training consists of learning to tense and release various muscle groups throughout the body.

c. An essential part of learning how to relax involves learning to pay close attention to the feelings of tension and relaxation in your body.

d. Learning relaxation skills is like learning other motor skills.

e. We employ tension in order to ultimately produce relaxation.

   1. Strong tension is noticeable, and you will learn to attend to these feelings.

   2. The initial production of tension gives us some "momentum," so that as we release the tension, deep relaxation is the result.

PROCESS

Present the rationale to the group.

Ask if anyone has any questions.

Note: In order to prepare for the session, leaders should read through Attachment B. Leaders should take themselves through progressive relaxation if they have not had this experience.

The leader may want to use additional images in the progressive relaxation process. For example, participants can be asked to imagine they are squeezing a ball or an orange.

If clients claim that, even after a relaxation session, they still feel tense, it is helpful to have them imagine relaxing scenes such as lying on a beach in the warm sun.

*From Bernstein and Borkovec, *Progressive Relaxation Training*, p. 162.

Content and Process Description

TPO No.: **2**

EO No.: **3**   To demonstrate progressive relaxation (continued)

EQUIPMENT: Mats or blankets, copies of Form I, Relaxation Data Sheet, Attachment B

CONTENT	PROCESS
2. See Attachment B for Form I. As the participants go through the relaxation process, they will be scored using Form I. The self-report section is to be filled in after the progressive relaxation process is completed. This section is intended to measure the overall sensation the client is having after participating in progressive relaxation. Honesty in completing this portion of the form should be stressed. Progressive relaxation may not produce complete relaxation during the first few sessions. For some people, the process does not work at all. Form I is only intended to provide a record of what has happened during the progressive relaxation sessions.	Present Form I to clients. Review the purpose of the form and the scoring process. If the participants have difficulty understanding the form, the leader may use demonstrations. For example, the leader may tense a muscle group, and not relax it, then have the participants score the performance.
3. Progressive Relaxation Process[†] "This is an activity that can help us learn to relax our bodies and minds by tensing and releasing muscles. We cannot be tense and relaxed at the same time, so if we learn to relax, we avoid wasting energy through muscle tension. If you ever feel tense, while asking a question or taking a test or any time, you can use the feeling of relaxation to feel better." "Let's begin by lying on your backs on the floor and not touching anyone else. Wiggle around a little until you find a way of lying down that is completely comfortable.	Instructions: Leaders provide narrative directions as written under Content.

[†]From The Centering Book by Gay Hendricks and Russell Wills; pp. 41–45. Copyright © 1975 by Prentice-Hall, Inc. Published by Prentice-Hall, Inc., Englewood Cliffs, NJ 07632.

Now close your eyes and think of your hands. Feel the bones inside them, feel the muscles that move the bones, feel the weight of them on the floor. Now make a fist with your hands and clench tightly. Hold your hands tightly (10 seconds). Now relax and feel the soothing, tingling feeling of relaxation come into your hands." (Pause 10 seconds or so between instructions.)

"Now draw up your arms and tighten your biceps—making muscles like a strongman. Hold them tightly (10 seconds). Now relax and feel the tension drain out of your arms." (Pause)

"Shrug your shoulders now, pushing them as if to push them through your ears. Hold them tightly there (10 seconds). Now let them go and feel all the tension drain out of your shoulders." (Pause)

"Continuing to keep your eyes closed, open your mouth as far as it will go, stretching the muscles at the corners of your mouth. Hold it tightly (10 seconds). Relax and enjoy the tingling feeling as the tension dissolves in your mouth." (Pause)

"Now press your tongue against the roof of your mouth and tighten your jaw muscles. Press tightly and hold it (10 seconds). Now let go and relax. Let the peaceful feeling of relaxation flow through your jaw." (Pause)

"Now tighten the muscles of your chest, stomach, and abdomen. Draw all of the muscles in tightly and hold them tense (10 seconds). Now let them go, feeling the soothing feeling of relaxation pour in." (Pause)

"Now tense the backs of your legs by straightening your feet. Hold your legs tensely (10 seconds). Now relax them and let all of the tension go." (Pause)

"Now tense your feet by curling the toes. Keep them curled tightly (10 seconds). Now relax your toes and feel the delicious feeling of relaxation come into your feet." (Pause)

Content and Process Description

EQUIPMENT: Mats or blankets, copies of Form I, Relaxation Data Sheet, Attachment B

TPO No.: ___2___

EO No.: ___3___   To demonstrate progressive relaxation (continued)

CONTENT	PROCESS
"Your whole body is feeling loose and relaxed now. Feel yourself completely supported by the floor and breathe deeply. As you breathe in, let each breath fill your body with deeper and deeper feelings of relax- ation." (Pause)	PROCESS
"Let the soothing feeling of relaxation fill your body. Each breath takes you deeper and deeper into relax- ation."	
(Pause 30 seconds to 1 minute.)	
"Now you will be coming out of relaxation in a moment, and you will feel rested and alert. I will count backward from ten to one, and as I do, feel your body becoming alert at your own rate."	
"Ten, nine, eight, feel the alertness returning to your body. Seven, six, five, feel your toes and fingers begin to move. Four, three, move your arms and legs. Two, eyes. One, get up slowly, feeling completely rested and alert."	*Instructions:* Leader provides narrative directions as written under Content.
4. Instant Relaxation—Whole Body*	
This relaxation exercise can be done sitting, standing, or lying down. It gives an individual a skill to counter ten- sion in all kinds of situations.	
"Let's close our eyes."	
"Now tense every muscle in your body at the same time. Legs, arms, jaws, fists, face, shoulders, stomach.	

*Ibid., pp. 46–47.

Hold them . . . tightly. Now relax and feel the tension pour out of your body. Let all of the tension flow out of your body and your mind . . . replacing the tension with calm, peaceful energy . . . letting each breath you take bring calmness and relaxation into your body." (Pause)

"Now tense your body again and hold it for a few seconds. Then let go, relaxing and feeling all of the tension flow out of your body." (Pause)

"And now tense every muscle in your body and at the same time, take a deep breath for a few seconds. Then say 'Relax' to yourself, and when you do, let your breath go and relax." (Pause)

"Take a deep breath and hold it about ten seconds. Then say 'Relax' to yourself and let yourself go." (Pause)

"When you feel like relaxing, just take a deep breath, hold it a few seconds, say 'Relax' to yourself, and let it all go. You can do this wherever you are, because nobody can hear you or see you. Practice this again by yourself two or three times." (Pause)

"Now let's open our eyes slowly, feeling calm and alert."

5. Instant Relaxation—Specific Parts*

"Now we are going to go through various parts of the body, telling each part to relax; as you tell each part to relax, you will be able to feel a soothing feeling of relaxation enter that part of your body. Now let your attention go to your feet." (Pause) "Tell your feet to relax."

This process is repeated for selected parts of the body.

Instructions: Leader provides narrative directions as written under Content.

Discuss: "This is another instant exercise. How well did it work for you? Do you think you could use this technique successfully now, or do you feel you need more practice?" (Focus: personal reactions to the exercise.)

*Ibid., pp. 48–51.

Content and Process Description

TPO No.: __2__

EO No.: __4__   To demonstrate the centering technique

EQUIPMENT: __Mats or blankets__

CONTENT	PROCESS
1. An introduction to centering. a. There is powerful energy in our bodies. This energy may be focused by concentration. We can learn to use this energy to our advantage through centering.	*An Experiment in Centering* Have participants find partners near to their own body build. (The leader may want to pair participants.) The leader introduces this activity by telling participants that just by thinking about it they can make themselves heavier or lighter. Tell one member of each pair to stand tall and light. Suggest to them to send all of their thoughts upward. Next have their partners take them around the waist and try to lift them. Caution participants to get a firm hold and lift slowly and gently. Now have those participants who were thinking light, think heavy. Tell them to imagine themselves nailed to the floor. Now have the participants' partners try to lift them again. It should be harder. The participants should feel heavier than before. The best way to insure this effect is to give strong images for light and heavy and allow plenty of time to let participants concentrate. Have participants reverse roles and try the exercise again. *Discuss:* "What do you think made your weight seem to change?" (Focus: our conscious will, energy, or body tension can be focused.) *Explain:* In the next session, we will learn something called centering. With centering, we focus our energy on our centers and that helps us to feel good about ourselves and gives a sense of strength.

2. Centering is a way to gain a feeling of solidness by concentrating on the center of the body.

3. Activities in centering.

Feeling the Center—Centering Activity A*

Instructions:

"Most of the time we use only a small part of our lungs when we breathe. If we can learn to fill our bodies with breath by breathing more deeply and smoothly, we can increase the energy that flows through our bodies. Let's begin by letting our bodies relax . . . becoming very comfortable and closing our eyes."

"And now, becoming aware of your feet and moving them around a little to become aware of how they feel, send them a message to relax. Let all of the tension go out of them and feel them rest comfortably on the floor."

"Now relax your legs. Let go of them and let them sink into the floor, feeling relaxed and heavy."

"Let the feeling of relaxation enter your chest and stomach. Feel the middle of your body become soothed and relaxed. Breathe deeply and smoothly, letting all of the tension go out of your body."

"Now let your neck and face relax. Feel the tension draining out of your face as you feel the soothing feeling of relaxation enter your face and your neck."

"Relax your arms and your hands, feeling them resting comfortably, completely supported. Breathe deeply, sending the feeling of relaxation to your arms and hands." (Pause 30 seconds.)

Present the concept of centering to the group.

Take participants through the centering exercises.

Have participants lie on the floor.

Note: The beginning portion of this exercise combines centering with diaphragmatic breathing. It is therefore suggested that it be used in its entirety for the first session. A shortened version, which may be used in subsequent sessions, is indicated by the bracket on the following page.

*From *The Centering Book* by Gay Hendricks and Russell Wills, p. 123. Copyright © 1975 by Prentice-Hall, Inc. Published by Prentice-Hall, Inc., Englewood Cliffs, NJ 07632.

Content and Process Description

TPO No.: __2__

EO No.: __4__   To demonstrate the centering technique *(continued)*

EQUIPMENT: Mats or blankets

CONTENT	PROCESS
"The center of your body is where it balances. For many people, the balance point is just below the navel. As you breathe in, imagine that your breath is pouring into your body through the center of your body. Let yourself feel the energy rushing into your body through the center, just below the navel. Feel your breath flow into your body, up through your chest, filling your head. Hold the breath inside you for a moment, then let it flow out, carrying with it any tension you feel. Breathe through your center, filling your body with energy, then let the breath flow out of you, relaxing your body completely." (Pause 10 breaths) "Let yourself feel the center of your body, so that you can come back to it when you want to relax and feel balanced. Anytime you have something in your head that you don't like, breathe it out and then replace it with pure, clean energy when you breathe in." "Now feel the alertness coming back into your body. Feel your feet and hands begin to stir. Feel your muscles begin to move. Open your eyes, feeling rested and full of energy."	This section comprises the essential images of centering. If used alone, a few moments of breathing before and after should be provided for participants to relax and breathe at their own pace.

Quick Centering Breath—Centering Activity B*

Instructions:

"Focus all of your attention on your center. Send all of your thoughts and feelings down to that point below your navel." (Pause)

"Now begin sending each breath all the way down to your center." (Pause)

"Each time you breathe, send the breath to your center." (Pause)

"Now that you know how to get in touch with your center, you can focus on that point when you feel nervous or angry, or whenever you want to feel better . . . it's always there when you need it."

This activity may be done in any position.

The leader should take the group through this activity verbally. Pauses should be about 10 seconds in duration.

Instant Centering—Centering Activity C†

Instructions:

Have the participants put all their thoughts in an elevator up in their heads. Then have them punch the button and send the elevator down to their centers.

Have the participants imagine an hourglass inside them, the top in their heads, the bottom in their centers. Have them let the sand slowly fill up the bottom.

Have the participants imagine a light shining out from their centers, and have them vary the intensity of the light.

The leader should present these images to the group as tools to use when centering.

Discuss: Ask, "Can you think of any other images that might help you in centering?" (Focus: the best images to use in centering are the ones that work best for the individual.)

Participants may present their ideas to the group.

The leader may ask the group to try and think of an image to present to the group at the next session.

*Ibid., pp. 24–25.
†Ibid., pp. 25–26.

		Sequence Sheet*		
TPO	**EO**	**DESCRIPTION**	**SESSION NO.**	**TIME (MIN)**

		Introduction to course
		    General overview of what the course will
		    cover
		    Format of sessions:
		        Sessions will be 50 minutes long.
		        There will be a warm-up, introduction
		        or review of a technique, discussion of
		        practice, a final relaxation activity
		        before leaving.
		        Participants may be asked to prepare
		        for the next class by observing some-
		        thing to report to the class, doing a
		        reading, home practice, etc.
			1	10

2	2	A. Purpose of warming up; warming up activities A and B		10
2	4	B. An experiment in centering		10
1	4	C. Identification of physical manifestations of stress		15

1	2	D. Give assignment: Tell participants to look
		     out for a situation when they feel tense for
		     next session's discussion. Take a few
		     minutes to listen quietly to music.
				5

2	2	A. Warm-up activities A and B (review) Warm-up activities C, D, and E introduced.	2	10
2	1	B. Diaphragmatic breathing		10
1	2	C. Discussion of Parts 1 and 2: "Identifying sources of stress"		20
2	4	D. Concept of centering Centering activity A		10
2	4	Evaluation of centering		
2	2	A. Warm-up activities A, C, and D (review) Warm-up activities E, F, and G	3	5 10
1	2	B. Discussion Part 3		20
2	1	C. Review diaphragmatic breathing		3
2	4	D. Quick centering breath		5
1	1	E. Discussion of practice		7
		Observe half of participants for evaluation of breathing and centering		

		Sequence Sheet* *(Continued)*		
TPO	**EO**	**DESCRIPTION**	**SESSION NO.**	**TIME (MIN)**
2	1	A. Warm-up activities E, F, and G (review)	4	5
		Warm-up activity I introduced		10
2	3	B. Progressive Relaxation, parts 1 (rationale) and 2 (basic process)		20
1	1	C. Discussion of practice		10
2	4	D. Clients choose a centering activity		5
		Observe second half breathing and centering.		
2	2	A. Warm-up activities E, F, and I (review); repeat 15 times	5	15
2	3	B. Progressive Relaxation, part 2		20
1	1	C. Discussion of practice		10
2	4	D. Choose centering activity		5
		Evaluate centering if necessary		
2	2	A. Warm-up activities E, F, G, and I repeat 15 times	6	20
2	3	B. Progressive Relaxation, part 3 Instant Relaxation		20
1	1	C. Discussion of practice		10
2	2	A. Warm-up activities E, F, G, and I repeat 15 times	7	20
2	3	B. Progressive Relaxation, part 3 Instant Relaxation		15
1	1	C. Discussion of practice		15
		Check evaluations for TPO 1		
2	2	A. Warm-up activities E, F, G, and I	8	15
2	4	B. Progressive Relaxation, part 4 Talking to your body		15
1	1	C. Discussion of practice		15
		D. Present closure		5

*Evaluation should take place on an ongoing basis. Performance Measures should be reviewed prior to each session, and clients' progress should be recorded during or directly after groups.

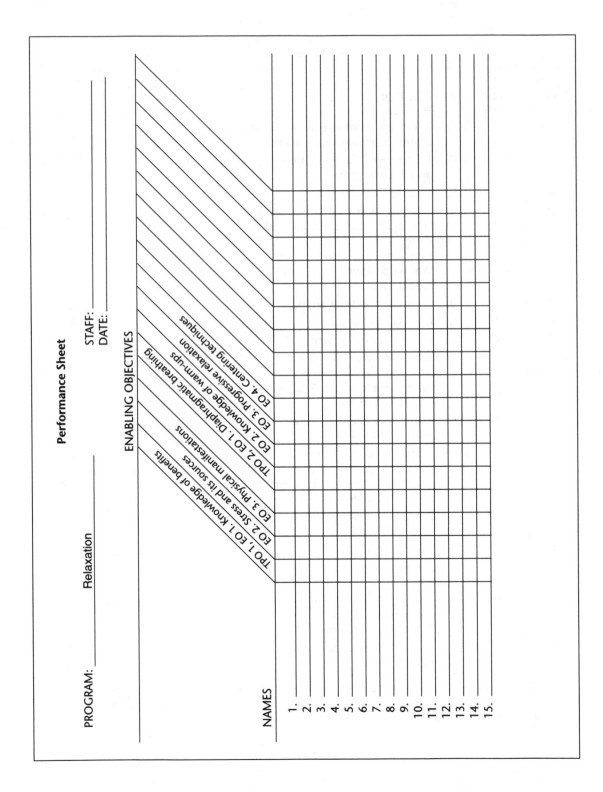

Performance Sheet

PROGRAM: _____   Relaxation

STAFF: _____
DATE: _____

ENABLING OBJECTIVES

TPO 1, EO 1. Knowledge of benefits
EO 2. Stress and its sources
EO 3. Physical manifestations

TPO 2, EO 1. Diaphragmatic breathing
EO 2. Knowledge of warm-ups
EO 3. Progressive relaxation
EO 4. Centering techniques

NAMES

1.
2.
3.
4.
5.
6.
7.
8.
9.
10.
11.
12.
13.
14.
15.

SUGGESTED REFERENCES

Benson, H. (1975). *The relaxation response*. New York: William Morrow & Co.

Bernstein, D. A., & Borkovec, T. D. (1973). *Progressive relaxation training*. Champaign, IL: Research Press.

Hendricks, G., & Wills, R. (1975). *The centering book*. Englewood Cliffs, NJ: Prentice-Hall.

Hewitt, J. (1977). *The complete yoga book*. New York: Schocken Books.

Stein, M. L. (1976). *Good and bad feelings*. New York: Morrow Junior Books.

Tanner, O. (1978). *Stress*. Alexandria, VA: Time-Life Books.

Form II: Cues for Tension and Anxiety Survey Schedule (CTASS)[1]

Individuals have different ways that indicate to them that they are tense or anxious. Check below the ways that apply to you. (This form is for you to keep. You don't have to share it with anyone if you don't want to.)

1. You feel tense in:
   a. your forehead (   )
   b. back of your neck (   )
   c. chest (   )
   d. shoulders
   e. stomach
   f. face (   )
   g. other parts _____

2. You sweat (   )

3. Your heart beats fast (   )

4. You can feel your heart pounding (   )

5. You can hear your heart pounding (   )

6. Your face feels flush or warm (   )

7. Your skin feels cool and damp (   )

8. You tremble or shake in your:
   a. hands (   )
   b. legs (   )
   c. other _____

9. Your stomach feels like you are just stopping in an elevator (   )

[1] Reprinted with permission from J. R. Cautela and D. Upper, "The Behavior Inventory Battery: The Use of Self-report Measures in Behavioral Analysis in Therapy," in *Behavior Assessment: A Practical Handbook,* ed. M. Hersen and A. S. Bellak (Elmsford, NY: Pergamon Press, 1976).

10. Your stomach feels nauseous (   )

11. You feel yourself holding something tight (like a steering wheel or the arm of a chair) (   )

12. You scratch a certain part of your body (   ) Part you scratch: _____

13. When your legs are crossed, you move the top one up and down (   )

14. You bite your nails (   )

15. You grind your teeth (   )

16. You have trouble with your speech (   )

Relaxation Data Sheet[1]
Form I

---

[1] Adapted from a handout provided by Mark Anderson and Glenn Riske in "Clinical Applications of Relaxation Techniques," National Parks and Recreation Congress 1981, Minneapolis, Minn.

NAME: _____

	Session I	Session II	Session III	Session IV	Session V
Is the face relaxed and smooth?					
Is the jaw slack?					
Are the shoulders down and at rest?					
Is the small of the back off the floor?					
Are the legs relaxed and at rest?					
Are the feet tilted out and at rest?					
Is the body motionless (not restless)?					
Average Score					
Self-Report n/r = no relaxation R = relaxation (+, −) T = tense					

0 = no response to instructions
1 = tenses, no relaxation
2 = relaxation, no tension
3 = tenses and relaxes

Score at least three sessions for each participant.

Comments:

Social Behaviors: A Program System
Mary E. Hess, MS, CTRS[1]

Introduction

The following pages contain a complete systems-designed program, utilizing the methods presented in Chapters 4 and 5. Frequent reference is made in those chapters to this appendix for illustrations and application of all parts in appropriate format and sequence.

[1] Materials used with the permission of the designer, Mary E. Hess.

PROGRAM: Social Behaviors

Purpose: To provide education and training on basic social behaviors necessary for positive socialization.

Program Objectives

TPO 1. To demonstrate knowledge and use of socially acceptable behaviors.

EO 1. To demonstrate the ability to recognize positive social behaviors.

EO 2. To demonstrate the ability to recognize and model appropriate verbal and body language when interacting with others.

EO 3. To demonstrate the ability to use appropriate conversation skills.

EO 4. To demonstrate the ability to show good sportsmanship when engaging in recreation activities.

IMPLEMENTATION DESCRIPTION

Population

This program is for individuals having difficulty with emotional, behavioral, or social functioning. The content was developed to serve individuals 14 years of age and older. Ideally, the program should be limited to no more than six individuals. The program must contain at least two individuals so that social interaction can be practiced.

Program Length and Duration

This program is designed to be implemented in six sessions. The sessions will vary in length: educational sessions last approximately one hour; video presentation sessions will be dependent on the choice of video. One session should occur every day.

Program Context

This program can be used in a variety of settings: clinical, community, or school.

Staff

As noted above, it is suggested that this program be limited to six individuals. Under these guidelines, one therapeutic recreation specialist will be sufficient to lead each session. The TRS should be familiar with the diagnoses of the clients being served, age-specific developmental milestones, and social skills.

Facility

The size of the room should be large enough to accommodate seating for everyone and ample room to stand to perform role-playing exercises. On one occasion, a large room will be needed for activity stations to be set up.

Equipment

This will vary based on the activities the leader chooses to do for each session. On the following pages, you will see that some program sessions contain "suggested activities."

ADDITIONAL IMPLEMENTATION INFORMATION

A Note on Population Considerations

When teaching social skills training, there are a variety of considerations that need to be made regarding the population being served. Stumbo (1994/1995) highlighted the factors that have been suggested by other researchers: "(a) developmental level of the individual (chronological vs. adaptive age), (b) primary or secondary disability problems (e.g., speech or communication delays), (c) magnitude or type of social skill problems (e.g., withdrawn to aggressive), (d) appropriateness to clients' peer group, (e) appropriateness to clients' culture, (f) socioeconomic or social class determinants, (g) gender, (h) physical environment and orientation of the instructional settings, and (i) continuance of reinforcement from peers."

Program Content and Process

If necessary, additional enabling objectives and performance measures can easily be added to incorporate more basic or more advanced skills training.

Evaluation of the Performance Measures

Evaluation of client performance should be conducted on an ongoing basis. Clients will be meeting most of the criteria stated in the performance measures during discussions. It is important that the TRS record the progress made by each client during or after sessions. In addition to the TRS recording client performance, other staff may be trained to do this. For example, if this program is being implemented in a clinical inpatient setting, it may be that the sessions take place during the daytime hours. The TRS may choose to educate other staff members (especially evening staff members) on the objectives of the social behaviors program and the client performance measures. Then, while evening programming is occurring, the evening staff can observe clients' social behaviors and offer redirection when necessary. This continuum of care will greatly benefit the clients.

Objectives and Performance Measures

PROGRAM: SOCIAL BEHAVIORS

TERMINAL PROGRAM OBJECTIVE: 1. To demonstrate knowledge and use of socially acceptable behaviors

ENABLING OBJECTIVE	PERFORMANCE MEASURE
1. To demonstrate the ability to recognize positive social behaviors.	1a. When given a combined list of positive and negative social behaviors, the client will demonstrate knowledge of the behaviors that contribute to developing positive relationships as evidenced by correctly identifying the behaviors as (a) positive social behavior, or (b) negative social behavior, as judged appropriate by the therapeutic recreation specialist.
	1b. While watching a video that shows others acting out various social behaviors, the client will demonstrate knowledge of the behaviors that contribute to developing positive relationships as evidenced by correctly identifying the positive social behaviors and the negative social behaviors, as judged appropriate by the therapeutic recreation specialist.
2. To demonstrate the ability to recognize and model appropriate verbal and body language when interacting with others.	2a. Upon completion of the social behaviors program, the client will demonstrate the ability to utilize appropriate body language while engaging in a dyad conversation as evidenced by:
	a. maintaining a distance of approximately 3 feet or one arm's length away from the person she or he is interacting with
	b. looking at person she or he is interacting with and maintaining a pleasant facial expression; smiling when appropriate

c. maintaining open body language (standing/sitting up straight, arms at side or on lap, leaning in slightly toward speaker)

as judged appropriate by the therapeutic recreation specialist.

2b. Upon completion of the social behaviors program, the client will demonstrate the ability to exercise appropriate verbal language while engaging in a dyad conversation as evidenced by:

a. speaking at an audible level

b. speaking in a firm yet relaxed tone

c. using voice inflection

d. using suitable and polite words

as judged appropriate by the therapeutic recreation specialist.

3. While interacting in dyad conversation, the client will demonstrate the use of appropriate conversation skills as evidenced by using the following mannerisms when engaging in conversation:

a. looking at person (when speaking and listening)

b. speaking in complete sentences, using a pleasant tone of voice, adequate volume, and moderate rate of speech

c. asking questions that are relevant to topic

d. allowing others to make comments and complete statements before talking (not attempting to control conversation)

e. responding to others' questions and/or comments

f. staying on topic

as judged appropriate by the therapeutic recreation specialist.

3. To demonstrate the ability to use appropriate conversation skills.

ENABLING OBJECTIVE	PERFORMANCE MEASURE
4. To demonstrate the ability to show good sportsmanship when engaging in recreation activities.	4. While participating in a recreation activity, the client will demonstrate the ability to show good sportsmanship as evidenced by: a. assisting in the assembly/take-down of equipment b. playing the game fairly (taking turns, following rules, accepting consequences, etc.) c. displaying courteous behavior to teammates/opponents d. graciously accepting defeat or victory as judged appropriate by the therapeutic recreation specialist.

Content and Process Description

TPO No.: __1__

EO No.: __1__   To demonstrate the ability to recognize positive social behaviors

EQUIPMENT: Dry erase board and markers, pencils for clients

CONTENT	PROCESS
The purpose of the social behaviors program is to assist clients in increasing their chances of experiencing success in their future social endeavors. Positive social behavior training provides individuals with practical tools that will assist them in interacting positively with others, taking control of various emotions, dealing with the problems and stressors they face daily, and making good choices about personal behaviors. It is crucial for an individual to understand and exercise positive social behaviors in order to develop and maintain appropriate peer relationships (with family, friends, and authority figures); experience success in the educational and workplace settings; and maintain functioning in the day-to-day activities that require some degree of socialization.	Present material in opposite column to the group. This should be done using age-appropriate terminology. Hold a discussion on the value of developing positive relationships.
Definitions:	Through a group discussion, define relationships, friendships, and social behaviors. In addition, provide examples of the different kinds/levels. Write definitions and examples on board to appeal to visual learners.
• Relationship—"the mutual exchange between two people or groups who have dealings with one another." Two levels: (1) casual and (2) intimate	Instruct clients to close their eyes and think about relationships/ friendships they currently have and relationships that have ended (casual and intimate). Now instruct clients to think about the individuals involved in their closest relationships. Instruct clients to make a mental list of the qualities that strengthen or weaken these relationships or qualities that prevent them from developing relationships with particular individuals altogether.
• Friendship—"a relationship of mutual affection and good will"	
• Social Behaviors—the conduct one uses when interacting with or communicating with other individuals	

CONTENT	PROCESS
	Test the clients' knowledge of social behaviors by using two methods:
	(1) Distribute one social behaviors worksheet to each client (Attachment B). Read the directions aloud to the group: "By using a smiley face or a frown face, identify each behavior as either negative or positive. Next, using the rating scale, identify how often you tend to utilize each behavior and with whom."
Identification of positive social behaviors and negative social behaviors (Attachment A)	As a group, go over the list of behaviors and classify each behavior as positive or negative. While doing this, ask the clients to provide specific examples of each behavior. This is done to provide/clarify understanding by all group members. Encourage questions to be asked.
	Completed worksheet is to be given to TRS to review.
	(2) Provide each client with paper and a pencil. Inform clients they are going to watch a video and conduct an assignment simultaneously. The instructions of the assignment are to log the social behaviors they witness the characters exercising and identify the behavior as positive or negative. NOTE: If deemed appropriate by the therapeutic recreation specialist, provide the group with a minimum or maximum number of social behaviors to identify or give each client one character to keep track of.
	After the video has ended, discuss the social behaviors that were observed in the video. If appropriate, discuss any consequences that occurred in the story as a result of a character exercising negative social behaviors.

Content and Process Description

TPO No.: 1

EO No.: 2   To demonstrate the ability to recognize and model appropriate verbal and body language when interacting with others

EQUIPMENT: Assortment of magazines, scissors, large pieces of construction paper, glue, markers

PROCESS

Using the explanation in the opposite column, explain to the group what body language is.

Explain to the group that body language messages usually fit into one of three categories: (1) passive, (2) assertive, and (3) aggressive. Emphasize that the most desired behavior of the three is assertive behavior.

Describe each of the three behaviors by using the definitions below and descriptions in the opposite column:

Passive: aim is to please others and avoid conflict at any cost—results in loss of self-respect

Aggressive: aim is to achieve or maintain control over people or situations—results in others left feeling humiliated, put down, and angry

Assertive: aim is to leave feeling satisfied with interactions—allows one to stand up for personal rights and express thoughts, feelings, and beliefs in direct, honest, and appropriate ways which do not violate the rights of others

CONTENT

Verbal messages and body language are the two primary ways people communicate their feelings. The way individuals express themselves through body language is generally an accurate reflection of their current mood. People are not always aware of the messages they are giving out through their body language and this can cause conflict with others. When a person wants something or is trying to get a message across, it is important that they use their nonverbal language in addition to their verbal language to convey their message accurately.

Passive Body Language

- Voice: weak, hesitant, soft, sometimes wavering

- Eyes: avoids eye contact, looking down toward feet, teary

- Posture: stooped, sagging, excessive head nodding

- Hands: fidgety, clammy

- Feet: shuffling, restless motions, tucked under chair, toed in, swinging back and forth

CONTENT	PROCESS
	To assist the clients in understanding how body language affects others, the leader demonstrates each behavior in a role-playing exercise. When done with the demonstration, have clients express how each reaction made them feel. **Leader will need to choose someone to play the "friend." The following dialogue occurs:
Aggressive Body Language	
• Voice: tense, shrill, loud, shaky, cold, demanding, "deadly quiet," authoritative, dominating	Friend: "Hey Patty, I forgot my lunch money today, could you lend me $5.00?"
• Eyes: narrowed, cold, staring, looking through you, rolling	Passive Patty's thoughts: I only have $5.00 for myself. My stomach has been growling all morning because I skipped breakfast this morning. I am really hungry.
• Stance: hands on hips or arms crossed, feet apart	
• Posture: stiff, rigid, rude	Passive Patty says in a soft voice with her head pointed toward her feet: "Sure, I guess I can lend you $5.00. I'm not that hungry today anyway."
• Hands: clenched, abrupt gestures, finger pointing, fist pounding	
• Feet: tapping, firmly planted	Friend: "Hey Angie, I forgot my lunch money today, could you lend me $5.00?"
Assertive Body Language	Aggressive Angie shouts while pointing her finger in the face of the friend: "How can you be so stupid! It's not my fault that you are such an airhead! There is no way that I am giving you money! I know that you would never pay me back anyway! Too bad for you— you'll just have to starve today!"
• Voice: firm, warm, good inflection, relaxed	
• Eyes: open, frank, direct eye contact but not staring	
• Stance: well balanced, straight at ease, approximately 3 feet or one arm's length away from person speaking with	Friend: "Hey Ashley, I forgot my lunch money today, could you lend me $5.00?"
• Posture: facing, erect, relaxed, occasional head nods	Assertive Ashley looks directly at her friend and says in a pleasant tone: "Well, I just have $5.00 myself so I can't really afford to give it all to you. We can do one of two things: we can pick out some food together and split it between us, or I can lend you $2.50. Either way we will both get to eat today."
• Hands: relaxed, warm, smooth motions	
• Feet: relaxed comfortable position	

To conclude the session on body language, allow the clients the opportunity to practice the three different behaviors through role-playing exercises. In order to do this, the leader should come to the session prepared with cards that have scenarios and behaviors written on them. The client should react to the scenario using the behavior written on the card. The scenarios contained on the cards should be situations that are age-appropriate for the clients as well as situations that are realistic (see Attachment C for examples).

Each client should practice/role-play assertive behavior at least once. The leader should provide necessary coaching to the clients.

* Additional suggested "hands-on" activity: Body Language Collages

Supplies: Assortment of magazines, scissors, large pieces of construction paper, glue, markers

Activity Directions:

1. Tri-fold the construction paper so that there are three columns

2. Label the columns "Passive, Aggressive, and Assertive"

3. Find and cut out pictures of people showing passive, aggressive, and assertive body language and glue the pictures into the appropriate column

4. When everyone has completed their collage, discuss the pictures or have clients make up a story to go along with their pictures.

Content and Process Description

TPO No.: __1__

EO No.: __3__   To demonstrate the ability to use appropriate conversation skills

EQUIPMENT: Chalkboard/dry erase
board

CONTENT	PROCESS
The purpose of the conversation skills training is to teach clients how to engage in brief and pleasant conversations with a variety of people in a variety of settings (acquaintances, neighbors, and co-workers).	Using the explanation in the opposite column, explain to the group what a conversation is and why it is important to use appropriate conversation skills.
Conversations are an important part of everyday living; they are a great way to build knowledge and develop understanding of others and ourselves. By using effective conversation skills you can improve day-to-day social interactions, fulfill daily needs, and possibly enlarge your circle of friends.	Review the basic guidelines of conversations (listed on the opposite column). Provide clients with their own list of Do's and Don'ts OR write them on a board to appeal to visual learners.
There are some basic guidelines that need to be followed while conversing with others:	Reinforce the need to use assertive verbal and body language in conversations.
Conversation DO'S	Provide a visual demonstration of both appropriate and inappropriate conversation skills (using either clients or staff).
• Look at the person or people you are talking to.	To conclude the conversation skills training session, allow the clients the opportunity to practice their conversation skills through role-playing exercises. To assist clients in practicing conversation skills through role playing, it may be necessary for the leader to prepare cards suggesting topics to converse on as well as situations where one would be required to introduce himself or others.
• If you haven't met before, introduce yourself and ask their name.	
• Use a person's name when talking to them.	
• Ask questions when you don't understand something.	
• Stick to the subject and keep the conversation topic appropriate for the environment.	

- Say nice things about people and praise those who deserve it.

- If you need to leave, end the conversation by saying something polite and letting the person know you will be leaving ("It's been good talking to you, but I need to get going." or "I've enjoyed talking with you today. Take care of yourself. Good-bye.").

- It's fine to disagree, but disagree politely.

Conversation DON'TS

- Don't fidget, look elsewhere, or wander off while someone else is talking.

- Don't listen in on conversations you aren't part of.

- Don't interrupt when someone else is talking.

- Don't whisper in front of another person.

- Don't whine, tattletale, brag, or say mean things about others.

- Don't ask personal questions such as how much things cost or why someone looks or dresses the way they do.

- Don't discuss personal topics or ask personal questions of people you do not know very well.

- Don't point or stare.

- Don't just walk away from a conversation abruptly.

- Don't argue about things that aren't important.

Content and Process Description

TPO No.: __1__

EO No.: __4__   To demonstrate the ability to show good sportsmanship when engaging in recreation activities

EQUIPMENT: Chalkboard/dry erase board; other equipment will vary

CONTENT

Sportsmanship refers to the way an individual behaves when participating in competitive activities. People generally associate sportsmanship with "structured sports" (basketball, football, tennis), but sportsmanship goes beyond the well-known structured sports. Sportsmanship is present during board games, card games, yard games, and even video games. Sportsmanship can be divided into two categories: good sportsmanship and bad sportsmanship.

- DO play fair, play by the rules; DO NOT cheat to win.

- DO take loss or defeat without complaint (DON'T make excuses), or victory without gloating (DON'T rub it in).

- DO talk politely and act courteously toward everyone before, during, and after games and events. That includes your teammates, your opponents, your coaches and theirs, the officials presiding over the game, and even spectators (who can sometimes be loud about their opinions).

- DO include everyone in the game, work as a team, and have respect for others regardless of their ability.

- DO exercise self-control, be courteous, and accept the results of your own actions.

PROCESS

Using the explanation in the opposite column, explain what the term sportsmanship means. Go on to explain that a large number of our interactions with others (peers) are likely to occur through participating in leisure/recreation-related activities (after-school activities, extracurricular activities, neighborhood play, weekend activities). Emphasize that using good sportsmanship skills will prove to be a valuable positive social behavior since we will be judged (to some degree) based on our behavior during such leisure/recreation situations. Likewise, we will judge others by the way they conduct themselves in these situations.

As a group, identify good and bad sportsmanship qualities. Use the list in the opposite column as a guide for sportsmanship qualities. List the identified qualities on a board to appeal to visual learners.

Ask the group to identify the negative effects poor sportsmanship has on a game/recreation activity. Clients should be encouraged to provide examples of personal leisure experiences that are memorable because of good sportsmanship or experiences that were spoiled by poor sportsmanship.

Leader may also choose to make a video (or show a movie; i.e. *Remember the Titans*) with various clips depicting individuals showing good/bad sportsmanship. Show the video to the group and ask them to identify alternative ways situations could have been handled.

**Suggested activity to allow clients to practice sportsmanship skills:

In a large open area arrange 3 or 4 stations. At each station set up an activity. If possible, offer a variety of activities that are slightly competitive in nature. Have clients engage in the games while the leader observes the clients' display of sportsmanship skills.

- DO stay cool. Even if others are losing their tempers, it doesn't mean you have to. Remind yourself that no matter how hard you've practiced and played, it is, after all, just a game.

- DO avoid settling disputes with violence. If you're in a difficult situation or someone's threatening you, seek help immediately from your coach, an official, or any other adult nearby.

- DO cheer your teammates on with positive statements and avoid talking negatively about other players or the other team.

- DO offer encouragement to teammates; if they make a mistake, do not criticize them.

- DO acknowledge and applaud good plays (of your own or the opponent); do this even if the opponent doesn't.

- DO accept the calls of officials; accept it gracefully even if you disagree with the call. Remember that referees may not be right every time—but they're people who are doing their best, just as you are.

- DO play the game until the end. DO NOT quit because you are not winning.

- Whether you win or lose, DO congratulate your opponents on a game well played.

- DO remember that the real winner is the one who had fun.

- DO share in the responsibilities of the game (setting up/taking down equipment).

- DO follow the directions of the leader or the coach.

- DO try to learn from mistakes that you make during games. DO NOT pout or make excuses.

Sequence Sheet

TPO	EO	DESCRIPTION	SESSION	TIME (MIN)
1	1	Introduction to social behaviors program and explanation of the program purpose	1	5.
		Definition of related terms		5
		Clients complete worksheet "Social Behaviors Identification Exercise" (Attachment B)		20
		Group constructs list of positive and negative social behaviors and behaviors are further defined through modeling		30
1	1	Social behaviors video presentation and exercise	2	varies
		Discussion on social behaviors and associated consequences		
1	2	Introduction to communication methods	3	5
		Education on the three behaviors		15
		Demonstration of the three behaviors		10
		Clients participate in role-playing exercises		30
		*Optional: Body Language Collages Activity		

Sequence Sheet *(continued)*

TPO	EO	DESCRIPTION	SESSION	TIME (MIN)
1	3	Introduction to conversation skills	4	5
		Education on conversation guidelines		25
		and		
		Demonstration of conversation skills		
		Clients participate in role-playing exercises		30
1	4	Introduction to sportsmanship	5	5
		Education on positive vs. negative sportsmanship qualities—group works together to construct list		30
		Demonstration of sportsmanship skills		20
		Discussion on the effects of positive vs. negative sportsmanship conduct		15
1	4	Sportsmanship video presentation	6	varies
		Discussion on observations and suggestions for alternative sportsmanship conduct		
		*Optional: Activity stations		

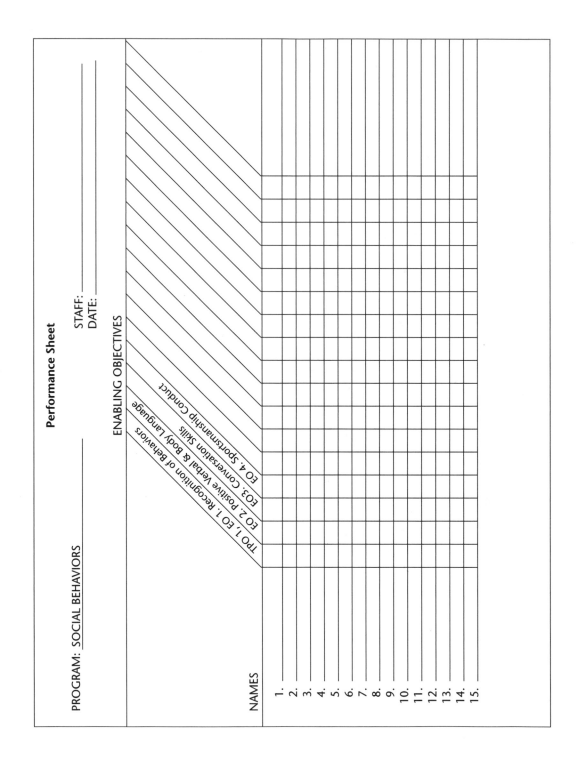

Performance Sheet

STAFF: _____
DATE: _____

PROGRAM: SOCIAL BEHAVIORS

ENABLING OBJECTIVES

TPO 1. EO 1. Recognition of Behaviors
EO 2. Positive Verbal & Body Language
EO 3. Conversation Skills
EO 4. Sportsmanship Conduct

NAMES

1.
2.
3.
4.
5.
6.
7.
8.
9.
10.
11.
12.
13.
14.
15.

ATTACHMENT A
Social Behaviors

Examples of positive social behaviors

- Taking turns
- Sharing
- Expressing feelings
- Cooperating
- Making eye contact
- Starting conversations
- Being assertive
- Listening to others
- Complimenting others
- Accepting compliments
- Following rules of play
- Refusing to cooperate with peers' negative behavior
- Apologizing to others
- Asking questions
- Telling others about self
- Playing fair
- Ignoring when appropriate
- Asking others about their interests/desires
- Talking in a brief manner
- Asking for what one wants/needs
- Helping others
- Refusing to do negative things asked by peers
- Respecting the personal space of others

Examples of negative social behaviors

- Physical aggression (hitting, kicking, etc.)
- Playing unfair/cheating
- Arguing
- Interrupting
- Name calling
- Bossing others
- Whining and/or complaining
- Using vulgar language
- Taking others' possessions
- Breaking others' possessions
- Dominating the activity
- Making poor eye contact
- Being a poor sport
- Being too loud
- Showing off
- Teasing
- Being intrusive
- Bugging others
- Getting into others' space
- Withdrawing and isolating self
- Being passive
- Listening poorly
- Hoarding toys, food, and so forth
- Talking too much
- Disobeying rules of play
- Being too rough in play
- Not handling peer pressure well (allowing peers to influence you to do things you shouldn't)
- Lying/spreading rumors

ATTACHMENT B

Social Behaviors Identification Exercise

Directions: (1) In the left column identify each behavior by drawing a smiley face for positive behaviors or a frown face for negative behaviors.

(2) Rate how often you tend to utilize each behavior and with whom.

1 = use every time   2 = use on a fairly regular basis   3 = use sometimes   4 = have never used

☺or☹

Offering to help others	1	2	3	4	With:
Being argumentative	1	2	3	4	With:
Talking in a brief manner/allowing others to talk	1	2	3	4	With:
Interrupting others when they are talking	1	2	3	4	With:
Being physically aggressive (hitting, kicking)	1	2	3	4	With:
Complimenting others	1	2	3	4	With:
Bossing others around	1	2	3	4	With:
Whining and/or complaining	1	2	3	4	With:
Asking for what one wants/needs	1	2	3	4	With:
Using vulgar language	1	2	3	4	With:
Behaving in an assertive manner	1	2	3	4	With:
Being verbally aggressive (shouting, name-calling)	1	2	3	4	With:
Listening to others speaking	1	2	3	4	With:
Playing unfair/cheating to get ahead or to win	1	2	3	4	With:
Accepting compliments	1	2	3	4	With:
Breaking others' belongings	1	2	3	4	With:
Following the rules of play	1	2	3	4	With:
Refusing to go along with peer's negative behavior	1	2	3	4	With:
Apologizing to others when appropriate	1	2	3	4	With:
Taking others' belongings without asking	1	2	3	4	With:
Asking questions	1	2	3	4	With:
Telling others about yourself	1	2	3	4	With:
Playing fair	1	2	3	4	With:
Asking others about their interests/desires	1	2	3	4	With:
Respecting the personal space of others	1	2	3	4	With:
Dominating an activity	1	2	3	4	With:

Behavior					With
___ Taking turns with others	1	2	3	4	With: _____
___ Avoiding eye contact with others	1	2	3	4	With: _____
___ Being a poor sport when playing	1	2	3	4	With: _____
___ Cooperating	1	2	3	4	With: _____
___ Lying/spreading rumors	1	2	3	4	With: _____
___ Starting conversations	1	2	3	4	With: _____
___ Teasing others	1	2	3	4	With: _____
___ Getting into others' space	1	2	3	4	With: _____
___ Withdrawing and isolating yourself from others	1	2	3	4	With: _____
___ Behaving in a passive manner	1	2	3	4	With: _____
___ Sharing your things with others	1	2	3	4	With: _____
___ Listening poorly	1	2	3	4	With: _____
___ Abruptly leaving conversations	1	2	3	4	With: _____
___ Hogging toys, food, and so forth	1	2	3	4	With: _____
___ Expressing feelings through words	1	2	3	4	With: _____
___ Talking excessively	1	2	3	4	With: _____
___ Making eye contact with others	1	2	3	4	With: _____
___ Not following/disregarding rules of play	1	2	3	4	With: _____
___ Being physically rough in play when not necessary	1	2	3	4	With: _____
___ Giving in to peers, participating in activities you shouldn't	1	2	3	4	With: _____

Stumbo, N. J. (1994/1995). Assessment of social skills in therapeutic recreation practice. *Annual in Therapeutic Recreation, 5,* 68–82.

Examples of Social Scenarios

- You lend a friend one of your books. She or he returns it with pages missing.

- A friend calls you late at night just to talk. You are tired and have to get up early in the morning.

- Your friend comes to you with a problem you don't know how to handle. You know your friend has a counselor that she or he likes and you suggest that she or he talk to them, but your friend repeatedly asks you what she or he should do.

- Someone in the car pool you are riding in decides to sing and does so for 15 minutes. It begins to get on your nerves and you politely ask him or her to stop, but he or she doesn't.

- The new shoes you bought three weeks ago are already starting to fall apart. You take them back to the store where you bought them.

- You bring your car to a repair shop for service. You ask the mechanic to call and let you know how much it will cost before doing the work. He doesn't call and when you call him he tells you he has already done the work and your bill is $250.

- You are assigned a group project for your science class. You come to your group meeting sessions prepared and ready to work. Your fellow group members come to the session with uncompleted work. They spend the hour talking about the latest school gossip. You need to get a good grade on this project or you won't get an A in the class.

- Someone in your class asks you to work with him on his homework after the teacher has specifically told the class that the assignment should be done without any help.

- You are being interviewed for a job in a new field and the director asks, "Why should I hire you when you have no experience?"

Suggested Reference

Stumbo, N. J. (1994/1995). Assessment of social skills in therapeutic recreation practice. *Annual in Therapeutic Recreation, 5,* 68–82.

Therapeutic Recreation Assessment Instruments

Leisure Attitudes and Barriers

Brief Leisure Rating Scale (BLRS: Ellis & Niles, 1985)

Ellis, G., & Niles, S. (1985). Development, reliability and preliminary validation of a brief leisure rating scale, *Therapeutic Recreation Journal, 19*(1), 50–61.

Ellis, G., & Niles, S. (1989). Development, reliability and preliminary validation of a brief leisure rating scale. In National Therapeutic Recreation Society (Ed.), The best of the Therapeutic Recreation Journal: Assessment (pp. 153–164). Alexandria, VA: National Recreation and Park Association.

Comprehensive Leisure Rating Scale (CLEIRS: Card, Compton, & Ellis, 1986)

Card, J., Compton, D., & Ellis, G. (1986). Reliability and validity of the comprehensive leisure rating scale. *Journal of Expanding Horizons in Therapeutic Recreation, 1*(1), 21–27.

Lindsey, S. P., & Card, J. A. (1990). Inter-rater reliability of the comprehensive leisure rating scale (CLEIRS). In G. L. Hitzhusen and J. O'Neil (Eds.), *Expanding horizons in therapeutic recreation XIII* (pp. 54–67). Columbia, MO: University of Missouri.

Leisure Attitude Scale/Measurement (Beard & Ragheb, 1982)

Burlingame, J., and Blaschko, T. M. (2002). *Assessment tools for recreational therapy and related fields,* 3rd ed. (pp. 237–242). Ravensdale, WA: Idyll Arbor, Inc.

Ragheb, M. G. (1980). Interrelationships among leisure participation, leisure satisfaction and leisure attitudes. *Journal of Leisure Research, 12,* 138–149.

Ragheb, M., & Beard, J. (1982). Measuring leisure attitude. *Journal of Leisure Research, 14*(2), 155–167.

Leisure Diagnostic Battery (LDB: Witt & Ellis, 1982)

Burlingame, J., and Blaschko, T. M. (2002). *Assessment tools for recreational therapy and related fields,* 3rd ed. (pp. 268–275). Ravensdale, WA: Idyll Arbor, Inc.

Dunn, J. (1986). *Generalizability of the leisure diagnostic battery.* Unpublished doctoral dissertation. University of Illinois at Urbana-Champaign.

Ellis, G., & Witt, P. (1982). *The leisure diagnostic battery: Theoretical and empirical structure.* Denton, TX: North Texas State University/State College, PA: Venture Publishing Co.

Ellis, G., & Witt, P. (1984). The measurement of perceived freedom in leisure. *Journal of Leisure Research, 16,* 110–123.

Ellis, G., & Witt, P. (1986). The leisure diagnostic battery: Past, present, future. *Therapeutic Recreation Journal, 20*(4), 31–47.

Ellis, G., Witt, P., & Niles, S. *The leisure diagnostic battery remediation guide.* Denton, TX: North Texas State University.

Witt, P., & Ellis, G. (1985). Development of a short form to assess perceived freedom in leisure. *Journal of Leisure Research, 17*(3), 225–233.

Witt, P. A., & Ellis, G. D. (1989). *The Leisure Diagnostic Battery: Users manual and sample forms.* State College, PA: Venture Publishing Company.

Witt, P. (1990). Overview and conclusions based on recent studies utilizing the Leisure Diagnostic Battery. In B. Smale (Ed.), *Leisure challenges: Bringing people, resources, and policy into play* (pp. 70–75). Waterloo, ON: Ontario Research Council on Leisure.

Leisure Motivation Scale (LMS: Beard & Ragheb, 1983)

Beard, J., & Ragheb, M. (1983). Measuring leisure motivation. *Journal of Leisure Research, 15*(3), 219–228.

Burlingame, J., and Blaschko, T. M. (2002). *Assessment tools for recreational therapy and related fields,* 3rd ed. (pp. 250–256). Ravensdale, WA: Idyll Arbor, Inc.

Leisure Satisfaction Scale/Measure
(LSS: Beard & Ragheb, 1980)

Beard, J., & Ragheb, M. (1980). Measuring leisure satisfaction. *Journal of Leisure Research, 12*(1), 20–33.

Burlingame, J., and Blaschko, T. M. (2002). *Assessment tools for recreational therapy and related fields,* 3rd ed. (pp. 257–262). Ravensdale, WA: Idyll Arbor, Inc.

Ragheb, M. G., & Beard, J. G. (1980). Leisure satisfaction: Concept, theory and measurement. In S. E. Iso-Ahola (Ed.), *Social psychological perspectives on leisure and recreation.* Springfield, IL: Charles C. Thomas.

Ragheb, M. G. (1980). Interrelationships among leisure participation, leisure satisfaction and leisure attitudes. *Journal of Leisure Research, 12,* 138–149.

Leisure Well-Being Inventory (McDowell, 1987)

McDowell, C. (1978). *Leisure well-being inventory.* Eugene, OR: SunMoon Press.

McDowell, C. (1983). *Leisure wellness: Concepts and helping strategies.* Eugene, OR: Sun-Moon Press.

McDowell, C. (1986). Wellness and therapeutic recreation: Challenges for service. *Therapeutic Recreation Journal, 20*(2), 27–38.

Life Satisfaction Scale (LSS: Lohmann, 1980)

Burlingame, J., and Blaschko, T. M. (2002). *Assessment tools for recreational therapy and related fields,* 3rd ed. (pp. 299–302). Ravensdale, WA: Idyll Arbor, Inc.

Over 50 (Edwards, 1988)

Edwards, P. (1988). *Guide to over 50.* Los Angeles, CA: Constructive Leisure.

Perceived Competence Scale for Children/
Self-Perception Profile for Children (Harter, 1982/1983)

Harter, S. (1979). *Perceived competence scale for children, Form O.* Denver, CO: University of Denver.

Harter, S. (1982). The perceived competence scale for children. *Child Development, 53,* 87–97.

What Am I Doing? (WAID: Neulinger, 1986)

Burlingame, J., & Blaschko, T. M. (1990). *Assessment tools for recreational therapy: Red book #1* (pp. 79–90). Ravensdale, WA: Idyll Arbor, Inc.

Hultsman, J. & Black, D. R. (1990). Baseline age norms for Neulinger's "What am I doing?" instrument. *Annual in Therapeutic Recreation, 1*(1), 37–47.

Hultsman, J. & Black, D. R. (1990). Baseline gender norms and cohort comparisons for Neulinger's "What am I doing?" instrument. *Annual in Therapeutic Recreation, 1*(1), 28–36.

Functional Abilities

Activity Therapy Assessment (Pershbacher, 1988)

Perschbacher, R. (1989). *Stepping forward with activities.* Asheville, NC: Bristlecone Consulting Company.

Perschbacher, R. (1993). *Assessment: The cornerstone of activity programs.* State College, PA: Venture Publishing Company.

Bond-Howard Assessment of Neglect in Recreation Therapy (BANRT: Bond-Howard, 1990)

Burlingame, J., & Blaschko, T. M. (1990). *Assessment tools for recreational therapy: Red book #1* (pp. 189–194). Ravensdale, WA: Idyll Arbor, Inc.

Bruninks-Oseretsky Test of Motor Proficiency (Bruninks & Oseretsky, 1972)

Bruninks-Oseretsky Test Kit. Circle Pines, MN: American Guidance Service.

Burlingame Software Scale (Burlingame, 1980)

Burlingame, J., & Blaschko, T. M. (1990). *Assessment tools for recreational therapy: Red book #1* (pp. 183–188). Ravensdale, WA: Idyll Arbor, Inc.

BUS Utilization Assessment (Burlingame, 1989)

Burlingame, J., and Blaschko, T. M. (2002). *Assessment tools for recreational therapy and related fields,* 3rd ed. (pp. 324–330). Ravensdale, WA: Idyll Arbor, Inc.

Communication Device Evaluation (Burlingame, 1990)

Burlingame, J., & Blaschko, T. M. (1990). *Assessment tools for recreational therapy: Red book #1* (pp. 195–200). Ravensdale, WA: Idyll Arbor, Inc.

Comprehensive Evaluation in Recreation Therapy— Physical Disabilities (CERT-PD: Parker, 1977)

Comprehensive Evaluation in Recreation Therapy— Psychiatric/Behavioral (CERT-Psych: Parker, 1975)

Burlingame, J., and Blaschko, T. M. (2002). *Assessment tools for recreational therapy and related fields,* 3rd ed. (pp. 342–350). Ravensdale, WA: Idyll Arbor, Inc.

Burlingame, J., and Blaschko, T. M. (2002). *Assessment tools for recreational therapy and related fields,* 3rd ed. (pp. 331–341). Ravensdale, WA: Idyll Arbor, Inc.

Parker, R. A., Ellison, C. H., Kirby, T. F., & Short, M. J. (1975). The comprehensive evaluation in recreation therapy scale: A tool for patient evaluation. *Therapeutic Recreation Journal, 9*(4), 143–152.

Parker, R., & Downie, G. (1981). Recreation therapy: A model for consideration. *Therapeutic Recreation Journal, 15*(3), 22–26.

Parker, R., Keller, K., Davis, M., & Downie, G. (1984). *The comprehensive evaluation in recreation therapy scale - rehabilitation: A tool for patient evaluation in rehabilitation.* Unpublished manuscript.

Fox Activity Therapy Social Skills Baseline (FOX: Patterson, 1977)

Burlingame, J., and Blaschko, T. M. (2002). *Assessment tools for recreational therapy and related fields,* 3rd ed. (pp. 351–368). Ravensdale, WA: Idyll Arbor, Inc.

Patterson, R. (1982). Development and utilization of an individualized assessment instrument for children and adolescents with severe and profound disabilities. In G. L. Hitzhusen (Ed.), *Expanding Horizons in Therapeutic Recreation X* (pp. 103–117). Columbia, MO: University of Missouri.

Patterson, R. (1985). *Activity therapy social skills baseline.* Dwight, IL: Wm. W. Fox Developmental Center. Unpublished manuscript.

Functional Assessment of Characteristics for Therapeutic Recreation (FACTR: Peterson, Dunn, & Carruthers, 1983)

Burlingame, J., and Blaschko, T. M. (2002). *Assessment tools for recreational therapy and related fields,* 3rd ed. (pp. 369–380). Ravensdale, WA: Idyll Arbor, Inc.

General Recreation Screening Tool (GRST: Burlingame, 1988)

Burlingame, J., and Blaschko, T. M. (2002). *Assessment tools for recreational therapy and related fields,* 3rd ed. (pp. 395–403). Ravensdale, WA: Idyll Arbor, Inc.

Idyll Arbor Reality Orientation Assessment (Idyll Arbor, 1989)

Burlingame, J., & Blaschko, T. M. (1990). *Assessment tools for recreational therapy: Red book #1* (pp. 211–216). Ravensdale, WA: Idyll Arbor, Inc.

Idyll Arbor Activity Assessment (Burlingame, 1989)

Burlingame, J., and Blaschko, T. M. (2002). *Assessment tools for recreational therapy and related fields,* 3rd ed. (pp. 404–420). Ravensdale, WA: Idyll Arbor, Inc.

Leisure Competence Measure (LCM: Kloseck, Crilly, Ellis, & Lammers, 1996)

Kloseck, M., & Crilly, R. G. (1997). *Leisure Competence Measure: Adult version professional manual and user's guide.* London, ON: Leisure Competence Measurement Data Systems.

Kloseck, M., Crilly, R., Ellis, G. D., & Lammers, E. (1996). Leisure Competence Measure: Development and reliability testing of a scale to measure functional outcomes in therapeutic recreation. *Therapeutic Recreation Journal, 30*(1), 13–26.

Maladapted Social Functioning Scale for Therapeutic Recreation Programming (Idyll Arbor, 1988)

Burlingame, J., & Blaschko, T. M. (1990). *Assessment tools for recreational therapy: Red book #1* (pp. 201–210). Ravensdale, WA: Idyll Arbor, Inc.

Mundy Recreation Inventory for the Trainable Mentally Retarded (Mundy, 1966)

Mundy, J. (1965). *The Mundy recreation inventory for the trainable mentally retarded.* Tallahassee, FL: Florida State University. Unpublished manuscript.

Ohio Leisure Skills Scales on Normal Functioning/Ohio Functional Assessment Battery (OLSSON: Olsson, 1988)

Burlingame, J., & Blaschko, T. M. (1990). *Assessment tools for recreational therapy: Red book #1* (pp. 175–182). Ravensdale, WA: Idyll Arbor, Inc.

Olsson, R. H. (1990). The Ohio leisure skills scales on normal functioning: A systems approach to clinical assessment. In G. L. Hitzhusen and J. O'Neil (Eds.), *Expanding horizons in therapeutic recreation XIII* (pp. 132–145). Columbia, MO: University of Missouri.

Olsson, R. (1994). *Ohio functional assessment battery: Standardized tests for leisure and living skills.* Tucson, AZ: Therapy Skill Builders.

Recreation Behavior Inventory (RBI: Berryman & Lefebvre, 1981)

Berryman, D., & Lefebvre, C. (1984). *Recreation behavior inventory.* Denton, TX: Leisure Learning Systems.

Recreation Early Development Screening Tool (REDS: Burlingame, 1988)

Burlingame, J., and Blaschko, T. M. (2002). *Assessment tools for recreational therapy and related fields,* 3rd ed. (pp. 451–459). Ravensdale, WA: Idyll Arbor, Inc.

Therapeutic Recreation Index (TRI: Faulkner, 1987)

Burlingame, J., & Blaschko, T. M. (1990). *Assessment tools for recreational therapy: Red book #1* (pp. 275–278). Ravensdale, WA: Idyll Arbor, Inc.

Faulkner, R. (1987). *TRI manual.* Seaside, OR: Leisure Enrichment Service.

Leisure Activity Skills

Cross Country Skiing Assessment (Peterson, 1990)

Burlingame, J., & Blaschko, T. M. (1990). *Assessment tools for recreational therapy: Red book #1* (pp. 241–244). Ravensdale, WA: Idyll Arbor, Inc.

Downhill Skiing Assessment (Peterson, 1990)

Burlingame, J., & Blaschko, T. M. (1990). *Assessment tools for recreational therapy: Red book #1* (pp. 237–240). Ravensdale, WA: Idyll Arbor, Inc.

Functional Hiking Technique (Burlingame, 1979)

Burlingame, J., and Blaschko, T. M. (2002). *Assessment tools for recreational therapy and related fields,* 3rd ed. (pp. 387–394). Ravensdale, WA: Idyll Arbor, Inc.

Leisure Interests and Participation

Constructive Leisure Activity Survey #1 (CLAS #1: Edwards, 1980)

Constructive Leisure Activity Survey #2 (CLAS #2: Edwards, 1980)

Edwards, P. (1980). *Leisure counseling techniques: Individual and group counseling step-by-step.* (3rd ed.) Los Angeles, CA: Constructive Leisure.

Edwards, P., & Bloland, P. (1980). Leisure counseling and consultation. *Personnel and Guidance, 58*(6), 435–440.

Family Leisure Assessment Checklist (FLAC: Folkerth, 1978)

Folkerth, J. (1979). Give the family flac. In D. J. Szymanski and G. L. Hitzhusen (Ed.), *Expanding horizons in therapeutic recreation VI* (pp. 174–179). Columbia, MO: University of Missouri.

Influential People Who Have Made an Imprint on My Life (Korb, Azok, & Leutenberg, 1989)

Burlingame, J., & Blaschko, T. M. (1990). *Assessment tools for recreational therapy: Red book #1* (pp. 279–282). Ravensdale, WA: Idyll Arbor, Inc.

Joswiak's Leisure Counseling Assessment (Joswiak, 1979, 1989)

Joswiak, K. (1975). *Leisure counseling program materials for the developmentally disabled.* Washington, DC: Hawkins and Associates.

Joswiak, K. (1980). Recreation therapy assessment with developmentally disabled persons. *Therapeutic Recreation Journal, 14,* 29–38.

Joswiak, K. (1989). *Leisure education: Program materials for persons with developmental disabilities.* State College, PA: Venture Publishing Company.

Leisure Activities Blank (LAB: McKechnie, 1975)

McKechnie, G. (1974). *Manual for environmental response inventory.* Palo Alto, CA: Consulting Psychologists Press.

McKechnie, G. (1974). The psychological structure of leisure. *Journal of Leisure Research, 6*(1).

McKechnie, G. (1974). *The structure of leisure activities.* Berkeley, CA: Institute of Personality Assessment and Research.

McKechnie, G. (1975). *Manual for leisure activities blank.* Palo Alto, CA: Consulting Psychologists Press.

Leisure and Social Sexual Assessment (Coyne, 1980)

Burlingame, J., & Blaschko, T. M. (1990). *Assessment tools for recreational therapy: Red book #1* (pp. 247–256). Ravensdale, WA: Idyll Arbor, Inc.

Leisure Pref (Edwards, 1986)

Edwards, P. (1986). *Manual for leisure pref.* Los Angeles, CA: Constructive Leisure.

Leisurescope/Teenscope (Nall & Schenk, 1983)

Burlingame, J., and Blaschko, T. M. (2002). *Assessment tools for recreational therapy and related fields,* 3rd ed. (pp. 278–298). Ravensdale, WA: Idyll Arbor, Inc.

Nall, C. (1983). *Instructional manual for leisurescope.* Colorado Springs, CO: Leisure Dynamics.

Nall, C. (1985). *Instructional manual for teen leisure scope.* Colorado Springs, CO: Leisure Dynamics.

Recreation Participation Data (RPD: Burlingame, 1987)

Burlingame, J., and Blaschko, T. M. (2002). *Assessment tools for recreational therapy and related fields,* 3rd ed. (pp. 573–579). Ravensdale, WA: Idyll Arbor, Inc.

State Technical Institute Leisure Assessment Process (STILAP: Navar, 1980)

Burlingame, J., and Blaschko, T. M. (2002). *Assessment tools for recreational therapy and related fields,* 3rd ed. (pp. 555–572). Ravensdale, WA: Idyll Arbor, Inc.

Navar, N. (1980). A rationale for leisure skill assessment with handicapped adults. *Therapeutic Recreation Journal, 14*(4), 21–28.

Navar, N., & Clancy, T. (1979). Leisure skill assessment process in leisure counseling. In D. J. Szymanski & G. L. Hitzhusen (Eds.), *Expanding horizons in therapeutic recreation VI* (pp. 68–94). Columbia, MO: University of Missouri.

Common Medical Abbreviations

ā	before	ASA	aspirin
āā	of each	asap	as soon as possible
abd	abdomen	ASD	atrial seotal defect
ac	before or with meals	ASHD	arteriosclerotic vascular heart
ACG	angiocardiography		disease
A.D.	right ear	A.T.	atrial tachycardia
A.D.A.	American Dietetic Association	ATL	achilles tendon lengthening
ADD	Average Daily Dose	A.U.	both ears
ADLs	activities of daily living	A-V	arteriovenous
ad lib	as desired	AWOL	absent without leave
Adm	admission, admitted	Ax	axilla
A.F.	atrial fibrillation		
AFB	acid-fast bacillus	B.A.	blood alcohol
AgNO$_3$	silver nitrate	BBB	bundle branch block
AIDS	acquired immune deficiency	BBS	bilateral breath sounds
	syndrome	B & C	board and care
AK	above the knee	BCP	birth control pills
AKA	also known as	BE	barium cncma
AKA	above the knee amputation	BIB	brought in by
ALL	acute lymphocyctic leukemia	bid	twice a day
am	morning or before noon	bilat	bilateral
AMA	against medical advice	BK	below the knee
AMI	acute myocardial infarction	BKA	below the knee amputation
amps	ampule	Bl. 1,2,3,4	Bland 1,2,3,4
amt	amount	BM	bowel movement
angio	angiogram	BMR	basal metabolic rate
ant	anterior	BP	blood pressure
ante-	before	BPH	benign prostatic hypertrophy
A & O	alert and oriented	BR	bathroom
A-P	anterior and posterior	Brady	bradycardia
Ap	apical pulse	BRN	Board of Registered Nursing
approx	approximate(ly)	BRP	bathroom privileges
ARDS	adult respiratory distress	BS	breath sounds, blood sugar
	syndrome	BSP	bromsulphalein
AROM	active range of motion	BUN	blood urea nitrogen
A.S.	left ear		

c̄	with	d/c	discontinue
C	Centigrade	D & E	dilation and evacuation
Ca	cancer or calcium	Dept	department
C & A	urine glucose test and acetest	Diab	diabetic
CABG	coronary artery bypass graft	DIC	disseminated intravascular
CAD	coronary artery disease		coagulation
cal	calorie	dil	dilute
CAPD	continuous ambulatory	Disc	
	peritoneal dialysis	or D/C	discontinue
caps	capsule	disp	disposition
CAT (EMI)	computerized axial tomograph	DJD	degenerative joint disease
cath	catheter	D.LR	dextrose in Lactated Ringer's
CBC	complete blood count	DM	Diabetes mellitus
cc	cubic centimeter	DNR	do not resuscitate
c/c	chief complaint	DO	doctor of osteopathy
CCU	coronary care unit, cardiac care	DOA	dead on arrival
	unit	DOB	date of birth
cert.	certification	DPAHC	durable power of attorney for
CHB	complete heart block		health care
CHD	coronary heart disease	DPT	diphtheria, pertussis, tetanus
chemo	chemotherapy		vaccine
CHF	congestive heart failure	dr	dram
chg	charge	Dr	doctor
CHO	carbohydrate	drng	drainage
Chol	cholestrol	drsgs	dressings
Clysis	hypodermoclycis	D/S	dextrose in saline
CNS	central nervous system	DSD	dry, sterile dressing
c/o	complaining of	DTR	deep tendon reflex
COLD	chronic obstructive lung disease	DTs	delirium tremors
Comp	compound	DUB	dysfunctional uterine bleeding
cond	condition	D/W	dextrose in water
cont	continuously	Dx	diagnosis
COPD	chronic obstructive pulmonary		
	disease	EBL	estimated blood loss
CP	cerebral palsy, chest pain	ECT	electroconvulsive therapy
Crani	craniotomy	ED	Emergency Department
CRF	chronic renal failure	EDC	estimated date of confinement
C & S	culture and sensitivity	EEG	electroencephalogram
CSF	cerebral spinal fluid	EENT	eye, ear, nose, and throat
CVA	cerebral vascular accident	EKG	
CVI	cerebral vascular insufficiency	or ECG	electrocardiogram
CVP	central venous pressure	elix	elixir
cysto	cystocopy	EMG	electromyogram
		ENT	ear, nose, and throat
d	day	EOM	extraocular movement
D & C	dilation and curettage	ER	emergency room

ESRF	end stage renal failure
EST	electroshock therapy
et or &	and
eta	estimated time of arrival
ETOH	ethanolism, alcoholism, under an intoxicated state
ETT	endotracheal tube
eval	evaluate, evaluation
exp	expiratory
extr	extract
F	Fahrenheit, female
FB	foreign body
FBS	fasting blood sugar
f/c	Foley catheter
fe	iron
F.F.	force fluid
F.H.	family history
FHT	fetal heart tones
FLB	funny looking beat
fld	fluid
FNP	family nurse practitioner
Fr	French
frq.	frequent
FSBG	finger stick blood glucose
FSBS	finger stick blood sugar
FSH	follicular stimulating hormone
ft	feet
FUO	fever of undetermined origin
FVC	forced vital capacity
Fx	fracture
G#, P#, SAB#, TAB#	gravida, para, spontaneous abortion, therapeutic abortion
GB	gallbladder
gd.	good
gen	general
GI	gastrointestinal
glu	glucose
glut.	gluteal
Gm	gram
GOT	glutamic oxaloacetic transaminase
GP	general practitioner of medicine

gr	grain
grav.	gravida
GSW	gunshot wound
GTT	glucose tolerance test
gtt.	drop
GU	genitourinary
G & W	glycerine and water
GYN	gynecology
H_2O	water
H_2O_2	hydrogen peroxide
H or "H"	by hypodermic
HA	headache
H.B.	heart block
hct	hematocrit
HCTZ	hydrochlorothiazide
hep A	hepatitis A
hep B	hepatitis B
hep C	hepatitis C
Hgb or Hb	hemoglobin
HHA	home health aide
h/o	history of
HOB	head of bed
HOH	hard of hearing
H & P	history and physical
hr	hour
HR	heart rate
HS	hour of sleep
h.s.	just before bedtime
ht	height
HTN	hypertension
hwb	hot water bottle
Hx	history
hyster	hysterectomy
I	iodine, iodide
IBC	iron-binding capacity
ICU	intensive care unit
I & D	incision and drainage
IDDM	insulin-dependent diabetes mellitus
IHD	ischemic heart disease
IM	intramuscular
Imp.	impression
in	inch
INH	isoniazide

inj.	injection		LLQ	left lower quadrant
I & O	intake and output		LMP	last menstrual period
IPPB	intermittent positive pressure breathing		LNMP	last normal menstrual period
irreg	irregular		LOC	level of consciousness
Isol	isolation		LP	lumbar puncture
iss	one and one half		ls	lumbosacral
IUD	intrauterine device		l. spine	lumbar spine
IV	intravenous		Lt., or L	left
IVP	intravenous pyelogram or push		LUE	left upper extremity
IVPB	intravenous piggyback		LUL	left upper lobe
IZ	immunization		LUOQ	left upper outer quadrant
			LUQ	left upper quadrant
JCAHO	Joint Commission on Accreditation of Healthcare Organizations		LVN	licensed vocational nurse
			L & W	living and well
J.H.S. 1,2,3	Jejunal hypersmolality syndrome		M	male
Jt.	joint		m	minimum
JVD	jugular vein distention		ma. or maj.	major
			MAE	moves all extremities
K+	potassium		max	maximal
KCl	potassium chloride		mcg	micrograms
kg	kilogram		MD	medical doctor, muscular dystrophy
KO	keep open		Mec.	meconium
KUB	kidney, ureter, bladder		Mech. Soft	mechanical soft
			med	medical
L	liter		med.	medicine
Ⓛor Lt.	left		meg	microgram
Lab	laboratory		MEQ	milliequivalent
Lac	lactose		mEq/L	milliequivalent per liter
lac.	laceration		mg or mgm	milligram
LAC	left antecubital		MgSO$_4$	magnesium sulfate
Lap	laporotomy		mgtts	microdrops
Lat	lateral		MHU	mental health unit
lb	pound		MI	myocardial infarction
LBBB	left bundle branch block		min	minimum or minute
LCSW	licensed clinical social worker		min.	minimum
L & D	labor and delivery		mitral	insufficiency
LE	lower extremity		ml	milliliter
lg	large		mm	millimeter
Lipo. 1,2,3,4	Hyperlipoproteinemia		mod	moderate
			M & R	measure and record
Liq	liquid		MR	may repeat
LLC	long leg cast		MRI	magnetic resonance imaging
LLE	left lower extremity		MS	multiple sclerosis, mitral stenosis
LLL	left lower lobe		mtg.	meeting

muc.	mucus		ortho VS	orthopedic vital signs
MVI	multiple vitamin injection		os	per mouth
			OS, o.s.	left eye
Na	sodium		OT	Occupational Therapy
n/a	not applicable		OTC	over the counter
NaCl	sodium chloride		O.U.	both eyes
n/c	nasal cannula		oz.	ounce
neg	negative			
Neuro.	neurology		p	pulse
NG	nasogastric		p̄	after, past
NKA	no known allergies		PAC	premature atrial contraction
NKDA	no known drug allergies		PACU	post anesthesia care unit
Nl/	normal		palp.	palpation
noc.	night, nocturnal		Pap Smear	Papanicolaou's Smear Test
N.P.	Nurse Practitioner		para	parous, having borne one or
NPN	non-protein nitrogen			more children
NPO	nothing by mouth		PAT	paroxysmal atrial tachycardia
NS	normal saline		Path.	pathology
N.S.	neurosurgery		PBI	protein-bound iodine
Nsg	nursing		p.c.	after meals
NSR	normal sinus rhythm		pcn	penicillin
N & T	nose and throat		PCV	packed cell volume
n.t.	nontender		PDR	Physician's Desk Reference
N.T.	nodal tachycardia		P.E.	physical examination
NTG	nitroglycerin		Ped.	pediatrics
N & V,	nausea and vomiting		per	through or by
n/v			perc.	percutaneous
			periph.	peripheral
O₂	oxygen		PERLA	pupils equally reactive to light
"O"	oral			and accommodation
OA	osteoarthritis		P.H.	past history
OB	obstetrics		P.I.	present illness
occas.	occasional		PID	pelvic inflammatory disease
OCp	oral contraceptives		PM	after noon
OD, o.d.	right eye		PMD	private medical doctor
oint.	ointment		PNC	premature nodal contraction
o.m.	every morning		pneumo.	pneumothorax
o.n.	every night		PNT	paroxysmal nodal tachycardia
OOB	out of bed		po, p.o.	by mouth
OP	outpatient, operation		P-O, PO	postoperative
OPD	outpatient department		P.O.	phone order
Opth.	opthamology		port	portable
OR	operating room		post-	after
ORIF	open reduction with internal		Post-op	after operation
	fixation		pp	postprandial
Ortho.	orthopedics		PPB	positive pressure breathing

O_2 for oxygen and $\bar{p}$ for after, past

PPBS	postprandial blood sugar	rec/d.	received
PPD	purified protein derivative (TB test)	reg, reg.	regular
		REM	rapid eye movement
pr	per rectum	res	residue
pre-	before	resp	respiration
pre-op	before operation	rest. fl.	restrict fluid
prep	preparation, prepare for	ret'd	returned
prn	whenever necessary	retro	retrograde
PRO	protein	RF	rheumatoid factor
Pro. Time	prothrombin time		rheumatic fever
procto	proctoscopy	Rh	Rhesus
Prog. Sip	Progessive Sippy	RHD	rheumatic heart disease
PROM	passive range of motion	RLE	right lower extremity
PSP	phenolsulfonaphthalein	RLL	right lower lobe
pt	patient	RLQ	right lower quadrant
P.T.	physical therapy	Rm	room
PTD	permanent total disability	r/o, R/O	rule out
PVC	premature ventricular contraction	ROM	range of motion
		ROS	review of systems
PVD	peripheral vascular disease	RR	recovery room
p/w/d	pale, warm, dry	rsp.	respirations or respiratory
		RSR	regular sinus rhythm
q	each, every	RUA	right upper arm
q 2h	every 2 hours	RUL	right upper lobe
q.am	every morning	RUQ	right upper quadrant
qd, q.d.	every day	R_x	prescription, treatment, therapy
qh	every hour		
q.h.s	every night	$\bar{s}$	without
qid (q.i.a.)	four times a day	S_3	3rd heart sound (ventricular gallop)
q.n.	every night		
qns	quantity not sufficient	S_4	4th heart sound (atrial gallop)
qod (q.o.a.)	every other day	sat.	saturated
qs	quantity sufficient	sc.	scant
qt	quart	Sed.	sedimentation
quad.	quadriceps	sens.	sensation or sensitivity
quan.	quantity	SG, sp. gr	specific gravity
		SGOT	serum glutamic oxalacetic transaminase
®or Rt.	right		
(R)	rectal	SGPT	serum glutamic pyruvic transaminase
R.A.	rheumatoid arthritis		
RAC	right antecubital	Sig	let it be labeled
RBBB	right bundle branch block	sl.	slight
RBC	red blood cells	SLR	straight leg raising
	red blood count	sm	small
RDS	respiratory distress syndrome	SMR	submucous resection
Re:	regarding, about	SNF	skilled nursing facility

SOAP	subjective, objective, analysis, plan		TPR	temperature, pulse, and respiration
SOB	shortness of breath		Tr	tincture
sol	solution		TSH	thyroid stimulating hormone
sos	if necessary		tsp	teaspoon
spec	specimen		TUR	transuretheral resection
spont.	spontaneous		TURP	transuretheral resection of prostate
sq or subq	subcutaneous			
s̄s̄	one half		Tw	tap water
SS	soap solution		tx	traction
SSKI	saturated solution of potassium iodide			
			U	unit
st	sterile		UA	urinalysis
ST			UE	upper extremity
or S. tach.	sinus tachycardia		UGI	upper G.I.
stat, STAT	at once, immediately		ung	ointment
STD	sexually transmitted disease		UOQ	upper outer quadrant
subl,			URI	upper respiratory infection
sub ling.	sublingual		Urol.	urology
subq	subcutaneous		UTI	urinary tract infection
supp	suppositories			
Surg	surgery, surgical		V-A	ventriculoatoneal
SVT	supraventricular tachycardia		vag	vaginal
syr	syrup		vd	voided
syst.	systolic		VD	venereal disease
sx.	symptoms		VDRL	venereal disease research laboratory test
T	temperature		V. Fib	ventricular fibrillation
t & a	time and amount		via	by way of
T & A	tonsillectomy and adenoidectomy		V.M.A.	vanilla mandelic acid
			VNA	Visiting Nurses Association
tab	tablet		V.O.	verbal order
TAB	therapeutic abortion		VS	vital signs
TAH	total abdominal hysterectomy		VSD	ventricular septal defect
TB	tuberculosis		VSS	vital signs stable
T & C	type and crossmatch		V.T.,	
TCDB	turn, cough, deep breathe		V. Tach.	ventricular tachycardia
TCU	transitional care unit or telemetry care unit			
			War. Blend	Waring Blender
TIA	transient ischemic attack		WBC	white blood cells
tid, t.i.d.	three times a day			white blood count
TKO	to keep open		w/c or W/C	wheelchair
TLC	total lung capacity		W & D	warm and dry
	tender loving care		WISC	Wechsler Intelligence Scale for Children test
T.O.	telephone order			
tol.	tolerate(d)		WNL	within normal limits

w/o	without
WPW	Wolff-Parkinson-White syndrome
wt	weight
x	times
yr	year
y/o	year old
Z/G, ZIG	zoster immune globulin

Symbols

@	at
+ or ^	increased, above, elevated, plus
↑	increased
– or ∨	decreased, below, negative, minus
↓	decreased
>	is greater than
<	is less than
≥	greater than or equal to
≤	less than or equal to
=	equal to
≠	not equal to
≅	approximately
±	plus or minus
?	questionable
∅	none
Δ	change
♀	female
♂	male
√	check
°	degree
1°	first degree
2°	second degree
3°	third degree
→	to, toward
2	secondary to
–	negative
∥	parallel
1:1	one-to-one

Glossary

Accountability is being responsible for the production and delivery of therapeutic recreation services that best meet client needs and move clients toward predetermined outcomes in the most timely, efficient, and effective manner possible.

Accreditation is the official recognition from a professional or governmental organization that a health care facility (or an educational institution) meets relevant standards.

Activity is a category of actions or program content, which may include experiences such as discussion, lectures, or written or cognitive exercises as well as traditional and nontraditional leisure activities.

Activity analysis is a process which involves the systematic application of selected sets of constructs and variables to break down and examine a given activity to determine the behavioral requirements inherent for successful participation and which may contribute to the achievement of client outcomes.

Agency plan includes all written communication that establishes and explains the standard of care for a particular agency.

Assessment is the systematic process of gathering and analyzing selected information about an individual client, and using the results for placement into a program(s) that is designed to reduce or eliminate the individual's problems or deficits with his or her leisure, and that enhances the individual's ability to independently function in leisure pursuits.

Assessment protocol is a document that provides clear information on the standardized procedures for preparing for, administering, scoring, interpreting, and reporting assessment information.

Causal is the result of an action; for example, intervention A causes outcome Z.

Centers for Medicare and Medicaid Services (CMS—formerly the Health Care Financing Administration [HCFA]) is a federal government body that is responsible for the regulatory review of health care agencies that bill for Medicare and Medicaid recipients.

Client documentation involves the written records that are kept regarding the actions taken for, with, and by the client; often becomes the official and legal record of client service.

    Treatment plans are documents that outline the action to be taken with, for or by the patient while receiving treatment; become part of patient's medical record.

    Progress notes are periodic updates of interventions and the patient's progression or regression; become part of patient's medical record.

Discharge/referral summaries contain documentation concerning the patient's entire length of stay and status at the end of treatment; may contain referrals to community agencies.

Follow-up or after-care records are documents of any care given to the patient after primary services are rendered.

Clinical or critical pathway (or care map or care track) is a documentation tool used in managed care and case management in which a timeline is defined for treatment of the patient's condition and for achievement of expected outcomes; can be used by staff to determine at any given time where patient should be in progress toward optimal health.

Clinical practice improvement is a method for examining the steps of a care process to determine how to achieve the best medical outcomes at the least necessary cost over the continuum of a patient's care.

Competence is the feeling an individual has when he or she is knowledgeable or skilled in some activity.

Confidence in client assessment means the specialist is relatively assured that the results of the assessment will lead to the correct decisions about placement of the client into intervention programs.

Content and Process Description is the specification of the content to be covered within the program as well as what processes or activities will be used to address that content.

Continuous improvement or performance improvement (or quality assurance or quality improvement) is a specified process of evaluation that health care agencies use to continually improve the services delivered to clients through self-inspection and on-site visitations by surveyors.

Criterion-referenced scoring is when each person is measured against a set standard. Being four feet high to ride a carnival ride is a criterion-referenced score; anyone below four feet tall cannot ride.

Database is the subjective and objective information about a patient collected during the initial assessment; may include health history, results of physical examination, and laboratory test results.

Diagnostic-related groups (DRGs) is the system of classifying or grouping patients according to medical diagnosis for purposes of reimbursement; pertains to the Medicare and Medicaid system for reimbursement of charges to private or public health care providers.

Disease is the failure of an organism's adaptive mechanisms to counteract adequately the stimuli and stresses to it, resulting in functional or structural disturbances at the cellular, tissue, and organ level.

Disability is a physical or mental impairment that substantially limits (past, present or future/real or perceived) one or more major life activities, having a record of such impairment, or being regarded as having such an impairment.

Effectiveness characterizes how an intervention works under everyday circumstances in routine clinical practice in a typical setting; the effectiveness of an intervention is the impact an intervention achieves in the real world, under resource constraints, in entire populations, or in specified subgroups of a population.

Effectiveness research attempts to address the degree to which clients improve under treatment as it is actually practiced in the field (i.e., with fewer controls and manipulations than in efficacy research designs). Effectiveness research compares different health care practices or interventions (e.g., medical technologies such as drugs, devices or procedures) covering the following areas: mortality, morbidity, symptoms, satisfaction, quality of life, preferences, and costs.

Efficacy characterizes how an intervention performs under ideal or more controlled circumstances. Efficacy is the improvement in health outcome achieved in a research setting, in expert hands, under ideal circumstances.

Efficacy research usually requires randomization to treatment and control groups, and a specific intervention for the treatment group, which usually has met criteria for a single diagnosis.

Enabling objectives (EOs) are a part of the specific program description that contain smaller behavioral units that specify the content to be covered within the larger terminal program objectives to be achieved through participation in the program; also called behavioral or instructional objectives.

Error in client assessment is the variance in scores caused by "unintentional" error that causes a score to deviate from its "true" score. Any condition that affects scores in ways that are "irrelevant" to the purpose of the assessment is considered error variance.

Evidence-based practice can be described as the selection of best available treatments for which there is some evidence of efficacy; evidence must be gathered through well designed and meaningful research efforts with client groups and be applicable to daily practice. Also known as **empirically validated treatment, empirically supported treatment, empirically evaluated treatment, empirical practice, research-based practice, research utilization, evidence-based treatment,** and **evidence-based health care.**

External locus of control means the person believes that something outside the individual (e.g., luck) is responsible for the outcome of a situation or an event.

Formative evaluation means that data collection is ongoing and occurs while the activity or program is in progress and is used to modify the program while it is implemented.

Functional abilities are baseline abilities that are usually prerequisite to typical leisure behavior that most individuals without disabilities would possess.

Functional intervention services help reduce functional limitations that prevent the individual from increasing leisure-related awareness, knowledge, skills, abilities, and involvement.

Goals are generic statements that describe basic direction in which the client is to improve.

> **Objectives** are usually specific statements about the direction of expected client improvement; contain: (a) condition, (b) behavior; and (c) criterion.
>
> **Condition** is the part of the objective that describes the circumstance under which the desired behavior will occur.
>
> **Behavior** is the part of the objective that identifies what action the client will demonstrate to prove he or she has achieved the desired knowledge, skills, or ability; must be observable and measurable.

Criterion in the behavioral objective delineates the exact amounts and nature of the behavior that can be taken as evidence that the objective has been met; a precise statement or standard that allows individuals to make judgments based on the observable, measurable behavior.

Health is the state of complete physical, mental, and social well-being, and not merely the absence of disease; healthfulness is a multifaceted phenomenon, encompassing physical, emotional, and social well-being.

Health Care Financing Administration (HCFA) (see Centers for Medicare and Medicaid Services).

Homeostasis is the process of seeking equilibrium or balance.

Illness is when a person's resources are imbalanced with the needed responses, and results in decreased ability to survive and to create higher standards for the quality of life. Illness is a state of being; the person's subjective experience of the disorder, either with or without objective physical and biochemical evidence of the disorder; the human experience of dysfunction and loss of well-being.

Incident reports are documents completed immediately following any variation, situation, or unusual occurrence in health care, mandated by JCAHO, to be used for quality improvement and patient review and evaluation of care.

Incidental orders are one-time, miscellaneous orders that break routine patterns of care.

Internal locus of control implies that the individual has the orientation that he or she is responsible for the behavior and outcomes he or she produces.

Intervention is an activity, a program, or a service that is designed and implemented to create some degree of client behavioral change (that is, behavioral change is the purpose of the program).

Intrinsic motivation is the impetus to do something for internally or personally rewarding reasons.

Joint Commission on Accreditation of Healthcare Organizations (JCAHO) is a private, nongovernmental agency that establishes guidelines for the operation of hospitals and other health care agencies, conducts accreditation programs and on-site surveys, and encourages attainment of quality patient care.

Leisure is defined by the main variables of perceived autonomy or freedom of choice and intrinsic motivation that reflects behaviors that are enjoyable.

Leisure awareness is the cognitive awareness of leisure and its benefits, a valuing of the leisure phenomenon, and a conscious decision-making process to activate involvement.

Leisure education is a broad category of services that focuses on the development and acquisition of various leisure-related skills, attitudes, and knowledge.

Leisure lifestyle is the day-to-day behavioral expression of one's leisure-related attitudes, awareness, and activities revealed within the context and composite of the total life experience. Leisure lifestyle implies that an individual has sufficient skills, knowledges, attitudes, and abilities to participate successfully in and be satisfied with leisure and recreation experiences that are incorporated into his or her individual life pattern.

Medicaid is a combined program of state and federal insurance and medical assistance for qualified needy individuals of any age.

Medicare is a federal health insurance program for individuals over the age of 65.

Mental health is positive functioning that consists of six dimensions of psychological well-being: self-acceptance, positive relations with others, personal growth, purpose in life, environmental mastery, and autonomy.

Minimum Data Set (MDS) is the recording format for a standardized assessment tool required by the federal government in long-term care facilities.

Narrative or source-oriented records are unstructured client records that require longhand written accounts of the chronology of client treatment and reaction to treatment; usually each discipline (source) completes its own section, independent of other disciplines.

National Committee for Quality Assurance operates a voluntary accreditation plan for managed care plans (health maintenance organizations [HMOs]) and employs a set of quality indicators called the Health Plan Employer Data and Information Set (HEDIS).

Norm-referenced scores provide benchmarks against which scores are judged according to how the client scores in relation to his or her peers; grading "on the curve" is an example of norm-referenced scoring.

Optimal experiences include feelings of intense involvement, clarity of goals and feedback, deep concentration, transcendence of self, lack of self-consciousness, loss of a sense of time, intrinsic rewarding experience, and a balance between challenge and skill.

Outcome criteria are standards by which measurable goals or outcomes are objectively measured and evaluated.

Outcome measurement is quantification of client outcome data in some way, either in absolute terms or in relative terms.

Outcomes are the documentable changes in the client's status, behavior, attitudes, skills, and/or knowledges that result from interventions and interactions; the difference in a person from entry into and exit from an intervention. May be positive or negative, intended or unintended.

Perceived freedom means that the activity or setting is more likely to be viewed as leisure when individuals attribute their reasons for participation to themselves (i.e., actions are freely chosen) rather than determined externally by someone else or by circumstances.

Performance measures (PMs) are behavioral objectives that clients are expected to achieve as a result of participating in the program.

Personal causality or attribution implies that an individual believes he or she can affect a particular outcome; his or her contribution to an outcome. For instance, when an individual experiences success, he or she can attribute that success either to personal effort (personal causality), or to luck or chance (situational causality).

Play is a basic human behavior that is inherent or a natural part of human existence and expression.

Policies and procedures are part of the agency's risk management plan and include written documents that set standards of care or operation for a given health care facility.

Practicality and usability is a nonstatistical concept that is concerned with the practicality of the assessment.

Predictable is being known in advance. For example, the outcomes of client participation in an intervention should be predictable, based on how the intervention is designed.

Problem-oriented medical records (POMR) focus on the problems of the patient rather than the source of information; many formats are available.

SOAP charting is a method of recording progress notes in which information is organized into Subjective data, Objective data, Analysis (interpretation), and Plan.

SOAPIE charting is a method of recording progress notes in which information is organized into Subjective data, Objective data, Analysis (interpretation), Plan, Interventions, and Evaluation.

SOAPIER charting is a method of recording progress notes in which information is organized into Subjective data, Objective data, Analysis (interpretation), Plan, Interventions, Evaluation, and Revision.

Focus charting is a method for organizing information in the narrative portion of the client's record to include data, action, and response for each identified concern.

Charting by Exception (CBE) is the charting system that departs from more traditional systems by requiring documentation only of significant, abnormal, or unusual findings.

The **P**roblem-**I**ntervention-**E**valuation **(PIE)** system involves flow sheets and allows care plans to be integrated within progress notes. PIE charting does not contain assessment data per se.

The **FACT** method of charting is named for its four key elements: (a) **F**low sheets individualized to specific services, (b) **A**ssessment with standardized baseline parameters, (c) **C**oncise, integrated progress notes and flow sheets documenting the patient's condition and responses, and (d) **T**imely entries recorded when care is given; closely resembles Charting by Exception.

The **Core** system focuses on the treatment process and consists of a database, plans of care, flow sheets, progress notes, and discharge summaries.

The **Outcomes** documentation system focuses on the process of care, especially the patient's behaviors and reactions to interventions and teaching; features a database, a plan of care, and expected outcome statements.

Program design is the written documentation of the strategy, intervention, or approach that will aid those who participate in the program to accomplish the stated goals.

Program evaluation can be defined as the systematic and logical process of gathering and analyzing selected information in order to make decisions about the quality, effectiveness and/or outcomes of a program, function, or service.

Protocols are documents that describe the "best practice" of a specific intervention as applied to a specific group of clients or client needs that have been standardized and result from recent research evidence, literature reviews, or professional consensus. Protocols document the purposeful procedures used to deliver intervention to clients, and provide a basis for evaluating the efficacy of those procedures. Either based on intervention or diagnostic groups/client problems.

Quality or **performance improvement** is the commitment to and actions taken by a health care facility or several health disciplines to work together to achieve an optimal degree of excellence in services rendered to each patient. Also known as **continuous quality improvement** and **quality assurance.**

Quality of life is the individual's perception of their position in life in the context of the culture and value system where they live, and in relation to their goals, expectations, standards and concerns. It is a broad-ranging concept, incorporating in a complex way a person's physical health, psychological state, level of independence, social relationships, personal beliefs, and relationship to salient features of the environment.

Recreation involves a vast variety of structured activities commonly sanctioned by the society and most frequently engaged in through some organized delivery system.

Recreation participation programs are opportunities for clients to select and engage in organized activities and leisure opportunities with others through a structured delivery system.

Rehabilitation Accreditation Commission (CARF) is a voluntary, not-for-profit accrediting agency that reviews a wide range of rehabilitation and human services programs in the United States, Canada, and Europe.

Reliability refers to the estimate of the consistency of the assessment results. Reliability of test results means that a sample of persons would receive relatively the same scores when reexamined on different occasions, with a different set of equal items, or under specific conditions.

> **Equivalent-form** (also called parallel-form or alternative-form) reliability is used to estimate the consistency between two forms of a test that have similar but not the same items.
>
> **Internal consistency** is important for tests that only have one form and it is intended to be given only one time. Internal consistency measures view each test as two halves that measure the same thing and can be compared with one another.
>
> **Inter-rater reliability** is calculated based on the number of agreements and disagreements between two observers.
>
> **Stability** of test results (as one measure of reliability) is estimated through the use of test-retest correlation coefficients. Test-retest statistics calculate the relationship between scores obtained by a group of people on one administration of a test with their scores on a second administration of the same test.
>
> **Replicable** is repeatability or reproduction. For example, client outcomes should be replicable over time from participation in a specific intervention.

Risk management includes the identification, analysis, evaluation, and then elimination or reduction of risks to patients, visitors, or employees; involves loss prevention and control, and handling of all incidents, claims, and other insurance- and litigation-related tasks.

Sampling technique refers to the method used to select the sample to be evaluated. There are two basic types of sampling techniques: **probability** and **nonprobability** or **purposive sampling.**

Scope of care or **scope of practice** includes the boundaries or limitations placed on the discipline's professional practice by legislative, legal, and professional groups.

For therapeutic recreation, the professional scope of practice includes functional intervention, leisure education, and recreation participation services.

Secondary disabilities are those limitations imposed by a primary disability, such as decubitus ulcers, atrophy, incontinence, etc.

Self-efficacy or **self-determination** or **competence** is the central or pervasive personal belief that an individual can exercise some control over his or her own functioning and over environmental events to reach some desired end; foundational to the individual's sense of competence and control. Individuals with higher self-efficacy believe their choices and actions will affect the outcome of a situation, those with lower self-efficacy believe their choices and actions have little relationship to the outcome.

Social well-being consists of at least two major concepts, social adjustment and social support. **Social adjustment** is a combination of satisfaction with relationships (or problems), performance in social roles (including social participation and behavior), and adjustment to one's social environment. **Social support** is the number of contacts in one's social network, and overall satisfaction with those contacts.

Specific program is a set of activities and their corresponding interactions that are designed to achieve predetermined goals selected for a given group of clients.

Statement of purpose is a one-sentence description of the program's intended focus.

Standards of care describe the degree and extent of care that a reasonably prudent person should exercise in the same or similar circumstances; in malpractice cases, applied to measure the competence of a professional.

Stress is a state that results from an actual or perceived imbalance between the demand and the capability of the individual to cope with and/or adapt to that demand that upsets the individual's short- or long-term homeostasis.

Stress-coping refers to any effort to master conditions of harm, threat, or challenge and bring the person back into equilibrium or homeostasis.

Summative evaluation is conducted at the end of the program and provides data that can be used to compare programs with one another or provide information for the next round of programming.

Terminal program objectives (TPOs) are general outcome statements that the client is expected to achieve.

Theory-based programming involves using theories to develop therapeutic recreation assessments, programs, and evaluations that lead to important client outcomes.

Therapeutic Recreation Accountability Model (TRAM) is a graphic representation of the various accountability and documentation procedures used by therapeutic recreation specialists to monitor and make decisions about the delivery of services for producing client outcomes; depicts inter-relationships between various decision or documentation points used by the specialist to provide and monitor appropriate, quality services.

Utilization review is a program usually initiated by reimbursement agents to maintain control over use of resources by patients and health care providers; may focus on length of stay, treatment regimen, validation of tests and procedures, and verification of the use of medical supplies and equipment.

Validity of an assessment refers to the evidence collected that describes the extent to which the test meets its intended purpose. It concerns what the test measures and how well it does so.

Concurrent validity concerns the relative ability to predict one set of scores from another set of scores measuring the same variable, that are taken at the same or nearly the same time (concurrently).

Construct validity is important when an unobservable "trait" is being measured to assure that it is being measured adequately.

Content validity is the degree to which the assessment content covers a representative sample of the content in question.

Criterion-related validity concerns the inferences or predictions made from a person's assessment results in relation to some other variable called an independent criterion.

Predictive validity is concerned with how accurately one set of scores measuring one variable predicts a second set of criterion scores measuring a second variable taken at some point in the future.

Wellness is a personal, positive, and proactive approach to health that emphasizes individual responsibility for well-being through the practice of health-promoting lifestyle behaviors. High-level wellness for the individual is an integrated method of functioning that is oriented toward maximizing the individual's potential within the environment in which she or he is functioning.

Index